TRAUMATIC RELATIONSHIPS AND
SERIOUS MENTAL DISORDERS

TRAUMATIC RELATIONSHIPS AND SERIOUS MENTAL DISORDERS

Jon G. Allen

Child and Family Center
The Menninger Clinic, Kansas, USA

JOHN WILEY & SONS, LTD
Chichester · New York · Weinheim · Brisbane · Singapore · Toronto

Reprinted May 2001, October 2002

Other Wiley Editorial Offices

John Wiley & Sons, Inc., 605 Third Avenue,
New York, NY 10158-0012, USA

WILEY-VCH GmbH, Pappelallee 3,
D-69469 Weinheim, Germany

John Wiley & Sons Australia, Ltd, 33 Park Road, Milton,
Queensland 4064, Australia

John Wiley & Sons (Asia) Pte Ltd, 2 Clementi Loop #02-01,
Jin Xing Distripark, Singapore 129809

John Wiley & Sons (Canada) Ltd, 22 Worcester Road,
Rexdale, Ontario M9W 1L1, Canada

Library of Congress Cataloging-in-Publication Data

British Library Cataloguing in Publication Data

A catalogue record for this book is available from the British Library

ISBN 0-471-49102-0 (cased)
ISBN 0-471-48554-3 (paper)

Typeset in 10/12pt Palatino by Best-set Typesetter Ltd., Hong Kong
Printed and bound in Great Britain by Antony Rowe Ltd, Chippenham, Wilts
This book is printed on acid-free paper responsibly manufactured from sustainable forestry,
in which at least two trees are planted for each one used for paper production.

To the women and men who have labored with me
in the effort to understand trauma
and who have sustained my hope
through their persistent and courageous efforts
to come to terms with it

CONTENTS

PART I   DEVELOPMENTAL FOUNDATIONS

PART III   TREATMENT AND LONG-TERM MANAGEMENT

TABLES AND FIGURES

ABOUT THE AUTHOR

Jon G. Allen is senior staff psychologist at the Menninger Clinic and project director of the Child and Family Center and the Clinical Protocols and Outcomes Center at Menninger. Dr Allen received his BA degree in psychology at the University of Connecticut and his PhD degree in clinical psychology at the University of Rochester. He completed postdoctoral training in clinical psychology at the Menninger Clinic. He conducts psychotherapy, diagnostic evaluations, consultations, and psychoeducational programs, specializing in trauma-related disorders. He has taught and supervised students at the University of Rochester, Northern Illinois University, the University of Kansas, Kansas State University, and Washburn University of Topeka, and he is also a member of the faculty of the Karl Menninger School of Psychiatry and Mental Health Sciences. He is immediate past editor of the *Bulletin of the Menninger Clinic*, a member of the editorial boards of the *Journal of Trauma and Dissociation* and *Psychiatry*, and serves as reviewer for several professional journals and book publishers. He is the author of *Coping with Trauma: A Guide to Self-Understanding* and co-author of *Borderline Personality Disorder: Tailoring the Therapy to the Patient*. He is the co-editor of *Diagnosis and Treatment of Dissociative Disorders* and *Contemporary Treatment of Psychosis: Healing Relationships in the 'Decade of the Brain'*. He has authored and co-authored numerous professional articles and book chapters on trauma, psychotherapy, hospital treatment, the therapeutic alliance, psychological testing, neuropsychology, and emotion.

FOREWORD

Both biological and psychosocial findings point to the importance of severe psychosocial privation and deprivation as a key component in the causation of mental disorder. The term trauma has somewhat reified these experiences and created almost a special cadre of mental health professionals whose concern is the treatment of traumatized individuals. The massive prevalence of such disorders in community samples reminds us of the very ordinariness of traumatic conditions. And it is perhaps because of this very ordinariness that we have a need to separate and make special a category of relationship experiences which are far more common than any of us feels comfortable with.

Those at the extreme end of early social adversity are perhaps as much as one hundred times more likely to develop severe psychiatric morbidity than those who were fortunate to have been at the opposite end of the spectrum. The average human mind is simply not equipped to assimilate or protect itself from environmental assaults beyond a certain level of intensity. By far the most intolerable of such assaults are ones that occur in the context of interpersonal relationships. But not just any relationship. Psychiatric sequelae are particularly associated with those conditions where adversity occurs in the context of a relationship biologically earmarked to provide the young mind with an experience of safety in the face of fear-provoking environmental impingements: attachment trauma.

Attachment trauma is the focus of this book and attachment trauma is the locus of the pathology of most individuals who come to seek our help in a wide variety of treatment contexts. Allen's book speaks to the problems which these individuals come with at the same time as addressing the clinician who is desperately trying to offer assistance. Allen offers the same remedy to both: understanding.

There are but a handful of professional books that could ever make the claim that they have the potential to change your life. There are many good books that inform, that provoke reflection, that may even shift professional practice in the direction of greater effectiveness or efficiency. But there are very few books like Bowlby's *Attachment and Loss* trilogy or Daniel Stern's *Interpersonal World of the Infant* that reframe an entire domain of phenomena to a point where readers are forced to change their habitual patterns of thinking about almost all aspects of their clinical work and rethink the basic assumptions of their common sense/professional psychology. For me, reading Freud's *The Interpretation of Dreams* as a first-year undergraduate psychologist was exactly that kind of destabilizing experience. Suddenly I realized that my experiences had meanings beyond those of which I was aware. The *Attachment* trilogy recast the assumption of unconscious meaning as cause in the context of real interpersonal relationships. Daniel Stern added a further twist, opening the window onto the interpersonal roots of the intrapsychic mental structures.

Allen's book for me belongs in the same category. He takes the story a step further and asks to what clinical use we can put our increased understanding of the interpersonal origins of mental structures that determine the experience of interpersonally traumatized individuals. His answer is simple, almost insultingly so: we can use it to help our patients understand and therefore cope with (or perhaps I should say learn to live with) their internal experiences.

The book in many respects is a wolf in sheep's clothing. In order to be able to enter into a meaningful dialogue with traumatized patients concerning their experience, the clinician must have a crystal-clear model of what the client is experiencing and why. Allen, in a remarkably integrative scholarly appraisal of thousands of clinical and empirical studies, provides the reader with this understanding. This is in itself a phenomenal achievement, but it does not stop here.

The text is beautifully sculpted in a manner to lend itself directly to a psychoeducational program. In my experience, psychoeducation has patronized the client, perhaps not invariably, but certainly in the vast majority of cases. This is not because psychoeducators in general have low opinions of their client group (although this may be true in some isolated instances), but rather because they have not been able to arrive at a coherent integration of the many thousands of 'known' facts concerning the nature and consequence of interpersonal trauma and, even if they have, they are quite unable to communicate this understanding in simple language.

In contrast, Allen's book is a genuine tour de force. Taking a developmental psychopathology orientation, it takes the reader from the nature of attachment relationships and their disorganization by trauma to the implication of these experiences for self-formation to the biological, cognitive and emotional aspects of traumatization. All the major trauma-related psychiatric conditions are reinterpreted in terms of this understanding, but this is not all. A comprehensive framework of the interventions which clinicians provide for trauma victims is integrated into the model, independent of orientation.

Throughout the book, then, there are two threads: one that concerns cutting-edge understanding firmly rooted in empirical evidence but never at the expense of clinical attunement, and the other that concerns how this understanding can be helpfully communicated to patients within the sometimes extraordinarily narrow windows of opportunity which professionals have within the early twenty-first-century healthcare system. The model that Allen constructs in this book is quite simply the most satisfactory integration of findings concerning interpersonal trauma which anyone has yet achieved. His review is comprehensive, and extremely valuable in that respect alone, but it is also original. Many contributions are cast in new light and are restated accurately, yet somehow more fully than they originally appeared. Restated in the context of other findings, the meaning of most research reviewed is enriched, made practically relevant and acquires new status and significance. Allen weaves a tapestry for the reader, a tapestry that tells a story which the clinician can remember and pass on to her or his patient. Thus the core implicit assumption that underpins Allen's enterprise is that an accurate understanding of their own mind empowers the patient to gain mastery over toxic internal experience. The capacity of the experience of meaning to cause behavioral and experiential change is harnessed in the service of healing.

There are no 'easy answers' when it comes to the consequences of trauma, nor does Allen offer any. The case that Allen builds is all about how relationship trauma infuses character, thus becoming integrated with the vitality of personality with all its tenacity for survival. Relationship trauma does not simply generate symptoms that can be treated, it generates the person who has to be accepted, related to and hopefully helped. Help may take a number of forms, but in all the forms that psychosocial intervention might take, the understanding of the underlying psychological processes is the *sine qua non* of adequate therapeutic help. Reading this book, you will come to appreciate the truth of this statement as well as making a giant step towards understanding the experience of the individuals who have turned to you for assistance.

Peter Fonagy
Freud Memorial Professor of Psychoanalysis, UCL
Director of Research, the Anna Freud Centre
Director, Child and Family Center and Center for Outcomes Research and Effectiveness, Menninger Foundation

PREFACE

At best, treating trauma is hard work; at worst, it can be traumatic. All of us who do this work need all the help we can get. Few of us have time to pore over the vast literature, relate it to our clinical experience, and pull it all together in a coherent way. I've had an opportunity to take on this task and find that what I've learned has greatly strengthened my clinical practice. I hope this book will also add to your knowledge and help you organize it in a way that enhances your work as a therapist.

But we have a dual task: as we gain professional knowledge, we also must learn to translate it into a language that everyone can understand. A main agenda of this book is to help you understand trauma in a way that you can also explain it to your clients. I focus on the severest trauma, which comes down to being frightened, hurt, and neglected in close relationships. And I emphasize its gravest effects, which include many of the more severe psychiatric disorders we treat. Yet trauma occurs on a continuum, and many of the matters addressed in this book pertain to the full spectrum of clinical work we do—not to mention our own lives. Most authors, quite wisely, take on this vast territory piecemeal, for example, focusing on post-traumatic stress disorder, dissociation, depression, relationship problems, or a particular treatment approach. But there is an advantage to covering the whole lot at once: we need a comprehensive and unified understanding of severe trauma and its treatment. And our clients need it too.

Before you embark on reading this book, you might want to know the story behind it. Oddly, I did not fully realize why I was writing it until it was nearly finished. As I was putting on the finishing touches, I picked up a copy of *How to Write*, by Pulitzer Prize-winning author Richard Rhodes—himself a trauma survivor. I was surprised when Rhodes admitted, 'The last thing I know, when I finish writing a book, is why I really wrote it.' It then dawned on me that, throughout the book, I was trying to come to terms with the sheer difficulty of treating trauma. At that point I connected this theme with a painfully instructive event that had occurred many months previously, when the book was in its early stages.

A restructuring of clinical services necessitated that I stop working with a trauma group to which I had become strongly attached. My colleague, Kay Kelly, and I had developed a group for patients with chronic mental disorders in a partial hospital program and had co-led the group for several years. In my last session, one of the patients seized the opportunity to put the ball on my side of the court by asking me to talk about how I felt at leaving the group. Without any forethought, I blurted out that I just wished I knew how to be of more help. To my chagrin, as I said this, tears welled up in my eyes. Quite discombobulated, I muddled through the rest of the session, carried by the patients' compassion. Later, mulling over the episode, I realized the obvious—how much helping meant to me and how distressed I had been by my limitations. Only as I neared the end of writing this book did I appreciate how determined I was to make sense of the emotional challenges posed by treating trauma.

If the title of this book has captured your attention and its size has not deterred you, I assume that you, too, are struggling conscientiously to help severely traumatized clients. How will this book help you with that struggle? We have a substantial professional literature on the *difficult-to-treat* client—where 'difficult' carries the connotations of the injunction, 'Stop being so *difficult!*' But I think we have not paid enough attention to this other stressful aspect of working with traumatized clients that, unbidden, became so painfully clear to me: They are *difficult to help*. Ironically, one of the most helpful things we can do is enable our clients to understand that there are good reasons for their difficulty in recovering from trauma. With this understanding, they feel more hopeful. They blame themselves less. They rightly proclaim, 'Knowledge is power!' With a legacy of trauma, they need nothing more than empowerment.

We therapists also can benefit from understanding why trauma is so hard to overcome. Except for indifference or outright rejection, nothing antagonizes traumatized patients more than therapeutic zeal. Such zeal minimizes the severity of their problems and the hard work they have been doing over the years. I still conduct a daily trauma group for patients admitted for acute inpatient treatment. Not infrequently, in the span of a few minutes, a patient will convey the gist of a horrendous history of trauma, enumerate a series of brutal recent stressors, describe a slide into desperate attempts to cope that made everything worse, and confess how it all culminated in suicidal despair. And yet the patient had been working hard in treatment for years. Despite knowing all that I do about trauma and its treatment, I cannot fix this. In fact, quite often I am left speechless. But understanding what I do about trauma, I can stay put without panicking or despairing. I convey that coping is difficult—often *extremely* difficult—but not impossible.

Similarly, treating such patients is difficult—often *extremely* difficult—but not impossible. To maintain hope and to protect ourselves from becoming as demoralized as our clients can sometimes be, we therapists must develop reasonable expectations. When we fully apprehend the challenges our clients face, we, too, can be more hopeful and less self-critical. We cannot circumvent the strain of our limitations. But we can find satisfaction in the relief our clients feel at being deeply understood, as well as in the benefits they receive from whatever additional help we can provide.

A cornerstone of all therapeutic approaches is our endeavor to understand our clients so as to help them understand themselves. Yet both facets of this endeavor are especially challenging in the field of trauma. To understand trauma, I have done what most clinical psychologists do—psychotherapy, consultations, psychological testing, and research, as well as a great deal of reading. But I have also done something else that few mental health professionals have an opportunity to do. I have conducted educational groups for traumatized patients for several hours a week over the course of several years. In the process, they have taught me as much as I have taught them and, with their help, I have hammered out many ways of better conveying our professional understanding to them.

Mastering the trauma literature and using it to help clients understand themselves is no small challenge. We are blessed with a vigorous community of scholars who have generated a wealth of information in the process of researching trauma and its treatment. To be of greatest help to our clients, we cannot overlook any source of knowledge. We not only must keep abreast of research findings but also must juggle a number of different theoretical perspectives. Accordingly, this book incorporates my clinical experience and extensive scientific literature into a broad theoretical framework that makes use of several perspectives: evolutionary, neurobiological, cognitive-behavioral, interpersonal, and psychodynamic.

Yet trying to master the vast trauma literature while facing the depth and complexity of our clients' problems can leave us therapists feeling as overwhelmed and fragmented as our clients. In *How to Write*, Rhodes noted, 'All stories are ultimately the same story: someone falls into a hole and has to find a way to get out.' Understanding shows the way out. Working on this agenda with the help of scores of traumatized patients over many years, I have constructed a coherent understanding of trauma that skirts none of its complexity. For several reasons, I rely on a developmental framework anchored in attachment theory to hold all this knowledge together. Attachment theory gives due weight to the developmental impact of childhood experiences and remains thoroughly grounded in empirical research. In addition, trauma that eventuates in serious mental disorders often takes place in the context of an attachment relationship, and trauma has been a major preoccupation of attachment researchers. Finally, attachment holds the key to therapeutic relationships. Thus attachment theory provides a unified framework for organizing our understanding of trauma, its developmental impact, and its treatment. For me, the flexibility of attachment is also the wellspring of hope, because traumatized persons continue seeking attachments, and they always can learn to become more securely attached, in therapy and in other relationships.

Synopsis

The first four chapters in Part I provide the developmental foundation essential to understanding the severe psychopathology that can stem from trauma as well as the rationale for trauma treatment. Chapter 1 presents core features of trauma and delineates a spectrum of relationship involvement, ranging from impersonal trauma (e.g., earthquakes) to interpersonal trauma (e.g., assaults), to attachment trauma (e.g., abuse and neglect). Chapter 2 documents the potentially traumatic impact of various kinds of maltreatment that may occur in attachment relationships, both in childhood and adulthood. Chapter 3 addresses the impact of trauma on patterns of attachment to clarify the process of trauma reenactment in interpersonal relationships. Chapter 4 considers the impact of maltreatment on the subjective sense of self and self-worth. One by one, these chapters gradually elucidate the depth of the impact of trauma in attachment relationships on the individual's capacity to regulate emotional distress.

The six chapters in Part II address a wide range of trauma-related psychiatric disorders, including post-traumatic stress disorder, dissociative disorders, and a host of potential comorbid disorders. Chapter 5 covers the psychology of PTSD and traumatic memories, taking up controversies about repressed memory and false memories. Chapter 6 examines PTSD from a biological perspective and considers the impact of trauma on physical health. Chapter 7 explicates dissociative detachment as a pervasive and potentially crippling trauma-related defense, while also making sense of dissociative identity disorder and examining how psychotic symptoms relate to dissociation and trauma. Chapter 8 covers a range of self-destructive behaviors that many traumatized persons employ largely to reduce tension, focusing on substance abuse, eating disorders, and self-harm. Chapter 9 addresses depression, a ubiquitous trauma-related problem that exemplifies challenges in recovery, construed here as the Catch 22s of depression. Chapter 10 tackles another controversial area, the diagnosis of personality disorders in the context of severe trauma.

Each of the first ten chapters addresses the bedrock of trauma treatment—how you can help your clients understand themselves. But the four chapters in Part III integrate the essential components of trauma treatment into the developmental foundation constructed in the first two parts of the book. Just as we must help our clients understand their problems, we must help them understand treatment. Because traumatic attachment relationships undermine the capacity to regulate emotional distress, trauma-focused interventions must be offered in the context of emotional containment. Chapter 11 spells out the nature and challenges of containment, which is provided by social support (secure attachment relationships), self-regulation, and a stable treatment frame. Chapter 12 reviews trauma-focused interventions that enable the client to create a coherent narrative of the trauma. Chapter 12 highlights exemplary cognitive-behavioral techniques with demonstrable effectiveness in the treatment of PTSD. Although each of the first 12 chapters explicitly provides guidance about educating clients, Chapter 13 addresses formal psychoeducational approaches. In this chapter, my colleagues AnnMarie Glodich and Kay Kelly join me in describing the diversity of educational groups that we have implemented throughout the Menninger Clinic and beyond.

When I was in the middle of writing this book and was educating professionals about the stressful impact of working with traumatized persons, it occurred to me that the conceptual framework I had been using to understand clients is equally applicable to us trauma therapists. We, too, have a history of adversity, a risk of developing psychiatric disorders, and a need for prevention and intervention. Chapter 14 spells out how the understanding of trauma and its treatment developed throughout the book can inform us about our own risk, and how we must use all our own medicine to protect ourselves. To be of help to our clients, we must stay healthy. And to stay healthy, we need the same things our clients need: social support in attachment relationships, self-regulation skills, an opportunity to talk about the traumatic impact of our work, and education.

I have interspersed clinical material and vignettes throughout the text. To preserve confidentiality, I have used pseudonyms and excluded or altered biographical details to preclude identification of individuals.

Acknowledgments

I have had a great deal of help in writing this book. The Helen Malsin Palley Chair in Mental Health Research funded much-needed time for writing as well as essential support services. The Menninger Professional Library has been an invaluable resource, and I am appreciative of Judith Kash's expert literature searches and Karen Flynn's help with acquiring and checking references as well as other secretarial assistance. I am particularly grateful to my colleagues in the Menninger Division of Scientific Publications, Mary Ann Clifft and Philip Beard, who provided expert consultation on innumerable editorial matters and helped edit the manuscript. Mary Ann's support and counsel have played a significant role in my development as an author.

The practical value of this book comes straight from the patients who have taught me about trauma and helped me to work out sensible explanations. I have also learned from many colleagues who have taken an interest in co-leading patient education groups. Kay Kelly and I have taught together for many years, and she initiated the application to family work. AnnMarie Glodich engaged me in the adolescent work and initiated its extension into the community. I have also benefited from the chance to work alongside many other colleagues who have joined me in leading groups, including Cindy Arnold, Miki Doron, Maria Holden, Janis Huntoon, Meredith Sargent, and Ella Squyres.

In many ways, this book owes its existence to Michael Coombs, my editor at Wiley, whose vision and expertise were invaluable. He encouraged me to write the best book I could and provided sound editorial advice from its conception to its completion. Several colleagues have graciously reviewed and critiqued portions of this manuscript, including Alice Brand Bartlett, Throstur Bjorgvinsson, Glen Gabbard, George Gergely, Peter Graham, Lisa Lewis, and George Thompson. I am particularly grateful to Kathryn Zerbe, who, in the process of reviewing several chapters, encouraged me to write with a strong voice.

Although my interest in attachment theory came from within, my expertise is largely a reflection of years' long collaboration with my colleagues in the Menninger Child and Family Center, Helen Stein and Peter Fonagy. Their fine minds and generous hearts have sustained me throughout the writing of this book. The opportunity to work with Helen in research and writing and to confer with her about clinical work has deepened my understanding of the role of attachment in trauma. Helen's careful review of the whole manuscript was both helpful and encouraging. Peter was the intellectual progenitor of this work, not only in his inspiring leadership of the Child and Family Center but also in his guidance throughout the writing. His substantial contributions to attachment theory and research have shaped my understanding of trauma. His unflagging enthusiasm for this book as he reviewed two full drafts has been a powerful incentive to see it through. Peter also has brought a treasure-trove of expertise across the Atlantic. I have learned much from our colleagues, Antonia Bifulco, George Gergely, Jonathan Hill, and Mary Target, and I hope that some of their thinking shines through.

It is ironic that writing a book extolling the virtue of family attachments takes a toll on the author's family life. I thank my wife, Susan, for her forbearance and encouragement, and for graciously allowing me the time and psychological space I needed to do this work.

Part I
Developmental foundations

Chapter 1

A DEVELOPMENTAL APPROACH TO TRAUMA

Experiencing trauma is an essential part of being human. (van der Kolk & McFarlane, 1996, p. 3)

Soon after being admitted to the hospital for an episode of severe depression, Mary came into one of my inpatient trauma education groups presenting herself apologetically as an 'imposter.' She said she had heard from other patients that the group was helpful; yet she did not really belong, because she had not experienced trauma. I responded by encouraging her to stay in the group, mentioning that we generally talk about coping with stress, which many patients find useful. I indicated that she could determine for herself if the group would be helpful to her. Over the course of a few weeks in the group, she began to connect her personal experiences to the educational material, and she gradually revealed some of her history.

Mary was an only child. Her mother had a serious mental disorder, and her father was emotionally unavailable and often away on business. Mary's mother was hospitalized for the first time just after Mary started school, in what was to be the first of many abrupt separations. For several months after her mother's first hospitalization, Mary stayed with her grandparents, with whom she'd had little prior contact. Mary's memories were sketchy, but she recalled being frightened and confused by her mother's sudden departure and by being shipped off to her grandparents' home in a distant city. Although the separation was extremely distressing, she remembered being treated well.

Mary never knew her mother's psychiatric diagnosis, but her description of her mother's behavior suggested a severe mood disorder, possibly with psychotic features. As Mary reflected on her history, she was able to acknowledge how frightened she was by her mother's erratic moods and violent rampages. One facet of the educational framework really hit home: *the essence of trauma is feeling terrified and alone*. With her mother's illness, her father's emotional and physical distance, and her own penchant for social isolation, Mary gradually recognized how feeling afraid and alone was a theme throughout much of her childhood. Prior to her own hospitalization, Mary had been relatively isolated and had been burdened by a series of stressors—the last straw being her mother's severe stroke, which left her uncommunicative. Mary recognized that her mother's recent illness was doubly stressful because it resonated with her mother's first hospitalization when Mary was a child.

Of course, Mary's feeling like an 'imposter' was not just a problem relating to the trauma education group. She had felt that there was no basis for her own difficult struggle with a mood disorder. She merely viewed herself as a 'poor coper.' She was able to use the group to understand the meaning of her depression and the basis of her difficulty overcoming it.

Mary's presentation is not unique. Many clients minimize their trauma. In essence, they think, 'It wasn't that bad, so I have no reason to be having all these problems.' Clients also see some types of trauma as more acceptable than others are. One client referred to her history of sexual abuse as an 'illegitimate trauma'—contrasting sexual abuse with being a combat veteran.

Our traumatized clients know better than anyone does what 'trauma' means. For many, however, this knowledge is intuitive rather than explicit. A major part of our clinical work entails helping clients construct a coherent narrative framework for their disturbance. As it was for Mary, understanding the concept of trauma can be an important part of that framework. And to help our clients develop that understanding, we therapists must have a clear grasp of some core concepts. Because trauma spawns such confusing mental states—in us therapists as well as our clients—clear thinking is a cornerstone of treatment. Thinking of trauma as 'feeling terrified and alone' may be one good place to start with clients, but there are several other fundamental aspects of trauma that we must clarify.

This chapter begins by spelling out core distinctions that pertain to many types of traumatic events. In brief, *trauma* refers to the enduring adverse impact of extremely stressful events. Much of this book is devoted to delineating this adverse impact from the perspective of developmental psychopathology, and this chapter provides a preview of that perspective. Having pinned down the concept of trauma, we will be in a position to tackle *interpersonal* trauma. Then I introduce the concept of a spectrum of interpersonal trauma based on the extent of interpersonal relatedness involved.

Impersonal trauma is at one end of the spectrum, and trauma in attachment relationships—what I will call *attachment trauma*—is at the other end. My thesis is simple: interpersonal involvement is a major contributor to severity of trauma, and attachment trauma is the worst.

This chapter delineates the range of impersonal and interpersonal trauma, and the next chapter focuses on attachment trauma in particular. As will be done throughout the book, the chapter closes with suggestions for educating clients.

CORE FEATURES OF TRAUMA

Trauma, like any other abstract concept, has fuzzy boundaries and is often used loosely. The Oxford English Dictionary (Brown, 1993), for example, lists its general usage as 'distress' or 'disturbance,' as in 'Finding the right desk on the first morning was the major trauma' (p. 3377). In such everyday usage, trauma becomes synonymous with stress. To be somewhat more specific, trauma can be conceptualized usefully as *extreme* stress, lying at the end of a continuum, with no bright line demarcating trauma from non-traumatic stress. To sharpen the understanding of trauma, I distinguish between potentially traumatic *events* and the trauma *response* and highlight the fundamental role of *controllability and predictability* in traumatic events.

Distinguishing events from responses

We often use the word trauma, like the word stress, in a way that blurs event and response. It is helpful to distinguish the event from its impact (Yuille & Tollestrup, 1992), but not as easy as it may seem. Events can be described objectively, from the position of an observer (one man pointed a gun at another and demanded money), but they are experienced subjectively (the terrified victim feared that he was about to die). Thus an event is partly defined subjectively on the basis of the individual's perception, interpretation, and emotional response. It is not the objective event, but rather the subjective experience—based largely on the meaning the event has to the individual—that determines whether the event will be traumatic. Individual differences play a major role in the outcome of exposure to potentially traumatic events, largely owing to the role of subjectivity. Of course the subjective response itself may be a reflection of a prior trauma history.

But what does it mean for an event to be traumatic? Webster's dictionary (Webster, 1979) offers two useful definitions. In the context of general medicine, trauma refers to 'an injury or wound violently produced.' In the context of psychiatry, a trauma is an 'emotional experience, or shock, which has a lasting psychic effect' (p. 1492). In a similar vein, the Oxford English

Dictionary (Brown, 1993) elaborates the meaning of trauma in the context of psychoanalysis and psychiatry: 'A psychic injury, *esp.* one caused by emotional shock the memory of which may be either repressed and unresolved, or disturbingly persistent; a state or condition resulting from this' (p. 3377). These dictionary definitions make two important points. First, in both general medical and psychiatric contexts, the trauma is not the event but its result. Second, trauma is an *enduring adverse response* to an event. From this perspective, the individual who has a horrific experience that did not have lasting adverse effects would not have been traumatized.

What kinds of events are liable to be traumatic? The *Diagnostic and Statistical Manual of Mental Disorders (DSM-IV)* (APA, 1994) defines trauma in the context of post-traumatic stress disorder (PTSD). To qualify for the diagnosis of PTSD, one must have experienced an event defined by Criterion A:

> The person has been exposed to a traumatic event in which both of the following are present: (1) the person experienced, witnessed, or was confronted with an event or events that involved actual or threatened death or serious injury, or a threat to the physical integrity of self or others; (2) the person's response involved intense fear, helplessness, or horror. (pp. 427–428)

Inherent in this DSM-IV definition is the distinction between objective events (that pose a threat or actual injury) and subjective response (fear, helplessness, horror). Both the objective event and the subjective response must be present for an event to be considered traumatic.

The account of a youngster referred to our trauma education group for adolescents illustrates the wisdom of including subjective as well as objective aspects of potentially traumatic events in DSM-IV. In the first session, he protested that he had no reason to be in the group. When asked why his doctor had sent him to the group, he enumerated a litany of violent events that he had witnessed in the context of drug dealing, including multiple homicides. He had witnessed and experienced events that involved actual or threatened death or serious injury, or a threat to the physical integrity of self or others. He maintained convincingly, however, that he was unfazed by these events. Given his antisocial bent, he felt a sense of excitement and invulnerability, rather than intense fear, helplessness, or horror. As his experience illustrates, blurring the distinction between event and response obscures individual differences that are a paramount contributor to trauma.

Albeit useful for diagnostic clarity and objectivity, I think the *DSM-IV* definition of potentially traumatic events is seriously off the mark. The exclusive focus on *physical* injury and on threat to *physical* integrity is too narrow. No doubt interpersonal trauma is often associated with physical threat or injury. Yet in the context of interpersonal trauma in general and attachment trauma in particular, threatening events need not pose physical danger to be traumatic. As I will discuss in Chapter 4, a threat to the integrity of the *psychological* self—in the absence of physical contact—is also potentially traumatic. Imagine the impact of screaming at a child, year after year, 'I hate you! I wish you had never been born!' Such attachment trauma may undermine the development of the self and related mental capacities, which constitutes trauma of the worst sort.

Uncontrollability and unpredictability

I launch discussion of trauma by asking clients, 'How would you define trauma?' In asking this question, therapists are likely to discover one way in which DSM-IV is right on the mark. 'Feeling helpless' will be high on any client's list. Another common reply is 'lack of control.' Down the list a bit will be 'unpredictable' or 'I never knew when it was going to happen.'

Consistent with clients' experience, Foa and colleagues (Foa, Zinbarg, & Rothbaum, 1992) synthesized extensive experimental research that points to lack of control and unpredictability as core aspects of stressful experience with traumatic effects. More specifically, they contend that uncontrollability and unpredictability of events of vital importance to the individual are traumatizing. *Loss* of control is even more stressful than *lack* of control.

Predictability and controllability may vary independently (e.g., one can predict but not control father's tirades after his regular bout of Friday night drinking). Yet unpredictability and uncontrollability often compound one another (e.g., mother's rampages come out of the blue). Unpredictability exacerbates uncontrollability, because the inability to predict danger leads to a generalization of fear. Predictability depends on cues that signal danger. Without any such cues, many facets of the general environmental context come to be associated with danger (e.g., mother might blow up anywhere at any time).

Foa and her colleagues marshaled extensive evidence that uncontrollability and unpredictability—albeit each in somewhat different ways—relate to four animal analogues of PTSD symptoms. In varying degrees, uncontrollability and unpredictability are associated with persistent increased arousal, heightened conditioned fear responses (analogous to reexperiencing symptoms), numbing, and avoidance. Although their review antedated *DSM-IV*, the literature on uncontrollability and unpredictability provides an apt framework for understanding the subjective experience of helplessness in the second part of Criterion A. Uncontrollability and unpredictability will be strong undercurrents throughout my discussion of interpersonal trauma. Moreover, in the realm of interpersonal (and attachment) trauma, being overpowered is a crucial relationship dimension of uncontrollability. The abuse of power is a major undercurrent in interpersonal trauma.

TRAUMA, PSYCHOPATHOLOGY, AND DEVELOPMENT

As a glance at the Contents will reveal, Part II of this book approaches trauma from the standpoint of psychiatric disorders. PTSD (Chapters 5 and 6) is the prototype of a trauma-related psychiatric disorder, and dissociative disorders (Chapter 7) are thoroughly intertwined with trauma and PTSD. Yet the potential psychiatric sequelae of trauma go far beyond PTSD and dissociation, and I will review several other psychiatric disorders and symptoms to which trauma may make a significant contribution. These problems include substance abuse, eating disorders, and self-harm (Chapter 8); depression (Chapter 9); and personality disorders (Chapter 10).

Comorbidity

Clients with a history of interpersonal trauma typically meet criteria for multiple psychiatric disorders, and the term *comorbidity* is often applied to this concomitance of diagnoses. For example, depression is frequently comorbid with PTSD. Widely accepted as it may be, this usage of comorbidity is technically incorrect. To be truly comorbid, two disorders should be independent of one another (Alarcon, Glover, & Deering, 1999; Winokur, 1990)—having one should not increase the probability of having the other. For example, hypertension and a sinus infection might be truly comorbid. Depression and PTSD are not.

We are not just splitting conceptual hairs here. An important agenda for examining myriad psychiatric disorders in relation to trauma is to understand their developmental progression. Alarcon and colleagues (Alarcon et al., 1999) elaborated a cascade model of PTSD in which symptoms, disorders, impairments in functioning, and environmental stressors are intertwined in a multitude of vicious circles. To take a simple example, a man with a history of severe physical abuse who develops PTSD in the aftermath of a beating uses alcohol to control the intrusive symptoms; his alcohol abuse leads to unemployment and fuels marital conflict, both of which in turn exacerbate his alcohol abuse; depression ensues and is further compounded by ongoing marital conflict and alcohol abuse; and so on. The cascade model entails a dysfunctional interaction between the individual and environment, with a snowballing of impairments and stressors that contribute to a downhill course of illness. This book provides a coherent framework for understanding such a dynamic interplay of myriad problems. Without such a framework, we therapists and our clients are left with a hodgepodge of diagnostic labels that make little overall sense.

By concentrating on traumatic relationships and serious mental disorders, this book carves out a circumscribed niche of the trauma field. Although persons with such extensive comorbidity comprise a relatively small segment of the clinical population, they account for the major burden of psychiatric disorder, for example, in terms of chronicity and resource utilization (Kessler & Zhao, 1999). They are difficult to help.

Biopsychosocial thinking

Although we have left the decade of the brain, the biopsychosocial perspective will remain. It is easy to give lip service to the value of a biopsychosocial framework, but it is difficult to live up to the standard of integrative thinking that this framework entails. The complexity of the neurobiology of PTSD is daunting. For many therapists, the *bio* part is more challenging than the *psychosocial* part. On the other hand, it is easy for the psychosocial perspective to fall by the wayside in the current penchant for biological reductionism, which is fueled by economic pressures to treat all ills with drugs in hope of a quick fix. Understandably, many clients are quick to grab onto the hope of a readily treatable 'chemical imbalance.' Many of our clients benefit from medication, but we can hardly treat attachment trauma without a psychosocial orientation.

Yet the biology of trauma is as important as it is daunting. I am convinced that we therapists must embrace biological thinking to understand our clients and, moreover, they must think biologically to understand themselves. Two biological perspectives are crucial: evolutionary biology and neurophysiology. Evolutionary thinking was at the heart of Bowlby's (1973, 1982) theory of attachment. And evolutionary thinking can illuminate our understanding of psychopathology. The lens of evolution enables us to grasp most fully that, no matter how pathological they may seem, our clients' trauma symptoms often can be best understood as adaptive efforts. Our continual focus on adaptation, informed by evolutionary thinking, can help us maintain a sympathetic attitude toward our clients' behavior and, ideally, help them become more compassionate toward themselves.

Without setting aside our psychosocial understanding, we therapists and our clients must also understand that trauma may adversely affect adaptation on the neurophysiological level as well as the behavioral level. Recent research is yielding bad news in this regard, and we should not give in to the temptation to sweep it under the rug. I will make a case for construing trauma as a *chronic physical illness* and explaining it as such to clients. This perspective helps trauma survivors develop a more compassionate attitude toward their struggles. Paradoxically, understanding the physical basis of trauma-related illnesses can provide a sense of relief. Recognizing that one has a chronic physical illness need not be a prescription for hopelessness but rather may clarify the importance of ongoing treatment and self-care.

Developmental psychopathology

In attending first to psychopathological outcomes, I have put the cart before the horse. Trauma is best understood from the perspective of developmental psychopathology (Cicchetti & Cohen, 1995; Rutter, 1989; Sroufe, 1997), which is concerned with the origins and course of individual pathways to adaptation and maladaptation. This perspective not only covers the full lifespan of the individual but also takes into account multigenerational processes. Developmental psychopathology aspires to integrate biological and psychosocial thinking. Developmental continuities and discontinuities, in both the individual and the environment, are lawful outcomes of dynamic balances among risk, vulnerability, protective, and buffering factors, all of which may be enduring or transient. *Resilience*—successful adaptation despite adversity—is just as pertinent as pathology, and change for the better is always possible, although constrained by prior adaptation. Attachment theory figures prominently in developmental psychopathology. Attachment shapes maladaptation and adaptation as a vulnerability or protective factor that exerts its influence over the course of the lifespan and across generations.

Nowhere is developmental psychopathology more pertinent than in the domain of trauma (Pynoos, Steinberg, & Wraith, 1995). At any age, trauma affects developmental pathways. Attachment trauma in childhood, however, is likely to have particularly devastating effects, because it produces a dual liability (Fonagy, 1999b; Fonagy & Target, 1997a). Attachment trauma not only generates extreme distress but also, more importantly, *undermines the development of mental and interpersonal capacities needed to regulate that distress.* This dual liability is the single most important theme running throughout this book, because it relates crucially to both psychopathology and treatment. Accordingly, after delineating the types of trauma that may occur in attachment relationships (Chapter 2), I will establish the foundation for the review of trauma-related psychopathology and treatment by examining attachment relationships (Chapter 3) and the impact of attachment trauma on the development of the self (Chapter 4). This developmental foundation sets the stage for psychopathology (Part II) and treatment (Part III).

Before embarking on this venture, I put attachment trauma into perspective by spelling out the full spectrum of trauma. Trauma can be arrayed along a spectrum of interpersonal relatedness. At the low end of involvement is impersonal trauma, for example, earthquakes and tornadoes. In the middle of the spectrum is trauma inflicted in an interaction with a stranger— a criminal assault or rape. At the high end of interpersonal involvement is trauma in the context of an attachment relationship, exemplified by father–daughter incest and wife battering.

Although attachment trauma may be the most pernicious in its contribution to serious mental disorders, other forms of interpersonal trauma as well as impersonal trauma are also crucial to our agenda. Many of our clients will have experienced multiple forms of trauma that cover the whole spectrum. Quite often a relatively impersonal trauma, such as major surgery, precipitates an acute episode of psychiatric disorder, owing in part to its meaning in relation to a history of interpersonal trauma, including attachment trauma. A woman with a history of incest may have an exacerbation of post-traumatic symptoms when she is faced with the prospect of anesthesia and surgery to be performed by a male physician.

RELATIVELY IMPERSONAL TRAUMA

In the spectrum of interpersonal involvement in trauma, the low end is exemplified by natural disasters, such as tornadoes, hurricanes, floods, fires, earthquakes, and volcanoes. Such events fulfill DSM-IV Criterion A insofar as they threaten death or physical integrity of self and others. Exposure to disasters is astonishingly common (McFarlane & De Girolamo, 1996). During 1967–1991, disasters worldwide killed seven million people and affected three billion. The lifetime exposure to disaster is estimated to be 13%, and there is a shocking differential exposure to disasters in the Third World as compared to developing countries: a ratio of 166:1.

Although PTSD is not a normative response to disasters, ample evidence indicates that such events are traumatic for many persons and pose a significant risk for psychopathology (Bolin, 1993; Green, 1993; Koopman, Classen, & Spiegel, 1997; Rubonis & Bickman, 1991). The Mount St Helen's volcanic eruption provided one of the clearest demonstrations of psychiatric morbidity associated with natural disasters (Shore, Tatum, & Vollmer, 1986). A community directly exposed to the eruption showed an onset rate of stress-related psychiatric disorders 11 to 12 times higher than that of an unexposed control community. Although this book focuses on interpersonal trauma, therapists should keep in mind that many clients who present with a history of interpersonal trauma also have undergone one or more impersonal traumas (Allen, Huntoon, & Evans, 1999b), which should not be overlooked.

To refer to impersonal trauma is to refer to the precipitating *cause* of the trauma as impersonal, for example, the weather. A tornado is an impersonal threatening agent. But many disasters are also associated with a *gruesomeness factor* (e.g., witnessing grotesque death or injury) that can be highly traumatic (Hartsough & Savitsky, 1984; Wright, Ursano, Ingraham, & Bartone, 1990). And the wake of devastation after disasters often includes traumatic interpersonal effects, such as traumatic loss and bereavement, which contribute significantly to post-disaster psychopathology (Rubonis & Bickman, 1991). Moreover, the interpersonal effects of such disasters go beyond bereavement to include loss of social support systems (Koopman et al., 1997). The aftermath of the Buffalo Creek dam collapse and flood in New York, for example, included demoralization, disorientation, and loss of connection associated with the dissolution of tightly knit communal groups and disruption of community support (Erikson, 1976). These interpersonal effects—along with the dam collapse itself—were attributable to human error and misjudgment that also contributed to long-term symptomatology (Green, Lindy, & Grace et al., 1990).

Tornadoes and earthquakes aside, there are multiple levels of human involvement in many disasters (Rubonis & Bickman, 1991), ranging from deliberate (e.g., arson) to indirect (e.g., a fire caused by faulty electrical wiring). Whereas natural disasters may lead to a sense of solidarity, technological disasters may lead to divisiveness, conflicts, and disputes over blame and responsibility that polarize neighborhoods and communities (Bolin, 1993). To complicate matters further, the devastating effects of an (impersonal) earthquake can lead to severe interpersonal stress owing to the contributing role of shoddy building construction. The impact of traumatic bereavement is compounded when the death is seen as preventable (Hartsough & Savitsky, 1984). Loss of faith in experts is another factor that compounds post-traumatic symptoms (Prince-Embury & Rooney, 1995).

Yet the extent to which interpersonal causation pervasively contributes to the traumatic impact of disasters remains unclear. Rubonis and Bickman's (1991) careful meta-analysis of 52 studies that employed quantitative measures of psychopathology showed significantly *higher* rates of impairment for *natural* as compared to human-caused disasters. Highlighting the role of uncontrollability and unpredictability, these authors noted the uncertainty and unexpected threat that exist for natural disasters. They pointed out that the ability to assign blame to other persons might pinpoint responsibility in a way that implies a solution and ultimate controllability.

Automobile accidents are prototypical of the intermingling of interpersonal and impersonal trauma. A sizeable minority of persons in these accidents develop PTSD (Blanchard, Hickling, Mitnick et al., 1995; Blanchard, Hickling, Vollmer et al., 1995; Ursano, Fullerton, & Epstein et al., 1999). Although automobile accidents are associated with a lower risk of PTSD than interpersonal trauma, they contribute substantially to the incidence of PTSD owing to their sheer frequency (Norris, 1992; Ursano, Fullerton, & Epstein et al., 1999). Moreover, a large class of motor vehicle accidents has a relatively high titer of interpersonal causation, namely, those associated with drunk driving. Some statistics for the United States are shocking (Sprang & McNeil, 1998). In one year, nearly 20,000 people were killed by drunk drivers, and nearly half of all 16- to 20-year-olds who were killed in motor vehicle accidents were killed by drunk drivers. In a recent decade, four times as many persons were killed by drunk drivers than were killed in the Vietnam war. Motor vehicle crashes associated with intoxication may be viewed as crimes rather than accidents, and research points to comparable rates of lifetime and current

PTSD in surviving family members and friends of victims of vehicular and other criminal homicide (Amick-McMullan, Kilpatrick, & Resnick, 1991). A related emerging area of clinical concern is PTSD in the wake of injury and dysfunction associated with medical negligence (Bradley, 1998; Reader, 1998).

Not only do relatively impersonal traumatic events have varying degrees of interpersonal involvement, but also a history of interpersonal trauma is no protection from impersonal trauma. Many individuals are victims of both interpersonal and impersonal trauma that may interact. As I will elaborate later (Chapter 6), trauma may accumulate in the form of sensitization. Thus a relatively impersonal trauma may be the last straw that precipitates overt symptoms in an individual with a history of severe interpersonal trauma. For example, in working with clients with a history of severe interpersonal trauma and associated psychopathology, I have been struck by the frequency with which psychiatric hospitalizations are precipitated by motor vehicle accidents. Although relatively impersonal (when not involving a drunk driver), these accidents—as well as a host of other traumas—evoke a core feeling of helplessness. Even in a relatively impersonal context, a sense of helplessness and the feeling of being out of control may constitute a reminder of prior interpersonal trauma.

INTERPERSONAL TRAUMA

As just discussed, the extent to which trauma is impersonal or interpersonal is a matter of degree. Without minimizing the impact of relatively impersonal trauma, I emphasize interpersonal trauma as most problematic and especially likely to lead to an array of serious mental disorders. Interpersonal trauma not only occurs in the context of an interpersonal interaction but also has the characteristic of deliberateness. As Gelinas (1993) put it,

> It is one thing to have a leg broken, or an eye put out in an auto accident; it is a very different thing to have someone intentionally break one's leg or put out one's eye. That injury didn't just happen, it was done. (p. 2)

Defining interpersonal trauma as a deliberate threat or injury in the context of an interpersonal interaction highlights the nature of the interpersonal relationship as an important dimension of trauma. Although attachment trauma may be the worst, ample evidence demonstrates that interpersonal trauma occurring outside close or intimate relationships also can be profoundly damaging. Tragically common forms of such trauma include criminal assaults, rape, and sexual harassment, as well as combat and other forms of political violence.

Criminal assault

Although statistics vary depending on samples and methods (Breslau, Davis, Andreski, & Peterson, 1991; Kilpatrick & Resnick, 1993; Norris, 1992), criminal violence is not rare by any standard. Illustratively, Resnick and colleagues (Resnick, Kilpatrick, Dansky, Saunders, & Best, 1993) assessed trauma exposure in a sample of over four thousand adult women in the United States, taking into account the type of trauma (e.g., rape versus other physical assault), fear of death or injury, and the degree of physical injury sustained. They found a lifetime prevalence of 10% for physical assault and of 13% for homicide of a family member. When sexual assault was included, over 35% had been exposed to some form of criminal victimization. Moreover, more than half those who reported a history of criminal victimization had been exposed to more than one incident. These data also attest to the high level of morbidity associated with criminal assault. Of those reporting physical assault, 38.5% had a lifetime history of PTSD. Of those experiencing homicide of a family member or close friend, 22.1% had a history of PTSD. The rate of lifetime PTSD rose to greater than 45% when the assault involved both life threat and injury.

As recent history attests, criminal assaults are not limited to one-on-one interpersonal interactions. A longitudinal study of a mass shooting in a small Texas town (North, Smith, & Spitznagel, 1997) illustrates the morbidity associated with such events. A man crashed his truck through the wall of a restaurant, held more than a hundred persons hostage, and walked around the dining room shooting victims at point-blank range, killing 23 individuals before he shot himself. Among survivors, the prevalence of PTSD in the six- to eight-week period after the shooting was 28.4%, and it remained relatively high (17.7%) a year later. Notably, women with a prior history of psychiatric disorder were a particularly high-risk group; 76% developed PTSD after witnessing the shooting.

Rape

Like the statistics for other forms of criminal assault, those on the prevalence of rape vary widely from study to study (Foa & Riggs, 1993; Kilpatrick & Resnick, 1993; Resnick et al., 1993). Moreover, rape is notoriously underreported and underdetected (Koss, 1993). A report from the Crime Victims Research and Treatment Center (1992) estimated that 1 out of every 8 women in America had been the victim of forcible rape. Of those women, 39% had been raped more than once, with an additional 5% being unsure how many times they had been raped.

Before PTSD came into the diagnostic lexicon, Burgess and Holmstrom (1974) identified a *rape trauma syndrome*. They conducted emergency room interviews of nearly a hundred victims of forcible rape and followed up the interviews with telephone contacts or home visits. An acute phase of disorganization was prototypical, and only a small minority of women were symptom free at follow-up. Using contemporary diagnostic criteria, Resnick and colleagues (Resnick et al., 1993) found an alarmingly high prevalence of PTSD associated with rape (32.0% lifetime and 12.4% current). Attesting to the traumatic impact of interpersonal violence relative to impersonal events, these authors found that persons with a history of criminal assault were three to four times more likely to have a lifetime history of PTSD compared to those who experienced non-assault Criterion A events (e.g., disasters, accidents, or witnessing someone being injured or killed).

Similarly Breslau's (1998) extensive review of the epidemiological literature on trauma exposure and prevalence of PTSD indicated that, of various kinds of traumatic events, assaultive violence (including rape and other sexual assault) is associated with the highest risk for developing PTSD. Moreover, females have an especially high risk of developing PTSD in the aftermath of assault. Yet, even learning of the sudden unexpected death of a close friend or relative constitutes a potential trauma. Although the risk of developing PTSD in the wake of this potentially traumatic event is relatively low (14% compared to 49% for rape in Breslau's review), the sheer prevalence of sudden unexpected death is so high that this kind of event accounts for a substantial proportion of persons with PTSD.

Sexual harassment

Sexual harassment covers a wide range of behavior. A great deal of sexual harassment (e.g., offensive remarks by co-workers), albeit stressful and destructive, is not traumatic in the strict (DSM-IV) sense of threatening physical integrity and evoking terror. When there is threat to physical or psychological integrity—coupled with fear, helplessness, or horror—sexual harassment itself can be a trauma in the strict sense. Rape by a supervisor would be at this extreme end of the spectrum where sexual harassment becomes a criminal assault.

Research on sexual harassment is limited. Generalizing from the trauma literature (Allen, 1997), the following factors are liable to increase the risk that sexual harassment will reach traumatic levels: (1) the extent of coercion, for example, making a job contingent on sexual compliance (e.g., *quid pro quo*); (2) the power differential in the relationship (e.g., supervisor versus co-worker); (3) the degree of physical contact involved; (4) the extent to which the harassment is embedded in a context of aggression, violence, and sadism; and (5) the extent to which the harassment is repetitive and prolonged. As these criteria make plain, abuse of power plays a central role in sexual harassment, as it does in rape. Compelling evidence shows that men who are prone to harass and aggress against women experience power as sexually arousing, often nonconsciously (Bargh, Raymond, Pryor, & Strack, 1995).

As would be the case with any severe stressor, a wide range of symptoms have been observed in conjunction with sexual harassment (Charney & Russell, 1994; Fitzgerald, 1993; Hoyer, 1994; Lenhart, 1996; Murdoch & Nichols, 1995). These symptoms may include anxiety, helplessness, and feelings of vulnerability; anger, hostility, and irritability; depression; feelings of humiliation; substance abuse; and somatic disturbance (e.g., headaches, gastrointestinal and cardiovascular symptoms, sleep and appetite disturbance, susceptibility to infection, and sexual dysfunction). Perhaps most important, sexual harassment commonly erodes self-esteem, undermining self-efficacy and leaving the individual filled with self-doubt. Eroded self-esteem, distrust, and sexual dysfunction can coalesce to destabilize the individual's close relationships.

PTSD is one potential consequence of sexual harassment (Fitzgerald, 1993; Hoyer, 1994). Although research to date is extremely limited, there is some evidence that a history of childhood or adulthood sexual abuse is associated with a higher risk of sexual harassment (Frazier & Cohen, 1992; Wyatt & Riederle, 1994). Thus a trauma history may not only sensitize an individual to the stress of harassment but also may increase the *risk of exposure* to harassment. Wyatt and Riederle (1994) speculate that a prior history of abuse may contribute to behavior that leads the individual to be perceived as vulnerable, may lead the individual to expect (and perhaps tolerate) victimization, and may impair judgment about the trustworthiness of others. These observations about the context of harassment are consistent with a large trauma literature on vulnerability to revictimization (Chu, 1991; Herman, 1992b; van der Kolk, 1989), which I will discuss further in the context of attachment and reenactment (Chapter 3).

Unfortunately, as is common with rape and other criminal assaults, a host of stressors may stem from the harassment and compound the individual's reaction. The process of filing complaints and the ensuing legal proceedings are notoriously stressful (Gutek, 1993). These proceedings may contribute to a sense of further revictimization at the hands of institutions and the courts. Harassment also commonly eventuates in the individual's loss of a job, coursework, or a major field of study. Thus the stress of sexual harassment is often compounded by many severe losses.

War and political violence

War is interpersonal (intergroup) violence on a massive scale, although the nature of the interpersonal involvement is as varied as the gamut of trauma. The US Army's motto, 'Steel on target,' renders the violence more impersonal, as do the increasingly common telecasts of laser-guided missiles in nighttime depictions with a greenish cast. In the realm of interpersonal assault are trench warfare and hand-to-hand combat. Terrorist bombings are a form of mass assault, and they exemplify on a horrific scale the uncontrollability and unpredictability at the core of trauma. At the extreme end of interpersonal trauma is prolonged torture in the context of an intense sadistic interpersonal relationship.

In its varied traumatic forms, war is staggeringly prevalent. McFarlane and De Girolamo (1996), for example, reported that there had been 127 wars and 21.8 million confirmed war-related deaths since World War II. The traumatic impact of war is all too plain. Combat entails continual exposure to destruction, injury, and—often grotesque—death on a massive scale over a long time period. Traumatic loss is rampant, for example, as soldiers contend with the death of buddies to whom they have become deeply attached under conditions of extreme stress. Combat also may do traumatic violence to one's identity insofar as it entails becoming a killer (Brende, 1983).

Given the extreme level of exposure, it is not surprising that the trauma field evolved in relation to the psychological devastation of major wars (Grinker & Spiegel, 1945). It was in the aftermath of the Vietnam war that PTSD was defined in DSM-III (APA, 1980). And it is in the context of the Vietnam war that we have some of the most grim findings about the scope and chronicity of combat trauma. The National Vietnam Veterans Readjustment Study (Kulka et al., 1990) showed a lifetime PTSD prevalence of 30.6% for men and 26.9% for women who served in the Vietnam theater. Nearly two decades after the war, the prevalence was 15.2% for men and 8.5% for women. The current prevalence of PTSD for World War II prisoners of war ranges as high as 50% (Blank, 1993).

EDUCATING CLIENTS ABOUT TRAUMA

Many clients ask for a definition of trauma, often ambivalently, with the intention of determining if their experience qualifies. I define trauma most simply as extreme stress, emphasizing intense fear, feelings of helplessness, and a sense of being overpowered and out of control. I pair feeling alone with feeling fear, for reasons that will become clear in the discussion of attachment trauma (Chapter 2).

In explaining trauma, I often distinguish between the objective events and the subjective experience as well as noting individual differences in response to potentially traumatic events. Clients are keenly aware of individual differences—most poignantly so when a sibling has gone through a similar experience with a seemingly better outcome. The notion of different responses to potentially traumatic events can be a sore spot, grounds for self-blame, and interpreted as proof of personal deficiency (e.g., 'I'm weak'). My educational goal is to foster the substitution of self-understanding and self-acceptance for self-blame and self-denigration. Often the client's self-denigration stems from a minimization of the traumatic events. I also bring up the concept of the dose–response relationship (Chapter 5), noting that the more severe and prolonged the trauma, the more the impact will be. There are individual differences in vulnerability, but each one of us has a breaking point.

I have found a way to present clients with a quick overview of trauma that encompasses much of the content of this book (see Figure 1.1). Borrowing from the family systems literature (Koch-Hattem, Hattem, & Plummer, 1987; Olson, Lavee, & McCubbin, 1988), I start with the concept of *stress pile-up*, wherein recent stressors reverberate with past trauma. As I will elaborate in the context of the biology of PTSD (Chapter 6), I note that a history of past trauma can sensitize persons to stress, such that they become more reactive than they would be without such a history. The reverberation of innumerable past traumas and recent stressors culminates in unbearably painful emotional states (including intrusive symptoms of PTSD), from which the individual understandably seeks immediate relief. Efforts to escape from emotional pain may include a retreat into isolation, dissociation, or depression. Or they may entail behaviors such as substance abuse, self-

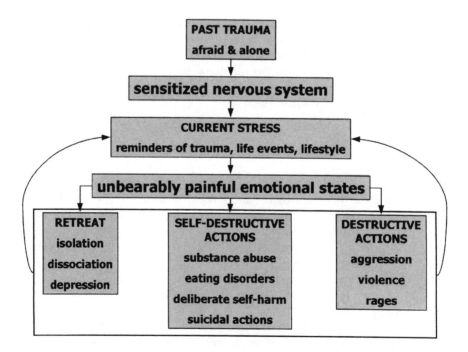

Figure 1.1 Stress pile-up, unbearable states, and vicious circles

starvation, bingeing and purging, deliberate self-harm, or suicide attempts. Or they may take the form of violent eruptions. All these efforts to alleviate distress, while sometimes powerfully effective in the short run, sooner or later backfire and contribute to additional stress, creating vicious circles. Rejection by the spouse leads to a feeling of rage, which is temporarily alleviated by self-cutting, which alarms and angers the spouse, leading to further rejection, and so on. Furthermore, by further sensitizing the central nervous system, the stressful consequences of destructive behavior may go beyond the interpersonal turmoil it creates.

Thus we have one pathway: stress pile-up (past trauma plus recent stress) → unbearable emotional states → maladaptive coping. We therapists endeavor through treatment to cultivate another pathway. We must help our clients to make the unbearable bearable. As will be discussed in Part III, we may do this by fostering a capacity for containing emotions through a stable treatment structure, self-regulation, and secure attachments (Chapter 11). Constructing a coherent trauma narrative, often a focal part of trauma treatment (Chapter 12), requires the capacity for containment and fosters it. Our broad educational agenda (Chapter 13) similarly contributes to containment.

I can present this whole framework to clients in a few minutes—not much more time than it took you to read it. Then we can get into the details.

Chapter 2

TRAUMA IN ATTACHMENT RELATIONSHIPS

> When mammals opted for a family way of life, they set the stage for one of the most distressful forms of suffering. A condition that, for us, makes being a mammal so painful is having to endure separation or isolation from loved ones. (MacLean, 1985, p. 415)

Attachment trauma occurs in an attachment relationship (Adam, Sheldon Keller, & West, 1995). Attachment trauma is especially detrimental because it undermines the primary function of attachment, which is to provide protection. Bowlby (1982) argued cogently that attachment evolved because of the relatively prolonged dependency of mammalian offspring on mothers. Given that we humans require the longest period of parental care, the development of human attachment is relatively prolonged and complex. For any mammalian species, Bowlby postulated that the overriding survival function of attachment is providing safety, with protection from predation being the driving force in evolution. Main (1995b) enumerated other survival functions, including protection from starvation, unfavorable temperature changes, natural disasters, attacks of conspecifics, and risks associated with separation from the group. Broadly speaking, attachment behaviors are evoked by danger, and their goal is to establish proximity to a protective attachment figure.

As Bowlby (1982) described, attachment behavior in humans not only provides physical safety but also is reinforced by a *feeling of security*. Thus attachment serves the function of comforting. Ainsworth and colleagues (Ainsworth, Blehar, Waters, & Wall, 1978) delineated the range of conditions that activate attachment behavior as including both environmental situations and internal states. The environmental conditions include separation and reunion with the attachment figure as well as any alarming events. The internal states include physical and emotional distress. Construing the main purpose of attachment as 'the provision of emotional security and protection against stress' (Rutter & O'Connor, 1999, p. 824) places attachment center stage in coping with trauma.

Parental caregiving is reciprocal with infant attachment (Bowlby, 1982; Cassidy, 1999; George & Solomon, 1999). Caregiving behavior evolved for the same purpose as attachment, to provide protection and, ultimately, to enhance reproductive fitness (Belsky, 1999b). The fundamental relationship between caregiving and reproductive fitness is chillingly illustrated by the hundred-fold increase in neglect and abuse associated with stepparents as compared to biological parents (Simpson, 1999). Although shaped by evolution and biology, the psychosocial development of caregiving is every bit as complex as the development of attachment, and the two are thoroughly intertwined. There are significant individual differences in the quality of attachment and parallel individual differences in the quality of caregiving that shape attachment. Although there is room for fairly wide latitude for caregiving to be good enough, there is little room for compromising the basic function of providing adequate protection. When caregiving falls short in this regard, development is liable to go awry (George & Solomon, 1999). Attachment trauma is the most extreme example of the failure of good-enough caregiving, because it not only constitutes a failure of protection but also places the child in danger. Imagine the fate of the child who needs *protection from the attachment figure*. Many do.

If attachment were confined to infancy, its role in trauma would be limited to etiology. But Bowlby (1982) adamantly maintained that attachment not only helps ensure security in infancy but also plays a key role in well-being and mental health throughout the lifespan. Of course, as Bowlby himself and Ainsworth (1989) later delineated, attachment follows a complex course of development beyond infancy. The range of attachment figures expands dramatically (i.e., beyond a mother figure to father, alternative caregivers, siblings, extended family, friends, partners, spouses, and even groups), and the expression of attachment changes markedly. Over the course of infancy, close body contact (e.g., molding to the mother) is supplemented by general proximity (e.g., having the mother in sight or nearby). As attachment relationships become internalized in the form of representations or internal working models, the feeling of security becomes further divorced from the physical presence of the attachment figure. As Ainsworth put it, these representations enable individuals 'to sustain a bond across time and distance' (Ainsworth et al., 1978, p. 714). But the growing capacity to tolerate separations never replaces the need for reunions, and this is nowhere more evident than in the context of trauma.

It should now be obvious that if we were only interested in impersonal trauma, such as natural disasters, attachment theory would be profoundly useful in working with survivors. Just bring to mind innumerable television newscasts of tragedies where tearful survivors find comfort in holding and hugging each other. But consider the importance of attachment theory for interpersonal trauma. Interpersonal trauma can drive a wedge of fear between survivors and other persons that prompts isolation, undermining the benefits of attachment. Just contemplate the plight of the rape survivor who needs the security of loving closeness but who is too frightened to tolerate being touched by her husband.

Now consider trauma inflicted in attachment relationships. Attachment trauma is likely to engender a fear of *closeness* to other persons. Think of attachment trauma not only as trauma that occurs in the context of an attachment relationship but also as a *trauma to the attachment system itself.* Keep in mind that attachment is a deeply rooted biological need. From the evolutionary perspective, attachment trauma is injurious to an individual's survival capacities. In this usage, attachment trauma is akin to head trauma, kidney trauma, and the like. Attachment trauma damages the safety-regulating system and undermines the traumatized person's capacity to use relationships to establish a feeling of security. To reiterate the central thesis in Chapter 1, attachment trauma creates a dual liability by creating extreme distress and undermining the development of the capacities to regulate that distress.

Throughout this book, I will discuss the potentially profound impact of attachment trauma on the self, relationships, and personality. To provide a foundation for this material, I will delineate the prototypical forms of attachment trauma and document their prevalence. I will show how the concept of attachment trauma in childhood illuminates our understanding of interpersonal trauma in adulthood. Although specific forms of adult psychopathology will be the focus of subsequent chapters (Part II), this chapter includes findings on diverse psychopathological outcomes to document the potential traumatic impact of profoundly disturbed attachment relationships.

This chapter provides a clear conceptual framework for organizing clinical narratives of attachment trauma. Attachment trauma has been overwhelming for our clients. But bearing witness to our clients' accounts of their trauma also can be overwhelming to us therapists. We therapists and our clients need an organized framework to help us make whatever sense we can of this experience. Just having some words, concepts, and categories to associate with otherwise unfathomable traumatic experience can alleviate some confusion and help us gain much-needed detachment and perspective. We need a detailed cognitive map.

ATTACHMENT TRAUMA IN CHILDHOOD

Attachment trauma in childhood can be construed as *maltreatment*—abuse and neglect. Clinical researchers generally agree more on the parental behaviors that comprise maltreatment than on how these behaviors should be classified. I use the conceptual framework developed by Bifulco and colleagues in their assessment of childhood maltreatment (Bifulco, Brown, & Harris, 1994; Bifulco & Moran, 1998). Bifulco's structured interview, Childhood Experience of Care and Abuse, is a retrospective measure that invites adults to convey their early experiences as stories. Open-ended questioning clarifies the nature and severity of maltreatment (Bifulco, Brown, & Harris, 1994). Bifulco's interview hews close to the clinical process, in some respects not being very far removed from trauma therapy. Using this interview, trained raters reliably classify the type and severity of maltreatment (Bifulco, Brown, & Harris, 1994). This assessment tool has demonstrated considerable validity in the form of corroboration of abuse by sisters (Bifulco, Brown, Lillie, & Jarvis, 1997) and in its ability to predict adult depression (Bifulco, Brown, Moran, Ball, & Campbell, 1998; Bifulco & Moran, 1998). Although Bifulco developed the interview for a community sample in London, we have found this assessment of maltreatment equally applicable to a community sample in a small city in the US Midwest (Fonagy & Stein, 1999) as well as to women referred for specialized inpatient treatment for severe trauma-related psychopathology (Stein, Allen, Brand Bartlett, & Gabbard, 1999).

There is no dispute that physical and sexual abuse, as well as gross physical neglect, are core categories of childhood maltreatment. Less theoretical and empirical attention has been paid to various forms of emotional or psychological maltreatment and their potentially traumatic consequences (Gorey & Leslie, 1997; Thompson & Kaplan, 1996), although much careful thought has been devoted to their definition (Barnett, Manly, & Cicchetti, 1991, 1993; Hart & Brassard, 1987, 1991; McGee & Wolfe, 1991; O'Hagan, 1995). In Bifulco's assessment, acts of emotional maltreatment are captured in two dimensions: parental antipathy (rejection, including verbal abuse) and psychological abuse (cruel and sadistic acts). The evaluation also includes a systematic appraisal of discord and violence in the home.

Physical abuse

Kempe and colleagues' (Kempe, Silverman, Steele, Droegemueller, & Silver, 1962) report on the *battered child syndrome* dramatically documented the appalling extent of physical abuse. Kempe's nationwide survey of hospitals in the United States found that 71 institutions reported 302 cases, with 33 fatalities and 85 instances of permanent brain injury. Battering was often associated with neglect and with a pattern of intergenerational transmission. Parents typically claimed innocence. Children under age three were at greatest risk, a pattern also observed in Malaysia (Kasim, Cheah, & Shafie, 1995).

Physical punishment can be distinguished from abuse (Wolfner & Gelles, 1993) but is often a precursor to abuse (Whipple & Richey, 1997). Bifulco's

(Bifulco, Brown, & Harris, 1994; Bifulco & Moran, 1998) assessment of physical abuse teases out some of the complexity of the abusive behavior and its psychological context. The interviewer evaluates the overall threatfulness of the abuse on the basis of the degree of violence, extent of injury, frequency of the incidents, and relationship to the perpetrator. Threatfulness also takes into account the perpetrator's state of mind, as illustrated by this interview excerpt:

> You could really gauge my father because his expression would change—his eyes would become quite manic. He definitely lost control without a doubt. You could see it happen. He would be sitting there and he would be annoyed. Then there would be an explosion and he was completely different. It would be very frightening. (Bifulco & Moran, 1998, p. 69)

It is impossible to provide exact estimates of prevalence of physical abuse, given widely varying methodologies and samples employed in research (Kaplan, 1996). Any single study must be considered illustrative rather than definitive, but a number of large-scale surveys attest to the magnitude of the problem. A telephone survey of over three thousand US households found that the prevalence of severe violence toward a child in the previous year was 11% (Wolfner & Gelles, 1993). Severe violence consisted of kicking, biting, or hitting with a fist; hitting or attempting to hit with an object; beating up; burning or scalding; threatening with a gun or knife; or using a knife or gun. A similar telephone survey recently conducted in Hong Kong revealed that 46.1% of parents reported severe violence in relation to a child in the year prior to the survey (Tang, 1998). A survey of nearly ten thousand residents over the age of 14 in Canada (MacMillan et al., 1997) found severe abuse to be reported by 10.7% of males and 9.2% of females. A survey of nearly two thousand US high school students revealed a lifetime prevalence of 31.5%, with 16.3% reporting physical abuse in the previous year alone (Nelson, Higginson, & Grant-Worley, 1995). Bifulco and Moran (1998) found that 18% of women in their London sample reported a history of physical abuse with 75% of the abuse occurring before age 10 and 41% before age 5. They noted, however, that this figure may be an underestimate because adults are unlikely to recall abuse in infancy or very early childhood.

Physical abuse has been associated with greater risk for a wide range of psychiatric and behavioral problems in inpatient (Brown & Anderson, 1991; Bryer, Nelson, Miller, & Krol, 1987), outpatient (Stein et al., 1996), and community samples (Briere & Runtz, 1990; Duncan, Saunders, Kilpatrick, Hanson, & Resnick, 1996). An extensive literature review (Malinosky-Rummell & Hansen, 1993) shows relatively consistent associations between childhood physical abuse and aggressive and violent behavior from childhood into adulthood, as well as an increased risk of substance abuse, self-injurious, and suicidal behavior. A study of physically abused adolescents referred to the New York State Department of Social Services documented the dramatic increase in risk for psychiatric and behavioral disorder associated with physical abuse, even when sexual abuse was excluded (Kaplan et al., 1998). Compared to a control group, the abused adolescents were seven times as likely to develop major depressive disorder or dysthymia, nine times as likely to show conduct disorder, and 19 times as likely to abuse drugs. Bifulco and Moran (1998) found a strong relationship between severity of physical abuse and adulthood depression: 33% of women reporting moderate physical abuse and 41% of women reporting marked abuse were depressed in the year prior to the interview, compared with a 14% rate of depression in non-abused women. In a careful prospective study employing court records documenting maltreatment, Widom (1999b) found that about a third of individuals with a history of physical abuse met criteria for a lifetime diagnosis of PTSD.

Sexual abuse

The scope of sexual abuse of women in the United States first became clear in the 1980s. Herman's (1981) summary of research indicated that between one fifth and one third of women reported some childhood sexual encounter with an adult male. Finkelhor's (1984) study estimated the prevalence of abuse of prepubertal boys to range from 2.5% to 5%. When early adolescent boys were included, the prevalence rose to 8.7%. Since these landmark studies, a host of surveys have been conducted (Feldman et al., 1991; Finkelhor, Hotaling, Lewis, & Smith, 1990; Goldman & Padayachi, 1997; MacMillan et al., 1997). In contrast to physical abuse, where both males (e.g., fathers) and females (e.g., mothers) may be abusive, sexual abuse—whether of males or females—is perpetrated far more often by males.

The widely varying prevalence rates of sexual abuse reflect differences in samples and methodologies. As Bifulco's (Bifulco, Brown, Neubauer, Moran, & Harris, 1994) assessment attests, a wide range of parameters characterize sexual abuse, including age inappropriateness, the stressful and threatening nature of the activities, extent of physical contact, frequency and duration of abusive events, extent of coercion, abuse of power and trust, and the relationship with the perpetrator. Moreover, the relationships among these parameters are themselves complex (Trickett, Reiffman, Horowitz, & Putnam, 1997). It is little wonder, as Gorey and Leslie (1997) commented, that disparate studies defy coherent summary. These authors reviewed 16 surveys of community samples and found that response rates and operational definitions of sexual abuse accounted for half the variability in reported prevalence rates. Aggregating across 25 samples and adjusting for response bias and operational definitions (excluding non-contact abuse) yielded prevalence estimates of 14.5% and 7.2% for males and females, respectively.

Consistent with an earlier study (Feldman et al., 1991), adjusted prevalence estimates gave no indication of an increase in the rate of sexual abuse over time.

Estimating the prevalence of sexual abuse in attachment relationships is extraordinarily difficult. Prevalence varies as a function of the relationship of the perpetrator to the child. Herman's early report indicated that 4% to 12% of sexual abuse of girls involved encounters with relatives, and 1% with fathers or stepfathers. Russell's early study found that 16% of women reported having had an incestuous experience whereas 31% reported sexually abusive experiences with a non-relative. In Finkelhor and colleagues' (Finkelhor et al., 1990) national survey in the United States, 27% of women and 16% of men reported childhood sexual abuse, but less than 2% of women and none of the men reported sexual abuse with a parent or stepparent. In their London sample, Bifulco and Moran (1998) found that sexual abuse involving physical contact was reported by 9% of women, with about one third perpetrated by a father or a surrogate father, and the majority perpetrated by other relatives, acquaintances, and strangers.

Of course, identifying the perpetrator's role (e.g., as a family member, relative, stranger) does not determine the *quality* of relationship between the child and the perpetrator (Trickett et al., 1997). Abuse in the context of a relationship with a caregiver, and a parent in particular, is likely to constitute attachment trauma. Ordinarily, attachment is the basis of incest avoidance (Erickson, 1993, 1999). Trickett and colleagues (Trickett et al., 1997) have documented that sexual abuse by biological fathers is especially traumatic, likely because it is embedded in an attachment relationship and thereby constitutes a greater betrayal of trust and exploitation of love.

Even if the percentages for abuse in attachment relationships are *relatively* low, the absolute numbers of women with a history of sexual abuse in attachment relationships are high. Inside or outside attachment relationships, sexual abuse poses a major clinical and public health problem. An extensive research literature (Browne & Finkelhor, 1986; Kendall-Tackett, Williams, & Finkelhor, 1993; Kluft, 1990b; Nash, Hulsey, Sexton, Harralson, & Lambert, 1993a; Polusny & Follette, 1995), details innumerable potentially adverse consequences of childhood sexual abuse. In their London sample, Bifulco and Moran (1998) found that sexual abuse had a high rate of association with depression, with half the women who had a sexual abuse history showing depression in the year prior to the study's interview. Widom's (1999b) prospective study showed that about a third of individuals with a documented history of childhood sexual abuse had a lifetime history of PTSD. Kendall-Tackett and colleagues (Kendall-Tackett et al., 1993) reviewed 45 studies of the effects of sexual abuse on children and estimated that abuse accounted for 15% to 45% of the variance in symptoms. Although common symptoms included fear, post-traumatic stress, behavior problems, and sexualized behavior, the authors emphasized that no single symptom was characteristic. Pertinent to attachment trauma, a close relationship with the perpetrator was associated with increased symptomatology.

Although the adverse effects of sexual abuse are now plainly demonstrated, the relationship between sexual abuse and psychopathology is not invariant. For example, Kendall-Tackett and colleagues (Kendall-Tackett et al., 1993) observed that one third of abused children were symptom free, whereas Browne and Finkelhor (1986) noted that less than one fifth of women with a history of childhood sexual abuse showed serious psychopathology in adulthood. Of course the literature includes an extremely wide range of severity of abuse, and severity as well as the relationship to the perpetrator plays a substantial role in the impact of the abuse. Furthermore, it is difficult to disentangle the effects of sexual abuse from the family pathology in which it is often embedded (Nash et al., 1993a; Rind, Tromovitch, & Bauserman, 1998). Dinwiddie and colleagues (Dinwiddie et al., 2000), for example, found a wide range of psychopathology to be associated with a reported history of childhood sexual abuse. Yet they failed to find significant differences in psychopathology between abused and non-abused co-twins, suggesting that shared family environment accounted for the symptomatology. Notably, abuse of both co-twins was associated with the highest rates of psychopathology in each.

Moreover, sexual abuse is often accompanied by other forms of abuse and neglect. Thus Zanarini and colleagues (Zanarini et al., 1997) aptly concluded that sexual abuse is not only a trauma in its own right but also can be viewed as a *marker* for severe family dysfunction. Hill and colleagues (Hill, Davis et al., in press) were able to disentangle childhood sexual abuse from quality of parenting as risk factors for adulthood depression. Although poor parental care was associated with a history of sexual abuse, and poor maternal care was associated with adulthood depression, these researchers found that a history of sexual abuse increased the risk of depression both in the presence *and absence* of poor maternal care. Even one incident of sexual abuse by a non-relative contributed independently to risk of depression.

Antipathy and psychological abuse

Antipathy entails parental rejection and hostility as manifested, for example, by criticism, disapproval, verbal abuse, coldness, ignoring the child, or favoritism (Bifulco, Brown, Neubauer et al., 1994). Severity of antipathy is indicated by its pervasiveness and the extent to which it is directed toward the child's character or the child as an individual (as opposed to the children as a group). The extreme of antipathy is the expression of hatred toward the child. Bifulco and Moran (1998) found that 33% of their London sample reported significant antipathy from at least one parent, but only 5% experienced antipathy from both parents. Antipathy from both parents predicted adult depression (i.e., 54% of women reporting such antipathy showed current depression, compared with 16% of those without this history).

At the extreme, antipathy shades into psychological abuse, and definitions of psychological maltreatment typically include antipathy (e.g., rejection and verbal abuse). Psychological abuse goes beyond antipathy in entailing cruelty, often with malevolent intent (Moran, Bifulco, Ball, & Jacobs, 2000). There is some consensus that the core of psychological maltreatment is frustrating the child's basic needs (Barnett et al., 1991; Hart, Binggeli, & Brassard, 1998). Because psychological abuse is often intertwined with other forms of abuse and is likely to be the most traumatic of the abuses (Hart et al., 1998; Hart & Brassard, 1987; McGee & Wolfe, 1991), it should be a top research priority and a major clinical concern. Bifulco and Moran (1998) observed,

> If neglect and loss of mother were the focus of study in the 1970s and physical and sexual abuse in the 1980s, it is psychological abuse that is likely to be seen in the future as the contribution of the studies of the 1990s. While the identification of psychological abuse marks the latest evolution of our own assessments of childhood experience, we also hope it is the last. (p. 115)

Psychological abuse encompasses a wide range of behavior and is especially challenging to define, although researchers have distinguished several types (Hart et al., 1998; McGee & Wolfe, 1991). Bifulco and colleagues (Bifulco, Brown, Neubauer et al., 1994; Moran et al., 2000) enumerated a comprehensive set of categories of psychological abuse: deprivation of basic needs (e.g., food, light, and sleep, as well as contact with other persons), deprivation of valued objects (e.g., belongings, toys, a pet), callous inflicting of marked distress or discomfort (e.g., being forced to eat something that makes the child vomit), cognitive disorientation (e.g., brainwashing), humiliation (e.g., public shaming), extreme rejection (e.g., telling the child of a wish for him or her to die and describing a horrible death), cruel threats of abandonment, terrorizing (e.g., playing on the child's fears), emotional blackmail (e.g., threats to harm others if the child fails to comply), and corruption and exploitation (e.g., forcing the child to take part in illegal activities). Moran and colleagues (Moran et al., 2000) found a history of childhood psychological abuse to be reported by 18% of women in their high-risk community sample. Psychological abuse most often consisted of repeated instances (at least weekly in almost half of those abused), was evenly distributed across all age groups, and rarely occurred in isolation from other forms of maltreatment. Psychological abuse was perpetrated almost exclusively by parents or parent surrogates, and there was a trend for the most extreme instances to be perpetrated by males.

Goodwin (1993a, 1993b) highlighted the extreme end of the spectrum of psychological abuse in her term, *sadistic abuse*. As Fromm (1973) also argued, *the core of sadistic abuse is terrorization for the purpose of gaining absolute control over the victim*. Although professional and scientific concern with psychological abuse is recent, Goodwin documented many historical precedents for sadistic abuse, including the Marquis de Sade and numerous serial killers. Various shades of sadistic psychological abuse can be distinguished according to the type of sadism involved. On the basis of associated personality characteristics and disorders, Millon (1996) distinguished four types of sadists: *explosive* (e.g., volatile, borderline), *tyrannical* (e.g., cruel, calculating, cool, menacing, psychopathic, paranoid), *enforcing* (e.g., compulsive, righteous, as might be associated with cruel discipline), and *spineless* (e.g., insecure, cowardly, counterphobic). Thus perpetrators of psychological abuse might be characterized as cruel, controlling, demeaning, nasty, vindictive, mean, malicious, menacing, malevolent, brutal, callous, and evil. Millon lamented the decision to exclude sadistic personality disorder from DSM-IV: 'How ludicrous it will appear to clinicians in the next decade when they reflect on a course of action that essentially "ran away" from perhaps the most significant personality problem of the 1990s' (p. 474).

Hart and colleagues (Hart et al., 1998; Hart & Brassard, 1991) reviewed substantial evidence for the adverse effects of psychological maltreatment, including a multitude of negative developmental consequences. Of course the effects of psychological abuse are often difficult to disentangle from other forms of abuse with which it is often intertwined (Moran et al., 2000). Briere and Runtz (1990), for example, found psychological abuse (including antipathy) to be highly correlated with physical abuse. Although all forms of abuse (sexual, physical, and psychological) were associated with symptomatology, psychological abuse was uniquely associated with low self-esteem. Excluding those with a history of childhood physical and sexual abuse, Ferguson and Dacey (1997) found that, compared to a non-abused control group, women with a history of psychological abuse showed higher levels of depression, anxiety, and dissociation. In their community series, Bifulco and colleagues (Bifulco, Moran, Stanford, Baines, & Bunn, 2000) found that childhood psychological abuse related strongly to chronic and recurrent depression, as well as suicidal behavior, in adulthood. A clear dose–response relationship was evident: the more severe the psychological abuse, the higher the risk of depression and suicidal behavior. A dose–response relationship was also evident in the finding that the higher the number of *types* of maltreatment (psychological, sexual, and physical abuse; neglect), the higher the likelihood of depression and suicidal behavior. Although psychological abuse was often confounded with other forms of maltreatment, it bore a stronger relation to depression and suicidal behavior than any other childhood adversity.

Complex abuse

Throughout this discussion, I have noted that it is often difficult to disentangle the effects of one type of abuse from those of another and that multiple forms of abuse increase the level of adversity (Bifulco & Moran, 1998; Bifulco et al., 2000). Our evaluations of childhood trauma (Bifulco, Brown, Neubauer et al., 1994; Stein, Allen, Allen, Koontz, & Wisman, 2000) also include consideration of an especially pernicious form of abuse: *complex abuse entails multiple forms of abuse in the same incident*. For example, physical and sexual abuse co-occur when a child is sexually assaulted and beaten. At worst, physical, sexual, and psychological abuse co-occur when a child is deliberately terrorized in the course of sexual violence. Fortunately, such episodes are sufficiently infrequent that results of systematic research on their impact are not available, although our research group is in the process of accumulating horrific data (Stein, Allen, Brand Bartlett et al., 1999).

Witnessing violence

As indicated earlier, the DSM-IV (APA, 1994) Criterion A definition of trauma includes not only directly experiencing traumatic events but also witnessing trauma. Extensive literature attests to the detrimental effects to children of witnessing violence in the home (Osofsky, 1995). Witnessing violence not only may evoke feelings of helplessness and horror but also may threaten the child with the loss of an attachment figure (Lieberman & Zeanah, 1999). This is attachment trauma. Bifulco's (Bifulco, Brown, Neubauer et al., 1994) assessment distinguishes among *discord* (e.g., arguments), *tension* (e.g., family members not speaking to one another), and *violence*, the latter including both interpersonal and non-personal violence (e.g., breaking things).

Jaffe and colleagues (Jaffe, Sudermann, & Reitzel, 1992) summarized early studies indicating that marital violence does not typically occur behind closed doors but rather is witnessed by children. Children may not only witness violence but also be injured in the course of it. For example, infants may be injured while being held, whereas adolescents are likely to be injured when attempting to intervene in fights (Christian, Scribano, Seidl, & Pinto-Martin, 1997). And children also are involved in calling for help and as the perceived precipitants of spouse abuse (Fantuzzo, Boruch, Beriama, Atkins, & Marcus, 1997). Furthermore, witnessing domestic violence is confounded with a host of potential developmental adversities, not least of which is physical abuse. Evidence suggests a direct relationship between frequency of spouse abuse and likelihood of child physical abuse, with a virtual certainty that chronically violent husbands will physically abuse a child and a high likelihood that violent wives will do so (Ross, 1996).

Witnessing marital violence is associated with a wide range of emotional, social, and behavioral problems (Jaffe et al., 1992; Osofsky, 1995). Given the confounding of witnessing marital violence with other forms of trauma, it is challenging to determine if witnessing violence per se is associated with adversity. Maker and colleagues (Maker, Kemmelmeier, & Peterson, 1998) made a start in disentangling the effects of witnessing violence from other adversities in their study of a wide range of symptomatic behavior in a sample of college women. Witnessing domestic violence was associated with violence in dating relationships, antisocial behavior, depression, and trauma-related symptoms. Witnessing violence was also associated with a history of physical and sexual abuse. When history of sexual abuse was controlled for, witnessing violence continued to relate significantly to violence in dating relationships as well as depression, although the relation to trauma symptoms diminished, and the relation to antisocial behavior disappeared. Furthermore, when controlling for physical abuse history, only the level of violence in dating relationships remained significant. That is, women with a history of witnessing domestic violence not only behaved more violently but also were more often victims of violence in dating relationships. Although Bifulco and Moran (1998) found hostility between parents to be highly associated with neglect and abuse, only neglect and abuse bore a significant relation to adult depression.

Neglect

Just as multiple forms of abuse may go together, abuse is often compounded by neglect. Whereas abuse generally consists of acts of *commission*, neglect generally consists of acts of *omission*. Numerous authors have commented on the relative neglect of neglect, not only in the research literature (Bifulco & Moran, 1998; Wolock & Horowitz, 1984) but also in referrals for child protective services (Ards & Harrell, 1993) and mental health services (Garland, Landsverk, Hough, & Ellis-MacLeod, 1996). Observing that not only childhood abuse but also neglect increased the risk of PTSD, Widom (1999b) commented, 'neglected children represent the largest component of official cases of child maltreatment confronting our child protective services systems today' (p. 1228).

The neglect of neglect is especially troubling in light of evidence that its adverse impact may equal or even exceed that of abuse (Egeland, 1997; Erickson & Egeland, 1996; Hart & Brassard, 1991). One particularly dire potential consequence of neglect is failure to thrive, evident in stunted growth, dejection and passivity, and impaired cognitive functioning (Erickson & Egeland, 1996; MacCarthy, 1979; Mackner, Starr, & Black, 1997). And the potential impact of neglect extends into adulthood. Bifulco and Moran (1998) found that neglect more than doubled rates of adult depression in their samples. Although van der Kolk and colleagues (van der Kolk, Perry, & Herman, 1991) found that sexual abuse was the strongest predictor of self-destructive behavior, neglect was a potent predictor of the failure to give up such damaging behavior despite ongoing treatment. Thus neglect may be a particularly pernicious form of child maltreatment insofar as it relates to imperviousness to care.

In the realm of *physical neglect*, Barnett and colleagues (Barnett et al., 1993) distinguish between failure to provide and lack of supervision. *Failure to provide* for physical needs includes the areas of food, clothing, shelter, health care, and hygiene. *Lack of supervision* compromises the child's safety and includes consideration of time left unsupervised, danger present in the physical environment, and adequacy of substitute caregivers, all taking into consideration the developmental needs of the child. Egeland and Erickson's (Egeland, 1997; Erickson & Egeland, 1996) prospective longitudinal study of mothers and children at risk revealed especially serious consequences of physical neglect in the four- to six-year-old age group. Compared to other maltreated (abused and emotionally neglected) groups, physically neglected children showed prominent symptoms of anxiety, aggression, unpopularity, and cognitive impairment. Neglect by itself was associated with academic failure extending into adolescence. At worst, physical neglect is fatal.

Although emotional and psychological neglect are somewhat more difficult to define and assess than physical neglect, they have been recognized in the literature on emotional and psychological maltreatment (O'Hagan, 1995). We construe *psychosocial neglect* as a superordinate term that covers a failure to support psychosocial development (Stein, Allen, Allen et al., 2000). Subcategories include *emotional neglect* (lack of responsiveness to the child's emotional states), *cognitive neglect* (failure to nurture and support cognitive and educational development, also labeled 'educational neglect' in the literature), and *social neglect* (failure to support interpersonal and social development).

Egeland and Erickson's (Egeland, 1997; Erickson & Egeland, 1996) findings from their prospective longitudinal study underscore the potentially profound adverse developmental consequences of emotional neglect. They use the term *psychologically unavailable* to describe parents who are unresponsive to their children's signals, particularly pleas for warmth and comfort. They describe psychologically unavailable mothers as detached and unresponsive, interacting mechanically, and taking little pleasure within the relationship. As these authors pointed out, physically neglected children are often emotionally neglected also, whereas the reverse is not true. Emotional neglect frequently occurs in the context of adequate provision for physical needs.

Stern (1985) gave a chilling example of psychologically unavailable caregiving in the face of meticulous attention to the infant's physical needs. Called in to evaluate the relationship between a mother diagnosed with chronic paranoid schizophrenia and her 10-month-old daughter, he observed the following behavior:

> When we first observed the baby arriving for one of her visits, the child was asleep. The mother gently took her sleeping baby and began to lay her on the

bed so she would stay asleep. The mother did this with enormous concentration that left us closed out. After she had ever-so-slowly eased the baby's head onto the bed, she took one of the baby's arms, which was awkwardly positioned, and with her two hands carefully guided it to a feather-like landing on the bed, as though the arm were made of eggshells and the bed made of marble. She poured herself into this activity with complete and total participation of her body and preoccupation of her mind. (p. 205)

When this mother was formally evaluated, she was observed to be the least attuned of all the mothers ever observed:

> In the course of two observations on different days, she performed no behaviors that met our criteria for affect attunement. . . . Yet at the same time she was attentive to the baby, overly so; she hovered to make sure that no harm befell her, tried to anticipate all her needs, and was totally absorbed by these tasks. (p. 206)

In Erickson and Egeland's (1996) longitudinal study, the impact of psychological unavailability in infancy was even more profound than that of physical neglect and other forms of maltreatment. They found nearly all children from this group to be insecurely attached, with adverse effects observable from infancy into elementary school. Developmental difficulties for these children included anger, non-compliance, lack of persistence, negativism, impulsivity, dependency, nervousness, and self-abusive behavior. They also noted a steep decline in performance on the Bayley Scales of Infant Development between 9 and 24 months. They concluded that this form of maltreatment was the most subtle, but its consequences were the most severe.

Although the consequences of neglect can be grave, they are not necessarily irreparable. Hill (Hill, Pickles et al., in press) examined the role of good adult love relationships in mediating between childhood neglect, as well as childhood sexual abuse, and adulthood depression in women. Both neglect and sexual abuse were associated with a lower likelihood of establishing a good adult love relationship, as well as being associated with depression. Absence of good love relationships in adulthood also increased the risk of depression. Yet establishing a good love relationship despite a history of neglect lowered the risk of depression (although the same was not true for sexual abuse).

ATTACHMENT TRAUMA IN ADULTHOOD

Bowlby insisted that attachment plays a vital role in life 'from the cradle to the grave' (Bowlby, 1982, p. 208). Just as the need for secure attachment does not end with adulthood, neither does attachment trauma. Abuse in adulthood has an overwhelming gender bias, consisting predominantly of attacks on women by men. And abuse in adulthood encompasses every form of attachment trauma discussed in childhood. Although the home is the wellspring of attachment, as Rose (1993) sadly commented, 'The home, thought of in our culture as a refuge, is actually the most dangerous place to be' (p. 465).

Physical abuse

Without doubt, battering has an ancient history. Lystad and colleagues (Lystad, Rice, & Kaplan, 1996) noted that a long tradition of domestic violence includes the 'rule of thumb,' which 'comes from an old common-law statute that imposed a limitation on men's disciplinary authority of "their" women by enjoining husbands from hitting wives with a stick wider than their thumbs' (p. 140).

In her classic work, *The Battered Woman*, Walker (1979) delineated the prototype of adult abuse akin to Kempe and colleagues' seminal paper on the battered-child syndrome (Kempe et al., 1962). Walker developed a profile of battering relationships based on detailed interviews of over a hundred women who volunteered to talk with her or her assistants. She construed battering as *repeated coercion in intimate relationships.*

Walker's observation of a three-phase cycle of violence common to battering relationships underscores the pertinence of attachment trauma to these relationships. In phase one, tension gradually escalates around minor battering incidents, with both members of the couple attempting to keep the violence under control. Phase two consists of the acute battering incident wherein controls give way. Phase three, the aftermath of the battering incident, is characterized by kindness and contrite loving behavior. Together with the observation that battering relationships often begin in the context of kind and gentle caregiving by the man, the phase-three interactions cement the battering relationship as a powerful attachment relationship: 'The women interviewed consistently admitted, although somewhat shamefacedly, that they loved their men dearly during this phase. The effect of their men's generosity, dependability, helpfulness, and genuine interest cannot be minimized' (p. 69).

When Walker wrote *The Battered Woman* in the late 1970s, she estimated that about 50% of women are liable to be battered sometime during their lifetime. As it is with any other form of abuse, the prevalence of battering is impossible to know with certainty. Rates vary in relation to samples and methods, as well as depending on whether recent incidence or lifetime prevalence is assessed (Bachman & Pillemer, 1992; Browne, 1993). Moreover, a large survey of US couples (Schafer, Caetano, & Clark, 1998) found a high level of disagreement between men and women about whether there had been a violent incident in their relationship in the year before the interview.

In this study, the lower-bound estimate of violence (both members agreeing) was 5.2%, and the upper-bound estimate (either member reporting) was 21.5%. On the other hand, a review by Holtzworth-Munroe and colleagues (Holtzworth-Munroe, Smutzler, Bates, & Sandin, 1997) suggested a 50% rate of violence in couples seeking marital therapy. Abbott and colleagues (Abbott, Johnson, Koziol-McLain, & Lowenstein, 1995) found a similar life-time prevalence among women seeking emergency department treatment (with 11.7% of these visits precipitated by domestic violence). Accumulating evidence indicates that marital violence has its antecedents in adolescent relationships, with estimates of dating violence ranging from 20% to 67% (Burgess & Roberts, 1996; Holtzworth-Munroe et al., 1997). As with other forms of attachment trauma, the injuries stemming from domestic violence are not only physical—at worst, fatal—but also psychological. Sequelae include somatic symptoms, depression, suicidal behavior, PTSD, and sub-stance abuse (Browne, 1993; Kemp, Rawlings, & Green, 1991; Lystad et al., 1996; Rose, 1993).

Although a great deal of research on domestic violence has been con-ducted in the United States, a notoriously violent country, domestic violence is garnering worldwide attention (Ellsberg, 1999; Fawcett, Heise, Isita-Espejel, & Pick, 1999; Horne, 1999; Kozu, 1999; McWhirter, 1999; Walker, 1999). Horne (1999) reported domestic violence rates as high as 60% in some developing countries, and Ellsberg (1999) reported a 52% lifetime prevalence of domestic abuse in Nicaragua, with 70% of the reports of significant emo-tional distress among ever-married women stemming from domestic abuse. Horne (1999) reported a high level of domestic violence in Russia, where 14,000 women are killed annually by their male partners. Walker's (1999) international perspective on domestic violence not only emphasizes the critical role of cultural factors but also underscores that domestic violence should be viewed as a human rights issue that is intertwined with state-sanctioned violence: 'rape and brutal physical beatings of the enemy's women have been considered the just spoils of war' (p. 22).

The relation of gender to physical abuse between intimate partners is complex. It is widely reported that women are as physically aggressive as men in intimate relationships (Bachman & Pillemer, 1992; Holtzworth-Munroe et al., 1997; Lystad et al., 1996; Schafer et al., 1998). But these statis-tics are misleading. Although the occurrence of an incident may be roughly equivalent, the frequency and severity of aggression (as well as the severity of injury, the likelihood of death, and psychological sequelae) show an extremely strong gender bias. Male aggression toward women is far more intense and damaging than female aggression toward men. Moreover, the motivation is different. Whereas men are more likely to resort to aggression to dominate and control, women are more likely to use aggression for self-defense, retaliation, and expression of anger (Bachman & Pillemer, 1992; Browne, 1993; Holtzworth-Munroe et al., 1997; Lystad et al., 1996).

Sexual abuse

In *The Battered Woman*, Walker wrote, 'When I first conceived this book, I did not plan to include a chapter on sexual abuse, since I wanted to avoid the sensationalism which might result from describing sexual behavior in a violent relationship' (Walker, 1979, p. 107). But sexual violence in intimate relationships should not be ignored—although it has received relatively little attention in relation to physical abuse, and it is underreported in the extreme. Walker gave many detailed examples of bizarre and horrific sexual abuse, and she provided ample evidence that sexual coercion and battering alternate with loving and exciting sexual behavior (often in courting and in phase three).

A number of reviews of domestic violence include reference to sexual abuse (Browne, 1993; Burgess & Roberts, 1996; Lystad et al., 1996; Rose, 1993). Current evidence suggests that marital rape occurs in 10–14% of intimate relationships (Mahoney & Williams, 1998). The prevalence of rape in intimate relationships increases in high-risk populations, for example, ranging from 20–30% in couples seeking treatment, to 34–59% in couples where battering occurs, and 50–70% of women seeking shelter from battering (Browne, 1993; Mahoney & Williams, 1998). Walker (1979) reported that most women in her study considered themselves to have been raped.

As Mahoney and Williams (1998) documented, women are far more likely to be raped by an intimate partner than by a stranger. And marital rapes are by no means less severe. Roughly the same proportion of women raped by husbands fear for their life during the rape as do women raped by strangers, and these rapes are often prolonged, going on for hours. As with stranger rapes, marital rapes are often intertwined with violence and threats of violence. As in other instances of domestic violence, children often witness marital sexual assaults. Furthermore, unlike rapes by a stranger, marital rape is repeated, with half of women reporting a history of 20 or more marital rapes. It is not surprising that psychological consequences of marital rape are likely to be more severe than those of stranger rape. Not only does the victim of marital rape live with the rapist and experience repeated assault, but also this assault occurs in the context of an attachment relationship, which should be—and at times is—comforting and safe.

Psychological abuse

Like physical and sexual abuse, psychological abuse is not confined to parent–child interactions. Although physical and sexual assaults have captured most of the attention of researchers, verbal assaults (the adult counterpart of parental antipathy toward children) can be highly detrimental in adulthood as well as childhood (Holtzworth-Munroe et al., 1997). Kemp and colleagues (Kemp et al., 1991) compared physically battered and verbally abused women and found a surprisingly small disparity between the two samples in PTSD (81% for physically battered and 63% for verbally abused but not physically battered women).

Therapists who underestimate the damage done by verbal assaults do so at their peril. In a psychoeducational group, I advised drawing the line at physical aggression in an intimate relationship, and many members took umbrage at this criterion. They protested that verbal assaults were far more destructive to their well-being than physical assaults. Their protest would not have surprised Walker:

> Verbal battering may well be the most powerful coercive technique experienced in a battering relationship. Despite having suffered severe physical injuries, most of the women interviewed in this sample reported that verbal humiliation was the worst kind of battering they had experienced. (Walker, 1979, p. 172).

In adulthood as well as childhood, verbal abuse often is only the tip of the iceberg of psychological maltreatment. Recall that, in Walker's (1979) view, the essence of a battering relationship is coercion. As described earlier, coercive power is at the core of sadistic abuse. Walker commented that, during phase one of battering, the psychological torture is most problematic. As she described, physical and psychological abuse are typically inseparable, with the resulting terror contributing to pervasive physical and psychological problems, including suicide. Of course the psychological coercion and terrorization are also backed up by the threat of physical and sexual violence. Moreover, Walker documented the severe emotional and economic deprivation that also may be employed in the service of coercion. Hence, as it often does with children, neglect may compound abuse in adult attachment relationships.

Herman (1992b) delineated the multifaceted aspects of psychological abuse in the context of captivity—whether that captivity is in prisons, concentration camps, slave labor camps, religious cults, brothels, or families. LaMothe (1999) captured the pernicious effects of such abuse in his concept of *malignant trauma*. Echoing Fromm's (1973) description of the sadistic personality, Herman characterized the perpetrator's motivation as the intent to create a willing victim. Repetitively inflicting psychological trauma establishes control. Herman underscored how violence and psychological abuse are intertwined but also pointed out that threats of violence are more frequent than actual resort to violence. Moreover, threats against others—children, parents, and friends—are common forms of coercive control. As Herman's delineation of the various forms of captivity in which psychological abuse occurs attests, psychological abuse in adulthood is not confined to attachment relationships. Yet, as she also elaborated, this form of abuse often eventuates in traumatic bonding, which exploits attachment needs (see Chapter 3).

Relatively little research has been conducted on the prevalence of psychological abuse in adult attachment relationships. Consistent with Walker's observations, Holtzworth-Munroe and colleagues (Holtzworth-Munroe et al., 1997) confirmed an extremely high prevalence of psychological abuse in the context of physical abuse. Prevalence figures for psychological abuse ranged from 33% to 58% in their national survey, suggesting that psychological abuse is characteristic of physically abusive relationships and normative in our culture. In a related vein, Mahoney and Williams' (1998) review noted the frequent intertwining of psychological and sexual abuse in marriage. That is, sexual abuse often occurs in the context of interpersonal coercion (e.g., threats to leave), with such coercion being more distressing than physical threats.

Elder abuse

The developmental perspective on attachment trauma not only may be extended into adulthood but also applies to old age. Although elder abuse is a relatively new focus of research, it is likely to become an increasingly prevalent problem with the aging of the population.

Sadly, all forms of abuse and neglect that pertain to the early end of the developmental spectrum apply as well to the late end of the spectrum. Furthermore, in old age, as in childhood, neglect takes on particularly grave import. As Goldstein (1996) noted, the frail elderly and those with dementia are at particularly high risk. Goldstein's review of the literature found that abuse is perpetrated primarily by spouses but also by adult children and siblings as well as by others. Among adult children, sons are more frequently abusive than daughters. Prevalence data for a range of nations are accumulating (Bachman & Pillemer, 1992; Comijs, Pot, Smit, Bouter, & Jonker, 1998). Although statistics vary depending on the sample and type of abuse, prevalence rates for elder abuse in the range of 2–5% have been reported. Elder abuse and neglect are associated not only with emotional distress, physical injury, and financial loss but also with an increased risk of mortality (Lachs, Williams, O'Brien, Pillemer, & Charlson, 1998).

ATTACHMENT TRAUMA AND PSYCHOPATHOLOGY

All sorts of traumas are risk factors for psychopathology, and it is challenging to find any specificity in the trauma–psychopathology relationship. As clinicians and researchers have documented, abuse and neglect in childhood and adulthood have far-ranging effects. Herman (1992a) captured these devastating effects in her concept of *complex PTSD* that results from prolonged interpersonal trauma—often in the context of attachment relationships.

Among the hallmarks of complex PTSD are a multiplicity of symptoms (e.g., somatization, dissociation, prolonged depression), relationship disturbance (e.g., vacillations between close attachment and isolation), and a risk for experiencing repeated harm at the hands of oneself and others.

We will grasp the potentially devastating impact of attachment trauma on the self and relationships more fully in subsequent chapters. Here I point out how some generic features of traumatic events are especially characteristic of attachment trauma. Foa and colleagues (Foa et al., 1992) proposed that PTSD is most likely to result from trauma in a previously safe or pleasant environment or despite behavior that previously produced feelings of safety or pleasure. They cited Masserman's (1943) animal research indicating that pairing an aversive stimulus with an appetitive response (reward) is especially stressful. Indeed Masserman construed this experimental paradigm as *emotional trauma*. As Foa and colleagues (Foa et al., 1992) found, *loss* of control is potentially more traumatic than *lack* of control. Attachment trauma contains all these problematic features. Feelings of security, comfort, protection, and safety alternate with feelings of lack of control, helplessness, and terror. This interplay is characteristic not only of childhood maltreatment but also of the cycle of violence that Walker (1979) identified as prototypical of adulthood battering relationships.

Dose–response relationship

The well-demonstrated dose–response relationship noted in Chapter 1 also underscores the potentially devastating impact of attachment trauma. The more extensive the trauma exposure, the more severe the associated psychopathology is likely to be (March, 1993; Weiner, 1992). This relationship holds whether the extent of exposure entails proximity to a volcano (Shore et al., 1986) or a schoolyard shooting (Pynoos & Nader, 1989), or the level of involvement in combat (Goldberg, True, Eisen, & Henderson, 1990).

Although many interpersonal traumas are single events (e.g., criminal assaults), many exposed individuals tend to be victims of multiple traumas. Furthermore, although the magnitude, frequency, and duration of events that make up attachment trauma vary widely, attachment trauma is typically repeated because it occurs in the context of an enduring relationship. Moreover, as discussed earlier, trauma occurring in attachment relationships often entails multiple forms of abuse combined with neglect. Bifulco and Moran (Bifulco & Moran, 1998; Bifulco et al., 2000) found clear evidence of a dose–response relationship for childhood abuse. The more types of abuse, the higher the risk of adult depression. For example, in one series, they observed a clear 'gradient, with 38% of those with two types of abuse becoming depressed, 26% with one and 14% with none' (Bifulco & Moran, 1998, p. 124). As noted earlier in this chapter, one episode of complex abuse may entail multiple forms of abuse. Disentangling the effects of different types of maltreatment, singly and in combination, is a high priority for research (Cicchetti & Toth, 1995).

Zanarini and colleagues' (Zanarini et al., 1997) study of the relation between childhood abuse and borderline personality disorder (BPD) illustrates the inextricable association between attachment trauma and the dose–response relationship. These authors found a wide range of experiences of abuse and neglect to be characteristic of patients with BPD, and these various forms of trauma typically occurred in combination. They noted that sexual abuse rarely occurred in a vacuum but rather was associated with more chaotic environments that involved emotional, verbal, and physical abuse, as well as emotional and physical neglect. In such instances, the attachment relationships simultaneously generate distress and fail to provide needed protection, security, and comforting.

Individual differences and resilience

A counterpoint to the robustness of the dose–response relationship is the paramount role of individual differences in mediating reactions to stress and trauma (Weiner, 1992). Substantial evidence links childhood adversity to poor adult outcomes (Rutter & Maughan, 1997) but, as noted in Chapter 1, resilience is often intertwined with psychopathology. Therapists who treat clients with a history of severe interpersonal trauma naturally assume that severe psychopathology is a universal outcome. Most therapists are unlikely to have systematic experience with exposed individuals who have a relatively good outcome.

This point has been driven home in my colleagues' prospective study of the relation between childhood experience and adult outcome for a sample of individuals seen in a preschool setting for emotionally disturbed children (Fonagy & Stein, 1999). They are accumulating a series of cases in which extent of childhood adversity documented in medical records and in Bifulco's (Bifulco, Brown, Neubauer et al., 1994) retrospective interview can be compared with adult outcome assessed by psychiatric diagnosis and measures of adult functioning (Hill, Fudge, Harrington, Pickles, & Rutter, 1995; Hill, Harrington, Fudge, Rutter, & Pickles, 1989). The research team's endeavors to infer adult outcome from knowing the childhood history (and vice versa) has been a humbling experience. The sheer diversity of outcomes associated with adversity, coupled with the staggering array of factors that appear to mediate these diverse outcomes—often seemingly idiosyncratic— is daunting. Particularly important in this research is the possibility that trauma in one or more attachment relationships may be offset by security in other attachment relationships (Stein, Fonagy, Ferguson, & Wisman, 2000). More generally, such factors as positive temperamental features, early competence, a supportive alternative caregiver, good school experience, an organized home environment, and a good adulthood love relationship are likely to foster resilience (Egeland, 1997; Hill, Pickles et al., in press; Rutter, 1999). Sadly, however, attachment trauma is likely to impinge adversely on such resilience-promoting factors.

EDUCATING CLIENTS ABOUT ATTACHMENT TRAUMA

Of all the topics we teach, attachment trauma is the most fraught with peril. A core symptom of PTSD is reexperiencing the trauma on exposure to reminders of it. Delineating the various forms of trauma—interpersonal trauma in general and attachment trauma in particular—invariably evokes painful memories. I learned the hard way in conducting psychoeducational groups for inpatients in specialized trauma treatment.

Although it is not the rule, discussions of attachment trauma can be overwhelming. A particularly difficult session illustrates the hazards of delving into a discussion of trauma. A patient's question about 'emotional abuse' prompted me to describe psychological abuse, including the concepts of cruelty and coercion. One of the group members responded by giving a horrific example of being tormented in childhood as well as her response to it. Two other group members quickly became highly distressed. One went into a dissociative state, and another abruptly left the room. At this juncture, I belatedly reiterated the request that individuals refrain from describing the details of their individual trauma history to avoid evoking undue anxiety in other group members. This prompted a strong protest that I was stifling participants' need to disclose their individual traumas, notwithstanding the adverse impact on other patients. Although this sort of distress and conflict can ensue from the discussion of details of any type of trauma, I realized belatedly that the focus on psychological abuse was especially difficult for patients to manage.

You might think that talking about abuse would be more problematic than talking about neglect. Not so. I still recall an extremely distressing experience from many years ago when I first talked about emotional neglect in a psychoeducational group. I focused on the failure to meet attachment needs and, in particular, the experience of never feeling special or loved, as emphasized in van der Kolk and colleagues' work on self-destructive behavior (van der Kolk et al., 1991). The entire group sank into a state of despondency that I could not alleviate. This experience drove home the idea that the reexperiencing of neglect can be even more painful than the reexperiencing of abuse. It is not uncommon for patients with a history of horrific abuse to report that feeling unloved was the worst part.

In teaching patients, I generally focus on generic aspects of trauma, such as the dose–response relationship and the role of uncontrollability and unpredictability. I enumerate the different types of interpersonal and attachment trauma in a relatively cursory fashion to avoid excessive provocation of traumatic memories. Having learned the hard way, rather than dwelling on neglect per se, I mention neglect in the context of frightening (e.g., abusive) events. I present the thesis that it is the combination of frightening experience (abuse) and the absence of restorative comforting (emotional neglect) that can be most traumatic. Yet even the briefest reference to neglect can quickly evoke extremely painful feelings. Toward the end of one group session, for example, I was prompted by a patient's question about trauma to write 'afraid and <u>alone</u>' on the blackboard, underscoring the latter. Suddenly a woman who had appeared calm and composed throughout the group up to that point began to cry. She described her sense of desperation about relentless episodes of depression, stating that she could no longer 'fight it.' But the most painful part of this experience was feeling alone, as her husband was unable to comprehend her pain or to provide adequate comfort.

If teaching about different aspects of trauma is so fraught with peril, why do it? Clients tend to minimize the trauma they have undergone—'It wasn't that bad!' Consequently they blame themselves for the adverse outcome they have experienced. Thus one message is: 'It *was* that bad.' Of course we therapists are walking a tightrope in endeavoring to help clients understand the severity of their experience without further demoralizing them or evoking overwhelming reexperiencing symptoms. But it is important to counter the view that only certain kinds of trauma, such as sexual or physical abuse, count.

In teaching clients about the impact of trauma, one of the most helpful interventions is to help them see that their responses are natural. The intent of this straightforward and seemingly universal educational intervention is to diminish self-blame for the adverse outcome. But here again we walk a tightrope. As I put it previously in a book for patients, 'You'll notice that I keep insisting that various forms of difficulty are *natural* reactions to traumatic experience. To say that reactions are natural and understandable is not to say that they are *inevitable*' (Allen, 1995a, p. 16). As noted in Chapter 1, although therapists may lose sight of it, patients are keenly aware that other individuals have undergone trauma without a severe adverse outcome. Many patients document this contrast by giving accounts of siblings who have fared better or friends who have had similar traumatic experiences but are not experiencing such severe disturbance.

I point out that many mediating factors contribute to diverse outcomes, including genetic factors and temperament, as well as potentially buffering factors such as social support. With a few such leads, many patients are able to reflect on factors that may differentiate them from their ostensible counterparts. For example, one group member who was chronically depressed and suicidal compared herself to a sister who was also physically abused.

She described herself as characteristically compliant and submissive, but she observed that her sister was temperamentally more 'feisty'—indeed, combative. She noted, however, that her sister's outcome was not entirely benign. Although her sister was not suicidal, her impulsive aggressiveness continued into adulthood and contributed to significant problems in relationships.

In talking with clients about trauma, I continually emphasize individual differences in trauma history, trauma-related problems, and response to treatment interventions. In this chapter I have emphasized how trauma may undermine the role of attachment in providing protection and reducing distress. In the next chapter I will discuss how trauma relates to individual differences in patterns of attachment in childhood and adulthood.

Chapter 3

ATTACHMENT, RELATIONSHIPS, AND REENACTMENT

If hoping is developmentally based on having experienced the mutuality of trust and having received some benevolent care, a person may be prepared by such experiences for meeting adverse circumstances with quiet courage. (Pruyser, 1987, p. 472)

This chapter and the next delve more deeply into the main theme I have begun to develop: *attachment is the foundation for distress regulation*. This chapter examines different patterns of attachment as they bear on distress regulation, and the next chapter shows how the self evolves out of different patterns of attachment relationships so as to foster distress regulation—or fail to do so.

As it is in clinical practice, our task in this chapter is one of pattern recognition, identifying recurring themes in interactions. The logic is simple: interactions generate mental representations that underpin subsequent interactions. This propagation of representations is intergenerational as well as developmental, passed on from one generation to the next as well as evolving from childhood into adulthood. Nowhere is the developmental and intergenerational propagation of relationship patterns more evident than in the realm of attachment theory. And attachment theory usefully classifies the representations that underlie traumatic relationships. This is no accident, because Bowlby developed attachment theory in the context of maltreatment and neglect, and trauma continues to preoccupy attachment researchers. Moreover, I find attachment theory especially useful in educating clients, because its core concepts make intuitive sense and attachment patterns are elegant in their simplicity.

ATTACHMENT AND PHYSIOLOGICAL REGULATION

Chapter 2 presented the biological function of attachment in terms of its survival value—protection from predators and other dangers. The survival value of attachment is intertwined with distress regulation. Danger, including vulnerability occasioned by separation, heightens attachment needs with concomitant physiological arousal. The aroused offspring emits distress signals that draw the attention of the caregiver and prompt reestablishment of proximity and protection (Field, 1985; Hofer, 1995). *Reunion reduces physiological arousal and associated emotional distress.* When a frightened monkey reestablishes ventral–ventral contact with the mother, hypothalamic–pituitary–adrenal axis activity and sympathetic nervous system arousal rapidly decrease (Suomi, 1999). These neurobiological systems play a key role in stress and the physiology of PTSD (see Chapter 6).

Although separation and reunion are associated with multiple neurochemical and neuroendocrine changes, the involvement of the endogenous opioid (narcotic) system is particularly instructive (Field & Reite, 1985; Hofer, 1995; Panksepp, Nelson, & Bekkedal, 1999). Opioids mediate the comforting experience of attachment, such that separation is akin to opiate withdrawal and reunion akin to opiate administration. Thus attachment is anchored in powerful reinforcement at the neurobiological level, and it is little wonder that narcotics can be a powerful substitute for attachment.

Evolution has engineered a clever arrangement that powerfully reinforces attachment behavior to promote survival. But the biological function of attachment does not end there. Mother–infant interaction also plays a central role in neurobiological development. As Kraemer (1999) put it, 'being mothered . . . is the most important thing for the psychobiological development of the infant' (p. 376). Hofer's animal research (Hofer, 1984; Hofer, 1995; Polan & Hofer, 1999) has teased apart a multitude of physiological regulators in mother–infant interactions. For example, mother–infant contact provides warmth and nutrients as well as a range of olfactory and tactile stimuli. Through such stimulation, mother–infant interactions establish what has been called a *psychobiological synchrony* that entrains the infant's physiological and behavioral rhythms (Field & Reite, 1985; Suomi, 1999; Taylor, 1992). Although much neuroanatomy is hard-wired at birth, the development of functional competence of neurobiological systems depends on early mother–infant interactions (Kraemer, 1999). Thus the infant's capacity for physiological self-regulation depends on synchrony with a caregiver. The crucial point is this: the precursors of attachment in mother–infant interaction that initially foster *physiological* regulation lay the foundation for attachment relationships that subsequently promote *emotional* regulation. What begins as a sensorimotor relationship that modulates physiological arousal evolves into an attachment relationship that regulates emotional arousal through psychological attunement.

Hofer (1995) emphasized how mother–infant interaction provides physiological containment and, conversely, separation entails an escape of physiological systems from containment. This *loss of containment provides a basis for understanding separation distress.* From this vantage point, consider the impact of failure to establish the needed psychobiological synchrony in the caregiver–infant interaction. This failure may lay a faulty foundation for neurobiological development, physiological regulation, and the capacity to regulate emotional distress. We might consider such a failure in early neglect and abuse to be *pre-attachment trauma* that compromises neurophysiological development. Extensive evidence indicates that a failure of early mother–infant regulation promotes a failure of subsequent self-regulation, evidenced by increased stress vulnerability (Hofer, 1995; Kraemer, 1999; Taylor, 1992). As will become increasingly clear throughout this book, many trauma-related symptoms can best be appreciated through the lens of attachment disturbance and the consequent failure of psychobiological self-regulation (van der Kolk & Fisler, 1994).

Although I will leave physiology in the background to focus on the psychology of attachment, keep in mind that attachment relationships continue to play a role in physiological regulation over the lifespan. Physiological synchrony occurs in close adult relationships as it does in mother–infant interactions (Field, 1985; Hofer, 1995; Taylor, 1992). Here is the link to treatment: the most prominent trauma-related disorder, PTSD, exemplifies neurobiological dysregulation (Chapter 6), and the secure attachment we (belatedly) promote in therapy and other relationships fosters containment (Chapter 11). But our immediate agenda is to understand variations in attachment patterns and their relationship to attachment trauma.

ATTACHMENT PATTERNS IN INFANCY AND CHILDHOOD

On the basis of social interactions, human infants form specific attachments by the third quarter of their first year of life in all but extremely anomalous rearing conditions. Furthermore, infants unquestionably take maltreating parents as attachment figures (Main, 1995a). On the basis of mother–infant observations in the home and in the laboratory, Ainsworth and colleagues (Ainsworth et al., 1978) elucidated a prototype of secure attachment and distinguished two common patterns of insecure attachment: avoidant and resistant. Viewing maternal caregiving and infant attachment as complementary systems, she described the intertwining of caregiver behavior and the child's corresponding attachment strategy in relation to that behavior.

Ainsworth (Ainsworth et al., 1978) developed a separation–reunion paradigm, the *Strange Situation*, to elucidate patterns of attachment behavior. The infant and mother are brought into an unfamiliar room filled with toys. A stranger enters, and the mother subsequently leaves the room, leaving the infant with the stranger. Then the mother comes back into the room, pausing to allow the infant a chance to respond to her return. After a while, the stranger leaves the room. Then the mother leaves the infant alone in the room. The mother then returns a second time and picks the infant up. Ainsworth devised this laboratory situation to elicit attachment behavior, and exposure of innumerable parent–infant dyads to this situation has evoked clear prototypes.

Researchers have discovered four patterns of attachment: secure, avoidant, resistant, and disorganized. This chapter explains how each attachment pattern is an adaptation to a particular style of caregiver behavior and delineates some key developmental sequelae of each pattern. Underscoring the contribution of parental behavior to infant attachment, researchers consistently find that patterns of attachment to the mother and father are somewhat independent of one another; whereas the predictors of attachment security are similar for each parent (Belsky, 1999a; Belsky, Rosenberger, & Crnic, 1995; Goldberg, 1991; Main, 1995b; Main, Kaplan, & Cassidy, 1985). Yet, consistent with attachment theory's emphasis on the mother–infant bond as the prototype of attachment, research findings suggest that maternal attachment exerts the greater developmental influence (Main, 1999; Steele, Steele, & Fonagy, 1996).

Secure attachment

Ample research shows that secure attachment characterizes the majority of infants in the Strange Situation (Slade & Aber, 1992; Solomon & George, 1999). Securely attached infants are highly sensitive to their mother's presence. Depending on their temperament, secure infants may be more or less distressed when the mother leaves the room and they are left alone with the stranger. When their mother returns, they make eye contact, approach, or greet her. They are reassured and return quickly to exploratory play. In short, they use their mother as a *secure base* wherein they are comforted if distressed and from which they derive a feeling of confidence in autonomy (Bowlby, 1988). Thus securely attached infants show a smooth alternation between exploratory behavior and attachment behavior (Main & Solomon, 1990). They explore the environment as long as proximity to the parent is assured; attachment is activated when proximity is threatened; they show attachment behavior directly upon reunion; and then they return once more to exploration. Notably, secure babies display relatively little anger in the home and, when they show anger, they are promptly comforted (Crittenden, 1995; Main, 1995b).

Ainsworth (Ainsworth et al., 1978) and others (Carlson, Cicchetti, Barnett, & Braunwald, 1989; Crittenden & Ainsworth, 1989) observed that the key maternal contribution to secure attachment is accessibility and sensitive responsiveness to the infant's attachment needs. Mothers of secure infants show such characteristics as cooperativeness, warmth, involvement, and interactional synchrony (Belsky, 1999a; Belsky et al., 1995; Goldberg, 1991; Main et al., 1985; Weinfield, Sroufe, Egeland, & Carlson, 1999). Hence the interactional synchrony that characterizes secure attachment sustains the psychobiological synchrony in the pre-attachment relationship.

The developmental benefits of secure attachment are legion. Ainsworth (Ainsworth et al., 1978) observed that secure attachment is associated with being more socialized, cooperative, willing to comply, positively outgoing, competent, effective in exploration, receptive to learning, enthusiastic, affectively positive, and persistent, as well as less easily frustrated in problem-solving. Extensive subsequent research has confirmed the association between attachment security and a wide range of positive psychosocial and cognitive attributes, as well as showing that secure attachment is a protective factor in relation to psychopathology (Goldberg, 1991; Main, 1995b; Slade & Aber, 1992; Weinfield et al., 1999).

Avoidant attachment

In the Strange Situation, the avoidant infant appears unconcerned with the mother's whereabouts, not at all distressed by her absence, and indifferent to her return. Avoidant infants tend to focus on the toys and ignore their mother. Commenting on this pattern of behavior in the Strange Situation, Ainsworth and colleagues (Ainsworth et al., 1978) noted that the avoidant infant 'appears to many . . . as a robust, friendly, independent child' but that instead 'this is an unusual way for a 1-year-old to behave in separation and reunion episodes in a strange environment' (p. 320).

Ainsworth and colleagues (Ainsworth et al., 1978) associated avoidant behavior with maternal rejection of the infant's attachment needs and behavior. She observed that mothers of avoidant infants were angry at their baby's demands, yet rigid and compulsive, suppressing their expression of anger. Subsequent research has confirmed that caregiving patterns associated with avoidance include aversion to close bodily contact and absence of cuddling and soothing; insensitivity to infants' signals; rejection of attempts to gain access; and intrusive and controlling behavior (Belsky, 1999a; Crittenden & Ainsworth, 1989; Main, 1995a; Main et al., 1985; Weinfield et al., 1999).

Avoidance is an adaptive strategy to cope with the caregiver's rebuff of attachment behavior (Crittenden & Ainsworth, 1989; Main, 1995a). Ainsworth (Ainsworth et al., 1978) referred to avoidance as defensive *detachment* behavior. The infant attempts to minimize attachment behavior and to shut down the attachment system so as to avoid rejection. Thus the infant shifts attention away from the mother in an effort to regulate distress, for example, by avoiding the frustration of rejection. Although the avoidant infant appears immune to the mother's whereabouts, unabated physiological arousal after reunion and return to play belies the defensiveness of this strategy (Fox & Card, 1999; Main, 1995b).

Crittenden (1995) observed that avoidant attachment is associated with compliance. With the rejecting parent, the avoidant child may develop a sophisticated pattern of inhibition—being cool, proper, and polite. The child elicits attention in indirect ways to avoid rejection, for example, by falsifying affect, reassuring the parent that everyone is happy, engaging in compulsive caregiving, and showing bright affect to draw the parent closer. With the hostile, demanding caregiver, the avoidant child may be compulsively compliant, attempting to please in every detail and trying to do everything exactly right. This compliance may be associated with a pattern of overachievement, as well as shame and self-blame, along with a sense of responsibility for parental behavior. In contrast, the frustration may be expressed overtly in peer relationships, where avoidant attachment is associated with hostility, aggressiveness, and conduct problems (Sroufe, 1997; Weinfield et al., 1999).

Resistant attachment

Ainsworth and colleagues (Ainsworth et al., 1978) observed that the resistant (ambivalent) attachment pattern is the least common in the Strange Situation. The resistant infant is preoccupied with attachment to the exclusion of interest in exploration and play. In contrast to the avoidant infant, who appears oblivious to the mother's presence, the resistant infant is highly attuned to separation and becomes distressed when the mother leaves. Yet, in contrast to secure infants, resistant infants are not easily comforted by their mother's return. Their attachment behavior is fraught with ambivalence and anger. They may protest if they are not picked up when they want to be, or if they are put down when they want to be held. They seek proximity but then angrily resist comforting. They are slower to be soothed, even when picked up, and owing to their accumulated frustration, they mingle angry resistance with clinging.

The resistant pattern relates to maternal unresponsiveness or inconsistent responsiveness rather than overt rejection (Belsky et al., 1995; Carlson et al., 1989; Crittenden & Ainsworth, 1989; Main, 1995b; Main et al., 1985). This pattern of inconsistent responsiveness may include insensitivity to the infant's needs, regarding the infant as a nuisance, being withdrawn, and providing insufficient stimulation. The resistant baby is the mirror image of the avoidant baby. Avoidance is a minimizing strategy, whereas resistance is a maximizing strategy (Main, 1995a, 1995b). In the Strange Situation, the resistant baby focuses intensely on the mother rather than on the toys. Resistant behavior is an adaptive strategy to cope with an under-responsive caregiver.

To elicit responsiveness from the inconsistent caregiver, the resistant infant increases the expression of signaling, crying, and proximity seeking. In essence, the infant escalates distress to solicit caregiving that might reduce it. With all their attention fixed on attachment, resistant infants have little time for exploration and play.

Although resistant attachment is associated with angry rejection of the caregiver, its developmental sequelae relate more to anxiety than aggressiveness (Sroufe, 1997). Notably, resistant children are liable to be victimized, for example, by avoidant children (Weinfield et al., 1999). Crittenden (1995) usefully elaborated the pattern of resistant behavior seen at the preschool level, which she characterizes as coy and coercive, aimed at disarming the parent's anger by submissiveness and feigned helplessness:

> Imagine a two-year-old who signals her desire for her mother. Her mother is attending to other things and does not respond. The girl intensifies her demand. Then she screams angrily and throws a toy toward her mother. Her mother now probably responds. Her response, however, is a matter of uncertainty. She might recognize her oversight and respond soothingly to her child, or she might respond with anger. In the first case, the child is reinforced for heightening her affective signal; because the reinforcement is unpredictable and intermittent, the child's learned response will be more prompt and intense next time and very difficult to extinguish. In the second case, maternal anger, the girl is partly reinforced by achieving her mother's attention and partly punished by the anger. In response to the anger, however, she can display coy behavior. This both terminates her mother's aggression and elicits nurturance. Once she has terminated the mother's anger (and, thus, regained safety), the girl's anger can safely be expressed. She fusses, and her mother tries harder to soothe her; she makes new demands. This continues until her mother becomes fed up and angry, whereupon the child once again displays disarming behavior. (p. 374)

Crittenden's example attests to the interactive development of attachment patterns as well as the role of vicious circles in escalating attachment-related conflicts.

Good-enough caregiving and attachment

Belsky (1999b) cogently argued that caregiving and attachment patterns evolved not for the purpose of fostering mental health or happiness but to maximize reproductive fitness. Sensitive responsiveness is an ideal that does not take into account the inherent conflict of interests between the needs of the parent and those of the child. The optimal caregiving–attachment strategy will vary depending on environmental and cultural conditions, and sensitive responsiveness will not always be in the best interests of the parent or child (e.g., in harsh conditions where resources are scarce). Not only secure but also avoidant and resistant attachment are adaptations to specific patterns of caregiving.

George and Solomon (1999) characterized secure, avoidant, and resistant patterns as reflecting *good-enough* caregiving (Winnicott, 1953). In the secure pattern, the mother flexibly balances her own needs with those of the child, providing the level of protection appropriate for environmental and developmental needs. In contrast, avoidance and resistance are somewhat out of balance. The avoidant pattern is associated with mild rejection and distancing, with the mother tending to dismiss the child's attachment needs and to place more emphasis on her own needs. The resistant pattern is associated with more closeness, with the balance tilted in favor of the child's needs, heightening the emphasis on attachment, albeit with a sense of uncertainty and some ineffectiveness in responding to the child's needs. All three patterns, however, fulfill the core function of attachment by providing the child with needed protection.

Disorganized attachment and trauma

Researchers observing Strange Situation interactions consistently struggled with anomalous unclassifiable cases, particularly in high-risk and maltreated samples. These infants seemed insecure but could not be classified in any single traditional category. To capture these cases, Main and her colleagues (Main, 1995b; Main & Solomon, 1990) delineated a disorganized (or disoriented) attachment classification that is assigned alongside the best-fitting alternative category (i.e., secure–disorganized, avoidant–disorganized, or resistant–disorganized).

The distinctive *lack* of a consistent attachment strategy made disorganized behavior elusive to classification in the Strange Situation (Main & Solomon, 1990). Disorganized behavior is contradictory and confusing, with alternations among proximity seeking, avoidance, and resistance. Disorganized infants may show simultaneous approach and avoidance behavior (e.g., backing toward the mother), or sudden eruption of aggression may intrude on their proximity seeking. Odd and bizarre behavior includes interrupted movements and expressions, stereotypies, anomalous postures, and direct indications of apprehension regarding the parent. Freezing, stilling, and dazed expressions suggest dissociative states. Physiological markers (e.g., heart rate and salivary cortisol) indicate that disorganized infants are especially alarmed by the stress of separation and that their lack of an effective coping strategy perpetuates their alarm (Spangler & Grossman, 1999; van IJzendoorn, Schuengel, & Bakermans-Kranenburg, 1999).

The disorganized classification crystallized in the context of research with high-risk samples, and disorganization and is especially characteristic of maltreated children (Carlson et al., 1989; Main, 1995a; Main & Solomon, 1990; van IJzendoorn et al., 1999). As elaborated later in this chapter, however, maltreatment is not the sole contributor to infants' disorganized attachment. The *caregiver's* trauma history also is associated with infant disorganization (Lyons-Ruth & Jacobvitz, 1999; Main, 1995b; Main & Hesse, 1990; Schuengel, Bakermans-Kranenburg, & van IJzendoorn, 1999; van IJzendoorn et al., 1999). This history may include unresolved loss of important figures through death, unresolved experiences of physical or sexual abuse, or more recent traumas.

Main and Hesse (1990) proposed that *the essential determinant of infant disorganization is frightened or frightening behavior on the part of the caregiver.* Either maltreatment or the caregiver's frightened post-traumatic states alarm the infant and pose an unsolvable dilemma: *the safe haven is alarming* (Main & Hesse, 1990; Main & Solomon, 1990), and the infant is placed in a state of *fright without solution* (Main, 1999). In contrast to caregiving associated with secure, avoidant, and resistant attachment, frightening or frightened caregiver behavior falls short of good enough, as it is an abdication of the caregiving role and a failure to provide protection (George & Solomon, 1999).

Disorganized attachment is indicative of the most profound insecurity and is most likely to be associated with the development of psychopathology (Lyons-Ruth & Jacobvitz, 1999; Sroufe, 1997; van IJzendoorn et al., 1999). Disorganized infant attachment predicts cognitive impairment; lack of social competence; externalizing, aggressive, and controlling behavior; and themes of helplessness and fear in preschool years. As will be elaborated in Chapter 7, dissociation is among the most striking psychopathological outcomes (Carlson, 1998; Main & Morgan, 1996).

Contextual contributors to attachment patterns

Researchers have focused primarily on the caregiver's contribution to infant attachment classification. What determines the caregiver's behavior? I have already noted some contextual factors, such as harsh environments and unresolved loss or trauma. Individual differences among infants that bear on attachment have also been studied, temperament most prominently. The role of infant temperament in attachment has been debated (Belsky et al., 1995; Kagan, 1989; Slade & Aber, 1992; Vaughn & Bost, 1999), and temperament's potential contribution is supported by findings showing commonality in the infant's attachment to both parents above and beyond each parent's individual contribution (Steele et al., 1996). For example, distress-prone infants may be insecurely attached because they are especially irritable and difficult to soothe.

Although some evidence indicates that insecurity is associated with distress proneness, and it is plausible to conclude that temperament makes some contribution to attachment security (Rutter, 1995), assessments of temperament generally relate only weakly to attachment classification (Vaughn & Bost, 1999). In particular, disorganized attachment is unrelated to temperamental, constitutional, or physical characteristics of infants (van IJzendoorn et al., 1999). Moreover, temperament will always become immediately intertwined with parental behavior (Belsky et al., 1995; Steele et al., 1996; Vaughn & Bost, 1999). For example, it is plausible that parental security will minimize the likelihood that irritable infants will develop insecure attachment (Steele et al., 1996).

Myriad factors influence the parent's capacity to behave in a way that promotes the infant's attachment security. Focusing on maternal caregiving, extensive research documents the importance of individual characteristics as well as social support (Belsky, 1999a; Belsky et al., 1995; George & Solomon, 1999; Lyons-Ruth & Jacobvitz, 1999). Numerous positive personality characteristics and indices of psychological health contribute to caregiving ability that promotes secure attachment. Conversely, parental psychopathology, such as severe and chronic mood disorder, impinges on caregiving and is a risk factor for insecure attachment. In addition, social support for the mother, especially the support of her spouse, contributes to caregiving and secure attachment. A secure partner may provide the mother with a safe haven and secure base in attachment that promotes her sensitive caregiving (George & Solomon, 1999).

In sum, attachment reflects the interactions among a host of risk and protective facts in the child, the caregiver, and the wider environment. Yet ample research demonstrates that the caregiver–child interaction is the final common pathway for attachment.

MENTAL REPRESENTATION AND INTERNAL WORKING MODELS

In teaching patients about trauma and relationships, I start by conveying the general principle that ways of relating are learned. As I state it, 'If you've been hurt repeatedly in the past, it's natural to be distrusting in the present.' Learning from the past and generalizing to the future are inevitable and adaptive. Then I raise the issue of faulty generalization. Past learning is maladaptive when the fit between the past and the present is poor. Then new learning is needed. This is a hopeful perspective, because new learning is always possible.

These simple notions are predicated on an underlying structure of mental representations that have been conceptualized and labeled in numerous ways in the psychoanalytic and developmental literature (Blatt, Auerbach, & Levy, 1997; Levy, Blatt, & Shaver, 1998). Diverse theories have employed many terms for such representations, including schemas (Horowitz, 1991b), scripts (Singer & Salovey, 1991), representations of interactions that have been generalized (Stern, 1985), self and object representations (Compton & Goldberg, 1985; Kernberg, 1976), ego states (Allen, 1977), and relationship formats (Seligman, 1999). In the future, we may be talking in terms of neural networks (Main, 1999). For now, I find Bowlby's term, *internal working model*, to be most straightforward to use with clients. In Bowlby's (1982) view, constructing mental models enables the child to predict the accessibility and responsiveness of attachment figures. Because these mental representations model attachment relationships, they also include self-representations—most importantly, a sense of acceptability and worthiness of support from attachment figures.

Internal working models are constructed on the basis of repeated interactions with caregivers. Stern (1989) meticulously described how specific interactions become generalized into more abstract representations. He proposed that lived moments are encoded into episodic memories that can be categorized together to form prototypes of relationships. These prototypes are the basis for expectations and predictions about relationships. Also, discourse between children and caregivers that gives interactions meaning will shape the development of working models (Thompson, 1999). This is a situation in which the rich get richer, insofar as attachment security fosters more coherent discourse about attachment experiences (Bretherton & Munholland, 1999).

Working models are akin to working memory. These models are activated to predict and interpret interactions with attachment figures, and coherent working models help stabilize one's state of mind in these interactions (Horowitz, 1991a). *Without coherent models, interactions become unpredictable, chaotic, and frightening—precisely the situation in disorganized attachment.* In addition, stable working models afford the opportunity to activate mental representations of attachment relationships *in the absence of the attachment figure.* For example, when they are distressed, securely attached preschoolers may engage in inner conversations during which they reassure themselves (Bretherton & Munholland, 1999). But it is important to keep in mind that working models may be more or less conscious (Bretherton & Munholland, 1999). Working models consist not only of explicit memories and conscious narratives ('My mother was always there for me') but also of implicit, procedural memories—in effect, skills and habits that shape interactions nonconsciously. And, as is true of all realms of mental life, conscious models may be incompatible with nonconscious models (Stern, 1989). The assertion, 'My mother was always there for me,' for example, may be a superficially reassuring party line that conceals unmet longings for nurturance.

The concept of *working* model implies a hopeful sense of tentativeness. Optimally, working models balance stability with change. On the side of stability, working models allow the individual to generalize through assimilation, interpreting present experience in relation to the past. As are all cognitive structures, working models are inherently self-perpetuating. Moreover, interactions stemming from working models also perpetuate them (e.g., when distrusting behavior alienates others, reinforcing the distrust).

The application of old working models to new situations fosters reenact-ments—for better, in the case of secure attachment, and for worse, in the case of traumatic relationships.

On the side of change, the process of accommodating to new experience allows for the updating and revision of working models (Bretherton & Munholland, 1999; Thompson, 1999), such as we endeavor to do in psy-chotherapy (Bowlby, 1988). Over the course of development, we all construct multiple—and often contradictory—working models, and we are challenged to employ them in a discriminating way according to the interactional reality of the moment.

DEVELOPMENTAL CONTINUITY AND DISCONTINUITY IN ATTACHMENT

Two facets of continuity in attachment are central to trauma. First, attach-ment plays a key role in distress regulation throughout life. Second, the four patterns of attachment identified in infancy—secure, avoidant, resistant, dis-organized—have conceptually analogous counterparts in adulthood. Thus we can use our understanding of different patterns of adult attachment to understand individual differences in the capacity to regulate distress in relationships.

Any continuity in attachment across the lifespan will take place in the face of rapid and radical change on two fronts. First, as we have already glimpsed, early in life there is a monumental change in the shift from physiological and behavioral regulation to mental representation. Second, the range of potential attachment figures expands markedly over the course of development (Ainsworth, 1989; Collins & Read, 1994; Hazan & Shaver, 1994; Howes, 1999; Shaver & Hazan, 1993). Hence researchers must employ radically different measures to assess attachment at different developmental stages (Crowell, Fraley, & Shaver, 1999; Hesse, 1999; Solomon & George, 1999). Thus in longitudinal research evaluating stability versus change, it is always difficult to tease apart changes due to development from those asso-ciated with measurement. In addition, as Main (1999) pointed out, we must distinguish between the predictive power of attachment classifications (e.g., the extent to which secure attachment in infancy predicts prosocial behav-ior in preschool) and their stability (e.g., the extent to which secure infants develop into secure preschoolers).

The combination of the developmental robustness of attachment, on the one hand, and the structural change of attachment and its measurement over the course of development, on the other hand, has yielded an enormously complex array of longitudinal findings. Yet the benefits of secure attachment for psychosocial development are legion (Allen & Land, 1999; Grossmann, Grossmann, & Zimmermann, 1999; Thompson, 1999; Weinfield et al., 1999), and there are astonishing examples of predictive power, such as the finding that attachment disorganization in infancy relates to dissociative disturbance in adolescence (Carlson, 1998). And there are equally remarkable demonstrations of stability in attachment classification, such as Main's (1999) report of continuity in secure versus insecure classifications from infancy to 19 years of age. More generally, a number of authors have reviewed evidence demonstrating some continuity of attachment classifications over the course of development (Blatt et al., 1997; Goldberg, 1991; Main, 1995b; Stein, Jacobs, Ferguson, Allen, & Fonagy, 1998), and a number of long-range longitudinal studies are in progress (van IJzendoorn, 1995). Yet continuity over the course of adulthood has been little researched. One study of the stability of attachment styles across a 25-year span in adulthood (Klohnen & John, 1998) showed an increase in the prevalence of secure attachment, along with a decrease in preoccupied attachment and no change in avoidant attachment. Persons with avoidant attachment may not have an opportunity to change, whereas those with preoccupied attachment may find stable and loving partners or seek out therapy that enables them to change.

Discontinuity matches continuity. Alongside demonstrations of continuity from infancy to late adolescence are examples of change in attachment classification over the short span of six months from 12 to 18 months of age (Weinfield et al., 1999). Not surprisingly, stability versus change in attachment classification will reflect stability versus change in the family environment and circumstances (Goldberg, 1991; Main et al., 1985; Slade & Aber, 1992). To reiterate, working models afford both stability and capacity for change. Extensive research showing consistent relationships between caregiving behavior and infant attachment classifications attests to the adaptability of working models to the environment, as do reliable findings of a substantial degree of independence between attachment classifications associated with one caregiver versus another. Thus contemporary attachment researchers seek evidence for *lawful* continuities and discontinuities in attachment classification (Thompson, 1999; van IJzendoorn & Bakermans-Kranenburg, 1996), as in other areas of development (Rutter & Rutter, 1993).

Enormously important for clinical purposes is the finding that an opportunity to form a close relationship with a responsive caregiver offers the possibility of change from insecure to secure attachment (Howes, 1999; Stein et al., 2000). We therapists are banking on discontinuity when we help patients update working models in the direction of greater security by the manner of our nonconscious interactions with them as well as our conscious discourse about attachment relationships (Bowlby, 1988; Main, 1999).

ATTACHMENT PATTERNS IN ADULTHOOD

Hazan and Zeifman (1999) marshaled compelling evidence that adult romantic attachments (pair bonds) share the core defining features of infant attachment: the need to maintain proximity, distress upon separation, and reliance on the partner as a safe haven and secure base. Although mental representations of attachment afford individuals a sense of connection over distance, Ainsworth (1989) asserted that 'the attachment is not worthy of the name if they do not want to spend a substantial amount of time with their attachment figures—that is to say, in proximity and interaction with them' (p. 14). As Ainsworth stated, bodily contact with the attachment figure will be desired when attachment is intensely activated by fear. Of course, as is the case in infancy and childhood, the value of attachment in providing a safe haven and secure base will depend on the adult's attachment classification. Two different approaches to characterizing individual differences in adults have been developed: the Adult Attachment Interview and self-report measures of attachment style.

Adult Attachment Interview classifications

Main (Main, 1995b; Main & Goldwyn, 1994) developed the Adult Attachment Interview to investigate how parents' attachment experiences relate to their infants' attachments to them. Main designed the interview to assess the adult's current state of mind with respect to attachment, posing two central tasks: (a) producing and reflecting on memories involving early relationships as well as any potentially traumatic experiences while (b) simultaneously maintaining coherent, collaborative discourse. The hour-long, structured semiclinical interview entails giving five adjectives describing relationships with each parent and documenting each adjective with pertinent autobiographical memories. Respondents are asked what they did when they were upset, hurt, or ill; whether their parents were threatening; why their parents behaved as they did; how they reacted to deaths and setbacks in development; and how their childhood experiences affected their personality.

A multidimensional scoring system yields adult categories that parallel infant attachment classifications: secure/autonomous (secure), dismissing of attachment (avoidant), preoccupied by past attachments (resistant), unresolved/disorganized with respect to loss and trauma (disorganized). Highly trained raters are able to classify individuals reliably and, as it was designed to do, the interview shows excellent predictive validity with respect to the infant's attachment classification (Hesse, 1999; Main, 1995a; Main & Goldwyn, 1994; van IJzendoorn, 1995; van IJzendoorn & Bakermans-Kranenburg, 1996). Most convincing are prospective studies showing this parent–infant correspondence in which Adult Attachment Interviews were administered to first-time parents prior to the birth of their infant, and Strange Situations were administered in the second year of the infant's life (Fonagy, Steele, & Steele, 1991; Steele et al., 1996; Ward & Carlson, 1995).

Secure adults value attachment relationships, regard attachment experiences as influential in their life, and acknowledge their need to depend on others. They freely explore their thoughts and feelings, remember childhood events clearly, and examine these events afresh in the interview. They collaborate well in the interview and give coherent accounts with little self-deception. They are at ease with their own imperfections and show neither idealization nor extreme anger in relation to their attachment experience. Parents who are classified as secure in the interview are likely to have infants who show secure attachment to them in the Strange Situation.

Dismissing adults attempt to limit the influence of attachment in their relationships. They are likely to report few or superficial memories of attachment experiences in childhood, and they may idealize their parents, glossing over negative aspects of the relationships. Alternatively, they may devalue their parents and derogate attachment relationships. At the same time, they are likely to deny dependency and instead to claim normalcy, personal strength, independence, and absence of distress. Main (1995b) noted that dismissing adults are like avoidant infants in the Strange Situation insofar as they reject the task and the interviewer, while giving the appearance of lack of distress and invulnerability.

Preoccupied adults show intense involvement in attachment relationships, remaining entangled in early relationships and malignant experiences. Their discourse is likely to be rambling, confusing, and highly emotional. They are preoccupied, angry, fearful, or overwhelmed by traumatic events, failing to separate past from present. Main (1995b) drew a parallel to the behavior of resistant infants in the Strange Situation: preoccupied adults overwhelm the interviewer and are unresponsive to interventions.

As is the case with infant attachment classifications, the unresolved/disorganized category reflects lapses in functioning rather than an organized attachment strategy. Hence, as it is in infancy, this classification is assigned in conjunction with the best-fitting alternative adult category. Disorganization is evident in lapses of reasoning and coherence of discourse in the context of unresolved experiences of loss and abuse. Persons who fit this classification find insistent questioning about trauma and loss to be disorganizing and disorienting. As is the case with infant disorganization in the Strange Situation, the observed lapses may be relatively brief—for example, spanning a few sentences. In effect, evoking traumatic memories pertaining to attachment relationships is disorganizing, in part by interfering with working memory (Main, 1999).

As will be elaborated later (Chapter 7), there are striking parallels between adult and infant attachment in the realm of dissociative experiences (Hesse, 1999; Main & Morgan, 1996). In the Adult Attachment Interview, brief dissociative states associated with traumatic memories may account for lapses in monitoring. Disorganized parents also may display dissociative states in the Strange Situation, and dissociative states are suggested as well by infants' dazed and disoriented expressions in the Strange Situation.

Adult attachment styles

In contrast to the Adult Attachment Interview, which explores adults' state of mind with respect to their own attachment history in their family of origin, research shaped by social psychology employs self-report measures to study attachment in current romantic relationships. Hazan and Shaver (1987) wrote brief descriptions of different attachment styles (parallel to secure, dismissing, and preoccupied) and asked respondents to indicate which category best characterized their romantic relationship. Since this ground-breaking study, other researchers have developed a spate of self-report measures—so many that sorting out their empirical and conceptual relationships has become a major task (Brennan, Clark, & Shaver, 1998; Crowell & Treboux, 1995; Sperling, Foelsch, & Grace, 1996; Stein et al., 1998; Stein, Koontz, Allen, Fultz, Brethour, Allen, Evans, & Fonagy, 2000). This line of research on adult attachment style also followed the path of the Strange Situation and Adult Attachment Interview by belatedly adding a fourth category, fearful, which I view as analogous to the disorganized category in being associated with relatively severe impairment and trauma.

The social-psychological research on adult attachment styles has added another layer of complexity to the conceptualization of attachment by bringing a dimensional perspective into the assessments. That is, in addition to placing themselves into one category, respondents can be assessed with regard to the *degree* to which they fit various categories (Bartholomew & Horowitz, 1991; Collins, 1996; Collins & Read, 1990). Two broad dimensions run through these measures of adult attachment styles: *anxiety and avoidance* (Brennan et al., 1998; Collins & Read, 1990; Fraley & Waller, 1998; Kobak, Cole, Ferenz-Gilles, Fleming, & Gamble, 1993). It is possible to derive attachment classifications from scores on these dimensions (Collins, 1996). Secure attachment entails low anxiety and low avoidance; dismissing combines low anxiety with high avoidance; preoccupied involves high anxiety and low avoidance; and fearful reflects high anxiety and high avoidance. Bartholomew and colleagues (Bartholomew & Horowitz, 1991; D. Griffin & K. Bartholomew, 1994; D. W. Griffin & K. Bartholomew, 1994; Scharfe & Bartholomew, 1994) have taken a somewhat different tack to the dimensional perspective, emphasizing positive versus negative concepts of self and others rather than anxiety and avoidance. Secure attachment entails a positive view of self and others; dismissing, a positive view of self and a negative view of others; preoccupied, a negative view of self and a positive view of others; and fearful, a negative view of self and others.

Although extensive research attests to the validity of self-report measures of attachment styles in predicting relationship characteristics, these measures are minimally related to Adult Attachment Interview assessments (Crowell et al., 1999; Hesse, 1999). This is not surprising, given their differences in focus (current romantic relationships versus family of origin), purpose (studying interpersonal relationships versus infant attachment), and methodology (conscious self-report versus relatively nonconscious discourse style). Thus researchers have developed two valid and relatively independent approaches to assessing adult attachment, which have the potential to be used in complementary ways in future research (Main, 1999).

Adult attachment styles and trauma

The assessment of adult attachment styles evolved in the field of social psychology and personality assessment, and relatively few studies have related attachment styles to trauma. Whereas fearful attachment characterizes only a small minority of persons in normative samples, Alexander and colleagues found that fearful attachment predominated among women with a history of sexual abuse in a nonclinical sample (Alexander, 1993; Alexander et al., 1998). Muller and colleagues (Muller, 2000) also reported a predominance of insecure attachment styles in a community sample of adults with a childhood trauma history, with avoidant styles (dismissing and fearful) predominating. We also found a predominance of fearful attachment in women in specialized inpatient treatment for trauma-related disorders (Allen, Coyne, & Huntoon, 1998a). In addition to assessing attachment styles, we have found it clinically useful to ask patients about their *current attachment network*, that is, the numbers and types of relationships that provide at least some degree of attachment security in the present. Women in inpatient treatment for trauma reported fewer secure current attachments than a community sample, but the absolute numbers may be more important than the relative difference. Traumatized patients reported an average of four secure attachment figures, compared to six reported by women in the community sample (Allen, Huntoon, Fultz, Stein, Fonagy, & Evans, in press). These are hopeful findings: *most patients are extremely persistent in seeking secure attachments, despite a history of attachment trauma.*

Attachment to pets

When discussing attachment in educational groups, I invariably include reference to pets. Human–animal bonds are ubiquitous and multifaceted, with attachment being one potentially important dimension (Melson, 1988). Although attachment to pets may reduce stress and promote health (Brown & Katcher, 1997), it may also relate inversely to human social support and thus adversely affect well being (Stallones, Marx, Garrity, & Johnson, 1988). Our clinical experience suggests that—for better or for worse—attachments to pets are particularly prominent in the life of traumatized persons. When discussing attachments to pets, I reiterate that attachment is a mammalian phenomenon, sometimes referring to MacLean's (1990) rooting of attachment in the limbic system, which we humans share with all mammals.

Our clinical impressions were confirmed by the results of our study of current attachment relationships (Allen, Huntoon et al., in press). Our instructions explicitly indicated that pets could be included as attachment figures. We found that, in comparison to a community sample, patients in a trauma sample were significantly more likely to list one or more pets as current secure attachment figures. Notably, Brown and Katcher (1997) found a relationship between attachment to pets and clinically significant levels of dissociation. They speculated that, for such individuals, dissociation and attachment to pets may both be a reflection of trauma. These researchers also proposed that persons with a history of interpersonal trauma may use attachments to animals as a substitute for human relationships as well as a way to seek a reparative relationship.

Aware of the potential benefits of attachments to pets, I am supportive of such attachments. But the extent to which they can be a hindrance (avoidance) or a benefit (buffer) in childhood and adulthood remains to be tested. In our retrospective assessments of childhood adversity (Stein, Allen, Allen et al., 2000), we have developed a pet attachment scale that ranges from none, to mild (contact with pets in the household), to moderate (pets as significant companions), to marked (pets providing tactile stimulation and solace in times of distress). Thus we will be able to examine the relation of these attachments to adult outcome. Meanwhile, in educational groups, I support comforting attachments with pets as a potentially helpful means of distress regulation while emphasizing the importance of developing a wider attachment network involving other persons.

REENACTMENT

Secure attachment provides a safe haven and secure base that enable relationships to regulate distress. Attachment trauma, by undermining security, blocks that avenue of distress regulation to varying degrees. But the trouble does not end there. Working models tend to be self-perpetuating. When the working models are based on traumatic interactions, trauma tends to beget trauma. Here I will examine revictimization and the intergenerational transmission of abuse and tie them to attachment relationships. I will also consider the processes whereby other persons are drawn into reenactments and the reasons why many persons have difficulty extricating themselves from abusive relationships in adulthood.

Revictimization

No doubt adults with no prior trauma history can be victims of assaults and abuse. Tragically, however, a history of interpersonal trauma confers a higher risk of later interpersonal trauma, a phenomenon known as *revictimization* (van der Kolk, 1989). In a longitudinal study of women, for example, Acierno and colleagues (Acierno, Resnick, Kilpatrick, Saunders, & Best, 1999) found that a lifetime history of victimization (sexual or physical assault) increased the risk of subsequent victimization. Most striking is their finding that prior victimization increased the risk of being raped by a factor of seven. In part such revictimization may reflect environmental continuity, to the extent that a woman is unable to extricate herself from a dangerous situation or high-risk environment.

Sadly, the risk of revictimization can be established early in life, as evidence relating childhood maltreatment to self-endangering behavior and assault in adulthood attests. As van der Kolk (1989) described, for example, persons with a history of childhood sexual abuse are vulnerable to involvement in pornography and prostitution. In addition, childhood sexual abuse may also increase the risk of pregnancy in adolescence, leading to yet another generation of high-risk children (Stevens-Simon & Reichert, 1994). Yet the precise relation between childhood abuse and self-endangering behavior merits further research. Widom and Kuhns' (1996) prospective study failed to demonstrate a significant relationship between childhood victimization and promiscuity or teenage pregnancy, although childhood sexual abuse—as well as physical abuse and neglect—increased the likelihood of prostitution for females.

Extensive evidence demonstrates that childhood maltreatment increases the risk of adulthood assault. Nishith and colleagues' (Nishith, Mechanic, & Resick, 2000) retrospective study found that childhood sexual abuse, but not physical abuse, related strongly to risk of adulthood physical and sexual assault. On the other hand, Widom's (1999b) prospective study indicated that all forms of court-documented maltreatment (childhood sexual abuse, physical abuse, and neglect) were associated with a high risk of exposure to rape in adulthood.

Cloitre and colleagues (Cloitre, 1998; Cloitre, Scarvalone, & Difede, 1997; Cloitre, Tardiff, Marzuk, Leon, & Portera, 1996) provided substantial evidence that a history of childhood abuse substantially increases the risk for sexual assault in adulthood. One of these studies (Cloitre et al., 1997) focused specifically on the detrimental impact of revictimization. Women assaulted in adulthood were divided into a revictimized group (women with a history of childhood sexual abuse, often accompanied by physical abuse) and a group assaulted in adulthood only. Both groups with adult assaults showed high rates of PTSD and major depression, but there were substantial differences among them in other respects. Revictimized women were more likely to have had multiple sexual assaults in adulthood, to have been assaulted by an acquaintance, to have experienced nonrape violent assaults, to show higher levels of dissociation and suicide attempts, and to have pervasive interpersonal problems. Cloitre (1998) viewed the elevated risk as reflecting the repetition of traumatic attachment patterns as well as the defensive compromise of alertness to danger. Consistent with Cloitre's conclusion, laboratory evidence indicates that, compared to those without such a history, sexually revictimized women are slow to conclude that a sexual interaction has gone too far for comfort (Wilson, Calhoun, & Bernat, 1999).

Although I am emphasizing the adulthood reenactment of childhood abuse, keep in mind that this pattern of repetition has a long developmental trajectory. Illustratively, physically abused boys, when exposed to a stranger expressing anger toward their mother in a laboratory situation, were more reactive than nonabused boys (Cummings, Hennessy, Rabideau, & Cicchetti, 1994). They showed more aggression and tended to jump into the fray, a pattern of behavior that might increase their risk of subsequent exposure to trauma. Similarly, research shows that community violence, maltreatment, and children's externalizing behavior are interrelated (Lynch & Cicchetti, 1998). Level of externalizing behavior measured at one point was associated with the risk of subsequent exposure to community violence (a year later). The children in this study were preadolescent, attesting to the likelihood that vulnerability to revictimization begins early.

Intergenerational transmission of violence and abuse

Victimization leads not only to revictimization but also to perpetration of trauma. As Widom (1989) argued, the *cycle of violence* has become a truism: 'Abused children become abusers and victims of violence become violent offenders' (p. 244). In her large-scale study based on examination of official records, Widom investigated how childhood abuse and neglect relate to rate of delinquency, adult criminal behavior, and violent behavior. A history of physical abuse was associated with a higher risk of arrests for delinquency, crime in general, and violent crime in particular. Neglect was similarly associated with a higher rate of delinquency, crime, and violent crime. Yet the link between childhood abuse and crime is not inevitable. The vast majority of abused and neglected children did not commit criminal offenses.

The extent of intergenerational transmission of abuse has been widely researched, with highly variable results. Kaufman and Zigler (1987) reported estimates ranging from 18% to 70% and concluded that a 30% intergenerational transmission rate was the best estimate. This 30% rate, albeit a minority of persons, is six times the base rate of abuse in the general population. Oliver's (1993) comprehensive and critical review of the literature came to a more refined conclusion. Pointing out that the extent of intergenerational transmission is bound to vary widely according to the nature of the sample, Oliver concluded that 'one-third of the children will continue the pattern, one-third will not, and the last one-third will continue to be vulnerable, their eventual parental behavior depending on extrafamilial pressures' (p. 1321). And it is not just a parent's childhood trauma that places the next generation at risk; so does adulthood trauma. For example, not only was a history of childhood abuse related to the prospective father's participation in abusive violence in Vietnam, but also his participation in abusive violence in particular was associated with behavioral disturbance in his children (Rosenheck & Fontana, 1998).

A host of factors besides trauma history contributes to parental abusiveness: social stressors, stressful life events, extent of social support in childhood and adulthood, attitudes toward punishment, and the health and behavior of the child (Albarracin, Repetto, & Albarracin, 1997; Bower & Knutson, 1996; Kaufman & Zigler, 1987; Zeanah & Zeanah, 1989). A properly comprehensive approach to intergenerational transmission of abuse requires many perspectives, from the biological to the sociopolitical (Buchanan, 1998). At the psychological level, however, Oliver (1993) pointed to awareness of one's own abuse history as a crucial mediating factor: 'The single most important modifying factor in intergenerational transmission of child abuse is the capacity of the child victim to grow up with the ability to face the reality of past and present personal relationships' (p. 1322). This finding attests to the wisdom in Freud's (Freud, 1914/1958, 1920/1955) recognition that repetition in action can substitute for remembering.

Herein lies an important source of hope for traumatized parents who fear they are damaging their children. I inform them that, while there is ample reason to be concerned about the perpetuation of trauma, there is clear evidence that many persons are able to break this cycle. Their work on gaining awareness of their trauma is a crucial step. In the context of such discussions, a number of clients express satisfaction and pride in their efforts to break the cycle. I point out that conflict and anger between parents and children are normal and inevitable, but that efforts to discuss and resolve conflicts can make a considerable difference. For many traumatized persons, understanding and reconciliation were missing in their childhood. I affirm their efforts to communicate more openly with their own children, which will offer their children the resources of attachment security.

Intergenerational transmission of attachment trauma

It seems obvious that intergenerational transmission of trauma is based on social learning. For example, the angry parent who assaults the child not only provokes the child's anger but also provides a model of behaving aggressively when angry. Evidence exists for transmission of abuse on the basis of role modeling, although the patterns transmitted from one generation to the next go far beyond imitating specific behaviors (Simons & Johnson, 1998). Zeanah and Zeanah (1989) argued persuasively, however, that specific types of maltreatment are not necessarily repeated across generations. Rather, 'child maltreatment is a kind of *relationship disorder* whose intergenerational transmission is mediated by the internal working models of parent and child' (p. 183, emphasis added). No doubt, maltreatment may be repeated directly, but recent attachment research demonstrates how the intergenerational transmission of trauma need not entail direct abuse.

As noted earlier, the intergenerational transmission of attachment is demonstrated by a high correspondence between parents' and infants' attachment classifications (Main, 1995b; van IJzendoorn, 1995), as well as indications of relatively high matching of attachment classifications across three generations (Benoit & Parker, 1994). Secure parents tend to have secure infants; dismissing parents have avoidant infants; preoccupied parents have resistant infants; and unresolved parents have disorganized infants. The evidence of correspondence is weakest for the preoccupied–resistant match, however, in part due to the relative infrequency of these categories.

How are attachment patterns transmitted from parent to infant? Sensitively responsive caregiving promotes secure attachment, and less than optimal caregiving is associated with insecurity (Ainsworth et al., 1978; van IJzendoorn, 1995). Yet the parent–child correlation is only partly mediated by sensitivity, and we must look beyond specific caregiving behavior to consider the influence of parents' internal working models. As Main (1995b) stated, 'It has long been presumed that the parent's representation of his or her own life history shapes the way in which the infant is conceptualized and, concomitantly, the way in which the infant is treated' (p. 97). Main discovered that disorganized infant attachment may not only be a direct reflection of maltreatment but also can be an indirect, second-generation effect of the parent's own traumatic experiences. The key contribution to infant disorganization is frightened or frightening behavior on the part of the caregiver (Main & Hesse, 1990). Such behaviors might include unusual movement patterns (e.g., looming, invasion of space, timidity, sensitivity to infant rejection, direct expression of fear of the infant), unusual speech content (e.g., frightening games), and parental dissociative behavior such as trance-like states (Main, 1995b). Importantly, the link from unresolved loss to frightening maternal behavior and infant disorganization may hold only for mothers whose pattern of adult attachment is insecure (Schuengel et al., 1999).

Lyons-Ruth and colleagues meticulously examined how maternal trauma history and attachment classification relate to mother–infant interactions that promote disorganized infant attachment (Lyons-Ruth & Block, 1996; Lyons-Ruth, Bronfman, & Atwood, 1999; Lyons-Ruth & Jacobvitz, 1999). Extending Main's observations that either frightened or frightening maternal behavior may be associated with infant disorganization (Main & Hesse, 1990), Lyons-Ruth emphasized the adverse impact of *unbalanced relational models*. Two main dimensions of maternal behavior are associated with infant disorganization: *hostile–intrusiveness* (frightening) and *helpless–withdrawal* (frightened). Infants whose disorganized behavior is intermingled with insecure attachment (avoidant or resistant) are more likely to have frighten*ing* mothers, whereas infants whose disorganized behavior is intermingled with secure attachment are more likely to have frighten*ed* mothers. Although hostile-intrusive behavior is more obviously frightening to the infant, helpless–withdrawal (frightened and unresponsive behavior) also can be alarming. Frightened–inhibited mothers tend to be hesitant, gentle, timid, and fragile—or awkward and distancing. Both frightening and frightened patterns entail seriously misattuned caregiving in which the infant has no control over the mother's behavior and no means of using the attachment relationship to regulate the fear engendered by that relationship—or any other source.

Lyons-Ruth's research showed that, whereas hostile–intrusive behavior is associated with a mother's history of physical abuse, helpless–withdrawal is associated with her history of sexual abuse. Translating these findings into the framework of this book, gross parental misattunement to the infant's attachment behavior stems from the parent's post-traumatic reaction to attachment-related cues, which serve as a reminder of the parent's attachment trauma (Schuengel et al., 1999). These post-traumatic reactions may include fear, anger, and dissociative responses. More specifically, Lyons-Ruth proposed that the mother's traumatic childhood (i.e., her own attachment trauma) makes it difficult for her to empathize with her infant, because empathy puts her in touch with attachment concerns that are painful for her. At worst such attachment concerns might stir up post-traumatic intrusive symptoms. Both emotional withdrawal and hostile intrusiveness are defensive insofar as they minimize the mother's emotional contact with her infant. For the infant, the maternal aversion to attachment is distressing, because the affective interaction between mother and infant is disrupted, and the attachment behavioral system is non-functional. Notably, outside the context of attachment theory, Nader (1998) found that children exposed to a potentially traumatic event were more likely to have symptoms if a parent also had been traumatized. Attachment research is helpful in understanding such findings, because it emphasizes the importance of the parent's capacity to respond to the child's trauma-related attachment needs. Yet not just post-traumatic reactions but also anything that overwhelms the parent in the caregiving role and that leads to feelings of helplessness and fear of losing control may foster behavior that promotes infant disorganization (George & Solomon, 1999).

The course of disorganized attachment beyond infancy is noteworthy in relation to reenactment. Lyons-Ruth observed that unbalanced relationship models are associated with an *asymmetry of power* in which one individual is more controlling and the other more helpless. Furthermore, disorganized infants are at risk for becoming controlling with parents (in either a punitive or caregiving way) as well as being aggressive and incompetent with peers. Thus the intergenerational transmission of attachment trauma—with or without overt maltreatment—places the child at risk for subsequent victim–victimizer relationships. Not only does this increase the likelihood of revictimization but also it decreases the ability to resolve later-occurring trauma.

Does parental trauma invariably lead to frightened–frightening or hostile–helpless behavior that fosters the intergenerational transmission of insecure attachment? As is the case with the cycle of violence and abuse, it is possible to break the cycle of transmission of insecure attachment. Recall Freud's (Freud, 1914/1958, 1920/1955) dictum that reenacting can substitute for remembering and Oliver's (1993) finding that a key factor in breaking the cycle of abuse is the awareness of one's trauma history. As will be discussed further in conjunction with the development of the self (Chapter 4), Fonagy and colleagues (Fonagy et al., 1995) showed how *parents' capacity to reflect on mental states—their own thoughts and feelings as well as those of their child—serves as a protective factor by decreasing the likelihood of transmitting disturbed attachment across generations.* By virtue of their capacity to reflect, parents can be receptive to their infant's attachment behavior despite their own trauma history. Recognizing that various forms of family stress are liable to promote insecure infant attachment, Fonagy and colleagues examined the potential mediating role of the mother's reflective function in ameliorating these effects. They found that all the mothers in a highly stressed, deprived group who were highly reflective had securely attached children. In contrast, virtually none of the stressed mothers who lacked reflective function had securely attached infants. These are hopeful findings, because they allow for therapeutic leverage in relation to the intergenerational transmission of attachment trauma. Therapy promotes reflective capacity and, thereby, attachment security. As will be a theme in the treatment of trauma, it is not the *content* of the insight but rather the *capacity* for insight that matters.

Contagion and projective identification

Reenacting trauma is a dyadic process that requires retraumatizing behavior on the part of the traumatized individual's partner. How are partners—be they friends, spouses, or us therapists—drawn into such reenactments?

Reenactment begins with emotional contagion. Our seemingly innate capacity to resonate with the emotional states of others has its prototype in the behavior of infants in the nursery (Simner, 1971), wherein contagious crying has been demonstrated experimentally in one-day-old babies and interpreted as evidence of rudimentary empathic distress (Sagi & Hoffman, 1976). Hatfield and colleagues (Hatfield, Cacioppo, & Rapson, 1994) reviewed extensive research indicating that individuals readily *catch* emotions from other persons. They define *emotional contagion* as 'the tendency to automatically mimic and synchronize expressions, vocalizations, postures, and movements with those of another person and, consequently, to converge emotionally' (p. 5). They document the startling rapidity with which dyads are able to synchronize a wide range of movements and emotional states. Facial cues are especially prominent in emotional states and their contagion (e.g., through facial imitation and proprioceptive feedback from movements of facial musculature). Moreover, the authors note that the extent of synchrony increases with the closeness of the relationship (i.e., attachment). The continuous synchronizing of behavior is procedural and nonconscious, and emotional states associated with feedback from synchronizing behavior may be more or less conscious. But the ubiquity of nonconscious emotional contagion may account for our unwitting propensity to be drawn into reenactments.

Going a step beyond emotional contagion is the phenomenon of projective identification, which has a defensive aim. Through *projective identification*, individuals attempt to rid themselves of intolerable mental contents (aspects of the self) by projecting them into other individuals, who then identify with these contents, experiencing and expressing them. Projective identification is a largely nonconscious form of interpersonal influence (Horwitz, 1983; Seligman, 1999; Silverman & Lieberman, 1999). Seligman (1999), for example, emphasized how 'one person pressures another to experience as part of herself something that the first person cannot accept within his own experience' (p. 143). He also described how projected mental contents can include traumatic experience and thus may contribute to the intergenerational transmission of trauma.

Silverman and Lieberman (1999) provided a dramatic example of this process. A mother who had experienced severe physical abuse at the hands of her alcoholic father and who had witnessed extremely violent interactions between her parents was determined to protect her daughter from such violence. In the service of attempting to protect her daughter, the mother repeatedly frightened her daughter with injunctions and lessons about how dangerous men could be. Consequently, her daughter was not only pervasively frightened but she also felt helpless—'infuriatingly ineffective' in coping with danger (p. 171). Silverman and Lieberman noted how the parent attributes certain qualities to the child and then influences the child to behave in a way that conforms to those attributions. Defensively, the parent can attempt to control something external (i.e., the child's behavior) rather than something internal (the dreaded emotional state). Although the attributions are relatively conscious, the phenomenon of projective identification is not.

To reiterate, interpersonal reenactments are likely to be supported by two nonconscious phenomena: emotional contagion and projective identification. The former is the most primitive in the sense that it entails an immediate emotional resonance and synchrony—akin to the contagion of crying in the nursery. The latter, likely operating in concert with the former, is more active and elaborate insofar as there is a defensive effort to influence the behavior of another person to correspond with certain attributions, to attempt to control the resulting behavior, and thereby to stay out of a dreaded mental state (e.g., of fearfulness or aggressiveness). Of course emotional contagion and projective identification do not just occur in parent–child interactions; they also occur in our clients' interactions with peers, spouses, and us therapists—all of whom may become partners in reenactments and revictimization.

Partner susceptibility

The likelihood of reenacting trauma reflects the traumatized individual's propensity to reexperience ordinary interactions as traumatic (e.g., in the form of attributions of malevolence or neglect), the inclination to communicate emotion in a way that promotes contagion, and the proclivity toward projective identification in which the traumatized individual influences or coerces the partner into behavior that confirms the disavowed attribution, projection, or role. Of course the partner's penchant for reenactment also plays an important role in the extent to which internal working models of relationships, and the corresponding role enactments, are reaffirmed or modified for the better.

Many traumatized clients, especially women, lament their penchant for picking abusive partners. Of course, therapists might infer an unconscious masochistic wish to reenact the history of abuse. Yet my discussions of this pattern of reenactment with clients reveal a more typical conscious intent to pick partners in such a way as to *escape or avoid* further abuse. A prototype is as follows. A woman who has been abusively dominated by a father and who feels inadequate and ineffectual as a result (the hostile–helpless pattern) seeks a man who is strong and protective. As Walker (1979) documented, such men are often highly attentive and affectionate (i.e., rescuing)—early in the relationship. Gradually or more suddenly (e.g., after marriage), these relationships become reenactments, as the imbalance of power turns into overt domination and outright aggression. For some women, such relationships are more extremely abusive and traumatic than their childhood precursors. As Walker described, these relationships are highly unstable, as the abuse is followed by a period of reconciliation, tension building, and then further abuse. Then the full-blown role reenactment pattern occurs, rescuing–rescued, abusing–abused, and neglecting–neglected. As is well documented in the domestic violence literature (see Chapter 2), the abusing–abused roles go both ways, although women—owing to lesser power—typically bear the brunt of the violence.

Given the evidence for intergenerational transmission of attachment insecurity and abuse, those partners who are most prone to engaging in reenactment themselves have a history of abuse and attachment insecurity. Just as the risk of abusing children is increased by a history of abuse, so is the risk of abusing adult partners. But this conspicuous pattern of repetition should not overshadow the partner's proclivity to engage in other roles as well. The partner with a history of attachment trauma—abuse and neglect— is likely to be especially responsive to emotional contagion and projective identification. This vulnerability entails a propensity not only to be abusive but also to feel abused, to desire rescue, to defensively engage in rescue, and to withdraw and feel neglected. Not uncommonly, reenactments involve two persons with a trauma history who resonate at every level—to emotional contagion, projective identification, and enacting the various roles at traumatic levels.

Traumatic bonding

We therapists must thoroughly understand why patients have so much difficulty extricating themselves from such abusive relationships. Invariably, the question arises, 'Why can't I (she) leave him?' Clients as well as their friends and therapists are often astounded by what Walker (1979) called the *miracle glue* that seems to perpetuate these relationships. Plainly, there are many practical reasons for a woman's inability to leave a battering partner, economic dependence prominent among them. Most compelling is the (often realistic) fear of being harmed worse or being killed—and the same happening to her children—if she leaves.

The practical arguments for remaining in abusive relationships can be overpowering. But many authors emphasize relationship dynamics over practical reasons when attempting to understand the motivation for remaining in abusive relationships (Allen, 1996; Dutton & Painter, 1981; Graham, Rawlings, & Rimini, 1988; Henderson, Bartholomew, & Dutton, 1997; Herman, 1992b; Walker, 1979). Key elements of such relationships are an imbalance of power, isolation from other sources of support, and low self-esteem (the latter often associated with a feeling of deserving no better). Moreover, in the context of reenactment, many persons refer to the relative 'security' of the familiar (albeit abusive) in contrast to their fear of the unknown (albeit safer).

Adults who remain in abusive relationships are often met with incredulity from others, who see the behavior as vexingly irrational. Common sense dictates that persons seek pleasure and avoid pain (setting the stage for resorting to naïve explanations of masochism). Such views fail to consider attachment. The concept of traumatic *bonding*, wherein attachment phenomena play a role in perpetuating abusive relationships, goes to the heart of the seeming paradox that abusiveness cements relationships. Traumatic bonding has been observed not only in relation to adulthood battering relationships but also in relation to childhood maltreatment (Bowlby, 1982), hostage-taking situations, as in the Stockholm Syndrome (Strentz, 1982; Symonds, 1982), and in many species of animals (Scott, 1987).

From the perspective of traumatic bonding, the explanation of remaining in abusive relationships is quite simple—although extricating oneself from such relationships is anything but. *Abuse escalates distress (e.g., fear), and distress heightens attachment needs.* Given isolation from other sources of support, the individual with heightened attachment needs will turn to the available attachment figure—particularly the individual who is in a position of power. Hence escalating abuse abets traumatic bonding. The greater the fear, the greater the attachment. Moreover, as many authors have emphasized, and as Walker (1979) has documented graphically, the loving-respite phase of battering relationships provides the illusory haven of security that further heightens attachment.

Periods of loving respite have deep evolutionary roots. De Waal's (de Waal, 1989; de Waal & Aureli, 1999) primate research amply documented the role of reconciliation and peacemaking in regulating aggression. De Waal proposed a relational model in which

> nonhuman primates engage in nonaggressive reunions between former opponents not long after an aggressive confrontation. Depending on the species, these reunions include mouth-to-mouth contact, embracing, sexual contact, grooming, holding hands, clasping the hips of the other, and so on. Opponents thus engage in rather intense mutual contact following conflict. (de Waal & Aureli, 1999, p. 119)

Such post-aggression reconciliation is especially likely in relationships that both partners have a high incentive to preserve, and it serves to regulate arousal and anxiety in these relationships. Thus reconciliation buffers the deleterious effects of aggressive interactions by alleviating anxiety and repairing valuable relationships. At moderate levels of conflict, reconciliation is adaptive. At abusive levels of conflict, the loving-respite phase can provide extreme levels of relief—and sometimes excitement—that perpetuate the traumatic reenactments.

Henderson and colleagues (Henderson et al., 1997) documented the connection between attachment styles and bonding in abusive adult relationships. To examine the fate of the abusive relationship, these authors measured attachment styles in women assessed shortly after leaving their abusive partners and then again after six months. They found, on initial assessment, that the overwhelming majority of women showed either preoccupied or fearful attachment patterns, both of which are associated with negative self-images. They also found that women with preoccupied attachment styles tended to have relationships of shorter duration and, after separation, tended to remain more emotionally and behaviorally involved with their abusive partner. They continued to feel love for them, remained sexually involved with them, and felt a desire to get back together with them. This continuing engagement reflects the ambivalent relationship-seeking aspect of the preoccupied attachment style. In contrast, women with a fearful style, although tending to remain in abusive relationships for a long time, were more inclined to want emotional distance and to avoid further contact after leaving their abusive partner.

Although much clinical and research attention has focused on the battered woman, clinicians also must understand the complementary dynamics in the battering man. De Waal (de Waal & Aureli, 1999) noted that aggression serves as a 'tool of negotiation within well-established relationships' (p. 127). What instigates the use of this tool? Like the battered woman, the battering man's attachment needs are at the heart of the traumatic (traumatizing) bond. Men in battering relationships often use power to cover up their dependency and fear of abandonment, and their aggressive threats and behavior are part and parcel of their jealousy and possessiveness, serving to avert abandonment (Dutton & Painter, 1981). The combination of aggression and peacemaking is powerfully effective in staving off abandonment. The traumatic bond outlives the physical separation, because the likelihood of return remains high (Henderson et al., 1997).

As I have described elsewhere (Allen, 1996), we therapists are tempted to join the cheering squad of family members, friends, and co-workers who cajole the patient to leave the abusive relationship. No doubt, in situations of grave danger, we must do everything possible to urge separation and the seeking of a safe haven. Yet, as clinical observations and research attest, this will be a short-term solution. Rather than attempting to persuade patients to leave such relationships, which is likely to fuel yet another power struggle, we therapists might better acknowledge the depth of the attachment and the paradoxical sense of security it affords.

The ideal approach, albeit easy to preach and well nigh impossible to practice, is one of relative neutrality in which we do not put pressure on the patient to leave but rather leave the onus for separation on the patient. Paradoxically, we can focus on the *difficulty* of giving up the attachment and can highlight the myriad factors that prompt the patient to stay in the relationship (not the least of which will be her keen appreciation of her partner's vulnerability and dependency, and her protectiveness of him). A solid therapeutic alliance founded on our empathy and acceptance counters the patient's isolation and may contribute to her capacity to reach out for other sources of support. Then, if she elects to leave the abusive relationship, she is less likely to have a sense of plunging into the void.

EDUCATING CLIENTS ABOUT ATTACHMENT AND REENACTMENT

Nothing beats attachment theory as a way to help clients understand the role of relationships in distress regulation. Attachment theory is easy to explain, and it makes intuitive sense to traumatized persons. I sometimes illustrate attachment patterns by referring to infant behavior in the Strange Situation, but more often I use the model of adult attachment styles. With attachment concepts as a backdrop, I introduce the concept of reenactment in terms of role relationships.

Attachment styles

Figure 3.1, modeled after the work of Brennan and colleagues (Brennan et al., 1998), can be drawn on a blackboard or a writing tablet, depending on the clinical situation. This diagram provides a straightforward overview of attachment classifications and dimensions. The secure attachment quadrant, which entails comfort with closeness, serves as a reference point—and a treatment goal. I present dismissing attachment as avoidance of closeness and relative comfort with distance. As I emphasize in teaching, it is understandable that persons who have been repeatedly hurt by others would aspire to this interpersonal stance. But it is defensive, *counter-dependent* rather than truly independent. Yet, as research findings described earlier suggest, for many severely traumatized patients, distance from others is not associated with comfort. Rather, the fearful quadrant typically fits much of their experience. As had been the case during trauma, they feel anxious and alone. Finally, the ambivalent (preoccupied) quadrant represents the anxiety they feel in times of relative closeness.

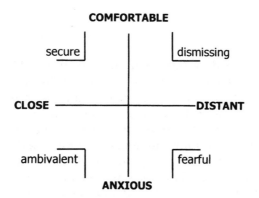

Figure 3.1   Attachment styles and relationship dimensions

Figure 3.1 is useful not only in depicting the different attachment styles but also in emphasizing differences in degree and the possibility of continual dynamic changes. The attachment categories are best presented as prototypes or idealizations (D. W. Griffin & K. Bartholomew, 1994), recognizing that individuals typically do not uniquely fit just one classification (Bartholomew & Horowitz, 1991). Patients readily confirm the view that attachment patterns not only vary in degree but also change over time and differ from one relationship to another (Allen, Huntoon et al., 2000; Rutter, 1995; Stein et al., 1998; Stein, Koontz et al., 2000).

In describing movement among categories, I point out that a person who attempts to move from the fearful position toward greater security is likely to become ambivalent—anxious about being hurt or abandoned. I also discuss anger about dependency in this context. It is easy to see how one could oscillate back and forth between ambivalent closeness and fearful avoidance, particularly when reenactments in relationships eventuate in hurtful interactions and disappointments. I also note how an individual may feel more or less comfortable with distance from one time to another. Many individuals attempt to move from fearful to dismissing insofar as they endeavor to feel comfortable in their isolation. When they are doing relatively well, they may be able to maintain this dismissing position, but because they are unable to rely on secure attachments, they are vulnerable to slipping back into the fearful quadrant when they are more distressed or ill.

Explaining different types of attachment and varying degrees of approximation to them sets the stage for helping clients to think about their current attachment relationships. As we have done for clinical assessment (Allen, Huntoon et al., in press), I invite them to list their current attachment figures on a sheet of paper. This list is the basis for two major treatment agendas: making use of current attachments as well as expanding the range of attachments and the depth of security in those attachment relationships.

Role enactments

As many others have done (Davies & Frawley, 1994; Gabbard & Wilkinson, 1994; Saakvitne, Gamble, Pearlman, & Lev, 2000; Twemlow, Sacco, & Williams, 1996), I find it easiest to discuss patterns of reenactments with patients in terms of a small set of roles revolving around victimization, rescue, and neglect. Over the course of several psychoeducational groups, I worked with patients and my colleagues, Kay Kelly and Janis Huntoon, to refine a diagram that presents the gist of these relationship patterns (see the outer shell of Figure 3.2). These roles are diagrammed so as to be dyadic, with the more active stance on the left and the more passive stance on the right. When discussing the desire to be rescued, I emphasize its universal-

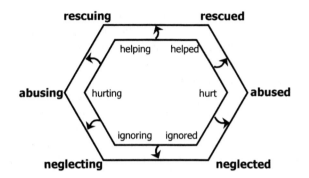

Figure 3.2   Relationship roles and reenactments

ity, and patients invariably assent. I present this desire to be rescued as often evident in childhood and utterly natural. Many patients describe fantasies of the ideal family or even daydream about being taken off to another world. For many, especially those who were fantasy prone (see Chapter 7), such fantasies were highly elaborate and vivid. Many patients report past relationships that held out the promise of rescuing, and therapists are readily cast into contemporary roles of rescue (Davies & Frawley, 1994). Of course the premise of this diagram is that roles shift, so any given role is temporary. Individuals also are prone to occupying all positions. Hence many persons not only wish to be rescued but also overextend themselves in an effort to rescue others through relentless caregiving. Some persons make a conscious effort to provide others with what they themselves did not experience, attempting to satisfy their attachment needs vicariously.

The abusing–abused dyad is the centerpiece of this diagram. It is here, of course, that the most blatant forms of reenactment occur—a prototype being the battering relationship. Here also, both sides of this dyad—abused and abuser—are likely to be enacted. This is ground where we therapists must tread carefully. The most loathsome self-attribute is that of abuser, and clients are extremely sensitive to recognizing in themselves the behavior they most despise.

At the lower end of the diagram is the neglecting–neglected dyad. Having emphasized repeatedly the dual role of frightening experience in combination with feeling alone, neglected, and abandoned, I often find that this facet of the diagram comes as no surprise. I argue that the relationship dynamics in this diagram tend to sink downward from top to bottom: from hoping for rescue, to feeling victimized, to feeling alone and neglected. As I present it, the neglecting–neglected aspect of this diagram is the black hole into which traumatic interactions tend to gravitate.

Although this sort of diagram is widely used in the trauma literature, I have added a new twist to it by inserting a parallel inner set of interactions that consist of toned-down versions of the potentially traumatic reenact-ments. The toned-down versions are: helping–helped versus rescuing–rescued; hurting–being hurt versus abusing–abused; and ignoring–ignored versus neglecting–neglected. This diagram ties in the PTSD perspective (Chapter 5) with the reenactment perspective. Reminders of trauma evoke PTSD symptoms. Many of the reminders that evoke post-traumatic intrusive symptoms are *interpersonal*. Figure 3.2 categorizes these interpersonal reminders.

I present the inner set of roles as ubiquitous in day-to-day interactions, stating that individuals not only routinely help each other but also hurt and ignore each other. Then I emphasize how, with a history of trauma, these ordinary interactions can evoke traumatic levels of responsiveness, because they may constitute reminders of trauma. I draw outward-pointing arrows to underscore the common pattern of sensitization wherein ordinary inter-actions trigger post-traumatic reexperiencing.

Starting at the top of the inner diagram, I note how common helpfulness is. Although many patients, unfortunately, do not share this view, they often can realize how they have built hopes of rescue on others' ordinary helpful behaviors and responses (e.g., expressions of sympathy and understanding as well as practical help). Such unrealistic hopes for rescue then lead to dis-illusionment (and sinking into the black hole). Alternatively, unsustainable efforts to help (then rescue) others also lead to disillusionment (e.g., feeling exploited, exhausted, and abused).

I state flatly that ordinary interactions involve people hurting each other—again, in the inner part of this diagram, at toned-down levels. I ask patients to give examples and often refer to hurtful behavior as critical, insensitive, tactless, annoying, aggravating, and so forth. Such ordinary behavior may be more or less deliberate or inadvertent—but it is ubiquitous. Severely traumatized persons will have no difficulty proffering many exam-ples. In emphasizing that it is normal and ordinary for persons to hurt each other in these ways, I attempt to normalize the client's involvement in the hurting–abusing side of this diagram. I draw attention to the distinction between abusive behavior (and feeling abused) and ordinary hurtful inter-actions. Here I am reiterating the pervasive theme of distinguishing the present from the past.

Similar to the arguments for helping and hurting, I emphasize that indi-viduals ordinarily neglect each other to mild degrees. This comes in the form of ignoring, distancing, withdrawing, and so forth. I also include in this domain the ordinary phenomenon of one individual not understanding, empathizing with, or being sensitively responsive to another. Another common example is ordinary detachment or preoccupation. Most trauma-tized persons can readily identify the active side of this dyad in their own behavior—they are often withdrawn, distant, and detached. Again, I point out how the ordinary levels of feeling ignored can trigger powerful feelings of aloneness, neglect, and abandonment. On the basis of our clinical observations and the emphasis I give to the role of neglect in trauma, I argue that *neglect is a common form of reexperiencing and reenacting traumatic relationships* (and, as described in Chapter 10, it is the core dynamic of borderline personality disorder).

Although Figure 3.2 depicts two levels of enactment—a traumatic level and an ordinary level—this is a gross simplification. We could fill in the space between the inner and outer levels with shades of gray: ignoring shades into neglecting, hurting into abusing, helping into rescuing. Our therapeutic challenge is to promote inward movement toward the center of the diagram rather than outward velocity toward the periphery.

The attachment classification and role enactment diagrams (Figures 3.1 and 3.2) stand on their own. Traumatized persons readily identify with both diagrams. It is possible, however, to explicitly link the attachment perspective and the role-enactment perspective. Insecure attachment styles constitute a propensity to experience and influence interactions in such a way as to enact the dyadic patterns in Figure 3.2. A fearful style is likely to be associated with a feeling of neglect. A dismissing style may be associated with abuse. I see the ambivalent style as generating a particularly high level of action and interaction in this diagram. Ambivalent attachment is associated with high levels of closeness and fear. Ambivalent individuals are liable to be drawn into interactions where they long for rescue and then are vulnerable to disillusionment. They enter into relationships with high anxiety. They are prone to feeling hurt and neglected, and they are particularly likely to be embroiled in volatile relationships (Henderson et al., 1997).

Figure 3.2 also illustrates unbalanced relationships akin to Lyons-Ruth and colleagues' emphasis on the hostile–helpless pattern associated with disorganized attachment. In Figure 3.2, the asymmetry is evident in the two sides, active and passive. The hostile–intrusive side would be associated with a proclivity to hurting–abusing, with the other member of the dyad (infant or adult) feeling helpless and intruded upon—hurt or abused. The helpless–frightened side would be conducive to withdrawing, with the other member of the dyad feeling ignored or neglected. This one diagram reflects the interactional wellspring of attachment as well as the interactional manifestations of insecure attachment in adult relationships.

In drawing clients' attention to repetition of problematic patterns, I endeavor to foster awareness and reflection so as to point them toward developing more supportive and stable relationships. Yet promoting a full appreciation of the power of reenactment in relationships, as well as means of interrupting these patterns, requires that we also help patients understand the impact of trauma on the self.

Chapter 4

THE TRAUMATIZED SELF

No more fiendish punishment could be devised, were such a thing physically possible, than that one should be turned loose in society and remain absolutely unnoticed by all the members thereof. (James, 1890/1950, p 293)

This chapter elaborates the thesis that attachment trauma undermines the development of the capacity to regulate distress. I have shown in Chapter 3 how traumatic attachment relationships engender alarm and fail to alleviate it. Sadly, formative experiences of the 'fiendish punishment' that James envisioned are not uncommon. The distressed infant goes 'absolutely unnoticed,' for example, in the presence of a psychologically unavailable caregiver who is in a post-traumatic dissociative state. James was making the point that the existence of the self depends on social recognition, and this is nowhere more true than early in life when the self comes into being. This chapter shows how attachment trauma undermines the development of the self and, thereby, the capacity for self-regulation. Here I am staking out the main territory for treatment (Chapters 11 and 12), because therapy must belatedly further the development of the self so as to facilitate self-regulation.

We therapists encounter the greatest depths of trauma in the realm of the self, and these depths are the hardest for us and our patients to fathom. Appreciating the full impact of trauma on the self has been elusive, in part because the self has been enormously challenging to conceptualize in psychology and philosophy. Neisser (1988a) delineated five core aspects of the self, Josephs (1992) listed twenty, and Dennett (1991) questioned if there is any sense at all in the concept of self. But we cannot be deterred by this controversy, else we will fail to tackle what we most need to grasp. I rely on one global distinction that has a century's worth of support in psychology: the distinction between the 'I' and the 'me' (Harter, 1999; James,

1890/1950; Mead, 1934; Sartre, 1957). The 'I' is the aspect of the self that most vexes philosophers and introspective psychologists. The 'I' is the self-as-agent, and the actions of the 'I' are associated with an admittedly elusive subjective sense of self (Damasio, 1999). By comparison, the 'me' is easy to understand. The 'me' is the objective self as evident in the self-concept or self-representation.

To convey the potential impact of attachment trauma on the 'I' and the 'me,' I will explore how these two aspects of the self come into being. Here is the question: How is mind created? I would approach this intellectual challenge with unalloyed excitement were it not for the subtext of trauma. But we therapists have a more pragmatic agenda, as we must glean all we can from current theory and research to guide us in our effort to right developmental wrongs.

After addressing trauma to the 'I' and the 'me' from a developmental perspective, I will suggest ways this understanding can be used in educational groups. At best, we can only scratch the surface in educating clients about this deep trauma to the self. No doubt, making therapeutic inroads into this domain of trauma entails far more than education. I am convinced that healing the self requires the most ambitious of interpersonal therapies. Regardless of how much we can explicate with them, our clients may benefit from our efforts to understand this relatively unfathomable trauma if we can use our understanding to empathize with their sense of depletion, helplessness, and passivity—and begin to help them out of it.

THE TRAUMATIZED 'I'

Developmental research clarifies how trauma may hamper emotional regulation by undermining the ability to relate to other persons as selves with minds. The capacity to become a self—an 'I'—depends on apprehending mental states. Most of us are fortunate to be able to take our *mind-reading ability* for granted, at least until we are perplexed by someone's behavior —or our own. But this mind-reading ability is a product of a complex developmental trajectory with a long evolutionary history.

Like developmental research, current evolutionary thinking underscores the need for the mind-reading ability that we may take for granted but our traumatized clients cannot. Tradition has it that practical problem solving and tool making drove the evolution of human intelligence. But relating to other autonomous—and rather unpredictable—individuals is far more challenging than tool making. Extensive primate research now supports the thesis that the evolutionary arms race that drove the expansion of the human neocortex is based on the need for social intelligence (Byrne & Whiten, 1988; Humphrey, 1988; Whiten & Byrne, 1988). We humans share with many species what Bogdan (1997) construed as the capacity for *interpretation*, 'organisms making sense of each other in contexts where this matters bio-logically' (p. 10). In his view interpretation becomes uniquely human in its psychosocial core, 'characterized as *engaging others psychologically in sharing experiences, information, and affects'* (p. 94). Although much interpre-tation is done consciously, more is done nonconsciously 'on automatic pilot' (p. 208).

I draw your attention to our evolutionary origins merely to emphasize the necessity of interpretation. As a social species, understanding each other is critical for our survival. Trauma in early attachment relationships can com-promise this fundamental adaptive capacity. As a therapist, you will devote considerable time and energy to nurturing it. To lay the foundation for this work, I will delineate the developmental steps toward the interpreting mind, examine how secure attachment facilitates these steps, and then discuss how attachment trauma impedes them.

Steps to the development of mind

Dennett (1987) proposed that we use the *physical stance* to predict the behavior of physical objects and the *design stance* to predict the behavior of artifacts (e.g., alarm clocks and computers) with minimal knowledge of their physical properties. But we cannot rely on the physical or design stances to predict each other's behavior. Our capacity to interpret human behavior— to make sense of each other—requires the *intentional stance:* 'treating the object whose behavior you want to predict as a rational agent with beliefs and desires' (p. 15).

Yet there is a transitional developmental step between grasping physical-mechanical causality and understanding mental causality, namely, the perception of action as goal directed (Leslie, 1994). Infants are attuned to goal-directed action long before they have any conception of mind (Gergely, Nadasdy, Csibra, & Biro, 1995). Csibra, Gergely, and colleagues (Csibra & Gergely, 1998; Csibra, Gergely, Biro, Koos, & Brockbank, 1999) construed this transitional step between the physical and intentional stances as the *teleo-logical stance*. The physical stance is exemplified by external causality—one billiard ball moves after being hit by another. The teleological stance, or naïve theory of rational action, is reflected in the capacity to interpret actions as efficiently achieving goals within the constraints of physical reality. Laboratory experiments show that, by nine months of age, infants inter-pret behavior as rational in the sense of being efficiently goal directed, even when the behavior is that of computer-generated animations. The capacity to adopt the teleological stance is adaptive because, whereas the physical–causal stance allows for the prediction of behavior of physical *objects*, the teleological stance allows for the prediction of the behavior of goal-directed *agents*.

The mentalistic intentional stance goes a big step further, taking us into the realm of mind. The intentional stance builds on the teleological stance by interpreting rational, goal-directed behavior as *guided by mental states*. Mental states include *desires* that represent goal states and *beliefs* that represent the constraints of reality. The capacity to grasp mental states becomes evident in the second year of life and is increasingly refined over the whole course of development. To reiterate, we come equipped to develop these stances because they allow us to predict the behavior of physical objects and other beings. The teleological stance works not just for non-human agents like insects (and computer animations) but also for human beings—to a point. But we need to invoke the mentalistic intentional stance when human actions are not superficially rational.

Consider a concrete example. A battering husband shoves his wife out of his way into a corner, and we comprehend her behavior from the physical stance. He has treated her as a physical object. Alternatively, he rushes toward her in a rage, and she jumps out of the way, then huddles in a corner. We grasp her behavior from the teleological stance. But what do we do if she is in a therapy group where other patients are talking about physical abuse, and she anxiously gets up from her chair, then huddles in the corner in a daze? We can only comprehend her behavior by invoking the intentional stance, for example, inferring that she is responding to a memory—a flashback that has put her into a post-traumatic dissociative state.

These various stances allow us to apprehend behavior from the outside. Now let us consider the experience of developing a self with a mind from the inside. Relationships require that we do more than understand other persons; we must understand ourselves as well. The 'I' is first a physical agent. Stern (1985) considered self-agency, 'the sense of authorship of one's own actions' (p. 71), to be one of several facets of the core self. In early infancy, being an author of actions entails a sense of controlling one's body in space. Neisser (1988a) observed that the sense of agency involved in initiating movements and perceiving their consequences produces pleasure in *effectivity*. Watson and Gergely (Gergely, 1999; Gergely & Watson, 1996, 1999; Watson, 1994) pinpointed how the road to a sense of self-as-physical-agent is paved with contingency detection. Infants actively seek contingent relationships and find a high degree of causal control to be extremely rewarding. Just like the rest of us, they like to make things happen. In the first three months of life, infants pay most attention to events that are *perfectly* contingent on their own actions—for example, watching their limbs move (Bahrick & Watson, 1985). This perfect response–stimulus contingency provides self-calibrating information that fosters the progressive differentiation of the self from the external world (Watson, 1994). When I move my arm, the chair across the room stays put! Part and parcel of developing such contingent relationships is constructing the primary representation of the body as a distinct object in the environment (Gergely, 1999, in press; Gergely & Watson, 1999).

Reflect on the centrality of your sense of will, agency, and efficacy to your well being. Then consider the potential impact of trauma in early life on the sense of self as physical agent in light of Foa and colleagues' (Foa et al., 1992) assertion that uncontrollability and unpredictability are at the heart of trauma. Loss of control and predictability undermine the bedrock of the self. And much of trauma—impersonal and interpersonal—entails a loss of control over the body and physical actions. Hence uncontrollability and unpredictability can be traumatic at any age. But trauma may have especially grave consequences early in life, when the infant is just becoming a *physical* agent. And, to go from the frying pan into the fire, we must also consider the impact of trauma on becoming a *mental* agent.

As Fonagy and Target (1997a) explicated, the intentional stance requires the ability to *mentalize*. To a large degree, mentalizing is a nonconscious interpretive skill, as riding a bicycle is a nonconscious perceptual-motor skill. We do it without thinking about it. We mentalize continually when we interact with others, apprehending and responding to their desires, feelings, expectations, and beliefs, and the like. Of course, when interactions fail to run smoothly, we benefit from consciously reflecting on mental states. '*What* was he thinking—feeling, wanting, imagining?' And we are not just perplexed by other persons; we perplex ourselves: '*What* was *I* thinking—feeling, wanting, imagining?' Fonagy and Target (1997a) construed our ability to consciously interpret human behavior in this way as *reflective function*, defined as 'the developmental acquisition that permits the child to respond not only to other people's behavior, but to his *conception* of their beliefs, feelings, hopes, pretense, plans, and so on' (p. 679). Thus the sense of subjective self begins on the basis of physical agency, then evolves into the experience of mental agency. Fonagy and Target pointed out that mentalizing and reflective function enhance the sense of self-agency insofar as 'action is intimately tied to the mental state (belief or desire) which initiated it' (p. 692). We are moved by mind, and we feel it.

The adaptive functions of mentalizing and reflective function are legion, as are the detrimental effects of trauma to these capacities (Dunn, 1996; Fonagy, 1995; Fonagy & Target, 1997a; Gergely, 1999; Target & Fonagy, 1996). Reflective function makes other persons' behavior meaningful and predictable, and reflective *self*-function (Fonagy, Target, & Gergely, 2000) makes our own behavior intelligible. In early childhood, reflective function supports pretend play, fosters conversations about feelings and the reasons for actions, and facilitates interactions with peers. Your reflective function also allows you to influence the behavior of others, for example, by deliberately influencing their desires, feelings, beliefs, and expectations. Your capacity to influence your own actions, modest as it may be, rests on the same process, reflectively treating yourself as a mental agent.

Reflective function should command your therapeutic attention most for its potential to allow your clients to experience their traumatic past as mental states rather than as currently occurring events. Your capacity for mentalization allows you to decouple your mental states from the reality in which they are embedded (Leslie, 1987). The client who cowers in the corner in a dissociative state has lost this capacity to decouple her mental state from reality. She cannot apprehend that the danger is *mental*—a frightening memory—instead experiencing it as *real*. Attachment trauma has compromised her reflective function, and it is our therapeutic job to help restore it.

Attachment and the development of mind

Stern's (1985) pioneering theory of the development of the self provides a foundation for recent research on trauma. Stern argued that, from the beginning, caregivers actively foster the sense of self. Parents treat infants as if they had a sense of self: 'It is almost impossible to conduct social interaction with infants without attributing these human qualities to them. These qualities make human behavior understandable, and parents invariably treat their infants as understandable beings' (p. 43). The infant's core self includes a sense of self-with-other, based on highly coordinated interactions between the infant and the caregiver. Because these interactions foster self-regulation, Stern viewed the 'other' as a 'self-regulating other' (p. 102).

Stern proposed that affect attunement plays a key role in the development of intersubjectivity, and he referred to parental mirroring and empathic responses as 'interaffectivity.' On the grounds that basic emotions are universal and innate, Gergely and Watson (1996) raised the possibility that 'emotions are among (if not the) earliest mental states that infants attribute to minds' (p. 1183). Consider that trauma entails overwhelming emotional states, involves the antithesis of emotional attunement, undermines the capacity for emotional regulation, and eventuates in intrusive post-traumatic emotional upheaval. The developmental link between emotion and the self warrants careful attention, because we therapists ultimately take on the therapeutic task of becoming a 'self-regulating other' by providing the kind of emotional attunement that fosters internalization of self-regulating capacities. This sounds like a tall order but, thanks to the mentalizing capacity we can (usually) take for granted, we therapists are doing this intuitively, much of the time.

Watson and Gergely (Gergely & Watson, 1996; Watson, 1994) discovered how infants gravitate toward the emotional attunement needed for development of the self. In the first two months of life, infants demonstrate a preference for perfect response–stimulus contingencies. For example, they pay close attention to their body movements. But a cardinal shift in contingency preferences takes place around three months of age. At this time, infants switch from a preference for a perfect degree of response–stimulus contingency to a preference for a high—but imperfect—degree of contingency. The adaptive consequence of this switch is a major reorientation of attention with a momentous result. *Infants switch from focusing on their own actions to attending to the emotionally responsive social environment* (Gergely & Watson, 1999). Specifically, three-month-old infants develop a high degree of interest in their mothers' responses to their emotional states. We therapists are making use of this three-month-old capacity whenever we bank on our clients' interest in our emotional responses—and their soothing effects. The term *mirroring* is misleading in this context to the extent that a mirror implies a perfectly contingent response (Gergely, in press). Optimal maternal (or therapeutic) responsiveness is inherently highly, but not perfectly, contingent—yet perfectly matched with the infant's newfound attentional preferences. And the infant's increasing attention to the mother's responsiveness has crucial developmental consequences for distress regulation. In the first months of the infant's life, the mother can soothe the infant only by her direct physical ministrations. After the infant prefers to focus on her emotional responses, however, the infant can be soothed by her emotional communications. The high level of contingency gives the infant a sense of control over the mother's emotional expressions, and this sense of control affords a rewarding sense of self-efficacy that helps counter the infant's distress—just as it may do for the adult in therapy.

Maternal emotional responsiveness also promotes emotional containment by contributing to the development of infants' sense of self by engendering representations of their own emotional states. But to convey the difference between emotional trauma and emotional attunement, I must clarify the difference between *raw emotion* and *empathic emotional communications*. As Gergely and Watson (1996) described, when they are in the empathic mode, mothers respond to infants' emotional states with *marked emotion* (not marked in the sense of 'intense' but rather in the sense of 'marked for sale'). In effect, these empathic maternal emotional expressions are tagged as such, for example, taking the form of exaggerated responses that are intended to communicate or reflect the infant's emotional state. Special features of this tagged emotion distinguish it from *realistic emotion* that is based on the mother's direct emotional response to provocation. Thus the mother might respond either angrily to her infant's fussiness (realistic emotion) or with an empathic response that communicates her apprehension of the infant's irritable state (marked emotion).

Fonagy and Target (1997a) refer to such empathic emotional responses as *complex affects*. For example, the mother may amalgamate smiling, questioning, or a mock display into her facial reflection of her infant's emotion. Just think of how you express distress on your face when someone tells you about an ominous diagnosis they have just been given. Such complex emotional expressions are potentially soothing to the infant (or adult), because they differ from direct emotional responses in subtle external features that signal benevolent intent. Whereas the mother in a state of realistic anger may be hostile toward her infant, the mother displaying 'marked' (empathic) anger has a prosocial aim, that is, to comfort and communicate (Gergely, personal communication, April 14, 1999). The infant's capacity to discriminate between these two kinds of maternal emotion hinges on complex expressive features that mark or tag the empathic states as such. Think of your capacity to tell if your friend is angry *at* you or angry *along with* you. Big difference—and quite a subtle one for the infant to learn.

Once able to discriminate the mother's empathic emotion from her raw emotion, the infant is in a position to transform soothing interactions into self-soothing capacities through a process of *internalization*. This transforming internalization entails the development of *mental representations* of emotional states—representations that ultimately will allow the individual to reflect and experience emotional states as such, rather than being totally at their mercy as if in the midst of traumatic events. We therapists bank on this capacity whenever we encourage our clients to put their feelings into words.

Our adult intuition might suggest that infants learn first to identify their emotional states from *internal* cues. On the contrary, Gergely and Watson (1996, 1999) argued cogently that infants first learn to differentiate their internal states on the basis of *external* cues, namely, others' empathic emotional responses to those states. Gergely and Watson drew a helpful analogy to the teaching function of biofeedback, for example, where a thermometer affixed to the tip of your finger signals relaxation as the warmth from increasing peripheral blood flow indicates a decrease in sympathetic nervous system activation. Observing an external stimulus that monitors an internal state can gradually sensitize one to that internal state and thereby enable one to regulate that state without the external cues. As they explained, 'parental affect-mirroring provides a kind of *natural social biofeedback training* for the infant that plays a crucial role in emotional development' (Gergely & Watson, 1996, p. 1190). Empathic emotion comprises social biofeedback insofar as the mother's expressiveness is yoked to the infant's emotional states. We therapists also can consider ourselves to be natural social biofeedback devices—when we are not in the throes of raw emotion.

The concept of social biofeedback helps explain the process of maternal containment of infant affect—how external regulation becomes internal regulation. This process plays a key role in therapy with traumatized persons, so its development in infancy merits our attention. Keep in mind the distinction between raw emotion and empathic emotion. The infant expresses raw emotion, which Gergely and Watson (1996) label *primary representations*, 'implicit, procedural representations of pre-wired automatisms of the basic emotion' (p. 1189). In interactions that provide containment, the infant's raw emotion meets with empathic responsiveness that allows the infant to find herself, in effect, in the face of her mother. More technically, in Gergely and Watson's terms, the infant internalizes the mother's empathic expression by developing a *secondary representation* of her expression of the infant's emotional state (in effect, if the infant could verbalize, *'That's* what I feel!'). Then the infant's emotion is no longer just raw physiological arousal and motor expression; it is mentalized. Mentalization tempers raw emotion, for example, by associating it with an image of the mother's expression ('That's what I feel!'), a feeling of control over the mother's expression ('She's responding to me!'), and a feeling of comfort in relation to her empathic responsiveness and benevolent disposition ('She cares what I feel!'). Thus, paralleling Stern's reference to a 'self-regulating other,' Gergely and Watson hypothesize that 'successful emotion-regulative interactions involving parental affect-mirroring may provide experiential basis for the establishment of a *sense of self as self-regulating agent'* (p. 1196). Concomitantly, these secondary representations separate the experience and communicative expression of emotion from action (Gergely & Watson, 1999). The child can feel angry without hitting and can perceive anger without expecting to be hit—a distinction sometimes lost on traumatized clients. Ultimately, these secondary representations of emotional states can become ensconced in language ('I am feeling angry'), which further bolsters the child's capacity for reflection and self-regulation.

Empathic responsiveness is crucial to the development of mentalization, but it is only part of a broader relevant relationship context. Fonagy and Target (1997a) reviewed a wide range of factors that contribute to the capacity for mentalization, with secure attachment being pivotal. They presented evidence that the quality of the caregiver's reflective function prior to the infant's birth predicts the infant's attachment security at one year of age. The process is this: the caregiver's attachment security fosters reflective function that, in turn, promotes coordination of representations of self and other:

> Unconsciously and pervasively, the caregiver ascribes a mental state to the child with her behavior, treats the child as a mental agent, which is perceived by the child and used in the elaboration of teleological models, and then in the development of a core sense of mental selfhood. (Fonagy & Target, 1997a, p. 690)

Conversely, the infant's secure attachment fosters the development of reflective function as evidenced, for example, by the relationship between security of attachment at 12–18 months and performance on theory of mind tasks at five years.

Here we have a two-way street in which attachment security fosters a meeting of minds. As Fonagy (1999d) put it, a secure attachment relationship provides a congenial context for the child to explore the mind of the caregiver so as to learn about minds: 'most important for the development of mentalizing self-organization is that exploration of the mental state of the sensitive caregiver enables the child to find in her mind an image of himself as motivated by beliefs, feelings, and intentions, in other words, as mentalizing' (Fonagy & Target, 1997a, p. 691). We therapists ultimately take on this developmental role, because attachment trauma has created an aversion to exploring minds, thereby impeding mentalization, the sense of self, and self-regulation. We can help our traumatized clients by creating an accepting climate in which they can find and explore themselves in our mind.

Attachment trauma and mentalization

If social biofeedback through empathic emotion is required to transform raw emotion into controllable mental states, then consider the potential impact of caregivers' indifference, neglect, and psychological unavailability on the development of the self and the capacity for emotional regulation. Gergely and Watson (1996) noted evidence that maternal depression is associated with a lower level of contingent emotional interactions, as well as maternal intrusiveness and negative emotions. As discussed in the context of attachment (Chapter 3), post-traumatic dissociative states in caregivers also constitute a form of attachment trauma by nullifying infants' control over their caregivers' responsiveness. Certainly, gross neglect could have devastating consequences for the development of affect regulation. But pervasive neglect is not necessary. *The core failure is episodic unresponsiveness when the infant is in a state of heightened attachment needs.*

We are wired to take an interest in the mental-emotional world by our orientation to our caregivers' responsiveness to our emotional states. Yet Fonagy and Target (1997a) described how neglect and abuse impinge on the sense of self-agency and promote a *defensive withdrawal from the mental world.* Apprehending the mind of the abuser will be terrifying to the child, because 'he will be confronted with attitudes towards himself which are extremely painful to recognize: hatred, cruelty, indifference' (Fonagy & Target, 1997a, p. 693). Recognition of hatred and murderousness in a parent's abusive behavior forces children to see themselves as worthless and unlovable (Fonagy, 1999b)—as is abundantly evident in the self-concepts of traumatized women I will describe shortly.

Albeit self-protective, the retreat from the mental world impairs the child's reflective capacities, for example, as shown by poor performance on theory-of-mind tasks, curtailed capacity for pretend play, and the relative absence of language referring to internal states (Fonagy & Target, 1997a). Moreover, by virtue of diminished interpretive ability, the child who cannot mentalize will have difficulty influencing others—for example, being less able to interact with the abuser so as to minimize the abuse or its impact. Fonagy and colleagues described how the maltreated child's defense against mentalization and compromised coping create a vicious circle in development:

> Poor comprehension of mental states associated with maltreatment amplifies distress, activating the attachment system. The need for proximity persists and perhaps even increases as a consequence of the distress caused by abuse. Mental proximity becomes unbearably painful, and the need for closeness is expressed at a physical level. Thus, the child may paradoxically be driven physically closer to the abuser. The child's ability to adapt to, modify, or avoid the perpetrator's behavior is likely to be constrained by limited mentalizing skills, and exposure to further abuse is likely to occur. The paradox of proximity seeking at the physical level concurrent with psychological avoidance lies at the root of the disorganized attachment consistently seen in abused children. (Fonagy et al., 2000, p. 111)

Fortunately, maltreatment does not completely curtail mentalization. Fonagy and Target (1997a) advocated a *dynamic skills theory* wherein mentalization is context dependent. Reflective function is tied to specific relationships so, for example, may be curtailed within the family but not in extrafamilial relationships. Or it may be inhibited in relation to the family's private interactions but not in their public behavior.

An alternative to curtailing mentalization is splitting, which can be adaptive in the context of maltreatment. As Gergely (in press) explained, the young child's theory of mind is predicated on the assumption of coherence. That is, persons are viewed as rational agents whose intentions and actions can be integrated into coherent representations that ensure the predictability of their behavior across a wide range of situations. When abuse alternates with caring behavior, the child is faced with contradictory intentions (persecutory and benevolent) that cannot be integrated into a coherent overall representation. Consequently, mentalization no longer renders behavior predictable, and the child is faced with uncertainty, anxiety, and helplessness. By assigning different identities to the abuser in different contexts, the child can maintain an assumption of rational agency, can see behavior as predictable again, and can restore the possibility of rational action in specific relationship contexts. But the price can be a mind torn apart (Freyd, 1996).

Subjective sense of self in gut feelings

Mentalization brings forth a sense of self as mental agent. How can we link this form of self-agency more explicitly to our clients' conscious experience? To put it concretely, what does it *feel like* to be a self with a mind? Conversely, what does it *feel like* when this sense of self as mental agent has been fundamentally traumatized? Consider again how trauma impinges on the *feeling* of being an embodied self-as-mental-agent. By undermining controllability and predictability, trauma places the individual in a helpless and passive position, countering any sense of agency.

Much interpersonal trauma entails being treated not as a person with needs, desires, feelings, beliefs, and values—as an intentional being—but rather as an object or a non-person. Whereas emotional attunement fosters mentalization, objectification abets a subjective sense of *non*-self. Such trauma leads to an existential void, which clients may express by declaring that they feel 'empty.' Or they wonder, 'Who *am* I?' Or, as Ehlers and colleagues (Ehlers, Maercker, & Boos, 2000) described in the context of political imprisonment, being completely overpowered can lead to a feeling of *mental defeat*, evident in feeling totally at the will of another, having no resistance, giving up caring about oneself, and ceasing to feel human.

Damasio (1994) firmly anchored the feeling of selfhood in the body. On the basis of neuropsychological observations, he developed the hypothesis that somatic markers—more prosaically, *gut feelings*—come to be associated with rewards and punishments and then continuously guide our actions. Without such anchoring in gut feelings (e.g., as a result of damage to the ventromedial frontal lobes), you would be left adrift, lacking a critical basis for knowing how to respond, decide, and interact. Damasio (1999) further proposed that the sense of agency—the core self—is continually constructed in pulses of consciousness on a moment-to-moment basis. Your consciousness is anchored in your body, such that you *feel* yourself being influenced by the environment (e.g., other persons) as you react and interact, whether or not you are aware of the source of influence. Rooted in your body, your sense of agency always has a feeling tone, be it subtly evident (tension, harmony) or obvious in strong emotion (fear, anger, joy).

Damasio provided a concrete direction for responding to the question, 'Who *am* I?' I believe that this question arises not just broadly from identity confusion but also more narrowly from the lack of a substantial moment-to-moment sense of core self anchored in feelings. It is no accident that, when I am confronted with the 'Who *am* I?' question in psychoeducational groups, I soon find myself focusing on feelings. 'Who *am* I?' quickly becomes 'What do I *feel*—or want, need, desire, care about?' I am not referring to the self-concept here—I will get to that shortly. Rather, I am drawing attention to the continually constructed nonverbal sense of self that takes the form of a succession of impelling mental states grounded in gut feelings. If this sense of self is elusive to those of us therapists who are enamored with mental states and emotions, imagine how opaque the sense of self must be to our traumatized clients. Many such clients feel profoundly dissociated from both the inner and outer world (Allen, Console, & Lewis, 1999; Allen, Coyne, & Console, 1997) and complain of feeling 'numb.' Some say they feel as if they do not exist from the neck down. Numbing detachment from the body contributes to a depleted sense of subjectivity, often expressed aptly as a feeling of 'emptiness' or 'deadness.' Continuing down this path, clients confront us therapists with another bedeviling question, 'How do I *start feeling*?' Then we have come full circle, back to the need for a secure attachment relationship that fosters mentalization and reflective function.

THE TRAUMATIZED 'ME'

Whereas the sense of subjective self may be frustratingly elusive to traumatized clients, the objective self is often painfully conscious. Janoff-Bulman (1992) observed that trauma may shatter one of the fundamental assumptions every person holds: The self is worthy. 'This assumption involves a global evaluation of the self, and, in general, we perceive ourselves as good, capable, and moral individuals' (p. 11). She provided ample evidence that trauma—and particularly interpersonal trauma—undermines the fundamental assumption of self-worth: 'Personal autonomy, strength of will, pride of self-possession are broken, and in their place are personal violation, loss of self-respect, and lingering doubts about one's self-worth' (p. 80).

To clarify the trauma to self-worth, I will describe some findings from our clinical assessment of traumatized women and then review others' research. Finally, I will consider some developmental origins of these traumatic adult outcomes.

Trauma and self-worth

The full extent of trauma-related damage to self-worth became evident in our psychological evaluations of women with a history of childhood maltreatment who were admitted for specialized inpatient treatment (Allen, Coyne, & Console, 2000). My colleagues Janis Huntoon, David Console, and I asked patients to fill out a questionnaire in which they were to articulate their most troubling intrusive images and thoughts, and we included the following item: 'Please describe briefly any negative views of yourself or disturbing thoughts about yourself that you have in conjunction with these intrusive images.' We administered this questionnaire to more than a hundred traumatized women, many of whom vividly conveyed the extent of their negative self-images. Examples of some responses will convey the scope of assaults to self-worth.

We found ample evidence for extremely impaired global self-worth. Patients commented explicitly on 'feeling worthless' or their 'lack of self-esteem.' Some referred to themselves as 'no good,' 'a loser,' or 'a bad person.' Even more extremely, others stated 'I have nothing of value inside me,' 'No one else is as bad as me,' and 'I'm evil and will go to hell.' Some expressed frank self-hatred (e.g., 'I hate myself,' 'self-loathing') or the desire to attack themselves (e.g., 'I want to cut my guts out').

Feelings of inadequacy are part and parcel of damaged self-worth. Examples include: 'I have been a failure,' 'I'm incapable of doing things,' 'I'm no good at anything any more,' 'I'm not able to function,' 'I amount to nothing,' and 'I'll never achieve my goals.' Patients described themselves as 'awkward,' 'dumb,' 'immature,' 'pathetic,' 'wimpy,' 'lazy,' and 'a fool.' Many expressed an impaired sense of self-efficacy: 'helpless,' 'weak,' 'can't cope,' 'out of control,' and 'constantly making bad decisions.' One stated, 'He took my control away, and I can't get it back.' Some expressed inability to cope with the trauma: 'I'm not strong enough to get over these thoughts and feelings,' 'I feel very stupid about my overreactions,' and 'I'm impatient with myself for allowing this stuff to impact my life so much, being sick all the time.'

More specifically, the domains of physical attractiveness and gender identity are adversely affected. Patients described themselves as 'ugly,' 'hopelessly fat,' 'disfigured,' and stated 'I hate my body' and 'I feel and look dirty, can't get clean.' Others expressed negative views about their sexuality and role functioning: 'I'm asexual,' 'I don't look or act like a woman,' 'I have been a bad mother, wife, and cook,' and 'I'm a failure as a daughter and spouse.'

Many patients expressed explicit feelings of shame (e.g., 'lots of shame,' 'embarrassment,' 'humiliation'). Some expressed a profound sense of degradation and repugnance, describing themselves as 'disgusting,' 'cheap,' 'a dirty little whore,' 'a freak,' 'tainted and used garbage,' and 'an inhuman monster that repulses everyone.' A number referred explicitly to guilt feelings (e.g., 'deep sense of guilt,' 'I believe everything I do is wrong'). Many blamed themselves for the traumatic events: 'I blame myself for them all,' 'It was my fault,' 'I'm bad, causing these things to happen,' 'Something must be wrong with me or he wouldn't do these things,' 'I was never good enough to make him stop,' 'They saw my evil and responded in kind,' 'I let them do it and could have said no,' 'I'm stupid because I told no one and therefore I wasn't protected,' and 'I should have had my guard up.' Guilt feelings and self-blame translate into a sense of deserving punishment: 'I have sinned and need to be punished,' 'I deserve to be hurt and to be in pain,' 'I deserve torture for my flawed personality,' 'I would like to go to hell,' and 'I have the urge to have others hurt me.' A number of patients described themselves as undeserving: 'I don't deserve good things,' 'I'm not deserving of anyone's love,' 'I don't deserve to have a good life,' and 'I don't deserve to live.'

In conjunction with the negative self-images and guilt feelings, many patients expressed a sense of being rejected and unloved: 'unwanted,' 'abandoned,' 'unlikable,' 'unlovable,' 'a person nobody would want to know,' 'No one will ever want to be close,' 'No one could possibly love me,' and 'Who is going to want me now?' One stated, 'Even God hates me.' Some expressed a sense of isolation and alienation: 'loneliness,' 'I cannot get close,' 'I am different,' 'I have no place on this earth,' 'I am the anti-Christ.' Also evident is extreme alienation from the self: 'I am non-existent,' 'I am invisible or waiting to be,' 'I can't stand living in my body knowing what was done to it,' and 'I want an exorcist to get rid of the evil spirits.'

Not surprisingly, intertwined with low self-worth and guilt feelings is profound hopelessness: 'I am hopeless,' 'I can't get better,' 'I won't ever be well,' 'I'll never be my old self again,' 'I've always been this way and will stay this way,' 'I'll never amount to anything good,' 'I'll never be able to trust or go on living a life with some comfort and stability,' 'I never will be adequate,' 'I'll never survive this depression,' and 'I'm too beaten down to fight anymore.' With hopelessness often comes suicidal thinking: 'Death is my only option,' 'I want to kill myself because of the pain,' and 'I need to die to get better.'

Consistent with our clinical observations, extensive research has documented a relation between maltreatment and low self-worth (Harter, 1999). A few studies will illustrate. Janoff-Bulman (1992) demonstrated how trauma can shatter three fundamental assumptions: the world is benevolent, the world is meaningful, and the self is worthy. Her research showed that trauma survivors express more negative views than their non-traumatized counterparts, even many years after the traumatic events. The fundamental assumptions of benevolence, meaningfulness, and self-worth are liable to be transformed into a world pervaded by 'malevolence, meaninglessness, and self-abasement' (p. 63). Survivors of deliberate interpersonal trauma held the most negative views: 'the world is viewed as more malevolent and the self is viewed more negatively, as if one mirrors the other' (p. 77). Foa and colleagues (Foa, Ehlers, Clark, Tolin, & Orsillo, 1999) also found that, compared to accident victims, assaulted persons showed more negative trauma-related beliefs in three domains: negative beliefs about the self, negative beliefs about the world, and self-blame. Moreover, the extent of negative beliefs discriminated sharply between trauma victims with and without PTSD. Andrews and colleagues (Andrews, Brewin, Rose, & Kirk, 2000) also found that shame after violent assault predicted subsequent PTSD.

Compared to physical and sexual abuse, psychological abuse may contribute uniquely to low self-worth (Briere & Runtz, 1990). Yet childhood sexual abuse is particularly likely to be associated with concerns about body image as indicated, for example, by Rorschach Test responses of abused women that reflected 'a distressing sense that something about them is fundamentally damaged' (Nash et al., 1993a, p. 282). Of course damage to self-worth also may stem from later interpersonal trauma. For example, women who had been date raped reported several areas of lowered *sexual self-esteem*, for example, in their judgments of the morality of their sexual behavior, the compatibility of their sexuality with other life goals, and their ability to control their sexual feelings, behavior, and relationships (Shapiro & Schwarz, 1997).

The development of low self-worth

Damaged global self-worth in adulthood is the culmination of a long course of development. As soon as the child is capable of reflection, maltreatment can begin to erode self-worth. In their review of the adverse effects of abuse and neglect on the self, Cicchetti and Toth (1995) noted that maltreated toddlers' lack of positive response or aversion to seeing their images in a mirror may be 'an early precursor to a generalized low sense of self-worth' (p. 550).

As Harter (1999) reviewed, the structure and organization of the 'me' changes markedly over the course of development in tandem with growing cognitive capacities. In early childhood, the self-concept is relatively disjointed and, barring maltreatment, tends to be relatively positive—indeed, unrealistically so. By middle childhood, when social comparison comes to the fore, children are more attuned to discrepancies between the real and ideal self and are more self-critical. Concomitantly, the self-affects of shame and pride become more evident. By adolescence the self-concept becomes more differentiated and integrated, and self-worth is increasingly relational, varying across different relationship contexts. Thus there are multiple developmental pathways to global self-worth. Individuals differ in domains of real–ideal self discrepancies that are important (e.g., physical appearance, likability, or academic competence) as well as in what aspect of relational self-worth (e.g., peers or parents) contributes most to global self-worth. In broad strokes, *global self-worth will be determined conjointly by perceived competence in various domains of importance and extent of supportive approval in valued relationships.*

Parental approval plays a major role in global self-worth throughout childhood and adolescence, and early experience often establishes a foundation of global self-worth that is highly resistant to change (Harter, 1999). As Bowlby (1973) recognized, the internal working model of the self is congruent with treatment by caregivers. Although the findings are not entirely consistent across studies, compared to insecure attachment, secure attachment is generally associated with a more positive and realistically balanced self-concept across developmental levels (Crowell et al., 1999; Harter, 1999; Thompson, 1999). Insecure attachment may be one mediator between maltreatment and low self-worth. By undermining attachment security, maltreatment may adversely affect the development of various competencies as well as the formation of supportive relationships, both of which contribute to self-worth.

When I talk with patients in psychoeducational groups about the development of their low self-worth, a few themes predominate. First, patients report that they *explained* the abuse and neglect on the basis of their being bad. Inferring that their badness was responsible for their plight was preferable to a view of their world as utterly meaningless and unpredictable. As Janoff-Bulman (1992) described, individuals assume that the world is meaningful, that events happen for a reason, and that good and bad outcomes are distributed on the basis of the goodness of the individual. From this perspective, misfortune—and especially maltreatment—is readily explained by one's badness.

Many patients recognize that explaining the maltreatment on the basis of their own failings provided an illusion of control that was preferable to utter helplessness. Perhaps if they could be different or better, the abuse might stop. As Janoff-Bulman (1992) argued, the assumption of meaningful action–outcome contingencies implies order and comprehensibility, whereas the alternative is randomness and the sense that there is nothing one can do to protect oneself. Yet the price for avoiding a feeling of uncontrollability and unpredictability is guilt feelings, whether in childhood or adulthood. As Walker (1979) observed, the battered woman not only suffers guilt-inducing attacks but also believes that she can change her partner's behavior by changing her own behavior. Yet she actually has little control over him, such that she feels an even greater sense of failure.

In identifying the locus of responsibility for childhood abuse, many patients state flatly, 'It was me or them.' Nathanson (1992) pointed out that the neglected child has two alternatives, namely, recognizing that the parents are incapable of love and will not provide protection or developing 'the creative but false theory that his or her parents are really okay and that their unpleasant behavior is the reasonable response of good people to a bad or defective child' (pp. 340–341). Patients readily agree with Nathanson's conclusion: 'Clearly, logic most often commands the second choice, which offers far greater emotional safety than the harsher reality.'

Herman (1992b) pointed out that the internalized sense of badness *preserves the attachment relationship* and thus the individual is reluctant to give it up even after the abuse has stopped. Thus in adulthood many patients are loath to give up their sense of badness because it would rearrange their whole internal world, and they would feel even more guilty if they were disloyal to their parents.

Sadly, many individuals did not need to infer their responsibility for maltreatment. They were told directly that it was their fault—or they were screamed at. Internalizing such critical attacks in attachment relationships in childhood (Briere & Runtz, 1990) and adulthood (Walker, 1979) leads to chronic self-criticism and self-doubt.

Most devastating to self-worth is the experience of active participation in abuse. Ehrenberg (1992) described the particularly damaging effects of sexual abuse when the child—to his or her horror—is gratified or sexually aroused: 'Where the sexual involvement with the parent was experienced as a fulfillment of the child's own fantasies, longings, and desires . . . the child may feel the full responsibility lies with himself or herself' (p. 160). As Herman (1992b) pointed out in this context, 'Any gratification that the child is able to glean from the exploitative situation becomes proof in her mind that she instigated and bears full responsibility for the abuse . . . these sins are adduced as evidence of her innate wickedness' (p. 104). And abuse can be carried even further when the child is coerced into active participation in the abuse of others. As Herman (1992b) described, the child 'believes that she has driven the most powerful people in her world to do terrible things. Surely, then, her nature must be thoroughly evil' (p. 105). Similarly, active participation in atrocities in combat damages self-worth (Brende, 1983; Janoff-Bulman, 1992).

But the child or adult need not engage in overtly abusive behavior to *feel* abusive and therefore blameworthy. The identification with an abusive parent or partner, and the internalization of the role of perpetrator—reinforced by anger, rage, and vengeful feelings and fantasies—also fuel the sense of badness.

EDUCATING CLIENTS ABOUT THE TRAUMATIZED SELF

Repairing damage to the traumatized 'I' requires an enormously complex and lengthy process of providing empathic attunement. And repairing damage to the traumatized 'me' requires attention to many areas of competence as well as supportive relationships. I have no illusion that these ambitious goals can be met through education, but I do think that education can help by articulating key problems and goals. Being more conscious, the problems with the 'me' are easier to address than those with the 'I.' After suggesting some educational strategies, I will introduce the concept of self-dependence, which neatly captures how the self and attachment relationships are optimally integrated.

Complexity of the self-concept

A discussion of self-esteem is easily launched by asking, 'How do you view yourself?' 'What thoughts do you have about yourself?' 'How do you feel about yourself?' Consistent with findings reported earlier, patients invariably generate a long list of words such as 'stupid,' 'dirty,' 'worthless,' and so forth. Then I invite them to consider the reasons that they developed such negative concepts. This question generates discussion that pertains to inferences ('They did it because I deserved it; I was bad'), internalizations ('They told me hundreds of times that I was worthless and should never have been born'), and loyalty conflicts ('I'd rather see myself as bad than think badly of my parents').

I emphasize how self-blame provided some hope of prediction and control, referring back to the core role of predictability and controllability in trauma. Consistent with Janoff-Bulman's (1992) concept of shattered assumptions, I also discuss how it is essential for us humans to make sense of our experience and to see it as meaningful. The intentional stance construes behavior as rational. It is preferable to see the self as bad, blameworthy, and deserving of maltreatment and neglect than to face meaninglessness—irrationality, unpredictability, and uncontrollability. Depending on the depth of discussion that emerges in the group, it may be possible to broach the issue of guilt and shame in relation to active participation in abuse as well as guilt feelings about one's own abusiveness. Typically, however, these extremely sensitive and painful conflicts are better addressed in the privacy of individual psychotherapy—and even there, only after a great deal of trust has developed.

Having generated a list of negative attributes and discussed how these self-concepts developed in the context of trauma, I draw a big circle, placing a large number of minus signs inside it to represent the diverse array of negative self-attributes. Paradoxically, validating patients' felt shortcomings in a supportive climate may bolster self-worth by engendering a sense of being accepted despite faults (Swann, 1997). Having given the negatives their due, I put in a few plus signs (far fewer than the minus signs) and ask if any patient has any positive views of himself or herself. Ideas such as 'kind,' 'caring,' 'sensitive,' 'artistic,' often come to the fore. Invariably, however, patients protest that 'the bad outweighs the good' and 'the positives don't count.'

Mere education will not counter these ingrained views. But I do endeavor to heighten patients' awareness of alternative ways of thinking. The self-concept is a construction, in effect, a theory (Harter, 1999; Neisser, 1988a)—and often a bad one. I point out that our concepts of ourselves, like our concepts of other persons, are gross oversimplifications of complex realities. There is no reason why they should be particularly accurate. On the contrary, with a history of attachment trauma, the self-concept is likely to be highly distorted. Fostering insight into the origins of low self-worth is one source of therapeutic leverage (Harter, 1999).

I also question the conviction that the bad is 'more real' than the good, or that having bad attributes means the good attributes 'don't count.' I present the notion that all persons are a mixture of good and bad attributes in varying proportions. Occasionally I bring up the idea that there are few saints among us who are all good. Some patients raise the question as to whether the saints *were* all good. Some patients then acknowledge that they see other persons who present themselves as all good as being 'boring' or 'unreal.' Whatever tack the discussion takes, I intend merely to raise a bit of skepticism about patients' grossly biased theories of themselves.

Resistance to change

Negative self-concepts of severely traumatized persons often seem impervious to change. If a fundamental assumption of non-traumatized persons is 'the self is worthy,' a fundamental assumption of maltreated persons is 'the self is unworthy.' Expressing anything but gentle skepticism about this assumption will meet with great resistance. Cognitive conservatism maintains beliefs that have made sense of the self and the world (Harter, 1999; Janoff-Bulman, 1992), and the desire for approval and praise is often overridden by the need for others to verify the negative self-view (Swann, 1997).

Many patients resent superficial attempts to alter their self-concept by having them repeat *affirmations* (e.g., 'I am a good person')—which they may perceive as phony or not counting in light of all the badness inside them. We therapists might think of our efforts to shatter this fundamental assumption, the self is unworthy, as potentially traumatic. We can be perceived as challenging a view of the self that provides stability and is, in a paradoxical sense, comfortable in its familiarity. Clients describe how feeling good about themselves—for example, when they catch themselves feeling pride and pleasure about their accomplishments—may boomerang. A feeling of pride is often followed by anxiety and then self-recrimination—at worst, self-harm. A substantial number of clients describe scenarios where success and pleasure precipitate a suicidal crisis. Sympathetic to such resistance, I elicit discussion of the anxiety associated with positive feelings about the self. I warn clients of the potential dangers of feeling too good about themselves. I urge them to 'go slow with pleasure' (Allen, 1995a). Taking this sympathetic tack in relation to their resistance diminishes the resentment that can be associated with naïve approaches to cognitive therapy. Respecting the ingrained assumption of low self-worth, I emphasize that sudden wholesale change—from the sense of self as predominantly bad to the sense of self as predominantly good—makes no psychological sense.

To foster gradual change, I find it helpful to shift to a temporal perspective, consistent with emerging consensus that situational fluctuations in self-worth occur on top of a more stable baseline (Harter, 1999). From this vantage point, the self-concept is not a static totality, but rather is manifested in moment-to-moment conscious reflections. I then draw a horizontal series of little circles (as if across time), pointing out that a positive circle (representing a moment of seeing the self in a somewhat positive light) may be interspersed among a string of negative circles. I quickly note how this positive circle—a blip of positive self-experience—may itself precipitate a string of negative circles (i.e., the boomerang). I point out that—saints perhaps *not* excepted—no one experiences an unending string of positive experiences. Rather, therapeutic success in working with traumatized self-worth entails *increasing the tolerance for moments of feeling good about the self*, while recognizing their transience. In this climate geared toward tempering resistance, those patients who have made some headway in treatment feel free to describe some instances in which they felt good about themselves.

Traumatized subjectivity

Trauma to the 'me' is far more accessible to discussion than trauma to the 'I.' I use the concepts of self-agency, assertion, and vitality to get to the 'I.' Occasionally I ask if clients can identify any sense of 'self-feeling.' Clients find these concepts to be elusive, because maltreatment contributes to a selfless, passive, and submissive stance in relationships. Of course, as with pride, a feeling of active assertiveness and vitality is often anathema. Like pride, assertiveness and vitality can be frightening. For example, in the context of discussing active assertion, a group member gave an example of a difficult and *successful* confrontation in a relationship with a close friend. He was effective in putting his point of view across, and his friend not only validated his experience but also agreed to change the offensive behavior. The client was enormously pleased with his effectiveness, but then he reported having become increasingly depressed and symptomatic over the ensuing days. His assertiveness, vitality, and efficacy were unfamiliar and frightening to him.

As I do in the arena of self-worth, I respect the power of resistance to feelings of self-agency. Paradoxically, I counsel patients to go slowly with their efforts at self-assertion, underscoring how risky it can be for them to allow themselves to become carried away with their successes. But I find it helpful to draw the contrast between passivity and activity in the subjective sense of self so as to chart the course toward more frequent experiences of vital selfhood.

Self-dependence

Blatt and Blass (1990, 1992) argued that most developmental theories are unbalanced in placing primary emphasis either on development of the self (separation) or on relatedness (attachment). Instead they proposed that self and relatedness are two separate but linked developmental lines, with progress in each dependent on progress in the other. More specifically, these two lines are: '(1) the achievement of a differentiated, consolidated, stable, realistic, and essentially positive identity; and (2) the establishment of the capacity to form stable, enduring, and mutually satisfying interpersonal relationships' (Blatt & Blass, 1990, p. 110).

Attachment theory illuminates how the self and attachment relationships emerge in concert with one another. Intrinsic to Bowlby's (1988) concept of the secure base was his conviction that secure attachment fosters autonomy and exploration—a proposition now supported by ample developmental evidence (Grossmann et al., 1999). When I discuss the four quadrants in the dimensional view of attachment (see Figure 3.1), I emphasize that true independence belongs in the secure quadrant—not in the dismissing quadrant, where counter-dependence lies.

Lichtenberg's (1989) concept of *self-dependence* elegantly bridges the dialectic between relatedness and autonomy in the context of attachment. As Lichtenberg characterizes it,

> To be self-dependent is not to be independent, without reliance on the attachment. Rather, to be self-dependent is to be able to rely on the self to evoke the other in a period of absence, to bridge the gap until reunion or restoration of the attachment. (p. 104)

As I paraphrase it, to be self-dependent is to be able to *bridge the gap between separation and reunion.*

I find it useful to discuss *how* clients attempt to bridge the gap as well as *how long* they are able to bridge the gap. Many clients rely on transitional objects—an object from the therapist's office, a picture, an audiotape, a card, a prescription—to feel connected. Even better, some clients report a capacity to evoke a mental image of the therapist (hearing the therapist's voice or picturing the therapist's warm smile) or a comforting memory of being with the therapist. Ideally, this evoked sense of secure attachment with the therapist sustains clients until the next contact (or until they make contact with another attachment figure).

With a history of attachment trauma, this capacity to evoke a helpful image or memory is a hard-won accomplishment. Generating images and memories can activate conflicts that nullify the sense of connection (e.g., when awareness of absence evokes angry feelings of neglect or abandonment). Moreover, the capacity to evoke a feeling of security in attachment in your mind requires mentalization and reflective function, to which the maltreated patient may be averse. Thus I point to self-dependence on the basis of secure attachment as a long-range goal, recognizing that an ambitious treatment process is likely to be required to get there (Chapters 11 and 12) and that a great deal of psychopathology must be addressed along the way (Chapters 5–10).

Part II
Trauma-related disorders

Chapter 5

PTSD AND TRAUMATIC MEMORIES

> There is never anything but the present, and if one cannot live there, one cannot live anywhere. (Watts, 1957, p. 124)

PTSD, the most conspicuous trauma-related disorder, adds insult to injury. Persons with PTSD not only have suffered through actual traumatic events but also continue to be traumatized repeatedly by the mental reexperiencing of those events. You should not breeze past the horror of this scenario: *exposure to traumatic events can result in an illness that is continually retraumatizing*—day and night. Thus persons with PTSD cannot live in the present because they are continually haunted by the past.

This chapter covers the various forms and symptoms of PTSD, then tackles controversies regarding the accuracy of memories of childhood abuse. We therapists must understand the gist of current memory research, because we must educate our clients so they do not become embroiled in misguided therapies and ill-advised family confrontations.

PTSD

PTSD (APA, 1994) is a complex syndrome that includes a combination of exposure to potentially traumatic events and a constellation of three dynamically intertwined symptom clusters: reexperiencing, avoidance and numbing, and hyperarousal. DSM-IV distinguishes between acute PTSD, with symptom duration from one to three months, and chronic PTSD, with symptom duration of three months or more. Symptoms of PTSD may be relatively continuous since the time of the trauma, or their onset may be delayed. DSM-IV also includes as a new category acute stress disorder, which may be diagnosed within the first four weeks after a trauma. Finally, although not a diagnostic entity, *peri*traumatic symptoms—those that occur right around the time of the trauma—are garnering increasing research attention. Thus the temporal succession of symptoms and disorders is: peritraumatic symptoms → acute stress disorder → acute PTSD → chronic PTSD.

The extent to which it is feasible or useful to educate clients about the details of diagnosis will vary with the clinical context, but the essence of PTSD can be boiled down to two points. First, the *post* in post-traumatic stress disorder highlights that the individual has been traumatized in the near or distant past, and the fundamental problem is the mental persistence of the trauma in the present. Second, the core of PTSD is the alternation between intrusive reexperiencing and avoidance.

Course of post-traumatic symptoms

The *post* in post-traumatic symptoms may range from days, weeks, and months to years and decades. As with many other psychiatric disorders, symptoms and impaired functioning may be relatively continuous or waxing and waning. Furthermore, the post-traumatic symptomatology may include the full or partial PTSD syndrome.

The potential evolution of PTSD begins with *peritraumatic symptoms*. The extent to which these symptoms should be construed as normal versus pathological—or harbingers of disorder—is a question under active investigation. By definition, a potentially traumatic event is likely to be extremely distressing to most persons. How this peritraumatic distress evolves into trauma (lasting adverse effects) is a matter for research. Horowitz (1997) characterized the normal acute (peritraumatic) response as the *outcry phase*, comprised of fear, sadness, and rage. He also noted the presence of immediate denial and the fact that the outcry may consist of 'only a stunned stare and the feeling of inability to comprehend the trauma' (Horowitz, 1986, p. 241). Because they are indicative of a poor prognosis, peritraumatic dissociative symptoms (e.g., the 'stunned stare' Horowitz described) have captured the lion's share of attention in recent research (see Chapter 7).

Yet there is also evidence that other aspects of the acute stress response besides dissociation signal risk for subsequent disorder. Solomon and colleagues (Solomon, Laror, & McFarlane, 1996) commented on the sheer diversity of acute stress reactions. Hence researchers have observed and studied many experiences, such as sense of threat, anxiety, fearfulness, helplessness, loss of autonomy, agitation, insomnia, irritability, aggression, paranoia, depression, apathy, numbing, confusion, disorientation, and physical symptoms (Koopman, Classen, & Spiegel, 1994; Roemer, Orsillo, Borkovec, & Litz, 1998; Shalev, 1996; Shalev, Peri, Canetti, & Schreiber, 1996; Solomon et al.,

1996). Although research on peritraumatic symptoms has focused primarily on adults, Pynoos and colleagues (Pynoos, Steinberg, & Goenjian, 1996) found that children who feared dying, felt their heart beating fast, and were very upset about how they acted during an earthquake could be predicted to exhibit symptoms of PTSD several months later.

Peritraumatic symptoms, when sufficiently severe and impairing, shade into *acute stress disorder*, a diagnosis that requires symptoms that cause significant distress or impaired functioning and last a minimum of two days and a maximum of four weeks. The symptoms of PTSD and acute stress disorder overlap substantially, but there is an important difference between the two disorders besides the time of onset. Acute stress disorder includes prominent dissociative symptoms, along with the PTSD symptoms of re-experiencing, hyperarousal, and avoidance. The dissociative symptoms include detachment, diminished awareness of surroundings, derealization, depersonalization, and amnesia for aspects of the trauma. Thus PTSD and dissociative disorders are combined in the first month in the diagnosis of acute stress disorder and then split into separate categories after the first month. Just as peritraumatic symptoms may shade into acute stress disorder, acute stress disorder may evolve into PTSD. As it was intended to do, a diagnosis of acute stress disorder predicts subsequent PTSD, as has been demonstrated for the impersonal trauma of motor vehicle accidents (Harvey & Bryant, 1998b, 1999) and the interpersonal trauma of assaults (Brewin, Andrews, Rose, & Kirk, 1999).

Yet Marshall and colleagues (Marshall, Spitzer, & Liebowitz, 1999) compellingly criticized the evidence and rationale for classifying the first months of post-traumatic symptoms as a separate acute stress disorder. Instead they proposed that PTSD be diagnosed at any point after trauma and that dissociative symptoms be noted as associated features. Although initial symptom severity generally predicts subsequent disorder, the wide variability in outcomes raises questions about specifying precise timelines for transition from one discrete disorder to another. As Marshall and colleagues stated, the current classification 'creates an illusion of pseudo-exactness regarding longitudinal course' (p. 1683).

Three months is the dividing line between *acute PTSD* (symptoms persisting from one to three months) and *chronic PTSD* (symptoms persisting beyond three months). This distinction is based on research showing that the proportion of symptomatic individuals decreases relatively sharply over the first three to four months and then levels off, such that continuation of symptoms beyond the first few months is somewhat predictive of chronicity (Foa & Rothbaum, 1998; Rothbaum & Foa, 1993). Yet no precise point in time separates those who recover from those who do not. Kessler and colleagues (Kessler, Sonnega, Bromet, Hughes, & Nelson, 1995) found a continuing— albeit gradual—decline in the prevalence of PTSD symptoms over the course of *several years* post-trauma. They found the steepest decrease over the course of the first 12 months after symptom onset with a continued decline over the course of six years (with median time to remission being 36 months for treated and 64 months for untreated subsamples). Attesting to the potential chronicity of PTSD, they found that symptoms failed to remit in over one third of the sample even after several years—regardless of treatment status.

Other studies also attest to the potential chronicity of PTSD. In a five-year follow-up study, Zlotnick and colleagues (Zlotnick, Warshaw et al., 1999) found that the probability of full remission from chronic PTSD, when accompanied by another anxiety disorder, is extremely low—0.18 for their full sample and 0.05 for the subsample with a history of childhood abuse. Notably, Kulka and colleagues (Kulka et al., 1990) found PTSD in over 15% of male and 8% of female Vietnam theater veterans nearly two decades after the war. Predictors and correlates of chronic PTSD include a family history of psychiatric disorder, severity of the trauma, severity of the PTSD syndrome, presence of other psychiatric disorders, concurrent life stressors, and absence of social support (Simon, 1999). Importantly, even partial (subsyndromal) PTSD can be associated with substantial impairments in functioning. A large-scale survey of a random sample of Canadian adults found that, although full PTSD was associated with greater impairment than partial PTSD in the area of vocational functioning (work or school), partial PTSD was associated with an equivalent level of impaired functioning at home and in social relationships, as well as with equivalent rates of treatment seeking (Stein, Walker, Hazen, & Forde, 1997).

Like many other chronic illnesses, PTSD has an extremely variable course, with symptoms potentially persisting, resolving, recurring, or fluctuating (Blank, 1993). Even when some symptoms subside, functional impairment may persist. For many patients with a long history of interpersonal trauma, the delayed onset of PTSD is profoundly demoralizing. Many such patients have gone through a period of relatively good functioning and then decompensate into severely symptomatic states. Often in a state of anguish and perplexity they ask, 'Why now?' I identified a prototype of this course of illness to address this question (see Figure 5.1).

Many persons leave home and function relatively well after a history of childhood trauma. Indeed, many become extremely successful—although the trauma may be masked by chronic inhibition of processing rather than being resolved (Brewin, Dalgleish, & Joseph, 1996). Yet stressors in adulthood take their toll. As indicated by the downward arrows in Figure 5.1, many individuals presenting for inpatient treatment in a severely decompensated state report a series of stressful events (e.g., death of a loved one, separation or divorce, general medical illness, or accident), some of which may be of traumatic proportions. The final stressor before the decompensation is the last straw. Further exploration typically reveals, however, that these discrete stressors occur on top of a chronically stressful lifestyle.

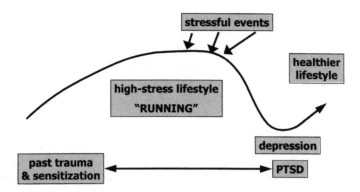

Figure 5.1   Stress pile-up and course of illness

Patients describe themselves as being always on the go or 'running,' as well as being involved in continual caregiving or being 'workaholics'—or all of these. As I will discuss further in Chapter 6, the trauma history may have sensitized such persons to stress, to the extent that the combination of a stressful lifestyle and discrete stressors in adulthood becomes overwhelming, and the individual decompensates (in patients' words, 'hit the wall' or 'crash'). The chronic 'running' may partly serve a defensive function, keeping past trauma out of mind. But the crash into depression, for example, undermines these defenses and may open the floodgates to traumatic memories. Of course the stressful events themselves may reverberate with past trauma (e.g., as reminders), and this reverberation may also contribute to the slide—and eventual crash—into depression.

For example, a sudden incapacitating depression and intrusive memories bewildered a patient who believed she had dealt with her history of childhood abuse. Relating her experience to the diagram, she revealed that she had been raising children, holding down a job, going to school, and taking care of an ill parent. In the context of this chronic stress, the last straw was writing a paper on child abuse for one of her school courses. Sadly, although many clients have indeed dealt with their trauma effectively, they remain vulnerable to exacerbations in the face of such stress pile-up.

Intrusive reexperiencing and flashbacks

Going through potentially traumatic events is a horrific experience. In the context of attachment trauma, these horrific experiences can be continual and prolonged—at worst, occurring over the course of many years. Yet, for many exposed persons, the agony does not stop with termination of the events, however brief or prolonged their duration. The tragedy of this illness is most glaring when the individual with PTSD is currently in a safe, loving attachment relationship. For example, a patient in a psychoeducational group who had a long history of trauma in her relationship with her father demanded—poignantly, tearfully, and bitterly—to know how she could be so distrusting and frightened of her husband of many years, who was steadfast in his kindness and support. Whenever they were intimate, she became frightened by intrusive memories.

DSM-IV (APA, 1994) lists a broad range of symptoms in the reexperiencing cluster, including distressing memories, images, and dreams; acting or feeling as if the events were recurring; and intense psychological distress and physiological reactivity to internal or external cues that are reminders of the event. Research is inconsistent regarding the extent to which physiological reactivity is tied directly to reminders or instead reflects generalized stress reactivity. For example, studies have shown that persons with PTSD respond selectively to reminders of the trauma (Casada, Amdur, Larsen, & Liberzon, 1998), that they respond to reminders of stressful experience that did not incite the trauma (Shalev, Peri, Gelpin, Orr, & Pitman, 1997), and that there are differences among trauma populations in their responsiveness to different kinds of cues (Kinzie et al., 1998).

Intrusive reexperiencing of trauma is the hallmark of PTSD, and clients readily identify *flashbacks* as the prototype. Flashbacks are extremely distressing not just because they are emotionally intense but also because they are disorganizing. Flashbacks are dominated by isolated sensory images (Bryant & Harvey, 1996; Kline & Rausch, 1985; Mellman & Davis, 1985; van der Kolk, 1996; Witvliet, 1997)—often to the exclusion of coherent meaning (Brewin et al., 1996)—and they are frequently intertwined with dissociatively altered states of consciousness (Krystal, Bremner, Southwick, & Charney, 1998).

Patients invariably implore, 'How do I stop the flashbacks?' The answer to this question entails the whole of trauma treatment (see Chapters 11 and 12). I distinguish the short-term goal of aborting them from the long-term goal of preventing them. Flashbacks are best aborted by *grounding* techniques (Saakvitne et al., 2000; Torem, 1989) that direct the patient's attention to the concrete external world, often by increasing sensory input. Therapists and others intuitively attempt to ground clients by calling their name, asking that they open their eyes, and attempting to engage them in conversation. Clients may also be asked to get up and walk around the room, walk in the fresh air, splash cold water on their face, and the like. As with any such intervention, what works for one client might not for another. In therapy groups, I ask clients to share their experience about grounding techniques. To the extent that the client is able to anticipate flashbacks, grounding may serve not only to abort them but also to prevent them from escalating.

Reexperiencing neglect

As described in Chapter 2, neglect is potentially traumatic, and it is often intertwined with abuse. I include neglect among post-traumatic reexperiencing symptoms. Reexperiencing neglect, albeit perhaps less terrifying than reexperiencing abuse, can be excruciatingly painful. Clients who reexperience neglect feel alone, abandoned, and unprotected. As DSM-IV (APA, 1994) criteria indicate, reexperiencing is liable to be triggered by 'cues that symbolize or resemble an aspect of the traumatic event' (p. 428). Reexperiencing neglect may be triggered by any reminder of feeling neglected and abandoned, or simply being alone may do so. As therapists well know, separations, miscommunications, and failures of attunement often prompt the reexperiencing of neglect. Also, because abusive events are intrinsically intertwined with—and followed by—emotional neglect, intrusive reexperiencing of abuse may be intertwined with—and followed by—a feeling of neglect.

I incorporate neglect into the reexperiencing domain to draw clients' attention to the distinction between past and present. To the extent that it is a reexperiencing symptom, the feeling of neglect, like that of abuse, is an emotional memory, not a current reality. Compared to the past, the present may be more conducive to making use of secure attachments to develop a sense of reconnection.

Hyperarousal

Hyperarousal, an aspect of PTSD that overlaps with other anxiety disorders, is manifested in irritability or outbursts of anger, difficulty concentrating, hypervigilance, sleep disturbance, and exaggerated startle response. The startle response is instructive. Persons with PTSD show an elevation in fear-potentiated startle (Grillon & Morgan, 1999; Prins, Kaloupek, & Keane, 1995), a state-dependent response that disposes them to startle intensely when they are frightened or anxious—as they are especially prone to be. Startle responses are not only disquieting in their own right but also are likely to escalate into flashbacks (van der Kolk, 1994). The startle response exemplifies non-conscious automatic responses for which many clients with PTSD may blame themselves—as if they should be able to prevent their reactions by proper thinking. I point out that the time between stimulus and startle is a fraction of a second—as short as 14 milliseconds (Rauch, Geyer, Jenkins, Breslin, & Braff, 1994). This short latency is merely an extreme case of a more general phenomenon (LeDoux, 1996). Conditioned fear responses occur fast—far outpacing the capacity for thought. I explain to clients that they cannot prevent startle and fear responses. Nevertheless, it is possible in principle—albeit often difficult in practice—to nip these reactions in the bud (e.g., by using relaxation or cognitive techniques) to prevent their escalation into full-blown panic or flashbacks.

Many clients ask about panic attacks in the context of trauma. Many symptoms of panic attacks, including not just physiological arousal but also depersonalization and derealization, are frequent concomitants of flashbacks. In principle PTSD is distinguished from panic disorder on the basis of such attacks being triggered by a reminder of trauma rather than coming out of the blue. In practice the distinction is difficult to make. Many persons who suffer from panic attacks also have a history of trauma (Falsetti, Resnick, Dansky, Lydiard, & Kilpatrick, 1995). The first panic attack may have been part and parcel of the peritraumatic stress response. Thus what subsequently appears to be a *spontaneous* panic attack may instead be reexperiencing symptoms associated with subtle reminders of trauma. At worst, as explained in Chapter 6, sensitization may lead to flashbacks and panic becoming spontaneous, with no obvious trigger.

It is little wonder that persons with PTSD are hypervigilant, and many refer to being constantly 'on guard.' PTSD entails a demonstrable cognitive bias toward threat (Brewin et al., 1996). Clients are hypervigilant not only because they anticipate further trauma but also because they are wary of the intrusive symptoms of PTSD. Patients with PTSD, like those with panic disorder, have a high level of anxiety sensitivity, worrying that their anxiety will have grave consequences (Taylor, Koch, & McNally, 1992). The *fear of fear* creates a snowballing of anxiety in response to ordinary stressors. Thus, in therapy, we must help clients reduce their excessive anxiety while also helping them to increase their *tolerance* for ordinary anxiety.

Fight or flight

I bring the fight-or-flight response into the discussion of hyperarousal or on any occasion when clients bring up their intense reactivity to threat. Cannon (1953) did not mince words in proposing the survival value of the fight-or-flight response: 'The business of killing and of avoiding death has been one of the primary interests of living beings throughout their long history on the earth' (p. 377). His work on stress was a forerunner of our current understanding of PTSD; he recognized that the fight-or-flight response could be triggered not only by actual danger but also by memories. Clients intuitively grasp the concept of the fight-or-flight response and can readily articulate its adaptive, self-protective significance. I expand on their understanding by explaining how the fight-or-flight response prepares the individual for vigorous action (e.g., by oxygenating the blood, increasing blood flow, diverting blood to large muscles, and making glucose available for needed energy).

Although they intuitively grasp the adaptive aspects of the fight-or-flight response, clients may not have a full appreciation of some of its key ramifications. The fight-or-flight response usefully exemplifies the naturalness of anger and rage. As Cannon put it, 'Anger is the emotion preeminently serviceable for the display of power' (Cannon, 1953, p. 342). Thus clients can be reminded that hyperarousal in PTSD includes irritability and outbursts of anger as well as anxiety symptoms. Of course many persons with a history of physical and psychological abuse in childhood or adulthood are terrified of anger as well as anxiety symptoms. Their models for expressing anger have been extremely destructive, and they have found others' anger to be dangerous. Many believe that their own anger is dangerous as well, because any overt expression of anger escalated the abuse. And they fear that any experience or expression of their own anger may quickly escalate to destructive rage. Many learned to go a step beyond suppressing the expression of anger to block their *feelings* of anger. Others are distressed by their irritability and feel guilty and ashamed about it. But traumatized persons need to cultivate anger because, as the fight-or-flight response attests, anger can be a source of power to employ in the service of self-protection and necessary confrontations.

Trauma-related sleep disturbance

The hyperarousal symptoms of PTSD include sleep disturbance. Unfortunately, sleep does not necessarily provide respite from reexperiencing trauma. Just as the flashback is the prototypical reexperiencing symptom during the waking state, the nightmare is the prototypical reexperiencing symptom during sleep. Although difficulty falling or staying asleep is listed among the hyperarousal symptoms in DSM-IV (APA, 1994), it may be useful to consider difficulty *falling* asleep among the hyperarousal symptoms and difficulty *staying* asleep among the intrusive (reexperiencing) symptoms (Weiss & Marmar, 1997). Therapists should also be aware that sleep disturbance in clients with PTSD may be caused or exacerbated by sleep-disordered breathing (e.g., sleep apnea) and sleep movement disorders (Krakow et al., 2000), the possibility of which should be evaluated medically.

We distinguish between intrusive and phobic aspects of trauma-related sleep disturbance, both of which contribute to insomnia (Allen, Console et al., 2001). *Intrusive* sleep disturbance in PTSD reflects the intrusion of fear and associated mental contents into sleep. Under the current view that REM sleep (dreaming) serves to process and consolidate daily events of emotional significance (Cartwright, 1981; Hobson, 1994), it is plausible that intrusive phenomena experienced during waking will continue to be processed during sleep, with concomitant hyperarousal. In this context, Hartmann (1998) construed traumatic nightmares as aiding processing by providing pictorial context for the dominant emotional concern in the aftermath of trauma.

Yet intrusive sleep symptoms are not limited to nightmares. Ross and colleagues (Ross, Ball, Sullivan, & Caroff, 1989, p. 698) distinguished post-traumatic nightmares ('a long, frightening dream that awakens one during REM sleep') from night terrors ('distinguishable from the nightmare on the basis of its genesis during non-REM sleep, its prominent autonomic accompaniments, and its tendency to be poorly recalled'). *Individuals with PTSD frequently awaken in a state of fear without being aware of a dream or nightmare* (Mellman, Kulick-Bell, Ashlock, & Nolan, 1995). These fearful awakenings also may be associated with physiological arousal akin to a panic attack (Mellman et al., 1995). Such nocturnal panic is common among patients with anxiety disorders (Craske & Rowe, 1997), and it is noteworthy that a higher proportion of panic disorder patients with nocturnal panic report a history of trauma than those without nocturnal panic—even when controlling for PTSD (Freed, Craske, & Greher, 1999). Moreover a number of authors have reported an exceptionally high level of abnormal movements during sleep in persons with PTSD (Inman, Silver, & Doghramji, 1990; Mellman et al., 1995; Ross et al., 1994). Thus PTSD is associated with problems in sleep continuity that include frequent awakenings and complaints of nonrestorative sleep (Mellman et al., 1995; Woodward, 1995).

Owing to the distress associated with sleep, many patients with PTSD become *phobic* about sleeping. Their anticipatory anxiety may include dread or fear of falling asleep (Hudson, Manoach, Sabo, & Sternbach, 1991; Inman et al., 1990). Not only do patients fear sleep because they anticipate nightmares and panic but also, for some patients, being in bed is associated with traumatic experience (e.g., sexual abuse or rape) and thus is a trauma-related cue. Such patients may be unable to sleep in a bed, or they may find it difficult to sleep at night but easier to sleep during daylight hours.

As illustrated in Figure 5.2, trauma-related sleep disturbance may entail two vicious circles (Allen, Console et al., in press). First, intrusive symptoms spawn phobic anxiety, which increases hyperarousal and then the likelihood of intrusive symptoms during sleep. Second, intrusive and phobic symptoms may enter into a vicious circle with insomnia. On the one hand, phobic symptoms contribute to initial insomnia and intrusive symptoms contribute

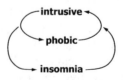

Figure 5.2   Vicious circles in sleep disturbance

to middle insomnia. On the other hand, by impairing anxiety regulation, insomnia may exacerbate intrusive and phobic symptoms. Furthermore, nightmares and daytime intrusive symptoms may escalate each other (Burnstein, 1985).

Addressing sleep disturbance is especially important in treating clients with PTSD. Disrupted sleep in any psychiatric, general medical, or situational context profoundly disrupts many areas of functioning (Dement, 1999; Hobson, 1994). Insomnia is not only frequently symptomatic of psychiatric disorders; it also may be part of their pathogenesis (Billard, Partinen, Roth, & Shapiro, 1994). Sleep deprivation undermines the quality of life and interferes with coping and treatment efforts (Craske & Rowe, 1997). Simply understanding how these various forms of sleep disturbance relate to PTSD can be reassuring to clients, as well as underscoring the importance of sleep hygiene in their treatment (Dement, 1999).

Avoidance and numbing

I present reexperiencing and avoidance to patients as a couplet. Avoidance is natural and inevitable. Anyone who has suffered the terror of a flashback would want to avoid another one, just as anyone who experiences one panic attack would want to avoid others. Horowitz (1997) documented that phases of intrusion and denial are a universal reaction to highly stressful life events. At best, the alternation of intrusion and denial is a controlled process associated with working through and resolution. At worst, oscillation between extremes of intrusion and denial perpetuates post-traumatic symptoms.

DSM-IV (APA, 1994, p. 428) combines 'avoidance of stimuli associated with the trauma and numbing of general responsiveness' in one symptom cluster. The criteria for avoidance include 'efforts to avoid thoughts, feelings, or conversations associated with the trauma,' as well as 'efforts to avoid activities, places, or people that arouse recollections of the trauma.' Criteria for numbing include 'markedly diminished interest or participation in significant activities,' 'detachment or estrangement from others,' and 'restricted range of affect.'

Foa and colleagues (Foa, Riggs, & Gershuny, 1995) argued, however, that avoidance and numbing involve different mechanisms and should be sharply distinguished from each other. From their examination of the clustering of post-traumatic symptoms in female assault victims, these authors concluded that numbing is a relatively passive and automatic process that occurs when more active, strategic efforts at avoidance are unsuccessful in failing to diminish hyperarousal. Subsequent studies of combat veterans (Litz et al., 1997) and victims of motor vehicle accidents (Taylor, Kuch, Koch, Crockett, & Passey, 1998) have confirmed the close association between hyperarousal and numbing.

Extrapolating from the DSM criteria, I explain social isolation to clients as one particularly problematic form of avoidance. With a history of interpersonal trauma, clients may find that *other persons* are reminders of trauma. Moreover, clients with a history of attachment trauma may find that depending on and feeling close to others reminds them of trauma. Numbing may also contribute to social isolation insofar as it fuels a sense of alienation and inhibits lively interactions.

Although clients readily identify with the processes of avoidance and numbing, discussing these topics can bring up painful feelings and defensiveness. Some clients feel criticized about avoidance. Many feel pressured by therapists' encouragement to work on their trauma, which their fear prevents them from doing. I point out that avoiding danger is always adaptive and that avoiding painful emotional states is also adaptive—most of the time. Likewise, many patients feel extremely frustrated by numbing. They want to work on their trauma but are emotionally blocked from doing so. They can talk about it only in a detached way, unable to experience any of the associated emotions. As Foa and colleagues observed (Foa, Riggs, & Gershuny, 1995), treatment strategies that target arousal and effortful avoidance may not affect numbing, particularly when numbing has become functionally independent of hyperarousal in persons with chronic PTSD.

Although avoidance and numbing have adaptive aspects, they also have a high cost in the context of PTSD. Because avoidance blocks learning, it can perpetuate PTSD and leave patients feeling stuck in the reexperiencing–avoidance cycle. Both avoidance and numbing block the working through process, as Horowitz (1997) described it. Brewin and colleagues (Brewin et al., 1996) made a convincing case that, even if avoidance suppresses active symptoms of PTSD, it contributes to other psychiatric disorders as well as to a persistent vulnerability to the eruption of active PTSD symptoms.

PTSD and grief

Bereavement is one of myriad stressful life events that prompted Horowitz's phase model of intrusion and denial, and there is considerable overlap between symptoms of grief and PTSD (Horowitz, 1986, 1997; Horowitz et al., 1997; Worden, 1991). Including the sudden, unexpected death of a loved one as a traumatic event in DSM-IV (APA, 1994) has shown this to be the most prevalent type of trauma, and one that accounts for a large burden of PTSD in the community (Breslau, 1998). Yet Jacobs (1993) also included among traumatic losses any death associated with 'chronic, disfiguring, painful diseases that horrify the survivors and break down their usual denial or other defenses used to cope with death' (p. 87). Although PTSD and grief intersect directly in the context of traumatic loss and bereavement, Jacobs

(1993) argued cogently that traumatic stress should be distinguished from separation distress, with the former better encompassed within trauma theory and the latter within attachment theory. Both are involved in traumatic loss.

Of course the relationship between PTSD and grief is not limited to traumatic losses. A history of trauma entails many losses. Many persons with a history of childhood maltreatment feel that they lost the opportunity to have a normal childhood or to *be* a child. In addition, functional impairment associated with trauma-related disorders brings numerous losses. Traumatized persons not only feel the loss of their childhood but also the loss of a normal adulthood. Moreover, many persons feel the loss of a hoped-for future. Posttraumatic grief may shade into depression, which Brewin (Brewin et al., 1996) and colleagues construed as resulting from

> an emotional reaction to the actual or symbolic loss consequent to the trauma. This may consist of the loss of another person or type of relationship, a highly valued role, health, physical and mental capacities, a future goal, or a sense of a good and effective self. (p. 681)

Thus healing from trauma entails mourning past losses and future hopes, and reconfiguring a new future that takes limitations in functioning into account.

TRAUMATIC MEMORIES

Most traumatized persons have no reason to question the accuracy of their memories of traumatic events. Yet many clients understandably question the meaning of intrusive traumatic images that come out of the blue, seem unbelievable, and cannot be integrated into their memory of their past. Then accuracy cannot be taken for granted, and we therapists find ourselves in a quagmire.

The terms 'reexperiencing,' 'reliving,' and 'flashback' are misleading insofar as they imply a literal reproduction of a traumatic event in memory rather than a reconstructive process subject to all the same limitations and distortions as any other form of remembering (Brewin & Andrews, 1998; Frankel, 1994a). Similarly, nightmares in the aftermath of an acute trauma do not necessarily depict traumatic events literally but rather may express the emotional impact metaphorically (Hartmann, 1998). Furthermore, we must distinguish between objective events and subjective experiences of those events, the latter affected to varying degrees by the individual's developmental level, level of functioning during the events, and interpretation of the events. Subjective experiences may or may not be remembered for varying periods of time. When they are remembered, they may be remembered with varying degrees of detail, coherence, and accuracy. We cannot confidently infer history from intrusive reexperiencing, whether it is in the form of fragmented memories of long-past trauma, flashbacks, or nightmares—no matter how vivid and compellingly veridical they may seem.

Educating clients about limitations in the accuracy of traumatic memories is important, because a lack of knowledge can render them vulnerable to misguided therapies and ill-considered actions, such as premature confrontations or cut-offs from family members. But we therapists educate in an emotionally charged climate, owing to the highly politicized controversy about repressed memories, recovered memories, and false memories. In the early 1990s, a social movement in the United States organized as the False Memory Syndrome Foundation evolved in the context of legal battles about the credibility of childhood sexual abuse memories ostensibly engendered by psychotherapy. A parallel organization, the False Memory Society, subsequently formed in the United Kingdom. This history has been reviewed by Brown and colleagues (Brown, Scheflin, & Hammond, 1998), as well as by others (Gutheil, 1993; Loftus, 1993; Loftus & Rosenwald, 1993; Morton, Andrews, Bekerian, Brewin, & Mollon, 1996; Schouten, 1994; Wakefield & Underwager, 1992). The focal point for the controversy is the putative *false memory syndrome*, construed by Kihlstrom (1998) as akin to a personality disorder in which a survivor identity is adopted in relation to an erroneous conviction in a history of trauma that undermines the person's functioning and relationships. At best, the False Memory Syndrome Foundation has provided support to falsely accused parents and countered misinformed treatment of trauma. But it also has had a highly divisive impact on the field.

To transcend the controversy, therapists must come to grips with the burgeoning scientific literature on memory. In this domain more than any other, to impart even a few sound ideas to clients requires substantial technical knowledge. Yet, if the American Psychological Association's working group on memories of childhood abuse (Alpert et al., 1996) is representative, we have yet to achieve consensus about what constitutes sound knowledge in the field of traumatic memory. One person's science may be another's illusion, and science cannot be divorced from political agendas (Brown, 1996; Freyd, 1998). Nonetheless, the working party of the British Psychological Society (Morton et al., 1996) was able to achieve a reasoned consensus on recovered memory. When educating patients, we therapists must take responsibility for our individual conclusions while acknowledging that much of what we believe remains controversial. I find patients quite receptive to this state of affairs—which is hardly unique to psychology.

We are likely to be confronted with two questions. First, how could a person not remember trauma? Second, how do fragmented or long-forgotten traumatic memories relate to the client's history? Confidently addressing these questions requires some basic knowledge about memory. I will briefly review how memory can be disrupted at different stages, and then I will elaborate the distinction between explicit and implicit memory. Firmly establishing these distinctions in your mind will take some effort. But the distinctions are crucial to helping your clients understand how they can be so overwhelmed by traumatic memories, yet be so confused about what actually happened to them.

Stages of memory

Four stages of memory include encoding, consolidation, storage, and retrieval (Schacter, 1996; Squire, 1987). Encoding and consolidation lead to durable storage, and storage makes retrieval possible. Memory can be disrupted at any of these stages.

As Schacter (1996, 1999) described, establishing coherent and detailed memories requires *elaborative encoding*, that is, paying attention to events and thinking about them in such a way as to integrate new information with prior information. Encoding failures are a prominent and under-appreciated contributor to impaired memory for trauma (Allen, Console et al., 1999). Consider Bower and Sivers' (1998) comment that 'during the trauma victims are probably not talking to themselves, conducting an internal monologue describing what is happening to them. After all, traumatic events are often characterized as unspeakable' (p. 642).

Without encoding, consolidation, storage, and retrieval are not possible. *Consolidation* is the slow neurobiological process by which information that is encoded becomes relatively resistant to disruption (Moscovitch, 1994). The result of elaborative encoding and consolidation is durable *storage* that supports retrieval. *Retrieval* may be relatively deliberate or involuntary, in either case depending on cues such as percepts, thoughts, feelings, or states of mind that comprise a fragment of the memory (Bower & Sivers, 1998). By virtue of associative processes, such retrieval cues (reminders) can activate a complex memory network.

Explicit personal event memories

To understand the disorganized mental state of the patient struggling to make sense of intrusive traumatic images, we must distinguish between implicit and explicit memory. To remember is to have an *explicit* memory. Episodic and semantic memory are two types of explicit memory (Tulving, 1972). Episodic memory is memory for an event that can be pinpointed in space and time. Semantic memory represents the meanings and abstractions derived from events. Explicit traumatic memories may have both episodic and semantic aspects, such as images of an attacker and beliefs about failure to defend oneself.

Questions about accuracy pertain to *autobiographical memories*, that is, explicit memories for information significant to the self (Brewer, 1986; Nelson, 1993). Autobiographical memory includes semantic memory (e.g., knowledge of facts about one's life, such as birthplace), but episodic autobiographical memory is the primary focus of concerns about accuracy. I prefer Pillemer's (1998) term, *personal event memory*, because it is more precise than autobiographical memory and especially pertinent to memory for traumatic events:

> The memory represents a *specific* event that took place at a particular time and place, rather than a general event or an extended series of related happenings. The memory contains a *detailed* account of the rememberer's *own personal circumstances* at the time of the event. The verbal narrative account of the event is accompanied by *sensory images*, including visual, auditory, olfactory images or bodily sensations, that contribute to the feeling of 'reexperiencing' or 'reliving.' Memory details and sensory images correspond to a particular *moment* or moments of phenomenal experience. The rememberer *believes* that the memory is a truthful representation of what transpired. (pp. 50–51)

I find it helpful to distinguish between personal event memories and *autobiographical narrative*, that is, what we say about what we remember (Allen, Console et al., 1999). To varying degrees, autobiographical narrative is supported by personal event memories. Memories supporting autobiographical narrative may vary in extent of detail, sensory modality (e.g., auditory versus visual), and coherence (i.e., fragmented, disjointed, or contradictory versus well organized). In addition, personal event memories and the associated narrative vary in accuracy. Personal event memory is only one source of autobiographical narratives. Autobiographical narratives also may be based on semantic memory (e.g., what you have been told about your past). In addition, autobiographical narrative may be influenced to varying degrees by more or less conscious conjecture or filling in of gaps. Autobiographical narrative also can be inaccurate by virtue of confabulation and lying. As Moscovitch (1995) put it, 'What distinguishes confabulation from lying is that typically there is no intent to deceive and the patient is unaware of the falsehoods. It is an "honest lying"' (p. 226). Although the concept of confabulation evolved primarily in relation to neurological damage, it is also applicable to cognitive impairments associated with traumatic memories. What you don't know, you can make up.

Personal event memories and associated autobiographical narratives have a complex developmental history. Although evident in rudimentary forms early in life (Schacter, 1996), narrative personal event memory is a highly sophisticated developmental achievement that begins to consolidate around the second and third years of life (Howe & Courage, 1993; Pillemer, 1998; Pillemer & White, 1989; Schacter, 1996). In part, the developmental complexity of personal event memory is intertwined with its dependency on the development of a sense of self (Howe & Courage, 1993). As MacLean (1990) aptly put it, 'Without an integrated sense of self, there is, so to speak, no place to deposit a memory of ongoing experience' (p. 578). Furthermore, like the sense of self, personal event memory is a social construction and thus tied to social discourse and reminiscence (Neisser, 1988b; Nelson, 1993; Pillemer, 1998; Pillemer & White, 1989).

Personal event memory is highly constructive—a point not always appreciated by either patients or professionals. Many clients, like the majority of psychologists, implicitly or explicitly hold something akin to a video recorder model of memory, an erroneous but popular view that the brain stores prior experience accurately and permanently (DuBreuil, Garry, & Loftus, 1998; Loftus & Loftus, 1980; Payne & Blackwell, 1998). But, unlike video recorders, we actively interpret experience (Neisser, 1986). Furthermore, personal event memories are not replayed, they are reconstructed, as Bartlett (1932) articulated many decades ago:

> Remembering is not the re-excitation of innumerable fixed, lifeless and fragmentary traces. It is an imaginative reconstruction, or construction, built out of the relation of our attitude towards a whole active mass of organised past reactions or experience, and to a little outstanding detail which commonly appears in image or in language form. It is thus hardly ever really exact, even in the most rudimentary cases of rote recapitulation, and it is not at all important that it should be so. (p. 213)

In a related vein, Kihlstrom (1998) added a twist to the library metaphor of memory: 'In the final analysis, memory is not analogous to reading a book; it is more like writing a book from fragmentary notes' (p. 18). Edelman and Tononi (2000) provide a geological metaphor: '*memory is more like the melting and refreezing of a glacier than it is like an inscription on rock*' (p. 93). They went beyond Bartlett's view of memory as a reconstruction: 'every act of memory is, to some degree, an act of imagination' (p. 103).

Research on the accuracy of personal event memories for non-traumatic events has burgeoned, and there are a number of reviews available for interested clinicians (Allen, 1995b; Brewin, Andrews, & Gotlib, 1993; D. Brown et al., 1998; Pillemer, 1998). Here are some conclusions from research to date. Not surprisingly, memory for recent events is more accurate than memory for remote events (Barclay, 1986; Barclay & Wellman, 1986; Rubin, 1982). Furthermore, personal event memories are self-knowledge, and what you recall is consistent with your self-concept at the time of recall (Barclay, 1986; Brewin & Andrews, 1998; Sanitioso, Kunda, & Fong, 1990). Unique events are more accurately remembered than generic events (Brewer, 1986; Neisser, 1988b; Nelson, 1993), inasmuch as the latter tend to be schematized (Schacter, 1989). Up to a point, emotion contributes to the salience of an event and thus increases the probability of recall (Bower & Sivers, 1998; Brown & Kulick, 1977). At moderate levels of arousal, stress-related neurotransmitter and neurohormone levels contribute to enhancement of memory, likely in conjunction with heightened attention (McGaugh, 1995; Thompson, 1993). On the other hand, as is likely to be the case for traumatic events, neurophysiological changes associated with extreme levels of emotion may impair memory (Bower & Sivers, 1998; van der Kolk, 1994). Finally, as Pillemer's (1998) defining characteristics of personal event memory attest, people's confidence in the accuracy of their memories is generally high (Brewer, 1986). Yet level of confidence is minimally correlated with the accuracy of memories (Barclay, 1986).

Although sources of distortion abound, the most significant overall conclusion from research on the accuracy of personal event memories for nontraumatic events is this: *although your memories may contain inaccurate details, the* gist *of your memories is likely to be accurate* (Barclay, 1986). An important caveat, however, is that what you recall spontaneously is likely to be more accurate than what you recall when you try to force yourself to remember or when you are under external pressure to remember details, such as when giving eyewitness testimony (Neisser, 1988b).

Because systematic research on accuracy of adults' memory for childhood abuse is relatively limited, Widom and colleagues' prospective studies are particularly noteworthy. These researchers compared adults' retrospective reports of childhood physical abuse (Widom & Shepard, 1996) and childhood sexual abuse (Widom & Morris, 1997) with court records of abuse documented 20 years previously. These studies showed substantial accuracy as well as discriminant validity for retrospective reports of abuse, along with a consistent bias toward *underreporting* abuse.

Implicit emotional memories

Schacter (1996) defined *implicit memory* generally as evident 'when people are influenced by a past experience without any awareness that they are remembering' (p. 161) and more technically as referring to 'facilitations of performance, generally known as repetition or direct priming effects, that need not and frequently do not involve any conscious recollection of the prior experience' (Schacter, 1989, p. 695). Thus, in contrast to explicit memory, implicit memory is expressed in performance rather than being accessible by conscious, volitional recall. Implicit memory is also called *procedural* memory, a term that is particularly apt for memory for motor skills, such as playing the piano or riding a bicycle. Typically, motor skills are performed without any explicit memory of the events during which they were acquired. Unlike explicit memories, which are initially encoded in a single instance, implicit memory for skills and habits is acquired gradually over many learning trials. Motor skills can be learned by persons with amnesia who are incapable of (explicitly) remembering the occasions on which they acquired these new skills (Schacter, 1996).

Priming is a key example of being influenced by past experience without any awareness of this being so. Consider post-traumatic triggers in light of Schacter's (1994) definition of priming as 'the facilitated identification of perceptual objects from reduced cues as a consequence of specific prior exposure to an object' (p. 234). The important point is that you do not know you have been primed. A client, for example, might have overheard a couple arguing in a store and not thought much of it at the time. Yet, on top of her history of witnessing marital violence in childhood, this event might prime her to react antagonistically to her husband's criticism—all without awareness.

Thus priming applies to emotional responses, which can reflect a history of exposure to traumatic events without any explicit memory for those events. Tobias and colleagues (Tobias, Kihlstrom, & Schacter, 1992) cited several classic examples from the clinical literature. A patient with Korsakoff's amnesia was pricked with a pin when he shook hands with an experimenter; subsequently, he refused to shake hands again with the experimenter, although he had no explicit memory of the earlier encounter. An amnestic patient was traumatized by some men who placed her drunken husband on her doorstep and told her he was dead. Without understanding why, she froze with terror whenever she passed the door. Another woman who had no comprehension for her phobia of running water ultimately learned that, as a child, she had strayed from a picnic and been trapped under a waterfall. A woman who was inexplicably depressed after surgery blurted out in hypnosis that she was told of a malignancy; she subsequently learned that the possibility of a malignancy was discussed while she was anesthetized. Tobias and colleagues conclude:

> In each of these cases, the person shows a change in emotional response—refusing to shake hands, freezing at a doorway, fearing running water, or feeling depressed—that is directly attributable to some previous experience; yet in each case, the experience itself is not remembered. In principle, this dissociation between the person's emotional response and his or her conscious recollection is analogous to the dissociation between implicit and explicit memory observed in the laboratory. (p. 70)

Thus *a perceptual cue associated with a previously threatening or traumatic event may evoke the fight-or-flight response without any explicit memory of the trauma*. The question of accuracy does not pertain to implicit emotional responses. Yet these conditioned emotional responses can be highly maladaptive in their overgeneralization—they are 'not conditional enough' (van der Kolk, 1994, p. 254).

Neurobiological dissociation of implicit and explicit memory

Knowing that there are brain-based reasons for their bewildering reactions helps patients. The distinction between implicit and explicit memory is anchored in neurobiological research (Schacter & Tulving, 1994), and the neurobiology of traumatic memory is crucial to understanding PTSD (van der Kolk, 1994). Consider fear conditioning, a form of subcortical emotional learning that yields indelible memory (LeDoux, 1996; LeDoux, Romanski, & Xagoraris, 1989). Conditioned fear responses are mediated substantially by the amygdala, which links unconditioned and conditioned stimuli and orchestrates multiple components of the fear response within fractions of a second (Davis, 1992; Halgren, 1992; LeDoux, 1992; McGaugh, Introini-Collison, Cahill, Kim, & Liang, 1992; van der Kolk, 1994). Thus long-term memories can be triggered non-consciously in milliseconds by sensations and perceptions (Cowan, 1988). These rapid, subcortical responses not only can be elicited and influence behavior non-consciously but also may be followed by minimal conscious elaboration. The client is blindsided and bewildered.

Extensive research has elucidated the cerebral circuitry associated with explicit memory (Schacter & Tulving, 1994; Squire, 1987; Squire & Zola-Morgan, 1991). The hippocampus occupies center stage in an amalgam of medial temporal lobe structures that organize highly processed information from sensory cortices into durable episodic memories. The hippocampus plays a major role in encoding situational context (i.e., the amygdala links a stimulus with fear, and the hippocampus embeds the fear conditioning into the broader situational context). The medial temporal lobe system interacts with the prefrontal cortex in the encoding of episodic memories (e.g., specific time–place contexts); remembering events likewise entails integrated prefrontal and medial temporal processing (Squire, 1987). Furthermore, whereas the hippocampus plays a key role in the automatic retrieval of memories (i.e., activation by cues), the frontal cortex plays a key role in deliberate, strategic memory retrieval (Schacter, 1995, 1999).

Ordinarily, the neurobiological systems supporting implicit and explicit memory operate in concert to produce meaningful emotion-laden memories (LeDoux, 1996). Yet, because these systems can be dissociated by neurological damage or by psychological trauma, they can operate independently such that implicit emotional memories may be unaccompanied by any explicit representation of the events in which they occurred. Moreover, the sheer speed of implicit memory mandates that feelings are likely to precede an explicit understanding of their basis.

Implicit memories in search of explicit memories

Many persons' memories of traumatic events—however intrusive and painful—match Pillemer's (1998) criteria for personal event memories. They pertain to specific events, are detailed, are accompanied by a sense of reexperiencing, represent particular moments of experience, and are believed. Such coherent emotional memories exemplify the parallel and unified functioning of the amygdala system and the hippocampal–prefrontal system (instigating fear with associated physiological arousal and providing explicit memory for details and context, respectively).

But many clients with intrusive symptoms do not complain of such well-articulated personal event memories of trauma. Their reexperiencing symptoms are far more fragmented and confusing. For example, compared with other emotionally charged memories, memories of rape are less clear and vivid, less ordered, less well remembered, less thought about, and less talked about—yet *more* emotionally intense (Koss, Figueredo, Bell, Tharan, & Tromp, 1996; Tromp, Koss, Figueredo, & Tharan, 1995). But the emergence of fragmented memories of long-forgotten events is liable to be most distressing and disorganizing (D. Brown et al., 1998; Cameron, 1996; Williams & Banyard, 1997). Cameron (1996), for example, found that the dawning awareness of childhood sexual abuse was often associated with a crisis marked by horror, disillusionment, and a suicidal state—with ensuing flipflops between intrusive symptoms and denial. Such emerging memories are often the impetus for seeking therapy.

Neither emerging traumatic memories nor recurrent flashbacks are personal event memories as Pillemer defined them. In the context of PTSD, a perceptual cue associated with a traumatic event serves as the trigger that evokes an emotional response—an implicit emotional memory. But, unlike a unified personal event memory, the explicit memory may not be forthcoming. This experience reflects an amalgam of too much (implicit) memory and too little (explicit) memory (van der Kolk, 1994). Brewin and colleagues (Brewin et al., 1996) noted that situationally accessible (implicit) memories in the absence of verbally accessible (explicit) memories are the hallmark of inadequately processed traumatic experience.

Implicit memory is the provocateur of intrusive post-traumatic memories, and explicit memory may or may not follow in its wake (Brewin et al., 1996). Implicit memories will prompt a search for explicit memories. As van der Kolk (1996) commented, 'People seem to be unable to accept experiences that have no meaning; they will try to make sense of what they are feeling' (p. 296). Of course, the explication is a complex construction with a potentially wide range of coherence and accuracy. As Squire (1995) put it, 'one could say that the neocortex is available to interpret any conscious mental content that is produced. It is then a separate question whether such content refers to a memory or not, and, if a memory, whether the memory is accurate or inaccurate' (pp. 210–211).

REPRESSED MEMORIES?

Incredulity about the possibility of repressing memories of childhood trauma has been a fulcrum for the false memory debate (Loftus, 1993). Ironically, repression is a minor player in traumatic memory impairment. Sorting out four questions avoids a hopeless muddle. First, how common is not remembering? Second, how accurate are long-forgotten memories? Third, what prompts remembering? Fourth, what role does repression play in not remembering?

How common is not remembering trauma?

Ample evidence indicates that many individuals do not remember or think about traumatic events for long periods (D. Brown et al., 1998). Substantial proportions of individuals in many samples report periods of not remembering trauma, with figures ranging from 19% (Loftus, Polansky, & Fullilove, 1994) to nearly 60% (Briere & Conte, 1993) as well as in between (Binder, McNiel, & Goldstone, 1994). But not remembering is a matter of degree (Brewin & Andrews, 1998; Freyd, 1998). Herman and Schatzow (1987), for example, found full recall in 38%, partial recall in 36%, and severely limited recall in 14% of a sample of patients. Williams (1994) found that 38% of women with a documented history of childhood sexual abuse did not remember the documented incident, although only 12% reported that they had never been abused. Williams (1995) further found that 16% of women who recalled the abuse reported recovering memories of it after a period of forgetting.

Failure to remember extends beyond childhood sexual abuse. In a sample of psychologists reporting a history of sexual or physical abuse, 40.5% had reported some period of forgetting (Feldman-Summers & Pope, 1994). Elliott (1997) surveyed a random sample from the general population, asking about a wide range of traumatic events and distinguishing continuous recall from partial and complete memory loss. She found evidence for delayed recall in 32% of the subjects who reported some form of trauma (17% reporting a period of partial memory and an additional 15% reporting a period of no memory). Elliott also found that delayed recall was especially high for interpersonal trauma. Although the data are not entirely consistent across studies, a common finding is more limited recall in the context of more severe abuse (Cameron, 1996).

Therapists should keep in mind, however, that failing to remember per se is not indicative of trauma. We fail to remember benign events as well as traumatic events. Moreover, as is true of traumatic events, we remember more about benign events after making an effort to do so (Read & Lindsay, 2000).

Are long-forgotten memories accurate?

High proportions of persons who have gone through a period of not remembering trauma are able to find external corroboration for their memories

(Feldman-Summers & Pope, 1994; Herman & Schatzow, 1987). Chu and colleagues (Chu, Frey, Ganzel, & Mathhews, 1999) found that the majority of patients who reported a period of complete amnesia for childhood sexual and physical abuse attempted to find corroboration, and the vast majority who attempted were successful. Kluft (1995) reported that more than half of a series of patients with dissociative identity disorder were able to find corroboration for traumatic events, many of which were remembered for the first time in hypnosis. Kluft also found a small number of patients for whom the memories could be conclusively disproved and concluded that his findings 'confute both the extreme credulous and the extreme skeptical positions on the recovery of memory of traumata' (p. 255).

Williams's research (Williams, 1994, 1995; Williams & Banyard, 1997) is especially noteworthy because she related lack of memory in adulthood to documented sexual abuse in childhood. Notably, Williams found no difference between the amnestic and non-amnestic groups in the extent of accuracy of their current accounts in relation to their documented histories. For both groups, Williams (1995) concluded, 'When one considers the basic elements of the abuse, their retrospective reports were remarkably consistent with what had been reported in the 1970s' (p. 662). Also important, the level of clarity or vagueness of adult memory was not related to the level of accuracy.

Cheit (1998) took a novel approach to the debate about recovered memory by gathering relatively unequivocal cases of documented trauma associated with a period of failure to remember and posting them on the Internet. To be included, a case must 'involve a traumatic event that was not remembered in the time shortly after it occurred, was recalled later in life, and has subsequently been corroborated in a meaningful fashion' (p. 143). He outlined 35 cases in his paper, and he is accumulating more on his website on the World Wide Web.

What cues prompt remembering?

Given concerns that false memories are elicited by suggestive memory recovery techniques in therapy, therapists should be aware that a wide range of contexts serve as retrieval cues (Brewin & Andrews, 1998). Williams (1995), for example, observed that recovered memories were triggered by a wide range of reminders generally unrelated to therapy. Chu and colleagues (Chu et al., 1999) observed that most trauma patients reported their first recollection of abuse while alone at home, and nearly half of those who remembered sexual or physical abuse were not in any treatment at the time. Few recalled any overt suggestion as a trigger for memory recovery. Elliott (1997) found the most common triggers for recall to be media presentations (54%), an experience similar to the original trauma (37%), and conversation with a family member (37%). Psychotherapy was a comparatively uncommon trigger (14%). Elliot also found the cue for delayed recall was similar to the original trauma. For example, delayed recall of sexual trauma was more likely to be cued by another sexual experience, whereas delayed recall of violent trauma was more likely to be cued by another violent experience.

What role does repression play in not remembering?

Skepticism about repression (Holmes, 1990) has cast doubt on delayed memories of trauma—notwithstanding that understanding and treating traumatic memories can proceed well without the concept of repression (Bonanno & Keuler, 1998). Also, even if one believes in it, there is no consensus that repression defends against memories, for example, as opposed to meanings (Mollon, 1998).

Setting repression aside, there is no doubt that traumatized clients 'wish to avoid unpleasant, overwhelming, or out-of-control states of mind' (Horowitz, 1988, p. 6). Thus not remembering trauma, at least at some junctures, is likely to result from *motivated inhibition*. Some individuals report using deliberate strategies to avoid remembering and thinking about abuse (Brewin & Andrews, 1998; Cameron, 1996; Koutstaal & Schacter, 1997). These strategies fit Erdelyi's (1996) concept of 'intentional not-thinking of target materials,' for example, by 'else-thinking' (p. 188). Such conscious efforts to block out traumatic memories can be construed as *suppression*, which is more likely to be effective for explicit than implicit memories (Erdelyi, 1996). Questioning the phenomenon of unconscious defense, Erdelyi pointed out that individuals might not remember (consciously) suppressing memories and then mistakenly infer that they (unconsciously) repressed them. Complicating matters further, individuals might forget that they have remembered trauma (Brewin & Andrews, 1998; Read & Lindsay, 2000). Given the fallibility of memory for external events (Schacter, 1999), we should not be surprised at inability to remember our mental processes.

I do not think it is plausible to limit all inhibition of painful remembering to conscious cognitive strategies. Elliott (1997) explained delayed recall of traumatic memories in terms of avoidance conditioning, 'whereby access to memory is punished by the negative affect that accompanies the recall, thereby motivating the development of memory-inhibiting mechanisms' (p. 812). Brewin and Andrews (1998) construed *repression* as an *active inhibitory process that prevents aversive information from entering working memory*. Thus repression involves selective attention, which entails a flexible integration of facilitatory and inhibitory processes, both deliberate (conscious) and automatic (non-conscious). Moreover, relatively stable individual differences may play a role in attention, for example, as persons with a repressive cognitive style avoid attending to negative information. Also, as discussed in

Chapter 3, persons with a dismissing attachment style show relatively limited memory for childhood adversity.

In sum, stable traits as well as deliberate and more reflexive inhibitory processes block painful remembering. Whether or not we invoke the concept of repression in this mix, we have only just begun to answer the question: How could a person not remember trauma?

FACTORS THAT IMPAIR PERSONAL EVENT MEMORIES OF TRAUMA

Many factors besides repression may contribute to inability to remember trauma and to distorted memories of trauma. These factors include the passage of time, developmental level, social context, fantasy proneness, dissociation, neurophysiological impairment, and failure of mentalization. In varying degrees and combinations, these factors—along with conscious and non-conscious inhibitory processes that limit information in working memory—contribute to a wide spectrum of detail and accuracy in memories of trauma.

Time

Because the false memory controversy centers on adults' memories of childhood sexual abuse, time is particularly important. Like other forms of explicit memory, autobiographical memory declines as time passes (Rubin, 1982). Technically put, 'The probability of remembering an event is a negative function of the length of time between encoding and retrieval' (Kihlstrom & Barnhardt, 1993, p. 90). A *use it or lose it* phenomenon is pertinent insofar as memories that are not retrieved and rehearsed may slowly dissipate (Schacter, 1999). Not thinking about trauma may erode memory. Moreover, erosion of accurate detail over time sets the stage for introducing distorted detail (Riccio, Rabinowitz, & Axelrod, 1994).

Developmental level

Whereas implicit memory is operative from birth, a relatively dense *infantile amnesia* before age two stems from the fact that narrative personal event memory only begins to develop at 18–36 months in tandem with the evolution of a sense of self and the capacity for language. The disjunction between implicit and explicit memory is evident in Terr's (1988) observation that preschool children may behaviorally reenact traumatic events that they experienced in infancy, even if they cannot narrate them. Although the cognitive capacity for narrative autobiographical memory develops in the third year of life, personal event memories in the preschool years tend to be relatively rudimentary and loosely organized, gradually becoming more detailed with age (Hudson & Nelson, 1986; Pillemer & White, 1989). Even so, there are significant individual differences in the age of earliest memories as well as variations in memorability between different types of childhood events (Usher & Neisser, 1993).

Most clients will understand that people generally remember little from their early years, and that such a failure to remember is not a sign of trauma. Inevitably, however, some clients will insist that they can remember very early events in considerable detail. While acknowledging that there are individual differences, therapists can state that this is not the norm and that persons can form vivid, memory-like images from what they have heard or believe. In light of wide individual differences, however, dogmatically insisting on the absence of veridical memories for early life is not justified. Arguing for open-mindedness is an intriguing report of an extraordinarily precocious 30-month-old boy having some memories of his own birth (Mollon, 1998).

Social context

Personal event memories are partly a social construction, and social processes may contribute to the lack of memory as well as to memory distortion. Conversations about events are a form of rehearsal that facilitates elaborative encoding. Secrecy associated with childhood abuse is prohibitive of discourse (Spence, 1994). Moreover, traumatic experience may be actively denied as it occurs (Saunders & Arnold, 1993). Thus a sense of unreality may be fostered by the family milieu (Ferenczi, 1949; Modell, 1991; Sluzki, 1993): 'It didn't happen; it happened but it wasn't important and has no consequences; it happened but (s)he provoked it; it happened but it's not abusive' (Reiker & Carmen, 1986, p. 363). At worst, abused individuals may doubt whether they know anything (Modell, 1991).

Research demonstrates the importance of social context for encoding personal memories. Goodman and colleagues (Goodman, Quas, Batterman-Faunce, Riddlesberger, & Kuhn, 1996) studied memories of children exposed to a painful medical procedure involving genital catheterization. Children whose mothers were more emotionally supportive and who discussed the experience with them showed fewer inaccuracies (and less suggestibility to misleading information) than those whose mothers did not converse with them or who had no time to attend to them. Research on abuse also suggests that emotional neglect may contribute to memory failure. In her study of adult memories of documented instances of childhood sexual abuse, Williams (1995) found that, compared to those with continuous memories, women with recovered memories of sexual abuse received less support from their mother. Similarly, Cameron (1996) found that, compared to women who did not have amnesia for childhood sexual abuse, those with a history of amnesia were three times as likely to report that there was no adult on whom they could rely in childhood.

Social context may not only interfere with elaborative encoding but also may abet confabulation—or lying. Antagonistic parents can pressure a child to construct memories of abuse. Emphasizing the power of parental authority, Terr (1994) documented a dramatic example of a mother brainwashing her daughter into constructing wholly false memories of sexual abuse. Brown and colleagues (D. Brown et al., 1998) made a convincing case that naturalistic research on interrogatory suggestion (e.g., police interrogations) and coercive persuasion (brainwashing) is far more pertinent to therapy than is the extensive laboratory research demonstrating pockets of unreliability in memory. These authors cited evidence that extreme social pressure brought to bear on an individual who is uncertain about past events could spawn *false beliefs* about the past. As they pointed out, whether such pressure can create *false memories* is another matter, although it is clear that individuals can create memory-like images from such false beliefs. These authors also reviewed the extensive literature on individual differences in *suggestibility* that relate to a propensity to generate false beliefs about the past under social pressure. Notably, suggestion is most likely to engender false memoirs for events that could plausibly have happened to an individual (Pezdek, Finger, & Hodge, 1997). Hence, *the combination of sparse detail, uncertainty, suggestibility, plausibility, and social pressure is fertile ground for memory distortion.*

The level of social coercion that Brown and colleagues described only fits seriously misguided therapy and, even then, would interact with the individual's suggestibility and uncertainty about the past. Yet the authors note how self-help and therapy groups that emphasize the recovery of memories of sexual abuse may approximate conditions conducive to false beliefs.

Fantasy proneness

Many traumatized clients report having retreated into fantasy in childhood to cope with trauma, neglect, and isolation. Fantasy-prone individuals (Lynn & Rhue, 1988; Wilson & Barber, 1983), as few as 4% of the population, report that they live their lives through fantasy. As children, they populate their make-believe worlds with imaginary companions, and they endow their dolls and stuffed animals with feelings and personalities. Many confuse memories of their fantasies with memories of events. Trauma, along with isolation and loneliness, abets fantasy in predisposed individuals. Therapists might be tempted to question a trauma history in a fantasy-prone individual. Ironically, fantasy may be a concomitant of trauma, and the presence of extremely unrealistic (fantasy-based) memories does not rule out a history of severe trauma.

Dissociation

Dissociation may impair encoding and retrieval of memories. As I will elaborate in Chapter 7, dissociative detachment at the time of trauma may limit the process of elaborative encoding needed to establish personal event memories, and it may also contribute to the patchy quality of memories (Allen, Console et al., 1999). Dissociation also separates realms of experience—sensation, affect, behavior, and knowledge—(Braun, 1988) in a way that may contribute to the fragmentation of traumatic memories.

Whereas dissociative detachment and fragmenting of experience may impair encoding, dissociative amnesia interferes with the *retrieval* of traumatic memories that have been encoded. Dissociative amnesia of varying duration and extent is well established in the trauma literature (Cohen, 1996; Loewenstein, 1991, 1996; Schacter & Kihlstrom, 1989; Spiegel, Frischholz, & Spira, 1993), and Steinberg (1995) identified amnesia as the central feature of dissociative disturbance. It is remarkable how much skepticism there has been regarding women's delayed memories of abuse in light of the well-accepted phenomenon of men's amnesia for combat (Freyd, 1998; McFarlane & van der Kolk, 1996). Paradoxically, although dissociation accounts for failures of retrieval, it also can be a retrieval cue to the extent that a dissociative state was part of the traumatic memory (Loewenstein, 1996). Not infrequently, dissociative defenses may backfire when a client retreats from current stress into a dissociative state that activates a traumatic memory.

Neurobiological impairment

The relation between emotion and memory is extremely complex, not only because the level of emotional arousal interacts with the nature and complexity of the task or event to be remembered but also because arousal may have different effects on encoding and retrieval (Revelle & Loftus, 1992). Whereas moderate levels of emotional arousal may enhance encoding, states of extreme emotional arousal are associated with neurotransmitter changes that may adversely affect encoding, consolidation, and retrieval. Confusing and fragmented intrusive memories (e.g., flashbacks) reflect disrupted encoding of declarative information at the time of trauma (Krystal, Southwick, & Charney, 1995). van der Kolk (1996) noted that 'the very nature of a traumatic memory is to be dissociated, and to be stored initially as sensory fragments that have no linguistic components' (p. 289).

As the neurobiology of trauma becomes better understood, the basis of encoding impairments is becoming clearer. For example, extreme fear can trigger large volleys from the amygdala and thalamus that block hippocampal activity, resulting in a failure of encoding and memory impairment for immediately preceding and subsequent events (Feindel, 1961; LeDoux, 1996; van der Kolk, 1994). In addition, the production of endogenous opioids, which have an analgesic effect (McCabe & Schneiderman, 1985), may also impair encoding of explicit memories (McEwen, 1995). We speculated that the dissociative quality of consciousness may reflect the impairment of information processing associated with this constellation of neurophysiological changes (Allen, Console et al., 1999).

The fragmented quality of many traumatic memories may also be associated with disruption at the stage of retrieval. Chronic stress-related changes in neurotransmission are associated with structural brain changes. Given the pivotal role of the hippocampus in encoding explicit memories (Schacter & Tulving, 1994), the increasing evidence of stress-related hippocampal damage is particularly noteworthy, although the neurophysiological changes underlying this damage remain to be clarified (McEwen, 1995; Sapolsky, 1997). A series of studies show decreased hippocampal volume associated with trauma and PTSD (Bremner, 1999; Bremner et al., 1995, 1997; Gurvits et al., 1996; Stein, Koverola, Hanna, Torchia, & McClarty, 1997). More broadly, other biological factors such as seizures, substance abuse, and head trauma may also contribute to memory impairment (Pope & Hudson, 1995). These findings bear not only on impaired memory for trauma but also on generalized memory deficits, especially in verbal memory, for patients with PTSD (Bremner, 1999; Bremner, Scott et al., 1993). Yet there remain many unanswered questions about the relationship between PTSD and memory impairment (Wolfe & Schlesinger, 1997). Although the finding of reduced hippocampal volume is consistent across studies, the findings regarding the relationship between extent of hippocampal volume and memory impairment are less so.

Flashbacks may be the upshot of the neurophysiological impairments that disrupt encoding and retrieval. Functional neuroimaging studies of regional cerebral blood flow in participants with PTSD (Rauch et al., 1996; Shin et al., 1997) show increased activation in the right-sided paralimbic cortex (including the amygdala) concomitant with decreased activation in left frontal cortex (Broca's area, which mediates speech), as well as in the left-middle temporal cortex. van der Kolk and colleagues (van der Kolk, Burbridge, & Suzuki, 1997) noted that deactivation of higher cortical structures involved in language production is especially significant. They referred to reexperiencing trauma as 'speechless terror,' and concluded that, when a traumatic memory is activated, 'the brain is "having" its experience. The person may feel, see, or hear the sensory elements of the traumatic experience, but he or she may be physiologically prevented from translating this experience into communicable language' (p. 109).

Reexperiencing and failure to mentalize

Mollon (1998) linked the fragmented and intrusive quality of traumatic memories to a failure to mentalize:

> Such patients typically have difficulty knowing what they feel, experience their minds as fragmented, and report physical sensations and bodily pain rather than mental pain. They may be somewhat puzzled by minds, both their own and other people's. . . . Actually, the term 'experience' carries connotations of more coherence than is the case in the realm of the unmentalised. It is 'experience' which cannot really be experienced, but instead exists as a sort of proto-experience, sensation which cannot be thought about or given words or repressed. Instead it lurks as a persecutor, preying on the mind, threatening invasion with particles of meaningless anxiety, dread, and perplexity. (pp. 156–157)

Elaborative encoding of personal event memories entails mentalization and reflection, in effect, a sense that 'I am having this experience.' Thus attachment trauma and the associated disorganized states of mind lay the foundation for inability to establish coherent memories of frightening experience. And all the memory-impairing factors just reviewed may become intertwined with—and contribute to—the failure to mentalize and reflect. As Mollon (1998) recognized, the danger of memory distortion may be especially great for those patients whose capacity to mentalize is pervasively impaired.

In therapy, we help our clients develop the capacity to mentalize this fragmented experience. Consider Brewin and Andrews' (1998) account of what it takes to integrate flashbacks into autobiographical memory:

> the person must be able to consciously edit and manipulate the information provided by the flashbacks within working memory. That is, they must retain awareness that they are experiencing the flashback, be able to reflect upon the experience as it is happening, and create ordinary autobiographical memories of the experience. (p. 965)

Given the various factors that impinge on mentalization, this is a daunting task for us and our clients.

A SPECTRUM OF ACCURACY IN PERSONAL EVENT MEMORIES OF TRAUMA

Because multiple factors in varying degrees and combinations may contribute to memory impairment, there is a wide spectrum of accuracy in any kind of personal event memory, and especially in personal event memories for trauma (Allen, 1995b). Consistent with research reviewed earlier, we should consider two continuous dimensions of potential memory impairment in combination: accuracy and persistence (Freyd, 1998). Thinking in shades of gray rather than black and white—true versus false—helps diffuse clients' defensiveness in relation to the false memory controversy.

Therapists can assume a relatively high level of accuracy for personal event memories of trauma that have been fairly continuous, especially when these memories have been elaboratively encoded with the aid of rehearsal—thought about and talked about. Of course corroboration adds further weight to confidence in such memories. Ordinarily, the question of accuracy in relation to continuous personal event memories—corroborated or not—does not arise.

In the middle ground of confidence about accuracy are fragmented, poorly articulated, and confusing memories of traumatic events, where implicit memory predominates over explicit memory. Such memories would include emerging images associated with long-forgotten events, flashbacks, and intrusive images in dissociative states. In some cases, the desire to explicate a trauma scenario consistent with intense emotional responses and fragmented imagery may prompt an intermingling of history and fantasy. Examples include memories of children who embellish traumatic events with developmentally natural fantasy (Terr, 1988), as well as memories of adults who confabulate from fiction and fantasy to generate recollections of bizarre trauma. At the extreme would be elaboration of bizarre memories of abuse in cult rituals (Qin, Goodman, Bottoms, & Shaver, 1998) and UFO abductions (Newman & Baumeister, 1998). Ganaway (1989) noted that highly fantasy-laden memories of trauma may serve the defensive function of obscuring more unthinkable abuse in the family. Corroboration is most desirable in these instances of partial memories, where the need for construction and the potential for confabulation are substantial.

At the inaccurate end of the spectrum are predominantly false memories, where confabulation renders even the gist of the memory off the mark. Justifiable alarm has been raised over the prospect that therapists abet such memories. Consider a worst-case scenario. A suggestible and fantasy-prone patient with a penchant for highly vivid visual imagery presents with psychiatric symptoms (e.g., depression, nightmares, panic attacks, low self-esteem, and social isolation). The therapist—without any evidence other than such ubiquitous symptoms with a host of possible etiologies—infers childhood sexual abuse to be the cause. Over the patient's protest, the therapist insists that memories of such childhood sexual abuse must be recovered through aggressive exploration. Gradually, images consistent with this putative trauma history begin coming to the patient's mind (e.g., a shadowy figure entering the bedroom) and, eventually, personal event memories are constructed—essentially out of whole cloth. Unfortunately, this process is not a fictional scenario; clinical horror stories akin to it have been documented in the literature (Esman, 1991; Loftus, 1993; Loftus & Rosenwald, 1993).

Of course therapists are not the only persons who might foster predominantly false memories in such scenarios. Peers, members of self-help and therapy groups, and family members might do so as well. Furthermore, another person's complicity is not necessary for the construction of inaccurate memories. Hypothetically, reading popular literature and being aware of the prevalence of psychiatric symptoms related to sexual abuse could lead a person to suspect a history of sexual abuse, to begin having nightmares, to construct images of abuse, and to develop false memories. One could speculate that anger toward the ostensible abuser might contribute to such scenarios, just as it might contribute to deliberate false accusations. Ironically, the anger and confabulated history of sexual abuse could be grounded in a history of other forms of maltreatment, such as physical and psychological abuse or neglect.

Furthermore, *an individual with a complex history of childhood maltreatment might have memories spanning all levels of accuracy*. For example, continuous, corroborated personal event memories of physical abuse discussed with siblings could be intertwined with partial memories of terrorizing psychological abuse intermingled with frightening fantasy. Binder and colleagues (Binder et al., 1994) gave a dramatic example of the intermingling of true and false memories. A woman with partial memories of childhood abuse who believed in astral projection reported that she had seen a flying saucer. She also had a history of being abused by a man who was convicted and imprisoned for child molestation. Thus implausible beliefs do not rule out a history of childhood trauma.

Also important, false *details* do not constitute false *memories* (Morton et al., 1996; Spiegel & Scheflin, 1994). Freyd (1998) gave a hypothetical example: 'if someone who was exposed as a child to anal rape and forced to watch pornography of vaginal rape later incorrectly remembered she was vaginally raped . . . we would presumably not count this as a false memory' (p. 110). Ironically, given that trauma may undermine the capacity for mentalization and abet fantasy, relatively false memories may be counted among the unfortunate outcomes of childhood maltreatment.

With respect to the spectrum of accuracy in memories of childhood abuse, it is fair to assume that anything can happen (Wylie, 1993). Yet this proposed spectrum raises a compelling empirical question: What is the prevalence of these various levels of accuracy and inaccuracy? Given the well-documented vulnerability of explicit memory to distortion from many quarters (Schacter, 1996, 1999), therapists should not lightly dismiss concerns about false memories. Yet, while false details are likely to be the rule, essentially false memories are likely to be the exception. Brewin and Andrews (1998) systematically reviewed evidence for the plausibility of recovered memories by taking into consideration the range of typical content, age at the time of remembered events, extent of corroboration, context of recall, and associated therapeutic techniques. Although the authors made a strong case for plausibility of memories, they also documented exceptions to the rule. While the prevalence of essentially false memories of childhood abuse remains unclear, the alarming prevalence of exposure to maltreatment is documented throughout the research literature. As I concluded previously, 'There is a false memory problem of unknown proportions and a more-or-less accurate memory problem of staggering proportions' (Allen, 1995b, p. 90).

Does accuracy matter?

A decade before the false memory controversy, Spence (1982) characterized the psychoanalyst's task in a way that has remarkable parallels—which he later (Spence, 1994) drew explicitly—to the therapeutic challenge of making sense of fragmented memories of childhood abuse. The psychoanalytic process generates *narrative truth*, which cannot be equated with *historical truth*. Like the therapist working with disconnected intrusive images and ideas, the analyst working with free associations engages the patient in an interpretive process that 'enables the patient gradually to see his life as continuous, coherent, and, therefore, meaningful' (Spence, 1982, p. 280). The psychoanalyst's theoretical predilections influence the interpretative process and thereby shape what becomes narrative truth. The same process pertains to the elucidation of autobiographical narrative in relation to traumatic memories. Spence argued that there is no clear demarcation between construction and reconstruction, and he focused on the pragmatic aspect of narrative truth:

> An interpretation, then, may bring about a positive effect not because it corresponds to a specific piece of past but because it appears to relate the known to the unknown, to provide explanation in place of uncertainty. . . . Interpretations may be effective without necessarily being 'true' in a strict historical sense. (p. 290)

As I will elaborate in Chapter 12, construction of a coherent narrative is a cornerstone of trauma treatment. If narrative truth carries the weight of therapeutic change, can clinicians ignore historical truth? Hardly. Spence (1994) emphasized the dangers of confusing narrative and historical truth in the context of child abuse. Even if the proportion of essentially false to essentially true memories is small, the stakes are extremely high. False allegations stemming from narrative truths that conflict with historical truths may be most conspicuously damaging when they enter the public domain in a court of law. But it does not take a legal battle to damage family relationships—whether or not the abuse narrative leads to disclosure or confrontation within the family.

Therapists need not become detectives, giving up their role as collaborators in the construction of narrative truth and instead searching actively for historical truth. But they must remain mindful of the distinction between narrative and historical truth. Even with more facts at our disposal, narrative truth cannot merge with historical truth. As Spence argued, psychological history is not a set of facts but rather a process that revolves around the connections and meanings made of the facts. These connections—the subjective experience of objective events—are not observable facts; they are invisible.

Implications for practice

Although it is not the most common, therapy is one context in which persons begin remembering a history of abuse. We do not know the extent to which we therapists contribute to false memories. Poole and colleagues (Poole, Lindsay, Memon, & Bull, 1995) concluded from their survey of professionals in the United States and the United Kingdon that as many as 25% of psychotherapists may engage in risky practice by virtue of suspecting abuse of which the patient is unaware and employing specific techniques to enhance memory. Olio (1996) subsequently pointed out, however, that this study leaves unanswered the extent to which therapists use various techniques, the competence with which they employ the techniques, and the relation of their beliefs and techniques to patients' recovery of memories.

Regardless of the extent of false memories and the contributions of therapy to them, therapists must keep abreast of continually evolving standards of care and adhere to them (D. Brown et al., 1998; Scheflin, 2000). Therapists must be knowledgeable about the limitations of memory. Those who employ techniques aimed at enhancing memory—hypnosis most prominently—must develop specialized expertise and employ numerous safeguards (D. Brown et al., 1998). Carefully documenting clinical material and the associated therapeutic process is also essential (Scheflin, 2000), as is providing informed consent that educates patients about memory and the risks of treatment (Young & Young, 1996). Whatever techniques we employ, our neutrality is the critical factor in sound practice. The client must decide what to believe.

EDUCATING CLIENTS ABOUT TRAUMATIC MEMORIES

Clients need to be educated about grounding techniques to head off or abort intrusive traumatic memories in the short run. They also must be helped to understand that decreasing vulnerability to intrusive post-traumatic symptoms in the long run requires an ambitious and integrated treatment approach (Chapters 11 and 12).

Yet our greatest challenge is to help clients who are struggling with the accuracy of their memories to understand some of the complexities reviewed in this chapter. Many clients are keenly aware of the false memory controversy—some will have been accused of having produced false memories—so are understandably defensive about their memories. I find that some clients minimize obviously traumatic events they remember clearly, then search for something worse in their history that will explain their suffering. Such clients must be helped better to *appreciate the impact of what they do remember, rather than attempting to remember more*. As I will argue in the discussion of treatment (Chapters 11 and 12), the search for specific memory *content* misses the mark.

To defuse clients' defensiveness about the accuracy of their memories, I point out that we all have false memories, in the sense that we mix up time frames, get details wrong, and tend to fill in the blanks with educated guesses. I also try to move patients away from black-and-white thinking to appreciate gradations in accuracy. This approach helps disabuse patients of the video recorder model of memory. Sometimes I convey to clients that vivid images can be misleading, referring to Kosslyn's (1994) research demonstrating that the same cortical areas involved in perception are activated in generating imagery. I remind them that anyone who has ever dreamed can appreciate the power of such imagery. I also explain the difference between implicit and explicit memory. Almost all clients know something about conditioned responses, which are a model for implicit emotional memory. I point out that they may have too much implicit memory and too little explicit memory, and their challenge is to construct an autobiographical narrative.

Any or all factors that potentially impair explicit memory can be explained to clients quite straightforwardly. Time elapsed is a simple one. Infantile amnesia takes a bit more explaining, but the idea that emotional memories can be well established before the child learns language that permits autobiographical memories will be quite understandable. The idea that we remember best what we have gone over in our minds or in conversation is readily contrasted with the fact that much abuse is kept secret or denied. Clients also need to know that efforts to fill in gaps resulting from social pressure (or internal pressure) can lead to distortions. I regularly discourage clients from attempting to force themselves to remember.

I broach the problem of fantasy proneness by pointing out that a retreat into fantasy is a natural way of coping that reflects imaginative capacity. Some clients recall that their fantasies were associated with a sense of reality, which sets the stage for the idea that fantasies can be intermingled with memories. Here caution is in order, because clients are liable to hear, 'You're just imagining it'—an accusation that will be all too familiar for many. The point is not to challenge but rather to empathize with *clients'* difficulty making sense of their history. Although dissociation requires fairly elaborate explanation in its own right (Chapter 7), clients can understand that they are unlikely to remember something clearly if they were not paying attention because they were feeling unreal, spacey, or tuned out at the time. Finally, explaining that there is a biological basis for memory disturbance can be alarming but, done with care, may also be reassuring to the extent that it diminishes self-blame (see Chapter 6).

All this education conveys to clients that their autobiography is a construction. I advocate thinking of this *autobiography as a current draft that will be continually revised across the lifespan*. The autobiography may require some research, because history cannot necessarily be inferred from memory. Although it is not the job of the therapist to do detective work, clients who are so inclined may do it, searching for corroboration that will bring their narrative truth in closer correspondence with historical truth.

When we discuss this process in psychoeducational groups, some members give examples of successful detective work. On the other hand, the challenges to obtaining corroboration also become clear when clients describe, for example, that family members are deceased, unavailable, or defensive—or they have no family. As they struggle on the current draft of their autobiography, clients could benefit from the wisdom of Mollon's (1998) advice to us: 'It is important for the therapist to tolerate uncertainty and ambiguity and avoid illusions of knowing' (p. 194).

Chapter 6

TRAUMA AS CHRONIC PHYSICAL ILLNESS

Many of the problems faced by the brain . . . have been dismissed because no anatomical or biochemical abnormalities have been identified as their cause. Unlike the heart, which visibly beats, we cannot see the brain think; therefore, when thought is disturbed for reasons that are not apparent, there is a tendency to blame the thinker for not doing it right. (Gershon, 1998, p. 310)

I am convinced that we therapists must appreciate the biological basis of trauma to empathize with our clients. Many clients are told by friends and family members, 'Just put it out of your mind,' 'Put the past behind you,' 'Move on,' or 'Get over it!' They fervently wish to do this, but they cannot— and they blame themselves for their failure to do so. Appreciating the biological basis of PTSD can help clients understand why they have such difficulty doing as others implore. I present PTSD flatly as a *chronic physical illness*. This concept validates clients' daily experience. As Yehuda and McFarlane (1997) suggested, 'Establishing that there is a biological basis for psychological trauma is an essential first step in allowing the permanent validation of human suffering' (p. xv). But thinking of PTSD as a physical illness does not go far enough. Many clients with PTSD also suffer from a range of general medical complaints that are best addressed under the rubric of *ill health*.

There is a downside to telling clients that they have a chronic physical illness. This view of their disorder confirms their sense of having been damaged and may further undermine their fragile self-esteem and hope. Yet conveying the gist of emerging knowledge about the physiological effects of trauma also can foster clients' hope by validating the challenges they have faced in getting well and clarifying their treatment needs. This physical-illness perspective is consistent with the increasing rehabilitative focus in treating chronic PTSD and its extensive comorbidity, and it sets the stage for emphasizing the crucial role of self-care in long-term management.

PTSD AS A CHRONIC PHYSICAL ILLNESS

Compelling evidence now indicates that trauma persistently perturbs the physiology of several stress-response systems (hypothalamic–pituitary–adrenal axis, locus coeruleus–noradrenergic, dopaminergic, opioid) and that early trauma adversely affects neurophysiological development. As with all forms of psychiatric vulnerability, individual differences are pronounced, and genetic contributions to trauma exposure as well as risk of disorder following exposure have been demonstrated.

The upshot of physiology gone awry is sensitization—heightened stress reactivity. It is certainly bad news that trauma may result in a persistently sensitized nervous system. I find myself continually wanting to doubt these findings, while the evidence continues to mount up. But overcoming reluctance to face these findings is essential, because understanding sensitization helps clients feel less crazy and mitigates self-blame.

I present key neurobiological findings in some detail here primarily to document the solid empirical basis for viewing trauma as a physical illness. If you are less interested in the neurobiological findings than their implications, you can get the gist of the chapter by skimming over the neurophysiological details and concentrating on a few general concepts: *pathophysiology, sensitization,* and *ill health.* Although the details are bound to change with the rapid explosion of knowledge in the field, I believe the die is cast with respect to these three broad phenomena.

Pathophysiology

When it was introduced in DSM-III (APA, 1980), PTSD was construed as a normal response to an abnormal (traumatic) event. Biological research now dictates a shift in thinking more consistent with an illness perspective (Yehuda & McFarlane, 1997). Although a majority of adults have been exposed to a potentially traumatic stressor, only a small minority have ever developed PTSD (Breslau, 1998). Yehuda and McFarlane (1995) acknowledged that pathologizing goes against social currents that dispose us to normalize the status of victims. Yet I think deeper understanding of the pathological impact of trauma should only reinforce our mandate to advocate for the needs and rights of traumatized persons.

Although many psychosocial risk factors predispose individuals to PTSD after trauma, the large discrepancy between trauma exposure and PTSD has prompted a search for *patho*physiological processes, and these processes have important implications for prognosis and treatment (Shalev, 1997a; Yehuda & McFarlane, 1997). A half-century ago, Kardiner (1941) anticipated this perspective in referring to psychological trauma as a *physioneurosis*. When I think of the Trauma Center in a hospital emergency service, I picture the victims of shootings and automobile wrecks—physical injuries and uncontrolled bleeding. I used to think that psychological trauma was an *analogy* to such physical trauma—with psychological trauma indicating a psyche rent apart. Yet emerging neurobiological research suggests that *psychological trauma is transduced into physical trauma*, albeit more slowly and insidiously than a shooting or automobile accident. The analogy might be this: psychological trauma precipitates slow internal bleeding—in the form of alterations in neurotransmission, hormone secretion, and gene expression. At worst, these alterations may eventuate in structural brain damage.

The brain's trauma center

If there is an occasion to delve into the brain in educating clients, the locus coeruleus–norepinephrine (LC-NE) stress-response system is a good place to start. Krystal and colleagues (Krystal et al., 1989) dubbed the locus coeruleus (LC) the *trauma center* of the brain. Norepinephrine (NE) can be presented as a form of adrenaline that, by mediating the sympathetic nervous system response to stress, is at the heart of the fight-or-flight response.

The nucleus paragigantocellularis in the ventrolateral rostral medulla serves as a relay station that activates the central noradrenergic stress response (through the LC), in tandem with the peripheral sympathetic nervous system response (Aston-Jones, Valentino, Van Bockstaele, & Meyerson, 1994; Murburg, Ashleigh, Hommer, & Veith, 1994). The peripheral sympathetic nervous system response prepares the individual for vigorous action (i.e., fight-or-flight) by shunting blood to large muscle groups, increasing energy to skeletal musculature by mobilizing blood glucose, accelerating heart rate and increasing blood pressure, dilating the pupils to allow more light to enter the eye, and constricting skin vasculature to limit blood loss in the event of injury (Southwick, Yehuda, & Morgan, 1995).

The LC, a cell group located in the central gray of the caudal pons in the brainstem, mediates the central noradrenergic response. LC neurons receive multisensory input, and the LC has widespread and diffuse subcortical and cortical projections that support its general activating function. The LC-NE system plays a key role in attention and vigilance, increasing the signal-to-noise ratio in sensory input (Aston-Jones et al., 1994). LC activation has an alerting function, potentially disrupting ongoing behavior to orient the individual to high-priority stimuli. Thus LC activation coordinates cognitive processes (attention and decision making) with peripheral sympathetic activation that mobilizes adaptive behavior.

In short, the LC-NE system is the brain's alerting or vigilance mechanism that prepares individuals to respond to threat. The *patho*physiology is an adaptation gone awry. Repeated and extreme stress eventuates in an *exaggerated* central and peripheral noradrenergic response that plays a major role in the *hyper*vigilance and *hyper*arousal in PTSD. The term, hyper*arousal*, however, is somewhat off the mark, insofar as research is inconsistent in showing elevated baseline levels of arousal in clients with PTSD. More precisely, PTSD is characterized by hyper*responsiveness* of the LC-NE system to stress (Charney, Deutch, Southwick, & Krystal, 1995; Murburg, 1994; Southwick et al., 1997; Southwick et al., 1995; Zigmond, Finlay, & Sved, 1995), possibly in concert with diminished serotonergic regulation (Spivak et al., 1999).

Simson and Weiss (1994) elucidated a chain of neurophysiological events that contribute to the persistent hyperresponsiveness of LC neurons to excitatory stimulation. Uncontrollable stress causes increased NE release; NE concentrations in the LC decrease as release and degradation exceed synthesis; and resulting decreased NE stimulation of inhibitory alpha-2 autoreceptors that would otherwise decrease further NE synthesis constitutes a functional blockade that undermines regulation of LC responsiveness, rendering LC neurons hyperresponsive to excitatory stimulation. The role of the alpha-2 autoreceptors in PTSD is instructive in linking flashbacks with panic attacks. Yohimbine is an alpha-2 receptor antagonist that blocks the *inhibition* of NE synthesis. Administration of yohimbine commonly induces panic attacks in clients with panic disorder, and it frequently induces panic attacks and flashbacks in clients with PTSD (Southwick et al., 1995).

Clients' high anxiety levels reflect their continual exposure to ubiquitous reminders of trauma as well other stressors. Hyperreactivity and hypersensitivity are terms that clients readily understand, and there is no need for them to learn the neurobiological basis of LC-NE system dysregulation. But they can be encouraged to *view their hyperreactivity as a physical disorder* insofar as the responsiveness of the LC-NE system has been persistently altered by exposure to extreme stress. In effect, the LC-NE system has been traumatized.

Although the LC-NE stress-response system may suffice to give clients an example of the physiological basis of PTSD, you may wish to appreciate the full extent of the pathophysiology in this disorder insofar as this extensive pathophysiology justifies presenting clients with the idea that PTSD is a chronic physical illness.

Dopaminergic stress response

Like the LC-NE system, the dopaminergic system plays a major role in stress responsiveness, and alterations in the dopaminergic system are also implicated in the pathophysiology of PTSD (Deutch & Young, 1995). The dopaminergic system is more exquisitely sensitive to stressors than the LC-NE system. Dopaminergic innervation originates in the midbrain substantia nigra and the ventral tegmental area, which has widespread cortical, limbic, and brainstem afferents. Ventral tegmental area neurons project to the nucleus accumbens (anterior to the hypothalamus) and the medial prefrontal cortex. This system is modulated by excitatory and inhibitory amino acid transmitters and, in turn, has a modulatory (excitatory and inhibitory) influence on other components of the stress response.

Dopaminergic modulation of medial prefrontal activation plays an important role in psychological aspects of the stress response, including the experience of anxiety and the acquisition of coping strategies. PTSD is associated with a functional deficit in cortical dopaminergic tone that contributes to impaired stress modulation and may also relate to the poor neuroleptic (dopamine blocking) response in clients with PTSD (Deutch & Young, 1995). Furthermore, stress-induced alterations in the dopaminergic mesocorticolimbic system attenuate responsiveness to reward and may contribute to the anhedonia and depression associated with PTSD (Zacharko, 1994).

Opioid function

Many traumatized clients not only complain of numbing but also experience stress-induced analgesia, for example, in conjunction with deliberate self-harm (see Chapter 8). These responses may be influenced by stress-related changes in the endogenous opiates (Southwick et al., 1995; Stout, Kilts, & Nemeroff, 1995). The concept of the body's natural narcotics can provide some concrete anchoring of this experience for clients.

Although research is limited, baseline levels of endogenous opiates appear either normal or reduced in clients with PTSD. Yet Pitman, van der Kolk, and colleagues (Pitman et al., 1990; van der Kolk, Greenberg, Orr, & Pitman, 1989) demonstrated that exposing combat veterans with PTSD to combat-related stimuli decreased their pain sensitivity, which they interpreted as 'phasic opioid-mediated stress-induced analgesia in PTSD' (Pitman et al., 1990, p. 143). These authors related the opioid response not to euphoria but instead to the blunting of emotional responses and to numbing (van der Kolk et al., 1989). Southwick and colleagues (Southwick et al., 1995) observed that self-medication with opiates is understandable in persons with PTSD, insofar as opiates suppress both central and peripheral noradrenergic activity. Yet when opiates are decreased, noradrenergic activity increases, suggesting that PTSD symptoms can be exacerbated by opiate withdrawal.

Hypothalamic–pituitary–adrenal axis

The core neuroendocrine response to stress is mediated by the hypothalamic–pituitary–adrenal (HPA) axis. The HPA axis has received extensive attention in the PTSD literature (McEwen, 1995; Michelson, Licinio, & Gold, 1995; Stout et al., 1995; Yehuda, 1997, 1998; Yehuda, Giller, Levengood, Southwick, & Siever, 1995). The HPA axis operates in tandem with the LC-NE system, contributing to central and autonomic responses to stress. The paraventricular nucleus of the hypothalamus has a wide range of inputs from other hypothalamic nuclei, as well as from the brainstem and limbic system. The chain of activation in the HPA axis is as follows: corticotropin-releasing factor (CRF) from the hypothalamic paraventricular nucleus activates adrenocorticotropic hormone (ACTH) from the pituitary, which stimulates the production of glucocorticoids (cortisol) from the adrenal cortex. CRF not only activates ACTH but also is part of a positive feedback loop with the LC-NE system.

Glucocorticoids mediate catabolism to provide energy for somatic demands related to stress, and they also serve a multifaceted function of containment. That is, glucocorticoids regulate inflammatory and immune responses, and they provide critical negative feedback via the hippocampus to attenuate the further secretion of CRF in the hypothalamus. Thus, through the hippocampus, which is rich in glucocorticoid receptors, cortisol normally keeps the HPA axis in check. Similarly, cortisol serves to shut down sympathetic activation following stress. Yehuda (1998) concluded that cortisol serves 'to restrain all biologic stress responses by initiating the *termination* of the neural defensive reactions that are normally activated by stress. . . . Cortisol is more of an "anti stress" than a stress hormone' (p. 100).

As with the LC-NE system, the adaptive physiology of the HPA axis can evolve into *patho*physiology in the context of extreme and chronic stress. Stress is commonly associated with *elevated* cortisol. Paradoxically, clients with PTSD show *lower* basal cortisol levels, regardless of gender, type of trauma, age of traumatization, duration of symptoms, or age at assessment (Yehuda, 1998). Along with lower basal levels are increased numbers of glucocorticoid receptors, increased receptor sensitivity, greater fluctuations in cortisol levels, and enhanced negative feedback inhibition. Thus the HPA axis shows under-activity in conjunction with being hyper*dynamic* (Stout et al., 1995). Yehuda (1998) postulated that 'a system that can maintain low levels of cortisol over a longer period of time, while also maintaining its full dynamic range, may be better set up to respond, or perhaps hyperrespond, to stress' (p. 117). She related these HPA axis changes to the symptoms of hypervigilance, increased startle, and increased reactivity to reminders of the trauma (Yehuda, 1997). Underscoring the concept of the pathophysiology of PTSD, Yehuda (1998) commented, 'Because the HPA observations in PTSD are *not* redundant with classic descriptions of the biologic stress response, they clarify that PTSD is one specific type of response to extreme stress' (p. 123).

Research on the physiology of peritraumatic stress reactions highlights the role of individual differences in HPA axis functioning in vulnerability to PTSD after trauma. McFarlane (1997) advocated that PTSD be construed as a *disorder of transition* that reflects an inability to modulate the acute stress response. McFarlane's fine-grained analysis of the time course of symptoms showed that intrusion, avoidance, hyperarousal, and dissociation at two days post-trauma did not predict PTSD, but these symptoms at 10 days post-trauma did predict PTSD. On the other hand, cortisol levels at two days post-trauma predicted whether an individual developed PTSD (hypocortisolism) or depression (hypercortisolism). Thus, unlike the psychological response, the physiological response at two days post-trauma predicted the development of PTSD by six months post-trauma. Yehuda and colleagues (Yehuda, McFarlane, & Shalev, 1998) expanded on these findings, reporting that not only lower cortisol but also higher heart rate at the time of trauma predicted subsequent PTSD. They inferred that individual differences in HPA axis functioning determine how an individual will react to traumatic stress. In predisposed individuals, a failure of the HPA axis to contain sympathetic nervous system hyperreactivity may initiate a cascade of intrusive and hyperarousal symptoms that eventuate in PTSD.

Pathophysiology in the HPA axis also relates to the findings of hippocampal damage in traumatized persons. The hippocampus is not only rich in glucocorticoid receptors and highly sensitive to glucocorticoid secretion in the HPA axis stress response, but also plays a key role in containment of the HPA axis response to stress. As noted in Chapter 5, several studies demonstrate decreased hippocampal volume in clients with PTSD stemming from a wide range of traumas (Bremner, 1999; J. D. Bremner et al., 1995; Bremner et al., 1997; Gurvits et al., 1996; Stein, Koverola et al., 1997). Social stress (being placed repeatedly in a subordinate position) also has been shown to lead to hippocampal atrophy in tree shrews (Magarions, McEwen, Flugge, & Fuchs, 1996).

Yet the relationship of stress and glucocorticoids to hippocampal neurophysiology is extraordinarily complex (Duman & Nestler, 2000; McEwen, 1995; McEwen & Magarinos, 1997; Sapolsky, 1997). Cell death and neurogenesis are ongoing in the hippocampus, and low levels of glucocorticoids contain cell death. On the other hand, extreme stress and excess glucocorticoid secretion may synergize with excitatory amino acid release to promote cell atrophy and death. Yet atrophy is not necessarily a sign of impending cell death. Rather, atrophy may be an adaptive and reversible response of viable neurons that temporarily reduces synaptic connectivity in order to spare neurons from excessive excitatory input. Even reversible atrophy, however, transiently impairs learning. The finding of decreased hippocampal volume in PTSD appears paradoxical, given the decreased basal levels of cortisol associated with PTSD. Hence it is unlikely that glucocorticoid toxicity explains the hippocampal atrophy. Instead, atrophic changes may be due to the increased sensitivity of glucocorticoid receptors associated with enhanced negative feedback inhibition and overall hyperresponsiveness of the HPA axis (Yehuda, 1997).

Thyroid function

Although the HPA axis has received the lion's share of attention in PTSD, the hypothalamic–pituitary–thyroid axis also merits mention. Mason and colleagues (Mason et al., 1995) summarized research indicating subtle hyperthyroid signs in clients with PTSD (elevated total T_3 and free T_3), as well as data suggesting that thyroid abnormalities vary with the course of PTSD. They noted that 'the clinical picture of classical hyperthyroidism includes such psychiatric symptoms as sleep disturbances, restlessness, anxiety, irritability, explosive anger, jumpiness or increased startle, and difficulty in concentrating—in other words, both cognitive and affective disturbances commonly observed in PTSD clients' (p. 370).

Fear conditioning and the amygdala

The amygdala is a good neurobiological anchor for PTSD reexperiencing symptoms (LeDoux, 1996). The amygdala serves as an interface between sensory input and motor response, and its action is independent of any particular sensory or motor modality (LeDoux, 1995). The central nucleus of the amygdala orchestrates a 'hard-wired fear response network' (Armony & LeDoux, 1997, p. 260) that includes sympathetic activation, parasympathetic control, secretion of stress hormones, reflex potentiation, and emotional behavior.

As noted in Chapter 5, in addition to its role in the expression of fear, the amygdala mediates the acquisition of conditioned fear responses, forging connections between conditioned and unconditioned stimuli. The amygdala receives input directly from the thalamus, as well as indirectly through unimodal and polymodal association cortex, allowing for activation by low-level stimulus characteristics that may prepare the amygdala to process more complex information from the hippocampus and association cortex. High levels of glucocorticoids potentiate conditioned fear responses. Most important, these conditioned responses forged by the amygdala are thought to be relatively indelible.

Amygdala-based fear conditioning has obvious adaptive functions. Yet, in the context of extreme stress, amygdala-based conditioning can result in overgeneralized fear responses to specific elements of the traumatic situation. Moreover, these subcortical amygdala-based fear responses are extremely rapid, preceding cortical elaboration. Thus not only does emotion precede thought but also the individual may not be aware of the stimulus that provoked the fear (Armony & LeDoux, 1997).

Recent studies of cerebral blood flow are consistent with the hypothesis that failure of fear extinction contributes to PTSD. Although not a universal finding, increased amygdala activation during symptom provocation in

Vietnam veterans with PTSD has been reported (Liberzon et al., 1999). Findings of decreased cerebral blood flow to the medial prefrontal cortex on symptom provocation in combat veterans (Bremner, Staib et al., 1999) as well as women with a history of childhood sexual abuse (Bremner, Narayan et al., 1999) are noteworthy insofar as prefrontal cortex plays a significant role in inhibiting the amygdala. Such findings support the hypothesis that PTSD symptoms are associated with a failure of extinction of conditioned fear responses. There is a neurophysiological basis for clients' inability to 'Just get over it!'

Developmental pathophysiology and attachment

The bulk of research on biological substrates of PTSD has been conducted with adults—combat veterans in particular. Yet there is a growing literature on the neurobiology of trauma in children and adolescents that demonstrates many comparable findings regarding patterns of pathophysiology (Perry, 1994; Pynoos, Steinberg, Ornitz, & Goenjian, 1997). The finding of trauma-related pathophysiology in children has particularly grave implications. As Perry (1994) stated, 'Young children victimized by trauma are at risk for developing permanent vulnerabilities—that is, permanent changes in neuronal differentiation and organization. In this regard, childhood PTSD is a developmental disorder' (p. 240).

The work of three research groups illustrates the potential developmental neurobiological impact of trauma. Putnam and Trickett (1997) are conducting a longitudinal study of a group of sexually abused girls referred by child protective service agencies. The girls entered the study in preadolescence, and they are being studied in relation to a control group matched for many demographic variables. These authors found indications of elevated catecholamines (consistent with hyperactivity in the LC-NE system), dysregulation of the HPA axis, and immune system compromise. Teicher and colleagues (Teicher et al., 1997) conducted extensive electroencephalographic (EEG) studies of psychologically, physically, and sexually abused children and adolescents admitted for psychiatric inpatient treatment. They observed a range of differences between abused and control group children, and their findings consistently point to left hemisphere abnormalities and atypical patterns of hemispheric asymmetry. The relative impairment of left hemisphere functioning is particularly noteworthy in light of neuroimaging studies that show decreased activation of left frontal functioning ('speechless terror') in clients with PTSD who are reliving the trauma (see Chapter 5). Finally, when Pynoos and colleagues (Pynoos et al., 1997) studied HPA axis function in children and adolescents five years after exposure to an earthquake, they found altered physiological patterns (e.g., low basal cortisol) comparable to those seen in adults with PTSD. They also reported alterations in inhibitory startle modulation among school-aged children exposed to sniper fire and commented that findings of compromised information processing in children have important implications for attention and learning deficits.

Trauma may affect the development of the brain in myriad ways, and the impact of adverse experience is potentially most grave during critical developmental periods when the brain is most plastic (Nelson & Carver, 1998; Perry, Pollard, Blakley, Baker, & Vigilante, 1995; Post et al., 1998). Particularly noteworthy in light of controversy about memory for early trauma (Chapter 5) is the likelihood that extreme stress adversely affects the development of the hippocampus and related cortical structures that mediate explicit memory (Nelson & Carver, 1998). Moreover, consistent with developmental literature reviewed in Chapter 2, not just abuse but also deprivation and neglect may have severe neurodevelopmental consequences (Perry et al., 1995). Furthermore, the adverse impact of early trauma and deprivation on the central nervous system is likely to render PTSD for adulthood trauma more difficult to treat (Post et al., 1998).

Developmental pathophysiology provides an opportune context to make the point that, in treating clients with a history of attachment trauma, we therapists are contending with a *failure of containment* on two levels: psychological and physiological. I described in Chapters 3 and 4 how attachment, physiological regulation, and self-regulation are intertwined. This chapter shows how pathophysiology entails a failure of containment at the neurobiological level, evident in multiple sensitized stress-response systems. Consider that this failure of containment on the physiological level may be accompanied by—or engendered by—a failure of containment in attachment relationships. Fonagy and colleagues (Fonagy et al., 1995) argued that 'secure attachment is the outcome of successful containment' (p. 243), and this is a two-way street: secure attachment also *provides* containment. Think of yourself as helping your traumatized client by providing emotional containment through an attachment relationship that will also foster physiological containment. And think of your client's internalizing the capacity for psychological and physiological containment as the optimal outcome of treatment (Chapter 11).

Sensitization

Clients must understand only one biological concept, sensitization. Ask a group of traumatized clients, 'How many of you have been accused of "making mountains out of molehills"?' All hands go up. I explain that this is precisely what the sensitized nervous system does. Sensitization is adaptive in preparing the individual for a quick response to any hint of danger. But, like all other adaptive physiological responses to stress, sensitization may become highly maladaptive, transforming molehills into mountains, causing a great deal of distress, and further perturbing physiology—as well as perturbing relationships with others who criticize the mountain making.

I explain PTSD as a chronic disorder resulting from sensitization to stressors. *Sensitization* is the process by which an initial severe stressor enhances subsequent responsiveness to a stressor of similar or lesser magnitude. Post (1992) initially described the role of sensitization in recurrent mood disorders and then speculated that the concept might be extended to PTSD. Subsequently, Post and colleagues (Post et al., 1998; Post, Weiss, Smith, Li, & McCann, 1997; Post, Weiss, & Smith, 1995; Post, Weiss, Smith, & Leverich, 1996) elaborated the role of sensitization in PTSD. Sensitization has been demonstrated in a wide range of stress-response systems discussed earlier—noradrenergic, dopaminergic, opiate, and HPA axis (Charney, Deutch, Krystal, Southwick, & Davis, 1993). A process of sensitization is also suggested by exaggerated autonomic and muscular responses to startling stimuli that only become evident concomitant with the evolution of PTSD in the months after trauma exposure (Shalev et al., 2000). Perry and colleagues (Perry et al., 1995) also emphasized the importance of sensitization in the developmental pathophysiology of trauma.

Sensitization is intrinsically time dependent and inherently long-lasting. That is, stress may induce a lasting alteration in behavioral and physiological responding, and the changed responsiveness increases over time (Antleman & Yehuda, 1994). The initiation and expression of sensitization have distinct mediating neurobiological mechanisms (Post et al., 1995). The dopaminergic mesocorticolimbic system appears to make a distinct contribution to the *initiation* of sensitization, whereas noradrenergic and serotonergic systems play an important role in the *expression* of sensitization. The late expression of sensitization may result from the waning of early overriding effects of habituation or tolerance, as well as from time-dependent changes in gene expression following stress. *Extreme, repeated, and intermittent stressors are most likely to result in sensitization*, although a single stressor may also do so (Post et al., 1998). The extreme and repeated stress regimen is characteristic of many forms of trauma that lead to PTSD, including childhood maltreatment, battering relationships, and combat.

Post and colleagues proposed that sensitization progressing to kindling is a useful model for understanding the course of PTSD:

> The evolution of full-blown seizure episodes in response to repeated subthreshold stimulation, and their eventual spontaneous emergence in the absence of obvious electrophysiological stimulation, bear at least some temporal similarity to the ability of the memory-like PTSD episodes to replay and eventually emerge in initially triggered and then spontaneous flashbacks. (Post et al., 1997, p. 286)

Post and colleagues likened PTSD symptoms to 'affective seizures' (Post et al., 1998, p. 830) and speculated that 'alterations in virtually every neuronal system in the brain may be occurring in the extreme situation associated with the induction of PTSD' (Post et al., 1995, p. 216). The progression from sensitization to kindling may be crucial in the course of PTSD in the transition from exogenous (sensitized) to endogenous (kindled) triggers for intrusive symptoms. Many clients complain that flashbacks 'come out of the blue.' Although therapists and their clients can always speculate on imperceptible triggers, the prospect of kindling-like intrusive PTSD symptoms suggests that we might take clients' experience at face value insofar as escalating flashbacks may become increasingly autonomous from external provocation.

When discussing sensitization, I caution clients about potential risks of substance abuse in relation to PTSD. *Cross-sensitization* refers to the process by which exposure to one type of stressor enhances subsequent response to another type of stressor. Sorg and Kalivas (1995) explicated the implications of cross-sensitization between environmental and pharmacological stimuli. Psychostimulants (e.g., amphetamines and cocaine) and acute environmental stressors are similar in increasing levels of NE, dopamine, and serotonin. Exposure to either one of these challenges may enhance subsequent responsiveness to the other. For example, repeated daily stress enhances subsequent response to cocaine or amphetamine challenge. On the other hand, cocaine or amphetamine abuse may sensitize the individual to environmental stress. Hence psychostimulants may exacerbate symptoms of PTSD. Similarly, withdrawal from alcohol and opiate narcotics is associated with activation of the LC-NE system and may potentiate flashbacks (Stine & Kosten, 1995). Thus abuse of stimulants and erratic use of alcohol, other anxiolytics, and opiates may be tantamount to retraumatization.

The concept of sensitization is useful for understanding PTSD from a developmental perspective (Perry et al., 1995), because childhood adversity (e.g., abuse) may contribute to sensitization that increases vulnerability to stressors in adulthood (Post et al., 1995). A history of exposure to assaults in childhood, for example, increases the risk of developing PTSD after trauma in adulthood (Breslau, Chilcoat, Kessler, & Davis, 1999). A study of stress in primates illustrates how physiological mechanisms of such sensitization are coming to light (Rosenblum et al., 1994). Researchers studied adult macaques who had been exposed to stress from the third to sixth month of life. The infant stress consisted of making mothers' foraging requirements unpredictably demanding, which was inferred to make the mothers less consistently responsive to their infants. In adulthood, the stress-exposed macaques demonstrated hyperresponsiveness to yohimbine, a finding that prompts an analogy to clients with PTSD who respond to yohimbine challenge with panic attacks and flashbacks.

Segal and colleagues (Segal, Williams, Teasdale, & Gemar, 1996) extended Post's sensitization model beyond physiology to include the activation of cognitive structures. These authors drew a parallel between hyperresponsiveness at the biological level and the oft-observed downward spiral in persons vulnerable to recurrent depression. They postulated that the downward spiral is associated with having developed elaborate and readily activated networks of depressive cognition. Akin to the triggering of PTSD symptoms by minimal stressors after sensitization, depressive cognitive networks, once developed, can be activated by relatively mild dysphoric states of mind. Similarly, traumatic memory networks (e.g., flashbacks) are rapidly activated in response to minor stressors. Thus in educating clients about sensitization, I emphasize that physiological upheaval and intrusive psychological symptoms are two sides of the same coin.

Reexperiencing trauma as a medical emergency

As Duman and Nestler (2000) asserted, 'the distinction between psychiatric illness and neurologic disorders is becoming increasingly arbitrary' (p. 54). Thus I counsel traumatized clients to take care of their sensitized nervous system. Post and colleagues (Post et al., 1996) pointed out that, in the evolution of sensitization, 'episodes beget episodes' (p. 61). Consistent with this postulation, a past history of PTSD increases the risk of PTSD following trauma (Ursano, Fullerton, Epstein, Crowley, Kao et al., 1999).

Because of the danger of increasing treatment resistance, Post (Post et al., 1998) advocated considering the reexperiencing symptoms of PTSD a 'medical emergency' (p. 832). Hence clients must do what they can to keep themselves safe from further trauma and more generally to minimize stress as much as humanly possible. This includes avoiding retraumatization in treatment. Akin to the downward spiral of depression (to which they are also vulnerable), they are prone to an escalating spiral of post-traumatic stress symptoms. Clients often wish for highly expressive cathartic interventions that they imagine will allow them to 'get it all out' and rid them of their symptoms. Plainly, such aggressively expressive treatment approaches are liable to backfire for persons who have been sensitized to stress. Consider the potential destructiveness of poorly contained treatment in light of the observation that *episodes beget episodes*. Here I regularly reiterate Kluft's (1993) maxim, 'the slower you go, the faster you get there' (p. 42). Meanwhile, however, we must help our clients learn to cope with distress by making use of social support (including therapy) and various techniques of self-regulation (see Chapter 11).

Familial risk factors and genetic etiology of PTSD

Of all serious mental disorders, PTSD would seem the least likely candidate for a genetic diathesis. PTSD has an environmental etiology *par excellence—* traumatic events. As has become evident in this chapter, however, the pathophysiological basis of PTSD is becoming increasingly apparent, and individual differences in vulnerability are looming increasingly large. Granting that PTSD reflects a process of pervasive neurophysiological sensitization, what distinguishes those persons who become sensitized from those who do not?

Although the literature on familial predictors of PTSD is rife with inconsistencies that render conclusions tentative (Connor & Davidson, 1997), Davidson and colleagues' (Davidson, Tupler, Wilson, & Connor, 1998) study of rape trauma bears mention. These authors found that family history of major depression was predictive of PTSD (with comorbid depression) following rape. Finding depression but not anxiety in the family history of women prone to developing PTSD following rape is noteworthy inasmuch as PTSD is an anxiety disorder, and earlier research has demonstrated anxiety disorders in family members of persons with PTSD. Davidson and colleagues emphasized the likely heterogeneity of PTSD and made a case for considering at least one subtype of PTSD to be a mood disorder. Consistent with this speculation, Acierno and colleagues (Acierno et al., 1999) found that a history of depression increased the risk of women developing PTSD not only after rape but also after non-sexual physical assault.

In considering risk factors—be they genetic or environmental—we must distinguish the two broad realms of PTSD criteria: trauma exposure and symptomatic response. The risk factors for trauma exposure (e.g., impulsivity) differ from those associated with post-traumatic symptomatology (e.g., anxiety or depression proneness). Breslau (Breslau et al., 1991), for example, found family history of substance abuse problems to be related to risk of exposure to traumatic events, and family history of anxiety to be related to risk of developing PTSD following exposure. A number of other risk factors also differentiated the two facets of PTSD. Low education, male sex, early conduct problems, and extraversion predicted trauma exposure; whereas early separation from parents, neuroticism, and preexisting anxiety or depression predicted PTSD.

Two studies illustrate the contribution of genetic factors to risk of trauma exposure. Comparing monozygotic and dizygotic twin pairs, Kendler and colleagues (Kendler, Neale, Kessler, Heath, & Eaves, 1993) found a substantial genetic contribution to the likelihood of experiencing stressful life events (i.e., robbery, assault, illness, injury, marital problems, financial problems). They argued that genetically influenced personality traits (e.g., impulsivity, low frustration tolerance, and risk taking) increase the likelihood of exposure to stressful life events. When considering total life events, they found that genetic and familial–environmental factors each accounted for about 20% of the variance. Their conclusion about these risk factors is highly pertinent to trauma: 'The genetic or familial–environmental influences on mental illness may not "directly" increase vulnerability to illness, but may instead increase risk for psychiatric illness by predisposing individuals to create for themselves high-risk environments' (p. 795). More pertinent to PTSD, Lyons and colleagues (Lyons et al., 1993), in a comparison of monozygotic and dizygotic twins, found evidence that both volunteering for service in Vietnam and the extent of combat exposure had substantial genetic contributions—likely linked, at least in part, to personality characteristics.

True and colleagues (True et al., 1991) studied Vietnam veteran monozygotic and dizygotic twin pairs to examine the conjoint impact of genetic diathesis and combat exposure. They found evidence of a genetic contribution to combat exposure as well as a genetic contribution to the risk for PTSD with combat exposure controlled. Heritability contributed to up to a third of the variance in PTSD symptoms. The authors proposed a diathesis–stress model as follows: 'Symptoms are assumed to be expressed in individuals when exposure to traumatic stress exceeds some critical threshold that varies among individuals as a consequence of genetic factors' (p. 262). Foy and colleagues (Foy, Resnick, Sipprelle, & Carooll, 1989) previously had made a similar point in noting that family history played a more important predictive role in veterans with relatively low combat exposure than in those under high-combat conditions.

Recent genetic research has found more specific gene–environment interactions, by linking stress vulnerability to compromised dopamine metabolism associated with the A1 allele of the D_2 receptor. Initial studies of the D_2A1 allele focused on its association with increased risk of severe alcoholism and other substance abuse (Uhl, Persico, & Smith, 1992). Subsequent studies have shown the D_2A1 allele to be associated with a wide range of behavior disturbance, including a host of addictions (e.g., nicotine, gambling, obesity), aggressiveness, attention deficit disorder, and Tourette syndrome (Blum, Cull, Braverman, & Comings, 1996; Comings, 1998). Consistent with the demonstrable role of dopaminergic mediation of reward (Koob & Nestler, 1997; Muscat, Papp, & Willner, 1992; Zacharko, 1994), The D_2A1 allele has been associated with a *reward deficiency syndrome* (Blum et al., 1996). That is, owing to a diminished number of dopamine receptors, individuals with the D_2A1 allele are hypothesized to show lower levels of dopaminergic activity in brain areas that mediate the experience of reward. Consequently, they fail to derive pleasure from ordinary activities and are liable to engage in addictive or impulsive behaviors to evoke pleasure.

Comings and colleagues (Comings, Muhleman, & Gysin, 1996) proposed that the spectrum of behavior disturbances seen in persons with the D_2A1 allele also indicates impaired coping with stress. Hence these authors investigated the frequency of the D_2A1 allele in relation to PTSD in combat veterans. Their findings were consistent with those for a range of other disorders. That is, compared to a base rate of the D_2A1 in about 25% of the general population, the frequency of the allele in veterans who meet criteria for PTSD is close to 60%. Consistent with the stress vulnerability hypothesis, family stress has been linked to impaired cognitive functioning in boys with the D$_2$A1 allele (Berman & Noble, 1997). Although these findings regarding the association between stress vulnerability and PTSD with the D$_2$A1 allele are not consistently replicated (Gelernter et al., 1999), they are intriguing on several counts. They provide a significant lead with respect to finding some genetic specificity in the heritability of vulnerability to PTSD; they may shed light on the frequent comorbidity of substance abuse with PTSD; and they may also relate to the anhedonic (numbing) aspects of PTSD.

TRAUMA AND ILL HEALTH

PTSD is noteworthy for a high prevalence of comorbid somatic symptoms, such that treatment often requires an artful combination of psychological, psychiatric, and general medical care. Friedman and Schnurr (1995) argued that 'PTSD is distinctive among psychiatric disorders in terms of its potential to promote poor health because of both the physiological and psychological abnormalities associated with this disorder' (p. 520).

To the consternation of clients with this *mélange* of psychiatric and general medical symptomatology, their somatic symptoms are often difficult to diagnose. When their psychiatric status becomes evident to general practitioners, they are often given the message, 'It's all in your head.' Treating such clients' injuries and illnesses in primary care settings requires exceptional expertise and sensitivity (Zerbe, 1999). Merely to enable a traumatized client to seek medical evaluation and treatment may entail an extraordinary psychological treatment effort. Nayak and colleagues (Nayak, Resnick, & Holmes, 1999), for example, employed a combination of psychoeducation, systematic desensitization, and stress-inoculation training to enable a client with a history of childhood sexual abuse to undergo a gynecological examination.

Several studies illustrate the extensive evidence indicating that trauma and PTSD are associated with elevated risk for somatic problems. Golding (1994) found that women with a lifetime history of sexual assault reported more lifetime physical symptoms than did women without such a history. These symptoms included gastrointestinal, pain, cardiopulmonary, neurologic, sexual, and reproductive complaints. Moreover, the odds of having six or more symptoms were more than three times greater for women with a sexual assault history. Notably, the differences between sexually assaulted and non-assaulted women were as pronounced for medically explained symptoms as they were for symptoms that could not be accounted for by illness, injury, or drug use. Thakkar and McCanne (2000) found that women with a history of childhood sexual abuse were particularly vulnerable to increases in physical symptoms in conjunction with daily stressors. Heim and colleagues (Heim, Ehlert, Hanker, & Hellhammer, 1998) found a high prevalence of physical and sexual abuse, as well as PTSD, in clients with chronic pelvic pain. They found complex alterations in HPA axis function, and they related hypocortisolism to a spectrum of stress-related physical disorders and pain.

McCauley and colleagues (McCauley et al., 1997) systematically compared different types and ages of abuse for risk of physical symptoms. These authors found a far higher prevalence of physical symptoms in women with a history of childhood or adulthood physical or sexual abuse compared to those without such a history. Echoing Golding's (1994) findings, women who reported six or more symptoms were nearly four times as likely to report abuse than those with two or fewer symptoms. Symptoms associated with childhood abuse included:

> nightmares, back pain, frequent or severe headaches, pain in the pelvic, genital, or private area, eating binges or self-induced vomiting, frequent tiredness, problems sleeping, abdominal or stomach pain, vaginal discharge, breast pain, choking sensation, loss of appetite, problems urinating, diarrhea, constipation, chest pain, face pain, frequent or serious bruises, and shortness of breath. (p. 1364)

Childhood physical and sexual abuse were equally likely to be associated with higher levels of physical symptoms (although experiencing both forms of abuse was associated with a slightly higher number of symptoms). A history of childhood abuse was as predictive of heightened physical symptoms as current adult abuse, although the combination of childhood and adult abuse was associated with the highest level of symptoms.

PTSD also has been associated with a higher risk of somatic symptoms in combat veterans. Beckham and colleagues (Beckham et al., 1998) compared Vietnam veterans with and without PTSD on extent of self-reported and physician-rated health problems. They found that veterans with PTSD showed a greater number of health problems than those without PTSD, even when controlling for age, socioeconomic status, minority status, combat exposure, and history of cigarette smoking. Similarly, in a prospective study of members of a health maintenance organization, Andreski and colleagues (Andreski, Chilcoat, & Breslau, 1998) found that, compared with other psychiatric disorders, PTSD at baseline predicted increased risk for somatic symptoms five years subsequently. They noted, 'Persons with PTSD were worse off than those with other psychiatric disorders across all the somatization symptom groups' (p. 136).

In light of the pervasive pathophysiology demonstrated in conjunction with PTSD, it is not surprising that trauma is associated with adverse effects on a wide array of organ systems. Yet the specific mechanisms remain to be determined. Friedman and Schnurr (1995) presented evidence that PTSD is a primary mediator of the relationship between trauma and health, although they also found some direct effect for trauma exposure. They pointed out that an important mediating factor in the relation between PTSD and poor health is PTSD-related behavior that undermines health. For example, alcohol abuse and cigarette smoking are ways of alleviating distress that undermine health. Of course genetic factors are also likely to play an important contribution in physical symptoms. In a study of Vietnam veteran twins, Eisen and colleagues (Eisen et al., 1998) found that genetic and combat effects contributed additively to compromised physical status (hypertension, respiratory conditions, skin conditions, gastrointestinal disorders, and joint disorders). Whereas the genetic contribution was substantial, the contribution of combat exposure, although statistically significant, accounted for relatively little variance.

The clinical literature consistently emphasizes the relation between somatization and a failure to experience and express emotion (Zerbe, 1999). Thus it is not surprising that somatic symptoms are related to a pattern of avoidance and numbing in clients with PTSD (Brewin et al., 1996; Litz et al., 1997). Brewin and colleagues, for example, proposed that premature inhibition of processing trauma would be associated with somatization, among other effects (Brewin et al., 1996). This proposal is consistent with finding significant relationships between dissociative symptoms and somatization (Nijenhuis, Spinhoven, Vanderlinden, van Dyck, & van der Hart, 1998; van der Kolk, Pelcovitz et al., 1996). More broadly, the PTSD literature is consistent with a substantial literature on the relation of alexithymia (inability to put feelings into words) to physical illness, although the basis of the alexithymia–somatization relationship is anything but clear (Lumley, Stettner, & Wehmer, 1996). Conversely, there is accruing evidence that expressing emotional reactions to traumatic experiences, and putting the reactions into words, promotes improved physical health (Greenberg, Wortman, & Stone, 1996; Richards, Beal, Seagal, & Pennebaker, 2000).

Although ample research confirms that many trauma-related physical symptoms are associated with diagnosable injuries or illnesses, many others are not. These symptoms are no less physiological and, as stated earlier, clients are frequently chagrined—indeed insulted—when told (or when they infer) that their problems are 'imaginary' or 'all in your head.' I find Weiner's (1992) distinction between disease and *ill health* to be enormously helpful in this context. Fortunately, stress does not invariably lead to diagnosable disease, although the absence of positive physical findings may be cause for much consternation. Yet Weiner pointed out that stress is often associated with various forms of ill health—as the recent research literature well documents.

Consistent with symptoms presented in primary care (McCauley et al., 1997; Zerbe, 1999), ill health takes many forms and includes a wide variety of physical symptoms: sleep disturbance, hyperventilation, fatigue, nausea, weakness, dizziness, headache, abdominal pain, chest pain, heartburn, joint pain, stiffness, muscular pain, and fibromyalgia. Even in the absence of diagnosable disease, such symptoms can be so severe as to be incapacitating:

> The syndromes of ill health are the result of failures of adaptation to challenges, changes in the life of many kinds, threats, dangers, and violence (including childhood experiences, such as abuse). In all of them, no structural alterations can be discerned, or if they are, they do not account for the symptoms. In some of them, clear alterations of physiological, rhythmic motor functions, or sensory thresholds can be observed. The former consist of changes in the amplitude, frequency or wave forms of, or of sudden transitions in rhythms. Whatever they may be, the illnesses reduce the fitness to work or the 'quality of life.' (Weiner, 1998, p. 517)

Many traumatized clients are likely to concur with Weiner's (1998) assertion that ill health is 'poorly conceptualized, virtually ignored in Western medicine, and a major source of iatrogenic disease' (p. 517).

Presenting somatic symptoms to clients as an expression of stress-related ill health facilitates a therapeutic alliance. Clients often feel accused of being crazy. I use the concept of ill health to point out that stress-related symptoms are not only 'all in your head' (insofar as they are mediated by the brain), but also they are liable to be all throughout the body, insofar as the central nervous system is connected to all other organ systems. Asking a group of traumatized clients about physical symptoms will quickly generate a list comparable to those produced in research studies. And discussing medical care will quickly generate a litany of complaints (e.g., patients sent to general medical facilities with their medical records often feel dismissed once the physician discovers a psychiatric diagnosis).

Quite often, however, some patients will report a supportive and collaborative relationship with a primary care physician of the kind that Zerbe (1999) advocates. In the context of somatization, it is imperative for routine medical monitoring not only to rule out diagnosable disease and provide support and palliative care but also to remain open to the potential development of diagnosable disease. Consistent with Zerbe's view, the most important message for any patient who has had an organic disease ruled out is to *find expert ongoing care and not to dismiss new symptoms as being imaginary, thereby failing to diagnose treatable general medical conditions.*

Taking physical symptoms seriously and encouraging clients to develop a good working relationship with a primary care physician (including finding whatever palliative help may be available) fosters openness to the importance of psychosocial interventions (Zerbe, 1999). As Weiner (1998) made plain, while medical interventions may be targeted at specific symptoms, *the whole person is ill.* Nowhere is the biopsychosocial model more apt. In the context of severe interpersonal trauma, however, the psychosocial interventions must be no less comprehensive than the general medical interventions. Minimizing stress and learning better to cope with stress are of major importance, and clients need to hear this. But no less important is social support (secure attachment) as well as whatever headway can be made in processing trauma rather than inhibiting such processing (Brewin et al., 1996). Hence the whole of trauma treatment must be brought to bear on these somatic symptoms.

EDUCATING CLIENTS ABOUT CHRONIC PHYSICAL ILLNESS

Weiner (1992) concluded from his summary of the stress literature that 'the effects of separation on young rats are *permanent* and affect *every organ system* studied to date' (p. 155, emphasis added). He went on, 'One of the contentions of this book is that both young and adult organisms are *permanently* changed by an acutely stressful experience' (p. 159, emphasis added). Similarly, Rosenblum and colleagues (Rosenblum et al., 1994) concluded from their study of early adversity in macaques that the noradrenergic and serotonergic systems 'may be *permanently* altered by early experiential factors' (p. 221, emphasis added).

It is tempting to withhold such knowledge from traumatized clients who are already profoundly demoralized—and not infrequently enraged—about the *emotional* damage they have suffered. Many such clients enter treatment in a state of suicidal despair. I am repeatedly struck by clients' excruciating sense of frustration and demoralization resulting from continuing illness in the face of years of hard work in treatment. Their self-esteem has been assaulted in the course of the trauma—often violently and repeatedly. And the chronicity and severity of their *illness* continually assault their self-esteem—often violently and repeatedly. Many have lost jobs, homes, marriages, and children. Why add insult to injury by confirming their worst fear that they are permanently damaged physically as well? But consider the implications of failing to educate clients fully about the nature of their illness. Imagine discovering a diabetic condition and not telling the client about it. Clients must be educated about their vulnerability and need for self-care.

Consider further the prospect of further damage to self-esteem associated with educating the client about *patho*physiology. There are two sides to this coin. Clients' self-esteem has been eroded not only by their trauma and their illness but also by their sense of failure to overcome it. They are told repeatedly, 'Put the past behind you.' They cannot just do it by fiat. Here, too, their self-esteem takes a beating. They feel guilty and ashamed for not being able to do as others admonish. They berate themselves for not being able to just 'snap out of it.' Their inability to recover may be construed as willful resistance. Some clients accuse themselves of willful resistance: 'Maybe I just don't want to get well.' Indeed psychological resistances to getting well are profoundly important, but the physiological challenges to getting well are no less so. Lack of understanding carries the risk that internal or external pressure to 'snap out of it' will lead to desperate attempts at cathartic-like treatments that are liable to backfire by further abetting sensitization—with each episode begetting more episodes.

As is the case with any other chronic illness, understanding the pathophysiology of PTSD need not be a prescription for despair. The challenge of educating clients about chronic illness is not unique to PTSD, although it is complicated by the sense of having been damaged deliberately and unjustly, as well as by the ubiquitous concomitant of severe depression. Thus presenting a realistic view that fosters hope is crucial—but not easy. I explain that chronic means persistent rather than continuous and permanent. I also emphasize the waxing and waning course of symptoms, consistent with other chronic illnesses. The concept of persistent illness squares all too well with clients' experience, and it is consistent with the challenging and lengthy course of treatment many need. Denying the persistence of the illness and the difficulty of treatment only confirms clients' self-denigration ('I should have gotten over this long ago').

But I am also careful to distinguish between persistent *vulnerability* and persistent *illness*. Pathophysiology does not entail continuous PTSD. It does, however, entail long-term attention to self-care, which includes not only stress management but also social support in attachment relationships (Chapter 11).

Diabetes as a model of chronic physical illness

Shalev (Shalev, 1997b) likened trauma to insulin-dependent diabetes, and I find that the analogy to diabetes fosters realistic expectations and hope insofar as proper treatment can improve functioning and minimize relapses. When I present the view of PTSD as a chronic physical illness in psychoeducational groups, I sometimes bring in a copy of Nathan's (1997) *Diabetes*. I thumb through the book and read several passages bearing on grappling with the diagnosis, interpersonal relationships, and—most important—self-care. The parallels to trauma are remarkable.

Nathan addressed the confusion clients feel with the onset of symptoms as well as the pain of confronting the diagnosis: '"Why me?" is a question we often hear from clients and one for which we have few satisfactory answers' (p. 29). He also described initial denial of illness and refusal to deal with it, as well as the long time it may take to accept the diagnosis. He observed that the client may feel alone, isolated, alienated and humiliated, with a sense that no one else can understand. He noted that these feelings are not unrealistic to the extent that family members may also deny the illness, and other persons also may shy away from close relationships.

Others may fail to understand the illness, blame the individual for it, and give unwanted advice.

Yet the greatest value of the analogy to diabetes is the emphasis on *responsibility for self-care*. Nathan stated that diabetes is 'a self-managed, self-treated disease' (p. 4) and that self-care must be incorporated into the client's lifestyle. Consistent with stress vulnerability in PTSD, he pointed out that the 'diabetic walks the same road trod by people without diabetes—it's just that for people with diabetes, the road is narrower' (p. xvi). He concluded, 'the most common characteristic of people who do well with diabetes is their willingness to learn and adjust' (p. 31), an attitude I endeavor to foster by introducing clients to the physical-illness perspective.

After reviewing the parallels between PTSD and diabetes, I also acknowledge crucial differences. Although many persons may experience diabetes as shameful and humiliating, it does not have the unspeakable quality that much of severe interpersonal trauma does (e.g., sexual abuse and assault). Unlike diabetes, much of interpersonal trauma entails deliberately inflicted harm, and this brings a particular poignancy to the 'Why me?' question which, as discussed in Chapter 4, often is answered in terms of being blameworthy or despicable. Furthermore, PTSD is often accompanied by severe depression, which makes it especially challenging to sustain the highly motivated, upbeat attitude advocated for recovering from diabetes and other general medical conditions. And resistance to change is a profound obstacle in many traumatized clients. To tackle these problems, we must go beyond pathophysiology to psychopathology.

Chapter 7

DISSOCIATIVE DETACHMENT AND COMPARTMENTALIZATION

> I understand dissociation pragmatically as a defense in which an overwhelmed individual cannot escape [what] assails him or her by taking meaningful action or successful flight, and escapes instead by altering his or her internal organization, i.e., by inward flight. (Kluft, 1992, p. 143)

We must approach the topic of dissociation with humility. Dissociation is the modern-day legacy of *hysteria* that Charcot, Freud, and Janet grappled with a century ago (Ellenberger, 1970), and there is no dearth of hysteria around its reemergence into the field. Controversy reaches its most fevered pitch in the context of the most florid and notorious dissociative disorder, multiple personality disorder (MPD)—now dissociative identity disorder (DID). Yet setting DID aside, the concept of dissociation remains problematic (Frankel, 1990, 1994b; Kihlstrom, 1994). As Frankel (1990) stated, 'In reviewing the history of the use of the term "dissociation," it is apparent that clarity is conspicuous by its absence' (p. 827). Dissociation has been applied to diverse psychological and psychiatric phenomena. Consider the DSM-IV (APA, 1994) description of dissociation: 'a disruption in the usually integrated functions of consciousness, memory, identity, or perception of the environment' (p. 477). This is a huge territory. Moreover we have dissociative states, dissociative processes, dissociative mechanisms, dissociative defenses, and a set of continually redefined dissociative disorders.

We can hardly help our clients by throwing up our hands in despair. They are even more bewildered than we are. They feel crazy when they see the world through a tunnel, disappear into a void for hours, cannot remember what they have done or who they have talked to, or do not even know who they are. We must help our clients understand these experiences. Academic reservations notwithstanding, merely labeling these phenomena *dissociative* helps clients feel less frightened and crazy.

The daily challenge of explaining dissociation to clients has shaped my thinking. I adopt an approach of radical simplification by focusing on two facets of dissociation: detachment and compartmentalization. Detachment and compartmentalization are not explanations; they are descriptive metaphors. Detachment is the most pervasive form of dissociative disturbance, well captured by clients' terminology—'spacing out.' More technically, detachment encompasses depersonalization and derealization. Detachment also captures what Carlson (1994) called day-to-day *dissociativity*, as measured by the widely used Dissociative Experiences Scale (Bernstein & Putnam, 1986). Quite often, explaining detachment suffices to address clients' concerns about dissociation. Yet detachment does not capture the more dramatic and perplexing of the dissociative phenomena: amnesia, fugues, and DID. I approach these disorders from the perspective of compartmentalization.

Although two simple concepts, detachment and compartmentalization, form the framework of this chapter, I will cover a lot of ground. As is true of the false memory debate, you can best deal with controversy by arming yourself with knowledge. This chapter begins by reviewing the traumatic basis of dissociation and examining the intertwining of dissociation and PTSD. Then the evolutionary origins of dissociation set the stage for appreciating its adaptive functions as well as its maladaptive effects. Emerging genetic and neurobiological findings expand the biological perspective. With this foundation, I will discuss detachment, compartmentalization, and DID in more depth. I take up the relation between trauma and psychosis in this chapter, because psychotic symptoms are frequent concomitants to severe dissociative disturbance, and these symptoms cause no end of diagnostic confusion. The chapter concludes with comments on educating clients about detachment, compartmentalization, and psychosis.

THE TRAUMATIC BASIS OF DISSOCIATION

Trauma is intrinsic to the diagnosis of PTSD but not dissociative disorders. Yet, in clinical practice, trauma is just as prominent in dissociative disturbance as it is in PTSD. For this reason, I think of PTSD and dissociative disorders as the two primary trauma-related disorders, in contrast to other disorders to be discussed in subsequent chapters, wherein trauma may or may not play a prominent role.

Therapists typically become aware of the link between trauma and dissociation when their adult clients with dissociative disturbance report a history of childhood abuse. Many clients remember that they dissociated in childhood to cope with traumatic experiences. Much research literature supports these clinical observations, but it is based on retrospective reports of trauma and therefore it is open to skepticism. Research on peritraumatic dissociation in adulthood, however, links trauma to dissociation more definitively, inasmuch as the dissociative disturbance is assessed in closer proximity to traumatic events. Research on dissociative disturbance in childhood also demonstrates the proximal relation between trauma and dissociation, most poignantly in infancy.

Childhood trauma and dissociation in adulthood

Although many forms of maltreatment have been studied in relation to dissociation, childhood sexual abuse has received most attention. Researchers have gone beyond merely associating presence or absence of sexual abuse with dissociation to examine the extent to which severity of trauma relates to dissociative disturbance. Although most research focuses on women, some studies include both genders (Carlson, Armstrong, Loewenstein, & Roth, 1998; Draijer & Langeland, 1999; Lipschitz, Kaplan, Sorkenn, Chorney, & Asnis, 1996), and researchers have examined inpatient, outpatient, and community samples.

Although findings are quite consistent in showing that one or more parameters indicative of more severe sexual abuse are associated with higher levels of dissociation, the specific abuse parameters that relate to dissociation vary from one study to another. For example, severity of dissociation relates to earlier age of onset (Chu et al., 1999; Kirby, Chu, & Dill, 1993; Waldinger, Swett, Frank, & Miller, 1994), higher frequency of abusive episodes (Chu et al., 1999), longer duration of abuse (Draijer & Langeland, 1999), greater invasiveness (Draijer & Langeland, 1999; Kirby et al., 1993), greater number of perpetrators (Zlotnick et al., 1994), and abuse by fathers in particular (Lipschitz et al., 1996). Carlson and colleagues (Carlson et al., 1998) carefully quantified severity of sexual abuse in relation to frequency of events, intensity of the experiences, and use of force (with scores ranging from 0 to over 10,000) and found severity of sexual abuse to be highly correlated with severity of dissociative disturbance. Childhood sexual abuse also has been found to be more predictive of dissociative tendencies than sexual and physical assault in adulthood (Zlotnick, Shea, Pearlstein, Begin et al., 1996).

A history of physical abuse also relates to dissociative disturbance in inpatients (Carlson et al., 1998; Chu et al., 1999; Draijer & Langeland, 1999; Kirby et al., 1993), although both positive (Lipschitz et al., 1996) and negative (Waldinger et al., 1994) findings have been reported for outpatients. Severity of dissociation also relates to age of onset (Chu et al., 1999; Draijer & Langeland, 1999) and frequency of episodes (Kirby et al., 1993) of physical abuse. Findings regarding the relative contribution of physical and sexual abuse to dissociation are inconsistent. In a mixed-gender sample of inpatients, Draijer and Langeland (1999) found both sexual and physical abuse in childhood to be independently related to level of dissociation. Whereas Carlson and colleagues (Carlson et al., 1998) found sexual abuse more strongly related to dissociation than physical abuse in a sample of inpatients, Mulder and colleagues (Mulder, Beautrais, Joyce, & Fergusson, 1998) found only an indirect association between a history of childhood sexual abuse and dissociation in a large random sample of the general population. Childhood physical abuse and current psychiatric symptoms mediated the relation between sexual abuse and dissociation.

Of course the effects of different forms of abuse may be compounded. Draijer and Langeland (1999) emphasized the interrelationships among different types of childhood adversity and found that those clients who were sexually abused both inside and outside the family or who were both sexually and physically abused showed the most severe dissociation. Lipschitz and colleagues (Lipschitz et al., 1996) found that clients reporting a combination of childhood and adulthood abuse showed higher levels of dissociation than those reporting either childhood or adulthood abuse alone.

Although most studies on childhood antecedents of dissociative symptoms focus on sexual and physical abuse, Ferguson and Dacey (1997) studied psychological abuse in a group of women health care professionals without any history of sexual or physical abuse. Women with a history of childhood psychological abuse showed higher levels of dissociation than those without this history, and dissociation related to psychological abuse independently of anxiety and depression.

As with all research on adult outcomes of childhood maltreatment, it is difficult to tease out the impact of abuse from the family context in which the abuse occurred. Nash and colleagues (Nash et al., 1993a) argued that family pathology explains the relation between sexual abuse and dissociation, although their conclusion is debatable (Briere & Elliott, 1993; Nash, Hulsey, Sexton, Harralson, & Lambert, 1993b). Irwin found that dissociation relates to a history of loss (Irwin, 1994) as well as perceived unavailability of emotional support in childhood (Irwin, 1996). Yet intrafamilial sexual and physical abuse (as well as loss and extrafamilial assault) related to dissociation even when controlling for level of emotional support (Irwin, 1996). Conversely, Draijer and Langeland (1999) found that, although sexual and physical abuse were the strongest predictors of dissociation, maternal dysfunction related to dissociation independently from sexual and physical abuse. Nijenhuis and colleagues (Nijenhuis, Spinhoven, van Dyck, van der Hart, & Vanderlinden, 1999) emphasized the combination of neglect with abuse in the etiology of dissociation. These authors found that none of the clients with dissociative disorders reported any emotional consolation in relation to their abuse. Yet Zlotnick and colleagues (Zlotnick et al., 1995) did not find that close relationships inside or outside the family had any mediating effect on the relation between dissociation and childhood stressors.

Anderson and Alexander (1996) systematically examined attachment as a potential mediator of the relationship between incest and dissociation in adulthood in a non-clinical sample of severely abused women. A fearful–avoidant attachment style was associated with more severe dissociation, and a significant proportion of the variance in dissociation was explained by attachment, above and beyond sexual and physical abuse. A small subset of women with DID were noteworthy in experiencing more severe sexual abuse, more physical abuse, and less maternal nurturance, as well as being far more likely to be fearful and unresolved in attachment.

Peritraumatic dissociation in adulthood

As many therapists and researchers have observed, symptoms of dissociative detachment are common in the immediate aftermath of traumatic events. What Horowitz (1986) construed as denial symptoms included staring blankly into space, being in a daze, a clouding of perception, numbness, and a feeling of being dead. Dissociative symptoms persons reported in the immediate aftermath of an earthquake included experiencing events, sensations, and emotions at a distance; feeling detached from the body; surroundings seeming unreal; restricted emotional range and numbing; and alteration in time perception (Cardeña & Spiegel, 1993). Marmar and colleagues' (Marmar, Weiss, & Metzler, 1997; Marmar et al., 1994) systematic assessment of peritraumatic dissociation, although quite heterogeneous in content, includes many items indicative of detachment: blanking or spacing out; being on automatic pilot; what was happening seeming unreal, as if in a dream or watching a movie or play; feeling like a spectator, as if floating above the scene or observing it as an outsider; and feeling disconnected from the body. Other peritraumatic dissociative symptoms include confusion, disorientation, alterations in perception of time and spatial relationships, and memory impairment.

Peritraumatic dissociation has garnered attention primarily as a risk factor for the development of PTSD, as demonstrated in a number of prospective studies. Dissociative symptoms experienced during and immediately after exposure to a firestorm (and reported within one month of the trauma) predicted PTSD symptoms several months later (Koopman et al., 1994). Dissociative symptoms assessed within a week of clients' hospitalization for injuries sustained in accidents, terrorist attacks, or assaults predicted occurrence and severity of PTSD at six months (Shalev et al., 1996). Peritraumatic dissociative symptoms in motor vehicle accident survivors predicted acute and chronic PTSD (Harvey & Bryant, 1998b; Ursano et al., 1999). Poor retrieval of specific trauma memories at one month also predicted PTSD symptomatology at six months post-trauma, although this may reflect an avoidant cognitive style rather than dissociation (Harvey, Bryant, & Dang, 1998). Retrospective reports of Vietnam combat veterans also have shown a relationship between extent of combat exposure and peritraumatic dissociation (Zatzick, Marmar, Weiss, & Metzler, 1994) as well as a relationships between extent of peritraumatic dissociation and subsequent PTSD (Bremner & Brett, 1997; Marmar et al., 1994; Tichenor, Marmar, Weiss, Metzler, & Ronfeldt, 1996).

In a series of retrospective studies of emergency services personnel exposed to trauma, Marmar and colleagues (Marmar, Weiss, Metzler, & Delucchi, 1996; Marmar et al., 1999; Marmar, Weiss, Metzler, Ronfeldt, & Foreman, 1996) found substantial relationships between peritraumatic dissociation and PTSD as well as high stability in retrospective assessments of peritraumatic dissociation and distress. Individual risk factors for peritraumatic dissociation included overestimation of danger, shyness and inhibition, avoidant coping, wishful thinking, uncertainty about identity, a global cognitive style, and belief that the future is determined by circumstances beyond control.

Two research groups studied peritraumatic dissociation in conjunction with interpersonal trauma. Dancu and colleagues (Dancu, Riggs, Hearst-Ikeda, Shoyer, & Foa, 1996) assessed dissociation and PTSD symptoms in two groups of assaulted women (rape and non-rape criminal assault) within two weeks of the assault. Then they reassessed the women at four-week intervals thereafter, up to three months post-assault. Both groups of assault victims initially showed more dissociation than non-assault controls, and rape victims showed more dissociation than non-rape assault victims at all assessment points. At the final assessment, rape victims but not non-rape victims remained more dissociative than did the controls. Furthermore, subjects who reported childhood sexual assault (but not those who reported childhood physical abuse) showed elevated dissociation at each assessment point. Initial level of dissociation predicted PTSD for the physical assault group but not the sexual assault group, but there was little variation in PTSD in the sexual assault group, leaving little room for differential predictions. Griffin and colleagues (Griffin, Resick, & Mechanic, 1997) found that rape victims who showed high levels of peritraumatic dissociation also showed more acute PTSD symptoms. Rape victims prone to dissociation also reported higher levels of subjective distress while talking about the rape and afterward, despite showing suppressed physiological responding.

Trauma and dissociation in childhood

Putnam and colleagues (Putnam, Helmers, Horowitz, & Trickett, 1995; Putnam & Trickett, 1997) examined dissociation in relation to childhood abuse, comparing a sample of sexually abused girls (aged 6–15) with carefully matched controls. The abused girls, who suffered perpetration by a family member that involved genital contact, were recruited through child protective services. The researchers administered clinical interviews to assess level of dissociative symptoms as well as hypnotizability. Although the abused girls did not differ from controls in hypnotizability, they showed significantly higher levels of dissociation.

The authors investigated numerous parameters of sexual abuse, finding two to be associated with dissociation: more coercive physical force and number of different perpetrators. Although dissociative tendencies and hypnotizability were weakly related to one another, the authors identified a small subgroup of girls who were high on both assessments, whom they characterized as double dissociators. These girls had more perpetrators and an earlier onset of sexual abuse. This longitudinal study has replicated findings of a relationship between sexual abuse and dissociation across different time periods. Notably, dissociative symptoms are the single best predictor of inappropriate sexualized behaviors across time periods, an indication that dissociation may contribute to revictimization. Putnam's research also showed physical abuse independent of sexual abuse to be associated with dissociation (Putnam et al., 1995).

The most direct—and most troubling—link between trauma and dissociation is emerging in attachment research, where dissociation is part and parcel of disorganized attachment in infancy. This research demonstrates what could be construed as peritraumatic dissociation in infancy, and I will discuss it in the context of dissociative detachment and compartmentalization.

PTSD AND DISSOCIATION

As described in Chapter 5, the close association between PTSD and dissociation is exemplified in the diagnosis of acute stress disorder, which includes an amalgam of post-traumatic and dissociative symptoms. The avoidant symptoms of PTSD and dissociative symptoms are especially difficult to tease apart. Nijenhuis and colleagues (Nijenhuis, Vanderlinden, & Spinhoven, 1998) have contrasted *positive* and *negative* symptoms of PTSD, the former including intrusive and hyperarousal symptoms, and the latter including constriction, isolation, anhedonia, and estrangement. Avoidant PTSD symptoms entail inability to recall aspects of the trauma as well as numbing, the latter including diminished interest, feelings of detachment and estrangement, and restricted range of affect. These negative-avoidant symptoms of PTSD overlap with dissociative phenomena. Moreover Foa and colleagues (Foa, Riggs, & Gershuny, 1995; Foa et al., 1992) linked the numbing symptoms of PTSD to freezing and tonic immobility in animals, and these are evolutionary prototypes of dissociation that I will examine shortly. Illustrating the impossibility of separating dissociative and PTSD syndromes as currently defined, Foa and colleagues referred to psychogenic amnesia, detachment, and restricted affect as the 'dissociative symptoms of PTSD' (Foa et al., 1992, p. 231).

As the overlapping etiology and symptoms imply, clients with a diagnosis of PTSD have a high likelihood of being diagnosed with a dissociative disorder and vice versa. As part of the DSM-IV field trials for PTSD, van der Kolk and colleagues (van der Kolk, Pelcovitz et al., 1996) collected data on the prevalence of dissociative disorders in persons with current and lifetime diagnoses of PTSD, whom they compared with individuals without any history of PTSD. Of those with current PTSD, 82% had a current diagnosis of dissociative disorder, and 95% had a lifetime history of dissociative disorder. Of those with a lifetime history of PTSD, 66% had a current diagnosis of dissociative disorder and 83% had a lifetime history of dissociative disorder. Dissociative disorders were far less common in persons without a current diagnosis or lifetime history of PTSD. Nonetheless, of persons with no history of PTSD, 32% had a current diagnosis of dissociative disorder, and 44% had a lifetime history of dissociative disorder. Among persons with PTSD, the proportion of dissociative disorders varied according to the type of trauma. Of persons with a history of early-onset interpersonal trauma, 88% had a dissociative diagnosis, in comparison with 67% of those with late-onset interpersonal trauma and 47% of those exposed to a disaster.

High levels of dissociative symptoms also are evident in Vietnam combat veterans with PTSD (Bremner, Steinberg, Southwick, Johnson, & Charney, 1993), although only a small minority of clients with PTSD show stringently defined pathological dissociation on the Dissociative Experiences Scale (Waller & Ross, 1997). Just as persons with a diagnosis of PTSD have a high risk of dissociative disorder, those with a diagnosis of dissociative disorder have a high risk of PTSD. Saxe and colleagues (Saxe et al., 1993) found that 90% of inpatients with dissociative disorders met criteria for PTSD, and Ellason and colleagues (Ellason, Ross, & Fuchs, 1996) found that nearly 80% of a predominantly female inpatient sample with a diagnosis of DID met criteria for PTSD.

The links between PTSD and dissociation are conceptual as well as empirical. Spiegel (1990b, 1997) views dissociative mechanisms as intrinsic to the development of PTSD, construing the polarization of consciousness evident in alternating between numbing and intrusive reexperiencing as fundamentally dissociative (Spiegel, 1990b). A number of authors have commented on the dissociative quality of flashbacks (Chu, 1998; Maldonado & Spiegel, 1998; van der Hart, van der Kolk, & Boon, 1998). Moreover, dissociative defenses come into play not only during trauma but also to cope with post-traumatic distress (Brett, 1993). Illustratively, Carlier and colleagues (Carlier, Lamberts, Fouwels, & Gersons, 1996) found PTSD symptoms in police officers at three months after trauma exposure to predict severity of dissociation at 12 months, but not the reverse; they concluded that dissociation could be a form of adaptation to chronic post-traumatic symptoms such as hyperarousal.

EVOLUTIONARY ORIGINS OF DISSOCIATIVE STATES

We easily understand how the fight-or-flight response evolved to save our skins in the face of threat, but the value of dissociation is not so obvious. In a fascinating effort to understand the origins of dissociation, a number of authors have turned to the literature on animal defense—freezing and tonic immobility (Foa et al., 1992; Nijenhuis, Vanderlinden et al., 1998). This literature usefully illuminates the adaptive functions of dissociation as well as its potentially maladaptive consequences.

Limitations of the fight-or-flight response

The fight-or-flight response could be construed as a trauma prevention response. By definition, for the person who has been traumatized, the fight-or-flight response failed. The traumatized individual has been overpowered and made helpless—unable to avert trauma by defensive aggression and unable to escape. As much evolutionary value as it obviously has, the fight-or-flight response has relatively little adaptive value in the context of much of childhood trauma—and attachment trauma in particular (Perry et al., 1995). The maltreated child does not have the resources for fight or flight. The child cannot overpower the abuser with aggression, and when the child reflexively responds aggressively, the abuse often escalates. The child cannot flee, although many abused children fantasize about running away or even attempt it. And the fight-or-flight response is counterproductive in the context of post-traumatic reminders of trauma, where there is no current danger, and the individual is saddled with potentially destructive physiological hyperarousal.

Nijenhuis and colleagues (Nijenhuis, Vanderlinden et al., 1998) reviewed substantial evidence for the limitations of the fight-or-flight response in the context of child abuse. They cited evidence that a minority of women report having actively resisted sexual and physical abuse, inasmuch as action was perceived as useless or dangerous. Rather, passive defenses (freezing, paralysis, and retreating into fantasy) predominated. These authors also reviewed similar findings pertaining to women's behavior during rape.

Predatory immanence

Just as it is not effective in every threatening context for humans, the fight-or-flight response is not always effective for other animals. Fight-or-flight is only one facet of defensive behavior that evolved in relation to predatory immanence. Although predatory immanence might seem far removed from our clinical concerns, the predator–prey relationship is chillingly apt to interpersonal trauma. As Perry and colleagues (Perry et al., 1995) commented, 'Humans evolved over the last 250,000 years in the presence of two major predators: large cats (e.g., tigers, panthers) and, the most dangerous predators, other hominids, including humans' (p. 282).

Fanselow and Lester (1988) explicated a range of anti-predator strategies animals evolved to avoid being devoured. Predatory immanence reflects a continuum of threat that ranges from being completely safe from predation to being killed. Although it is all motivated by fear, defensive behavior takes strikingly different forms depending on where the animal perceives itself to be on the continuum.

At the point of *zero immanence*, when it is completely safe from predation, the animal goes about its ordinary routines, engaging freely in various appetitive behaviors (e.g., exploring, foraging, feeding, mating, and nesting). At the point of *pre-encounter*, the animal faces an increased likelihood of encountering a predator, for example, when the predator is likely to be in the vicinity. To minimize risk, animals forage less frequently and eat larger amounts to maintain intake. The human counterpart might be the child who restricts her activities (e.g., stays in her room or stays out of the house) when her abusive father is home.

Post-encounter freezing occurs when the animal has detected the predator. As Fanselow and Lester described, the adaptive functions of freezing include decreasing the likelihood of detection, increasing the likelihood that the predator will lose sight of the prey, causing the predator to shift attention away from the prey, and minimizing the movement cues that are important releasing stimuli for predatory behavior. Freezing is an unconditioned response that can be conditioned to cues associated with threat. Hofer (1970) noted that prolonged immobility in the face of threat has been observed throughout the phylogenetic range from insects to humans. He observed that freezing behavior is associated with systematic changes in physiological arousal, prominent among which are decreased heart rate, frequent cardiac arrhythmia, and increased respiratory rate. Although respiration rate is high, its depth is so limited as to be almost imperceptible, probably to further minimize the likelihood of detection. Although freezing is common among a wide range of species, Hofer found inter-species differences in the proclivity for freezing as well as individual differences within species. Kalin and colleagues (Kalin, Shelton, & Takahashi, 1991) also observed that freezing becomes increasingly differentiated from aggression over the course of development in infant rhesus monkeys.

When freezing fails to avoid detection by predators, contact is immanent, and the predator is about to strike, another abrupt and dramatic shift in behavior may occur. In the freezing state, the animal is tense and ready to erupt into what Fanselow and Lester (1988) term *explosive behavior*—for example, struggling, fighting, and biting. Such *circa-strike defensive behaviors* may enable the animal to escape in flight. If the explosive circa-strike behavior fails to permit escape, the animal may lapse into a state of *tonic immobility*. Tonic immobility may decrease the likelihood of continued attack and potentially allow for an opportunity to escape. If the animal survives the attack but has been injured and is safe from further attack, *recuperative behavior* ensues. For example, the animal attends to its injuries and rests, promoting healing.

Fanselow and Lester (1988) noted that, during a given episode of predatory immanence, movement back and forth along the continuum is possible. For example, if post-encounter defenses (freezing) fail, circa-strike behavior may succeed in enabling flight and escape, after which the animal may again freeze to escape further detection until the predator has left the vicinity. The striking qualitative differences among defensive behaviors, coupled with the back and forth movement that may occur in the course of predatory (traumatic) events, attests to the potentially adaptive function of dramatic switches from one behavioral state to another.

Freezing and dissociation

Nijenhuis and colleagues (Nijenhuis, Vanderlinden et al., 1998) explicitly linked the predatory immanence model to dissociation, which they liken primarily to freezing but also to tonic immobility. They related freezing to a wide array of dissociative behaviors including unresponsiveness to stimuli, trance-like states, inattentiveness, anesthesia, analgesia, paralysis, loss of feelings, and amnesia. They also noted the role of endogenous (opioid-mediated) analgesia in dissociation and in animal defense. These authors found that clients with dissociative disorders often display three behaviors akin to freezing in animals, namely, analgesia, anesthesia, and behavioral immobility, and that freezing and analgesia–anesthesia symptoms discriminated between clients with dissociative disorders and psychiatric controls (Nijenhuis, Spinhoven et al., 1998). Similarly, Perry and colleagues (Perry et al., 1995) related dissociative behavior to freeze and surrender responses. They noted that freezing may escalate into dissociation, construing dissociation as 'simply disengaging from stimuli in the external world and attending to an "internal" world' (p. 280). They observed several behaviors characteristic of traumatized infants and children consistent with a dissociative response pattern: 'Observers will report these children as numb, robotic, nonreactive, "day dreaming," "acting like he was not there," "staring off into space with a glazed look"' (p. 281). They also observed heart rate decreases in children prone to coping by dissociation, consistent with Hofer's (1970) findings.

Although the parallels between freezing and dissociation seem compelling, *there is a crucial difference between them.* As Perry and colleagues (Perry et al., 1995) noted, dissociation entails disengaging from environmental stimuli. Yet, as the animal literature makes plain, *anxiety in general and freezing in particular is associated with a narrowing but heightening of attention* (Allen, Console et al., 1999). The frozen animal is hypervigilant, riveting its attention on the predator. Albeit appropriately characterized by absorption, freezing is a highly engaged, not detached, state.

Tonic immobility and dissociation

Behavioral immobility is common to freezing and tonic immobility, and the literature on the relation between animal defense and dissociation does not consistently distinguish these two responses (Nijenhuis, Spinhoven et al., 1998; Nijenhuis, Vanderlinden et al., 1998). Yet Perry and colleagues (Perry et al., 1995) emphasized a continuum of dissociative responses ranging from freezing to surrender, the latter being consistent with tonic immobility. The focus on surrender is crucial because, while freezing shares some characteristics of dissociation, I think tonic immobility is a better prototype.

Gershuny and Thayer (1999) speculated that dissociation is a response to lack of control in general and fear of death in particular: 'like fears about lacking/losing control, fears about death may be potent during and after trauma and may help differentiate traumatized individuals who dissociate more and experience greater levels of trauma-related stress' (p. 649). We have ample reason to take this speculation seriously. Hofer (1970), crediting Darwin with the notion of a death feint, noted the similarity of feigned death to prolonged immobility (freezing). Yet, on the basis of his research on rodents, he also described how tonic immobility differs from freezing. Tonic immobility occurs suddenly during active struggling; the eyes are immediately closed, and the animal appears to have collapsed. Tonic immobility is associated with an even greater decrease in heart rate than freezing. Hofer noted that immobile behavior lulls the predator into inattention and allows sudden escape.

Gallup (1974) viewed tonic immobility as a terminal defensive reaction and observed it to be elicited by physical restraint (e.g., manual restraint, entrapment, harnessing, or confinement). Tonic immobility, which follows a brief period of struggling, may last from seconds to hours. In addition to immobility, the state is characterized by unresponsiveness to the environment and 'catatonic-like waxy flexibility' (p. 837). The state is terminated abruptly and discretely, with eruption into mobility. Intense stimuli, by sustaining fear, prolong rather then terminate immobility. Tranquilizers decrease it and stimulants increase it. Tonic immobility also appears to show a pattern of sensitization inasmuch as repeated aversive stimuli (e.g., uncontrollable shock) make it easier to induce and more prolonged. Although Gallup did not relate tonic immobility to dissociation, he criticized the notion that it was related to hypnosis or trance in humans. On the other hand, Ludwig (1983) saw the sham death reflex in animals as analogous to dissociation in humans.

Whereas Nijenhuis and colleagues (Nijenhuis, Spinhoven et al., 1998; Nijenhuis, Vanderlinden et al., 1998) saw analgesia as a link between freezing and dissociation, analgesia may pertain more to tonic immobility than to post-encounter freezing. Fanselow and Lester (1988) pointed out that endogenous analgesia decreases pain-related disruption of defensive (circa-strike) behavior and enhances tonic immobility. They noted that the analgesia can be activated in advance of injury and pain, and it is responsive to conditioning. Analgesia subsides and pain ensues when the animal is safe and moves into the recuperation phase. Consistent with this view, Nijenhuis and colleagues (Nijenhuis, Vanderlinden et al., 1998) observed that danger signals increase analgesia, whereas safety signals inhibit it.

Immobility and adaptation gone awry

An evolutionary perspective can be helpful in understanding behavior that has little contemporary adaptive value (Gazzaniga, 1992). Immobility is a glaring example. When we discussed dissociation and immobility in a psychoeducational group, a patient who was struggling with severe dissociative symptoms described how an episode of freezing put her in danger. She was driving into the parking lot of a grocery store, and a tractor-trailer was backing toward her. Apparently, the driver was not paying attention. She abruptly stopped her car and froze. She knew she should back up, but she was paralyzed. Fortunately, the truck driver noticed her and stopped just before smashing into her car. Only after he drove away did her fear subside to the point where she could move. Freezing may have protected her from being spotted by a predator, but it hardly prevented the truck from backing into her.

Krystal (1988) documented the potentially catastrophic consequences of immobility. Danger can lead to helpless surrender, evident in progressive paralysis. Immobilization has both dissociative and depressive aspects. Krystal likened the catatonic-like traumatized states to *primal depression* associated with devitalization, fatigue, weakness, and lack of resistance to illness. Krystal included a wide range of dissociative symptoms in this traumatized state, namely, depersonalization, derealization, numbing, analgesia, robotization, automatization, and 'a virtually complete suppression of all affect expression and registration' (p. 145). He described 'a progressive surrender of self-preserving initiatives through the *constriction and progressive blocking of mental functions such as memory, imagination, associations, problem solving, and so on'* (p. 153), which he likened to 'a walking death' (p. 145). The immobilized dissociative state itself can become a threat to survival. Krystal gave horrifying examples of passive surrender in the face of unavoidable and overwhelming danger:

> In this state, even military personnel, such as thousands of Polish officers in Katyn, obeyed orders leading to their mass murder. Many European Jews similarly obeyed orders in an automatonlike fashion, took off their clothes, and together with their children descended into a pit, lay down on top of the last layer of corpses, and waited to be machine-gunned. (pp. 143–144)

In such dire circumstances, Krystal proposes an adaptive function of dissociative states: 'We are dealing with a complex pattern of surrender, necessary and prevalent in the entire animal kingdom and carrying its own means of *merciful, painless death'* (p. 116).

Although dissociative states may make for a painless death, Krystal pointed out that they can be 'the ultimate surrender pattern, which may become a "self-destruct reaction"' (p. 118) manifested in psychogenic death. Seligman (1975) reviewed evidence that some animals never come out of tonic immobility—they die. He contrasted two types of psychogenic death. Deaths related to tonic immobility are associated with parasympathetic nervous system activation and lowered heart rate; they are relaxation, or *giving-up deaths.* In contrast, *emergency deaths* are associated with sympathetic nervous system activation and accelerated heart rate. In discussing giving-up deaths, Seligman emphasized uncontrollability, a fundamental aspect of trauma. These sudden psychogenic deaths are not limited to animals but also occur in humans. Here we reach the ultimate trauma, 'sudden death from helplessness,' in which 'an individual loses control over matters important to him. Behaviorally he reacts with depression, passivity, and submission. Subjectively, he feels helpless and hopeless. Consequently, unexpected death ensues' (pp. 187–188). Seligman's work, as well as Perry and colleagues' (Perry et al., 1995) emphasis on the extreme of the dissociative continuum being surrender, illustrates how dissociative states and depression may shade into one another.

Dissociation as maladaptive coping

Dissociatively altered states of behavior, physiology, and consciousness may have evolved because they protected all of us animals from predation. Dissociative states also protect individuals from unbearable emotional and physical pain by virtue of their affective numbing and analgesic concomitants. They provide a means of disengagement and detachment when engagement—and attachment—is unbearably painful. Even in potentially traumatic situations, however, by virtue of undermining coping, dissociative surrender can be profoundly maladaptive. Moreover many sensitized persons respond to daily stressors, anxieties, and irritations with dissociative defenses. Although, at best, there might be some adaptive function of dissociating in the face of current danger, there can be little adaptive value in dissociating in the face of ordinary affects. On the contrary, dissociation robs the individual of the adaptive aspects of affects.

Not only does dissociation potentially block coping with danger and everyday stressors and conflicts but also dissociation blocks resolution of trauma. Researchers consistently attribute the relation between peritraumatic dissociation and PTSD to the failure to process traumatic experience (Dancu et al., 1996; Griffin et al., 1997; Koopman et al., 1994; Marmar et al., 1999; Shalev et al., 1996). Marmar and colleagues (Marmar et al., 1999), for example, commented,

> Dissociation at the time of trauma may protect the victim for a full conscious appreciation of helplessness, grief, and terror, but at the price of long-term difficulties in integration and mastery of the traumatic events. Elements of unintegrated traumatic experiences may later express themselves as unbidden intrusive imagery, affect states, nightmares, obsessive ruminations, or behavioral reenactments. (p. 21)

Shalev and colleagues (Shalev et al., 1996) noted that, by splitting traumatic experiences off from other parts of the self, the reprocessing and integration of the trauma will be hampered. Koopman and colleagues (Koopman et al., 1994) also observed that dissociation may block necessary grief work following trauma and emphasized that 'treatment for trauma victims should address dissociative symptoms, helping them to come to grips with the reality of the traumatic event' (p. 892).

GENETIC AND NEUROBIOLOGICAL CONTRIBUTIONS TO DISSOCIATION

There are individual differences in propensity to dissociate in the face of trauma, and not all persons with PTSD develop dissociative disorders. While some researchers are exploring the parameters of trauma that increase the risk for dissociation, others are investigating the possibility of genetically based individual differences. Although lagging far behind PTSD, the neurobiology of dissociation is garnering increasing attention. Finally, as with most other psychiatric disorders, therapists should keep in mind possible organic contributions to dissociative symptoms.

Genetic contributions to individual differences

Some etiological models of dissociative disorders presume a genetic diathesis (Braun & Sachs, 1985; Kluft, 1991), but there is scant research on genetic contribution to dissociation. Two studies comparing identical and fraternal twins on the Dissociative Experiences Scale (Bernstein & Putnam, 1986) yielded contradictory findings. Focusing exclusively on items reflecting pathological dissociation, Waller and Ross (1997) found that from one third to one half of the variance in pathological dissociation in an adolescent sample reflected shared environmental experiences, and the remaining variance reflected non-shared environmental factors. Notably, consistent with evidence they cite that childhood maltreatment is more prevalent in families with twins, they found that pathological dissociation was considerably higher in their twin sample than in the general population. Yet these researchers found no evidence for heritability.

On the other hand, studying an adult sample, Jang and colleagues (Jang, Paris, Zweig-Frank, & Livesley, 1998) found genetic factors to account for half the variance in pathological and non-pathological dissociation. They concluded that there is 'a single dimension of vulnerability to dissociation, with environmental influences differentiating pathological from nonpathological dissociative experience' (p. 350). Also pertinent to heritability of a propensity to dissociate is Tellegen and colleagues' (Tellegen et al., 1988) finding that half the variance in absorption (a mild form of detachment) is explained by genetic factors. Thus absorption shows a level of heritability comparable to that of a wide range of other personality characteristics.

Neurobiology of dissociation

In contrast to PTSD, research on the neurobiology of dissociative disorders is barely underway. Researchers have long been interested in physiological differences among personality states in DID, but this literature is beset with contradictions and methodological challenges (Miller & Triggiano, 1992). Krystal and colleagues (Krystal, Bennett, Bremner, Southwick, & Charney, 1995; Krystal et al., 1998) reviewed research supporting global *cortical disconnectivity* in dissociative states, a concept with considerable intuitive appeal. More generally, trauma-related neurophysiological changes and dissociative symptoms are best conceptualized as two sides of the same coin (Allen, Console et al., 1999).

While the neurobiology of dissociation is being pinned down, therapists should keep in mind that dissociative symptoms, like a host of other psychiatric symptoms, may stem from organic brain impairment. Good (1993) reviewed extensive evidence for dissociative symptoms in conjunction with such organic contributors as substance abuse, psychotropic and other medications, head trauma, migraine, tumors and other cerebral disease, and sleep disturbance. Particularly noteworthy is the well-established finding of dissociative symptoms with temporal lobe epilepsy.

Yet we also must distinguish temporal lobe seizures from dissociative pseudoseizures. Bowman (1993) conducted a careful assessment of trauma history and a range of Axis I syndromes in a series of clients with EEG-documented pseudoseizures. The vast majority of these clients had a psychological trauma history and a current diagnosis of dissociative disorder, and a substantial minority had a current diagnosis of PTSD. Childhood and adulthood traumas were associated with pseudoseizures, and the seizure phenomena often expressed the trauma in the form of a symbolic reenactment. Trauma-focused psychotherapy resulted in reduction of pseudoseizures for some of these clients. Subsequent research (Bowman & Markland, 1999) demonstrated that a wide range of recent and remote stressors relate to pseudoseizures, a common pattern being current conflicts that evoke affects associated with a history of abuse. Interestingly, pseudoseizures are associated with a lifelong avoidance of emotion and interpersonal conflict. Of course clients who have epileptic seizures may also have a trauma history and dissociative pseudoseizures (Bowman & Coons, 2000).

DISSOCIATIVE DETACHMENT

Kluft (1992) neatly captured the gist of the difference between dissociation and defensive action in his notion that dissociation is akin to mental flight when physical flight is not possible. The concept of mental flight is one of the quickest ways to convey the essence of dissociation to clients, and it sets the stage for discussing dissociative detachment.

A continuum of detachment

When you are in a state of alert consciousness, you can be fully aware of the external environment, as well as having a sense of self that includes awareness of your body and your own actions. In a state of alert consciousness, you remain grounded by flexible awareness of both the outer and inner worlds. I contrast alert consciousness with three levels of detachment: mild (absorption), moderate (depersonalization and derealization) and extreme (unresponsiveness).

Mild detachment is evident in *absorption*, a prominent and non-pathological dimension in the Dissociative Experiences Scale (Waller, Putnam, & Carlson, 1996). Tellegen and Atkinson (1974) distinguished *reality absorption* (e.g., becoming totally involved in a movie) from *fantasy absorption* (e.g., becoming immersed in a daydream). Both forms of absorption result in a failure to notice external events and may also entail an altered sense of self. Tellegen and Atkinson demonstrated a relationship between absorption and hypnotizability, and absorption can have a trance-like quality. Absorption also relates to openness to experience, capacity for vivid imagery, and a tendency to direct attention inward (Roche & McConkey, 1990). Such normal detachment is pleasurable rather than distressing. It is associated with a sense of voluntary control, such that the absorbed individual easily returns to flexible awareness and grounding in the environment.

Absorption per se is not pathological (Waller et al., 1996). On the contrary, absorption can be associated with a highly *engaged*—not detached—state that is essential to high performance, creativity, and enjoyment. Yet clients with dissociative disturbance report extreme levels of absorption that become thoroughly intertwined with more severe detachment (depersonalization and derealization) as well as amnesia (Allen & Coyne, 1995; Allen, Coyne et al., 1997; Allen, Coyne, & Huntoon, 1998b). To be absorbed in any one facet of experience is to be detached from every other. It is not the absorption but rather the detachment that impairs adaptation. When absorption becomes pervasive, detachment predominates over engagement and becomes problematic.

Absorption in the inner world precludes engagement and coping with the outer world. Moreover, for clients with dissociative disturbance and PTSD, absorption in the inner world can be a slippery slope. Immersion in imagery and memory, along with the lessened grounding in outer reality, renders the client vulnerable to post-traumatic flashbacks and more severe dissociative states. Thus, for persons with a history of abuse, an inclination toward absorption increases the risk of PTSD and dissociative disturbance (Kunzendorf, Hulihan, Simpson, Pritykina, & Williams, 1998).

Moderate detachment entails a sense of unreality that includes *depersonalization* (feelings of unreality associated with the internal world, the self, the body, and one's actions) and *derealization* (feeling as if the external world is unreal). Some clients complain about feeling spacey, foggy, or fuzzy. They feel as if they are floating or drifting. Others feel as if they are acting in a play, watching themselves from a distance, or dreaming. Some feel as if they are automata, robots, or on autopilot. Some feel isolated as if in a shell, a bubble, or behind glass. Driven by anxiety and having lost a sense of control, clients often feel painfully alienated in such dissociatively detached states.

Extreme detachment goes beyond depersonalization and derealization, suggesting a state of tonic immobility. Clients with severe dissociative disorders say they 'go away,' are completely 'gone,' 'blank,' in the 'void,' or in the 'blackness.' They are *unresponsive*, sitting and staring, as if in a comatose or catatonic state. They seem beyond reach and are extremely difficult to engage. Some clients report being in such profoundly detached states for hours at a time. They describe a sense of 'coming to,' having had no self-awareness and no sense of the passage of time. They are disoriented when they notice that hours have passed since the lapse in consciousness. When they regain some degree of alertness, they may have difficulty resuming normal consciousness, continuing to feel extremely detached. Some clients report that they are able to regain a normal state of consciousness only after a period of sleep.

Depersonalization disorder

Depersonalization disorder is the one dissociative diagnosis where just detachment is involved; all others entail compartmentalization as well. The central criterion for depersonalization disorder in DSM-IV is 'persistent or recurrent experiences of feeling detached from, and as if one is an outside observer of, one's mental process or body (e.g., feeling like one is in a dream)' (p. 490). Depersonalization is reported by 80% of the general population and, as the third most common symptom (after anxiety and depression), it is a frequent concomitant of a wide range of psychiatric disorders (Coons, 1996). Depersonalization warrants diagnosis as a distinct disorder only when it is sufficiently severe in its own right as to cause marked distress or impairment of functioning. Notably, out-of-body experiences are relatively common in normal populations and, outside the context of dissociative disorders, they are typically pleasurable and distinct from depersonalization (Gabbard & Twemlow, 1984).

Although depersonalization has a complex etiology, conflicts, stress, and traumatic events are common precipitants (Coons, 1996). Depersonalization disorder is among the least studied of the dissociative disorders, but a carefully assessed case series (Simeon et al., 1997) revealed the typical onset to be in adolescence or early adulthood, with a treatment-refractory, chronic waxing and waning course. Clients who met criteria for depersonalization disorder typically had a wide array of other Axis I and II disorders, and depersonalization interfered primarily with interpersonal relationships. Trauma histories were common but not typically severe.

Derealization often accompanies depersonalization, and both can be subsumed under detachment (Spiegel & Cardeña, 1991). Derealization entails feeling that the external world is unreal or strange. Like depersonalization, derealization occurs in the context of a wide range of psychiatric disorders, and it is a common concomitant of trauma, including childhood abuse (Steinberg, 1995). Because derealization rarely occurs as a distinct symptom apart from depersonalization and other dissociative states, it is not included as a separate disorder in DSM-IV but rather listed as one basis for assigning a diagnosis of dissociative disorder NOS (not otherwise specified).

Detachment and memory impairment

Clients with severe dissociative disturbance frequently complain of memory gaps and 'lost time.' These complaints do not just pertain to the past but also to ongoing problems with memory impairment that hamper clients' functioning on a daily basis. They cannot remember what they have done, where they have been, or conversations they have held. Such memory gaps can be associated with *reversible* dissociative amnesia to be discussed later. But dissociative detachment may account for much *irreversible* memory impairment (Allen, Console et al., 1999).

As described in Chapter 5, laying down retrievable personal event memories requires elaborative encoding (Schacter, 1996). Dissociative detachment is not conducive to elaborative encoding. Encoding failure is easiest to understand in the context of extremely detached states, for example, when a person is 'in the void' for an extended period, just staring into space. But many clients also fail to encode ongoing experience when they are more active. They do not remember putting on clothes, writing a list, driving around town, or buying articles at a store. They may have gone about these activities in a highly detached, autopilot-like state, with a minimum of self-awareness and an absence of self-reflection. Schacter (1999) included this form of memory impairment under the category of *absent-mindedness*, an apt description for dissociative detachment. Detached states entail a suspension of self-awareness and the higher-order, reflective consciousness that is essential for establishing autobiographical memory (Armstrong, 1997). In a state of detachment, clients are not paying attention to what they are doing, they are not thinking about it, they are not talking about it, and they will not remember it. The same is likely to be true in the midst of traumatic events (Bower & Sivers, 1998) such that the events will not be encoded in the form of personal event memories.

I do not want to imply that it is easy to distinguish between reversible amnesia in conjunction with dissociative compartmentalization and irreversible memory impairment in conjunction with dissociative detachment. Yet I think we should attempt to *rule out detachment before concluding that compartmentalization (e.g., DID) is the cause of inability to remember*. Efforts to retrieve poorly encoded memories will be futile and may only abet confabulation. Research showing a substantial relationship between dissociative tendencies and proclivity to elaborate (relatively benign) false memories in response to suggestion (Hyman & Billings, 1998) underscores this concern.

Detachment, fantasy proneness, and hypnotizability

Understanding dissociation entails distinguishing it from closely related concepts. As just discussed, absorption (Tellegen & Atkinson, 1974) shades into dissociative detachment. Highly related to absorption is fantasy proneness (Wilson & Barber, 1983), as discussed in Chapter 5. Although not inherently pathological, absorption and fantasy proneness are commonly associated with a history of punishment, abuse, loneliness, and isolation. Thus predisposed persons may use fantasy defensively to cope with stress and trauma, and a subset of fantasy-prone persons show significant maladjustment (Lynn & Rhue, 1988; Rhue & Lynn, 1987; Wilson & Barber, 1983).

Wilson and Barber's studies of fantasy proneness, Tellegen and Atkinson's research in absorption, and Hilgard's (1970) related studies on *imaginative involvement* (e.g., having imaginary companions) were all part of these researchers' broader interest in hypnotic susceptibility. Hypnosis has long played a prominent role in the clinical investigation and theoretical understanding of the most extreme dissociative disorder, multiple personality disorder (Ellenberger, 1970), which Bliss (1986) construed as 'abuse of self-hypnosis' (p. 125). Yet there is no consensus on the extent of overlap between dissociation and hypnotizability, and this is a topic of ongoing theoretical debate and empirical investigation (Whalen & Nash, 1996).

Maldonado and Spiegel (1998) view hypnotic responsiveness as contributory to dissociative capacities and consider the hypnotic state to be a controlled form of dissociation. They refer to dissociative states as *trance-like*, a term that makes intuitive sense to clients. Yet Putnam and Carlson (1998) caution that hypnosis is a metaphor rather than an explanation for dissociation, the underlying mechanisms for which still need explication. Moreover the magnitude of the correlations between measures of dissociation and hypnotizability is generally quite low, suggesting that these are far from identical (Whalen & Nash, 1996), although the low correlations partly reflect substantial methodological differences between scales (Vermetten, Bremner, & Spiegel, 1998; Whalen & Nash, 1996). In addition, the evidence for a relationship between early trauma and hypnotizability is equivocal, although the relationship between trauma and dissociation is well demonstrated (Whalen & Nash, 1996).

Attachment, detachment, and peritraumatic dissociation in infancy

Bowlby (1973) observed defensive detachment as a common reaction of young children to separation, manifested in a temporary failure to recognize or respond to the mother upon reunion. As discussed in Chapter 3, Main and Morgan (1996) linked disorganized–disoriented attachment patterns to the approach–avoidance conflict that occurs when the attachment figure is frightening. The infant shows *disorganization* in the form of contradictory actions and, lacking an adaptive behavioral strategy, may also show *disorientation*, an alteration of attention to cope with fear. I believe that attachment researchers, without quite recognizing it as such, have discovered peritraumatic dissociation in infancy.

As I conceptualize it, attachment *disorganization relates to compartmentalization* and behavioral state switches, whereas attachment *disorientation demonstrates profound detachment* reminiscent of the animal defense literature. Lack of orientation is reflected in lapses of consciousness and awareness, for example as manifested in Main and Morgan's description of 'immobilized behavior accompanied by a dazed expression' (p. 115). In a number of one-year-olds, they observed 'freezing all movement for as long as 45 seconds, sometimes with hands in air. During this period the infant appears unresponsive to changes in the environment, with eyes unmoving and half-closed' (p. 108). They gave an example remarkably reminiscent of tonic immobility, complete with abrupt escape:

> Upon reunion, a mother picks up her very active son and sits down with him on her lap. He sits still and closes his eyes. His mother calls his name but he does not stir. Still calling his name, she bounces him on her knee and gently shakes him, but he remains limp and still. After several seconds he opens his eyes, slides off her lap, and darts across the room to retrieve a toy. (p. 124)

Main and Morgan (1996) also were struck by the parallels between infant disorientation and adult behavior in the Adult Attachment Interview. For example, 'some adults fall silent in the middle of a sentence discussing loss or trauma, that then complete the sentence, 20 seconds or more later, as if no time had passed.' Hesse (1999) also documented numerous examples of lapses in metacognitive monitoring during the Adult Attachment Interview associated with alterations of consciousness, absorption, and the intrusion of dissociated ideas and memories. Main and Morgan (1996) also commented on microdissociative states in the Strange Situation, for example: 'Some mothers of disorganized infants have been observed sitting immobilized with eyes half closed or blankly staring into space. In two of these cases, the infant immediately exhibited disoriented behavior' (p. 126). Lyons-Ruth and Jacobvitz (1999) described a mother classified as unresolved in the Adult Attachment Interview as showing profoundly detached behavior while feeding her infant. She

> appeared to enter a trance-like state, sitting immobilized in an uncomfortable position (with her hand in the air) and blankly staring into space for 50 consecutive seconds. She entered into what appeared to be an altered state on several occasions for a total of 5 minutes during a 20-minute feeding session. (p. 529)

As described in Chapter 3, such frightened maternal states frighten the infant and are associated with disorganized–disoriented attachment.

Thus dissociative disturbance exemplifies the potential intergenerational transmission of attachment trauma described in Chapter 3. The caregiver's trauma is manifested in dissociative states in the Adult Attachment Interview as well as in interactions with the infant, both of which may evoke memories of attachment trauma. These post-traumatic dissociative states in the caregiver are frightening to the infant who, in turn, shows peritraumatic dissociative symptoms that are part and parcel of disoriented attachment. Disoriented attachment becomes a diathesis for dissociative pathology in adulthood, which may then be perpetuated into the next generation.

Carlson's (1998) longitudinal research supports the link between inter-generational transmission of attachment trauma and dissociative pathology. Carlson showed that attachment disorganization measured in infancy pre-dicts dissociative traits in adolescence. Considering the infant's plight when the attachment figure is frightening, she viewed freezing, dazing and still-ing to be the result of mutual inhibition of proximity-seeking and avoidance behavior in an infant lacking well-developed capacities for self-regulation. She noted that caregivers' dissociative or trance-like states as well as mal-treatment may elicit such infant behavior. Using teacher ratings, diagnostic interviews, and self-report measures at different age levels, Carlson found that attachment disorganization in infancy related to dissociative symptoms in elementary and high school as well as late adolescence (e.g., as reflected in a significant correlation between extent of infant disorganization and Dis-sociative Experiences Scale scores at age 19). She concluded that attachment disorganization mediates the effects of early caregiving on later dissociative experiences and increases the child's risk for development of dissociative pathology.

Hesse and Van IJzendoorn (1998) found that a college student whose parents suffered a familial loss within two years of the student's birth showed high levels of absorption, which the authors linked to dissociative tendencies and inferred attachment disorganization in infancy. Liotti (1999) also found clients with dissociative disturbance to report that their mother experienced a loss around the time of their birth, which he too associated with disorganized attachment.

DISSOCIATIVE COMPARTMENTALIZATION

Consider dissociation shorthand for *dis*-association: the active undoing of association. Janet, who pioneered the study of dissociation a century ago, used the term *disaggregation* (van der Hart & Friedman, 1989). Detachment entails dis-association in the sense of disconnection from the external or internal world. Yet dis-association goes far beyond detachment in exclud-ing whole realms of experience from consciousness. *Compartmentalization* provides a useful metaphor for such exclusion. To understand dissociation, defined in DSM-IV as 'a disruption in the *usually integrated* functions of consciousness' (p. 477, emphasis added), we must first appreciate the sig-nificance of conscious integration. Although we therapists can take a fair degree of conscious integration for granted, our clients who dissociate cannot. Much of our therapeutic work amounts to fostering conscious integration by helping our dissociative clients to think about the unthink-able—and feel the unfeelable. Just enabling your client to feel angry or fright-ened without wrenching alterations of consciousness may be a major integrative feat.

Conscious integration versus dissociative compartmentalization

In the face of much disagreement about the nature and functions of consciousness (Guzeldere, 1997), there is considerable consensus on a fundamental distinction between lower-level and higher-level consciousness (Armstrong, 1997; Bowers, 1990; Edelman, 1989, 1992; Spiegel, 1990a). *Lower-level consciousness* is unreflective, immediate, and sensory, in contrast to *higher-order consciousness*, which entails self-awareness as well as a capacity to link present with past and future. Armstrong (1997), for example, described the functions of higher-order consciousness as follows:

> If we have a faculty that can make us aware of current mental states and activities, then it will be much easier to achieve *integration* of the states and activities, to get them working together in the complex and sophisticated ways necessary to achieve complex and sophisticated ends. (p. 726)

Higher-order consciousness does not require language but, with language and symbolization, it flourishes. Higher-order consciousness permits self-monitoring, and it allows us to cope with novelty and to engage in flexible problem solving (Baars, 1988). Dissociative detachment, with its autopilot-like quality, suspends higher-order consciousness. Reflective function, in contrast, entails higher-order consciousness in the service of self-awareness and adaptive interpersonal interactions.

When aspects of self-experience and interpersonal relationships are unbearably painful, reflective function is actively curtailed (see Chapter 4). Painful integration of conscious experience can be blocked, albeit temporarily and ineffectively, by dissociative compartmentalization. My focus on compartmentalization is consistent with Spiegel and Cardeña's (1991) characterization of dissociation as 'a structured separation of mental processes (e.g., thoughts, emotions, conation, memory, and identity) that are ordinarily integrated' (p. 367). These dissociated mental contents are incompatible such that one excludes the other from consciousness (Spiegel, 1990a). The dissociating client is unable to think about the dissociated contents in connection with one another but rather alternates between contradictory states.

Dissociative compartmentalization is a stopgap measure to preserve some sense of coherence and predictability, which are the bedrock of the developing self (Chapter 4). Unity and coherence are also fundamental properties of consciousness (Edelman & Tononi, 2000). Trauma threatens to undermine coherence, and drastic defenses are invoked to preserve it. Although dissociative compartmentalization and splitting can be distinguished from one another (Gabbard, 2000), they are both efforts to preserve coherent states of mind. Splitting sustains mental coherence and predictability in the face of contradictory relationship demands (Gergely, in press). How can a child be a devoted daughter and a sexual partner? Ludwig (1983) explicated the adaptive function of dissociative compartmentalization of mental functions in this connection:

> By automatically relegating one set of attitudes, wishes and values to one state of consciousness and a conflicting set to another, the individual at least has some basis for concerted action. Opposing drives or desires can be expressed in a sequential, but not integrated, way. (p. 96)

To maintain a semblance of coherence and predictability, dissociative compartmentalization separates aspects of the self into an alienated, not-me domain. Dissociation is closely linked to autobiographical memory (Kihlstrom, 1984; Kihlstrom & Hoyt, 1990). As emphasized in Chapter 5, personal event memories are intrinsically associated with a sense of self. In contrast, dissociated mental contents—memories, images, ideas, or affects—may be active and impinge on consciousness, but they are not consciously linked with the person's history or sense of self. Thus dissociated memories are likely to be fragmented, to make no sense in relation to the usual sense of self, and to intrude unbidden in a way that disrupts consciousness (Brewin & Andrews, 1998).

Attachment and compartmentalization

Interpersonal trauma, and attachment trauma in particular, entails a striking discontinuity in relatedness as well as in self-experience. To reiterate, the infant whose attachment figure is frightening is in an approach–avoidance conflict. The infant cannot reconcile proximity seeking and withdrawal, and is left with the alternatives of disorientation (detachment) and disorganization (compartmentalization).

Like detachment, compartmentalization is strikingly evident in infancy. Main and Morgan (1996) construed disorganization as entailing 'an observed contradiction in movement pattern, corresponding to an inferred contradiction in intention or plan' (p. 115). Consider this example of compartmentalization intermingled with detachment:

> Creeping rapidly forward to father as though to greet him in the doorway, the infant suddenly stops and turns her head 90 degrees to the side. Gazing blankly at the wall with face expressionless and eyes half-closed, she slaps her hand on the floor three times. These gestures appear aggressive, yet they have a ritualistic quality. The baby then looks forward again, smiles, and resumes her approach to the father, seeking to be picked up. (pp. 108–109)

Liotti (1999) viewed the inability to integrate such contradictory intentions into coherent working models as prototypically dissociative. He proposed that 'disorganized attachment is the *first step* in a developmental pathway leading, perhaps through a long sequence of dramatic or violent family interactions from infancy onward, to pathological dissociation in adult life' (p. 296).

Freyd's (1996) concept of *betrayal trauma* complements observations from attachment research. Freyd construed betrayal as a violation of trust that occurs in situations in which 'the person doing the betraying is someone the victim cannot afford *not* to trust' (p. 11). Incest is prototypical of betrayal trauma. As they do in infancy, conflicts in attachment relationships may spawn compartmentalization. In Freyd's view, *knowledge isolation*, the blocking of memory associated with betrayal trauma, is motivated by the need to maintain the attachment relationship. Some sexual abuse may be compartmentalized not because it is frightening but rather because *awareness of the betrayal would endanger the child by threatening the attachment relationship*. Thus Freyd emphasized the 'social utility of forgetting, in contrast to the more traditional explanations of forgetting to avoid being overwhelmed or to avoid unbearable pain' (p. 136). Of course these explanations are not mutually exclusive. Supporting her thesis that dissociation is adaptive in blocking awareness of betrayal in attachment relationships, Freyd reviewed evidence that amnesia rates increase in accordance with the closeness of the relationship of the perpetrator to the victim.

Freyd also pointed out how prohibiting the child from communicating about sexual abuse is paralleled by the child's need to keep this information isolated in her own mind. Freyd observed that information blockage (compartmentalization) can be abetted by several contextual factors: availability of alternative realities (e.g., nightly abuse with daily normality), social isolation during the abuse, reality-distorting statements by abusers (e.g., denying it happened), and absence of any explicit discussion of the events. Although she focused on childhood sexual abuse, Freyd maintained that betrayal blindness also occurs in the context of adulthood attachment trauma, such as in battering relationships.

Dissociative amnesia

Dissociative amnesia starkly exemplifies compartmentalization. Terr (1994) encountered a prototypical example of amnesia—interlaced with detachment—when she was called in to consult on a woman who was incarcerated for drunk driving and resisting arrest. Two highway patrolmen spotted Terr's client, Patricia, sitting in her car on the side of the highway early one evening. When they approached her to determine what was wrong, she was unresponsive—sitting there like a zombie. The officers inferred that she must be intoxicated. After failing to make any contact with her, they decided to arrest her. She suddenly became combative. When she awoke in jail the next morning, she had no idea where she was—or *who* she was. She could not remember her employer or the names of any friends or relatives. By the time

Terr was called in to consult, Patricia had recovered her sense of identity, although her memory surrounding the arrest was limited.

With careful interviewing, Terr helped Patricia recall the events leading up to the amnesia. She had discovered her boyfriend in her bed with another woman. After a confrontation, Patricia recalled going blank, not moving, not thinking, and losing a sense of time. She could only speculate about why she had driven where she did. In a dissociative state, she had misperceived the arresting officer as a killer, and she fought him to protect herself. With Terr's help in exploring her history, Patricia recalled other dissociative episodes dating back to age nine when she witnessed her intoxicated mother burning to death in a fire—after which Patricia went into the bathroom and became extremely detached as she 'drew the bathwater, put her clothes into the hamper, settled into the tub, and drifted into a weird shut-off never-never land' (p. 93).

Terr's description of Patricia fits the DSM-IV (APA, 1994) definition of dissociative amnesia: 'one or more episodes of inability to recall important personal information, usually of a traumatic or stressful nature' (p. 481). The amnesia is manifested in retrospectively reported memory gaps for periods of time ranging from minutes to years, and the memory impairment is potentially reversible. The amnesia may be localized to a circumscribed period of time surrounding a traumatic event (as in Patricia's case), or it may be selective (partial recall), generalized (failure to recall one's entire life), continuous (failure to recall events from a specific time up to the present), or systematized (failure to recall information in a particular category, for example, in relation to a particular person). Dissociative amnesia has been documented in relation to a wide range of traumas and in relation to impulsive behavior, such as sexual and financial indiscretions, as well as violent behavior (Loewenstein, 1996).

The inability to recall events, however, does not mean that these compartmentalized memories do not (implicitly) influence consciousness (Steinberg, 1995). On the contrary, as discussed in Chapter 5, memory fragments may come into consciousness unbidden, and affects associated with the experience may be triggered without any ability to retrieve a coherent personal event memory. Furthermore, although compartmentalized memories are *relatively* inaccessible, they are not permanently inaccessible. Kihlstrom and Schacter (1995) argued that 'in most cases the amnesia is reversible, and access to the autobiographical memories covered by the amnesia is eventually restored' (p. 341).

The reversibility of dissociative amnesia is based on encoding in altered states (Loewenstein, 1996), including an altered sense of self or identity. Returning to the altered mental state or sense of self in which the memory was encoded may enable the person to remember the event. From the vantage point of state-dependent memory (Bower, 1981; Bower & Sivers, 1998), the mental state (e.g., a mood) can become a retrieval cue. Spiegel

(1995) noted that 'To the extent that individuals do enter a spontaneous dissociative state during trauma, the memories may be stored in a manner that reflects this state. . . . Furthermore, retrieval should be facilitated by being in a similar dissociative state (e.g., hypnosis)' (p. 137). Thus dissociatively detached states can become compartmentalized, and episodic memories for these states (with however much or little detail was encoded in them) can be activated by reexperiencing detachment.

Dissociative fugue

Dissociative fugue, going one or two steps beyond amnesia, is characterized in DSM-IV (APA, 1994) by 'sudden, unexpected travel away from home or one's customary place of work, with inability to recall one's personal past' and 'confusion about personal identity or assumption of a new identity' (p. 484). The travel may entail anything from short trips lasting hours to wandering over long distances for months. Although assumption of a new identity is not the rule, when it does happen, it is often characterized by decreased inhibition or gregariousness. A fugue entails dissociative amnesia and, like amnesia, is often precipitated by stress or trauma (Cardeña & Spiegel, 1996).

Terr (1994) observed that Patricia's dissociative episode could have evolved into a fugue. I find that the line between detachment, amnesia, and fugue is often blurry. For example, I interviewed a client who was very frightened about an episode that was inexplicable to her. She had driven far from home in a detached state, and she found herself lost and disoriented. She eventually reoriented herself to the point that she was able to call her mother, who found her and brought her back home. The client and I were able to reconstruct a series of severe stressors that led up to the episode in which she took flight. I think of such dissociative episodes as *fugue-like* and find them quite common.

DISSOCIATIVE IDENTITY DISORDER (DID)

DID manifests dissociative compartmentalization most dramatically, going a step beyond fugue to entail the 'presence of two or more distinct identities or personality states' which 'recurrently take control of the person's behavior' (APA, 1994, p. 487). The diagnosis requires amnesia for events and behavior during at least some dissociated states. DID is typically the most severe of the dissociative disorders, as it combines detachment (depersonalization and derealization) and amnesia with fugue-like behavior and identity fragmentation (Steinberg, 1995). Moreover, DID often occurs as part of a constellation of other psychiatric disorders and in conjunction with severely impaired functioning, including self-destructive behavior. Consistent with their severe psychopathology, many clients with DID report multifaceted and repeated childhood maltreatment.

Dissociative disorder not otherwise specified (NOS) is a relatively common dissociative diagnosis with symptoms overlapping DID (Steinberg, 1995). For example, many clients exhibit altered states associated with amnesia that are not sufficiently elaborate to be construed as distinct identities. Conversely, a number of clients show dramatic shifts in identity that are not associated with dense amnesia. Dissociative disorder NOS also includes trance states indigenous to particular cultures and dissociative states resulting from prolonged coercive persuasion (e.g., thought reform and brainwashing).

Controversy

Although DID has a venerable history (Ellenberger, 1970), the resurgence of interest in this disorder in the United States in the 1980s sparked professional skepticism. There is no dearth of scholarly critiques (Fahy, 1988; Frankel, 1993; Ganaway, 1989; Merskey, 1992; Piper, 1994; Spanos, 1996) and useful debates (McHugh, 1995a, 1995b; Putnam, 1995a, 1995b). Among skeptics' more prominent concerns are the vagueness of the diagnosis, doubt about the etiological role of childhood sexual abuse, doubt about the veracity of memories of childhood abuse, and the potential iatrogenic basis of the disorder. Skeptical clinicians suspect that therapists' fascination leads to the creation of the disorder by means of suggestion and reinforcement of behavior consistent with the diagnosis, often abetted by hypnosis.

The true prevalence of DID is unclear. For example, whereas Ross and colleagues (Ross, Anderson, Fleisher, & Norton, 1991) estimated that 5% of general psychiatric inpatients are likely to warrant a diagnosis of multiple personality disorder, Rifkin and colleagues' (Rifkin, Ghisalbert, Dimatou, Jin, & Sethi, 1998) careful diagnostic assessments of 100 randomly selected women admitted to an acute psychiatric hospital revealed only one who met criteria for DID.

Controversy prompted systematic research on the nature and extent of professional skepticism. Cormier and Thelen (1998) found that 79% of psychologists considered multiple personality disorder to be a valid diagnosis. Although 62% believed it to be extremely rare, 38% believed that they had encountered someone with the condition, and 85% believed it to be the result of severe child abuse. The bimodal distributions of responses on a number of items reflected the polarization in the field, and psychologists with a cognitive-behavioral orientation were more skeptical than those with a psychodynamic orientation. Pope and colleagues (Pope, Oliva, Hudson, Bodkin, & Gruber, 1999) surveyed board-certified American psychiatrists regarding their beliefs about dissociative disorders and found little consensus regarding the scientific validity of DID or dissociative amnesia. The modal (albeit minority) response was that both diagnoses should be included in the DSM as *provisional*. More specifically, 15% thought DID should not be included at all, 43% thought it should be included with reservations, and 35% thought it should be included without reservations. Psychodynamically oriented psychiatrists were less skeptical than biological psychiatrists.

Skepticism regarding the role of childhood sexual abuse in the etiology of DID is intermingled with concern about false memories. The context of DID, however, raises the ante inasmuch as the severity of the psychopathology and the extreme accounts of trauma often strain credibility (Ganaway, 1989). Moreover, the common use of hypnosis in the treatment of clients with DID adds fuel to the fire of criticism, although the relation of hypnosis to confabulation is highly complex and widely misunderstood (D. Brown et al., 1998). As described in Chapter 5, Kluft (1995) found that many clients with DID were able to corroborate memories that emerged in hypnosis, although some false memories also came to light.

I have no doubt about the potential role of iatrogenic influences in DID. I have evaluated clients, for example, whose therapist has suggested that they give names to dissociative or regressed states (e.g., 'Why don't we call the part of you that curls up in a corner and hides, "Heidi"'). This kind of intervention encourages the kind of role enactment that Spanos (1996) described as characteristic of DID. Clients who have experienced this sort of therapy are legitimately perplexed about whether they truly have 'multiple personality disorder.' I have also seen clients whose dramatic, ego-syntonic presentations of florid DID strain credibility as well as clients with severe identity disturbance who gravitate toward a diagnosis of multiple personality disorder because it provides some organization to their otherwise inchoate experience.

Iatrogenesis?

My clinical introduction to multiple personality disorder (Davidson, Allen, & Smith, 1987) left me with the unalterable conviction that this is not invariably an iatrogenic condition. Rather than suggesting that the patient had the disorder, I was oblivious to what most therapists would now consider blatant signs.

A patient whom I had been seeing in psychotherapy for several months began complaining of 'blackouts' lasting several hours, and she displayed a brief dissociative episode in my office. Customarily quite reserved, she suddenly cursed. When I attempted to draw her attention back to this uncharacteristic behavior moments later, she was totally oblivious to it, denied that it had happened, and accused me of playing a therapeutic game to provoke her anger. As I recounted the events, she began to question her conviction that I was lying, and she became very frightened.

Not long after this session, she did something that penetrated my own obliviousness. She rushed into my office in an agitated state, handed me a bag containing whiskey and assorted pills, and implored, 'Here, take these quickly and hide them! She's going to kill herself with them.' I did as she asked, and then she prevailed upon me not to tell her—that is, in her ordinary state of mind—what had just transpired between us. Then she switched her state of mind, was completely perplexed and disoriented, and identified the experience as being like her other recent blackouts. Although her symptoms were prototypical, we continued to downplay the diagnosis until it became incontrovertible, and then we explained it to her as such (Davidson et al., 1987). Thus, rather than encouraging the development of DID, in hindsight it is clear that I was under the grips of a combination of ignorance and denial. In effect, she had to hit me over the head with it before I saw it.

Having gone through such an experience made it easier to recognize subsequently. I continued to be impressed, however, by patients' fear and confusion about the disorder—their inclination to hide it rather than flaunt it. In one striking example, a patient had traveled a long distance for a diagnostic evaluation. She entered my office and appeared completely lucid. Yet some hints of disorientation led me to suspect that she was in a dissociative state. I asked her some questions about where she was and what she was doing in my office. It turned out that she had no idea, but having been in similar situations she inferred that she was in the midst of some sort of psychological evaluation. As the disorder came to light, she acknowledged that she was attempting to pass for someone who was fully oriented. Then she recounted experiences in which she would suddenly find herself in a dangerous situation (e.g., in a hotel room with a strange man and having no recollection of how she got there) and would cleverly talk her way out of it.

Switching among behavioral states

Putnam (1992) warned,

> The implicit and mistaken assumption made by many people is that the alter personalities are separate people. This is a serious conceptual error that will lead to therapeutic error. Alter personalities are not separate people! Rather, I think that they are best conceptualized as examples of a fundamental and discrete unit of consciousness, the behavioral state. (p. 96)

The DSM-IV (APA, 1994) criteria teeter on the edge of reification by referring to 'distinct identities or personality states (each with its own relatively enduring pattern of perceiving, relating to, and thinking about the environment and self)' then go over the edge in stating that 'these identities or personality states recurrently take control of the person's behavior' (p. 487). This definition captures the client's experience of being taken over by an alien force. But we therapists must empathize with the client's perspective without also adopting it. We should think of one behavioral state taking over another behavioral state. This happens in all of us all the time from infancy onward, ideally with a growing sense of continuity. Only in persons with DID are these states radically compartmentalized.

Putnam (1988, 1991) took Wolff's (1987) infancy studies as the model for his focus on changes in behavioral states. Putnam regarded dissociative disorders as only one instance of *behavioral state disorders* associated with precipitous and radical state switching. He defined switches as follows:

> The psychobiological events associated with shifts in states of consciousness as manifest by changes in state-related variables such [as] affect, access to memories, sense of self, cognitive and perceptual style, and often reflected in alterations of facial expression, speech and motor activity, and interpersonal relatedness. (Putnam, 1988, p. 26)

Putnam noted that such switches occur not only in trauma-related disorders but also in panic attacks, catatonic states, and bipolar disorder. Others have described switching in the context of depression (Gilbert, 1992), Tourette syndrome (Bercez, 1992), and paranoid states (Vinogradov, King, & Huberman, 1992). Yet *amnesia amplifies the discontinuity in behavioral state switches in DID*. Putnam (1988) observed that switches in DID typically occur within five minutes, although they may occur within a matter of seconds. These dissociative switches are triggered by an extremely wide array of stimuli, and the psychopathology entails not only the dysfunctional nature and lability of the states themselves but also the counterproductive nature of the individual's attempts to modulate the states and switching (e.g., by alcohol and drugs).

Switching among working models of relationships

To understand DID, we must go beyond switches in behavioral states to *switches in patterns of relatedness*. Here attachment theory is beginning to get a promising foothold in thinking about DID (Anderson & Alexander, 1996; Barach, 1991; Liotti, 1995, 1999; Schwartz, 1994). Barach (1991), for example, construed the core problem in multiple personality disorder as 'the *alternation* between intrusion/assault and abandonment' (p. 120). In their study of women with DID and disorganized attachment, Anderson and Alexander (1996) commented on the challenge of adapting to unpredictable violence alternating with periods of nurturance. From the vantage-point of attachment theory, 'personalities,' 'alters,' and 'identities' can be replaced with *working models*. Discontinuous behavioral state switches are part and parcel of contradictory models of relatedness. Over time, these working models accrue a history on the basis of a long series of interactions in certain contexts. Thus working models become components of identity or, when dissociated, become associated with an illusory sense of separate identity.

The contradictory relationship demands of the frightening attachment figure (Main & Morgan, 1996) and the experience of betrayal trauma (Freyd, 1996) make plain how a child would develop prominent and utterly incompatible working models of relationships. But we all have contradictory working models, and the dissociative processes that sustain rigid compartmentalization of these models remain to be understood. It is not simply a matter of the client's feeling that one working model (e.g., the most typical, depressive, compliant state of mind) is the core self and all others are not-me. Rather, from the vantage-point of any one working model, all others are not-me. In the compliant state, the client feels as if the aggressive state is not-me. In the aggressive state, the client feels as if the compliant state is not-me.

DID, with its contradictory working models, each of which becomes *the* self when activated, exemplifies the extreme failure of integration of higher-order consciousness. Psychotherapy aims to restore these integrative functions:

> In severe dissociative disorders, the client displays an inability to tolerate affective tension, including the emotions produced by confusion or ambiguity, and vehemently resists the restoration of paradoxical experiencing. Instead of a healthy, vibrant maintenance of the tension between mutually informing opposites, a collapse into polarized experience takes place. . . . Relational psychoanalytic treatment of MPD must reflect efforts to restore the tension between opposites. The client learns to hold these tensions in one central consciousness and eventually learns to negotiate and 'play' with these opposites. (Schwartz, 1994, p. 208)

The perspective of incompatible mental states—and the working models of relationships embedded in them—helps to empathize with clients as well as to normalize their experience. Most of us adults know what it is like to feel like a frightened child or to have more or less disguised temper tantrums. With encouragement, most of us could engage in the kind of role enactments (Spanos, 1996) encouraged in Transactional Analysis (Berne, 1961), for example, where you engage in dialogues among your *Child, Adult,* and *Parent ego states* to elucidate your conflicts. Higher-order consciousness or reflective function enables us to 'hold these tensions in one central consciousness,' as Schwartz (1994) aptly put it. But amnesia and the lack of access to various working models and the histories of interactions embedded in them cannot be normalized. It would have been one thing for my client with DID to have entered my office saying, 'Please take these so *I* don't kill *myself* with them.' When, instead, she said, 'Take these so *she* doesn't kill *herself'* and then soon afterward failed to remember what just transpired between us, we were struggling with a level of compartmentalization that is far harder to grasp.

Switching among memories

A proper understanding of DID and other dissociative phenomena will require help from cognitive science (Allen, 1998; Bower & Sivers, 1998; Brewin & Andrews, 1998). Illustratively, Morton (1991, 1994) took a stab at applying his *headed records* theory of autobiographical memory to the understanding of amnesia in DID. Morton likened memory to a filing cabinet full of *records* (memories). To facilitate retrieval, each record has a *heading* that contains information relevant to the contents of the record. Headings are searched by forming a *description*. When the description matches a heading, the record becomes conscious.

Think of records in terms of personal event memories with a sense of self being intrinsic to each memory (see Chapter 5). Then Morton's (1994) analysis of DID makes intuitive sense. He argued that the self is a core component of record headings and that 'we could imagine each personality having its own set of records, headed by individual ⟨self⟩ markers' (p. 395). The cognitive mechanism for setting up these dissociated memory systems has yet to be clarified, and it will require a developmental approach. 'The assumption would be that the process of consolidation of ⟨self⟩ and its use in the organization and retrieval of event memory would have been disrupted by the severe early abuse' (p. 396). This perspective takes us from state-dependent memory to self-dependent memory (or, in terms of attachment theory, working-model-dependent memory) in which dissociated senses of self are associated with different working models of relationships.

I present these speculations merely to underscore the need to avoid incorporating clients' reifications into our theoretical models. We must aspire eventually to replace these reifications with well-documented psychological processes (Brewin & Andrews, 1998).

A model for therapy: switching as a defensive process

Kluft (1996) delineated nearly a dozen current theoretical models of DID, so it should come as no surprise that there is no consensus on the optimal treatment approach. Sound treatment of DID, like that of any other severe trauma-related disorder, entails educating the client, establishing a therapeutic alliance, maintaining a therapeutic frame and appropriate boundaries, managing challenging transference and countertransference reactions, and helping the client to process the trauma in the context of adequate support and self-regulation strategies (Kluft, 1993; Schwartz, 1994; van der Hart et al., 1998).

Yet this consensus on basic principles of sound psychotherapy is offset by considerable divergence with respect to focus on trauma and working with alters. Some therapists make extensive use of hypnosis (Peterson, 1996), while critics express concern that hypnosis may contribute to iatrogenesis and false memories. If hypnotic accessing of a spate of alters is one extreme, avoiding acknowledgement of the disorder is the other (McHugh, 1995a).

Many therapists search for middle ground. Van der Hart and colleagues (van der Hart et al., 1998), for example, stated,

> Some therapists of clients with DID tend to contact as many identities as possible to map the inner system of identities and to gain a sense of what to expect later in treatment. However, we think that this approach may cause too much upheaval, and we tend to focus more on the states of mind that play an active role in the client's daily life. (p. 267)

This approach fits with my own preference to work with the client's current state of mind while endeavoring to expand the client's tolerance—in that state of mind—for a wider range of affects and memories. I am convinced that encouraging switching, actively pursuing alters, and attempting to recover memories of abuse can exacerbate dissociation, promote regression, and undermine functioning. As Gabbard also emphasized,

> The memory dysfunction typical of patients with dissociative disorders actually makes them less-than-ideal subjects for therapy aimed at recovering memories. A more reasonable goal is to help them recover normal mental functions, particularly the capacity to reflect and mentalize, so that they can develop a more coherent representation of self and others. (Gabbard, 2000, p. 274)

I consulted with a colleague whose client was becoming increasingly depressed. He spent the bulk of his sessions working with her in altered states, for which she had amnesia. In her ordinary—and increasingly isolated—state of mind, she was feeling neglected and abandoned. Given her amnesia, it was as if *she* had little contact with her therapist. Her therapy was dissociated from her usual experience and her daily life. I encouraged my colleague to work more with the client in her usual state of mind without encouraging her to switch into altered states so as to restore needed balance into the therapy.

Of course, when a client with DID does switch into another state of mind—or working model—we must work with the client to understand the conflict and anxiety that evoked this defensive maneuver (Gabbard, 2000). Not uncommonly, for example, a client who becomes irritated with the therapist switches into an aggressive state, or a client remembering childhood trauma switches into a childlike frightened state. Dissociating these states upon resumption of ordinary consciousness prevents clients from being overwhelmed by affects and conflicts that cannot be integrated in higher-order consciousness. Viewing DID as an ongoing defensive process rather than an inherently enduring condition helps avoid reification. I think of DID as an episodic condition, like a mood episode or psychotic decompensation. Of course, like depression or psychosis, a DID episode may be protracted.

Much of the time, persons with a history of DID remain in their ordinary (albeit constricted) state of mind, without any indication of dissociative identity disturbance. During these remissions, the treatment approach can be therapy as usual. As with a host of other episodic psychiatric disorders, however, stress can precipitate a recurrence of dissociative compartmentalization. And, with their history of trauma and PTSD, clients with DID are especially reactive to stressors. Yet improved interpersonal functioning, affect tolerance, and coping skills diminish the need for the dissociative defenses, and the client can remain in ordinary (albeit expanded) states of mind more of the time, without identity confusion and alteration.

DISSOCIATION, PTSD, AND PSYCHOSIS

Many clients with severe dissociative disturbance and PTSD present with disorganized thinking, impaired reality testing, paranoid ideation, and hallucinations in multiple sensory modalities. Descriptively, these symptoms are properly labeled *psychotic*, but they place the client at risk for misdiagnosis.

Dissociative detachment and psychosis

Our series of studies of women in inpatient treatment for trauma-related disorders demonstrated strong correlations between dissociative detachment and psychotic symptoms on psychometric tests (Allen & Coyne, 1995; Allen, Coyne, & Console, 1996; Allen, Coyne et al., 1997). Dissociative detachment undermines the individual's anchoring in the outer world, thereby hampering reality testing and rendering the individual with post-traumatic symptoms vulnerable to the nightmarish inner world. Dissociative detachment not only deprives individuals of external anchors but also robs them of internal anchors—the sense of being connected to one's body, a sense of self or identity, and one's own actions. The consequence may be not only profoundly impaired reality testing but also severe confusion, disorientation, and disorganization. Dissociative detachment and psychotic states also overlap in feelings of profound alienation, which many of the psychoticism scales on psychometric tests reflect. Dissociative detachment entails not only alienation from the outer world and relationships with others, but also alienation from the self.

Dissociative identity disorder and psychosis

Because DID is the most severe of the dissociative disorders, and clients with this disorder are likely to have a wide range of post-traumatic symptoms as well as several related psychiatric disorders, we clinicians should not be surprised that psychotic symptoms are prevalent in this group. Several authors have addressed the overlap between DID and schizophrenia (Greaves, 1993; Kluft, 1987; Ross & Joshi, 1992; Ross et al., 1990), and Ross and colleagues (Ross et al., 1990) concluded that pathognomonic Schneiderian symptoms 'are better described as first-rank symptoms of MPD than of schizophrenia' (p. 117). Consider Greaves's perspective:

> When a 38-year-old client 'switches' in one's office, believes earnestly that she is a 13-year-old boy at her uncle's house in St. Louis and that the year is 1965, and then spontaneously reenacts an anal rape (which is why, in trance logic, 'she' believes she is a 'boy'), hallucinating the therapist as the uncle, the client is disoriented as to person, place, time and situation on mental status. That is what 'psychosis' is known to mean in the examination of psychiatric clients: a gross breakdown in reality and orientation, whether transient, episodic, or chronic. (Greaves, 1993, p. 375)

Hence Greaves argued that multiple personality disorder is a 'transient, episodic, recurrent dissociative psychosis of traumatic origin' (p. 375).

Although Greaves noted a wide range of psychotic symptoms in conjunction with this traumatic psychosis, I highlight one facet he does not mention: delusional thinking. The belief that a person encompasses many distinct selves of different ages, genders, temperaments, histories, and names could be viewed as a theory and, as argued above, a misguided theory that we therapists should not also adopt. But the term, theory, is far too tentative to capture the sense of reality that clients maintain about their self-organization. DID represents a *delusion about the self*. I am not using the term, delusion, loosely. Persons with DID may believe, for example, that ingesting poison will kill one of the selves while leaving others intact. Schwartz (1994) referred to such beliefs as reflecting a 'delusion of separateness' (p. 205). And delusions about the self can be extremely elaborate, often accompanied by maps and drawings, for example, with different alters living in different parts of a dwelling.

No doubt the term, delusion, has negative—indeed frightening—connotations, and it is unlikely to be a helpful explanation for most clients. But we therapists may think of delusions sympathetically as an *effort after meaning*. Albeit overly inferential, *delusions reflect the need to make sense out of confusing and frightening experience*. Consider the plight of persons whose experience is punctuated by gaps, who find evidence of actions they do not remember, who are told that they have behaved in uncharacteristic ways, and who hear voices. Is it utterly unreasonable for such persons to make the inference—however patently unrealistic to others—that they are inhabited by different personalities, alters, demons, or some such? Just as paranoid delusions meaningfully explain frightening events, so do delusions of multiple personalities explain bewildering sequelae of severe dissociative states. The cognitive scientist sees the client's consciousness being altered by 'modular, informationally encapsulated processes that are spontaneously triggered by internal or external stimuli' (Brewin & Andrews, 1998, p. 965). The client has a simpler—albeit delusional—explanation: an alter did it.

Psychotic symptoms in PTSD

Psychotic symptoms also are common in patients with PTSD. Butler and colleagues (Butler, Mueser, Sprock, & Braff, 1996) found that combat veterans with PTSD showed significantly elevated hallucinations, delusions, and bizarre behavior in the absence of thought disorder. The content of some psychotic symptoms did not qualify as reexperiencing trauma. Yet the patients did not meet criteria for schizophrenia. Similarly, Hamner (1997) found that 36% of a sample of treatment-seeking combat veterans with PTSD reported hallucinations, delusions, or both in the absence of thought disorder. For the vast majority of these patients, at least some of the psychotic symptoms did not have content indicative of reexperiencing combat trauma.

Hamner and colleagues (Hamner, Frueh, Ulmer, & Arana, 1999) conducted an exceptionally thorough study of psychotic symptoms in combat veterans with PTSD who did not have a primary psychotic disorder. They examined the severity of the various PTSD symptoms as well as positive and negative psychotic symptoms, and they categorized psychotic symptoms as combat or non-combat related. Nearly half the patients had psychotic symptoms, all reporting hallucinations and most reporting delusions. Only one patient had a thought disorder. Most patients' hallucinations involved themes that were both combat and non-combat related, whereas only one patient with delusions reported a combat-related theme. Severity of PTSD and severity of psychotic symptoms were strongly correlated, although the relation was mediated by negative rather than positive symptoms. In the PTSD patients with psychotic symptoms, the severity of global psychosis was comparable to that reported for schizophrenia. Although these patients did not meet criteria for schizophrenia, they responded positively to antipsychotic medication.

PTSD in patients with primary psychotic disorders

Having a primary psychotic disorder is no protection against trauma and PTSD. Mueser and colleagues (Mueser et al., 1998) studied trauma histories and PTSD symptoms in a large sample of inpatients and outpatients with serious mental disorders. They found an extraordinarily high prevalence of trauma exposure (98% reported at least one trauma with an average of 3.5 different types of events) as well as a high rate of current PTSD (43%). Yet a diagnosis of PTSD was recorded in only 2% of the patients' medical charts. Although PTSD was highest in patients with depression (54%) and borderline personality disorder (47%), it was also prevalent among patients with bipolar disorder (40%), schizoaffective disorder (37%), and schizophrenia (28%). Zimmerman and Mattia (1999) found PTSD to be four times more prevalent among outpatients with psychotic depression than among those with non-psychotic depression.

Shaw and colleagues (Shaw, McFarlane, & Bookless, 1997) argued convincingly that psychotic episodes themselves can be traumatic and eventuate in post-psychotic PTSD. Consistent with my own view (see Chapter 1), they proposed that the DSM emphasis on threat to *physical* integrity is too narrow, and that a threat to *psychological* integrity also may be traumatic. They pointed out that psychosis entails extreme threat as well as a feeling of helplessness associated with the impossibility of escape. Delusions include fears of killing or being killed, and hallucinations can be tormenting. Furthermore, circumstances surrounding hospitalization can be extremely stressful. For example, patients endure loss of control when admitted involuntarily, and they are exposed to many stressful interactions in the hospital. Hence the acute psychotic episode and its sequelae are potential traumatic stressors that may provoke subsequent intrusive, avoidant, and hyperarousal symptoms. To test these hypotheses, the researchers recruited patients with a diagnosis of a primary psychotic disorder who were nearing discharge from the hospital, and they interviewed the patients about PTSD symptoms connected with their psychosis and hospitalization. About half the sample met criteria for post-psychotic PTSD, and the majority met the individual criteria sets. The authors concluded that post-traumatic sequelae of psychotic episodes often have a considerable impact on the disease process, especially exacerbating the negative symptoms of withdrawal and detachment.

EDUCATING CLIENTS ABOUT DISSOCIATIVE STATES

Traumatized clients frequently raise questions about dissociation, often equating dissociation with multiple personality disorder and asking explicitly if they are 'psychotic.' In this section, I will describe the role of diagnostic assessment in client education and then comment on the process of explaining detachment, compartmentalization, and psychosis.

Assessment and client education

Steinberg's Structured Clinical Interview for DSM-IV Dissociative Disorders (Steinberg, 1993, 2000; Steinberg, Rounsaville, & Cicchetti, 1990) groups dissociative experiences into five broad categories: amnesia, depersonalization, derealization, identity confusion, and identity alteration. Steinberg collected and organized a wealth of clinical examples that are extremely useful for educating therapists about dissociative phenomena (Steinberg, 1995). But the interview also familiarizes the client with various facets of dissociation. The inclusion of various questions immediately conveys to clients that others have had such experiences. For example, 'Have you ever felt as if there were large gaps in your memory?' (amnesia), 'Have you ever had the feeling that you were a stranger to yourself?' (depersonalization), 'Have you ever felt as if familiar surroundings or people you knew seemed unfamiliar or unreal?' (derealization), 'Have you ever felt as if there was a struggle going on inside of you about who you really are?' (identity confusion), and 'Have you ever acted as if you were a completely different person?' (identity alteration). This systematic and comprehensive interview enables clients to articulate experiences that they are likely to have associated with being crazy and that they may never have discussed with anyone before.

The Dissociative Experiences Scale (Bernstein & Putnam, 1986) is the most widely used self-report measure in research on dissociation and shows substantial empirical validity (Carlson, 1994; Carlson & Armstrong, 1994; Carlson & Putnam, 1993; Steinberg, Rounsaville, & Cicchetti, 1991; van IJzendoorn & Schuengel, 1996). When used in a clinical setting, the content of the 28 items immediately conveys to clients by implication that their dissociative experiences are not unique. The scale can be used as the basis for a structured interview in routine clinical assessment (Allen & Smith, 1993). For items to which they have responded positively, I ask clients to give examples of the experiences. For example, 'You indicated that quite often you find yourself in a place and have no idea how you got there. Can you tell me about a time when that happened?' 'You indicated that you sometimes feel as if you're looking through a fog. Can you tell me more about what that's like?' Such exploration clarifies the dissociative symptoms for both the therapist and the client, and it provides a springboard for explaining different aspects of dissociation to the client.

Explaining dissociative detachment

Whenever a client asks about dissociation, I describe the continuum of dissociative detachment ranging from alert consciousness to being in the void. Detachment is likely to be the most pervasive dissociative problem, and it is almost certain to be among the dissociative experiences included in DID. I emphasize several points in relation to this continuum. First, most persons experience dissociation to some degree. Second, stress, anxiety, or reminders of trauma often prompt dissociation, and detachment is a form of mental flight in the face of this stress. Third, alert consciousness is more easily regained from a point of mild detachment than from a point of extreme detachment. Fourth, although detachment may be an effort to escape stress, it can readily backfire. Having given up moorings in reality, the client is vulnerable to frightening flashbacks. Ironically, mental flight from a minor stressor places the client at risk for a re-traumatizing post-traumatic state. Fifth, the antidote to dissociation is grounding or anchoring oneself back in external reality. I acknowledge, however, that grounding goes against the grain inasmuch as it entails returning to the outer reality from which the client has taken mental flight.

Quite often clients ask, 'Why shouldn't I do it?' I characterize dissociation as a blessing and a curse. In the original trauma, where fight-or-flight was not feasible, dissociation helped the client to survive emotionally. Yet current stressors or post-traumatic reminders are not real dangers and ultimately must be mastered rather than escaped. Dissociative detachment undermines functioning in several ways. Detachment not only puts the client at risk for post-traumatic flashbacks but also, because of lack of attentiveness to the outer world, renders the client oblivious to real current dangers. Detachment also compromises cognitive functioning—attention, concentration, and memory. Not least, dissociative detachment during trauma puts persons at greater risk for developing PTSD.

While sympathizing with the natural and adaptive functions of avoidance, I emphasize that severe and persistent detachment blocks active coping with current problems, conflicts, and stressors, such that it becomes a self-perpetuating problem. Of course the client cannot just stop dissociating by an act of willpower. The continuum underscores that milder detachment is more easily reversed than extreme detachment. By cultivating awareness of detachment, clients can ground themselves in response to early signs when they have more control and before they become unresponsive.

I also alert clients to the possibility that dissociative detachment impairs memory. I describe how severe detachment precludes attending to events and behaviors as well as thinking about what one is doing. Thus I note how detachment is not conducive to establishing memories. I point out how this might have been true at the time of trauma and how it may also be an ongoing problem—in either case, potentially accounting for memory gaps and lost time. I explain how, if the information does not get into memory, it cannot possibly be retrieved. Clients find this concept both frustrating and relieving. Memory enhancement techniques may never enable them to remember some events. Yet they need no longer engage in a futile exploration for memories that are not there.

Explaining DID

I draw clients' attention to the change in terminology in DSM from multiple personality disorder to dissociative identity disorder. I explain that these two labels neatly capture the difference between the client's point of view and the therapist's point of view—the perspective from the inside and the perspective from the outside. I acknowledge that many clients with this disorder feel as if they have different people or personalities inside. That is their psychological reality. Yet I point out that others see them as being one person with one personality. Thus we therapists see them as having an identity disorder (believing they are composed of many persons or personalities) that is based on trauma-related dissociation. This distinction respects clients' experience while also introducing them to another point of view (dissociatively based identity disturbance).

I help clients think about compartmentalization by drawing a large circle with several smaller circles inside. I state that the self (large circle) is comprised of many different states of mind (smaller circles), pointing out that it is normal for any person to cycle through a wide range of states. I ask clients to give examples of such states, and they typically label them with feelings (e.g., frightened, angry, happy, depressed). I point out that all of us have the capacity to regress to states of mind in which we feel childlike (e.g., feeling like an intimidated or frightened child, or displaying childlike temper tantrums). I point out that DID is characterized by a relatively rigid separation among these states of mind—compartmentalization. I link these states of mind to different demands in traumatic relationships, for example, the abrupt 180-degree changes that occur when a loving parent becomes abusive or neglecting. I explain that this compartmentalization reflects a lack of access to some states of mind when in other states of mind. This lack of access includes amnesia for events and behaviors associated with some states of mind. I point out how such compartmentalization had an adaptive aim at its inception during trauma (avoiding states of mind incompatible with daily functioning) and afterward (avoiding dreaded post-traumatic states of mind).

The concept of compartmentalization normalizes DID. The problem is not having various states of mind; we all do. To stay focused, we all must compartmentalize. It is the *rigid and extreme* compartmentalization of the various states that is problematic. The goal of treatment—admittedly frightening to the client—is to increase flexible access to these various states (memories and ways of feeling in relationships) so as to alleviate the discontinuity in daily experience and to enhance the potential for conscious control. Thus treatment aims to help clients expand their awareness and tolerance for emotions, for example, enabling them to feel angry and to remember events associated with angry feelings without a dissociative switch. Ultimately, integration entails being able to relate in contradictory ways—lovingly and angrily—while keeping both in mind.

Sometimes clients raise questions about their responsibility for behavior in dissociative states. For example, the client may not remember an incident of self-injurious behavior and feel no sense of control over it or responsibility for it. Sometimes clients express this explicitly: 'It wasn't my fault. I couldn't help it. My alter did it.' I empathize with the client's feeling of lack of control but emphasize that treatment aims to enhance awareness and control. While accepting that exerting control can be extremely difficult, with DID as well as with many other psychiatric disorders, we therapists must consider clients responsible for their behavior. As others have done (Bears, 1994; Halleck, 1990), I point out the alternative. The most frightening—and counter-therapeutic—stance imaginable would be to convey that clients cannot be responsible for their behavior. Their investment in treatment, including their efforts to prevent dissociative episodes, exemplifies this sense of responsibility.

Explaining psychotic symptoms

I became interested in the relation between dissociative and psychotic symptoms not only because of diagnostic challenges but also in response to recurrent questions. 'What does it mean that I hear voices?' 'Am I psychotic?' 'Is this schizophrenia?' 'Are my hallucinations schizophrenic or dissociative?' 'My doctor wants me to take antipsychotic medication—does that mean I'm psychotic or schizophrenic?'

I respond to such questions by distinguishing between psychotic *symptoms* and *disorders*. I ask clients what the term, psychotic, means to them. They quickly get to the concept of being 'out of touch with reality,' a core feature of psychosis (Beer, 1996). I point out how extreme dissociative detachment and post-traumatic flashbacks—where the present is confused with the past—fit this concept of psychosis. I acknowledge that this is a frightening term—it connotes being crazy or insane, and perhaps irrevocably so (Beer, 1996). Hence I emphasize psychotic *symptoms and states* rather than *conditions*. But there is no denying the psychotic aspect of these states: the experience is frightening *because it is out of touch with reality*.

I also inform clients that psychotic experiences such as hallucinations occur in a wide range of contexts—grief reactions, for example. I explicate that having a psychotic *symptom* does not indicate a primary psychotic *disorder* such as schizophrenia or schizoaffective disorder. I acknowledge that misdiagnosis of post-traumatic psychotic symptoms is not uncommon, although we may hope that it will become less so as these disorders are better understood. And I explain to clients that sometimes antipsychotic medication can be helpful for persons with trauma-related disorders who are experiencing psychotic symptoms. But, ultimately, the undoing of dis-association through therapy—the reclaiming of alienated memories, feelings, and relationships into the self—will help the client feel less psychotic.

Chapter 8

SUBSTANCE ABUSE, EATING DISORDERS, AND SELF-HARM

Whereas I do believe that emotions have the capacity for short-circuiting all concern for consequences and alternatives, I am not sure that addictive cravings do. What seems abundantly clear, however, is that these cravings can undermine the agent's capacity for making rational choices. (Elster, 1999, p. 169)

Nowhere is the failure of self-regulation more evident than in traumatized clients who abuse substances, binge, purge, starve, and engage in self-injurious behavior. Consider a prototypical adult outcome of attachment trauma. Throughout her childhood, the client felt frightened and unprotected by those upon whom she depended. She hates herself, blames herself whenever anything goes wrong, feels she deserves nothing good, and believes that she must suffer. Generally distrusting and isolated, when she enters into close relationships she becomes desperately dependent and sacrifices her own needs. Then she feels mistreated, exploited, and resentful. She is exquisitely sensitive to misunderstandings, criticism, and rejection. Conflicts in her primary attachment relationships continually remind her of her traumatic past, implicitly or explicitly. PTSD avoidance mechanisms—not thinking about the trauma, not talking about it, staying away from reminders—are ineffective in the face of relationships that involve continual reenactment and reexperiencing. Repeatedly, she finds herself in unbearable emotional states and feels compelled to take action. She must *do something*, however potentially destructive, to change her state of mind. Throughout her adult life she has resorted alternately to alcohol abuse, bingeing and purging, and self-cutting to provide temporary respite from emotional pain.

Substance abuse, eating disorders, and self-harm are stopgap measures, desperate attempts to reduce distress. At best these behaviors terminate unbearable emotional states in the short run. But these stopgap measures are patently self-defeating in the long run. Sooner or later they precipitate precisely the unbearable emotional states they are intended to abort. This chapter examines the developmental contribution of trauma to substance abuse, eating disorders, and self-harm, while focusing on their role in regulating unbearable emotional states. The chapter concludes with a model for educating clients about self-destructive behavior in a way that respects its adaptive intent while confronting its counterproductive impact.

SUBSTANCE ABUSE

The prevalence of substance abuse in persons with PTSD is high. The US National Comorbidity Survey showed highly elevated rates of alcohol and drug abuse/dependence among men and women with PTSD compared to those without PTSD (Kessler et al., 1995). For men with PTSD, the lifetime prevalence of alcohol and drug abuse/dependence were 52% and 34%, respectively (compared to 34% and 15% among men without PTSD). For women with PTSD, the lifetime prevalence of alcohol and drug abuse/dependence were 28% and 27%, respectively (compared to 13% and 8% among women without PTSD). Moreover, the prevalence of substance abuse may be even higher in persons with PTSD who seek treatment (Friedman, 1990). Conversely, the prevalence of PTSD in substance abusers is also high (Ruzek, Polusny, & Abueg, 1998; Stewart, Pihl, Conrod, & Dongier, 1998) and, among substance abusers, those with PTSD are likely to show an especially high level of other comorbid clinical syndromes and personality disorders (Najavits, Gastfriend et al., 1998; Ruzek et al., 1998). Yet the extent to which childhood trauma apart from PTSD increases the risk for substance abuse is less clear. Retrospective reports of childhood maltreatment are highly predictive of drug abuse. But prospective research fails to confirm that childhood abuse and neglect (documented in court records) increase the risk of a drug abuse diagnosis (Widom, Weiler, & Cottler, 1999), although a documented history of childhood neglect does increase risk of alcohol abuse among women (Widom, Ireland, & Glynn, 1995).

Despite their frequent co-occurrence, the assumption that substance abuse and PTSD are causally linked has not gone unquestioned (Bremner, Southwick, & Charney, 1995), and multiple potential developmental pathways may link the two disorders (McFarlane, 1998; Ruzek et al., 1998; Stewart et al., 1998; Stine & Kosten, 1995). The PTSD–substance abuse links are likely to be affected by the type of trauma, the specific PTSD symptoms, and the type of substance abused. Prominent gender differences are intertwined with type of trauma and substance abuse history. In addition, the two sides of substance abuse, intoxication and withdrawal, relate to PTSD symptoms in different ways.

In educating clients, I always start with substance abuse to illustrate stopgap measures for dealing with trauma-related distress. Clients readily grasp the self-medication pathway, wherein substances abuse quells PTSD symptoms and unbearable emotional states. Yet clients need to appreciate that substance abuse increases risk of trauma exposure and may also exacerbate PTSD symptoms. Then trauma and PTSD intertwine in a vicious circle.

Substance abuse alters unbearable emotional states

Substance abuse alters states of mind (McFarlane, 1998). Patients report that alcohol and heroin are helpful for intrusive and hyperarousal symptoms, and that benzodiazepines and marijuana are helpful for hyperarousal symptoms; whereas cocaine exacerbates hyperarousal symptoms (Bremner, Southwick, Darnell, & Charney, 1996). Consistent with these reports, substance abuse may be both positively and negatively reinforced (McFarlane, 1998; Ruzek et al., 1998; Stine & Kosten, 1995), with euphoric mental states being positive reinforcers and the termination of the aversive mental states being negative reinforcers.

Clients are on solid neurobiological grounds in using central nervous system depressants (e.g., alcohol, opiates, and benzodiazepines) to alleviate hyperarousal. These agents decrease noradrenergic activity (Friedman, 1990; McFarlane, 1998). Research consistently shows a relationship between the hyperarousal cluster of PTSD symptoms and increased risk of substance abuse. Alcohol dampens startle responses as well as other symptoms of hyperarousal (Stewart et al., 1998). Accruing evidence indicates that PTSD more often precedes substance abuse than follows it (Kessler et al., 1995; Stewart et al., 1998), which supports construing substance abuse as an avoidant symptom of PTSD (Friedman, 1990; Ruzek et al., 1998).

Yet individual differences loom large. Some persons struggling with numbing symptoms of PTSD abuse substances to *increase* the experience and expression of emotions (Ruzek et al., 1998), relying on disinhibiting effects to allow access to blocked emotions. A client in a psychoeducational group, for example, described how alcohol abuse enabled her to express anger toward her husband. Insightfully, she also acknowledged the counterproductive effects: her drunken tirade, although cathartic, damaged her relationship more than it helped. Confirming that generalizations are risky, McFarlane's (1998) longitudinal study of firefighters showed that PTSD led to increased alcohol consumption for some individuals and decreased consumption for others. He concluded that the state of mind 'associated with PTSD seemed to either discourage or increase the alcohol consumption of these men in the early stages of the disorder, suggesting that there may be either a self-medication effect or a dysphoric effect of alcohol in this disorder' (p. 817).

Research on the longitudinal course of PTSD in relation to the course of substance abuse supports the self-medication hypothesis. Bremner and colleagues (Bremner et al., 1996) conducted a retrospective study of combat veterans in treatment for chronic PTSD. They tracked the course of PTSD symptoms and substance abuse from two years prior to combat to 24 years afterward. PTSD symptoms generally increased sharply over the first few years after combat and then plateaued. Moreover, the course of alcohol and drug abuse paralleled PTSD symptomatology, although there was some decline in consumption in midlife. Epstein and colleagues (Epstein, Saunders, Kilpatrick, & Resnick, 1998) interviewed women who reported a history of childhood rape and compared them to women without this history. Women reporting childhood rape had twice the number of alcohol abuse symptoms and, among childhood rape victims, those with PTSD had double the alcohol-related symptoms. PTSD, and not childhood trauma, predicted alcohol abuse, and twice as many women recalled that their PTSD preceded alcohol abuse than the reverse. Chilcoat and colleagues (1998) also found that PTSD dramatically increased the risk of substance dependence (on prescribed psychoactive drugs), but exposure to traumatic events in the absence of PTSD did not.

Insofar as substance abuse is triggered by negative emotions, PTSD may exacerbate it. Persons with PTSD are sensitized to stress and hyperresponsive to reminders of trauma. Ordinary interpersonal conflicts can spiral into traumatic levels of reexperiencing and reenactment. Consider what happens when substance abuse is thrown into this mix. Ruzek and colleagues (Ruzek et al., 1998) pointed out that the kinds of events preceding relapse in substance abusers—interpersonal conflict, intimacy, failure experiences, and physical pain—may generate especially strong emotional responses in persons with PTSD and render them highly vulnerable to relapses. As Ruzek and colleagues also observed, persons with PTSD anticipate that anxiety will trigger their symptoms and thus are quick to resort to substance abuse whenever they begin to feel anxious.

Substance abuse increases trauma exposure

Although PTSD typically precedes substance abuse, the reverse occurs in a significant minority of cases (Epstein et al., 1998). Substance abuse may contribute to trauma exposure (Cottler, Compton, Mager, Spitznagel, & Janca, 1992; McFarlane, 1998), although not all research is consistent on this point (Chilcoat & Breslau, 1998). Intoxication can promote high-risk or reckless behavior that precipitates traumatic events with risk for developing PTSD

(Ruzek et al., 1998; Stewart et al., 1998). Drunk driving is a prime example, and motor vehicle accidents account for a substantial proportion of PTSD in the general population (Norris, 1992; Ursano, Fullerton, Epstein, Crowley, Kao et al., 1999). In the realm of interpersonal trauma, a substantial minority of women who have been raped report alcohol use proximal to the time of the assault (Resnick, Yehuda, & Acierno, 1997). Intoxication may impair judgment and capacity for self-protection, and intoxicated women are likely to be viewed by others as more sexually available (Ruzek et al., 1998).

Brady and colleagues (Brady, Dansky, Sonne, & Saladin, 1998) found important individual differences in the developmental sequence of PTSD and substance abuse. These researchers contrasted clients whose PTSD symptoms *preceded* cocaine abuse (primary-PTSD group) with those whose symptoms *followed* it (primary-cocaine group). The primary-PTSD group consisted primarily of women with a history of childhood abuse, and they showed a greater number of additional clinical syndromes and personality disorders than the primary-cocaine group. In contrast, the primary-cocaine group consisted of persons with a history of physical assault and witnessing trauma. The researchers inferred that clients in the primary-cocaine group incurred trauma and PTSD as a result of activities related to the procurement and use of cocaine.

A poor prescription: substance abuse exacerbates PTSD

Although PTSD increases the risk of substance abuse, and substance abuse contributes to trauma exposure, evidence is mixed as to whether substance abuse increases the risk of developing PTSD after trauma exposure (Acierno et al., 1999; Chilcoat & Breslau, 1998). Yet therapists have ample reason to be concerned that substance abuse will exacerbate current PTSD symptoms. In addition, substance abuse may reactivate PTSD symptoms that have been in remission, and may also contribute to chronicity in PTSD (Stewart et al., 1998). *If substance abuse is self-medication, it is a poor prescription.*

Understanding the complex relationships between substance abuse and PTSD requires distinguishing intoxication from withdrawal. The immediate (self-medicating) effects of depressants (e.g., alcohol, opiates, benzodiazepines) may dampen PTSD symptoms. Yet withdrawal from these substances engenders noradrenergic activation that may exacerbate PTSD symptoms (Stewart et al., 1998; Stine & Kosten, 1995). Alcohol withdrawal mimics PTSD arousal symptoms, and clients may misattribute their alcohol withdrawal symptoms to PTSD. Moreover, chronic alcohol use exacerbates sleep disturbance and heightens startle reactions. Opiate withdrawal, too, increases central noradrenergic activity and may worsen PTSD symptoms (Stine & Kosten, 1995).

Paralleling withdrawal from central nervous system depressants, psychostimulants have noradrenergic activating properties that may exacerbate PTSD symptoms (Stewart et al., 1998; Stine & Kosten, 1995). Cocaine and opiate abusers are especially vulnerable to PTSD after trauma exposure (Stine & Kosten, 1995). Therapists and their clients must be mindful of the phenomenon of cross-sensitization between environmental stress and psychostimulants. That is, psychostimulants act as pharmacological stressors with neurophysiological effects akin to environmental stressors. These effects have been demonstrated across a wide range of neurotransmitter systems (Sorg & Kalivas, 1995). In effect, a dose of a psychostimulant is akin to a dose of environmental stress. Hence stress-sensitized clients with PTSD must be warned about the risks of stimulant use.

Even by patient report, substance abuse is self-medication that backfires. Brown and colleagues (Brown, Stout, & Gannon-Rowley, 1998) queried patients undergoing detoxification in an inpatient setting about the relation between their PTSD and substance abuse symptoms. Substance abuse did not ameliorate PTSD. On the contrary, patients reported that when one disorder worsened, so did the other. Conversely, when one disorder improved, so did the other. Changes in PTSD symptoms had a greater impact on substance abuse than the reverse, confirming that PTSD tends to drive substance abuse. Similarly, Dansky and colleagues (Dansky, Brady, & Saladin, 1998) studied the course of untreated PTSD symptoms in patients in pharmacological treatment for cocaine abuse, finding that improvement in PTSD symptoms occurred in tandem with improvement in substance abuse symptoms (although they did not find improvement in intrusive symptoms of PTSD).

Although substance abuse exacerbates PTSD, therapists must bear in mind that there are individual differences. McFarlane (1998) reported evidence that alcohol use at the time of exposure to potentially traumatic stressors may lessen the intensity of traumatic memories. Similarly, Stewart and colleagues (Stewart et al., 1998) presented evidence that alcohol, benzodiazepines, and marijuana, by virtue of memory-impairing effects, may block intrusive symptoms of PTSD. Cottler and colleagues (Cottler et al., 1992) also commented on a marginally significant trend for marijuana use to be associated with lower risk of PTSD following trauma.

Vicious circles

The various pathways between substance abuse and PTSD are not mutually exclusive, and researchers have pointed to the likelihood of vicious circles (Epstein et al., 1998; McFarlane, 1998; Stewart et al., 1998). As Stewart (Stewart et al., 1998) commented, PTSD and substance abuse each tend to be more severe in the presence of each other and, 'once the symptoms of both disorders are established, a vicious cycle comes into play where one disorder serves to sustain the other' (p. 808). McFarlane (1998) summarized his study of female prisoners in South Australia, a substantial proportion of whom had a history of PTSD and substance abuse:

> the typical history of these women was that they had been the victims of child abuse and their PTSD had been manifest in their early adolescence. A pattern of substance abuse then emerged which contributed to their criminal behaviour. A cycle of domestic violence, rape and assault followed. (p. 820)

Clients in my psychoeducational groups confirm the intertwining of trauma, PTSD, and substance abuse that McFarlane observed. I inform clients that substance abuse increases the risk of being traumatized, and I point out that the cycle of intoxication and withdrawal is akin to having their sympathetic nervous system on a roller coaster. I also draw their attention to the likelihood that, like other stopgap measures, substance abuse will contribute to interpersonal conflicts as well as a host of other stressors (e.g., marital conflict, legal problems and impaired work performance) that exacerbate PTSD. I emphasize that a history of sensitization increases their vulnerability to all these stressors.

Combined treatment

Viewing substance abuse as self-medication for PTSD is misleading if trauma-oriented therapists and clients infer that, if PTSD is treated, the substance abuse will resolve (Stine & Kosten, 1995). On the contrary, attempting to treat the PTSD without attending to the substance abuse may make both problems worse. Not only does each disorder tend to be worse in the presence of the other but also the presence of each complicates the treatment of the other (Ruzek et al., 1998). As Stine and Kosten (1995) stated, 'both disorders also can influence the resilience of the fundamental psychological and biological systems themselves. This results in disorders of self-regulation and compromises a client's ability to benefit from treatment' (p. 454).

By requiring withdrawal, treatment of substance abuse may exacerbate symptoms of PTSD (Stine & Kosten, 1995). Conversely, by requiring processing of trauma, treatment of PTSD may exacerbate substance abuse (Stewart et al., 1998). Thus clients with a history of substance abuse undergoing treatment for PTSD need appropriate supports and safeguards (Shapiro, 1995b). As Chilcoat and Breslau (1998) found, among the complications of pharmacological treatment of PTSD is abuse of psychoactive drugs, whether these are prescribed for PTSD or related disorders. Some therapists argue that a stable, relapse-free period should precede trauma-specific interventions (Ruzek et al., 1998).

PTSD and substance abuse should each be treated in their own right, and they should be treated simultaneously (Hoffman & Sasaki, 1997; Ruzek et al., 1998; Stine & Kosten, 1995). Brown and colleagues (P. J. Brown et al., 1998) found that most clients concur with this professional opinion, but a sizable majority of substance-abusing clients with PTSD were never referred for PTSD treatment. Encouragingly, the majority of those referred for PTSD treatment followed through, although a minority of clients refused PTSD treatment owing to distrust of professionals, apprehension that talking about their trauma would make it worse, and fear that their trauma would be revealed to others (e.g., family members).

Consistent with accruing knowledge about the relationships between PTSD and substance abuse, promising integrated treatment protocols have been developed and researched. Ruzek and colleagues (Ruzek et al., 1998) reported success with a treatment approach that includes psychoeducation, identification of high-risk stressors, and coping with violations of abstinence, which are often especially stressful for clients with PTSD. Najavits and colleagues (Najavits, Weiss, Shaw, & Muenz, 1998) reported findings of an uncontrolled study of their cognitive-behavioral treatment for women with PTSD and substance abuse. Their 24-session protocol focuses on cognitive, behavioral, and interpersonal coping skills. They found that substance abuse significantly improved from pre-treatment to post-treatment, although PTSD symptoms did not improve until the three-month follow-up assessment. They found a relatively high level of treatment compliance and satisfaction. Theirs was a severely impaired sample, with many clients being polysubstance dependent as well as having a history of severe and repetitive trauma along with poor functioning and personality disorders. Surprisingly, women with the severest impairment were most likely to complete treatment.

EATING DISORDERS

Given the frequent co-occurrence of trauma and eating disorders, therapists treating clients with trauma-related problems are likely to encounter many with eating disorders, and those treating clients with eating disorders are likely to confront trauma in conjunction with this disturbance (Zerbe, 1993a). The co-occurrence of sexual abuse and eating disorders is especially significant for women. Eating disorders are nine times more common in women than men (Zerbe, 1999), and women are at far higher risk for sexual abuse than men. Considering the role of shame in relation to sexuality and the body that is evident in women with eating disorders (Zerbe, 1993c, 1995), sexual abuse is a plausible contributor to these disorders. Recognition and treatment of eating disorders in trauma clients is crucial, because these disorders are associated with a high level of morbidity and mortality (Zerbe, 1999), with anorexia carrying a mortality rate of 8–18% over a 10- to 20-year period.

Eating disorders and childhood trauma

Trauma is just one facet of the potentially complex etiology of eating disorders in which biological, intrapsychic, interpersonal, and socio-cultural factors all play prominent roles (Wechselblatt, Gurnick, & Simon, 2000; Zerbe, 1993a). Trauma is neither a necessary nor sufficient cause for the development of an eating disorder. Researchers initially questioned whether rates of childhood sexual abuse are any higher among women with eating disorders than among women more generally (Pope & Hudson, 1992). Yet subsequent research (Fallon & Wonderlich, 1997; Welch & Fairburn, 1994; Wonderlich, Brewerton, Jocic, Dansky, & Abbott, 1997) has shown that childhood sexual abuse is higher in women with eating disorders than control samples, and there is modest evidence that childhood sexual abuse is more prevalent in women with bulimia than in women with restricting anorexia.

Yet there is no evidence that childhood sexual abuse is a specific risk factor for bulimia; rather, *sexual abuse is a non-specific risk factor for a wide range of psychiatric disorders—including eating disorders*. As with substance abuse populations, bulimic clients with a history of sexual abuse have higher rates of other psychiatric disorders than do bulimic clients without this trauma history. Moreover, although sexual abuse is not the cause of eating disorders, it may affect their nature and manifestations (Waller, 1991). Zerbe (1993a), for example, described a woman whose father's demand for oral sex created an abhorrence of fellatio that she concretized in her symptom of purging. For this client, eating repeated the trauma: 'Her father had forced her to "eat meat," so she found this staple particularly intolerable' (p. 204).

Although researchers have focused primarily on sexual abuse, other forms of childhood maltreatment and PTSD are also prevalent among clients with eating disorders, suggesting that these disorders may be part of a broader trauma response in some clients (Fallon & Wonderlich, 1997). Kent and colleagues (Kent, Waller, & Dagnan, 1999) systematically studied the full range of potential childhood abuse (sexual, physical, emotional) and neglect experiences in relation to disordered eating attitudes in a non-clinical population. Although all forms of childhood maltreatment were associated with overall eating psychopathology, maltreatment accounted for relatively little of the variance, and only emotional abuse made a significant independent contribution. Moreover, the relation between emotional abuse and eating pathology was mediated entirely by anxiety and dissociation, which were associated with the abuse history. Gleaves and colleagues (Gleaves, Eberenz, & May, 1998) studied not just trauma history but also PTSD in relation to different forms of eating disorder (bulimia, anorexia, eating disorder NOS) in patients in residential treatment. In this population, 74% reported a trauma history, and 52% met criteria for PTSD. Yet PTSD related minimally to the type and severity of eating disorder in these clients.

Eating disorders and adulthood trauma

Dansky and colleagues (Dansky, Brewerton, Kilpatrick, & O'Neil, 1997) examined trauma and PTSD in adulthood in relation to bulimia and binge eating disorder (in the latter, there is no compensatory behavior such as purging, exercising, or laxative abuse). In a representative sample of US women, respondents with bulimia reported a higher prevalence of rape, sexual molestation, aggravated assault, and direct victimization than women without eating disorders. Current PTSD bore a particularly strong relationship to eating disorders. Bulimic women were 13 times more likely than those with binge eating disorder to have had PTSD within six months prior to the interview. Among traumatized women, bulimia was more prevalent in those with PTSD than in those without PTSD. Even when controlling for PTSD status, bulimia was more prevalent among women who had been assaulted—sexually, physically, or both—than among those who had not been assaulted.

Given that trauma more often than not preceded the eating-disordered behavior, Dansky and colleagues concluded that the eating-disordered behavior serves a compensatory function. They speculated that subclinical symptoms may be exacerbated by the challenges of coping with victimization. More specifically, in light of its especially high relation to PTSD, they concluded that disordered eating may be a way of coping with heightened anxiety.

Eating disorders and unbearable emotional states

In educating clients with eating disorders about trauma, I focus less on etiology and more on the current function of the eating-disordered behavior. When I ask for examples of problematic means of coping with emotional distress, clients invariably mention overeating, bingeing and purging, and anorexia. Consistent with clients' reports, many clinicians and researchers have commented on the role of eating-disordered behavior in regulating emotional distress (Dansky et al., 1997; Kent et al., 1999; van der Kolk & Fisler, 1994; Zerbe, 1993a).

Although not in the context of trauma, Heatherton and Baumeister (1991) reviewed extensive evidence that binge eating (alone or in the context of bulimia) dampens aversive states by promoting an *escape from self-awareness*, and they view bingeing as part of an avoidant coping style. Women who binge have high self-expectations and are highly self-conscious, as well as being prone to low self-esteem and negative self-evaluations. High levels of self-awareness are therefore emotionally aversive, being associated with anxiety, depression, and generalized distress. Self-awareness is painful and difficult to control. Thus bingeing on food is one strategy to narrow the focus of attention to the immediate stimulus environment in an effort to block self-awareness. Bingeing is a powerful distraction.

Although many pathways lead to a desire to escape self-awareness, interpersonal trauma is a straight route. As detailed in Chapter 4, trauma can be associated with excruciatingly painful self-awareness, including a damaged body image. In addition, trauma is associated with feelings of helplessness associated with uncontrollability and unpredictability. From this perspective, consider the beliefs that Heatherton and Baumeister observed in persons who binge: 'distorted ideas about food and about their own bodies, as well as broader perceptions that life is dangerous and uncontrollable' (p. 96). Bingeing and purging may develop along somewhat different pathways, but both are associated with reduction of emotional distress. Of course substance abuse and self-harm may also foster an escape from self-awareness in a similar manner.

Rorty and Yager (1996) delineated how severe childhood abuse and neglect can contribute to a complex post-traumatic syndrome in which eating disorders may be embedded. Viewing disturbed eating behaviors as a means of regulating stress and painful emotional states, these authors argued that purging is motivated not only by the goal of undoing the caloric effects of a binge but also by its potential to reduce tension and restore a sense of equilibrium. They also noted that bingeing is often associated with dissociative states. In this context, Zerbe (1993a) commented on the calm bulimic clients feel after an episode, 'as if they are encased in a cocoon' (p. 220). Rorty and Yager pointed out that, after the dissociative experience of bingeing, purging may serve to reestablish a sense of groundedness. They, too, are powerful distractions.

Swirsky and Mitchell (1996) asked bulimic women with and without a history of childhood sexual abuse to report their subjective experiences at various points in the binge–purge cycle. The majority of women reported dysphoria prior to the binge, and about half felt soothed, relieved, or dissociated during the binge. The end of the binge often brought a resurgence of dysphoria (e.g., feelings of guilt and shame as well as disgust and self-hatred). After purging, the majority of women reported feeling relieved and soothed as well as feeling in control. Although negative feelings began to return after the whole cycle, the majority of women reported feeling better afterward than beforehand. Consistent with Heatherton and Baumeister's (1991) thesis that eating-disordered behavior promotes an escape from self-awareness, Swirsky and Mitchell noted, 'Participants repeatedly mention that during the binge, "nothing exists but the food"' (p. 24). Although differences between women with and without a sexual abuse history were generally minimal, the level of anxiety and self-hate after the binge and before the purge was highest in the abused group.

Rorty and Yager (1996) characterized purging as 'a form of violence against the self' which they linked to 'bodily shame, sense of worthlessness, and self-loathing' (p. 779) associated with a history of abuse. They pointed out how eating-disordered behavior not only provides a way of coping with damaged self-esteem but also organizes a system of meaning and identity:

> In the face of highly contradictory demands for female success in contemporary society, women lacking an internal sense of purpose are more vulnerable to adopting that offered by the culture: the meaning (often cast in an almost spiritual light) offered by purification and transcendence of the body via self-control of basic needs and physically manifested in a thin body. In a culture that presents the pursuit of slenderness as a legitimate life goal, these women find a system of meaning around which their identities, thoughts, and actions can be structured. (p. 781)

As these clinical and theoretical perspectives make plain, complex developmental pathways from trauma to eating disorders come together in the individual's discovery that bingeing, purging, and starving is a means to regulate her unbearable emotional states. The resort to eating-disordered behavior may stem partly from a failure to develop secure attachment relationships that provide the bedrock for self-regulation and enable the individual to reach out for support. Mallinckrodt and colleagues' (Mallinckrodt, McCreary, & Robertson, 1995) comparison of women with and without symptoms of eating disorders, all of whom reported an incest history, is noteworthy in this connection. As expected, a history of incest was associated with relatively insecure attachments, a lower sense of self-efficacy, and less social support. Given the incest history, however, women with eating disorders showed most difficulty in the realm of attachment and social competencies. They reported less warmth and support in relation to their mother, less secure attachment in adulthood, lower perceived social support, and more limited social networks.

Combined treatment

Trauma may complicate the treatment of eating disorders and vice versa (Rorty & Yager, 1996; Wonderlich et al., 1997). Moreover, clients with trauma and eating disorders are likely to have a wide range of other comorbid disorders as well as a general pattern of impulsivity (Rorty & Yager, 1996). Gleaves and Eberenz (1994) identified a subgroup of patients in residential treatment for eating disorders who were especially treatment resistant. This subgroup had extensive prior treatment, a history of suicidal or self-mutilating behavior, and substance abuse problems. In this treatment-resistant group, 71% of the clients reported a history of sexual abuse, in contrast to 15% of those in the comparison group.

Trauma-related disorders and eating disorders each must be assessed and treated in their own right, and the links between them should be addressed

(Dansky et al., 1997; Fallon & Wonderlich, 1997; Rorty & Yager, 1996). Consistent with Stine and Kosten's (1995) view that trauma treatment will not suffice to alleviate substance abuse, Pope and Hudson (1992) warned that 'the therapist should be wary of the assumption that the abuse is the cause of bulimia nervosa or that treatment addressing the abuse will necessarily alleviate bulimic symptoms' (p. 462). As Rorty and Yager (1996) observed, the traumatic material must be approached cautiously, with an eye toward safety and coping that will prevent harm from a possible exacerbation of the eating disorder.

Yet therapists must be mindful that preventing the client from engaging in the eating-disordered behavior may rob her of her way of coping with her unbearable emotional states. As Zerbe (1993b) pointed out, although others properly view eating disorders as self-destructive, from the client's point of view *the eating disorder is an attempt to preserve the self*. Consider Zerbe's suggested interpretation from the perspective of trauma: 'When you stay away from food, a part of you feels alive. You feel in charge of your own life' (p. 324). Thus fostering other means of establishing a sense of control is essential to the treatment of trauma-related eating disorders.

DELIBERATE SELF-HARM

Substance abuse and eating disorders are but two of myriad self-destructive behaviors clients employ to regulate their unbearable emotional states. Everyone easily understands how substance abuse serves this function. We professionals understand how eating-disordered behavior may do so. Understanding how deliberate self-harm regulates emotional states is not so easy.

Favazza and Conterio (1989) aptly commented that 'Clinically the most commonly encountered and vexing form of self-damaging behavior is the low lethality, direct, multiple-episode type as exemplified by persons who repeatedly cut and burn themselves over long periods of time' (p. 283). How can cutting and burning oneself provide emotional relief? Clients who engage in such behavior have learned that injuring themselves makes them feel better, even if they do not understand why this is so. It is little wonder that their friends and family members fail to grasp this point. I vividly recall my incredulity many years ago when a client who regularly cut herself told me how seeing the blood beading on her arm and feeling the warm sensation made her feel as if she was taking a soothing bath.

Several terms refer to the self-destructive behaviors to be considered here, including self-mutilation, self-injurious behavior, and parasuicidal behavior. Morgan and colleagues (Morgan, Burns-Cox, Pocock, & Pottle, 1975) introduced the term, *deliberate self-harm* to refer to 'a non-fatal act, whether physical injury, drug overdosage or poisoning, carried out in the knowledge that it was potentially harmful and, in the case of drug overdosage, that the amount taken was excessive' (p. 564). These researchers interviewed a large series of patients within a day after admission to an emergency room, the vast majority of whom had overdosed with prescribed medication. Only a minority of these patients had expected to die, and interpersonal conflict was the most common precipitant for their behavior.

Pattison and Kahan (1983) further elaborated a syndrome of deliberate self-harm on the basis of a large series of published case reports. Whereas Morgan and colleagues (Morgan et al., 1975) introduced the term primarily in the context of overdoses, Pattison and Kahan focused more on self-mutilation. These authors and others (Favazza & Rosenthal, 1993; Feldman, 1988; Haines, Williams, Brain, & Wilson, 1995; Menninger, 1938; Osuch, Noll, & Putnam, 1999; Walsh & Rosen, 1988) have documented the wide variety of clinical contexts in which deliberate self-harm occurs, including psychosis, mental retardation, organic brain syndromes, institutionalization, and incarceration.

I will focus on the prototypical form of deliberate self-harm that Pattison and Kahan articulated, because it relates most directly to interpersonal trauma. As they defined it, deliberate self-harm typically begins in adolescence, is low in lethality, is characterized by repetitive episodes over many years, and is often triggered by felt lack of social support. The syndrome entails:

> 1) sudden and recurrent intrusive impulses to harm oneself without the perceived ability to resist; 2) a sense of existing in an intolerable situation which one can neither cope with nor control; 3) increasing anxiety, agitation, and anger; 4) constriction of cognitive-perceptual process resulting in a narrowed perspective on one's situation and personal alternatives for action; 5) a sense of psychic relief after the act of self-harm; and 6) a depressive mood, although suicidal ideation is not typically present. (p. 867)

Although cutting is most common, deliberate self-harm takes many forms. Connors (1996) lists the following:

> cutting, burning, slapping, punching, scratching, gouging, skin-piercing, hair-pulling or plucking, harmful enemas and douches, interfering with the healing of wounds, inserting dangerous objects into the vagina or rectum, head-banging, picking at cuticles and nails until they bleed, poking the ear, pulling out eyelashes or teeth, digging into the gums, choking, hitting oneself with objects, chewing the inside of the mouth/cheeks, ingesting sharp objects (such as razor blades, staples, needles, and pins), using an eraser to 'burn' or tear the skin, and biting oneself. (pp. 199–200)

Often such acts of deliberate self-harm are embedded in a broad constellation of other self-destructive behaviors, which include substance abuse (Pattison & Kahan, 1983; Zlotnick, Mattia, & Zimmerman, 1999), eating-disordered behavior (Favazza, 1987; Zlotnick, Shea, Pearlstein, Simpson et al., 1996), and aggression (Romans, Martin, Anderson, Herbison, & Mullen, 1995; Simeon et al., 1992; Zlotnick, Mattia et al., 1999), as well as a wide range of other high-risk and impulsive behaviors (Favazza & Rosenthal, 1993; Romans et al., 1995; Zlotnick, Shea, Pearlstein, Simpson et al., 1996).

Self-mutilation in animals

Deliberate self-harm is not unique to humans but rather has been observed in a wide variety of non-human species. Favazza (1987) described the similarity between self-mutilation in humans and animals, noting that non-human primates engage in hair pulling, head hitting, and skin scratching, head banging, face slapping, eye and ear digging, and self-biting. As he commented, 'Animals use their claws and large incisor teeth for automutilation; during the course of evolution humans have substituted tools, such as knives and razor blades' (p. 51). As they do in humans, distressed states trigger self-harm in animals. Behaviors indicative of fear, anxiety, and agitation in pharmacologically stressed primates include skin picking so intense that it results in bleeding (Ninan et al., 1982). Social stress-related displacement activities in animals commonly include self-scratching (Maestripieri, Schino, Aureli, & Troisi, 1992). After reviewing the animal literature, Jones and Daniels (1996) construed self-injury as 'self-aggression' that often has its origins in a history of social isolation and is prompted by threat or frustration.

Deliberate self-harm versus suicidal behavior

Clients feel deeply misunderstood when therapists and others fail to distinguish deliberate self-harm from suicidal behavior. Simeon and colleagues (Simeon et al., 1992) defined self-mutilation as 'deliberate injury to one's own body tissue without conscious intent to die' (p. 222). Walsh and Rosen (1988) warned against referring indiscriminately to self-injurious behavior as 'suicide attempts' and 'suicide gestures.' They pointed out that self-harm may be construed as *anti-suicidal* behavior insofar as it can be employed to avert suicide—a point Menninger (1938) made over a half-century ago and one that has been reiterated by others since (Connors, 1996; Feldman, 1988).

Self-harm is intended to terminate an unbearable emotional state, whereas suicidal behavior is intended to bring permanent escape through death. Baumeister (1990) marshaled evidence for his thesis that suicide 'emerges as an escalation of the person's wish to escape from meaningful awareness of current life problems and their implications about the self' (p. 91). Like suicide, substance abuse, eating-disordered behavior, deliberate self-harm, and other self-destructive behaviors offer escape from painful self-awareness. To the extent that these other means are ineffective—and even exacerbate a sense of failure and self-hatred—the need to escape will become increasingly desperate. As Baumeister stated, individuals 'become receptive to stronger means of stopping the unpleasant feelings—with suicide as the ultimate weapon in this battle' (p. 103); hence suicide 'emerges as a fatal escalation of the person's efforts to escape' (p. 107). Traumatized clients readily concur with his conclusion that the main appeal of suicide is its promise of 'relief through oblivion' (p. 107).

To say that deliberate self-harm and suicidal behavior must be distinguished from one another should not imply that they are mutually exclusive. Dubo and colleagues (Dubo, Zanarini, Lewis, & Williams, 1997) found that 65% of inpatients with borderline personality disorder (BPD) who showed a pattern of extreme self-mutilation also had a history of frequent suicidal behavior. Favazza and Conterio (1989) noted that persons who become desperate over their inability to control their self-mutilative behavior may resort to suicide. Yet Sabo and colleagues (Sabo, Gunderson, Najavits, Chauncey, & Kisiel, 1995) found no correlation between deliberate self-harm and suicidal behavior across a five-year period in a series of women in inpatient treatment for BPD. Underscoring their distinctness, suicidal behavior declined significantly whereas self-harm did not decline but rather showed a fluctuating course.

Deliberate self-harm and childhood abuse

Although self-harm has been linked to adulthood trauma such as rape (Greenspan & Samuel, 1989), combat (Pitman, 1990), and lifetime trauma of any kind (Zlotnick, Shea, Recupero et al., 1997), most researchers have focused on its origins in childhood abuse. Most persons in Favazza and Conterio's (1989) survey of self-mutilators characterized their childhood as miserable and reported a history of abuse.

Although diverse forms of abuse have been reported in conjunction with deliberate self-harm, childhood sexual abuse has been a consistently prominent finding. Zlotnick and colleagues (Zlotnick, Shea, Pearlstein, Simpson et al., 1996) found a higher prevalence of reported childhood sexual abuse in female inpatients who engaged in self-mutilation than in those who did not (79% versus 49%). Boudewyn and Liem (1995) found a history of sexual abuse to be associated with suicidal and self-harm behavior for male and female college students, but the strength of association between sexual abuse and self-harm was especially great for females. Moreover, severity of sexual abuse was directly associated with extent of self-harm. Romans and colleagues (Romans et al., 1995) investigated deliberate self-harm in a random sample of women in the community, using a broad definition of deliberate self-harm in which overdosing was prominent. Women with a history of childhood sexual abuse were far more likely to engage in deliberate self-harm than those without this history, and severity of childhood sexual abuse related directly to extent of deliberate self-harm. Only one woman who engaged in deliberate self-harm did not report a history of childhood sexual abuse, and she reported having been sexually and physically assaulted in adulthood. Deliberate self-harm was rare in this community sample, even for those women with a history of sexual abuse (fewer than 10% of these women reported deliberate self-harm), and self-mutilation was extremely infrequent. In clinical populations, however, the prevalence of self-mutilation is far higher (Zlotnick, Mattia et al., 1999).

Deliberate self-harm and childhood neglect

Along with abuse, isolation and neglect play a major role in self-harm. As Favazza (1987) commented,

> A large number of human self-mutilators report pathological childhood experiences including physical and psychological abuse by parents and inadequate supplies of parental love, nurturance, and comforting physical contact. As children, self-mutilators often experience a sense of abandonment, of loneliness, and of unlovability, and they may carry these traits into adolescence and adult life. (p. 53)

Similarly, Kaplan (1991) and Novotny (1972) observed that self-cutting in clinical populations is almost invariably associated with a history of maternal neglect in the form of psychological unavailability.

Early social isolation and separation are also associated with self-injurious behavior in animals (Favazza, 1987; Jones & Daniels, 1996; Kraemer, 1999). As noted earlier, Jones and Daniels (1996) commented that animals with a history of isolation are prone to self-directed aggression when threatened or frustrated. Relating the animal literature to the clinical literature on deliberate self-harm, they noted the importance of the combination of physical and sexual abuse with neglect: 'the feelings of isolation and abandonment which arise from experiences of separation from parents, abuse and violence are similar to those experienced by individuals of other species which have been physically isolated' (p. 265).

Consistent with clinical observations, research supports relationships among abuse, neglect, and deliberate self-harm. Romans and colleagues (Romans et al., 1995) found that women with a history of sexual abuse who engaged in self-harm were more likely to report lack of care (and high control) by both parents. These women also were likely to have had parents who separated and to have lived away from their natural parents for a substantial period. Turell and Armsworth (2000) reported similar findings bearing on neglect for incest survivors who engaged in self-mutilation.

Van der Kolk and colleagues (van der Kolk et al., 1991) studied childhood trauma histories in patients with personality disorders and bipolar disorder in relation to self-cutting, other forms of self-destructive behavior, and suicidal behavior. They distinguished disrupted parental care (neglect, separations, family chaos) from physical and sexual abuse. Disrupted care and abuse related to all forms of self-destructive behavior. Yet abuse related more strongly to suicidal behavior, whereas neglect related more strongly to cutting. These authors were particularly struck by the strength of association between neglect and ongoing self-destructive behavior. They inferred that trauma contributes to the initiation of self-destructive behavior whereas lack of secure attachments (founded in a history of neglect) maintains it. Dubo and colleagues (Dubo et al., 1997) reaffirmed these findings in their study of inpatients with a diagnosis of BPD. Sexual abuse related strongly to suicidal behavior, but several facets of neglect played a more prominent role in self-mutilation than sexual abuse did. The findings for self-mutilation underscored the importance of emotional withdrawal, failure to protect, and inconsistent treatment on the part of the caregiver.

Confirming the cardinal role of neglect in the etiology of self-harm is the striking consensus in the clinical literature that rejection, separations, and feelings of abandonment often precipitate episodes of self-cutting (Favazza & Rosenthal, 1993; Feldman, 1988; Leibenluft, Gardner, & Cowdry, 1987; Pao, 1969). Kaplan (1991), for example, observed that 'The enactment is often precipitated by an unanswered phone call, the departure of a friend or lover or therapist, a caring face that turned away' (p. 384). In his series of inpatients, Novotny (1972) noted that disappointment in the therapist often triggered episodes of self-cutting. Also in the context of inpatient treatment, Pao (1969) observed that the patient's own moves toward independence also precipitated self-cutting. Hence clinical improvement is one common elicitor of self-harm.

I construe the reexperiencing of neglect as a prominent post-traumatic intrusive symptom, which is perhaps most conspicuous in clients with BPD. Thus I think of self-harm as one way of alleviating painful affects evoked by current reminders of this facet of attachment trauma.

Deliberate self-harm and unbearable emotional states

Although the literature on the functions of deliberate self-harm is striking mainly for the sheer multiplicity of motives and effects, tension reduction figures prominently in conceptualizing the syndrome (Favazza & Rosenthal, 1993; Pattison & Kahan, 1983). Kemperman and colleagues (Kemperman, Russ, & Shearin, 1997) put it simply: clients engage in self-injurious behavior to 'feel better' (p. 148). They listed a number of dysphoric states that precede self-harm: anxiety, rage, despair, emptiness, loneliness, and an absence of feeling. Walsh and Rosen (1988) aptly noted that, 'a primary goal for self-mutilators may be to alter their present states of mind, to "leap out" of anguish and tension into a revised, reconstituted, less pressured form of consciousness' (p. 45). Favazza (1987) also commented on the extremely rapid—sometimes instantaneous—sense of relief that self-harm provides.

Favazza and Conterio's (1989) survey of female habitual self-mutilators underscored the impact of self-harm on mood states. Two thirds of respondents reported feeling better immediately after self-harm. Respondents reported that self-harm helped control racing thoughts, alleviate depression and loneliness, induce relaxation, and enable them to feel real again. The researchers commented that the effectiveness of self-harm in reducing symptoms accounts for its developing into a repetitive syndrome. Of course engaging in *any* voluntary behavior that significantly alters your state of mind provides a sense of control, and the self-control deliberate self-harm affords is one of its most powerful incentives (Connors, 1996; Favazza & Rosenthal, 1993). Perhaps partly because of the emotional relief and sense of control it provides, self-harm often promotes a feeling of profound peace and well-being (Connors, 1996; Kaplan, 1991). Kaplan (1991) concluded that self-mutilators form comforting attachments to their implements: 'Along with their fuzzy animals they also have a fierce attachment to the slicing razors, scratching safety pins, pinching clothespins, abrading shards of glass—the tender-hurting caregivers that have the power to comfort, soothe, and bring relief of bodily tension' (p. 383).

A few systematic studies confirm clinical observations of the tension-reducing function of self-harm. Kemperman and colleagues (Kemperman, Russ, & Shearin, 1997) obtained retrospective reports on the relation between mood and self-harm by asking clients with BPD to rate various mood states before, during, and after typical episodes of self-harm. They found a significant decrease in ratings of negative affect along with a significant increase in ratings of positive affect following self-injury. Osuch and colleagues (Osuch et al., 1999) carefully assessed motivation for self-injurious behavior in a large series of inpatients. Their findings document the potential multiplicity of functions but underscore the prominent role of affect modulation as a central motive. Haines and colleagues (Haines et al., 1995) conducted an experimental demonstration of tension reduction in prisoners with a history of self-harm (employing prisoners without such a history as well as a non-prison control group). Using compelling personalized imagery scripts, they found that only the self-mutilation group showed a reduction in physiological arousal at the imagined point of self-mutilation. These authors also noted that psychological measures of tension reduction showed a time course lagging behind the physiological measures, and they inferred that the decrease in physiological arousal is a key reinforcer of the behavior.

Deliberate self-harm, anger, and aggression

Clinical observations and empirical research attest to the wide range of unbearable emotional states that self-harm may serve to regulate. Yet anger bears special attention inasmuch as self-mutilation is a patently aggressive act. Zlotnick and colleagues (Zlotnick, Mattia et al., 1999) recently found a high prevalence of deliberate self-harm in patients with intermittent explosive disorder. More than a half-century ago, Menninger (1938) commented on the aggression that self-harm entails, noting that this aggression is turned against the self in the form of self-punishment. He cited the instructive example of a man whose disturbed relationship with his aggressive and unsympathetic mother was the backdrop for an extreme example of self-mutilation. This 30-year-old high school principal was hospitalized for depression, holding the delusion that he was responsible for all sorrow in life. His mother precipitously insisted that he leave the hospital against medical advice, after which he beat his two-year old infant to death to spare the baby a lifetime of suffering. Subsequently, he thrust his arm into some machinery, causing an injury that necessitated the amputation of his right hand—with which he had murdered his infant.

Although the repetitive self-harm that we see more commonly in non-psychotic contexts is less extreme, the phenomena of rage, aggression, and self-punishment are no less prominent. Feldman (1988) noted that self-harm is prompted by rage, frustration, and a desire for retaliation. Novotny (1972) viewed self-cutting as a hostile–aggressive action, noting its association with frustration and rage—as well as guilt feelings. Yet the aggression is taken out on the self—a safe target—rather than the person on whom the client fears alienating by a direct expression of aggression. Self-harm indirectly expresses aggression and simultaneously metes out punishment for it. Consistent with this view, self-punishment was among the core motives for self-injury in a study of inpatients (Osuch et al., 1999).

Pao (1969) observed that feelings of abandonment and neglect typically trigger the rage that precipitates self-cutting. Jones and Daniels (1996) came to a similar conclusion in relation to the animal literature. An individual with a history of isolation is likely to respond to threat and frustration with self-directed aggression owing to an inability to express aggression socially:

> There is an implicit assumption in both the human and non-human models that a predisposition toward social aggression is a vital part of the behavioural repertoire of many biologically successful species. Self-injury may occur when the more usual avenues of expression are denied or this aggressive disposition is increased. (p. 264)

Thus these authors construed self-harm as redirected social aggression, consistent with Pao's (1969) linking self-cutting to fear of aggression.

For clients whose self-harm takes the form of cutting and bleeding, the experience of symbolically releasing anger may contribute to tension reduction. Favazza (1987) commented that the blood letting may symbolize ridding oneself of bad blood. As he stated, 'The implied metaphor is clear: in cutting their skin they provide an opening through which the tension and badness in their bodies rapidly escapes' (p. 194). Similarly Kaplan (1991) observed that self-cutters think of emotions as 'demonic substances' (p. 382) that can be expelled through blood.

Deliberate self-harm and dissociation

A number of therapists and researchers have linked self-injury with dissociation (Brodsky, Dulit, & Cloitre, 1995; Connors, 1996; Osuch et al., 1999; Turell & Armsworth, 2000; van der Kolk et al., 1991). Pao (1969) provided an exceptionally rich clinical description of dissociative phenomena in self-cutters, likening their altered ego states to fugues, depersonalization, and derealization. Pao described petit mal-like lapses in consciousness and the obliteration of self-awareness, noting that a typical client who engaged in self-cutting was often unaware of the act of cutting as well as the sensation of pain. Yet shortly after the act, she 'came to herself' as 'all of a sudden, she discovered that she had already cut herself' (p. 198).

A number of researchers have confirmed the link between self-harm and dissociation. Van der Kolk and colleagues (van der Kolk et al., 1991) found that ongoing dissociation correlates with sustained self-cutting over a period of years. Glover and colleagues (Glover, Lader, Walker-O'Keefe, & Goodnick, 1997) found that, like those with DID, female inpatients who engaged in self-injurious behavior had elevated numbing scale scores (in comparison with major depressive disorder controls). Zlotnick and colleagues (Zlotnick, Shea, Pearlstein, Simpson et al., 1996) found that female inpatients with a history of self-mutilation had higher levels of dissociative symptoms than those without this history. In a subsequent study of selected outpatient men and women (Zlotnick, Mattia et al., 1999), this research group found higher levels of dissociation in the self-mutilation group in comparison with the non-mutilating outpatient control group—even when controlling for BPD as well as history of sexual and physical abuse.

Dissociative detachment as an unbearable state of mind

Although self-harm serves predominantly to reduce dysphoria (Leibenluft et al., 1987), therapists should keep in mind that the dysphoria may not only involve a painful agitated state but also the opposite—a highly distressing sense of numbness and detachment. Ironically, while dissociative defenses protect against overwhelming affect, these same defenses can also lead to unbearable states of mind. Favazza (1987) pointed out that self-harm can be used not only to decrease arousal (e.g., the sensation of an impending explosion) but also to *increase* arousal to escape 'a perplexing feeling of numbness, strangeness, and unreality' (p. 192). Osuch and colleagues (Osuch et al., 1999) also observed that self-*stimulation* is a core motive for self-harm.

In discussing their finding that ongoing dissociation correlated with sustained self-cutting over a period of years, van der Kolk and colleagues (van der Kolk et al., 1991) commented, 'although dissociation provides protective detachment from overwhelming affects, it also results in a subjective sense of deadness, of disconnection from others, and of internal disintegration,' and they observed that 'many persons who cut themselves report that self-mutilation allows them to terminate this dysphoric state of mind' (pp. 1669–1670). In their study of emotional states surrounding self-injury, Kemperman and colleagues (Kemperman, Russ, & Shearin, 1997) found a significant decrease in dissociation from the beginning to end of the self-injurious behavior. By producing bleeding, self-cutting may be particularly effective in alleviating dissociative detachment. Favazza (1987) noted that the sight of blood can help restore a sense that the self-cutter is alive. Kaplan (1991) commented on how 'a deadened piece of flesh is brought to life by the cutting edge of the razor and the sight of blood' and that one client likened the blood to 'a voluptuous bath, a sensation of delicious warmth' (p. 381).

Although self-harm may be employed to terminate a disquieting dissociative state, it also may be employed to initiate a dissociative state. Connors (1996) deftly summarized the complex relation between self-harm and dissociative states:

> For some, self-injury may serve as a toggle switch for dissociative processes: It may keep someone from dissociating or switching, or it may facilitate a switch; some survivors describe both experiences. They sometimes injure themselves so that the pain can serve as an anchor to the present and allow them to avoid switching or 'going away.' Other times, or for other survivors, self-injury either causes or coincides with a switch to an altered state, helping the person to disconnect from current distress. (p. 204)

Deliberate self-harm and pain

Often self-mutilation is not associated with painful sensations, likely owing to numbing and perhaps endorphin-mediated stress-induced analgesia (Glover, 1992). In Favazza's (1987) survey of a large sample of self-mutilators, the majority reported little or no pain, whereas a small minority reported great pain.

Russ and Kemperman and their colleagues investigated differences between patients with BPD who experience pain during self-injury and those who do not. Initial evidence suggested that those who do not feel pain are likely to be more severely disturbed (Russ, Shearin, Clarkin, Harrison, & Hull, 1993). The pain-insensitive patients showed more extreme anxiety, depression, dissociation, impulsivity, and trauma-related symptoms; they also were more likely to report a history of sexual abuse. These researchers then conducted a series of studies to examine differences in pain sensitivity among these two subtypes of patients. For example, they asked women with BPD to rate the amount of pain they imagined they would feel in a variety of situations varying in likely pain intensity (Russ et al., 1996). Compared to women who did experience pain in the course of self-injury, those who did not showed a poorer capacity to discriminate between intensely painful and mildly painful stimulation. A subsequent study of response to potentially painful thermal stimulation (Kemperman, Russ, Clark et al., 1997) replicated the findings for imagined pain, with those patients who do not experience pain during self-injury showing poorer ability to discriminate among potentially painful stimuli. The authors attributed pain insensitivity to abnormal neurosensory processing, and they postulated that the analgesic subgroup of patients experienced particularly severe or early trauma. In all studies (Kemperman, Russ, Clark et al., 1997; Kemperman, Russ, & Shearin, 1997; Russ et al., 1996), the analgesic patients scored higher on the Dissociative Experiences Scale, which the authors related to a tendency to deny pain on a cognitive level or to block out the affective component of the experience (Kemperman, Russ, Clark et al., 1997).

We might readily understand how deliberate self-harm associated with analgesia may be tension reducing, especially to the extent that the endogenous opioid system is implicated. Yet clients who *do* feel sensory pain in conjunction with deliberate self-harm also report a sense of emotional relief. Pain may contribute to the self-punitive effort to assuage feelings of guilt or self-hatred. But, perhaps more important, many clients report that they can better cope with discrete physical pain than diffuse emotional pain. And to reiterate an earlier point, pain or no pain, by its dramatic ability to alter a state of mind, deliberate self-harm affords a powerfully reinforcing feeling of control. As discussed in Chapter 4, infant studies show how the experience of control provides a powerfully reinforcing source of pleasure (Gergely & Watson, 1996). More generally, behavior that reduces negative emotion yields positive emotion (Solomon, 1980). Hence even painful self-injury alleviates unbearable emotional states.

The interpersonal field of deliberate self-harm

Walsh and Rosen's (1988) emphasis on altering states of mind provides an ideal focus for discussing self-harm with clients. This emphasis fits clients' experience. Of course we therapists must also address the interpersonal context of self-harm, particularly insofar as clients are less aware of it. In addressing the interpersonal context, however, we should heed Leibenluft and colleagues' (Leibenluft et al., 1987) warning: 'Our experience leads us to believe that professionals are prone to attribute primarily hostile or manipulative intent to the behavior, and that they pay insufficient attention to the internal experience of the client' (p. 323).

Because getting out of unbearable emotional states is likely to be foremost on the client's mind, immediate confrontation of the 'manipulative intent' not only will elicit defensiveness but also will lead the client to dismiss the therapist as completely misunderstanding the basis of the behavior. On the other hand, commenting on the interpersonally coercive nature of self-harm as a central dynamic, Walsh and Rosen (1988) caution therapists: 'To exclude this dimension from the discussion because of its pejorative risks would seem to run another equally important risk: that of omitting a key element in defining the interpersonal field of self-mutilative acts' (p. 49). Osuch and colleagues (Osuch et al., 1999) reported a diverse array of conscious intentions to influence others by self-harm, ranging from soliciting support to seeking revenge. They also noted that many interpersonal intentions implied a sense of magical control.

One relatively neutral—and extremely important—interpersonal facet of self-harm is its communicative function. As Walsh and Rosen (1988) pointed out, many persons who self-mutilate have difficulty expressing their emotional experience verbally. Zlotnick and colleagues (Zlotnick, Shea, Pearlstein, Simpson et al., 1996) found alexithymia to be associated with self-mutilation in female inpatients. I have observed consistently that self-mutilating clients not only feel out of touch with their emotions but also believe that *words cannot possibly express the depth of their emotional pain*—only blood and scars will do.

Favazza (1987) was no doubt correct in stating that 'Sometimes self-mutilation can be a manipulative ploy to gain attention or to coerce others' (p. 197). As already stated, presenting this view to clients head on will provoke defensiveness and leave them feeling misunderstood. Many clients counter this confrontation by pointing out that they engage in the behavior in secret. Yet, by the time we therapists see them, the secret is usually out and the interpersonal field is conspicuous. Clients often are unaware of the impact of their behavior on others, and this impact needs to be brought to their attention and put in perspective.

As discussed next, I emphasize relief from unbearable emotional pain as a main effect of self-harm, which meshes with clients' experience. Then I can draw their attention to interpersonal side effects that eventuate in vicious circles. Although I developed this approach in the context of deliberate self-harm (Allen, Kelly, & Glodich, 1997), I employ the model more generally in relation to a wide range of self-destructive avoidant behaviors, including substance abuse and eating disorders.

EDUCATING CLIENTS ABOUT INTERPERSONAL EFFECTS AND VICIOUS CIRCLES

When I ask clients in psychoeducational groups to give examples of self-destructive behavior, they invariably include substance abuse, eating disorders, and self-harm. Substantial evidence shows that these three forms of self-destructive behavior often go together (Favazza & Conterio, 1989; Heatherton & Baumeister, 1991; van der Kolk & Fisler, 1994; Welch & Fairburn, 1996), and they are often combined with a wide range of other impulsive and self-destructive behaviors. Lacey (1993), for example, identified a subgroup of *multi-impulsive bulimics* who engaged in substance abuse and self-harm, as well as stealing. Compared to bulimics without this constellation of additional impulsive behaviors, members of the multi-impulsive group were more likely to report a history of sexual abuse. Regarding the multiplicity of destructive behaviors, Lacey commented,

> Clinically, the clients describe that each behaviour was associated with a *similar sense* of being out of control, and that the patterns of behavior fluctuated and were usually interchangeable. Usually the behaviours have a *similar function* of reducing or blocking unpleasant or distressing feelings. (p. 192)

Sabo and colleagues' (Sabo et al., 1995) observation that decreases in substance abuse can be followed by increases in deliberate self-harm confirms Lacey's point that different self-destructive behaviors alternate with one another. Of course, within each of these three arenas of self-destructive behavior, different forms may alternate with one another (e.g., an individual may migrate from one substance to another or from bulimia to anorexia). Most clients who engage in deliberate self-harm employ more than one method (Pattison & Kahan, 1983). A client in a psychoeducational group, for example, attempted to encourage another client by stating that she had been able to stop cutting herself. After a moment's hesitation, however, she went on to confess that she had instead begun to insert objects under her skin (albeit with less frequency than the self-cutting). I regularly acknowledge with clients that calling these behaviors 'self-destructive' misses the point. Other persons view the behavior as self-destructive, but its main purpose is self-preservative—to escape emotional pain. In this context, I bring up suicidal behavior as a desire to escape pain permanently (Baumeister, 1990).

Self-destructive behavior as addiction

Substance abuse, eating disorders, and deliberate self-harm by no means exhaust the domain of self-destructive behaviors. When I ask clients in psychoeducational groups to expand the list of stopgap measures, they include such behaviors as promiscuous sex, gambling, smashing objects, and excessive shopping. Quite often, clients refer to a wide range of these behaviors as 'addictions,' and I take this concept seriously. Favazza and Conterio (1989) noted that 71% of their sample considered their self-mutilation to be an addiction. Applying the concept of addiction to a broad range of self-destructive behavior underscores for clients and therapists how difficult it is to give up these behaviors.

Although it was not developed in the context of trauma, Elster's (1999) comprehensive theory of addiction highlights important features of self-destructive behavior. Chemical and behavioral addictions are not identical but overlap. Elster enumerated a constellation of characteristics common among addictions: *craving* is the most important explanatory concept; *tolerance* and *withdrawal* are essential to chemical addictions but only loosely applicable to behavioral addictions; *cue and belief dependence* refer to the fact that perceiving and believing the substance to be present provoke craving; and *crowding out* entails total preoccupation with the addiction. Also part of the addictive constellation are mood alterations, desire and inability to quit, denial, a struggle for self-control, relapse, and objective harm to the individual. Many of these criteria pertain not only to substance abuse but also to eating disorders, self-harm, and other destructive behaviors. Nothing is harder than giving up powerful reinforcers.

Interpersonal side effects

I use the diagram in Figure 8.1 to differentiate the *main effect* of tension reduction from the pernicious interpersonal *side effects* and to point out a problematic vicious circle. What first captures attention in Figure 8.1 is the following sequence: interpersonal stressors → unbearable emotional states → self-destructive behavior → relief. Consistent with the role of neglect in attachment trauma and self-harm, I emphasize feeling rejected, unloved,

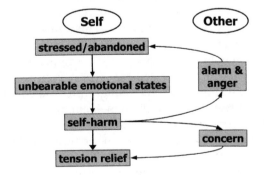

Figure 8.1 Interpersonal side effects of self-destructive behavior

abandoned, and alone as common interpersonal stressors. Having made it amply clear that I understand that relief is the main intent of their behavior, we can begin to examine its impact on others—typically attachment figures.

I start this line of exploration by asking clients to comment on the validity of the hypothesis, 'You're just trying to get attention.' I state my conviction that this accusation misses the point. Clients are not primarily concerned with others' attention but rather are understandably utterly preoccupied with their own unbearable emotional state and the means of terminating it—crowding out, in Elster's (1999) terminology. Indeed this self-preoccupation is precisely what I wish to counter. Of course this is not an either–or situation. Relieving tension and endeavoring to get attention are not mutually exclusive. On the contrary, to open an avenue for considering the attention-getting aspect of destructive behavior, I draw the lower-right arrow as a side effect. This feedback loop reflects the possibility that self-injurious behavior might sometimes elicit (positively reinforcing) concern from others. This arrow encompasses other interpersonal tension-reducing effects as well (e.g., preventing others from leaving).

Always mindful of the need to foster secure attachments, I emphasize that wanting attention is healthy and that behaving in ways that elicit attention from others is highly desirable. But clients must learn to get attention in ways that are effective. In a similar vein, I reframe manipulation. To manipulate means to 'Handle, esp. with (physical or mental) dexterity' (Brown, 1993, p. 1687). In this neutral sense, we all endeavor to manipulate or influence each other, using the intentional stance described in Chapter 4. Of course 'manipulation' has connotations of unfair and deceptive influence. To avoid being judgmental, I endorse the need for influence but emphasize the need for *effective influence*.

The upper-right arrow in Figure 8.1 highlights the ineffectiveness of self-destructive behavior as a potential source of interpersonal influence. Herein lies the main problem: self-destructive behavior alienates attachment figures. Self-destructive behavior—especially self-harm and suicidal behavior—is alarming and thereby provokes anger. To emphasize that anger is rooted in alarm, I use the analogy of the parent whose child runs out in the street. Quite often, energized by fear, the parent yells at the child. I point out that, the more other persons care about you, the greater their fear and anger are likely to be.

The alienating effect of self-destructive behavior creates a blatant vicious circle. At best, in the short run, others might provide comfort and concern that—along with direct tension reduction—reinforces the behavior. This is the side effect of getting attention. But, sooner or later, self-destructive behavior prompts others to withdraw—be it through direct hostility and rejection, threats of abandonment, or more covert and quiet distancing. Hence, through its interpersonal consequences, self-destructive behavior evokes precisely the unbearable emotional states that it is intended to quell.

It is little wonder that such behavior often escalates in relationships—including client–therapist relationships. Here we have a tragically common exemplar of reenactment of childhood trauma in contemporary attachment relationships. And, to reiterate the point made in the context of PTSD, reexperiencing neglect is often the trigger for this pattern of reenactment.

Stopgap versus constructive coping

I started this chapter by describing a prototypical client in dire straits, and I have only made matters worse. The client is not only plagued by unbearable emotional states but also is coping by further endangering herself and provoking others to behave in a way that escalates these states and her self-endangerment. We therapists must convey to clients our recognition that these are extremely hard problems. Addictions are notoriously tenacious. All these problems are difficult to treat, and deliberate self-harm is particularly challenging (Favazza, 1987). I make no attempt to shield clients from these realities—they live them, and they will not be misled by any pat answers or promise of easy solutions. I emphasize that clients resort to all these self-destructive behaviors because *they work*. Their effects are often dramatic and immediate. No wonder they are addictive and extremely difficult to give up.

Elster (1999) discussed the controversy about whether labeling behaviors 'addictive' is therapeutically beneficial or counterproductive. There is no simple answer to this question, given the complex relations between emotions and addiction, on the one hand, and responsibility, choice, and rationality on the other. At worst, the concept of being addicted can undermine the sense of responsibility or control and contribute to rationalizations for continued destructive behavior ('I can't stop myself'). At best, the concept of being addicted can undercut denial and support a determined effort to overcome the addictive behavior along with an appreciation of the need for whatever treatment support is available. As Elster observed, 'Many addicts try the naïve strategy of "just quitting" before they learn that more sophisticated techniques are needed. . . . What an addict learns in his failed attempts to quit is that he is what his culture labels as an addict. To be addicted is to be unable to "just quit"' (p. 132). Our clients need to know that we do not expect them to just stop. They will need considerable structure and support over a long period to be able to do so.

As Elster carefully documented, the trade-off between short-term relief and long-term damage is at the heart of clients' struggles to substitute adaptive coping for self-destructive behavior. In the throes of unbearable present emotion, the client is likely to ignore the future. Immediate desperation offsets the incentive of long-term well being. As Elster articulated in describing persons who discount the future, behavior with long-term self-destructive consequences may, for them, be their best option. We cannot expect them to take steps to reduce their rate of time discounting, because to want to be motivated by long-term concerns ipso facto *is* to be motivated by long-term concerns. (p. 146)

This statement is particularly worth considering in light of the DSM-IV (APA, 1994) diagnostic criterion for PTSD, 'sense of a foreshortened future' (p. 428). Furthermore, as Elster made plain, 'By virtue of the high levels of arousal and valence they induce, emotions and cravings are among the most powerful sources of denial, self-deception, and rationalization in human life' (p. 200).

We therapists and our clients are in an uphill battle with self-destructive behaviors. How can this struggle be won? As Elster made clear, discounting the future is most extreme when craving is at its peak, and craving is heightened by the ready opportunity to engage in the addictive behavior (e.g., the presence of the cocaine or the razor blade). The alcoholic will be more likely to consider future consequences when far removed from the pub. Criteria for the syndrome of deliberate self-harm include cognitive constriction and a narrow perspective (Pattison & Kahan, 1983). Suicidal states entail escape from self-awareness by a deconstruction of meaning, accomplished by focusing all attention on the concrete immediate present (Baumeister, 1990). In effect, faced with the unbearable emotional state and the opportunity to terminate it by means of self-harm, nothing else matters. As Elster (1999) put it, 'other considerations simply do not present themselves to the mind of the agent, or do so in a way that reduces their motivational power' (p. 198).

Prevention is the best medicine. Clients will have the best chance of resisting self-destructive behavior if they can avert unbearable emotional states, if they can block opportunities that fuel cravings, and if they can find means of coping through constructive alternatives to destructive behavior. I use Figure 8.1, when the client is not in the throes of craving, to draw attention to future consequences so as to decrease the incentives associated with self-destructive behavior. At best, this educational effort will facilitate prevention—avoidance of extreme emotional states and opportunities for destructive action.

When I draw clients' attention to adverse future consequences—interpersonal rejection and vicious circles—I acknowledge that these interpersonal dynamics are characteristic of relationships with therapists as well as with other attachment figures. Although therapists are trained to deal with such behavior, being human, they are also alarmed and frustrated by it. Therapists, too, are likely to withdraw. Clients readily give examples of therapists who have succumbed to the vicious circles and discontinued the treatment. We all must set limits, and we must help clients recognize their responsibility for making a treatment relationship viable.

When I discuss these destructive ways of coping with unbearable emotional states, I always contrast them with more constructive means of coping. Therapists not only must empathize with the difficulty of change but also must offer hope of change. I encourage clients to elaborate constructive means of coping, and most groups of clients can develop impressively long lists—exercise, hobbies, relaxation, music, taking warm baths, medications, and reaching out to other persons for help. But I flatly acknowledge that these constructive coping methods, which include many of the treatment interventions we offer, cannot compete with self-destructive behaviors in rapidly altering unbearable emotional states. To be more specific, our treatment interventions are some help, but their effects are often less immediate and dramatic than those clients have been using. If there were an equally effective, non-destructive alternative, clients surely would have discovered it long ago. When we advise clients to 'talk rather than act,' it can seem as if we are asking an alcoholic to settle for a thimble of beer rather than a fifth of whiskey.

With the vicious circles clearly understood, however, I emphasize that the alternative coping methods therapists endorse do not have the counterproductive effect of making the precipitating problems worse. The whole of treatment is the answer to how one overcomes these destructive patterns.

Chapter 9

POST-TRAUMATIC DEPRESSION

> Fear . . . is the most depressing of all the emotions; and it soon induces utter, helpless prostration, as if in consequence of, or in association with, the most violent and prolonged attempts to escape from the danger, though no such attempts have actually been made. (Darwin, 1872/1965, p. 81)

Our clients do not usually come for therapy stating that they have a history of trauma and wondering if they have PTSD. More often they seek treatment because they are depressed. If they are admitted for hospital treatment, they are likely to be suicidal.

Barbara came into a psychoeducational group after being admitted to the hospital in an acutely suicidal state. She indicated that she had been depressed and suicidal countless times, and she had been hospitalized numerous times previously. This time, she said, was different. Whereas before she had never lost her will to live, now she had completely given up. Many times, in telling her story, she mentioned that she was 'just tired.' She gave a history of physical abuse and extreme neglect in her childhood. Her alcoholic father terrorized the whole family, beating her and her brother as well as her mother. Her mother—herself abused and neglected in child-hood—was characteristically irritable and depressed, and she regarded her children as an annoying burden. She provided minimal physical care and little solace. As a girl, Barbara had depended for comfort on her mother's sister who lived down the street. Her aunt, like Barbara's mother, had grown up with abuse and neglect, but she was 'a fighter' with whom Barbara could identify. And her aunt managed to combine toughness with empathy and affection, which Barbara relied on into adulthood.

Barbara's depressive episodes began when her aunt died. Although she had been married three times, she had never found anyone besides her aunt in whom she could confide. She and her third husband divorced several months prior to this hospitalization. Barbara had a preadolescent son who had been diagnosed with attention deficit disorder and conduct disorder. To support him and herself, she worked long hours in a factory. Having been browbeaten for her inadequacies and failings since childhood, she was extremely self-critical, always teetering on the edge of self-hatred when she encountered any criticism. Yet she took pride in her capacity for hard physical work. Increasingly, however, she found herself exhausted at the end of the day, unable to meet the demands of raising her difficult son. At best, she had enough energy left in the evening only to engage in battles with him. She had no financial support and, since the death of her aunt, she had no confidant or emotional support. A week before her suicidal state, she had gone to a teacher–parent conference, after which she felt ashamed and guilty for not being able to help her son with his schoolwork, despite the teacher's sympathetic attitude. Eventually, Barbara revealed what made this current episode different: in an argument the evening before hospitalization, her son declared that he would be better off if she were dead, and then he could go live with his father. She felt that she no longer had reason to keep fighting against overwhelming depression.

As any therapist working with traumatized clients knows, Barbara's story is not unusual. It illustrates well, however, several points about the relation between trauma and depression. First, many clients with a trauma history seek treatment because they are depressed and suicidal. Second, the pile-up of stress that often precipitates their severe depressive episode consists of chronic stress coupled with discrete stressful events. Third, the client feels physically depleted as well as emotionally hopeless. Fourth, the client has minimal social support. Fifth, presented with such a situation, the therapist also may feel hopeless. There was one ray of hope, however, evident in the fact that Barbara was still alive. Rather than proceeding with her suicide plan, she had mentioned it to her son's counselor in a family conference, and the counselor had persuaded her to admit herself to the hospital.

Barbara's plight illustrates how the stressor that precipitates a suicidal state and hospital admission may be the last straw in a developmental sequence of stressors originating in childhood trauma and neglect. Depression is much like PTSD in being a disorder of cumulative stress. This chapter begins by examining the intertwining of depression and PTSD and considering the various ways in which trauma and stress play a part in the genesis of depression. To provide a basis for helping clients adopt a less self-critical attitude toward their depression, the chapter addresses the adaptive functions of depression as well as its costs. The discussion of depression also continues a theme begun in Chapter 7 in the context of dissociation: passivity is a prominent form of coping with interpersonal trauma. Like dissociation, depression can be construed as a form of surrender.

As the opening clinical vignette makes plain, recovering from post-traumatic depression is no small feat. I encourage clients to adopt a compassionate attitude toward their struggles by drawing their attention to a series of paradoxes, which I call the *Catch 22s of depression*. I emphasize not so much the obvious things that one should do to recover from depression but rather why doing these obvious things is so difficult. Freed from some of the self-blame for their symptoms, clients are more able to undertake the challenges of treatment.

DEPRESSION AND PTSD

In reviewing the literature on the relation between depression and other psychiatric disorders, Winokur (1990) suggested that therapists endeavor to determine if depression is primary or secondary to other psychiatric disorders. Optimally, this judgment is based on differences in the time of onset, with the primary disorder developing before the secondary disorder. When the relative timing is unclear, the disorder with the greater chronicity or severity is considered primary. Secondary depression is common in relation to a wide range of psychiatric and general medical illnesses, and depression adversely influences the prognosis for recovery from the primary illness. Pertinent to this chapter's agenda, Winokur noted that secondary depression is common in clients with a primary anxiety disorder (with proportions of anxiety disordered clients having depression ranging from 33% to 75%).

Comorbidity

Extensive research demonstrates that a history of PTSD substantially increases the likelihood of having depression and vice versa. The National Comorbidity Survey (Kessler et al., 1995) showed that 48% of men and 49% of women with a lifetime history of PTSD also had a lifetime history of major depression (versus 12% and 19% rates of depression for men and women without PTSD). A lifetime history of PTSD was associated with a 21% and 23% rate of dysthymia for men and women (versus 4% and 7% for men and women without PTSD). In their study of young adults, Breslau and colleagues (Breslau, Davis, Andreski, Federman, & Anthony, 1998) found that 37% with a history of PTSD also had a history of major depression (compared to 11% of those without a PTSD history).

Two studies tracked the co-occurrence of PTSD and depression longitudinally. Shalev and colleagues (Shalev et al., 1998) conducted repeated interviews of persons who were admitted for hospital treatment of traumatic injuries (predominantly due to accidents but also involving terrorist acts and combat). These researchers found major depression in over 40% of clients with PTSD at one month and again at four months after the injury. Clients with both disorders showed more severe impairment, and the combination of PTSD and depression at one month predicted PTSD at four months better than either PTSD or major depression alone. Blanchard and colleagues (Blanchard, Buckley, Hickling, & Taylor, 1998) conducted follow-up assessments of motor vehicle accident victims at a point ranging from one to four months after hospitalization. About half the participants with PTSD showed concurrent major depression. Through careful statistical analyses of the entire set of PTSD and depressive symptoms, these researchers concluded that a two-syndrome model better fits the data than a one-syndrome model. Replicating Shalev's findings, the combination of PTSD and depression (compared to PTSD alone) predicted higher distress, poorer role functioning, and higher likelihood of PTSD at reassessment six months after the initial assessment.

PTSD and depression overlap at the biological level as well as the psychological level. Although there are significant neurophysiological differences to be discussed shortly, Heim and colleagues (Heim, Owens, Plotsky, & Nemeroff, 1997) explicated how PTSD and major depression are both characterized by increased corticotropin-releasing factor (CRF) activity. As indicated in Chapter 6, hypothalamic CRF plays a major role in HPA axis activity by stimulating release of ACTH from the pituitary which, in turn, stimulates the release of cortisol from the adrenal cortex. More generally, CRF has anxiogenic effects by activating the central noradrenergic system. Thus PTSD and major depression both entail dysregulation of stress–response systems.

PTSD as the primary disorder

PTSD, like any other disorder, is a chronic stressor. The intrusive symptoms of PTSD are frightening. As Darwin (1872/1965) recognized, chronic fear is depressing. Kessler and colleagues' (Kessler et al., 1995) findings in the National Comorbidity Survey are consistent with the view that PTSD contributes to depression. They found that PTSD preceded more often than followed depression. Breslau and colleagues' (Breslau et al., 1998) study of young adults yielded similar findings. They tracked the 3.5-year incidence of depression following an initial determination of PTSD. For the group with PTSD at initial assessment, 21% showed major depression at follow-up (compared to 5% of those who did not have prior PTSD). Notably, exposure to trauma in the absence of PTSD did not strongly predict subsequent major depression. Boudreaux and colleagues (Boudreaux, Kilpatrick, Resnick, Best, & Saunders, 1998) also found that PTSD mediated the relation between rape and major depressive episodes in women. On the other hand, in their study of predominantly accident-related trauma, Shalev and colleagues (Shalev et al., 1998) did not find evidence that PTSD increased the risk of developing major depression.

Depression as the primary disorder

Although Breslau and colleagues (Breslau et al., 1998) found that PTSD often preceded depression, the reverse was also true. Preexisting major depression increased risk for PTSD after trauma exposure. Major depression also increased the risk for exposure to trauma (physical assault, rape, being threatened with a weapon, serious injury or accident). The researchers inferred that depression may increase the risk of trauma exposure by impairing attention, judgment, and interpersonal relationships. Acierno and colleagues (Acierno et al., 1999) also found that a history of depression increases the risk of women developing PTSD following rape or non-sexual physical assault.

In their longitudinal study of emergency room admissions associated with predominantly accident-related trauma, Shalev and colleagues (Freedman, Brandes, Peri, & Shalev, 1999; Shalev et al., 1998) assessed clients at one week, one month, four months, and one year after the trauma. They found that prior depression increased likelihood of PTSD, major depression, and both disorders following trauma. Depression predicted PTSD at one year even better than anxiety and PTSD symptoms assessed at one week, one month, and four months after the trauma. The authors attributed their findings to the likelihood that depressive cognitions interfere with recovery from trauma.

Davidson and colleagues (Davidson et al., 1998) compared rape survivors who developed PTSD with those who did not. Of those who developed PTSD, over half had past major depression or a family history of major depression, compared to fewer than a quarter of those who did not develop PTSD. These researchers found strong evidence for a family history of major depression but only weak evidence for family history of anxiety to be associated with risk of PTSD in rape survivors. They inferred that trauma exerts a modifying effect on the symptomatology of depression in those individuals predisposed to major depression. Specifically, they argued that trauma affects the presentation of depression and advocated thinking of PTSD as a mood disorder.

Is post-traumatic depression a unique disorder?

Research demonstrates the complexity of the relationship between depression and PTSD. PTSD may precede or follow the development of depression, and the two disorders may also develop in tandem. Post-traumatic depression differs from primary depression (Davidson & Fairbank, 1993; Davidson & Foa, 1993), and PTSD without depression might be considered atypical (Davidson et al., 1998)—or there may be a depressive subtype of PTSD (Friedman & Yehuda, 1995). Is post-traumatic depression a simple combination of PTSD and depression, or is it a unique disorder?

Yehuda (1997, 1998; Yehuda et al., 1995) documented a distinctive HPA axis neuroendocrine profile in PTSD as compared to the profile routinely observed in the classic animal model of stress and major depression. This finding is paradoxical inasmuch as PTSD is a stress-related disorder *par excellence*. The classic stress response evidenced by elevated cortisol has been replicated in thousands of investigations. Yet, as reviewed in Chapter 6, *lower* basal cortisol has been found consistently in studies of PTSD for all types of trauma (including childhood sexual abuse and rape) and in both genders. Thus, although they are similar in hypersecretion of CRF and blunted ACTH response, depression and PTSD are in many ways diametrically opposed stress responses. Depression is characterized by increased levels of cortisol and decreased glucocorticoid receptor responsiveness, as well as a progressive desensitization of the HPA axis, which may be associated with underresponsiveness to the environment. Conversely, PTSD is associated with an increased concentration and hyperresponsiveness of glucocorticoid receptors evident in the sensitization of the HPA axis, which may be associated with hyperresponsiveness to environmental stress. Notably, when PTSD and depression occur in conjunction with one another, the PTSD neurophysiological profile, not the depression profile, predominates.

Neurobiological differences between PTSD and depression go beyond the HPA axis. Friedman and Yehuda (1995) contrasted the *hyper*thyroidism found in PTSD (with augmented response to thyroid-stimulating hormone) with the *hypo*thyroidism found in depression (with blunted response to thyroid-stimulating hormone). Major depression and PTSD also differ in noradrenergic autoreceptor sensitivity (Maes et al., 1999; Southwick et al., 1995), with PTSD being characterized by greater noradrenergic activity. Notably, symptoms of depression in PTSD respond poorly to antidepressants compared with response in non-PTSD populations—notwithstanding improvement in PTSD symptoms. Hence in relation to the combination of PTSD and depression, the antidepressants may be construed to have a greater anti-PTSD than antidepressant effect (Friedman & Southwick, 1995).

PTSD also alters the symptomatic expression of depression. Constans and colleagues (Constans, Lenhoff, & McCarthy, 1997) found that, among combat veterans with major depression, the presence of PTSD greatly increased the proportion of those who qualified for the melancholic subtype. Numbing symptoms of PTSD predicted melancholia, and excessive guilt was closely related to emotional numbing. The authors concluded that clients with PTSD and depression are not showing true endogenous depression but rather a depressive subtype of PTSD.

In sum, the hybrid disorder, post-traumatic depression, is distinct from major depression in prognosis and treatment response. Many clients with a trauma history and PTSD present for treatment not with trauma-related complaints but with depression. The difference PTSD makes in the syndrome of depression attests to the importance of considering the possibility of trauma-related contributions to disturbance in clients who seek treatment for depressive complaints. Research to date suggests that post-traumatic depression is harder to treat and has a poorer prognosis than major depression apart from PTSD. Treatment that fails to address the trauma will miss the mark.

TRAUMA, STRESS, AND DEPRESSION

The notion that trauma plays a prominent role in the etiology of depression is not new. The learned-helplessness theory of depression is a trauma theory. This section examines how traumatic stress intertwines with less severe stress over the course of development to precipitate a depressive retreat.

Learned helplessness

Seligman's (1975) seminal work on learned helplessness demonstrates the close relationships among repeated stress, trauma, and depression. Seligman recounted how he serendipitously discovered learned helplessness in the course of studying how fear conditioning relates to instrumental learning. Dogs were placed in a shuttle box with two compartments. They could escape electric shock turned on in either compartment by jumping to the other. A warning signal preceded the shock, and the dogs learned to avoid the shock by jumping to the other compartment at the onset of the warning signal. After learning, the dogs were calm: 'After about fifty trials the dog becomes nonchalant and stands in front of the barrier; at the onset of the signal for shock it leaps gracefully across and never gets shocked again' (p. 22).

But a learning history of inescapable shock completely undermined this nonchalant coping style. Seligman described the typical procedure to induce learned helplessness. On the first day, the animal was strapped into a hammock, then given 64 inescapable shocks. The shocks were unpredictable, occurring at random time intervals without any warning signal. The next day, the animal was placed in the shuttle box where shock was signaled and could be escaped by jumping to the other compartment. About a third of the dogs behaved like naïve dogs; they learned to escape to avoid the shock. Most dogs with the history of exposure to inescapable shock, however, demonstrated learned helplessness. Seligman described the prototypical reaction as he first observed it:

This dog's first reactions to shock in the shuttle box were much the same as those of a naïve dog: it ran around frantically for about thirty seconds. But then it stopped moving; to our surprise, it lay down and quietly whined. After one minute of this we turned the shock off; the dog had failed to cross the barrier and had not escaped from the shock. On the next trial, the dog did it again; at first it struggled a bit, and then, after a few seconds, it seemed to give up and to accept the shock passively. On all succeeding trials, the dog failed to escape. This is the paradigmatic learned-helplessness finding. (p. 22)

Although he was constructing a theory of depression, Seligman character-ized learned helplessness as a *trauma response*, and he viewed controllability as a cornerstone of learned helplessness:

when a rat, a dog, or a man experiences inescapable trauma he first struggles frantically. Fear, I believe, is the dominant emotion accompanying this state. If he learns to control the trauma, frenetic activity gives way to an efficient and nonchalant response. If the trauma is uncontrollable, however, struggling eventually gives way to the helpless state I have described. The emotion that accompanies this state is, I believe, depression. (p. 54) [Furthermore,] when an organism has experienced trauma it cannot control, its motivation to respond in the face of later trauma wanes. Moreover, even if it does respond, and the response succeeds in producing relief, it has trouble learning, perceiving, and believing that the response worked. (pp. 22–23)

To understand post-traumatic depression, we must appreciate the pro-found passivity that characterizes learned helplessness. Seligman delineated six cardinal symptoms: lowered initiation of voluntary responses, difficulty learning, persistence of helplessness, lowered aggression and decreased dominance, loss of appetitive behavior, and physiological changes—all of which are prototypical of depression. He summarized, 'Learned helplessness is caused by learning that responding is independent of reinforcement; so the model suggests that the cause of depression is the belief that action is futile' (p. 93). It is little wonder, then, that depression, like PTSD, is a likely outcome of repeated exposure to uncontrollable traumatic events. And it is little wonder that PTSD itself is depressing. *I view post-traumatic intrusive symptoms as akin to unpredictable and uncontrollable shock in Seligman's learned-helplessness paradigm.* The illness is traumatizing.

Childhood trauma and vulnerability to adult stress

Childhood trauma, vulnerability factors, and stressful life events are syner-gistic in the etiology of post-traumatic depression. We now know that child-hood trauma has neurobiological sequelae. Considerable evidence in the human and non-human animal literature indicates that stress exposure early in life increases the risk of stress-related depression in adulthood, likely owing to a sensitized HPA axis (Heim et al., 1997; Weiss, Longhurst, & Mazure, 1999). This stress sensitization may be most evident in women

(Weiss et al., 1999). Recent research on intracellular changes associated with depression suggests that subtle structural neuronal damage associated with prior stress (not yet manifested in behavioral changes) may promote vulnerability to subsequent stress that manifests itself in depressive episodes (Duman, Heninger, & Nestler, 1997).

As reviewed in Chapter 2, Bifulco and Moran (1998) targeted depression in their study of adult outcomes of a wide range of forms of childhood maltreatment. Their work merits reiteration here, because it attests to the developmental intertwining of childhood trauma, associated stressors, and adulthood depression. Bifulco and Moran demonstrated that neglect, parental antipathy, physical abuse, and sexual abuse all increase risk of adulthood depression. These authors initially reported that, of all the abuses, sexual abuse places the individual at highest risk for depression in adulthood, and theirs is one among a long line of studies demonstrating a relationship between childhood sexual abuse and depression in adulthood (Browne & Finkelhor, 1986; Weiss et al., 1999). Yet Bifulco and colleagues subsequently found that psychological abuse is even more strongly associated with depression (Bifulco et al., 2000).

Bifulco and colleagues' work exemplifies a developmental model of adulthood depression. A history of childhood maltreatment in women increases the risk of depression in response to stressful life events in adulthood, and the impact of adversity is influenced by neglect. For example, Bifulco (Bifulco, Harris, & Brown, 1992) found that death of the mother prior to the child's sixth year predicted adulthood depression and anxiety. Yet the impact of the loss cannot be separated from the family context and the child's response. *The relationship between loss and subsequent symptoms was mediated by lack of maternal care prior to the loss, lack of paternal or substitute care after the loss, and childhood helplessness.*

Neglect also plays a role in the impact of sexual abuse. Bifulco (Bifulco, Brown, & Adler, 1991) found that childhood sexual abuse increased the risk for adult depression; sexual abuse was associated with chronicity of depression; and the highest rates of depression were associated with the most severe abuse. Yet neglect and physical abuse were also associated with adulthood depression. Moreover, neglect, physical abuse, and institutional stays were also associated with a higher *risk* of childhood sexual abuse. Hence neglect potentially has an impact in two different ways. Neglect prior to the abuse makes the child more vulnerable to maltreatment, and neglect subsequent to the abuse may exacerbate its effects. Childhood sexual abuse also was associated with increased risk of marital problems, thus heightening the risk of depressogenic life stressors.

Bifulco and colleagues (Bifulco et al., 1998) extended their earlier findings by conducting a study with both retrospective and prospective components. Depressive episodes during the study period were predicted not only by childhood maltreatment but also by prior depressive episodes, particularly in adolescence. Adolescent depression was almost universally associated with childhood maltreatment. Furthermore, vulnerability in the form of low self-esteem and relationship problems was associated with a higher risk of depressive episodes following stressors. The authors noted that these vulnerability factors are associated with a higher rate of stressful events as well as a higher sensitivity to such events.

To summarize, a wealth of research supports a developmental model in which childhood maltreatment not only may contribute to physiological sensitization but also may lead to impaired self-concept and interpersonal relationships. This biosocial vulnerability contributes to the likelihood of stressful interpersonal events in adulthood and to the risk of a depressive episode following such events. The risk of vicious circles in depression is especially noteworthy in light of the high likelihood of recurrence of depression (Angst, 1997; Montgomery, 1997) and the possibility that mood episodes themselves may be sensitizing with respect to subsequent relapses. As Post (1992) expressed it, episodes beget episodes (see Chapter 6).

Attachment and depression

Bifulco (Bifulco et al., 1992) proposed that it is not the childhood loss that confers a vulnerability to subsequent depression but rather the quality of the child's attachment. She speculated that the child's attachment security plays a role in the child's competence and capacity for mastery, factors that determine the child's capacity to cope with loss.

One can make a solid theoretical case that trauma-related attachment insecurity confers a risk for depression. Yet there is limited research relating attachment classifications to depression, and the findings from one study to another are not consistent, owing in part to the heterogeneity of the depressed samples (Dozier, Stovall, & Albus, 1999). Some evidence suggests that insecure attachment is associated with depressive symptomatology in childhood (Greenberg, 1999). Yet studies relating adolescent and adult attachment status to depression have yielded mixed findings, with preoccupied attachment relating to depression in some samples and dismissing and secure attachment related to depression in others (Dozier et al., 1999; Fonagy et al., 1996).

Blatt and Homann (1992) marshaled substantial theoretical and empirical support for their contention that different forms of attachment insecurity relate to different *types* of depression. Feelings of loneliness and helplessness as well as fear of abandonment characterize *anaclitic* (or dependent) depression; whereas themes of failure, low self-worth, and guilt characterize *introjective* (or self-critical) depression.

Vulnerability to both forms of depression stems from internal working models associated with disturbed attachment relationships. Blatt and

Homann proposed that maternal unavailability (or excessive availability) promotes ambivalent attachment and renders the individual vulnerable to anaclitic depression in response to loss, separation, or perceived abandonment. Exposure to high levels of control and harsh parental standards, on the other hand, promotes avoidant attachment and renders the individual vulnerable to introjective depression in response to personal failure or criticism. I find it helpful to keep in mind these two broad themes of *loss* and *failure* as I work with clients to explicate the meaning of the stressful circumstances that precipitate depressive episodes.

Stressful life events

We have seen how childhood trauma in attachment relationships contributes to post-traumatic depression. It is hardly surprising that attachment trauma in adulthood in the form of battering relationships is also associated with PTSD and depression (Watson, Barnett et al., 1997). When we work with clients who have post-traumatic depression, however, we must attend to a broad developmental series of stressors of varying severity. In short, having been sensitized by a history of childhood trauma, many adult clients have collapsed under the weight of chronic stress compounded by discrete stressful life events.

A fine literature attests to the contribution of stressful life events to depression (Dohrenwend, Shrout, Link, Skodol, & Stueve, 1995; Hammen, 1995; Kendler, Karkowski, & Prescott, 1999). The work of Brown's group is exemplary. Brown (1998) asserted that

> most cases of depressive disorder result from a failure to meet goals derived from evolutionary-based needs such as being admired, forming friendships, having a core adult attachment figure, having children, and so on. These goals are almost entirely social in nature, and in this sense rates of depression are likely to be largely the result of psychosocial processes. (p. 358)

A substantial number of studies demonstrate that the vast majority of depressive episodes occur in the aftermath of at least one life event that has long-term threatening implications.

Brown proposed that loss is a core feature of depressogenic life events, although he conceptualized loss in a broad fashion that also encompasses the experience of failure to attain high standards or valued goals. In Brown's view, loss entails not just loss of a person but also loss of a cherished idea. Loss often involves a core identity, and it reflects the 'likelihood of being cut off from a key source of self-value or the development of a grave impediment to carrying out a core activity' (p. 362). Although loss is prominent in depression, Brown also noted the significance of humiliation, defeat, and entrapment. Brown summarized the kind of severely threatening life events that may provoke the onset of depression as follows: 'high commitment to the role area involved in the event, loss—defined in a broad sense, devaluation in one's own or others' eyes, experience of defeat, entrapment, lack of a sense of control' (p. 365).

Although the kinds of severely threatening life events that provoke depression have been well defined, Brown noted that only a fifth of women exposed to such events become severely depressed. Two individual vulnerability factors predicted the onset of depression in response to stressful life events: negative psychological factors (low self-esteem or subclinical depressive symptoms) and negative environmental factors (negative interpersonal interactions or lack of a close confidant). Low self-esteem increases the likelihood of responding to a severe life event with defeat and hopelessness. Furthermore, neither stressors nor vulnerability factors alone are likely to provoke depression; it is the combination of the two that does so.

The individual's contribution to stressful life events varies. Whereas the loss of a home because of a tornado is independent of the individual, a divorce associated with mood and personality disturbance is dependent on the person's characteristics and behavior. Both types of stressful events are associated with a risk of major depressive episodes (Dohrenwend et al., 1995), but there is some evidence that events dependent on personal characteristics are particularly likely to provoke depression (Kendler et al., 1999). Hammen (1995), for example, found that conflict and negative interpersonal events were prominent precipitants of depression in women. Of course vulnerability factors such as low self-esteem and lack of social support are intrinsically intertwined with personal characteristics that may contribute to provoking stress.

The genetic basis of depression is well established (Hyman & Nestler, 1993), but it is noteworthy that genetic factors contribute not only to mood vulnerability but also to stress exposure and social support. Kendler and colleagues (Kendler et al., 1999) conducted a twin study to tease apart the role of genetic factors and stressful life events to depressive episodes. They found that part of the relationship between stressful life events and depressive episodes is mediated by genetic risk. The authors interpreted this finding to indicate that genetically influenced traits, such as difficult temperament, contribute to exposure to stressful events that are dependent on individual characteristics.

Chronic stress and the conservation–withdrawal reaction

Depressed clients with trauma-related disturbance readily identify with the notion that depression is akin to mental and physical exhaustion as a consequence of being burned out by accumulated stress. Consider Darwin's perspective that fear eventuates in 'helpless prostration' in light of the relentless internal assault of intrusive symptoms on top of a potential pile-up of external stressors. Extensive evidence indicates that chronic stress contributes to dysregulation of the HPA axis and the syndrome of depression (Chrousos & Gold, 1992; Hyman & Nestler, 1993). As research on learned helplessness attests, chronic stress produces depression-like symptoms in animals as well as humans. Bedi (1999), for example, reviewed evidence that 'in rats and mice, chronic exposure to uncontrollable distressful stimuli decreases hedonic responsiveness, escape performance, appetitive response, sexual behaviour and body weight and also results in sleep disturbances—symptoms quite similar to those of human depression' (p. 227).

In educating clients, I convey there is some purpose in their depression. I start with the simplest idea—their stress level is intolerable, and depression stops them in their tracks. The body refuses to keep going. They want to crawl into bed and pull the blankets over their head. I describe the protective function of depression in terms of the *conservation–withdrawal reaction*, that is, withdrawal conserves resources in the face of continuing demand. Infancy provides the prototype for the conservation–withdrawal reaction:

> it is possible to postulate that the quiet sleep that occurs with the prolonged continuation of stimulation or the absence of stimulation, i.e., pain, cold, hunger, etc., becomes an identifiable characteristic for the withdrawal reaction and for what will become associated with the affect of depression. (Schmale, 1972, p. 328)

Dubovsky (1997) contrasted the conservation–withdrawal reaction, mediated by the parasympathetic nervous system, with the fight-or-flight response, mediated by the sympathetic nervous system. In his view, the conservation–withdrawal response 'counterbalances the fight–flight response and is also called into play in any situation in which it is necessary to withdraw from a threat that is impossible to overcome, thus conserving energy until the situation changes' (p. 279). Hibernation is an example. Notably, Dubovsky viewed the tonic immobility response discussed in Chapter 7 on dissociation as a part of the conservation–withdrawal mechanism.

The conservation–withdrawal hypothesis is an appealing explanation for the adaptive function of depression. Unfortunately, depression is not particularly adaptive for many of the clients we treat. I tell clients that, if depression enforced rest and recuperation, it might be quite helpful. But most clients suffering from post-traumatic depression cannot rest. The conservation–withdrawal hypothesis is weakened by the common observation that depression is accompanied by hyperarousal (Dubovsky, 1997; Neese, 2000; Sloman, Price, Gilbert, & Gardner, 1994). Much of the time depressed clients are agitated. They cannot relax, and they cannot sleep restfully. This clinical phenomenon is a manifestation of the neurophysiology of depression discussed earlier; depression is a high-stress state. Furthermore, sleep disturbance is common to PTSD and depression. Hence post-traumatic depression is an example of the conservation–withdrawal reaction gone awry. Nonetheless the conservation–withdrawal hypothesis provides a rationale for encouraging clients to rest to the extent possible. Many feel guilty for trying to do so.

DEPRESSION AS INTERPERSONAL IMBALANCE

Therapists should readily agree with depressed clients who assert that they have a 'chemical imbalance.' But, intertwined with this chemical imbalance is a profound *interpersonal imbalance*. The conservation–withdrawal hypothesis addresses the potentially protective function of depression from a physiological perspective. A deeper look into the evolution of depression requires an interpersonal perspective.

Intermousal trauma

Although Seligman's (1975) work demonstrates that depressive states are not unique to humans, the use of electric shock as a model of trauma lacks a naturalistic ring. Consider instead a prototype of interpersonal trauma in mice (Kudryavtseva & Avgustinovich, 1998). Researchers exposed mice to varying numbers of social defeats. They allowed pairs of mice to interact aggressively, finding invariably that one would come out the winner and the other the loser. On successive days, they intermingled members of various pairs, consistently pitting losing members against winning members.

In the early stages of social confrontation, active defense predominated in the behavior of losers. After repeated defeat, however, active defense gave way to passivity. The repeatedly defeated mice no longer showed any aggression. They became submissive to the point of immobility (e.g., freezing or lying on their back). The defeated mice eventually adopted a submissive stance even in the absence of attacks by the opponent. Even when they were safe, they showed decreased exploratory behavior and lessened social interaction as well as generalized motor retardation. These depressive behaviors were associated with altered physiology (e.g., higher cortisol levels, immune deficiency, gastric mucosa damage, and weight loss). As in humans, the depressive symptoms were intermingled with anxiety symptoms, the latter manifested by increased alcohol consumption—not just a human proclivity. Depressive and anxiety symptoms in the mice were responsive to antidepressant treatment. Notably, this syndrome was evident in a strain of mice with a hereditary disposition to depressive-like states, whereas repeated social defeat was associated with more active defense in a different strain. Hence the animal model also follows the human findings in showing evidence of a genetic predisposition to depressive coping with defeat. The authors summarized the factors that produced the anxious–depressed state in mice: repeated social defeat, lack of social success, chronic negative emotion, and submissiveness. The parallels to interpersonal trauma are unmistakable.

The adaptive function of surrender

Gilbert, Price, and colleagues (Gilbert, 1992; Price, Sloman, Gardner, Gilbert, & Rhode, 1994; Sloman et al., 1994) developed an evolutionary theory of depression that applies directly to interpersonal trauma. From their perspective, depression is an *involuntary subordinate strategy* (Price et al., 1994) that has three adaptive functions: it inhibits aggression, communicates that the individual poses no threat, and facilitates a state of mind conducive to yielding and giving up. Depression signals, 'I am out of action' (Gilbert, 1992, p. 473). This involuntary subordinate strategy protects the individual by de-escalating conflict and aggression. As Sloman and colleagues (Sloman et al., 1994) put it, 'inhibition of self-assertion is at the core of the depressed state' (p. 402). Especially important is the inhibition of up-hierarchy aggression, where the individual is engaged in a confrontation with someone who is more powerful. This dyadic imbalance is intrinsic to attachment trauma, where an abused child is subordinate to a parent, or a battered woman is subordinate to her physically stronger partner.

Gilbert (1992) proposed that dominance hierarchies, with stable rankings of individuals in a group, evolved to minimize aggression. In such a social system, you know your place and—to some degree—stay there. The alternative is continual conflict and confrontation over resources. From the perspective of the involuntary subordinate strategy, an extraordinary range of interpersonal stressors can provoke depression. Low rank is associated with depression (i.e., an inhibition of self-assertion). Feelings of inferiority and low self-esteem often go with low rank. Loss of status is depressing. Put downs are depressing. Being threatened is depressing. Being humiliated is depressing. Above all, being overpowered, trapped, and defeated is depressing. Often entrapment or blocked escape is associated with uncontrollable closeness to a dominant individual. As Gilbert explicated, the interpersonal imbalance associated with involuntary subordinate status is also replicated internally, for example, in the form of a self-abusive internal dialogue that maintains a feeling of inferiority and subordination. As traumatized clients' self-descriptions presented in Chapter 4 attest, depressive ideation perpetuates a sense of being overpowered and defeated.

As the hypothesis of an involuntary subordinate strategy makes plain, *the main axis of depression is power*. Power is also the main dimension of interpersonal trauma. But power (and access to social and material resources) is intertwined with another axis of depression, belonging (Gilbert, 1992). Being in the in-group confers a sense of safety and of success, and the individual's degree of similarity to others is a key to rank and popularity. Persons who are depressed invariably see themselves as different. Feeling excluded—and being excluded—are depressing insofar as they constitute a lowering of status as well as decreased access to resources and help. Thus neglect, along with active abuse, reinforces the sense of inferiority and unworthiness.

This evolutionary perspective places anger and aggression in the forefront of depression, albeit by way of inhibition. As Gilbert (1992) argued, there are wide individual differences among depressed clients in the extent to which they feel and express anger. For many traumatized persons, not only behaving aggressively but also feeling anger has been dangerous. Some individuals have no awareness of their anger. Others contend with conscious anger and resentment, which they are loath to express. Still others struggle with angry outbursts. Because up-hierarchy aggression is likely to be dangerous, aggression is likely to be directed toward subordinates (e.g., children or others perceived to be lower in status). Plainly, the view of oneself as subordinate also is compatible with self-directed aggression.

The *involuntary* aspect of the involuntary subordinate strategy bears emphasizing. As Gilbert (1992) stated, the individual 'does not wish to be depressed but biologically the programme is up and running, the response rule is activated. Furthermore, in nonverbal animals these response rules and algorithms convey their instructions by changing the biological state of the organism' (p. 174). Voluntary submission and acceptance of defeat—giving in gracefully—can be adaptive without entailing depression. Depression is involuntary. The biological changes that underline motor retardation and lack of energy facilitate inhibition of potentially dangerous confrontation and aggression. Low self-esteem and negative cognitions also reinforce subordinate status. As Sloman and colleagues (Sloman et al., 1994) summarized: 'the depressed person is stuck in the [involuntary subordinate strategy]—expressed by a sense of personal failure, inferiority, inability, powerlessness, and hopelessness' (p. 405).

Gilbert (1992) also emphasized the close tie between depression and lack of safety. We saw in Chapter 3 how lack of safety associated with insecure attachment inhibits exploration. Active exploratory behavior puts the subordinate individual at risk for the aggressive attentions of the dominant individual. Consistent with the learned-helplessness model, the depressive retreat blocks new learning. Thus, while sympathizing with the plight of depressed clients, we should not give undue emphasis to the adaptive functions of their depression. Gilbert (1992) put it well:

> Maybe, in earlier evolutionary times depression was a self-protective response, but today when so much depends on self-presentation and the ability to maintain a flow in positively rewarding interactions and exchanges of reassurance signals, the depressed position of being 'out of action' often leads to further loss of support and help. . . . depression should not be glorified. Its consequences can often be serious not only to self but also to other family members (e.g., children). (pp. 473–474)

Dissociation, depression, and passivity

We examined dissociation from an evolutionary standpoint in Chapter 7, and we have just considered depression from a similar point of view. Both dissociation and depression entail passive surrender. I find it hard to avoid the conclusion that post-traumatic dissociation and depression are overlapping pathways to the same destination. The dissociative pathway entails an alteration of consciousness, whereas the depressive pathway entails an alteration of mood. In conducting diagnostic evaluations of severely depressed clients who dissociate, I often find it difficult to distinguish between the two symptoms. The client is completely lacking in vitality, feeling numb and dead. Is this dissociation, depression, or both?

Krystal (1988) viewed the catatonoid (dissociative) reaction as a 'primal depression' (p. 158). Consider the learned helplessness of depression in light of Krystal's view of trauma:

> *Catastrophic psychic trauma* is defined as a *surrender to what is experienced as unavoidable danger of external or internal origin*. It is the psychic reality of this surrender to what one experiences as an unbearable situation with no escape, no exit, that causes one to give up and abandon life-preserving activity. (p. 154)

Under the rubric of primal depression, Krystal continued in the same vein:

> Having *experienced* its own mortality and helplessness, no living creature is quite the same again. The reconstruction of one's feeling of security, or even faith, is never again complete. It is as if the encounter had provided a black background upon which the rest of one's life will be painted. Never again can one diminish the dark hues in one's emotional palette. (p. 158)

From an evolutionary standpoint, dissociation and depression deter further attack. Dissociative alterations of consciousness and the accompanying analgesia also serve to protect the individual in the throes of attack. In the worst-case scenario, as Krystal (1988) speculated, dissociative analgesia provides for a merciful, painless death. As dissociation abets detachment and thereby alleviates emotional physical pain, depression abets retreat and withdrawal, and thereby averts further assault.

The phenomenon I wish to underscore here, which I will amplify in the next chapter on personality disorder, is the *passivity* in dissociation and depression. As the learned-helplessness literature attests, passivity is among the greatest obstacles to change.

Alternatives to surrender

As Sloman and colleagues (Sloman et al., 1994) indicated, the evolutionary perspective can be helpful in allowing clients to appreciate the adaptive basis of their depression. Self-blame for depression can be countered with the view that depression is a naturally protective way of coping with feeling overpowered. Like Dubovsky (1997), Price and colleagues (Price et al., 1994) proposed the analogy of hibernation, for example, explaining to clients that 'depression is nature's way of helping certain humans to survive unfavourable social conditions' (p. 314). As they pointed out, the analogy 'is often acceptable to depressed clients, who may themselves feel like curling up into a ball in a hole in the ground and staying there for a long time' (p. 314).

Yet we therapists must help clients move from their depressive retreat back to active coping. Sloman and colleagues delineated five options to involuntary subordination: conflict resolution by reconciliation, winning the conflict (e.g., by increased assertiveness), voluntary yielding, leaving the arena, and reassessment of the value of the resource. This is the territory of interpersonal and cognitive therapies.

Zetzel (1965) also addressed the links between helplessness and depression in post-traumatic states. She, too, recognized the role of passivity in depression. But, with an eye toward recovery, she examined the adaptive function of depression *tolerance*. She viewed depression as a 'prerequisite for optimal maturation' (p. 248). Construing depression as a natural response to loss, disappointment, and frustration, Zetzel pointed out how tolerating depression is crucial in the process of accepting the limitations of the self and reality. To overcome depression, however, the acceptance of limitations must give way to adaptive action: 'passive acceptance must be followed by the active mastery which facilitates the development of object relations, learning, and ultimately the capacity for happiness' (p. 273). As all who have treated clients with post-traumatic depression well know, this is a tall order.

TRAUMA AND BIPOLAR DISORDER

When clients ask how their manic episodes relate to trauma, I respond with a disclaimer that this is relatively unexplored territory in the research literature. I know of no research indicating a role for trauma in the etiology of bipolar disorder. There is evidence, however, of greater overlap between bipolar disorder and PTSD than would be expected if these were unrelated disorders. Kessler and colleagues (Kessler et al., 1995), for example, found mania to be far more common in persons with PTSD than in those without (12% versus 1% for men and 6% versus 1% for women). Conversely, Mueser and colleagues (Mueser et al., 1998) found that 40% of patients with bipolar disorder had a history of PTSD.

Although we do not know the role of trauma and PTSD, if any, in the *etiology* of bipolar disorder, I find it plausible that trauma and PTSD play a role in the *course* of the disorder. Trauma and PTSD are associated with a process of sensitization that results in increased stress vulnerability. Like depressive episodes, manic episodes are often precipitated by stressful life events (Hammen & Gitlin, 1997; Johnson & Roberts, 1995). Hence, for patients with bipolar disorder who have a history of trauma and stress sensitization, one manifestation of their vulnerability might be mood episodes. As stressors, PTSD symptoms might also contribute to manic episodes.

Furthermore, many stressors that impinge on clients with bipolar disorders are partly or entirely dependent on the person, and many of these person-dependent stressors are interpersonal. Patients with bipolar disorder in my educational groups readily give examples of extreme stress and interpersonal conflicts resulting from their impulsive manic behavior. This is fertile soil for vicious circles. A potentially wide range of trauma-related interpersonal problems—not least of which is ongoing abuse—may contribute to manic episodes in clients with bipolar disorder, and these episodes compound the pile-up of stress.

EDUCATING CLIENTS ABOUT THE CATCH-22S OF DEPRESSION

In discussing the relation between stress and depression with clients, I use the same model developed to explain the course of PTSD (see Figure 5.1). I point out that many persons with a history of childhood trauma do well in adulthood—often for long periods of time. Yet stress accumulates. Most clients are keenly aware of the discrete stressors—life events—that precipitated their depression. Sometimes these life events are directly related to previous trauma, for example, when an assault awakens memories of childhood physical abuse. Sometimes the connection is more opaque, for example, when an automobile accident awakens memories of childhood abuse. Of course any uncontrollable stressor that renders the individual helpless has an intrinsic connection to childhood trauma. I point out that a chronically stressful lifestyle may underlie the discrete life events (e.g., overwork, compulsive caregiving, chronic interpersonal conflicts, or living in an unsafe environment). Not uncommonly, immersion in a wide range of stressful activities or relationships serves a defensive function; it is distracting, keeping the person's mind off past trauma. Yet the pile-up of discrete stressful life events on top of severe chronic stress ultimately becomes unbearable, and depression intervenes.

Before discussing ways of overcoming depression, I draw clients' attention to its adaptive value. They have felt overwhelmed by stressors, conflicts, and seemingly impossible situations. Depression stops them from running themselves further into the ground, as the conservation–withdrawal hypothesis would have it; and depression prevents them from engaging in losing battles, as the involuntary subordinate strategy would have it. More broadly, as Neese (2000) documented, depression potentially helps individuals disengage from unproductive or futile efforts. More specifically, depression serves to 'inhibit dangerous or wasteful actions in situations characterized by committed pursuit of an unreachable goal, temptations to challenge authority, insufficient internal reserves to allow action without damage, or lack of a viable life strategy' (Neese, 2000, p. 18). At best the depressive retreat from futile efforts at coping can set the stage for taking stock, rethinking goals, and redirecting one's efforts. Paradoxically, depressed mood also interferes with disengaging from unreachable goals and with adopting more effective strategies. While stopped, the depressed person is *stuck*.

Having delineated how and why clients get into depression, we come to the hard problem—how they can get out of it. When discussing the treatment of depression with traumatized clients, I indicate that they probably have received some or all of the following advice: 'have fun,' 'be active,' 'socialize,' 'think positively,' and 'decrease your stress.' I go through this list quickly so I can finish before clients start tuning me out, leaving the room, or glaring angrily at me. I quickly interject that, although this is good advice, depression undermines their capacity to follow it. And they are not just dealing with major depression; they are dealing with fear and post-traumatic depression, which compound the difficulty in doing what is needed for recovery. Next to each bit of good advice, I list a symptom or consequence of depression (see Table 9.1).

Once I have made it clear that I understand these catch-22s, clients begin to listen. This is an important discussion, because recovery from depression entails following some or all of this advice. I walk a fine line in presenting these catch-22s. I do not want to abet the client's sense of hopelessness. I convey that it is *difficult* to get out of severe depression, but it is not *impossible*. Traumatized clients *do* recover from severe depression. But recovery is not easy, and it is not quick.

Helping clients understand why recovery is so difficult promotes hope rather than hopelessness. Clients feel helpless partly because of their failure to do as others imply or implore: 'If you'd just . . . [have fun, get out more, exercise, etc.] . . . you would snap out of it!' I point out that, undoubtedly, they

Table 9.1 The catch-22s of depression

Good advice	Consequences of depression
Have fun	Diminished capacity for pleasure
Be active	Low energy
Socialize	Tendency to withdraw and isolate
Think positively	Negative thinking
Reduce stress	Stressful consequences

have been trying to do some or all of these things, but depression interferes with their efforts. They might adopt a more compassionate attitude toward their struggles if they understand the paradoxes in recovering from depression. To the extent that they are able to understand that there are good reasons for their difficulty, and they can develop realistic expectations regarding the challenges they face, clients feel relieved rather than more hopeless.

Unfortunately, because of the catch-22s, there is no way around having to force oneself out of depression. Understandably, depressed clients resent others' pressure to make this effort. They are told, 'Pull yourself up by your bootstraps!' 'Fake it till you make it!' They must row upstream to summon motivation, willpower, and hope. To avoid evoking their ire, we therapists must balance encouragement to make the effort to overcome depression with empathy for the difficulty in doing so. I review the challenges one by one.

Have fun

One of the most straightforward approaches to treatment is to view depression as reflecting a lack of response-contingent positive reinforcement and to encourage the client to engage in behaviors that increase the level of reinforcement (Lewinsohn, 1974). This is sound advice based on empirical evidence, but it is hard to implement. One of the core DSM-IV (APA, 1994) symptoms of a major depressive episode is 'markedly diminished interest or pleasure in all, or almost all, activities most of the day, nearly every day' (p. 327). This criterion is consistent with extensive personality research indicating that the *absence of positive affect is a distinctive feature of depression* (Clark, Watson, & Mineka, 1994; Watson, 2000). Moreover, just as depression is not conducive to pleasure, neither is post-traumatic fear.

To underscore the point that depression undermines the capacity for pleasure, I suggest to clients that the 'pleasure circuits' in the brain may not be working properly in post-traumatic depression. This view is based on evidence from animal models that uncontrollable stress is associated with decreases in dopaminergic transmission that interfere with brain reward mechanisms (Cabib & Puglisi-Allegra, 1996). Human studies also demonstrate a relation between positive emotionality and dopaminergic function (Depue, Luciana, Arbisi, Collins, & Leon, 1994), and Watson (2000) commented in this connection that genetic factors may contribute to diminished amounts of 'cerebral joy juice' (p. 228).

Thus, when depressed clients follow the advice to go out and have fun, they are liable to fail and then to feel even more inadequate and depressed. When they understand that depressive states, fear, and the capacity for pleasure run directly counter to each other, they are more likely to be tolerant of their difficulty in following the advice. Fortunately, this is not an all-or-nothing situation. Many clients will have a *diminished* capacity for pleasure rather than none at all. I encourage them to go slowly, suggesting that, as they improve, they might notice some interest or pleasure returning. I caution them that feelings of pleasure may not last and may be only intermittent. Some clients who discover that they begin to gain pleasure from an activity will then pursue the activity so desperately as an antidepressant that they soon tire of it or wear themselves out. I counsel patience and emphasize that change will be gradual.

Be active

Encouraging clients to be active is good advice. There is evidence, for example, that exercise can serve as an antidepressant (Dunn & Dishman, 1991; Sime, 1984), for example, by enhancing positive mood (Watson, 2000). Among the diagnostic criteria for major depressive episode, however, are 'fatigue or loss of energy nearly every day' (APA, 1994, p. 327) as well as psychomotor retardation. Consistent with these criteria, Watson and Clark (Watson, 2000; Watson & Clark, 1997) have demonstrated that decreased activity is part and parcel of the core dimension of depression, absence of positive affect. Moreover, the lack of a sense of safety that accompanies posttraumatic depression runs counter to exploratory activity and the active engagement with the environment essential to boosting mood.

We can only respect the challenge of this catch-22. Clients can best be encouraged gradually to be more active, as well as cautioned that if they push themselves too hard, they may only feel more exhausted, and the whole effort may backfire. Encouraged to do so in psychoeducational groups, many clients can give concrete examples of their gradual, step-by-step return to a more active life. One client described how an important step in recovery from depression was giving himself credit for getting out of bed, getting dressed, and getting something to eat. To reiterate, my main point is not to encourage the obvious, but rather to help clients understand why the obvious is so challenging.

Socialize

Encouraging clients to socialize is among the more complex and challenging prescriptions for depression. Clients are often admonished, 'Don't isolate.' This good advice goes against the grain. Fears and distrust associated with interpersonal trauma often contribute to a general propensity toward isolation. On top of this, interpersonal stress is a common precipitant of depressive episodes. Interpersonal conflict, disappointment, and a sense of social defeat propel clients into depression. Furthermore a disinclination to interact with others is part and parcel of the 'markedly diminished interest or pleasure' associated with depression. As Watson and Clark (Watson, 2000; Watson & Clark, 1997) have demonstrated, our capacity for positive affect is a core facet of a constellation of behaviors that involve extraversion (gregariousness and affiliation) as well as a more generalized propensity to be actively engaged in goal-oriented behavior. Active engagement with other persons enhances positive mood; it is an antidepressant. Yet depression undercuts the motivation for social behavior as well as other goal-directed behavior (e.g., work).

Social encounters are also fraught with vicious circles for depressed persons. Already feeling defeated, inferior, and excluded, they are likely to encounter further rejection as a consequence of their depression. *Their feelings of inadequacy and rejection are unlikely to be based solely on cognitive distortions.* To the extent that depression is contagious (Hatfield, Cacioppo, & Rapson, 1993), contact with depressed persons will be aversive to others. Several authors have reviewed research documenting that rejection is associated with the depressed person's impaired social skills (Gilbert, 1992; Lewinsohn, 1974; Segrin & Abramson, 1994). Segrin and Abramson (1994) attribute the rejection to several facets of depressed behavior. Humans and other animals have a preference for responsiveness in others, and depressed persons are strikingly unresponsive in many respects. They speak relatively little; their speech is hesitant and slow; and their voice is quiet and monotonous. They engage in less eye contact, and their facial expressions and gestures are less animated. In addition, depressed persons do not follow the rules of conventional politeness. For example, they are prone to focus on their own negative experience; they do not show interest in others; and they may be critical of others. Failure to attend to their appearance also elicits rejection. Finally others' feelings of responsibility and obligation engendered by depression may prompt them to withdraw.

Although the interpersonal perils of depression are evident even in interactions with strangers or acquaintances, they are even more pronounced in intimate relationships. As Coyne (1990) documented, marital conflict is prominent in persons with depression. These conflicts can be precipitants of depression as well as being exacerbated by depressive states. Coyne observed that 'Spouses may have precipitated many of the difficulties of depressed persons, and they may be actively involved in their perpetuation' (p. 43). For example, depressive behavior elicits criticism, and criticism is predictive of relapse. And the depression, which may be shared by both persons, plays a part in the vicious circles:

> depressed persons and their spouses may be involved in a cycle in which their unsuccessful efforts to resolve differences lead to withdrawal and avoidance and to negative affect, mistrust, and misgivings about each other. The accumulated effect of such interactions is to overwhelm the couple when they again attempt to settle specific differences, increasing their hopelessness about the possibility of improving their relationship. (pp. 42–43)

Coyne concluded that depression 'is more frequently a refractory problem than has been assumed' (p. 47), and there is ample recent evidence for this assertion (Akiskal & Cassano, 1997).

Keep in mind that these sobering accounts of interpersonal problems pertain to depression in general rather than post-traumatic depression in particular. Interpersonal stress can be far more extreme in the context of traumatic reenactments, and clients who have experienced attachment trauma are often pervasively distrusting. It is little wonder that the admonishment, 'Don't isolate!' may fall on deaf ears.

To reiterate, we can only respect the challenges that clients face in overcoming the obstacles to obtaining the social support they desperately need. Therapists should not automatically attribute clients' experience of rejection to cognitive distortions, although such distortions certainly make matters worse. Acknowledging that depression elicits rejection validates clients' perceptions. Pointing out the behaviors inherent in depression that others find aversive can draw clients' attention to their contributions to interaction difficulties in a non-judgmental fashion. Perhaps most useful is recognizing that their tolerance for interpersonal contact may be relatively low, and they may need to go slowly. I refer to the dangers of 'social overdoses.' For example, when depressed clients join a party of fun-loving people, they may feel only more alienated and depressed as a result. Contact with cheerful individuals is liable to be distressing, particularly if these individuals expect responsiveness and admonish the client to 'buck up' in some way or other. Not surprisingly, depressed persons are drawn to each other, but they run the risk that mutual contagion will plunge them further into depression. I advise clients to seek support from persons with whom they have some common ground that promotes understanding. Often clients will find such common ground with other persons who have struggled with depression, but the key point is finding persons who have a high *tolerance* for depression. Easier said than done.

Think positively

Perhaps the most global obstacle to thinking positively is the criterion 'diminished ability to think or concentrate' (APA, 1994, p. 327). A client in a psychoeducational group, for example, had a highly aversive reaction to a discussion of depression. She became progressively more distressed as the group went on and, when asked about the basis of her distress, she said that she could not grasp any of the discussion. She could not concentrate well enough to follow the train of thought. She was too overwhelmed to *think* about coping, much less to *engage* in any coping.

Of course, to the extent that depressed clients are able to think, they are likely to focus exclusively on negatives. Having positive thoughts about oneself goes directly counter to the DSM criterion, 'feelings of worthlessness.' More generally, depressed persons expect negative outcomes and believe that they have no control over these outcomes (Weary & Gannon, 1996). Accordingly, as Neese (2000) put it, the core challenge of cognitive therapy is 'increasing the person's expectations of the effectiveness of future actions' (p. 18).

In attempting to help clients shift their beliefs, however, therapists are liable to encounter another catch-22. Despite its demonstrable efficacy (Craighead, Craighead, & Ilardi, 1998; Roth & Fonagy, 1996), I find that many clients are antagonistic toward cognitive therapy, in part because they feel criticized for thinking negatively. This is quite a tangle. Clients' antagonistic reactions are especially likely in response to a naïve approach to cognitive therapy that focuses narrowly on errors in thinking—as if bad logic were to blame for depression. As Gilbert (1992) commented, 'in the hands of less skilled therapists, a "cognitive errors therapy" can be easily turned into an "it's your fault" approach' (p. 411). Feelings of inferiority are not entirely based on cognitive distortions. Depression is unattractive to others, and the depressed person encounters overt or covert rejection.

Furthermore, we should question the extent to which negative thinking precipitates depression. Brown (1998), for example, stated, 'Psychological research on depression has tended to place particular emphasis on the inappropriateness of negative cognitive sets. By contrast, I would emphasize their appropriateness and how such cognitions may be fully understandable in light of the person's current milieu' (p. 367). Low self-esteem is indeed a vulnerability factor for depression, but Brown pointed out how negative self-evaluations may well reflect realistic doubts about the person's ability to deal effectively with the consequences and implications of severe life events that precipitated depression. In a similar vein, Gilbert (1992) commented,

> A too liberal use of the dictum, 'It is not things in themselves that disturb us but the view that we take of them' is plainly wrong. What little we do know about the development of the nervous system suggests that (in the main) some negative life events and early experience that deviate from innate needs nearly always cause subsequent disturbance and this is true whether we look at animals or humans. (p. 412)

We face a chicken-and-egg problem in relating negative thinking to depression. If one implies that negative thinking causes depression, clients can feel blamed in that way. Notably, the progenitor of cognitive therapy, Beck (1991), pointed out that it is

> far-fetched to assign a causal role to cognitions because the negative automatic thoughts constitute an integral part of depression, just like the motivational, affective, and behavioral symptoms. To conclude that cognitions cause depression is analogous to asserting that delusions cause schizophrenia. (p. 371)

Nevertheless, by any account, the meaning (interpretation) of life events plays a prominent role in the depressive outcome (Brown, 1998). Yet Segal and colleagues (Segal et al., 1996) emphasize the triggering of negative thinking by dysphoric mood as opposed to the reverse. They argue that, as 'mood becomes more depressed, these dormant dysfunctional sets of cognitive biases become more active' (p. 376). Even if they do not cause or even trigger depressive episodes, negative cognitions contribute to the escalation and perpetuation of depression, once set in motion. As Segal and colleagues (Segal et al., 1996) stated,

> In depression, negative concepts and negative events are rehearsed, leading to an extensive elaboration of related mnemonic structures highly interconnected with depression. . . . This structure, which could alternatively be described as a 'depression schema', ties together the associated items so closely that experiencing the emotion in a variety of contexts may serve to activate the entire structure, and to call to mind notions of self-denigration, profound loss, and other cognitions commonly found in depression. . . . the increased activation of negative constructs in negative mood can lead to a 'downward spiral' of depression in vulnerable individuals, magnifying slight negative moods into persistent depressive feelings. (pp. 374–375)

When teaching groups of clients about these problems with depression, I often inquire as to how many have had experience with cognitive therapy and how helpful they have found it to be. There is considerable variability among clients, with attitudes ranging from highly positive to highly negative—just as it is with many different forms of treatment. Like any other form of therapy, cognitive therapy can be done well or poorly. I discuss negative thinking with depressed clients as akin to 'kicking yourself while you are down.' While recognizing the value of cognitive therapy, I also underscore the dangers of believing that they should succeed easily in changing their thinking and then feeling like a failure after finding it to be so difficult. Having many substantially positive thoughts may be quite unrealistic for many clients with post-traumatic depression. Rather, I emphasize gaining awareness of negative thinking and questioning negative assumptions rather than 'thinking positively.' Gilbert (1992) put it well:

> cognitive therapy . . . is not about 'retraining' in the sense that one might teach a dog new tricks. It is rather engaging with a person's internal constructions and meaning-making processes and helping them to explore alternatives, to treat beliefs as hypotheses and to test out ideas; to understand the relationship between thoughts (inner constructions and feelings and behaviour); and to acquire new skills. (p. 384)

Reduce stress

Depression, like PTSD and a host of other psychiatric disorders, is a reflection of stress vulnerability. Stress not only triggers depressive episodes but also maintains depressed states. Furthermore, depression is a high-stress state—conservation–withdrawal notwithstanding. Stress is evident in the physiology of depression, and it is evident in the typical intermingling of anxiety and fear with depression (Watson, 2000)—especially when depression is intertwined with PTSD.

Moreover, in addition to being a reaction to stressful life events, severe depression brings on additional negative life events (e.g., need for hospitalization, loss of a job, or breakup of a relationship). Suicidal behavior contributes to especially severe interpersonal conflicts, often in the form of vicious circles discussed in Chapter 8. That is, suicidal behavior frightens and angers persons who are in a position to support depressed clients, and the alienation that suicidal behavior evokes promotes rejection and distancing. This rejection often adds additional fuel to the feelings of abandonment and neglect that initiated the suicidal state.

Of all the catch-22s of depression, reducing stress may be the most important and the most difficult. I will discuss stress management in detail in Chapter 11, where we will also confront a number of paradoxes. Reducing stress, simple as it may sound, entails the whole of trauma treatment. Reducing stress requires reducing PTSD. It requires reducing all the destructive symptoms discussed thus far, particularly insofar as these symptoms exacerbate interpersonal conflict. And, above all, reducing stress requires developing more stable and secure attachments. To conclude with yet another challenge, developing secure attachments is complicated by the common problem of trauma-related personality disorders, the subject of the next chapter.

Chapter 10

POST-TRAUMATIC PERSONALITY DISORDERS

> Most people have no knowledge or understanding of the psychological changes of captivity. Social judgment of chronically traumatized people therefore tends to be extremely harsh. The chronically abused person's apparent helplessness and passivity, her entrapment in the past, her intractable depression and somatic complaints, and her smoldering anger often frustrate the people closest to her. (Herman, 1992b, p. 115)

Imagine hearing that you have a 'personality disorder.' You are 'borderline.' You have 'personality disorder not otherwise specified.' Debates in the professional literature attest to the challenges we therapists face in understanding these disorders, and explaining them to clients is no easy matter. Personality disorders are not easy to diagnose. Nor are they easily disentangled from myriad other psychopathological effects of interpersonal trauma discussed throughout this book. We are not dealing with transient problems and acute disorders but rather with chronic and recurrent problems that affect the whole person.

This chapter reexamines much of the material from earlier chapters from the perspective of personality disorders. This reexamination is important, because diagnosing personality disorders in the context of interpersonal trauma is controversial. Yet it is through its enduring impact on personality functioning that attachment trauma poses the greatest treatment challenges. For example, depressive episodes are often occasioned by stressful life events. Many such stressful events are interpersonal. And the individual's problematic interpersonal behavior plays a role in many of these interpersonal stressors. Hence the presence of personality disorder dramatically increases the risk of relapse in clients hospitalized for depression (Ilardi,

Craighead, & Evans, 1997). PTSD symptoms also may be exacerbated by interpersonal reenactments. Moreover personality disturbance indicative of impaired capacity for interpersonal relationships is associated with chronic post-traumatic symptoms after rape (Regehr & Marziali, 1999). As these examples illustrate, clinicians cannot ignore the personality disorder component of post-traumatic psychopathology, because personality disorders adversely affect the treatment of Axis I disorders (Target, 1998).

DSM-IV (APA, 1994) defines personality disorder broadly as an 'enduring pattern of inner experience and behavior that deviates markedly from the experience of the individual's culture, is pervasive and inflexible, has an onset in adolescence or early adulthood, is stable over time, and leads to distress or impairment' (p. 629). A number of authors focus on impaired interpersonal functioning (Parker & Barrett, 2000). Rutter (1987), for example, advocated an overarching view of personality disorder as a 'a persistent, pervasive abnormality in social relationships and social functioning generally' (p. 454). Researchers also focus on interpersonal disturbance in the psychometric assessment of personality disorders (Horowitz, Rosenberg, Baer, Ureno, & Villasenor, 1988; Kim, Pilkonis, & Barkham, 1997; Pilkonis, Kim, Proietti, & Barkham, 1996).

Is it possible to carve out discrete disorders from the broad territory of chronic difficulties in interpersonal relationships? DSM-IV certainly requires therapists to do so, but consensus is not easy to achieve. Although clinicians can agree relatively well on whether or not an individual has personality disorder, the reliability for discrete disorders is relatively poor, and different diagnostic methods do not yield comparable results (Bronisch & Mombour, 1998; Oldham et al., 1992). Moreover, there is extensive overlap among the ostensibly discrete categories. Using structured diagnostic interviews, Oldham and colleagues (Oldham et al., 1992) found that personality-disordered patients met criteria for an average of 3.4 different personality disorders. They argued for a two-level diagnostic system, recommending that specific personality disorders be diagnosed for patients who meet criteria for one or two categories and that a diagnosis of *extensive personality disorder* be made for those meeting criteria for multiple categories. Complicating matters further, the various personality disorders differ considerably in their breadth, for example, with borderline being relatively broad and obsessive-compulsive relatively narrow (Livesley, Jackson, & Schroeder, 1992).

Millon (1996) construed the discrete personality disorders as prototypes, recognizing that these ideal types are rarely seen in isolation from one another. The intermingling of characteristics from different prototypical personality disorders yields more individualized subtypes. One personality disorder may lend coloring to another as, for example, the tenor of narcissistic personality disorder may be altered substantially by the influence of histrionic, avoidant, or antisocial features. Recognizing empirical overlap among discrete disorders, DSM-IV groups them into three clusters. Cluster A, *odd or eccentric,* includes paranoid, schizoid, and schizotypal personality disorders; cluster B, *dramatic, emotional, or erratic,* includes antisocial, borderline, histrionic, and narcissistic personality disorders; and cluster C, *anxious or fearful,* includes avoidant, dependent, and obsessive-compulsive personality disorders. Yet whether assessed by structured interview (Oldham et al., 1992) or psychometric testing (Allen, Huntoon, & Evans, 1999a), individuals with extensive personality disturbance are likely to have disorders that cut across these clusters.

Should clinicians think in terms of discrete personality disorder categories or in terms of dimensions of personality disturbance with all shades of gray? From the most global dimensional perspective, I think in terms of *personality disorderedness* rather than personality disorder. Research on personality disorder from a dimensional perspective, however, has gone beyond a global dimension of personality disorderedness by deriving discrete factors from broad-band scales. Livesley and colleagues (Livesley et al., 1992), for example—despite using personality disorder descriptors in their scale—found 15 different dimensions of personality disorderedness that corresponded minimally to the DSM personality disorder categories. Moreover they did not find substantial differences between normal and clinical samples in the organization of personality problems, and there was continuous variability from normal to clinical populations rather than any clear dividing line. Consistent with much other literature (Parker & Barrett, 2000), these findings support a dimensional rather than categorical approach to personality disorders.

At present, we would do well to juggle the dimensional and categorical approaches by preserving a dimensional concept of personality disorderedness while striving to distinguish different forms of chronic difficulties in interpersonal relationships to the extent possible. The Inventory of Interpersonal Problems, for example, can be employed to measure the overall level of interpersonal dysfunction as well as more specific dimensions of disturbance (Kim et al., 1997; Pilkonis et al., 1996). Three subscales compose a measure of overall personality pathology: interpersonal sensitivity (or poor interpersonal boundaries), interpersonal ambivalence, and aggression. Two additional subscales—need for social approval and lack of sociability—show promise in distinguishing cluster C from other personality disorders. Yet the researchers advocated conceptualizing a global dimension of personality pathology in terms of attachment and interpersonal theories:

> The hypothesis is that a good general marker of [personality disorder] is chronic difficulties in interpersonal relationships; these difficulties are often manifested as an inability to develop a balance of attachment and autonomy. In the individual case, this lack of modulation can result in one of two different (skewed) developmental lines: exaggeration of concerns about autonomy, with a relative lack of attachment, or exaggeration of concerns about relatedness, with a relative lack of differentiation. (Kim et al., 1997, p. 293)

We should not be surprised that interpersonal trauma, and attachment trauma in particular, is associated with chronic difficulties in interpersonal relationships. Furthermore, the two broad domains of difficulty—problems with closeness and excessive distance—overlap conceptually with different patterns of insecure adult attachment (i.e., preoccupied versus dismissing and fearful). Most research on the relation between trauma and personality disorder has focused on borderline personality disorder (BPD). This is not unreasonable, inasmuch as BPD is prototypical of personality-based disturbance in relationships. While eschewing trait-defined personality disorders, Rutter (1987) viewed the dramatic cluster (borderline, antisocial, histrionic, and narcissistic) as exemplifying 'pervasive persistent abnormality in maintaining social relationships' (p. 453).

Before delving into the relation between trauma and personality disorder, this chapter examines the argument for diagnosing complex PTSD instead of personality disorder. The chapter reviews how trauma, PTSD, dissociation, and attachment relate to the full array of personality disorders. Although trauma contributes to a wide array of personality disturbances, BPD rightly occupies center stage, because so many facets of BPD pertain directly to the manifestations of trauma examined throughout this book. Nonetheless, after giving BPD its due, the chapter also highlights two other domains of personality disturbance that are highly problematic in clinical work: masochism and alienation. The chapter concludes with some suggestions for discussing personality disorders with clients.

PERSONALITY DISORDER OR COMPLEX PTSD?

Herman (1992a, 1992b) persuasively argued that the panoply of psychopathology frequently observed in the wake of extreme and repeated interpersonal trauma be construed as *complex PTSD*, which includes an array of symptoms along with pervasive personality disturbance. Typical personality disturbance includes pathological changes in relationships (e.g., oscillations between attachment and withdrawal), identity disturbance, and a propensity to experience repeated harm and injury at the hands of oneself and others. This syndrome is most likely to occur in the context of prolonged traumatic experience such as childhood abuse, battering, incarceration, or torture. Herman (1993) proposed that this multifaceted symptomatology and personality disturbance be diagnosed as *disorders of extreme stress not otherwise specified*. Zlotnick and Pearlstein (1997) developed a structured interview to assess cardinal dimensions of this complex psychopathology.

Rather than adding a new diagnostic category, DSM-IV (APA, 1994) included a wide array of symptoms potentially co-occurring with PTSD *as associated descriptive features* and mental disorders These associated features include

impaired affect modulation; self-destructive and impulsive behavior; dissociative symptoms; somatic complaints; feelings of ineffectiveness, shame, despair,
or hopelessness; feeling permanently damaged; a loss of previously sustained
beliefs; hostility; social withdrawal; feeling constantly threatened; impaired
relationships with others; or a change from the individual's previous personality characteristics. (p. 425)

Herman's formulation of complex PTSD and the associated descriptive
features delineated in DSM-IV are consistent with the impact of interpersonal trauma I have reviewed throughout this book. These descriptions
are heavily weighted toward the kinds of personality disturbance that will
be discussed throughout this chapter. The diagnosis of PTSD plainly fails to
capture the impact of repeated interpersonal trauma on symptomatology
and interpersonal functioning (Cloitre et al., 1997). Complex PTSD is apt
shorthand for emphasizing the potential contribution of severe interpersonal
trauma to diverse psychopathology wherein the narrowly defined syndrome
of PTSD may be prominent to varying degrees. Yet complex PTSD is inherently so broad that its diagnostic utility is limited, and there is substantial
heterogeneity within the complex PTSD client population (Allen, Huntoon,
& Evans, 1999a). From the standpoint of aspiring to improve diagnostic pre-
cision, complex PTSD goes in the wrong direction. The concept of personality disorder is murky enough, and combining it with a multiplicity of Axis
I symptoms only makes it more diffuse.

In part, the motivation for proposing that complex PTSD be diagnosed
instead of personality disorder is to avoid blaming the victim (Herman,
1992b) by explicitly acknowledging the traumatic basis of the disturbance.
Therapists should bear in mind, however, that diagnostic categories are not
inherently pejorative; rather, professionals and non-professionals may mis-
understand and misuse them in ways that are damaging. Inasmuch as DSM-
IV has only sanctioned the expansion of the PTSD diagnosis in a most
indirect way (through associated features), we cannot skirt the diagnosis of
personality disorder. Personality disorders require specific treatment and, as
stated earlier, they affect the prognosis for treatment of Axis I disorders. We
cannot ignore them. Moreover, the etiology of personality disorders is
extremely complex, and trauma may contribute to personality disturbance
in various ways and to varying degrees. Hence we must diagnose personality disorders as carefully as possible, and we must tackle the challenge
of explaining them to clients in a way that does not further damage their
self-esteem.

TRAUMA AND PERSONALITY DISORDER

Several studies underscore the lack of selectivity in personality disorders
associated with trauma, indicating a somewhat global relationship between

trauma and personality disorderedness. In a study of combat veterans with a primary diagnosis of PTSD, for example, Southwick and colleagues (Southwick, Yehuda, & Giller, 1993) employed a structured clinical interview to diagnose personality disorders and found several to be frequent: borderline, obsessive-compulsive, avoidant, and paranoid. Moreover, more than one third of the patients met criteria for at least two personality disorders. Modestin and colleagues (Modestin, Oberson, & Erni, 1998) employed structured clinical interviews to assess personality disorders in a mixed-gender sample of inpatients, and they examined the relation between diagnosis and history of childhood trauma. Patients with a diagnosis of any personality disorder were more likely than those without personality disorder to report a history of childhood physical abuse, sexual abuse, or both. Childhood trauma was most strongly associated with paranoid, borderline, dependent, sadistic, and self-defeating personality disorders. Although BPD was the most frequent diagnosis, there were no differences in severity of childhood trauma between clients with a diagnosis of BPD and those with other personality disorder diagnoses.

Our study of psychometric test findings in inpatient women with a history of childhood trauma (Allen et al., 1998a) is consistent with findings from structured clinical interviews. We found elevations on several personality disorder scales, including depressive, self-defeating, avoidant, dependent, and borderline. Findings from studies of combat trauma show a similarly wide array of personality disturbance on testing (Hyer, Brandsma, & Boyd, 1997). Shea and colleagues' (Shea, Zlotnick, & Weisberg, 1999) questionnaire assessment revealed highly similar patterns of personality disorder among female inpatients and outpatients with a history of childhood sexual abuse and male combat veterans with PTSD.

Johnson and colleagues (Johnson, Cohen, Brown, Smailes, & Bernstein, 1999) studied the relation between childhood abuse and neglect documented in an official US state registry and personality disorder in adulthood. Physical abuse was associated with elevated symptoms of antisocial, borderline, dependent, depressive, passive–aggressive, and schizoid personality disorder. Sexual abuse was associated with BPD, and neglect was associated with antisocial, avoidant, borderline, dependent, narcissistic, paranoid, passive–aggressive, and schizotypal personality disorder. Self-reported childhood maltreatment was also associated with a wide array of personality disorders, although the specific patterns of findings differed from those for documented maltreatment. Examining the findings as a whole, the researchers noted that persons with a documented history of childhood maltreatment were four times more likely to have an adulthood personality disorder than those without a trauma history. Although this study had many methodological strengths, it also has some significant limitations (Widom, 1999a), the most notable being the small number of cases of documented maltreatment.

Researchers are a long way from demonstrating that any specific forms of childhood trauma relate to specific types of adulthood psychopathology (Rutter & Maughan, 1997), so we cannot expect much specificity in the relation between trauma and personality disorder. There is a little specificity in the common finding that cluster B personality disorders are associated with childhood trauma (Johnson et al., 1999; Modestin et al., 1998; Wexler, Lyons, Lyons, & Mazure, 1997). More specifically, some studies suggest that childhood trauma relates more strongly to BPD than to other personality disorders. For example, Laporte and Guttman (1996) reviewed records of a large sample of inpatient women and found that, compared with those with another personality disorder diagnosis, clients with BPD had a more severe trauma history (e.g., childhood loss; adoption; multiple foster-home placements; parental divorce or separation; verbal, physical, and sexual abuse; and witnessing domestic violence). The women with BPD were more often verbally and physically abused by their mother, but they were more likely to have been sexually abused by someone outside the immediate family (in contrast to those with other personality disorders, who were more likely to have been abused by their father). Those with BPD were more likely to have experienced multiple abuses by multiple perpetrators and to have been abused by both parents. Sexual abuse, verbal abuse, physical abuse, and being adopted all contributed independently to the likelihood of a BPD diagnosis.

Although Zlotnick's (1999) study of incarcerated women found that childhood abuse was associated with a diagnosis of BPD but not antisocial personality disorder, there is substantial evidence that childhood adversity plays a role in the development of antisocial behavior. Luntz and Widom's (1994) carefully controlled prospective study of individuals with a documented history of childhood maltreatment (abuse, neglect, or both) showed that trauma predicted number of antisocial symptoms and diagnosis of antisocial disorder. Yet Cadoret and colleagues' (Cadoret, Yates, Troughton, Woodworth, & Stewart, 1995) study of adopted offspring of antisocial biologic parents demonstrated that environmental adversity interacts with genetic predisposition in the etiology of adolescent aggressivity and conduct disorder. An adverse adoptive family environment increased the risk of aggressivity and conduct disorder only for offspring of biologic parents with antisocial personality disorder. Underscoring the importance of attachment, the authors concluded, 'The adverse home environment factor described herein as interacting with the biologic background of antisocial personality disorder could have influenced the adoptee through such influences as altered parental affection, availability, and involvement' (p. 923).

Reiss and colleagues' (Reiss et al., 1995) study of same-sex siblings varying in degree of genetic relatedness further clarified the role of family environment in the etiology of adolescent antisocial behavior. While finding evidence for substantial heritability, these researchers demonstrated dramatic effects of non-shared environmental contributions, that is, differential treatment of siblings within families. It was not the general family climate but rather the level of conflict and negativity targeted at the individual child by mothers and fathers that predicted antisocial behavior. More specifically, the authors concluded

> It is not simply aggressiveness or punitiveness by the parent that plays a role, but also the parent's yielding to coercion by the child. Thus, what may lie at the core here is a toxic combination of sustained negative and disruptive affect and inconsistency in parental authority and direction. (p. 933)

Underscoring the role of differential treatment, problematic parenting directed toward one sibling decreased the likelihood of the other sibling's antisocial behavior, an effect the authors termed the 'sibling barricade' (p. 935).

As a number of authors have pointed out (Southwick et al., 1993; Widom, 1999a), finding an association between trauma and personality disorder leaves many etiological questions unanswered. It is often unclear, for example, whether PTSD or personality disorder is primary (Southwick et al., 1993). Personality disturbance such as impulsivity can increase the likelihood of trauma exposure. Thus we should consider *pre*-traumatic personality disorder alongside *post*-traumatic personality disorder. Personality disorder could also render the individual more vulnerable to PTSD in the aftermath of trauma exposure. Moreover, the PTSD syndrome itself may contribute to adverse changes in personality functioning.

Paris (1997, 1998a) argued persuasively that childhood trauma should be considered a *risk factor* for adulthood personality disorder in a diathesis–stress model that includes genetic contributions as well as family and environmental factors beyond maltreatment and protective factors. He emphasized that resilience is the rule, even in the context of traumatic stress. Consistent with Paris's point, Luntz and Widom (1994) found that, although abuse and neglect are demonstrable risk factors, 86% of the maltreated individuals did *not* develop antisocial personality disorder.

DISSOCIATION AND PERSONALITY DISORDER

Three questions regarding dissociation and personality disorder bear consideration. Is dissociation uniquely characteristic of BPD? How prominent is dissociation within clients with BPD? How does BPD relate to dissociative identity disorder (DID)?

DSM-IV (APA, 1994) includes 'severe dissociative symptoms' among the diagnostic criteria for BPD (p. 654). Are dissociative symptoms specific to BPD? In a large sample of inpatients, Modestin and colleagues (Modestin, Ebner, Junghan, & Erni, 1996) found Dissociative Experiences Scale scores to be associated with symptoms of several personality disorders: antisocial, schizotypal, dependent, and borderline, and passive–aggressive. Psychometric test findings consistently show clients with DID to score high on scales reflecting avoidant, borderline, self-defeating, passive–aggressive, schizoid, and schizotypal symptoms (Dell, 1998). Yet, using a structured clinical interview to diagnose personality disorders, Zweig-Frank and colleagues found that Dissociative Experiences Scale scores were substantially higher in women and men with BPD than those with other personality disorders (Zweig-Frank, Paris, & Guzder, 1994a, 1994b). Notably, in these personality disorder samples, severity of dissociation related only to BPD diagnosis and not to childhood adversity (loss, abuse, or problems with parental bonding).

Although dissociative symptoms are now built into the diagnosis of BPD, there is considerable variability among clients with BPD in the extent of dissociative pathology. Shearer (1994) studied a series of women inpatients with BPD, using clinical diagnoses (multiple personality disorder and dissociative disorder NOS) and Dissociative Experiences Scale scores to contrast clients with and without dissociative pathology. In clients with BPD, dissociative pathology was associated with more severe trauma (childhood physical and sexual abuse as well as adult assault), more impaired functioning (post-traumatic symptoms, behavioral dyscontrol, self-injurious behavior, alcohol abuse), and higher treatment utilization (younger entry into treatment, more frequent hospitalizations, and longer inpatient stays). These findings underscore the heterogeneity in BPD. The author noted that about a third of clients with this disorder have no significant trauma history, post-traumatic symptoms, or dissociative disturbance. Yet the substantial subset with post-traumatic disturbance poses significant treatment challenges.

As Shearer (1994) observed, DID and BPD can be diagnosed concomitantly, but there is no consensus among therapists about whether one or the other or both diagnoses should be given to clients with overlapping symptoms. This diagnostic problem may be finessed by construing DID not as an Axis I syndrome but rather as a form of character pathology in which dissociation is a prominent defense (Brenner, 1996). Most authors, however, endeavor to tease apart the similarities and differences between DID and BPD. Marmar and Fink (1994), for example, while reviewing evidence that many clients with DID meet criteria for BPD, delineated substantial differences between the two disorders in the nature of defenses and quality of the traumatic etiology.

Boon and Draijer (1993) compared clients with a diagnosis of DID or dissociative disorder NOS with clients diagnosed as meeting criteria for BPD in whom a dissociative disorder had been ruled out. They employed two groups with BPD: one composed of clients referred for consultation regarding dissociative symptoms and the other with no indication of dissociative disturbance. Not surprisingly, the clients with BPD who were referred for consultation regarding dissociative symptoms (and in whom DID and dissociative disorder NOS had been ruled out) were intermediate between the pure BPD group and the dissociative disorders group in extent of dissociative symptoms. Careful clinical interviewing, however, revealed subtle differences between the borderline and dissociative clients in extent and quality of amnesia, presence of psychotic symptoms, and severity of childhood physical and sexual abuse. Although not meeting criteria for DID or dissociative disorder NOS, the clients with BPD who were referred for evaluation of dissociative symptoms showed significant dissociative disturbance, which the authors relate to childhood trauma in this BPD subgroup. These findings are consistent with those of Shearer (1994) regarding the importance of identifying the subgroup of clients with BPD who have significant trauma-related dissociative disturbance.

INSECURE ATTACHMENT AND PERSONALITY DISORDER

Attachment disturbance is a natural link to enduring problems in interpersonal relationships. Although there are ample theoretical grounds to link attachment disturbance to personality disorder (Fonagy, 1998), surprisingly little empirical research has been conducted (Dozier et al., 1999).

Two studies of women with a history of childhood sexual abuse related attachment status to personality disorders. In a clinical sample composed of inpatients and outpatients, Stalker and Davies (1995) related Adult Attachment Interview classifications to personality disorders diagnosed on the basis of a structured clinical interview. They found a high rate of personality disorder (88%) as well as high rates of preoccupied (68%) and unresolved (60%) attachment classifications. Seven of the eight subjects with a diagnosis of BPD were classified as unresolved with respect to trauma and/or loss. Furthermore, patients classified as insecure were more likely to have a number of different personality disorder diagnoses. Alexander and colleagues (Alexander et al., 1998) assessed incest survivors with the Family Attachment Interview as well as a personality disorder inventory. The majority of survivors showed fearful attachment. Borderline, avoidant, and self-defeating personality disorder scales were associated with fearful and preoccupied attachment classifications; whereas dependent personality disorder was associated with the preoccupied classification.

Patrick and colleagues (Patrick, Hobson, Castle, Howard, & Maughan, 1994) administered the Adult Attachment Interview to two groups of patients: 12 with BPD and 12 with dysthymic disorder. The findings were striking: all 12 patients with BPD were preoccupied, and almost all of these fell into the subgroup characterized by appearing confused, fearful, and overwhelmed in relation to past experiences with attachment figures. Significantly more borderline than dysthymic patients were rated as unresolved with respect to loss or trauma. Notably, the borderline and dysthymic patients did not differ from each other with respect to extent of reported childhood trauma; it was the failure to resolve the trauma that distinguished the BPD group. As the authors put it,

> They were unable to locate or contain significant early experiences within a coherent mental framework or, indeed, to think about the significance or implications of particular experiences . . . whereas the dysthymic clients who also reported early traumatic experiences of a comparable severity and type had retained or had developed coherent strategies for dealing with thoughts, affects, and memories connected with such disturbing early experiences. (p. 386)

Fonagy and colleagues (Fonagy et al., 1996) paved the way toward understanding the mechanism by which BPD may stem from a failure to resolve trauma. These researchers studied the relation between attachment classification assessed by the Adult Attachment Interview and personality disorder assessed by structured clinical interview in a predominantly female sample of inpatients with severe personality disorders. They found that 75% of the patients with a diagnosis of BPD were classified as preoccupied, with a high proportion fitting the subclassification of fearful preoccupation with traumatic events. They also found a diagnosis of BPD to be significantly related to the unresolved attachment classification. A history of abuse as well as a perception of parents as more neglecting and less loving were more prevalent among patients with BPD than among those without this diagnosis. Patients with a diagnosis of BPD were generally lower on reflective self-functioning.

Most crucial, however, is the interaction between abuse, reflective functioning, and BPD. Abuse was highly associated with BPD for clients with minimal reflective functioning. Specifically, 97% of those with abuse and low reflective functioning met criteria for BPD; whereas only 17% of the clients reporting abuse in the group with high reflective functioning met criteria for BPD. Fonagy and colleagues (Fonagy et al., 1995, 1996) proposed that persons who developed BPD coped with abuse by avoiding conceiving of the contents of their caregiver's mind and, in particular, avoided awareness of the caregiver's wish to harm them. Thus the researchers inferred that failure to mentalize prohibited resolution of abuse experiences, as well as playing a part in many symptoms of borderline disorder (Fonagy et al., 2000).

TRAUMA IN THE ETIOLOGY OF BPD

The core characteristics of BPD are frantic efforts to avoid abandonment, unstable and intense interpersonal relationships, identity disturbance, self-damaging impulsivity, recurrent suicidal or self-injurious behavior, affective instability, feelings of emptiness, intense anger, paranoid ideation, and severe dissociative symptoms. With such a broad and heterogeneous set of characteristics that impinge on interpersonal functioning, BPD is a prototype of personality disorderedness. And the heterogeneity of these diagnostic criteria is only part of the picture. In a careful diagnostic study of psychiatric inpatients, Zanarini and colleagues (Zanarini, Frankenburg, Dubo et al., 1998) found that, compared to clients with other personality disorders, those with BPD were especially likely to show a pattern of complex Axis I comorbidity consisting of a mood disorder, an anxiety disorder, and an impulse disorder. Mood disorders were extremely prominent (90%) but did not discriminate BPD from other personality disorders; whereas anxiety disorders were nearly as prevalent (80%) and highly discriminating.

Finding organization in BPD

How can therapists and their clients make sense of the seeming hodgepodge of symptoms associated with BPD? Gunderson (1996) argued persuasively that the varied symptoms of BPD can be given some coherence by focusing on the client's fear of abandonment and aloneness. He linked this fear to attachment disturbance and the inability 'to evoke a mental representation of a soothing (responsive, empathic, and reliable) other' (p. 752). This deficit is consistent with the failure of reflective function that Fonagy and colleagues (Fonagy et al., 1996) identified. Accordingly, the client requires continual contact with the attachment figure, and anticipated separation may provoke frantic efforts to prevent abandonment. Gabbard summarized the core disturbance:

> Borderline patients are consumed with establishing exclusive one-to-one relationships with no risk whatsoever of abandonment. They may demand such relationships with an air of entitlement that overwhelms and alienates others. Moreover, when they do become close with another person, a set of twin anxieties are activated. On the one hand, they begin to worry that they will be engulfed by the other person and lose their own identity in this primitive merger fantasy. On the other hand, they experience anxiety verging on panic related to the conviction that they are about to be rejected or abandoned at any moment. (Gabbard, 2000, p. 413)

Complementing Gunderson's and Gabbard's view are Zanarini and colleagues' (Zanarini, Frankenburg, DeLuca et al., 1998) findings of extreme vulnerability to dysphoric states in clients with BPD. Compared to clients with other personality disorders, those with BPD reported experiencing a wide array of dysphoric states and associated cognitions far more frequently. Clients with BPD reported experiencing 25 different dysphoric states 50% of the time. The co-occurrence of three states at high levels best discriminated clients with BPD from those with other personality disorders: feeling betrayed, the perception of being out of control, and thoughts of self-harm. The conjunction of self-destructive impulses with dysphoria is consistent with substantial evidence that BPD can be construed as an impulse-spectrum disorder (Zanarini, 1993), albeit often intermingled with compulsive symptoms (Zanarini & Weinberg, 1996).

Feeling abandoned or alone is a common precipitant of the dysphoric, self-destructive, out-of-control states of mind that clients with BPD experience. Gunderson characterized intolerance of aloneness as 'a serious psychological deficit that seems to develop from basic failures in the early attachment to primary caretakers' (p. 756). I believe that this deficit is manifested not as a continuous aversion to being alone but rather in recurrent mental states in which aloneness has become a post-traumatic reexperiencing symptom. As I have emphasized throughout this book, the core of trauma is feeling helpless and frightened in conjunction with feeling alone (neglected, unloved, rejected, or abandoned). For the traumatized subgroup of clients with BPD, the post-traumatic reexperiencing of an unbearable emotional state of aloneness is liable to eventuate in self-destructive actions that alleviate dysphoria but also perpetuate the triggering interpersonal stressors.

Trauma and BPD

Much research on the impact of trauma on personality disorder has focused on BPD, and sexual abuse has been in the spotlight. Childhood maltreatment tends to be associated especially with cluster B personality disorders, of which BPD is the most extensively researched. Furthermore, the occurrence of PTSD in conjunction with BPD is substantially higher than with other personality disorders. Zanarini and colleagues (Zanarini, Frankenburg, Dubo et al., 1998) found that 61% of females and 35% of males with BPD met criteria for PTSD (whereas only 30% of females and 11% of males with other personality disorders had PTSD).

Childhood maltreatment is now a well-established—if neither necessary nor sufficient—etiological factor for BPD (Gabbard, 2000). Thus current research aspires to disentangle the contributions of different forms of maltreatment as well as the relative contributions of abuse, neglect, and other manifestations of family dysfunction to BPD. Weaver and Clum (1993), for example, studied depressed female inpatients, a subgroup of whom met criteria for BPD. The clients with BPD reported higher levels of sexual and physical abuse as well as witnessing violence. They also reported a more impaired family climate (less family cohesiveness, less expressiveness, more conflict, and more controlling parenting). Sexual abuse predicted BPD even when physical abuse and family environment were controlled. In addition, a high level of parental control remained a significant predictor of BPD even when the trauma variables were taken into account.

Zanarini and colleagues (Zanarini et al., 1997) conducted a more refined, large-sample study comparing inpatients with BPD to those with other personality disorders. These researchers found that different forms of abuse (emotional, physical, sexual), neglect, and family disturbance differentiated the borderline from the non-borderline group. Four facets of adversity independently predicted BPD: female gender, childhood sexual abuse by a male who was not a caretaker, denial of one's thoughts and feelings by a male caretaker, and inconsistent treatment by a female caretaker. Clients with BPD who were sexually abused also reported far higher levels of other adversity (abuse, neglect, and family disturbance) than those who were not sexually abused. These findings led the authors to conclude that 'childhood sexual abuse reported by borderline clients may represent a *marker of the severity of the familial dysfunction* they experienced, as well as being a traumatic event or series of events in itself' (p. 1104, emphasis added). The role of neglect in the etiology of BPD deserves particular mention:

> This finding concerning neglect by both of the parents and sexual abuse by noncaretakers makes intuitive clinical sense. It may be that neglect by both of the parents puts the preborderline child at risk for being sexually abused by making it clear to potential perpetrators that no one will notice or care if the child is abused. Such neglect may also put the preborderline child at risk for being sexually abused by leaving him or her with a strong unmet need for attention, care, and closeness that may be misinterpreted and/or manipulated by unscrupulous, sexually predatory individuals. (p. 1105)

These studies merely begin to document the complex role of sexual abuse and other childhood adversities in the etiology of BPD. Although multiple adversities are associated with BPD, and sexual abuse rarely occurs in isolation from other adversities, sexual abuse looms large as an etiological factor. Moreover, various parameters reflecting severity of sexual abuse are associated not only with the likelihood of BPD but also the severity of the disorder (Zanarini, 1997). Yet a meta-analytic review of the relation between childhood sexual abuse and BPD that incorporated 21 studies and 2479 subjects showed only a moderate effect size and some inconsistent findings regarding severity of trauma and extent of disorder (Fossati, Madeddu, & Maffei, 1999). Plainly, childhood sexual abuse leaves much variance unexplained, and the multifaceted nature of BPD and its associated psychopathology must be matched by an equally multidimensional view of its etiology.

Complex etiology of BPD

Like other psychiatric disorders, BPD is best conceptualized in terms of a diathesis–stress model. Many researchers are investigating potential neurobiological contributions to various dimensions of behavioral disturbance in

BPD. Impulsive expressions of anger and irritability evident in aggression directed toward the self or others have been associated with frontal lobe impairment (van Reekum, Links, & Federov, 1994) and dysregulation of the serotonergic system (deVegvar, Siever, & Trestmen, 1994). Controlled studies demonstrating the efficacy of selective serotonergic reuptake inhibitors in the treatment of impulsivity and aggression in the context of BPD (Markovitz, 1995; Salzman et al., 1995) and personality disorder more generally (Coccaro & Kavoussi, 1997) attest to the prominent role of serotonergic function in this regard. Affective instability also has been linked to increased sensitivity of the cholinergic system associated with dysphoria and hyperresponsiveness of the noradrenergic system associated with heightened reactivity and irritability (Steinberg, Trestman, & Siever, 1994). Impaired cognitive functioning has been linked to subtle deficits in visuospatial and memory tasks evident in neuropsychological testing as well as in neurological and laboratory findings (O'Leary & Cowdry, 1994; Zanarini, Kimble, & Williams, 1994). While these findings suggest a neurobiological diathesis for impaired emotional and behavioral self-regulation, it is important to remember that *childhood maltreatment may be one factor contributing to this biological diathesis* (Figueroa & Silk, 1997; Linehan, 1993a; Teicher, Ito, Gold, Schiffer, & Gelbard, 1994).

Linehan, who pioneered cognitive-behavioral treatment for BPD (Linehan, Armstrong, Suarez, Allmon, & Heard, 1991), proposed a comprehensive diathesis–stress model of etiology that includes two broad factors: emotional dysregulation and an invalidating environment (Linehan, 1993a; Wagner & Linehan, 1997). The diathesis includes a biological contribution to impaired processing of emotions, which may reflect a host of genetic, intrauterine, and developmental factors. Emotional dysregulation includes high sensitivity, emotional intensity, and slow return to baseline. The biological diathesis interacts with an invalidating environment, that is, 'one in which communication of private experiences is met by erratic, inappropriate, and extreme responses. In other words, the expression of private experiences is not validated; instead, it is often punished, and/or trivialized' (Linehan, 1993a, p. 49). The essence of invalidation is communicating that the child's actions and reactions are not appropriate responses to events.

Together with the biologically based impairment of emotional regulation, invalidation disrupts the child's learning to identify and modulate emotional states. The child also becomes self-invalidating. Vicious circles ensue when the child responds to being invalidated by extreme emotional displays that only exacerbate the family's invalidating behavior. Of course, child abuse is an extreme form of invalidation (Linehan, 1993a), but there are other forms as well. Park and colleagues (Park, Imboden, Park, Hulse, & Unger, 1992) conducted a careful clinical study of the reported family history of clients with BPD. These authors were struck by the exceptional interpersonal sensitivity of many of these clients, which often appeared to have been evident in childhood. Many of the clients reported encountering constant devaluation in childhood that included depreciation or failure to recognize their exceptional intuitive insights and access to feelings.

As noted earlier, Paris emphasized that childhood trauma is just one risk factor among many for the development of personality disorder. Paris (1994) proposed a comprehensive etiological model for BPD that takes into account the finding that severe sexual abuse characterizes the history of only a minority of clients. He reviewed research on a multitude of other potential adversities potentially contributing to BPD, including physical and verbal abuse, separation and loss, parental psychopathology, emotional neglect, and other forms of family disturbance. Paris also proposed that social disintegration (e.g., broken homes, absence of social associations and recreational opportunities, poverty, and crime) and rapid social change contribute to impulsive behavior. He viewed social disintegration as a risk factor and social integration as a protective factor, arguing that social integration provides containment of impulsive behavior. Hence multiple pathways to BPD stem from various combinations of different risk and protective factors.

In a similar vein, Zanarini and Frankenburg (1997) proposed that constitutional and environmental factors along with a triggering event contribute to the development of BPD. On the constitutional side is a vulnerable temperament resulting in the expression of extreme dysphoria. These authors distinguished three levels of potential environmental trauma in increasing severity. Type I includes separations, insensitivity to the child's feelings, and emotional discord in the family. Type II includes verbal and emotional abuse as well as neglect. Type III includes frank physical and sexual abuse, severe psychiatric illness in caretakers, and a chaotic home environment. The authors found that about half the clients with BPD experienced type I and/or II trauma, and about half experienced all three types of trauma. They noted that the final stage in the development of BPD is a triggering event (e.g., leaving home, starting an intimate relationship, or being assaulted) that evokes feelings of extreme dysphoria (e.g., rageful despair) that, in turn, trigger impulsive, self-destructive behavior.

Diathesis–stress models such as those proposed by Linehan, Paris, and Zanarini underscore how a host of adversities are likely to intertwine in complex ways over the course of development—at best offset to varying degrees by protective factors. Severe attachment disturbance is part and parcel of the developmental adversity. Zanarini's work neatly pinpoints extreme dysphoric states as a fulcrum for borderline pathology, and Fonagy's work demonstrates how adversity may be offset by a capacity to reflect on mental states that makes dysphoria bearable and prevents the need to cope by self-destructive action. With the help of a validating environment in the context of secure attachments, the client may acquire reflective ability that promotes self-regulation.

THE PROBLEM OF MASOCHISM

In the arena of personality disorders, the concept of masochism puts us at highest risk for adding insult to injury by blaming the victim (Herman, 1992b; Howell, 1997). Self-defeating personality, which also has been studied in relation to abuse (Viviano & Schill, 1996), has somewhat less pejorative connotations. Yet Millon (1996) argued cogently that all personality disorders entail self-defeating behavior. Accordingly, he suggested that the more specific term, masochism, should not be abandoned. Nonetheless, neither masochistic nor self-defeating personality disorder are included in the most recent iteration of the DSM (APA, 1994).

We can take the terms out of the diagnostic lexicon, but the phenomena will remain. An adolescent in an educational group reluctantly asked for help in understanding an impulse she considered 'crazy.' She described an argument with her boyfriend that put her into a rage. She then had a compelling urge to go out to a bar and get raped. How can we help her understand this? Do we tell her that she must *enjoy* being terrified, humiliated, and injured? No doubt, the history of the term, masochism, associates pleasure with pain (Howell, 1997), and there is no question that pleasure and pain can be intermingled (Krystal, 1988). Yet traumatized clients feel misunderstood and insulted if therapists imply that they want to suffer, like to suffer, or enjoy suffering. Ironically, however, some masochistic clients embrace this view in the service of self-denigration.

Taking the view that clients enjoy suffering expresses more frustration than understanding, and it leaves therapists and their clients stuck. I take the stance that clients are striving to *suffer less*—albeit often ambivalently and ineffectively. Herman's (1992b) focus on failure of self-protection and van der Kolk's (1989) emphasis on reenactment reframe masochism constructively and sympathetically. But we must also tackle masochism and suffering head on. Howell (1997) proposed that masochism be defined in behavioral terms as 'the tendency to be abused or tortured by oneself or others' (p. 240). Thus masochism entails a propensity toward suffering, the motivation behind which is far more complex than seeking pleasure through pain. Traumatized clients are in extreme conflict about pleasure and suffering—they seek and avoid both.

Motivated suffering

Traumatized clients do not enjoy suffering. But suffer they do. Enjoyment of suffering is off the mark, but motivated suffering is not. Many traumatized clients feel that they *must* suffer and that they must *not* feel unadulterated pleasure. They are often plagued by self-loathing. They feel guilty and deserving of punishment. They feel they deserve nothing good or valuable—pleasure included. Rather than thinking that the client finds pleasure in pain, I think of the need to dilute pleasure with pain and suffering. That is, the intermingling of pleasure and pain affords a grim compromise—to experience pleasure, the price of pain must be paid (e.g., as evident in our adolescent client's desire to be raped rather than to be loved).

Millon's (1996) review of masochistic personality highlights the sheer complexity of the associated motivation. Pervasive manifestations of masochism include not only abuse of the body but also self-denigration; taking on an inferior role; adopting a defenseless position that allows for exploitation and abuse; prohibiting enjoyment and self-enhancement; undermining of achievement and success; and shunning supportive relationships. In discussing the childhood origins of masochism, Millon pointed out how being injured or suffering may inhibit further hostile attacks. In addition, he described how children may learn that they can receive parental affection and support only when they are ill, injured or deficient:

> By defeating themselves, masochists seek not only to avoid being beaten and humiliated, but to elicit nurture and affection. The direct pursuit of pleasure threatens them by evoking experiences of anxiety and guilt. Whether these processes stem from 'internalized bad objects' is one analytic way to formulate the problem. What this means simply is that the person had internalized a punitive system that must be enacted when normal affectional desires are sought. One must suffer, therefore, to be loved. (p. 588)

The psychoanalytic literature describes well how the internalized self-torment inherent in depression may be externalized and transformed into masochistic reenactments whereby other persons are unwittingly enlisted in inflicting punishment and suffering (Asch, 1988; Kernberg, 1988). Perhaps most important in the context of trauma, masochism affords some sense of control insofar as the individual obtains a degree of power over suffering (Cooper, 1988; Millon, 1996). Although it is helpful to acknowledge that clients are endeavoring to suffer less, this is only a partial truth. They are *continually attempting to regulate and control their level of suffering.* Given that they must suffer, they strive to take charge of their suffering and to derive whatever gratification and advantage can be gleaned from it.

Cooper (1988) documented the thorough intermingling of narcissism and masochism, wherein a history of maltreatment and suffering can become the basis for a sense of self-importance and entitlement to special recognition and treatment. Yet this is not a pathway out of suffering but rather a means of perpetuating it in traumatic reenactments. The masochistic client escalates demands for special treatment to the point where the demands cannot possibly be met, and then suffers rejection and disappointment. Many clients state that perpetuation of suffering is 'comfortable' in the sense of being familiar. They recognize that breaking out of the familiar pattern will be anxiety provoking. Moreover, as Gabbard (1997) observed, positive feelings evoke anxiety when patients have learned that positive experiences and letting down their guard are followed by traumatic events. Anticipating misfortune is self-protective: 'The patient prepares herself for an ambush that she is certain will come, especially if she starts to feel safe or hopeful. This posture will not prevent the trauma from happening, but at least it prevents *unexpected* trauma from occurring' (p. 13). Thus actively provoking events that produce suffering reduces anxiety. Actively driving away an attachment figure, for example, is preferable to being abandoned unexpectedly.

As all these examples attest, the intrapsychic and interpersonal dynamics of masochism are self-perpetuating. Depressed–masochistic behavior is aversive to others, leading to criticism, rejection, and abandonment, thereby exacerbating self-loathing, depression, and suffering (Coyne, 1990; Kernberg, 1988; Millon, 1996; Segrin & Abramson, 1994).

Masochistic and depressive personality disorder

The closest remaining relative of masochistic personality disorder in DSM-IV (APA, 1994) is depressive personality disorder, which is included among criteria sets provided for further study. Disentangling the contributions of biologically based temperament, mood disturbance, enduring situational stressors, and personality disturbance to chronic depression has proved challenging. Yet there is little doubt that depression can become integrated into personality and interpersonal functioning (Akiskal, 1997; Klein & Miller, 1997; Roth & Mountjoy, 1997). As characterized in DSM-IV, depressive personality disorder is evident in a pervasive pattern of depressive cognitions and behaviors, as manifested by dejected, gloomy, and joyless mood; feelings of inadequacy and worthlessness; self-criticism; brooding, negativism, and pessimism; and proneness to feeling guilty. Although there is considerable overlap among depressive disorders, careful diagnostic assessment shows that most persons who meet criteria for depressive personality disorder do not have dysthymia or current major depression (Phillips et al., 1998).

Our psychological evaluations of women with a severe trauma history (Allen et al., 1998a; Allen, Huntoon, & Evans, 1999a) showed a triad of personality disorder scales to be most characteristic: masochistic, depressive, and dependent. We noted that masochistic and depressive behaviors, to the extent that they elicit nurturance, might gratify dependency needs—although they also become involved in traumatic reenactments in attachment relationships. Millon (1996) pointed out that masochistic and depressive personality disorders overlap in their passive and accommodating interpersonal orientation, but he argued for a subtle distinction between the two. Depressive personality reflects a thoroughgoing hopelessness and passivity, evident in giving up. Masochism entails a more active orientation, consistent with the effort to exert some control over suffering:

> there is a measure of both control and desirability in giving in to their suffer-ing and discomfort. For them, a measure of moderate anguish may be a prefer-able state, that is, it may be the best of all possible alternatives available to the person. Passivity, therefore, indicates an acceptance of pain as a realistic choice, given the individual's inescapable options, not a final and irretrievable state of hopelessness. (p. 584)

Surrender revisited

The phenomena just reviewed under the rubric of masochism should have a familiar ring. I have examined passive surrender from three angles: con-sciousness, mood, and personality. In the context of dissociation, I discussed how surrender (tonic immobility) can forestall further aggression. In the context of depression, I indicated how surrender is protective by inhibiting the expression of aggression. Although passive surrender may have been adaptive in evolutionary history and in the context of childhood trauma, it is utterly problematic when it becomes an ingrained personality disposition.

Masochistic surrender is dramatically evident in traumatic bonding (Chapter 3). And traumatic bonding exemplifies the complexity of masochis-tic behavior. The paradox of clinging to abusive relationships can be under-stood in the context of attachment theory. Instilling fear by abuse heightens attachment needs, and intermittent provision of protection and comforting strengthens the attachment. Traumatic bonding illustrates the motivation to balance suffering by endeavoring to preserve an attachment relationship at the cost of considerable pain. Moreover, as Howell (1997) pointed out in the context of discussing masochistic relationships, dissociation may facilitate the attachment by compartmentalizing the painful abusive aspects of the relationship. At the same time, by impairing judgment, dissociation abets failure of self-protection and thereby contributes to the perpetuation of abusive relationships.

In the context of trauma, masochism can be woven into the fabric of per-sonality structure in the identity of 'victim.' There is no question about the reality of victimization, the definition of which includes being 'subjected to cruelty, oppression, or other harsh or unfair treatment' (Brown, 1993, p. 3575). The maltreated child or adult is indeed a victim. But taking on the stance of victim as an ingrained aspect of identity consolidates and reinforces self-defeating passivity and helplessness (Gabbard, 1997). The cost is enor-mous, as Krystal (1988) indicated: 'Once the victim identity is established firmly, it may support the vicious circles of guilt, rage, and despair that drive post-traumatic persons into self-numbing and isolation' (p. 165). Given the reality of victimization, aspiring to eradicate the experience of being a victim from a client's identity is likely to be interpreted as minimizing the trauma and to meet with considerable resistance. While accepting victimization as one facet of identity, we may endeavor to help clients minimize ongoing reenactments of victimization. Encouraging traumatized persons to view themselves as 'survivors' and not just victims reinforces active coping in place of passive surrender. Thus, while not expecting clients to give up their feelings of passive victimization, we might aspire to help them tilt the balance increasingly toward a sense of active surviving.

Masochism as treatment resistance

Traumatized clients declare, 'There is nothing good about me,' 'I cannot think any positive thoughts,' 'I don't have any right to feel good,' 'I don't deserve to get better,' 'I only deserve to die.' Here therapists may feel that they have hit a brick wall. This is a two-pronged problem. The client must suffer and must not have anything good. Krystal (1988) documented how trauma may eventuate in prohibitions against caring for the self. And such prohibitions are especially likely in the context of attachment trauma, wherein basic capacities for emotional regulation and self-care are not nurtured. Fear of feeling good and inability to care for the self conspire against change for the better. *Masochism presents the ultimate catch-22: positive outcomes must be avoided.*

We therapists may take at face value the client's expressed wish for help, but the client is not free to take what we have to offer. When I was reviewing treatment of trauma, a woman in my inpatient educational group angrily protested, 'We wouldn't *be* here if any of this stuff worked!' Consider her plight: she must seek help in a place where nothing helps. A matter-of-fact inquiry into her current struggles led to a poignant discussion of her fear of her own anger in her relationship with her alternately supportive and explosive father. Not only was she afraid of him but also, whenever she accepted his support, she felt guilty because of her anger toward him. She felt the same ambivalence toward anyone in a position to help her.

We may be tempted to respond to masochistic protests that 'There is nothing good about me' with a cheerleading attitude—which is often adopted by group members. But cheerleading will not counter this entrenched masochistic stance. Paradoxically, heaping on praise and reassurance may only increase guilt feelings and self-hatred. Empathic education and confrontation are often an essential part of the challenging effort to interrupt these extremely damaging, self-perpetuating, and emotionally painful patterns (Asch, 1988; Coyne, 1990; Kernberg, 1988; Price et al., 1994). Some clients can only accept treatment on behalf of others (e.g., 'I am only refraining from suicide for the sake of my children'), a stance that therapists might best graciously accept rather than immediately confront.

Anger revisited

Fear of anger and aggression plays a key role in masochistic surrender, just as it does in depressive and dissociative surrender. Reclaiming anger, although frightening to the client, is a pathway out of masochism. Krystal (1988) pointed to this phenomenon in the context of self-destructive substance abuse, and it applies to masochism as well:

> The client must be able to experience with the therapist that which he has never before dared to face—his hatred. Instead of seeing himself as a victim, and by virtue of his 'victimhood' claiming innocence, now he is confronted with his murderous aggression. To do so, however, he must give up the treasured view of himself as the victim, which, again, has to be mourned. (p. 191)

As Parens (1992, 1993) articulated, therapists must help clients distinguish between constructive and destructive anger. Having experienced destructive anger and aggression, the concept of constructive anger may be anathema to traumatized clients. Parens' continuum is useful. At the benign end, he put irritability and anger—both of which are helpful and self-protective. Anger is a source of power—obviously a double-edged sword. Masochistic submission and self-attacks rob the individual of effective interpersonal power.

In discussing the power of anger with clients, I use the analogy of pulling open a door that is stuck. Frustration is energizing and provides power for pulling harder and getting the door unstuck. Similarly, anger can energize interpersonal influence. Anger may fuel self-assertion, confrontation, and self-protective behavior. Therapists must acknowledge, however, that regulating anger to employ it effectively in the service of influencing others is an extraordinarily complex social skill that takes extensive practice. How many of us are really good at it?

Many traumatized clients face the danger that their anger quickly can take a destructive turn. Parens (1992) proposed that 'excessive unpleasure experiences generate hostile destructiveness' (p. 75). In a similar vein, Lewis (1992) wrote, 'Probably the most powerful generator of aggression in animals and possibly in man is the repeated infliction of pain' (p. 384). Maltreatment promotes destructive hostility and anger. Parens (1992) distinguished three levels of destructive aggression: hostility, hate, and rage. Whereas anger is a transient response to an aversive situation, hostility makes for enduring antagonism. The extreme of hostility is hate. Rage, like anger, is transient, but extreme. In educating clients, I add 'temper tantrums' and 'bullying intimidation' to the list of common and counterproductive expressions of anger. I emphasize that bullying intimidation is difficult to give up, because it is often highly effective in getting your way. Yet I point out that this behavior is also highly ineffective with respect to the goal of having enduring, satisfying relationships.

Masochistic surrender may block the extremes of hate and rage. The self-sacrifice of suicide may be the ultimate surrender. The link to rage is sometimes blatantly conscious, when suicide is a means to avoid homicide. For example, a man in an educational group who had been severely beaten by his father throughout childhood described a telephone confrontation with him in adulthood. He was flooded with homicidal rage, and he got out his gun and drove toward his father's home. He stopped alongside the road before he arrived, and he was on the brink of killing himself. Instead he drove to the hospital emergency room. He was then profoundly depressed, feeling that he deserved nothing good and that he must die. Moving out of the position of masochistic surrender threatened him with the eruption of uncontrollable rage, which he then controlled by resuming his self-sacrificing stance.

Helping such clients with the problem of masochism is a difficult and lengthy process. The destructive expression of rage, albeit frightening and often ensuing in guilt and shame, also can be extremely gratifying. It can be hard to give up. But distinguishing healthy irritation and anger from hostility, hate, intimidation, and rage points the way between surrender and dangerous aggression.

ALIENATION

BPD and masochism capture clinical attention because they entail problematic forms of engagement. Yet no less important is a pattern of profound disengagement, where the traumatized client is essentially unreachable. Although there is no 'alienated personality disorder,' painful isolation can be a characteristic interpersonal pattern.

In psychological testing (Allen, Huntoon, & Evans, 1999a) we identified a group of trauma patients who scored extremely high on a cluster of scales indicative of isolation: avoidant, schizoid, schizotypal, and paranoid. This group also scored high on scales indicative of hostility (negativistic and antisocial personality disorder), as well as on the borderline scale, which likely reflected their anger as well as the severity of their disturbance and their self-destructiveness. In comparison to several other clusters, this alienated group scored extremely high on dissociative detachment. Moreover, as we had observed previously, this pattern of extreme alienation is most likely to be associated with psychotic symptoms (Allen & Coyne, 1995).

Extremely alienated patients may be so detached—from others and from themselves—that they are virtually unknowable in treatment relationships. I have worked with such alienated patients in a specialized inpatient treatment setting where they remain relatively enigmatic for months. This alienated pattern is inherently extremely slow to change, although with substantial safety over a long period of time, such patients are able gradually to establish some sense of connection in relationships. Of course this pattern of alienation does not exclude suffering, and moving into close relationships may then entail extreme conflict with hallmarks of borderline disorder. The treatment challenge is to provide some stability and to help the patient cope with interpersonal conflicts so as to avert yet another enduring retreat into alienated isolation.

EDUCATING CLIENTS ABOUT PERSONALITY DISORDERS

It is not uncommon—and not unhealthy—for clients to protest being pigeon-holed by psychiatric labels. Personality disorder is a particularly problematic label, because it readily translates in the client's mind to being a 'bad person.' Consider the impact of having a character disorder or character pathology. These terms can translate into having 'bad character.' Although complex PTSD can circumvent personality disorder diagnoses, this diagnosis has no official sanction and provides little diagnostic discrimination.

I tackle the problem of personality disorder head on. I ask clients directly how they view their diagnosis of personality disorder. If they do not bring it up, I ask if being told they have a diagnosis of personality disorder has connotations of being called a 'bad person.' Clients invariably assent. Explaining that the essence of personality disorder is *persistent difficulties in interpersonal relationships* sets the stage for helping the client to adopt a more reflective stance and to think about personality disorder from a developmental perspective. Clients readily understand that it is a small step from interpersonal trauma to persistent difficulties in interpersonal relationships.

Although one can question whether it is the best conceptualization (Rutter, 1987), viewing personality disorders as exaggerated personality traits (Paris, 1998b; Parker & Barrett, 2000) provides a ready explanation for clients. For example, many traumatized clients comment on their 'paranoia.' I point out that it is natural for someone who has been hurt by others to be distrusting and suspicious. Moreover, within limits, paranoia is universal and adaptive (Meissner, 1978). Indeed not being sufficiently paranoid can be a problem. Particularly with a history of interpersonal trauma, it is risky to be gullible and naïve, and it is prudent to be wary and cautious. In its full expression, of course, paranoia poses severe interpersonal problems. A similar line of reasoning pertains to avoidant personality disorder. It is hardly surprising that a person who has been badly mistreated would feel inferior, fear criticism and rejection, and shy away from others. Lest we take such normalization too far, we must also point out how paranoid or avoidant orientations are over-generalized responses that tend to be self-perpetuating by leading to actual rejection.

Dependent personality disorder is another relevant example. I point out that persons with a trauma history naturally tend to be distrusting and isolated. When they do form a close relationship, they may conclude that they have found the one trustworthy person on earth, and then they may become completely dependent on this one person. They must pay the price of self-sacrifice for their dependency. Of course such dependency places the person in an extremely vulnerable position, in which fears of abandonment loom large and hostility intrudes. Then we approach the territory of BPD.

BPD is especially difficult to explain because the term, borderline, does not refer to a personality trait but rather to a spectrum of personality impairment bordering on psychosis at one end and neurosis at the other (Grinker, Werble, & Drye, 1968). Thus the exaggerated-trait view of personality disorder does not apply to BPD. No simple explanation will do. Moreover, many clients have at least some degree of awareness of the close association between 'borderline' and 'difficult to treat' in the mind of the therapist. Many recount their experience of being dismissed or rejected for treatment as a result of being 'borderline.'

We should not shy away from these realities. Traumatized clients with BPD and other personality disorders are difficult to treat and difficult to help. Intense interpersonal conflicts are experienced in treatment relationships as in other close relationships, by the client and by the therapist. Consider Fonagy and colleagues' (Fonagy et al., 1995) portrayal:

> It takes but one patient with severe borderline pathology to shatter the equilibrium of the therapist's life with unending demands for 'special' treatment, round-the-clock availability, physical and sometimes sexual contact, perfect attunement, heroic efforts to prevent self-injury or suicide, and all the therapist's efforts are repaid only by contempt, reproach, hostility, and, at times, outright physical attack. (p. 259)

Most challenging is the struggle with clients' projections and inevitable reenactments:

> Once they see in us the hated alien other, once we have become who they want us to be, they are calm and safe and experience the coherence of self-representation, which was their goal. Unfortunately, in these states we are no longer able to offer therapeutic help. This is why these patients are difficult. Their treatment involves a paradox. In order for them to enter a therapeutic dialogue, to make their genuine self accessible to us, they have to shed the alien self-representation. Once this has been achieved, they have in all probability destroyed the very situation that might have helped them. (Fonagy, 1998, p. 162)

Fortunately, we have a fine clinical literature on countertransference to help us with such inevitable emotional struggles in treating these clients (Gabbard & Wilkinson, 1994). And, while we continually face seeming impasses, Fonagy (1998) argued that the therapist's mentalistic elaborative stance offers a way forward: 'The experience of intimate contact with another mind capable of recognizing the client's turmoil may be all that is needed for the recovery of a way of being that is essential to adequate functioning in the human world' (p. 164).

The best stance we can take is to acknowledge these relationship challenges and to help clients understand the basis of them. Virtually all the difficulties discussed in this book are pertinent to the phenomena seen in clients with BPD who have a history of severe interpersonal trauma. Thus I discuss how trauma-related problems contribute to enduring effects on personality—sense of self and relationships. I emphasize the attachment disturbance with a focus on fear of abandonment, as Gunderson advocated (1996). Gunderson's view fits with my continual emphasis on interpersonal trauma consisting of feeling frightened in conjunction with feeling alone. Zanarini's work on dysphoria (Zanarini, Frankenburg, DeLuca et al., 1998) and self-damaging impulsivity (Zanarini, 1993) is compatible with the conceptualization of destructive action as a means of escaping from unbearable emotional states (Chapter 8). Unstable relationships, identity disturbance, dysphoric mood, and anxiety are all part and parcel of the commingled disorders reviewed in this book.

In educating clients about their personality disorders, therapists must confront the misconception that personality disorders do not respond to treatment. Treatment is difficult but not impossible. Certainly, like other facets of trauma-related psychopathology reviewed throughout this book, personality disorders to not respond *quickly* to treatment. Although research is limited, and results vary widely from one study to another and one disorder to another, we can safely conclude that long-term treatment leads to substantial improvement in many clients with personality disorders (Gabbard, 2000; Gabbard, Coyne, Allen, Spohn, Colson, & Vary, 2000; Target, 1998). Perry and colleagues' (Perry, Banon, & Ianni, 1999) review of research showed that over half the clients who remained in psychotherapy for more than a year no longer met full criteria for personality disorder. These researchers estimated that a quarter of patients recover per year and that psychotherapy yields seven times the recovery rate found in the natural course of BPD.

Among the personality disorders, long-term course of BPD following extended treatment has been most thoroughly studied. Outcomes are generally favorable, with the caveats that drop-out rates are high and suicide rates are substantial—up to 10% in some studies (Gabbard, 2000; Linehan et al., 1991; Target, 1998). Particularly encouraging is the effectiveness of a psychoanalytically oriented partial hospital program that tracked improvement in patients with BPD over the course of 18 months (Bateman & Fonagy, 1999). Compared to those receiving standard psychiatric care, patients in the partial hospital program showed substantially reduced levels of self-harm as well as greater improvement in anxiety, depression, and social adjustment. A subsequent assessment of this same sample revealed not only stable gains but also evidence of continued improvement at 18 months follow-up, suggesting that the treatment set in motion a benign process of change (Bateman & Fonagy, in press). The authors concluded that essential to effectiveness is the *consistent application over time of a theoretically coherent treatment approach focusing on interpersonal relationships.*

Although we have no reason to be sanguine about treatment outcomes, particularly in working with clients whose BPD is intertwined with other trauma-related psychopathology, we can realistically encourage clients that substantial improvement is possible if they persist in a stable treatment process. As described in the next part of this book, treatment entails developing supportive relationships and improved capacity for self-regulation that must become part of a lifestyle devoted to self-care over the long haul. This is a tall order, particularly for clients whose personality disorder includes masochism and alienation.

Part III
Treatment and long-term management

Chapter 11

CONTAINING TRAUMA

> If many remedies are prescribed for an illness, you may be certain that the illness has no cure. (Chekhov, *The Cherry Orchard*)

A client in an educational group handed me a poem with Chekhov's quote at the top. I was first taken aback but then appreciated its aptness to trauma treatment. I do not know the source of the quote she gave me; the translation I tracked down (Chekhov, 1998) was a shade more bleak: 'Gaev: You know, when people suggest all sorts of cures for some disease or other, it means it's incurable. I keep thinking, racking my brains, and I come up with plenty of solutions, plenty of remedies, and basically, that means none—not one' (pp. 25–26). Many clients who come to us in a depressive crisis would readily identify with Gaev's plight. They have tried all we have to offer, and they are not cured. We cannot cure, but we can help.

The mental health profession's rediscovery of trauma in the 1980s generated enthusiasm for helping clients to uncover and talk about their trauma. Trauma-focused interventions remain crucial, if not curative (LaMothe, 1999). But growing appreciation of the severity and chronicity of post-traumatic disorders, in tandem with increasing awareness of the limitations of treatment—even with well-designed early intervention (Shalev, 1997c)—has shifted emphasis toward rehabilitation (Shalev, 1997b).

Clients will be the first to attest to the severity and chronicity of their illness as well as the limitations of treatment. We must be forthright with them. If we had a cure, we would provide it. Clients' wish for cure is natural and healthy, but it may not be realistic. We must offer hope while respecting reality. Forming realistic expectations is also crucial for us therapists. We, too, may become disillusioned and demoralized in the face of treatment challenges.

We must take a long view of progress while focusing on short-term goals. I tell clients they must work on many fronts, sometimes simultaneously, sometimes successively, sometimes recursively. I acknowledge flatly that each of the various interventions we offer may only help a little, and we will usually employ several in combination. In addition, rather than focusing on the elusive cure, we must endeavor to help clients develop the capacity to take care of themselves over the long haul.

CONTAINMENT

Treatment needs a focus. Faced with many problems and many interventions, our treatment approaches can become as fragmented and chaotic as our traumatized client's internal world. We must treat symptoms, and there are many symptoms to treat, as well as many symptom-oriented treatment approaches. But merely focusing on one symptom after another can leave us adrift. We may be tempted to plunge into intensive work on traumatic memories in response to clients' imploring us to get into the pain of the trauma so as to somehow 'get it all out' and rid them of all their problems. Yet, to the extent that they are unable to regulate emotion and resort to self-destructive means, this approach is liable to make clients worse. We need a conceptual compass to provide an overall direction for treatment while we attend to symptoms as best we can when they arise.

We must foster our client's *capacity* to work on the trauma before tackling traumatic memories. The first of these agendas is the focus of this chapter, and the second is the focus of the next. These differing agendas parallel the contrast between expressive and supportive approaches to psychotherapy (Horwitz et al., 1996; Rockland, 1989). Expressive or exploratory approaches are relatively unstructured, uncovering, and insight oriented; whereas, supportive approaches are relatively structured, directive, and reality oriented. Rockland (1989) argued cogently that, although it has been practiced for thousands of years, supportive psychotherapy has been a relatively neglected art that requires a great deal of skill. As a rule, the more impaired the client's functioning—especially in relation to reality adherence and affect regulation—the more supportive the treatment must be. Yet this principle is easily ignored in trauma treatment, particularly to the extent that the client presses for an expressive approach that will 'get it all out.'

Chu (1992) questioned the widespread belief that 'in any clinical situation where childhood abuse is discovered in the history, all efforts should be made to immediately explore and abreact those abusing experiences' (p. 353). The result of this exploration can be retraumatization. Excessively expressive (or insufficiently supportive) treatments can lead to deterioration. Expressive and supportive approaches are best interwoven in an optimal balance that takes into account such factors as the client's affect tolerance, impulse control, motivation for treatment, and capacities for relationships (Horwitz et al., 1996). Over the course of the past two decades, the field of trauma treatment has moved from a relatively expressive emphasis (e.g., with hypnotic uncovering of traumatic memories in the context of intense emotion) to a more supportive emphasis (e.g., focusing on rehabilitative aims).

I use the metaphor of *containment* for the supportive aspects of trauma treatment. Traumatized clients have experienced a failure of containment. They have been overwhelmed by trauma, and they have attempted to contain the painful emotions in ways that backfire, namely, avoidant defenses and self-destructive actions. Therapists must help clients establish means of containment before conducting interventions that re-evoke painful emotional states. Revisiting the thesis that secure attachment establishes the foundation for self-regulation, this chapter focuses on two mutually enhancing aspects of containment: supportive relationships and self-regulation. Together with a stable treatment frame, supportive relationships and self-regulation provide containment for truama-focused interventions, as diagrammed in Figure 11.1.

My proposal that containment be given priority is consistent with current consensus about the need for phase-oriented trauma treatment (Chu, 1992; Herman, 1992b; van der Hart et al., 1998; van der Kolk, McFarlane, & van der Hart, 1996), with supportive interventions preceding expressive interventions. Herman (1992b) wrote,

> Though the single most common therapeutic error is avoidance of the traumatic material, probably the second most common error is premature or precipitate engagement in exploratory work, without sufficient attention to the tasks of establishing safety and securing a therapeutic alliance. (p. 172)

She likened the recovery process to running a marathon, a test of endurance, which requires long preparation and repetitive practice. She proposed that recovery from trauma unfolds in three stages: establishment of safety, remembrance and mourning, and reconnection with ordinary life.

Figure 11.1   Containment in trauma treatment

Phase-oriented treatment is not a lock-step process but rather a matter of shifting emphasis over time, with much back and forth movement. We should not think of stabilization as something to be accomplished quickly so that we can get on with the real work on traumatic memories. For severely traumatized clients, this preliminary work may require months or even years, and some clients may never be able to tolerate much focus on traumatic memories (Chu, 1992). In my view, *the real work is in helping the client develop the capacities for close relationships, self-regulation, and self-care that will enhance adaptation and quality of life.* Work on traumatic memories is beneficial to the extent that it enhances these capacities.

STRUCTURING TREATMENT

A clear and stable structure plays a critical role in the containing function of treatment. This section covers several aspects of structuring treatment as they pertain to trauma: safety, boundaries, the therapeutic frame, and the therapeutic alliance.

Safety

Herman (1992b) proposed that 'The first task of recovery is to establish the survivor's safety. This tasks takes precedence over all others, for no other therapeutic work can possibly succeed if safety has not been adequately secured' (p. 159). Thus self-endangering behavior should always take top priority in therapy sessions (Linehan et al., 1991). Maintaining safety includes formulating concrete plans for self-protection in times of increased danger. As part of a safety plan, van der Hart and colleagues (van der Hart et al., 1998) recommend an *emotional 911*, that is, having persons or institutions that the client can contact immediately in times of extreme distress. Clients benefit from having a written list—the longer the better—complete with telephone numbers.

Establishing safety is a gradual process that can take months to years. Physical safety includes safety from others as well as safety from self-harm. More broadly, safety entails self-care (caring for health needs, including sleep, diet, exercise, as well as freedom from self-harm) and having a safe environment. Safety from others is a particularly important concern for persons who are vulnerable to ongoing abuse, whether in childhood or adulthood. In situations of domestic violence, a client, her family members, and even the therapist may be at grave risk. Thus treating battered women entails developing detailed plans for escape (Enns, Campbell, & Courtois, 1997). Ideally, such safety plans should not be imposed on the client by the therapist but rather negotiated collaboratively (Saakvitne et al., 2000). Yet, when the client's repetitive self-endangering behavior threatens to destroy the treatment relationship, the therapist may need to set limits unilaterally and discontinue the (ineffective) treatment if the client does not adhere to them.

Boundaries

Part and parcel of the client's—and therapist's—safety is the definition and maintenance of therapeutic boundaries and limits. The most glaring boundary violation is sexual contact, and clients with a history of sexual abuse are at high risk in this regard (Kluft, 1990a). Gutheil and Gabbard (1993) describe a slippery slope of boundary violations that may ensue in sexual contact:

> a common sequence involves a transition from last-name to first-name basis; then personal conversation intruding on the clinical work; then some body contact (e.g., pats on the shoulder, massages, progressing to hugs); then trips outside the office; then sessions during lunch, sometimes with alcoholic beverages; then dinner; then movies or other social events; and finally sexual intercourse. (p. 188)

Because boundary violations are intrinsic to abusive relationships, traumatized clients are particularly likely to have difficulty adhering to therapeutic boundaries, and attention to boundaries is a highly prominent aspect of treating trauma (Chu, 1992; Herman, 1992b; Kluft, 1993; Saakvitne et al., 2000). Particularly hazardous is the temptation to re-parent the client (Chu, 1992). Therapists should heed Gutheil and Gabbard's reminder, 'This is not love, it's work' (p. 192). Of course boundaries are not absolute, and much of the art of psychotherapy is balancing consistency with flexibility (Waldinger, 1994). Moreover, the nature of the boundaries will vary depending on the type of treatment as well as the context of the relationship (Gutheil & Gabbard, 1993).

The therapeutic frame

Contributing to therapeutic boundaries is a solid therapeutic frame, conceptualized as 'an envelope or membrane around the therapeutic role that defines the characteristics of the therapeutic relationship' (Gutheil & Gabbard, 1993, p. 190). A number of authors have addressed the importance of a well-articulated therapeutic frame in the treatment of trauma (Barach, 1993; Chu, 1992; Enns et al., 1997; Kluft, 1993; Lewis, 1996). There are many matters to be spelled out, including frequency, duration, and location of sessions; confidentiality; fees and payment arrangements; forms of address; telephone contact; procedures for emergencies; and policies in relation to vacations and other interruptions. Such aspects of the treatment frame can be supported by written informed consent (Scheflin, 2000; Young & Young, 1996).

Like boundaries, the therapeutic frame is not established once and for all at the outset of treatment but rather will be a matter for continual testing and negotiation. Nonetheless, fundamental aspects of the treatment frame should be agreed upon at the beginning of treatment, and therapists should not take for granted that a suitable agreement can be made:

> Therapists must be prepared to come to the conclusion that no psychotherapeutic work will be possible if the client is unable to agree to the treatment conditions. . . . Therapists of borderline clients must always remind themselves that there are much worse fates than termination of the treatment. It is better not to begin at all than to begin under grossly misguided circumstances. (Gabbard & Wilkinson, 1994, p. 39)

Therapeutic alliance

The therapeutic frame sets the stage for a therapeutic alliance, which Kluft (1992) aptly construed as 'the heart and soul of treatment' (p. 152). Two core components of the therapeutic alliance are the client's experience of the therapist as warm, supportive, and helpful; and the client's sense of working with the therapist in a joint effort (Luborsky, 1976; Luborsky, Crits-Christoph, Alexander, Margolis, & Cohen, 1983). In the treatment of BPD, we emphasize collaboration, defined as the client's making active use of the psychotherapy as a resource for constructive change (Allen, Newsom, Gabbard, & Coyne, 1984; Frieswyk, Colson, & Allen, 1984). Thus we highlight the client's active participation, responsibility, and control, which should be a precondition for working on traumatic memories (Kluft, 1993).

When embarking on treatment of severely traumatized clients, we should not assume that we can quickly establish a solid therapeutic alliance. Building a workable alliance may take months or even years. Clients with a history of being hurt and betrayed by others—often persons on whom they depended—are not likely easily to develop a realistic, positive relationship with a therapist. Furthermore, while the therapist might assume that being an active partner would appeal to the traumatized client, this expectation goes against the grain of a pattern of passive surrender evident in dissociation, depression, and masochism. Here is another catch-22: the client needs a good alliance to overcome trauma-related problems, but trauma-related problems preclude a good alliance.

The alliance is unlikely to develop rapidly, and it does not necessarily grow in a linear fashion. Our research on the therapy of clients with BPD demonstrated substantial fluctuations in the alliance, both within therapy sessions

(Allen, Gabbard, Newsom, & Coyne, 1990) and between sessions (Horwitz et al., 1996). Not uncommon is a honeymoon period in which the alliance is superficially positive, followed by a seesaw pattern that entails periods of disruption. I discuss this seesaw pattern with clients and help them articulate common precipitants of plummeting alliances. I ask, 'What plunges your relationship with your therapist into the pits?' One theme predominates: feeling abandoned. Common triggers include vacations, weekends, illnesses, lapses in empathy, or other kinds of therapist errors. Yet client resistance also plays an important role in such ruptures. Edging toward the brink of remembering or discussing trauma—or having gone over the brink and revealing too much—precipitates periods of withdrawal, remoteness, non-attendance, or destructive behavior that interrupts the therapeutic process. Whatever the precipitant of the disruption, the client's treatment-interfering behavior should be a high-priority agenda (Linehan et al., 1991).

I help clients understand that disruptions in the alliance do not signal treatment failure but rather provide opportunities for growth and further strengthening of the alliance. Repairing ruptures in the alliance is a cornerstone of therapy (Safran, Muran, & Samstag, 1994). By talking with the therapist about the disruption, the client can build confidence in being able to resolve interpersonal conflict, which can generalize to negotiation and conflict resolution in other relationships. In explaining how therapy may help, I also discuss the role of internalizing the therapeutic alliance (Horwitz, 1974). Internalizing the therapist's helpfulness and acceptance promotes self-care and self-acceptance. Internalizing the collaboration entails being able to carry on the work of problem solving and self-understanding without the direct help of the therapist.

Of course the therapeutic alliance is a two-way street. The therapist's contributions to the alliance are important, and it is a matter for research to discover how—even on a moment-to-moment basis—we therapists can foster the alliance (Horwitz et al., 1996). The therapist has primary responsibility for maintaining boundaries and the therapeutic frame, without which there can be no therapeutic alliance. Reliability, consistency, and predictability are crucial to the process of containment. We must remember that, if the alliance entails a realistic perception of the therapist as a helpful person, the therapist must be trustworthy.

In discussing this aspect of the alliance with clients, I acknowledge that, unfortunately, the trustworthiness of therapists cannot simply be taken for granted. We cannot sweep sexual abuse of clients by therapists under the rug. On the contrary, clients should be aware of this treatment risk, and I make it a topic of discussion in educational groups. Many clients are painfully aware of the risk of being abused by therapists on the basis of their personal experience. Unfortunately, defensive avoidance (e.g., dissociation) can place clients at greater risk for being exploited and abused, by therapists as by others.

THE HAZARDS OF SEEKING SOCIAL SUPPORT

Healing relationships are a cornerstone of trauma treatment, and secure attachment the basis of healing relationships. Yet another catch-22: trauma interferes with entering into healing relationships needed to overcome trauma. I bring this catch-22 to clients' attention, recognizing the obstacles to secure attachments and then thinking about ways to overcome them.

Benefits of social support

Extensive research backs therapists' encouraging traumatized clients to seek social support. Social support is adaptive from an evolutionary standpoint (Argyle, 1992; Kendler, 1997; Weiner, 1998) and is associated with higher levels of physical and mental health (Antoni, Millon, & Millon, 1997; Argyle, 1992; Kendler, 1997; Kessler, Kendler, Heath, Neale, & Eaves, 1992; Monroe & Steiner, 1986). In the domain of trauma, social support predicts better outcomes after adult victimization (Cutrona & Russell, 1990).

Yet merely encouraging clients to seek social support overlooks a host of complexities. Social support is multifaceted (Sarason, Sarason, & Pierce, 1990; Sarason, Levine, Basham, & Sarason, 1983), involving different kinds of relationships, for example, spouse, relatives, friends, and acquaintances (Argyle, 1992; Kendler, 1997; Kessler et al., 1992). Intimate or close relationships provide the most crucial support, and other sources of support cannot compensate for the lack of them (Coyne, Ellard, & Smith, 1990). Extent of support depends on both quality and quantity of relationships (Monroe & Steiner, 1986; Sarason et al., 1983), and there are different types of support (Argyle, 1992). Although we therapists tend to emphasize *emotional* support, *instrumental* support—such as practical help with everyday tasks—sometimes may be as important or more important in buffering stress (Coyne et al., 1990). Systematic assessments of support yield an amalgam of positive and conflictual relationships (Kendler, 1997), and there is considerable evidence that the negatives may outweigh the benefits of the positives (Coyne et al., 1990; Rook, 1992; Sarason, Pierce, & Sarason, 1990; Silver, Wortman, & Crofton, 1990). Finally, there are substantial gender differences in patterns of social support (Sarason et al., 1983).

Social support, personality, and attachment

Surprisingly, social support is more a personality attribute than an environmental factor (Argyle, 1992; B. R. Sarason et al., 1990). *Perceived* support predicts positive health outcomes whereas actual number of supportive interactions predicts negative health outcomes. This latter counterintuitive finding reflects the likelihood that the number of ostensibly supportive inter-actions is a function of the extent of distress, neediness, and inability to cope (Coyne, 1990; Monroe & Steiner, 1986; B. R. Sarason et al., 1990). What counts is the individual's *belief* that help will be available if needed rather than the actual amount of help received (B. R. Sarason et al., 1990). This belief is rela-tively stable and based on personality characteristics such as sociability and interpersonal skills (Kendler, 1997; B. R. Sarason et al., 1990). The important role of personality factors likely accounts for the substantial contribution that genetic factors make to extent of social support (Kendler, 1997; Kessler et al., 1992).

Sarason and colleagues (B. R. Sarason et al., 1990) concluded that *sense of social support* is crucial, and this is a stable characteristic related to perceived availability of support as well as to expectations that others' behavior will be supportive. These authors believe that sense of support is based on inter-nal working models of attachment. This assumption is consistent with find-ings that secure attachment is conducive to the development of positive and supportive interpersonal relationships, positive views of self and others, as well as social skills. Ample research shows that this benign developmental process emerges early in life, as secure attachment is conducive to develop-ing supportive peer relationships in early childhood (Thompson, 1999; Wein-field et al., 1999).

An interactional perspective

Although most persons find relationships satisfying and supportive (Rook, 1992), therapists must be mindful of potential pitfalls before simply encour-aging clients to reach out for support. Seeking support can be hazardous, even when psychopathology is not involved. Distress is contagious (Hatfield et al., 1993) and thus aversive to others. Silver and colleagues' (Silver et al., 1990) research on reactions to cancer patients' distress showed that other persons may feel vulnerable ('It could happen to me') as well as helpless, owing to awkwardness and confusion about how to respond and behave. Furthermore, it is harder to be supportive in relation to anger, rage, and bit-terness than depression and sadness. When adequate support is not forth-coming, the client's helplessness will increase. Then the supporter's sense of inadequacy increases, leading to withdrawal, rejection, and avoidance.

Here is a dilemma: you must communicate distress to receive needed emotional support, but expressing distress risks alienating your support network. Silver and colleagues also observed that the cancer victim's *self-presentation* played an important role. Support went to those whose forthright expressions of distress were counterbalanced by evidence of con-structive coping. Evidence of coping minimizes the supporter's feelings of helplessness, over-involvement, and potential burden. In contrast, when victims either fail to express distress or express distress along with a sense that they are floundering, supporters are more likely to withdraw. These authors recommend the following strategy of self-presentation: 'We believe that victims may thus benefit most by conveying that although they are distressed by what is happening to them, they are attempting to cope through their own efforts' (p. 418). This leaves supporters feeling less burdened, with a sense that they merely need to provide supplemental assistance. Although these authors conducted their research with strangers rather than intimate partners, they noted that ongoing distress might be even less tolerable to the latter. Although the research focused on cancer patients, the authors also cited parallel findings for rape victims.

Given the prospect for contagion, vulnerability, and a sense of helplessness, it is not surprising that what passes for support is often directed at *reducing the partner's distress*, which may result in counterproductive behavior. Coyne and colleagues (Coyne et al., 1990) studied couples in which one member (most often the husband) had suffered a myocardial infarction. They noted a common pattern of ineffective pep talks that failed to help the patient and then led the supportive spouse to feel rejected. Overprotective and intrusive responses also can undermine the self-efficacy of the survivor. These authors also observed that intensifying ineffective efforts to provide support may backfire and, 'What may be needed most is not "more social support" but a disengagement from efforts that are not working, based on an appreciation of the limits of social relationships and of one person's taking responsibility for the other' (p. 146).

Depression and problems with social support

The hazards of social support are glaringly evident in relation to depression. In their longitudinal research on women, Brown (1992) and Harris (1992) examined the role of social support as a potential buffer against depression in the wake of stressful events. An optimally supportive relationship fosters confiding in relation to the crisis and offers emotional responsiveness without substantial negative components. Harris (1992, p. 173) pointed to the importance of a close relationship, indicating that 'fire-engine support' (competent help from a stranger) is less helpful than 'milk-van' support (entailing closeness and regular care).

Harris identified many forms of unsupportive responses, including divided loyalties (e.g., jealousy and taking another person's point of view), criticism (e.g., blaming the person for the crisis), hard-heartedness (e.g., insensitivity and criticism for making too much of a fuss), self-protective responses (e.g., evading conversation about the crisis to avoid feeling distressed), lack of availability, and inappropriate responses (e.g., kindly attempts to distract the individual that attempt to hurry her through the

stress). Brown and Harris garnered substantial evidence that, whereas supportive responses to crises provide a buffer against depression, *unsupportive
responses dramatically increase the risk of depression*. Particularly detrimental are
let-down responses in marital relationships where, instead of reasonably
expected support, the woman feels criticized or neglected.

As Brown and Harris elucidated it, a series of interpersonal adversities
culminate in depression. Interpersonal stressors are most likely to set the
stage for depression, and unsupportive interpersonal responses—additional
interpersonal stressors—are likely to be the last straw. Both the stressor and
the unsupportive response contribute to low self-esteem and a sense of hopelessness in an escalating series. I present the sequence to clients this way:
stress pile-up → depression → reaching out for support → let down → utter
despair—the latter often involving suicidal states. This sequence is all too
plain to them.

Trauma, social support, and attachment

All of us face the catch-22 that expressing distress is necessary to obtain
support but risks driving away potential sources of support. Yet traumatized
clients face a more problematic catch-22: those who most need the support
have the least capacity to obtain and benefit from it, and they are at high risk
for alienating sources of support. Note Silver and colleagues' (Silver et al.,
1990) view in the context of cancer: 'those who express difficulties in coping
with a stressful life event may elicit more rejection from others than do those
who appear to be coping well . . . those in greatest need of social support
may be least likely to get it' (p. 398).

Coyne and colleagues (Coyne et al., 1990) challenged the assumption that
having '"low support" represents having less of something and "high
support" more of it' (p. 131). This leads to a naïve, more-is-better approach,
namely, 'what is most needed by persons who are doing badly in stressful
circumstances is more social support' (p. 131). In practice, low social support
often does not mean absence of relationships but rather presence of conflictual relationships. Negatives often outweigh positives. As Coyne and colleagues stated,

> what persons low in perceived support need is relief from relationships that
> are conflictive, demanding, or otherwise problematic. They might be able to
> find this relief by resolving some of the difficulties posed by these relationships
> or insulating themselves from them, rather than instigating more involvement.
> (p. 131)

Persons suffering from interpersonal trauma are disadvantaged in several
ways. They feel extremely distressed, and there is ample evidence for their
perception that others do not want to hear about their trauma, because it is

too distressing (Harber & Pennebaker, 1992). In addition, their symptoms—particularly self-harm and suicide—are extremely alarming to others. Traumatized persons are likely to be angry and bitter as well as sad and depressed. They are not likely to convey to prospective supportive partners that they are coping actively, the optimal strategy that Silver and colleagues recommended (Silver et al., 1990). On the contrary, they are likely to adopt a passive and self-defeating stance that may fuel others' sense of helplessness.

Intimate relationships have the potential to provide the greatest sense of support, as Sarason and colleagues noted (B. R. Sarason et al., 1990). Yet intimate relationships also are especially likely to be characterized by intense conflict, including anger and violence. Although secure attachment in intimate relationships offers the best chance of support, insecure attachment is most conducive to conflict. In particular, the ambivalent pattern of attachment (e.g., as characteristic of clients with BPD) is liable to produce intense turmoil and reenactments of traumatic relationship patterns. Hence the notion that negative interactions outweigh the benefits of support is particularly troubling in relation to attachment trauma. Although not concerned with attachment style, Tarrier and colleagues (Tarrier, Sommerfield, & Pilgrim, 1999) found that many clients with PTSD encounter hostility and criticism from their key relative, and those who encounter such negative responses benefit less from treatment.

Research demonstrates that trauma-related insecurity in attachment is likely to undermine potential sources of support. McCarthy and Taylor (1999) assessed adult attachment style and quality of adult love relationships in women with a history of childhood adversity. They found a strong relationship between childhood abuse and negative functioning in adult love relationships, which was mediated by insecure attachment. We compared women in inpatient treatment for trauma-related disorders with a sample of community women (Allen, Huntoon et al., in press) and found that the patients showed predominantly fearful attachment, whereas the community sample showed predominantly secure attachment. We also asked participants to list their current attachment figures, that is, persons whom they could count on for comfort and protection in times of distress. Traumatized women listed fewer attachment figures with whom they had a sense of security, and more figures with whom they felt somewhat insecure. Nonetheless, the average number of attachment figures for the trauma sample was about four—suggesting that, despite their predominantly fearful orientation, traumatized women typically are able to find some sources of support.

Three studies illustrate how adult relationships may serve as buffers by influencing whether childhood abuse and neglect eventuate in adult psychopathology. Whiffen and colleagues (Whiffen, Judd, & Aube, 1999) found that intimate relationships moderated the relationship between childhood sexual abuse and adult depression. That is, given a history of childhood sexual abuse, having an intimate adulthood relationship served as a protective factor with respect to depression, whereas the lack of an intimate relationship served as a risk factor. On the other hand, Hill and colleagues (Hill, Pickles et al., in press) found that good adult love relationships reduced the risk of depression associated with childhood neglect but not sexual abuse. Roch and colleagues (Roche, Runtz, & Hunter, 1999) found that the relation between childhood sexual abuse and a wide range of trauma-related symptoms (PTSD, dissociation, anxiety, depression, self-concept, sexual concerns, tension-reducing behavior) was mediated by adult attachment style. That is, given a history of childhood sexual abuse, symptoms were more likely in the context of insecure attachment than secure attachment. As would be expected, there is a double liability associated with childhood sexual abuse, because abuse was also associated with a higher likelihood of insecure attachment in adulthood.

Intervention in social support

There are four avenues of intervention with respect to problematic social support (Argyle, 1992; Rook, 1992): helping the client to lessen the conflict and strain in close relationships; helping the client to disengage from strained relationships; increasing social competence through social skills training; and helping the client to forge new ties. With respect to forging new ties, a noteworthy option is self-help groups (Argyle, 1992), which take advantage of the fact that similarly distressed persons are less likely to be unsupportive, despite problematic coping on the part of the person seeking support (Silver et al., 1990). Although therapists work on all four fronts, addressing trauma-related attachment problems that fuel interpersonal stress and undermine support is a useful fulcrum for psychotherapeutic efforts.

In discussing the hazards of social support, I also draw clients' attention to the challenges faced by those who endeavor to support them. In one educational group, we elucidated three tightropes that partners must walk simultaneously: they must encourage without pushing too hard; help without taking over; and be able to give the client space without completely withdrawing and giving up. Insightful clients recognized that their own depressive negativism made their partners' job even more difficult. I pointed out that they yank these tightropes back and forth as their partners attempt to walk them.

Given all the hazards traumatized clients face in seeking social support, it is not surprising that we therapists often play a key role in their support networks. By temperament and training, we are likely to have a high tolerance for distress and to understand the challenges our clients face. We mental health professionals also may play a backup role in relation to other social services. Campbell and colleagues (Campbell et al., 1999) found that rape survivors at highest risk of post-traumatic symptoms were those who received minimal help from the legal and medical professions and who were also subjected to secondary victimization in these contacts—particularly in relation to non-stranger rape. Some survivors were blamed or disbelieved, or the assault was minimized. Encouragingly, those survivors who received mental health counseling showed decreased post-traumatic symptoms, owing to the validation and support they received—not just in relation to the rape but also regarding their negative interactions with persons in the legal and medical professions.

SECURE ATTACHMENT IN PSYCHOTHERAPY

If traumatizing relationships are the problem, healing relationships must be the solution. Seeking social support is fraught with peril, and a supportive psychotherapy relationship may be required to help the client develop the capacity to make use of others' support. This section examines the process by which psychotherapeutic relationships can transform profoundly insecure attachments into more workable secure attachments. We will not be concerned with therapeutic technique but rather with understanding what we are endeavoring to accomplish with psychotherapy—and helping clients understand as well.

Psychodynamic psychotherapy

Psychodynamic psychotherapy is among the most popular forms of treatment for a wide range of disorders (McFarlane, 1994) and has long been applied to the treatment of trauma (Keane, 1998). In writing about psychoanalytic treatment of traumatic neuroses, Fenichel (1945), for example, commented on the need to balance supportive and expressive interventions and argued that the most direct help for trauma involved opportunity for 'repeated re-experiencing of the trauma and a verbalization and clarification of the conflicts involved' (p. 127). Yet he also recognized the need for a great deal of support, including reassurance and rest.

Although it is widely practiced, the effectiveness of psychodynamic treatments of PTSD rarely has been researched, and the few studies that have been conducted have methodological limitations that make them difficult to interpret (Foa & Meadows, 1997; Roth & Fonagy, 1996). The only pertinent well-controlled study (Brom, Kleber, & Defares, 1989) compared three brief treatments for PTSD: psychodynamic psychotherapy modeled after Horowitz's (1997) approach, systematic desensitization, and hypnotherapy. Compared to a wait-list control group, all three treatments were effective for

PTSD and a range of other symptoms, and there were only small differences among the three treatments in outcome. The effectiveness of psychodynamic psychotherapy in this study is roughly comparable to that found for a wide range of cognitive-behavioral treatments (Sherman, 1998). Yet the findings are difficult to generalize, because the sample consisted of clients who had experienced an extremely wide range of traumas and bereavements. Thus, widely applied as it is, psychodynamic psychotherapy is essentially untested in its efficacy for treating trauma.

Or is it? McFarlane (1994) pointed out that, while psychodynamic approaches place particular emphasis on the conscious and unconscious meanings of the trauma, they share many common elements with other therapeutic approaches that have been demonstrated to be effective (Chapter 12). These common elements include developing a realistic appraisal of the threat, overcoming avoidance, improving affect modulation, mastering intrusive recollections, moving from a sense of being a victim to that of being a survivor, developing a sense of a future, and engaging in rewarding social relationships. McFarlane added that trust is essential to the treatment relationship and that the client must feel secure in the conviction that the therapist is able to 'cope with bearing witness to the trauma and understanding its significance' (p. 402). Of course the value of psychotherapy is not just to treat the trauma but rather to help the traumatized *person*. Any techniques employed to work with traumatic memories must be embedded in a supportive therapy process that addresses the full range of problems with which the traumatized person struggles.

Group psychotherapy

Group psychotherapy is helpful in many ways pertinent to treating trauma. As Yalom (1970) demonstrated, group therapy naturally provides abundant opportunities for interpersonal learning, including learning how to express feelings and developing greater trust in other persons. Groups offer a unique opportunity for *universality*, a recognition that one's experiences are shared by others, a crucially important experience for traumatized clients. Yalom commented,

> Many clients enter therapy with the foreboding thought that they are unique in their wretchedness.... After hearing other members disclose concerns similar to their own, clients report feeling more in touch with the world and describe the process as a 'welcome to the human race' experience. (p. 10)

Van der Kolk noted that 'the essence of the trauma response is the severance of secure affiliative bonds' (van der Kolk, 1987, p. 153) and commented that cohesive and stable groups can provide a much-needed sense of safety and comfort. Groups can be a powerful forum for overcoming the prohibitions against talking about trauma, and they provide an opportunity for others to bear witness, thus potentially helping survivors overcome feelings of shame and guilt (Herman, 1992b; Talbot et al., 1998).

A diverse array of groups have been applied to the treatment of trauma (van der Kolk, 1987), with the composition of the group often depending on the type of trauma experienced (e.g., women's groups for incest survivors versus men's groups for combat veterans). Although there is some debate over the role of group therapy for clients with severe dissociative disorders (Barach, 1993), properly conducted group psychotherapy can have distinct advantages in overcoming the dissociative client's sense of alienation (Buchele, 1993; Caul, Sachs, & Braun, 1986; Coons & Bradley, 1985). Yet group therapy runs the risk of being over-stimulating and disorganizing, particularly to the extent that uncovering and disclosing details of traumatic experiences are emphasized. Hence group treatment for trauma must be conducted with attention to structure, safety, and support (Herman, 1992b; Talbot et al., 1998; Zlotnick, Shea, Rosen et al., 1997), and group therapy often should be preceded by individual therapy and other supportive interventions (Herman, 1992b).

Initial naturalistic studies suggested that group psychotherapy is a promising intervention for trauma. Herman and Schatzow (1984) conducted a six-month follow-up evaluation of women who had participated in a 10-week supportive group for incest survivors. The most consistent benefit was improved self-esteem along with lessened shame and guilt feelings. Attesting to the importance of universality, the authors noted, 'In [the clients'] unanimous opinion, the single most helpful thing about the groups was the contact with other incest victims' (p. 613). Hazzard and colleagues (Hazzard, Rogers, & Angert, 1993) reported widespread benefits evident on psychometric assessment after participation in a year-long therapy group for sexual abuse survivors. Notably, members who had been in previous individual therapy showed greater benefit than those who had not.

A small number of controlled studies lend further empirical support to group treatment of trauma. In their review of psychosocial treatments for PTSD, Foa and Meadows (1997) cited the results of an unpublished study that showed interpersonal process group therapy for survivors of childhood sexual abuse to be more effective in reducing PTSD symptoms than a wait-list control group. Stalker and Fry (1999) randomly assigned women with a history of sexual abuse to either individual or group psychotherapy and compared the results with a wait-list period. The 10-week individual and group interventions were similar in content, each having a substantial psychoeducational focus. The two interventions were comparable in effectiveness, with change evident in an array of post-traumatic and other symptoms, both at termination and one-year follow-up. Notably, Zlotnick and colleagues (Zlotnick, Shea, Rosen et al., 1997) found that adding group therapy to individual therapy for PTSD improved the outcome.

Resick and colleagues (Resick, Jordan, Girelli, Hutter, & Marhoefer-Dvorak, 1988) compared the effectiveness of three six-session group interventions for rape victims: stress inoculation, assertiveness training, and supportive–educational psychotherapy. Six-month follow-up showed that all three groups were effective—and equally so—with respect to a wide range of outcome measures. Alexander and colleagues (Alexander, Neimeyer, Follette, Moore, & Harter, 1989) compared two 10-week group formats for treating women with a history of childhood sexual abuse. The interpersonal transaction group involved participation in dyadic discussions of a range of topics pertinent to abuse. A process group focused more on members' interactions in the group. Although both types of groups yielded durable alleviation of depression and distress, the process group showed some advantage with respect to improved social adjustment.

I draw three general conclusions from the group psychotherapy literature. First, the client should begin group therapy only after developing some capacity to process the trauma in individual therapy. Second, the format of group therapy matters less than providing the client with an opportunity to learn from other persons who have been traumatized so as to feel less alone and ashamed. Third, when trauma is discussed, the emphasis should be on how it is affecting the client's current functioning (e.g., in the form of reenactment). Thus, rather than exploring details of group members' trauma history, groups should focus on enhancing the capacity for supportive relationships and current coping.

Trauma therapy from the attachment perspective

Bowlby (1988) provided a theoretical framework for psychotherapeutic treatment of trauma, construing the therapist's role as

> providing the conditions in which his patient can explore his representational models of himself and his attachment figures with a view to reappraising and restructuring them in light of the new understanding he acquires and the new experiences he has in the therapeutic relationship. (p. 138)

The foundation for this work is providing the client with 'a secure base from which he can explore the various unhappy and painful aspects of his life' (p. 138). Despite this solid lead, attachment theory has been underutilized in developing theories of psychotherapy (Rutter, 1995; Slade, 1999). Given that affect regulation is a core trauma problem, and attachment relationships are the wellspring for developing the capacity to regulate affect, the quality of the attachment relationship established in psychotherapy should have a major impact on affect regulation.

Clients will bring their attachment style into the relationship with the therapist, and clients with secure attachment make better use of therapy than those with insecure attachment (Dozier, 1990). Different insecure attachment styles pose different challenges for psychotherapy (Slade, 1999). Clients with a dismissing attachment style are likely to defend rigidly against the experience and expression of affect, and they show substantial treatment resistance (Dozier, 1990). In contrast, clients with a preoccupied attachment style will present with under-regulated affect, and the therapist's task will be to provide containment. Such clients are particularly difficult to help in psychotherapy (Fonagy et al., 1995, 1996). Many clients are likely to present with a combination of preoccupied and unresolved/disorganized attachment patterns—or vacillating among different insecure patterns—such that the therapeutic challenge goes beyond providing containment for dysregulated affect to helping the client to develop and maintain a coherent and organized state of mind.

Although Bowlby (1988) highlighted the need to revise internal working models, Fonagy and colleagues (Fonagy, Moran, Edgcumbe, Kennedy, & Target, 1993) argued persuasively that we must attend not only to the *content* of the client's mental representations but also to the mental *process of representing* relationships. More specifically, trauma may inhibit mentalizing, that is, apprehending the behavior of oneself and others on the basis of mental states—thoughts, beliefs, feelings, and intentions (Chapter 4). This inhibition prevents painful representations (e.g., the experience of being hated) from coming to mind but promotes a sense of emptiness and passivity, as well as a lack of vitality and initiative.

In the context of coping with past trauma, the defensive inhibition of mentalization puts the client in the position of leaping out of the frying pan into the fire. Fonagy (1995) described how, for the child as yet unable to mentalize, there is no clear distinction between ideas and reality; ideas are experienced as direct replicas of reality. Fonagy and Target (Fonagy & Target, 1997a; Target & Fonagy, 1996) have described the *psychic equivalence* mode of functioning wherein thoughts and feelings are experienced with all the intensity that would be associated with current external events. It is difficult—but critical—for those of us who can take mentalization for granted to imagine what it is like to function in the psychic equivalence mode. Perhaps we can find common ground with our clients in our experience of dreaming, where neurobiologically kindled mental states are experienced with the intensity of real events. Some of our traumatized clients aptly refer to their flashbacks as 'daymares.' Similarly, many traumatized clients who take the Rorschach Inkblot Test become frightened by what they see, as if they are not generating an imaginative association but rather perceiving something threatening or dangerous. Paranoid states provide another example, wherein the person is unable to recognize a fearful mental state as such but rather feels endangered by external reality. More mundane examples abound as clients equate thoughts and fantasies with actions—for example, feeling guilty for their mental states as if they had committed a crime when they merely had an image of assaulting someone. Another example is the client who cannot recognize his or her sexual wishes and fears as such but rather develops the unshakeable conviction that the therapy relationship will become a sexual one.

This distinction between the psychic equivalence mode (wherein mental states are not distinguished from real events) and the mentalizing mode (wherein internal mental states are apprehended as different from external events) goes to the heart of the difference between reliving and remembering trauma. Reexperiencing trauma, the core problem in PTSD, is a failure of mentalization, exemplifying the psychic equivalence mode. The client feels as if he or she is in current danger. The goal of therapy—be it psychodynamic or cognitive-behavioral—is to help clients remember trauma instead of reexperiencing it. Therapy helps clients to mentalize trauma, to experience it as a memory. A memory implies a mental state—thoughts, feelings, and images. Experiencing memories as mental states implies distinguishing between mental reality and external reality as well as between past and present. Moreover, as mentalized, memory can be experienced with an appropriate sense of fallibility, with a potentially wide range of accuracy (Allen, 1995b; Fonagy & Target, 1997b; Schacter, 1996).

Hence, as Fonagy and colleagues have argued (Fonagy, 1998, 1999b; Fonagy et al., 1993), therapists must not aspire simply to alter the *content* of mental representations, as Bowlby (1988) suggested, but also to foster the *capacity* for mentalization and reflective function. We must do more than interpret; we must provide developmental help (Fonagy, 1995). The capacity for mentalization originally develops in the context of secure attachment, or it becomes inhibited in the context of attachment trauma. Analogously, for the therapist to rekindle this ability, an attachment relationship must be established in which the client has a sufficient sense of security to be able to reflect. In the earlier psychoanalytic literature, this process was eloquently described as the ability to work in *potential space* (Ogden, 1985; Winnicott, 1971). We therapists tend to focus on helping the client *change* thoughts and feelings. More fundamentally, we must provide a relationship that *enables* thinking and feeling. This is the ground for change. As Fonagy and colleagues (Fonagy et al., 1995) found, increasing capacity for reflective functioning is associated with symptomatic improvement in psychodynamic psychotherapy.

Fostering the client's capacity to mentalize entails explicating mental states in the client and therapist (Fonagy, 1998, 1999b). The therapist clarifies changes in the client's mental state and encourages the client to think about his or her impact on the therapist's state of mind and behavior. Differences in perceptions can be addressed. Countertransference enactments are not to be avoided—they are inevitable—but they become occasions for explicating the mental states of the client and therapist. This approach to treatment requires that the therapist be able to maintain a reflective stance that ultimately enables the client to find himself or herself in the therapist's mind and to integrate this image as part of his or her self-representation. In successful therapy, the client gradually comes to accept that feelings can safely be felt and ideas may safely be thought about. (Fonagy, 1998, pp. 163–164)

As Fonagy and colleagues succinctly put it (Fonagy et al., 1993), the treatment process allows 'the experience of mental involvement with another human being without the threat of overwhelming mental anguish' (p. 43).

The capacity for mentalization and reflective functioning fostered by effective psychotherapy sets the stage for adaptive shifts in ways of relating. Therapeutic change does not come about by way of acquiring new mental contents—insights or recovered memories—but rather by way of acquiring procedural knowledge (Fonagy, 1999a; Fonagy & Target, 1997b). As Fonagy and Target (1997a) stated, 'attachment is a skill' (p. 97). Psychotherapy is more like a piano lesson than a history lesson. To conduct psychotherapy effectively is to foster relationship skills that promote openness to new possibilities—to be able to think, feel, and relate in new and fresh ways. Thus, 'change occurs in the implicit memory leading to a change of the procedures the person uses in living with himself and with others' (Fonagy, 1999a, p. 218).

Consider, for example, the client whose trauma left him overwhelmed by rageful annihilation fantasies. He is convinced that he will destroy the therapist, as he feels he has been destroyed. He may derive some help from verbalizing his fears and hearing the therapist verbalize her conviction that she will not be damaged. But interactions speak louder than words. Innumerable interchanges outside the focus of conscious awareness allow the client continually to see in the therapist's demeanor and hear in her tone of voice that she is not feeling endangered. Gradually, in the course of these interactions—thousands, perhaps—the client can come to experience himself as less dangerous. Although verbalizing this process may help by drawing attention to it, the change in implicit, procedural knowledge could arise without any conscious insight. Through implicit learning in a secure attachment relationship, the client has acquired new attachment skill.

Fonagy and colleagues (Fonagy et al., 2000) neatly summarized the commonalities among diverse schools of therapy, pointing out that they all

(1) aim to establish an attachment relationship with the patient; (2) aim to use this to create an interpersonal context where understanding of mental states becomes a focus; and (3) attempt (mostly implicitly) to recreate a situation in which the self is recognized as intentional and real by the therapist, and this recognition is clearly perceived by the patient. (p. 117)

Fortunately, you do not need to think about every step in this process of working with your clients; you can rely on your intuition. You provide a safe climate, remain open to your clients' thoughts and feelings (as well as your own), express (largely non-verbally) an attitude of interest and concern—and put a tiny bit of this process into words.

Stern and colleagues (Stern et al., 1998) articulated beautifully how the opportunity for implicit relational learning may arise in the context of *moments of meeting*. These authors view interactions as governed by implicit relational knowing. Along with whatever conscious and unconscious goals individuals may have in any interaction, they also will be pursuing non-consciously an intersubjective goal that entails 'mutual recognition of each other's motives, desires and implicit aims that direct actions, and the feelings that accompany this process' (p. 908). A sense of affective attunement exemplifies this intersubjective goal. Inevitably in the course of interacting there arise special moments of meeting wherein well-honed procedures for relating are interrupted, technique is beside the point, and client and therapist are without a script. Such moments of meeting provide an opportunity for genuine spontaneity and interactive creativity. When these moments are properly seized, the interchanges allow for therapeutic changes in the shared implicit relationship and thereby for the development of new procedural knowledge.

Countertransference from the attachment perspective

Slade (1999) described how the client's insecure attachment style is likely to pose relationship challenges for the therapist. On the one hand, dismissing clients 'lock the therapist out as they themselves were locked out by their attachment figures . . . And the therapist is left feeling much as the client once felt as a child: angry, unacknowledged, silly, and inept' (p. 588). On the other hand, with preoccupied clients, collaboration is difficult to achieve, and 'the therapist feels much the way the clients once did as a child: swamped, angry, helpless, confused, and dysregulated' (p. 588).

Therapists, too, bring their attachment styles into the treatment, as well as being drawn into attachment patterns by clients. Dozier (Dozier, Cue, & Barnett, 1994) found evidence that case managers with secure attachment styles were more likely to respond to clients in a way that positively influenced the client's attachment disturbance. Like clients, therapists can adopt a dismissing style, defending against affect and attachment. Alternatively, therapists can become entangled in a preoccupied style of relating that entails sharing the client's emotional turmoil. Yet, within bounds, therapists' deactivating and hyperactivating attachment styles can therapeutically counterbalance clients' complementary styles (Tyrrell, Dozier, Teague, & Fallot, 1999). Of course therapists' attachment experience will not always remain within bounds. The pulls into defensive distance or entangled closeness can be enormous, and there is no reason to believe that we therapists should be able to resist them entirely (Plakun, 1998). We, too, can experience incoherent and disorganized states of mind.

As with the client's disturbance, the therapist's situation is difficult but not hopeless. We can regain our equilibrium—sufficient balance between closeness and distance—and restore our own reflective function so as to provide a secure enough base for the client (Plakun, 1998). But we too need the kind of help we aim to provide for the client—the therapeutic frame, supportive relationships, and a capacity for self-regulation (see Chapter 14).

Psychotherapy as a bridge

In educating traumatized clients, I characterize psychotherapy as a bridge or stepping stone to secure attachments in other relationships. Clients quickly point out that they find it difficult to *get on* the bridge—in effect, to allow the psychotherapy to become an attachment relationship. Yet they consistently state that it is even more difficult to *get off* the bridge. They are keenly aware of their penchant to cling to whatever secure attachment they establish, as well as their aversion to letting go of this safety for the sake of establishing other attachment relationships. The client must keep one foot on the bridge while putting another foot off into other relationships. And clients are quick to point out that, having gotten off the bridge, they may need to return to it from time to time. Disappointment, betrayal, or trauma in a subsequent relationship puts them back to square one or worse—being unable to get back on the bridge again.

What do traumatized clients acquire on the bridge that allows them to move on to other more secure relationships? Attachment is a skill. *Working* models imply the possibility of change. The client who forms a secure attachment to the therapist will have a secure base, not only for exploring the internal world but also for deepening other attachment relationships. Of course what makes this goal of therapy easy to state in principle and extremely challenging to translate into practice is the client's profoundly insecure attachment in the therapy relationship. We cannot expect the client to make a quantum leap from insecure attachment to secure attachment. Rather the client may gradually develop greater attachment skill evident in modified relationship models that will provide a bridge into other relationships, perhaps with fits and starts and much jumping off and back onto the bridge.

PRINCIPLES OF SELF-REGULATION

I think of containment in terms of the overarching developmental lines of relatedness and autonomy (Blatt & Blass, 1992). Relatedness is the wellspring of autonomy, as secure attachment fosters autonomous exploration. In discussing treatment with clients, I always present supportive relationships and self-regulation as a pair. To prevent or to cope with unbearable emotional states, clients must find some balance of utilizing support from others and relying on their own capacities to calm and comfort themselves.

The integration of supportive relationships and self-regulation comes into play most directly in the phenomenon of self-dependence, as Lichtenberg (1989) defined it, namely, the capacity to bridge the gap between separation and reunion. Various self-regulation strategies could be construed as gap-bridging maneuvers. For example, internalizing the therapeutic relationship helps the client to bridge the gap. I focus on the extent to which clients are able to evoke a helpful memory of the therapist (or a memory of being with the therapist). I ask if they are able to form a visual image of the therapist, to hear the therapist's voice in their mind, or to evoke a sense of the therapist as a comforting mental presence. Such internalization is a high aspiration, because it requires a capacity for reflection as well as the ability to prevent the benign mental representation from being swamped by conflicts. That is, all the conflicts that pertain to the real interaction with the therapist may also intrude on the mental experience of the therapist. For example, thinking of the therapist may evoke feelings of abandonment rather than connection, or hostility and persecutory fantasies rather than a feeling of safety.

Reflective function and self-regulation

As secure attachment is a platform for reflection, reflection is a platform for self-regulation. Without reflection, the client is liable to go straight from unbearable affect to dissociation or self-destructive action. With the capacity for reflection—if only to experience and identify a painful emotion as such—the client has some capacity to sit with the emotion and think about ways of alleviating the painful state. Yet as we endeavor to foster such growth, we are rowing upstream. Encouraging openness to experience goes against the tide of the client's avoidance and disavowal. And encouraging self-care brings two additional resistances. Caring for the self—as opposed to harming or neglecting the self—goes against the tide of masochism. In addition, taking responsibility for self-care goes against the universal wish for instant maternal care, which will be transferred onto the therapist.

To regulate affect, one must be able to tolerate it. Conversely, to be able to tolerate affect, one must have confidence in being able to regulate it. Krystal (1988) stated,

> people who can comfortably experience a feeling generally feel secure that their state is justified by their life experience; that it makes sense; and that, having accomplished its purpose or run its course, it will stop. . . . One of the things that makes possible tolerance of painful affects is the ability to modify them periodically for some short period of gratification or respite. (p. 21)

He noted that the capacity for reflective self-awareness makes it possible to discern one's affective state and to use affects as signals for coping and self-regulation. Here is our job:

> Once we renounce the idea that we can help anyone to be *rid* of emotions, we are glad to find that we can be helpful in other ways—helping clients to name and identify their emotions and to obtain the maximum information from them. (p. 53)

To foster such openness to emotion we must also confront the second resistance: aversion to self-care. Secure attachment fosters self-regulation, and the prototype of self-care is the capacity to mother oneself. Healthy development ensures abundant means of alleviating distress (downregulation) as well as alleviating boredom by increasing stimulation and excitement (upregulation). Trauma interferes with the development of the capacity for self-regulation, and Krystal (1988) emphasized how trauma may interfere with the *permission* to care for the self. Self-solacing may be forbidden. The capacity to anticipate and avoid harm may be inhibited. The situation is difficult but not hopeless. Although clients have severe conflicts about self-care, most have attempted various constructive forms of self-regulation, however ambivalently, alongside the destructive forms.

We should not be too critical of our clients' ambivalence toward self-care; Krystal proposed that ambivalence about self-care is universal, which most of us can probably confirm by a little introspection. We simply need to recognize and respect this ambivalence as we encourage clients to take on self-regulation as a long-term project and teach them whatever we can about how they might go about it. We must teach what should have become a natural and automatic process. For example, I encourage clients to label their feelings ('I'm starting to feel panicky'), to validate them ('There must be some reason for this feeling'), and to invoke an explicit plan for alleviating them ('When I feel panicky, I must breathe more slowly').

Simple but difficult

I approach clients' resistance by framing self-regulation as *simple but difficult* (Allen, 1995a; Kabat-Zinn, 1994). But resistance is not the only problem. Techniques that are tried and true for non-traumatized persons are liable to backfire in various ways for traumatized clients. They must be approached with caution and awareness of the potential hazards, which I will discuss shortly.

But we should not blithely assume that self-regulation is easy for anyone, us therapists included. Behavior is regulated overwhelmingly by non-conscious automatic processes, including responsiveness to myriad environmental cues of which we are unaware (Bargh & Chartrand, 1999;

Baumeister, Bratslavsky, Muraven, & Tice, 1998; Kirsch & Lynn, 1999; Norman & Shallice, 1986). These automatic processes can work for good or for ill, but in general we should be grateful for them. Deliberate conscious control is slow and unwieldy, although necessary to cope with novelty and complexity, as well as to inhibit automatic responding when necessary (Norman & Shallice, 1986). We are aware of our conscious efforts at self-regulation, which we generally construe as willpower (Mischel, 1996). To refer to 'self-control' or even 'self-regulation' may be unwarranted hubris. We might more humbly—and accurately—think of ourselves as being able to *nudge* ourselves under optimal circumstances.

As is well documented in the technical literature and easily confirmed by a moment's reflection, influencing emotions can be extremely challenging, especially when they are intense (Elster, 1999). Given the powerful influence of the environment on our behavior and emotions (Bargh & Chartrand, 1999; Elster, 1999), one of the best ways to influence ourselves is to control our exposure to environmental cues. For example, the alcoholic must avoid situations where alcohol is available; the self-mutilator must not keep razor blades in her apartment; and the client prone to overdosing must not have a stash of pills handy.

In his work with young children, Mischel (1996) demonstrated the cardinal role of *self-distraction* in the ability to delay gratification. Many clients recognize the importance of distraction in calming themselves down as well as refraining from self-damaging behavior. They must direct attention away from fantasizing about how gratifying self-harm or other self-destructive actions might be. Yet such self-control takes energy, and trauma depletes the individual's resources (Baumeister et al., 1998). This is blatantly true in the context of post-traumatic depression, where the challenges are great and the ego resources are slim. I present this litany of difficulties only to make the point that we must first empathize with the challenges our clients face in attempting to regulate their painful states constructively; then they might listen to us when we offer some concrete strategies for doing so.

Goal setting

Carver and Scheier's (1998) careful analysis of goal-directed behavior contains several points pertinent to self-regulation in the treatment of traumatized clients. Emotion arises in conjunction with rate of progress toward goals. Goal-directed behavior entails both approach and avoidance. Progressing well toward approach goals engenders elation and joy, whereas progressing poorly toward these goals engenders depression. This point bears emphasis: *slow progress toward goals is depressing*. On the other hand, doing well with respect to avoidance goals (e.g., avoiding punishment) engenders relief, whereas doing poorly (e.g., anticipating punishment) engenders anxiety. For all of us, engaging in goal-directed activity entails a balance between confidence and doubt, engagement and disengagement, persistence and giving up.

Although we generally admire persistence and deplore giving up, Carver and Scheier argue that being unable to give up unattainable goals is a huge problem: 'the person experiences distress (because of an inability to make progress) and is unable to do anything about the distress (because of an inability to give up). . . . This situation—commitment to unattainable goals— is a prescription for distress' (p. 195). Many clients struggle with this plight in treatment. They courageously persist in treatment for years in the face of ongoing symptoms and relapses. In the midst of relapses, they become profoundly demoralized, often feeling as if they no longer have the will to keep trying. At these junctures, many become suicidal—the ultimate expression of disengagement and giving up. Working on trauma is a prescription for slow progress toward goals, the guaranteed precipitant of negative affect. If the client has adopted the completely understandable goal of cure, freedom from symptoms, and freedom from relapses, depression will ensue.

Particularly in the midst of relapses, clients long for wholesale and dramatic change. But we must help them go in the opposite direction. To ensure success and positive emotion that builds confidence in treatment, we must orient clients toward a view of improvement based on small, gradual changes (Kirsch & Lynn, 1999). Gollwitzer (1999) proposed a two-step strategy for goal attainment that I introduce to clients in the context of self-regulation. The first step is goal setting, an important challenge. What are realistic treatment goals? Over the long term, gradual improvement with ups and downs is realistic—but by no means guaranteed. But we must focus on the short term, where clients can experience concrete progress. Gollwitzer emphasized that goals must not only be achievable (within the person's capacity) but also be specific rather than general (e.g., 'Say "No!" when I do not want to do something' rather than 'be more assertive'). Goals should be proximal (near future) rather than distal (distant future). The combination of specific and proximal goals allows the individual to identify clear feedback that promotes self-monitoring. It is helpful to formulate *learning goals* (e.g., learning how to calm oneself or discovering capacities to distract oneself). Approach goals are preferable to avoidance goals. For example, rather than setting the goal of not feeling anxious, the client might adopt the goal of calming himself by listening to music at the initial signs of anxiety. The client must also eliminate distractions and temptations in the environment. Perhaps most difficult in light of clients' ambivalence and depression, *success requires high motivation to attain the goal and a strong sense of commitment to it.*

Gollwitzer made a convincing case that goal setting must be accompanied by *implementation intentions*, that is, specifying when, where, and how the goal will be implemented: when situation *x* arises, I will perform response *y*. This entails forming a clear idea of situation *x* in advance. Situation *x* could be an emotional state in an environmental context. For example, the client might formulate the implementation intention, when I am afraid and alone at home during the daytime, and I am tempted to cut myself, I will take a walk around the neighborhood. Mentally rehearsing implementation intentions is helpful, and adhering reliably to plans ensures that intentions become habitual.

EDUCATING CLIENTS ABOUT SELF-REGULATION STRATEGIES

I begin discussion of self-regulation by asking clients what methods they have tried. I am struck by wide variation. Whereas some clients have tried innumerable strategies, others say they have none. To address clients' resistances to self-regulation, I emphasize some of the potential hazards they face in employing seemingly tried and true methods. Before reviewing traditional methods, I alert them to an under-emphasized form of self-regulation: alonetime.

Alonetime

By training and perhaps by temperament, we therapists place an extremely high value on relatedness—as my attachment to attachment theory attests. But we must strike a proper balance between relatedness and autonomy, mutual regulation through attachment and self-regulation. And we must keep in mind that clients who have been traumatized in attachment relationships have relied extensively on isolation as a form of self-protection. This one-sided strategy does not work—the client's presence in our office attests to that. Yet we can also side with the client's desire for isolation, when kept in proper balance.

Buchholz and Helbraun (1999) articulated a concept of adaptive *alonetime* that helps clients feel understood. They defined alonetime as the 'individual's need to retreat psychologically and at times, physically, in order to constitute and reconstitute functioning and control stimulation so as to maximize perceptual and cognitive organization, emotional well-being, and homeostasis—by oneself' (p. 143). They construe the function of alonetime as follows: 'The alonetime need is psychobiologically based, has its roots in intrauterine experience, and is one aspect of behavior that supports the development of the self and inner coping strategies' (p. 154).

Thus construed, alonetime is a cornerstone of self-regulation. As Buchholz and Helbraun state, 'As mutual regulation is sister to attachment, self-regulation is akin to alonetime' (p. 144). The authors cite evidence for self-soothing behaviors in utero and note that infants not only have many means of engaging and making interpersonal contact but also many strategies for disengaging by regulating and breaking contact (gaze aversion, covering the ears, closing the eyes—and sleep). They suggest that infants communicate their need for alonetime by gaze aversion. As they point out,

> if we did not have this skill, we would not be able to fall back on choosing to be alone and content in the face of loss or disappointments in relationship. The baby, too, must be able to survive times when mutual regulation is not available or when it fails in a mismatch. (p. 150)

Manageable mismatches foster self-reliance. Thus we can empathize with our clients by adopting the authors' thesis that there is 'an ongoing motivation to be out of contact as well as connected' (p. 154)—and *not pathologizing this need*.

Focusing inward: relaxation, meditation, hypnosis, and sleep

Three commonly used techniques—relaxation, meditation, and hypnosis—promote an inward focus, and they share some potential benefits and risks. Relaxation is simple but potentially difficult for traumatized clients. The simple part, as outlined by Benson (1975), comprises several components: seeking a quiet environment, closing your eyes, attending to a mental focus, adopting a passive attitude, finding a comfortable position, engaging in deep breathing, and progressively relaxing your muscles. Such activities may be accompanied by guided imagery.

Relaxation is not considered an adequate treatment for PTSD but is often incorporated as an adjunct to cognitive-behavioral treatments. A relaxation group was included as a *control group* in a study of the effectiveness of an exposure and cognitive restructuring treatment protocol for women with a history of sexual assault (Echeburua, Corral, Zubizarreta, & Sarasua, 1997). Although both interventions showed significant benefit, exposure and cognitive restructuring was significantly more effective than relaxation, particularly at follow-up. Similarly, relaxation training showed only modest benefits in the treatment of Vietnam veterans with PTSD (Watson, Tuorila, Vickers, Gearhart, & Mendez, 1997).

Relaxation seems innocuous, but it poses hazards in the treatment of trauma. Many traumatized clients readily grasp the paradoxical phenomenon of *relaxation-induced anxiety* (Fahrion & Norris, 1990). Full-fledged relaxation as Benson (1975) advocates puts the client in a highly vulnerable position—it is the farthest imaginable state (short of sleep) from hypervigilance and being poised for fight or flight. Profound relaxation may leave the client feeling endangered. Moreover, relaxation instructions foster turning inward and giving up grounding in external reality, and this loss of grounding may precipitate intrusive memories and dissociative states (Fitzgerald & Gonzalez, 1994). Guided imagery also can take a wrong turn in a client with a mind full of traumatic images. A client may picture herself alone on a beach on a warm summer day, and then form images of an attacker stalking her.

For clients who do not encounter these hazards, so much the better. For those who cannot engage in this classic form of relaxation, I emphasize the need for greater alertness and grounding. For some, keeping their eyes open or relaxing while sitting up might suffice. An outward focus, such as listening to music, might also be helpful. For others, a still posture in itself may be conducive to dissociation. Thus I emphasize the potential value of *relaxing activities*, which entail alertness and engagement with the environment. These may include walking or hiking, or a wide range of hobbies and crafts.

Relaxation and meditation are close cousins, and Benson's (1975) relaxation instructions include a meditative focus. But meditation places greater emphasis on regulation of states of consciousness (Austin, 1998), and for that reason is particularly pertinent to trauma and dissociation. Shapiro (1982) defined meditation as a 'family of techniques which have in common a conscious attempt to focus attention in a nonanalytical way and an attempt not to dwell on discursive, ruminating thought' (p. 268). Meditation focuses more on the *process* of thinking than the *content* of thoughts. Meditation has been integrated into carefully designed stress management protocols (Kabat-Zinn, 1990) and has demonstrated effectiveness in decreasing anxiety, depression, and other symptoms in clinical (Kabat-Zinn et al., 1992) and non-clinical (Astin, 1997) populations.

Yet meditation cannot lay claim to superiority over other stress reduction approaches (Shapiro, 1982) and, to my knowledge, its contribution to the treatment of trauma is untested. In theory, meditation would be ideal for helping dissociative clients learn to regulate their states of consciousness. Moreover, fostering a non-defensive attitude of openness toward inner experience is consistent with Krystal's (1988) approach to trauma. Yet meditation is not without its hazards (Shapiro, 1982). Because of its inward focus, meditation runs the risk of fostering intrusive memories and dissociative states. Moreover, immersion in meditation practice may abet a cognitive avoidance strategy. Perhaps we should consider meditation a gold standard of conscious control to which relatively few traumatized clients should aspire. A small proportion of clients I have worked with report that they use it and find it helpful.

Much of the focus on hypnosis in the context of trauma has centered on memory enhancement, and hypnosis is included among the prime culprits in abetting false memories. No doubt, if hypnosis is employed as a memory enhancement technique, it must be done with great expertise and proper safeguards (D. Brown et al., 1998). Yet hypnosis may also be employed as a means of enhancing relaxation and self-regulation, and recent applications of hypnosis in the treatment of traumatic memory place greater emphasis on containment than abreaction (Brown & Fromm, 1986; Peebles, 1989; Smith, 1993a; Spiegel, 1988). Given its long history and the solid clinical rationale for its use in the treatment of trauma, it is unfortunate that the effectiveness of hypnosis in trauma treatment has garnered so little systematic research (Cardeña, 2000). Like meditation, hypnosis is potentially helpful for treatment of dissociation, because it entails learning how to regulate states of consciousness. As Smith (1993b) noted, *hypnosis can be construed as a form of controlled dissociation*. Yet hypnosis is conducive to an inward focus that carries hazards of affective dysregulation in relation to traumatic memories, and considerable skill is required to transform potentially retraumatizing hypnotic experiences into therapeutic outcomes (Peebles, 1989).

Sleep is perhaps the ultimate form of inward focus as well as the ideal form of relaxation and restoration. Sleep is also the prototype of alonetime. The physical and mental health benefits of sleep, and the corresponding detrimental effects of sleep deprivation, are well documented (Dement, 1999; Hobson, 1994). For traumatized and post-traumatically depressed clients, sleep may be the epitome of self-regulation that is simple but difficult. The inward focus of sleep leaves the traumatized client vulnerable to nightmares. Also contributing to insomnia and sleep deprivation are phobias that develop in relation to sleep (Allen, Console et al., 2001). I often think that the single most helpful intervention for trauma is a decent night's sleep—or many.

Biofeedback

Biofeedback, or *psychophysiological self-regulation*, provides an external gauge to facilitate monitoring of an internal state. It is commonly employed in conjunction with relaxation techniques and optimally included as part of a comprehensive program of self-regulation (Fahrion & Norris, 1990). In principle, biofeedback should be a particularly useful self-regulation strategy for many traumatized clients who not only struggle with physiological hyperarousal but also are alienated from their body and physiology (Krystal, 1988). Yet there is limited research on the value of biofeedback in the treatment of PTSD. Peniston and colleagues (Peniston & Kulkosky, 1991; Peniston, Marrinan, Deming, & Kulkosky, 1993) have demonstrated benefits of brainwave training in Vietnam veterans. On the other hand, Watson and colleagues (Watson, Tuorila et al., 1997) did not find any benefit of adding thermal biofeedback to standard relaxation instructions in the treatment of PTSD in Vietnam veterans. Without a range of comparison studies, biofeedback can only be included with many other legitimate contenders in the field of self-regulation, where no particular method can be demonstrated to stand out from the pack.

Exercise

Exercise does not entail an inward focus, and it increases rather than decreases arousal. Exercise is pertinent to trauma insofar as substantial research has shown it to be effective in decreasing anxiety and depression (Sime, 1984) and enhancing positive mood (Watson, 2000), although we await a convincing physiological explanation for these effects (Dunn & Dishman, 1991). Westerlund (1992) reported that many incest survivors find exercise to be a helpful way of gaining a sense of control over their body.

Although exercise does not have the hazards of strategies that promote an inward focus, it has risks of its own. Most problematic for trauma clients is the potential for exercise-evoked arousal to heighten anxiety and, at worst, lead to panic, flashbacks, and dissociation. Insofar as physiological arousal (e.g., elevated heart rate and labored breathing) is part and parcel of a traumatic memory network, the arousal can become a cue or trigger for a traumatic memory. Traumatized persons prone to anorexia may also become self-destructively addicted to exercise. Hence clients must be cautioned to go slowly with this technique, as they must do with all others (Allen, 1995a).

Medication

I present medication to clients as an adjunct to self-regulation. Medication treatment of trauma-related disorders is a vast territory, owing to the fact that severely traumatized clients may present with a wide array of psychiatric diagnoses and symptoms. Hence the full array of psychotropic medications has been employed in the treatment of trauma (Friedman, 1997; Marshall, Davidson, & Yehuda, 1998; Yehuda, Marshall, & Giller, 1998). These include antidepressants (selective serotonin reuptake inhibitors, tricyclic antidepressants, monoamine oxidase inhibitors); antianxiety (benzodiazepines) and antiadrenergic (alpha-adrenergic agonist and beta-adrenergic blocking) agents; mood stabilizers (lithium and anticonvulsants); and opioid antagonists. Antipsychotic agents, although not specifically indicated for treatment of PTSD, are often employed to treat associated psychotic symptoms.

The vast literature on pharmacological treatment of PTSD includes a remarkably small number of well-controlled studies. Although more extensive studies are now underway, the few controlled trials have focused predominantly on antidepressants, and the outcomes have not been encouraging. Yet the relative dearth of positive findings likely reflects researchers' focus on severely impaired and treatment-refractory combat veterans (Friedman, 1997). Results have been more promising in the treatment of civilian populations, for example, women with a history of sexual abuse (van der Kolk et al., 1994). Brady and colleagues (Brady et al., 2000) conducted a double-blind placebo-controlled trial employing a selective serotonin reuptake inhibitor (sertraline) in the treatment of a large sample of predominantly female subjects who had suffered a wide range of traumas, the most common being physical or sexual assault. The treatment relieved PTSD symptoms and improved social and occupational functioning as well as quality of life. By stringent criteria, 53% of the participants were classified as good responders (compared to 32% for placebo).

Friedman (1997) recently observed that there are compelling clinical grounds for focus on antidepressants that have shown efficacy in relation to both depression and anxiety. Yet he emphasized that, given how the pathophysiology of PTSD differs from anxiety and depression, 'the time has come to develop and test drugs that have been developed specifically for PTSD rather than to recycle pharmacological agents that have been developed to treat affective or other anxiety disorders' (p. 367). He advocates investigating agents that affect neuropeptides rather than biogenic amines, given the prominent role of HPA axis dysregulation in PTSD (Chapter 6). Moreover, different pharmacological interventions are likely to be needed for different symptom clusters, different subtypes of PTSD, different stages of disorder, and different individuals.

No cure, but many remedies

I am impressed by the sheer diversity of ways clients have to alleviate distress. I have merely noted the more conspicuous ones here—some ancient (relaxation, meditation, exercise), others modern (biofeedback, psychopharmacology). All in all, a good night's sleep is certainly the most ancient and probably the most important. In any group of clients, individual differences stand out. What works for one client backfires for another.

There is little research to consult when applying these methods to the treatment of trauma. Therapists are inclined to combine—if not pile on—techniques that work. Consider the domain of psychopharmacology. There is little controlled research on individual medications and none on combinations, despite the fact that polypharmacy is the rule. Imagine what it would take to research the possible components and combinations of stress management techniques. I think that some combination of deactivating (relaxation) and activating (exercise) techniques would be best—along with good sleep hygiene (Dement, 1999). But most important is consistency in whatever approach the client adopts.

This chapter's focus on containment provides the backdrop for the next chapter's review of a range of treatment approaches that focus on the core symptom of PTSD: reexperiencing the trauma. Naturally, these treatments draw most clinical and research attention. But the capacity for containment must undergird these treatments, and the need for ongoing containment through relationships and self-regulation will continue long after the focal treatments have been completed. And, as I will argue, the therapeutic benefits of trauma-focused interventions are best understood as promoting the capacity for containment.

Chapter 12

NARRATING TRAUMA

Delightfully and inescapably we have story-telling brains. (Roberts, 1999, p. 7)

The prescription for trauma is simple: talk about it. Simple, *but difficult.* The survivor must tell the story to a trusted confidant who bears witness (Herman, 1992b; Tedeschi, 1999). Doubtlessly, this trauma intervention is ancient, and contemporary trauma treatments are variations on this venerable theme. Cognitive-behavioral techniques, for example, structure the task of telling the story to enhance the benefits of doing so.

While touching on technique at various points, this chapter provides a rationale for trauma-focused interventions. Clinical researchers have developed effective protocols for treating PTSD. Yet treating severely traumatized clients with several psychiatric disorders calls for extensive improvisation. Employing structured protocols where applicable, we must help the client tell the story while providing needed support and containment. To forge a workable alliance in relation to this agenda, we must also help our clients understand what we are doing and why.

Encouraging clients to talk about their trauma runs headlong into their avoidance, and therapists must have a solid conviction in the wisdom of this approach. After putting avoidance into perspective, this chapter advocates going beyond catharsis to transforming traumatic experience. This framework sets the stage for reviewing exemplary cognitive-behavioral techniques for treating PTSD and complications that may interfere with their effectiveness—not least of which is their application to the trauma-related disorders reviewed throughout this book. The chapter elaborates the thesis that *treating attachment trauma entails fostering narrative capacity rather than discovering and elucidating any particular narrative* content. This footing puts therapists in a position to explain trauma treatment to clients.

AVOIDANCE REVISITED

PTSD entails alternating between intrusive reexperiencing and avoidance. This alternation may be rapid when the client actively struggles to put traumatic images out of mind, or it may be prolonged when the client goes through long phases of being plagued by intrusive symptoms and then suppressing them (Brewin et al., 1996). The costs of many avoidance strategies (suicide attempts, self-harm, substance abuse, eating disorders, dissociation, somatization) are high (Brewin et al., 1996), especially insofar as avoidance increases rather than decreases stress (Polusny & Follette, 1995). Avoidance is also self-perpetuating insofar as it blocks coping and new learning. Notably, survivors may be misled about the effectiveness of their avoidant strategies. Sexual abuse survivors reported employing denial and emotional suppression as their most common and helpful coping strategies; yet avoidant coping was associated with poorer psychological adjustment (Leitenberg, Greenwald, & Cado, 1992).

Avoidance is invariably a stopgap strategy. Traumatic memories are elaborate networks (Bower, 1981; Lang, 1977, 1985; Tryon, 1999), comprising stimulus, response, and meaning elements. These memory networks include relatively conscious autobiographical or personal event memories alongside relatively non-conscious implicit memories (Allen, 1995b; Brewin et al., 1996; van der Kolk, 1994). Given the complexity of these memory networks, and the fact that activating any one element may activate the whole network, traumatized individuals are likely to be exposed continually to internal and external cues that evoke intrusive symptoms. These cues may be obvious reminders of trauma, such as when a man who was beaten as a child witnesses a boy being slapped by his mother in a grocery store. But the cues need not be so obvious, because non-conscious aspects of the memory network may be primed outside of awareness (e.g., by environmental stimuli or physiological arousal). Any event that evokes a sense of helplessness or a feeling of being out of control may activate a traumatic memory network. As if the potential ubiquity of activating cues were not enough, avoidance is also fueled by anticipatory fear of anxiety, which is especially keen in persons with PTSD (Schoenberger, 1999; Taylor et al., 1992).

Hence the survivor will need to employ avoidance strategies continually, and the need for avoidance will escalate insofar as these strategies (e.g., substance abuse or self-harm) generate interpersonal conflicts that instigate reenactments and reexperiencing. Avoidance paradoxically fuels the phenomena to be avoided.

Ironic mental processes

Wenger and colleagues (Ansfield & Wegner, 1996; Wegner, 1994, 1997; Wegner & Erber, 1992) have demonstrated the irony that active efforts to suppress intrusive thoughts can increase the likelihood that such thoughts will become conscious. 'Don't think of a white bear!' is a paradoxical injunction, but this is just what the trauma survivor may try to do. As Wegner (1997) put it, 'the simple decision to try to control our minds can sometimes lead us wildly out of control—turning what we thought was an antidote for our mental malaise into the very poison that creates it' (p. 148). Wegner and Erber (1992) demonstrated experimentally that, compared to deliberately concentrating on particular thoughts, attempting to suppress the thoughts *increased* the likelihood that the suppressed thoughts would come to mind. Harvey and Bryant (1998a) demonstrated that persons suffering from accident-related acute stress disorder showed an *increase* in intrusive trauma-related thoughts after a period of actively suppressing such thoughts, a rebound effect also observed by others (McNally & Ricciardi, 1996).

Two competing processes explain the paradox that thought suppression may exacerbate intrusive symptoms (Wegner, 1994): (1) a conscious effort to keep the thought out of mind, for example, by absorbing oneself in a competing mental activity; and (2) a non-conscious, automatic monitoring process that scans for failure to suppress the unwanted intrusive thoughts. That is, to avoid thinking about something, you need to be alert to signs of its emergence, paradoxically, keeping your mind on it! Yet, with good concentration, the effortful process of thought suppression will win out, notwithstanding that the non-conscious monitoring process continually activates the suppressed thoughts. But any increase in *cognitive load* may undermine the effortful strategy and thereby enable the intrusive thoughts (kept active by non-conscious monitoring) to become conscious. Clients with severe trauma-related disorders are often experiencing extreme cognitive load owing to such factors as insomnia, dissociation, depression, substance abuse, and anxiety.

Furthermore, the ironic mental process involved in thought suppression also can be played out in interpersonal interactions, in which 'more of the solution leads to more of the problem' (Shoham & Rohrbaugh, 1997, p. 151). For example, admonishments such as 'Just don't think about it!' or 'Just put the past behind you!' may only fuel futile efforts at thought suppression, create additional anxiety and resentment (and cognitive load), and increase intrusive symptoms. Rather than directly trying to bolster clients' efforts at suppression, I emphasize the sheer difficulty of mental control so as to help them relax their unrealistic expectations.

The value of avoidance and distraction

Avoidance is problematic insofar as it blocks coping, often entails self-destructive actions, increases stress, and paradoxically undermines mental control. Yet avoidance is not all bad. Avoidance of real danger is adaptive. Of course, being exceptionally sensitive to anxiety (Taylor et al., 1992), clients with PTSD feel endangered by their intrusive symptoms, and we must help them experience these symptoms as distressing but not truly dangerous. Intrusive symptoms are truly dangerous only insofar as clients engage in self-endangering behavior to stop them.

Avoidance of distress is generally adaptive, and we must not criticize clients for it. For example, in an educational group when we were discussing self-regulation, a highly self-critical client asked if distracting herself by engaging in relaxing activity (playing the guitar) was unhealthy. I responded that, on the contrary, distracting oneself from distressing traumatic memories is appropriate *the vast majority of the time*. Bringing the trauma to mind is best done in the context of psychotherapy or a confiding relationship, although some time spent sorting it out afterwards is also healthy. The problem is not with avoidance or distraction, but rather with *exclusive* reliance on avoidance. Thus I emphasize the need to balance avoiding and remembering.

BEYOND CATHARSIS

In counterphobic fashion, flying in the face of their penchant for avoidance, many clients wish for a cure through catharsis. They hope that, by getting into painful memories, they can somehow rid themselves of painful feelings. Clients have a venerable precedent for their hope. As Breuer and Freud wrote a century ago:

> If the reaction is suppressed, the affect remains attached to the memory. An injury that has been repaid, even if only in words, is recollected quite differently from one that has had to be accepted. Language recognizes this distinction, too, in its mental and physical consequences; it very characteristically describes an injury that has been suffered in silence as 'a mortification' ['*Kränkung*', lit. 'making ill'].—The injured person's reaction to the trauma only exercises a completely 'cathartic' effect if it is an *adequate* reaction—as, for instance, revenge. But language serves as a substitute for action; by its help, an affect can be 'abreacted' almost as effectively. In other cases speaking is itself the adequate reflex, when, for instance, it is a lamentation or giving utterance to a tormenting secret, e.g. a confession. If there is no such reaction, whether in deeds or words, or in the mildest cases in tears, any recollection of the event retains its affective tone to begin with. (Breuer & Freud, 1895/1957, p. 8)

In many ways, this passage is compatible with contemporary thinking about narrating trauma. It is the explanation rather than the technique that we must question. Does catharsis cure? The abreactive approach reached its pinnacle in primal scream therapy (Janov, 1970). I recall decades ago participating in a primal scream workshop for therapists, in which there was much screaming but little screening. Participants were encouraged to emote intensely by various means. At the end of the day, when everyone was preparing to leave, one of the participants could not stop the abreaction. The leaders, as well as the rest of the participants, were alarmed and bewildered by her unremitting distress. Now that we better understand flashbacks and dissociative states, fewer clinicians would be puzzled.

When I discuss working on trauma with clients, I refer to 'thinking, feeling, and talking about it.' What is the role of the 'feeling' part? Not mere abreaction (Brown & Fromm, 1986; Peebles, 1989; van der Hart & Brown, 1992). Many clients, understandably, want to get rid of their emotions. This strategy overlooks the adaptive functions of emotions, well documented by Darwin (1872/1965) and reiterated by many others subsequently (Allen, 1980; Izard, 1977; Nathanson, 1992; Plutchik, 1962). Emotions evolved not only to energize behavior but also to facilitate communication. Psychoanalytic understanding of affects (Rapaport, 1953) underscored their role as a signal to the self. Emotional responses make us aware of a problem to be solved. Most of these affect-generating problems are interpersonal, and if interpersonal (and intrapsychic) conflicts are not resolved, the affect will be regenerated continually (Allen, 1980). In the domain of anger, for example, Mayne and Ambrose (1999) noted that 'Cathartic venting of anger can generate and reinforce negative thinking and behavior both in individuals and couples' and concluded that 'it may not be anger expression, but rather appropriate social responses to anger-producing situations, that ultimately diffuses damaging anger cycles' (p. 356). From a humanistic perspective (Greenberg & Safran, 1989; Krystal, 1988) affective experience is enriching and contributes to vitality, and this relatively subtle aspect of affect is hardly lost on our traumatized clients who complain of feeling 'dead,' owing to dissociative numbing.

Greenberg and Safran (1989) contrasted five types of therapeutic intervention in relation to affect: synthesizing emotion (bringing it into awareness), evoking emotion to motivate behavior (e.g., anger to fuel assertiveness), modifying emotional responses (e.g., fear of harmless stimuli), evoking emotions to access related pathogenic beliefs (e.g., guilt feelings that point to self-blame), and emotional restructuring. Although all five interventions play a role in trauma treatment, emotional restructuring occupies center stage. Littrell (1998) meticulously reviewed a wealth of empirical research on the effectiveness of evoking emotion in therapy, finding that therapists' facile assumptions about the value of emotional experience and expression in psychotherapy are remarkably hard to confirm.

She found no evidence that the experience and expression of emotion per se is therapeutic, arguing that all studies favoring the evocation of emotion are effective by virtue of restructuring experience.

TRANSFORMATION

Experiencing and expressing emotion in the context of bringing the trauma to mind is not sufficient for healing. Clients must *change* the experience of bringing the trauma to mind. This change requires emotional engagement and assimilating the trauma into one's view of oneself and the world.

Emotional engagement

Catharsis alone is not healing, but the idea that emotion must be part of the process of change has been reiterated many times since Breuer and Freud. In writing about combat trauma in the context of World War II, for example, Grinker and Spiegel (1945) noted the importance of 'release and uncovering of isolated, repressed, and suppressed emotions, memories and conflicts' (p. 373). Rachman (1980) proposed decades ago that emotional processing is critical to treating problematic fears, and that emotional processing requires exposure to the feared situation: 'Fear must be experienced before it can be reduced or eliminated' (p. 52).

Foa and Kozak (1986) described how the process of assimilating traumatic experience requires that the 'fear-relevant information must be made available in a manner that will activate the fear memory' (p. 22). Foa and colleagues (Foa, Riggs, Massie, & Yarczower, 1995) discovered that facial expression of fear during treatment predicted a good outcome. These researchers subsequently demonstrated that assault victims who had the best outcomes reported a high level of distress within sessions, and their distress habituated across sessions (Jaycox, Foa, & Morral, 1998). Research on anger management also underscores the need for activation of anger to promote change (Mayne & Ambrose, 1999). Of course the intensity of the emotion must be kept in manageable bounds to prevent retraumatization (Foa & Kozak, 1986; Rachman, 1980).

Assimilating and accommodating to the trauma

Therapeutic exposure provides an opportunity for the client to come to terms with the trauma. To use Piaget's (1962) terminology, adaptation requires a balance between *assimilation* (relating the trauma to existing cognitive structures) and *accommodation* (modifying existing cognitive structures to take the trauma into account). This adaptation through assimilation and accommodation must be a gradual process. Rachman (1980) speculated that 'the process of transformation is a matter of breaking down the incoming stimulation into manageable proportions and then absorbing it over an optimal period' (p. 58). Horowitz (1986, 1997) argued that the intrusive symptoms of acute trauma promote an integration of new and incompatible trauma-related information with enduring cognitive structures.

Using Lang's (1977, 1985) model of fear structures, Foa and colleagues (Foa, 1997; Foa & Kozak, 1986, 1991) proposed that clients adapt to trauma by altering its meaning in a way that reduces fear. The client can learn to see the feared situation as less dangerous or probable, or view her anxiety responses as less enduring or devastating. For example, a client in one of my educational groups who struggled with panic learned to reassure herself: 'Wait it out, and it will pass.' Foa also underscored the corrective impact of habituation within and across sessions, in which the feared stimulus becomes associated with a lower level of fearful responsiveness. Remembering becomes less frightening. Foa and colleagues (Foa, Rothbaum, & Molnar, 1995) concluded that 'any treatment that organizes the trauma memory, and either directly or indirectly alters the victim's schemas of self and world will help to ameliorate symptoms of PTSD' (p. 491).

Reviewing empirical evidence from both natural recovery processes and successful treatment, Foa (1997) neatly pinpointed three components essential to successful processing of traumatic experiences: (1) engaging emotionally with the traumatic memories, (2) organizing a coherent narrative of the trauma, and (3) modifying core beliefs about the self and the world (i.e., revising ideas that the world is extremely dangerous and that the self is extremely incompetent). These three components provide a handy framework for explaining trauma treatment to clients.

In a similar vein, Brewin and colleagues (Brewin et al., 1996) defined emotional processing as 'a largely conscious process in which representations of past and future events, and awareness of associated bodily states, repeatedly enter into and are actively manipulated within working memory' (p. 677). They also emphasized the need for clients to search for meaning, make judgments about cause and blame, and adjust their expectations about the self and the world. Much of this cognitive processing involves transforming fragmented memories or flashbacks into coherent narratives:

> If flashbacks are to become integrated with regular autobiographical memories, the person must be able to consciously edit and manipulate the information provided by the flashbacks within working memory. That is, they must retain awareness that they are experiencing the flashback, be able to reflect upon the experience as it is happening, and create ordinary autobiographical memories of the experience (Brewin & Andrews, 1998, p. 965)

Such processing does not create a new memory but rather creates the possibility of *remembering differently* by virtue of establishing new associations

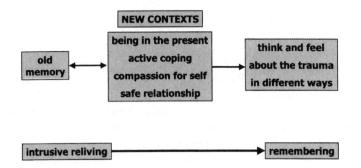

Figure 12.1   Transforming traumatic memories

with the traumatic memory. Successful processing enables the client to be reminded of the memory without being unduly distressed or disrupted (Rachman, 1980). We can help the client create a network of new associations to be activated in conjunction with the memory. As Brewin and colleagues (Brewin et al., 1996) stated, 'Reminders of the trauma will then, hopefully, lead to the accessing of more recent representations rather than the original traumatic memories' (p. 678). As diagrammed in Figure 12.1, I draw clients' attention to four broad domains of new associations that need to be established in relation to traumatic memories (Allen & Lewis, 1996): *temporal* (e.g., remaining aware of the present while thinking about the past), *behavioral* (active coping, for example, by keeping one's head up and eyes open rather than cowering), *cognitive* (e.g., establishing coherent narratives and thinking about oneself more compassionately in conjunction with the trauma), and— of paramount importance—*interpersonal* (e.g., thinking, feeling, and talking about trauma in the context of a secure attachment relationship). Establishing new contexts for bringing traumatic memories to mind enables the client to think and feel about the trauma in different ways, and it is the route from reliving to remembering.

SELECTED TECHNIQUES

Foa (1998) drew a valuable contrast between treatment of obsessive-compulsive disorder and PTSD. Exposure and response prevention is the treatment of choice for obsessive-compulsive disorder. In contrast, a wide variety of interventions have equivalent efficacy for PTSD—and therapists have adapted virtually all therapeutic techniques to its treatment (Meichenbaum, 1994). This section reviews three demonstrably effective approaches: prolonged exposure, cognitive restructuring, and Eye Movement Desensitization and Reprocessing (EMDR).

Prolonged exposure

Prolonged exposure (flooding) has a long and successful history in the treatment of anxiety disorders (e.g., phobias), and it has been extended into the treatment of trauma and PTSD. Single-case, quasi-experimental, and controlled studies indicate that prolonged exposure ameliorates traumatic memories and enhances adjustment (Saigh, 1998). Keane and colleagues, for example, demonstrated the efficacy of prolonged exposure with Vietnam veterans (Keane, Fairbank, Caddell, & Zimering, 1989) but also addressed the need for safeguards to prevent retraumatization. These safeguards include establishing a strong, supportive therapeutic relationship; providing relaxation training to facilitate mastery of anxiety; and including debriefing after the exposure to ensure that the client is settled and reoriented to the present (Lyons & Keane, 1989).

Foa and colleagues conducted extensive research demonstrating the efficacy of prolonged exposure for rape trauma (Foa, Dancu et al., 1999; Foa, Rothbaum, Riggs, & Murdock, 1991) and developed a refined treatment protocol (Foa & Rothbaum, 1998). The treatment includes systematic in vivo exposure as well as prolonged imaginal exposure. The in vivo exposure entails approaching situations associated with the rape that evoke moderate anxiety and progressing to situations that evoke maximum fear. For example, *under safe conditions,* a client returns to the vicinity of a rape and remains there for 30–45 minutes until her distress substantially abates. The imaginal exposure during therapy sessions entails having the client recall the trauma vividly, speaking into an audiotape recorder for 30–60 minutes, and recounting the trauma in the present tense. Then the client is instructed to listen to the audiotape as homework to augment the in-session exposure.

Like Keane and colleagues, Foa (Foa & Rothbaum, 1998) incorporates extensive supportive interventions into the treatment. These supportive elements include educating the client about trauma, PTSD, and exposure therapy; relaxation and breathing retraining; carefully graded in vivo exposure; therapeutic reassurance and cognitive reframing during the imaginal exposure; ensuring that the client is calmed and reoriented after the imaginal exposure; and offering availability by telephone between sessions. Although Foa's treatment focuses on assault in adulthood, many clients treated with prolonged exposure also have a history of childhood sexual abuse, and studies underway suggest that the protocol is also effective in treating childhood trauma (Meadows & Foa, 1998).

Despite safeguards, prolonged exposure is—by design—a highly stressful procedure. Pitman and colleagues (Pitman et al., 1991) presented a series of cases illustrating potential complications. They observed 'a clear connection between depressive exacerbations and the flooding's mobilization of guilt, shame, and feelings of inadequacy associated with traumatic memories' (p. 19). Yet Pitman and colleagues (Pitman, Orr, Altman, Longpre,

Poire, Macklin et al., 1996) subsequently did not find that evoking anger and guilt feelings contributed to a poor outcome. Of course complications of PTSD treatment are hardly unique to flooding; any technique that activates traumatic memories (e.g., talking about the past) may become problematic.

Frueh and colleagues (Frueh, De Arellano, & Turner, 1997) suggested that clients who are averse to prolonged exposure might be treated instead with systematic desensitization, wherein traumatic imagery is paired with a state of relaxation. Although maintaining a state of relaxation during imaginal exposure would seem contrary to the principles of exposure therapy articulated earlier, Foa and Kozak (1991) noted that relaxation may enhance imagery as well as attention to fear-relevant information. There is some evidence for the effectiveness of desensitization in the treatment of trauma (Blake & Sonnenberg, 1998; Brom et al., 1989), but it has not been employed as widely as prolonged exposure, because evidence increasingly supports the value of in vivo and prolonged imaginal exposure (Meadows & Foa, 1998).

Cognitive restructuring

Extensive evidence shows that trauma can eventuate in detrimental changes in cognitions, captured well in Janoff-Bulman's (1992) concept of shattered assumptions. Foa and colleagues (Foa, Ehlers et al., 1999) discerned three core domains of post-traumatic cognitions: negative cognitions about the self, negative cognitions about the world, and self-blame for the trauma. Such negative cognitions sharply distinguished between trauma survivors who developed PTSD and those who did not. Moreover, interpersonal trauma (assaults) was associated with more negative cognitions than was impersonal trauma (accidents). In their study of attachment styles, Muller and colleagues (Muller, 2000) found that negative views of the self were highly correlated with post-traumatic stress symptoms, but negative views of others were not. Dunmore and colleagues (Dunmore, Clark, & Ehlers, 1999) also identified a range of negative cognitions that contributed to the onset of PTSD as well as to the maintenance of PTSD symptoms. Most problematic is an appraisal of *ongoing threat*, which contributes to a life 'dominated by apprehension and uncertainty' (p. 825).

A wide range of cognitive interventions has been applied in the treatment of PTSD (Meichenbaum, 1994). Resick and colleagues' cognitive processing therapy developed for the treatment of rape-related PTSD provides an exemplary model of cognitive therapy. Cognitive processing therapy has a coherent theoretical rationale, carefully blends a range of therapeutic elements, and—not least—has demonstrated effectiveness (Calhoun & Resick, 1993; Resick & Schnicke, 1992, 1993).

The cognitive intervention begins with educating the client about trauma and the role of maladaptive cognitions in PTSD. Cognitive processing systematically integrates exposure and cognitive interventions. The exposure component begins with a homework assignment. The client writes a detailed description of the trauma and her reactions to it, and then she reads it aloud to herself. Then the client reads aloud her account of the trauma to the therapist. Having elicited the memories, the treatment directly explores and confronts the associated maladaptive cognitions, focusing particularly on themes of safety, trust, power, esteem, and intimacy.

Eye movement desensitization and reprocessing (EMDR)

EMDR (Shapiro, 1995b) is a popular and highly controversial treatment for trauma (Bower, 1995; Greenwald, 1999; Herbert & Mueser, 1995; McNally, 1999a, 1999b; Meichenbaum, 1994). EMDR exemplifies eclectic cognitive-behavior therapy, integrating exposure with cognitive restructuring. The EMDR protocol includes several components. Therapists and their clients identify core traumatic images with associated emotions and physiological sensations. Therapists target negative cognitions (e.g., negative views of the self or self-blaming) and help clients articulate more positive cognitions (e.g., how clients would prefer to think of themselves in conjunction with the trauma). Clients rate their subjective distress and their view of the validity of the positive cognitions to facilitate tracking progress within and between sessions. Desensitization proceeds by asking the client to bring the traumatic memory to mind while simultaneously moving the eyes from side to side, following the therapist's fingers moving back and forth in front of the face. After each cycle of bilateral stimulation, the client lets go of the traumatic images and verbalizes what comes to mind. When the subjective distress abates, the client brings to mind the traumatic memory in conjunction with the positive cognition while engaging in eye movements. Over the course of successful treatment, not only does distress in relation to the traumatic memories abate (desensitization) but also cognitions become more positive and adaptive.

Why is EMDR so controversial? One factor may be its extraordinary popularity among therapists, who can be taught to use it (at least in rudimentary form) in a weekend workshop (Shapiro, 1995a). Although its practitioners' sheer enthusiasm might be enough to raise eyebrows, other factors also promote skepticism. EMDR incorporates well-established principles and techniques of cognitive-behavior therapy, but Shapiro (1995b) presented it as a revolutionary discovery based on her experience walking in a park. She noticed that her rapid eye movements reduced distress associated with disturbing thoughts and memories. After developing the treatment protocol, she concentrated on the eye movements rather than the many conventional aspects of the treatment in her theoretical explanation of its effectiveness.

The employment of eye movements led Shapiro (1995b) to propose a neurobiological explanation for the effectiveness of the treatment, notwithstanding that moving one's eyes is no more neurobiological than speaking, listening, or thinking. Indeed a more compelling case can be made for the enduring neurobiological impact of talking (Vaughan, 1997). Not only is there no need for a neurobiological explanation for EMDR, but also Shapiro's (1995b) explanation is confusing and poorly integrated with contemporary neurobiological theory and research (Allen & Lewis, 1996).

Information-processing explanations focusing on the role of attention in relation to eye movements are more promising. Eye movements compete for limited cognitive resources, decrease the vividness of visual imagery in the visuospatial sketchpad component of working memory, and thereby decrease negative emotions associated with the visual images (Andrade, Kavanagh, & Baddeley, 1997). More generally, EMDR entails a paradoxical instruction to intentionally maintain the negative images and thoughts in mind while undermining this instruction by adding a substantial cognitive load (Kirsch & Lynn, 1999).

To cap off the controversy, research generally has failed to support a unique contribution of the eye movements or other bilateral stimuli to efficacy (Boudewyns & Hyer, 1996; Cahill, Carrigan, & Frueh, 1999; Devilly, Spence, & Rapee, 1998; Lohr, Tolin, & Lilienfeld, 1998; Pitman, Orr, Altman, Longpre, Poire, & Macklin, 1996; Renfrey & Spates, 1994). While continuing to adhere to the neurobiological theory, Shapiro (1995b) ultimately concluded that the eye movements are not essential to the protocol.

Notwithstanding this explanatory muddle, Shapiro developed EMDR in the spirit of cognitive-behavioral therapy by launching the intervention in the context of controlled research (Shapiro, 1989), which she has continued to advocate (Shapiro, 1996). Perhaps spurred by controversy and skepticism, clinical researchers have conducted an impressive array of controlled studies of the effectiveness of EMDR. The more recent studies tend to be better designed than the earlier ones. For example, employing a wait-list control group, Rothbaum (1997) showed EMDR to be effective for treatment of PTSD and depression in women who had suffered rape trauma, with further gains evident at 90-day follow-up. Marcus and colleagues (Marcus, Marquis, & Sakai, 1997) showed EMDR to be more effective than standard care with respect to PTSD and a wide range of other symptoms for clients treated in a Health Maintenance Organization setting. Scheck and colleagues (Scheck, Schaeffer, & Gillette, 1998) found EMDR to be superior to an active-listening control group in treating traumatic memories in young women with a history of severely dysfunctional behavior. Wilson and colleagues (Wilson, Becker, & Tinker, 1995; Wilson, Becker, & Tinker, 1997) showed EMDR (compared to a wait-list control) to result in significant gains that were maintained over a 15-month follow-up period in the treatment of 80 persons with varied trauma histories (46% of whom had PTSD). On the other hand, Macklin and colleagues (Macklin et al., 2000) found that initial gains from EMDR treatment of combat veterans were lost over a five-year follow-up period (although I would hardly expect any brief intervention to yield gains over a period of several years in this patient population).

After weighing the positive and negative results, many reviewers continued to voice caution and skepticism about EMDR (Cahill et al., 1999; DeBell & Jones, 1997; Foa & Meadows, 1997; Keane, 1998; Lohr et al., 1998; Roth & Fonagy, 1996). Cahill and colleagues, for example, concluded that EMDR is more effective than no treatment and as effective or more effective than non-validated interventions for PTSD. Yet there has been scant research directly comparing EMDR to other demonstrably effective treatments for PTSD. This is a particularly critical concern, because EMDR emerged into a field of well-established cognitive-behavioral treatments for anxiety disorders but was presented as revolutionary. As Lohr and colleagues (Lohr et al., 1998) stated, introducing EMDR merely as another variant of existing treatments may have circumvented much controversy. McNally (1999b) concluded, *'what is effective in EMDR is not new, and what is new is not effective'* (p. 619). Not only have the eye movements not been demonstrated to add to effectiveness, but also a recent study raised a question as to the unique contribution of the cognitive intervention (Cusack & Spates, 1999). Thus Cahill and colleagues' conclusion is representative: 'Our opinion is that the important procedural variable is repeated exposure to the traumatic memory under conditions of safety' (p. 29).

Some authors have commented on potential clinical advantages of the EMDR protocol. For example, the relatively brief exposure in EMDR may make the procedure more tolerable than prolonged exposure to both clients and therapists (Boudewyns, Hyer, Peralme, Touze, & Kiel, 1995; Pitman, Orr, Altman, Longpre, Poire, & Macklin, 1996). Furthermore, by virtue of the demand on attention, the eye movements may have the benefit of providing grounding in present reality for clients who are prone to dissociation (Allen, Keller, & Console, 1999). Given that a meta-analysis indicated comparable effectiveness of EMDR to other cognitive-behavioral interventions (Van Etten & Taylor, 1998), the relative brevity of EMDR compared to cognitive-behavioral treatments—*averaging 4.6 versus 14.8 sessions in studies reviewed*—is an enormous potential advantage, as a number of authors have commented (Blake & Sonnenberg, 1998; Marcus et al., 1997; Montgomery & Ayllon, 1994; Wilson et al., 1995, 1997). Hence research directly comparing EMDR with other effective treatments while controlling for duration of treatment would be especially valuable.

SOME HORSE RACES

A number of PTSD treatment protocols are effective, but therapists and clients have no clear basis for deciding which is best. Comparing treatments is complicated by the fact that they are more like blended whiskeys than single malts. Resick's cognitive processing therapy includes a major exposure component. EMDR incorporates exposure and cognitive therapy. Although Foa's prolonged exposure appears relatively pure on the face of it, she noted, 'In effect, we practice informal cognitive therapy during exposure, in that we help clients to examine ways in which they evaluate threat and to develop inferential processes that lead to more realistic conclusions' (Foa & Kozak, 1991, p. 45).

The blending of exposure and cognitive restructuring is only part of the eclecticism evident in various forms of cognitive-behavior therapy. All place a premium on educating the client. In addition, although the experience of emotional distress is part and parcel of the protocol, self-regulation techniques (e.g., relaxation and breathing retraining) are included to help clients master the distress. Anxiety management training, and stress inoculation training in particular, include an eclectic combination of self-regulation and cognitive interventions (Foa & Rothbaum, 1998; Meichenbaum, 1994). These approaches can be used as stand-alone treatments, and their various elements are often integrated into the exposure therapies. Moreover, the clinical descriptions of the various treatments highlight how the cognitive-behavioral interventions are embedded in highly supportive psychotherapy processes. Yet, as Meichenbaum (1994) put it, 'there is not sufficient evidence to suggest the superiority of one form of treatment over any other, nor an appreciation of how the various treatment components can be combined most effectively' (p. 284).

Given the extensive overlap among ostensibly distinct treatment approaches, demonstrating differences among them will be challenging. Although most research compares an intervention of choice to no treatment (e.g., waiting list) or non-validated treatment (e.g., relaxation), researchers increasingly are conducting horse races, pitting effective treatments for PTSD against one other. In one of the early studies, Foa and colleagues (Foa et al., 1991) compared prolonged exposure, stress inoculation training, and supportive counseling to a wait-list control in the treatment of rape trauma. All active treatments showed benefits, but prolonged exposure and stress inoculation training were the most effective. Yet stress inoculation treatment showed the greatest improvement immediately after treatment, whereas prolonged exposure showed the greatest improvement at three-month follow-up. The authors concluded that combining prolonged exposure with stress inoculation treatment might produce optimal outcomes. Surprisingly, this prediction was not borne out in a subsequent study comparing prolonged exposure alone, stress inoculation training alone, and the combination of the two protocols in the treatment of female assault victims (Foa, Dancu et al., 1999). Contrary to expectations, prolonged exposure alone was consistently superior not only to stress inoculation training but also to the combined treatment. The authors speculated that the combined treatment may have been less effective owing to its complexity (and information overload for participants). In contrast, prolonged exposure has the advantage of efficacy combined with simplicity.

Two studies are noteworthy for comparing prolonged exposure and cognitive restructuring. Tarrier and colleagues (Tarrier, Pilgrim et al., 1999) treated a mixed-gender sample of traumatized persons, most of whom were crime or accident victims. Both treatments were effective, and there were negligible differences between the two, with the exception that more clients in the imaginal exposure treatment worsened over the course of treatment (although this difference disappeared at follow-up). Marks and colleagues (Marks, Lovell, Noshirvani, Livanou, & Thrasher, 1998) treated a mixed-gender sample with PTSD, half of whom had been exposed to impersonal trauma, and half to interpersonal trauma. The study compared four interventions: in vivo and imaginal exposure, cognitive restructuring, combined exposure and cognitive restructuring, and relaxation training. Assessment of outcome included a six-month follow-up. Relaxation training showed modest benefits, whereas the other three interventions produced marked improvement but did not differ significantly from one another. Thus not only were there no differences between exposure and cognitive therapy but also combining them yielded no additional benefit.

To date, only one study has compared EMDR head-to-head with another effective treatment. Devilly and Spence (1999) compared EMDR with an eclectic cognitive-behavior protocol that combined elements of stress inoculation training, prolonged exposure, and cognitive restructuring. Clients were men and women who met criteria for PTSD and received either the nine-session eclectic protocol or up to eight sessions of EMDR. Follow-up at three months was conducted by mailed questionnaires. Both treatments resulted in improvement, but the eclectic protocol was consistently more effective than EMDR. The differences between the two treatments became more pronounced over time, with evidence of return of symptoms in the EMDR condition. These latter findings are puzzling insofar as they are inconsistent with previous studies showing relatively durable changes with EMDR (Rothbaum, 1997; Wilson et al., 1997).

This small set of studies confirms that there are a number of effective approaches to the treatment of PTSD and related symptoms and casts doubt on the more-is-better approach of adding one to another. In clinical practice, however, various aspects of the different approaches are blended, albeit in somewhat differing proportions. Yet significant effectiveness does not mean that the vast majority of clients improve substantially. Tarrier and colleagues (Tarrier, Pilgrim et al., 1999) found that, at six-month follow-up, nearly half the clients continued to meet criteria for PTSD, and a only a quarter returned to a level of symptoms expected in a normal population—and this was a sample in which the majority of participants underwent a trauma that lasted less than one hour. Marks and colleagues (Marks et al., 1998) reported that over a third of their treated subjects met PTSD criteria at the end of treatment and that about half or fewer (depending on treatment) showed marked improvement in terms of good end-state functioning. Foa and colleagues (Foa, Dancu et al., 1999) reported good end-state functioning for about half or fewer of the participants in active treatment at one-year follow-up (52% for prolonged exposure, 42% for stress inoculation therapy, and 36% for the combined treatment). In a naturalistic study of intensive specialized inpatient treatment for severe trauma-related psychopathology, we also found a mixture of substantial gains in functioning with continuing symptomatology at one-year follow-up (Allen, Coyne et al., 2000).

SOME COMPLICATIONS

The results of controlled studies can be viewed as a glass half full (marked improvement with effective treatments) or half empty (many clients continuing to be symptomatic). To expand the half-empty perspective, the limitations of these treatment trails are even more conspicuous in light of exclusion criteria. Foa and colleagues (Foa, Dancu et al., 1999; Foa et al., 1991) excluded clients on the basis of organic mental disorders, psychotic symptoms, depression severe enough to require immediate psychiatric treatment, severe suicidal ideation, bipolar disorder, substance abuse, assault by a spouse or other family member, and being in an ongoing relationship with an assailant. Tarrier and colleagues (Tarrier, Pilgrim et al., 1999) excluded persons with psychosis and organic brain syndromes, those with childhood sexual abuse as the primary trauma, and those with substance abuse as a primary problem. Marks and colleagues (Marks et al., 1998) excluded those with melancholia or suicidal intent, organic brain disease, psychosis, and alcohol abuse.

Dissociation

Dissociative disturbance is problematic in the treatment of trauma, because it interferes with emotional processing and thereby contributes to impaired functioning (Feeny, Zoellner, & Foa, 2000). In clients who are prone to it, dissociative detachment is likely to be evoked by any intervention that focuses on trauma—particularly exposure-based approaches. Dissociative detachment also blocks attention to the cues that are the focus of desensitization (Foa & Hearst-Ikeda, 1996). From the perspective of exposure therapy, dissociative detachment is a particularly problematic form of distraction (Allen, Keller et al., 1999). Foa and Kozak (1986) described how distraction during exposure may yield apparent short-term habituation (within sessions) but block long-term habituation (between sessions), and the latter is particularly crucial to outcome (Jaycox et al., 1998). Foa (1997) pointed out that dissociation is indicative of low emotional engagement, which blocks processing and benefit from exposure therapy. Consistent with these clinical–theoretical assumptions, Michelson and colleagues (Michelson, June, Vives, Testa, & Marchione, 1998) presented evidence that, among other trauma-related factors, dissociation impeded benefit from exposure treatment for panic disorder.

Of course, as a preeminent avoidant defense, dissociation will interfere with *any* form of treatment—not least psychotherapy, when the client remembers little of the process. Dissociative defenses also complicate EMDR and require special adaptations of the protocol (Allen, Keller et al., 1999; Paulsen, 1995; Shapiro, 1995b). Wagner and Linehan (1998) suggest helping dissociative clients to avoid undue exposure to environmental cues that remind them of trauma, bolstering their tolerance of negative emotions, and fostering their self-regulation skills so as to help them tolerate needed therapeutic exposure.

Anger and guilt feelings

Anger is a natural response to threat, trauma, and trauma-related cues. Yet, like dissociation, anger can interfere with trauma-focused interventions. Foa and colleagues found that, whereas fear during exposure enhances benefit from treatment, anger impedes it (Foa, 1997; Foa, Riggs, Massie et al., 1995). Feeny and colleagues (Feeny et al., 2000) found that, among female assault victims, level of anger assessed at one month after the assault predicted subsequent PTSD. The researchers proposed that anger, like dissociation, impedes emotional processing of the trauma. On the other hand, Andrews and colleagues (Andrews et al., 2000) found that, whereas both shame and anger with others predicted PTSD symptom severity at one month after victimization by violent crime, only shame independently predicted continuation of PTSD symptoms at six months.

Relative to its prevalence and prominence as a social and clinical problem (Deffenbacher, 1999; Robins & Novaco, 1999), anger has been neglected in the PTSD treatment literature. In part this neglect may reflect the difficulty of treating trauma-related anger and aggression. Yet Novaco and Chemtob (1998) developed a promising treatment protocol for combat veterans. They conceptualize trauma-related anger as 'context-inappropriate "survival mode" functioning' (p. 164). More specifically, 'In conjunction with trauma, anger is intrusive and is part of a dyscontrol syndrome involving heightened arousal, hostile appraisal, and antagonistic behavior activated as a survival response to severe threat' (p. 169). I find that clients suffering from interpersonal trauma also relate directly to the concept of *survival-mode functioning*. Making use of stress inoculation training, Novaco and Chemtob's protocol focuses on cognitive restructuring, arousal reduction, and behavioral coping skills. Initial results of its implementation with a highly treatment-resistant client population are promising, consistent with demonstrated effectiveness of anger management in other clinical contexts (Mayne & Ambrose, 1999).

Like anger, guilt feelings—often spawned by self-blame—are prominent in the symptomatology of trauma survivors. Pitman and colleagues (Pitman et al., 1991) cautioned that exposure alone may reinforce negative appraisals and exacerbate guilt feelings and depression, although subsequent experimental findings did not confirm this concern (Pitman, Orr, Altman, Longpre, Poire, Macklin et al., 1996). Foa and colleagues (Foa & McNally, 1996; Foa, Riggs, Massie et al., 1995) observed that exposure therapy may be more effective for fear than guilt feelings. Concern that exposure alone will not ameliorate guilt feelings underscores the potential value of integrating cognitive restructuring with exposure therapy, and guilt feelings related to self-blame are an important focus of cognitive techniques (Calhoun & Resick, 1993; Foa & Rothbaum, 1998). Kubany (1998) developed a comprehensive cognitive treatment protocol for trauma-related guilt feelings that shows considerable clinical promise.

Who benefits?

Consider the exclusion criteria employed in randomized controlled trials, along with a few of the more prominent complications just discussed, in light of the panoply of trauma-related psychopathology reviewed in this book. Do these interventions work for everyone but the clients we are treating? Even with the exclusion criteria, many clients fail to derive substantial benefit.

Of course the problem of generalizability is not unique to trauma; it applies to the full range of randomized controlled trials (Fonagy, 1999c). These limitations do not rule out the use of cognitive-behavioral interventions for clients with severe psychopathology in relation to attachment trauma. Yet the limitations underscore the need for judicious use of these techniques—particularly prolonged exposure—as well as the crucial role of containment as I described in Chapter 11.

NARRATING TRAUMA

To come full circle, consider Foa's (1998) observation that a range of treatment interventions are effective for trauma. Allowing for differences in blend, these interventions will include exposure and cognitive restructuring with attention to emotion regulation skills in the context of a containing supportive psychotherapy relationship. In principle, psychotherapy could accomplish these aims as well as cognitive-behavioral therapy. Yet, in contrast to more unstructured psychodynamic psychotherapy, cognitive-behavioral techniques structure the treatment such that neither the client nor the therapist can easily avoid the emotionally stressful work of exposure.

Foa's (1997) perspective on the core features of trauma treatment covers the full range of therapeutic approaches. The client must emotionally engage with the traumatic experience and construct a meaningful narrative that provides a balanced and realistic view of the self and the world. Thus written narrative has been found helpful in the treatment of trauma. Cognitive restructuring for rape trauma begins with a written narrative that the client reads to herself, then reads aloud to the therapist. Pennebaker and others have conducted extensive research with non-clinical samples demonstrating the health benefits of writing emotional accounts of traumatic experiences (Greenberg et al., 1996; Harber & Pennebaker, 1992; Pennebaker, 1997; Pillemer, 1998; Richards et al., 2000). Many trauma clients find journaling about their past and their daily emotional experiences to be a helpful adjunct to treatment.

Emerging evidence suggests that optimal processing of traumatic experience is associated with increasingly elaborate and coherent narratives (Foa, 1997; Pennebaker, 1997). Roberts (1999) argued that stories 'provide holding, containing structures of meaning' (p. 12) and further, 'Narrative responses to desperate circumstances offer a means of containing wild, threatening, and unpredictable experiences, and re-establishing some kind of order and relationship. . . . we see story-making, as a life-supporting process, a psychic resource, a defense against futility, emptiness, and formless terror' (p. 13). Roberts noted that stories can be toxic: 'Some are simply cursed—they live with a toxic story, which configures meaning in a pattern that saps rather than enhances life, these are stories that disconfirm, reduce, shackle, and snare' (p. 16). Toxic stories are not to be excised but rather rewritten. Habituation and extinction do not remove old connections but rather add new connections. Most important, in telling the story to a confidant who bears witness, the client not only feels less afraid but also feels less alone.

Thus we should not separate the storyteller from the listener, or the story from the relationship in which it is created—or not created. Consider Pillemer's (1998) recasting of repression: 'The reasons that an early trauma, such as a sexual assault, may not be remembered will include the child's incomplete understanding of the event and the absence of willing and nurturant adult conversational partners' (p. 134). This wonderfully plain prose epitomizes the job of the trauma therapist—to be a willing and nurturant adult conversational partner—whatever the theory or technique employed. Extensive research with the Adult Attachment Interview demonstrates that narrative incoherence is associated with insecure attachment (Hesse, 1999). From this perspective, Holmes (1999) construed psychotherapy as building up a 'story-telling function' (p. 57). He pointed out that

> secure attachment is marked by coherent stories that convince and hang together, where detail and overall plot are congruent, and where the teller is not so detached that affect is absent, is not dissociated from the content of the story, nor is so overwhelmed that feelings flow formlessly into every crevice of the dialogue. Insecure attachment, by contrast, is characterized either by stories that are overelaborated and enmeshed . . . or by dismissive, poorly fleshed-out accounts. (p. 58)

Different forms of insecure attachment correspond to 'three prototypical pathologies of narrative capacity: clinging to rigid stories; being overwhelmed by unstoried experience; or being unable to find a narrative strong enough to contain traumatic pain' (p. 59).

Just as we should be mindful of the relationship context in which trauma stories are told, we must keep in mind that *the content of the story is less crucial than the capacity to create, refine, and narrate the story in a secure attachment relationship over the lifetime.* Persons who have endured attachment trauma and its related psychopathology cannot take this capacity for granted, and they cannot simply use standard techniques for processing the trauma. The historical accuracy of the story is hardly inconsequential (Allen, 1995b), and whatever meaning can be found in traumatic experience will be tied to its content. And process depends on content—we cannot learn to tell the story unless there is some historical experience to construct it around. But obsession with content can lead us astray (Fonagy, 1999a; Fonagy & Target, 1997b), and our broader therapeutic mission should be to *cultivate the capacity to narrate* meaningful stories. This capacity is built around a secure attachment that fosters reflective function (Chapter 4). Whether the therapist employs psychotherapy, prolonged exposure, cognitive restructuring, or EMDR may matter less than the developmental help that the treatment provides (Fonagy, 1995). The goal is not catharsis or getting the proper story on the table; it is the development of the capacity to continually create and refine stories. Holmes (1999) put it well:

> psychological health (closely linked to secure attachment) depends on a dialectic between story-making and story-breaking, between the capacity to form narrative, and to disperse it in the light of new experience. . . . narrative capacity . . . moves between fluidity and form, between structure and 'destructuring', construction and deconstruction. This capacity ultimately depends on being able to trust both intimacy and aggression. (p. 59)

Tedeschi (1999) linked narrative construction to resilience, which depends upon the world becoming comprehensible and meaningful again. He described the processes whereby some fortunate survivors go beyond recovery to post-traumatic growth. Whereas psychopathology is evident in damage to the sense of self and identity, trauma also may prompt a sense of being a strengthened survivor with increased self-efficacy. I have emphasized the psychopathology of distrust and isolation, but Tedeschi pointed to the possibilities of greater empathy and intimacy. Trauma also may enhance spirituality and eventuate in a commitment to living each day to the fullest: 'participants may report greater emotional serenity (but not necessarily an absence of psychological distress) together with increased appreciation for life, and a quiet strength that can come from a recognition that the self is strong yet vulnerable' (p. 328). Of course we cannot know the extent to which the resilience that promotes such beneficial change was extant before the trauma or stemmed from it. As Tedeschi's account makes plain, however, openness to intense emotions and a capacity to wrestle actively and deliberately with complex meanings—reflective function—is required for growth.

Yet attachment trauma undermines the reflective capacity needed to resolve it. Consider LaMothe's (1999) perspective:

> In malignant trauma there is a horrifying void of an obliged, trustworthy, and faithful other and in this void there is consequently the absence of psychological organization and the very structures of subjectivity. It is not that these experiences continue to remain in the more primitive limbic lobe structures of the brain. It is, rather, that these experiences cannot be organized because the very symbols which human beings depend upon for psychological organization cannot represent the very absence of obligation, trust, and fidelity. . . . These 'unspeakable' experiences of malignant trauma can be partially communicated to those who listen and respond, which provides evidence for the claims made above. That is, a person may write, tell a story, or paint or sculpt their experience of the traumatic event, yet there is something, some black hole that remains outside of symbol and language. (p. 1205)

Reflect on the contrast between Tedeschi's (1999) concept of post-traumatic growth and LaMothe's (1999) appreciation for the unresolvable aspects of malignant trauma. Consider the contrast between significant gains and remaining psychopathology in the treatment outcome literature. We therapists and our clients must tolerate tension between optimism and pessimism, hopefulness and hopelessness, confidence and doubt. To reiterate Chekhov (1998), we offer many remedies with no cure. Trauma stories will always remain unfinished, works in progress.

EDUCATING CLIENTS ABOUT NARRATING TRAUMA

Talk about it. When? How? To whom? I expand the 'When?' question to 'If and when.' As van der Kolk and colleagues put it, 'There is no intrinsic value in dredging up past trauma if a client's current life provides gratification, and the present is not invaded by emotional, perceptual, or behavioral intrusions from the past' (p. 428). I deal with the 'When?' question by explaining the need for containment to precede trauma-focused interventions. Containment entails having established a durable treatment frame, supportive relationships, and capacities for self-regulation. Establishing adequate containment, of course, is easier said than done, and there is no guarantee that it *can* be done. Back to the 'If?' question: we cannot automatically assume that all clients will be able to work directly on their trauma (Chu, 1992). Absent a crystal ball, I temporize. I cannot say that a client will *never* be in a position to work on the trauma, but I can often see that this will not be indicated until a great deal of preparatory work is done. Containment before processing.

The 'How?' question entails good news and bad news. Many trauma treatments work, but there is no clear favorite. Moreover, many clients have extensive psychopathology that renders them less than optimally suited to demonstrably effective techniques (e.g., prolonged exposure). Most problematic, we lack empirical evidence that would allow us to base treatment decisions on individual differences. As Roth and Fonagy put it, the crucial question is not 'What works?' but rather 'What works for whom?' (Roth & Fonagy, 1996). The best we can do is to attempt rationally to tailor the treatment to the client's needs, capacities, preferences, and responses to interventions (Foa & Rothbaum, 1998).

I do not promote any particular technique but rather explain to clients some of the potential benefits of talking about their trauma. I discuss the problems with avoidance and continually emphasize the importance of openness to experience in the context of self-care. I describe Foa's research (Foa, 1997; Foa, Riggs, Massie et al., 1995) demonstrating the relation of emotional engagement to treatment outcome. I also point to the need to build new associations to the trauma so as to be able to remember it rather than reexperiencing it. I review the details of changing temporal, behavioral, cognitive, and interpersonal associations. When clients express interest, I describe the details of different treatments. I start with Foa's prolonged exposure, because it is the most straightforward intervention. Given its peculiar theoretical history, EMDR is challenging to explain, and my colleague, Michael Keller, developed a sensible rationale for distribution to clients (Allen, Keller et al., 1999). I often invite clients who have had experience with EMDR to describe it to others. I try to refrain from wincing when they include some pseudo-biological explanation they have been given, and I focus instead on the psychological principles reviewed in this chapter.

I highlight the importance of developing the capacity to think and feel about the trauma in the context of a secure relationship. This brings us to the 'To whom?' question. Finding a confidant who can tolerate distress is no small feat, and the challenge of finding persons who will bear witness to trauma is particularly great (Harber & Pennebaker, 1992). Groups for survivors are potentially enormously valuable but also may be retraumatizing. Containment before processing. I draw clients' attention to the potential hazards of disclosure to peers, family members, and groups. Often the 'To whom?' will be an individual therapist. As clients will attest, this is no simple recommendation. Finding a suitable therapist and a good match is no small challenge. Here, too, I advocate caution and gradual work on the trauma. Clients are in the best position to select therapists and treatments when they are well-informed consumers, which brings us to the topic of educational groups.

Chapter 13

PSYCHOEDUCATIONAL APPROACHES

> The function of education is to develop long-term, organized bodies of knowledge and generic problem-solving skills that will help the learner solve personal problems, both in the present and in the future. (Hatfield, 1994, p. 7)

I have never liked the term, *psychoeducation*. What does it mean? Sex education and driver's education make sense. I tell patients, 'This is a trauma education group.' 'Psycho' education is a misnomer. *Psychiatric* education would be better because, historically, the purpose of psychoeducation has been to educate lay persons about psychiatric disorders.

Psychoeducation evolved in the context of deinstitutionalization, when the responsibility for caring for the chronically mentally ill shifted back to families (Simon, 1997). At its inception, psychoeducation was a family-focused intervention in the treatment of schizophrenia, and it continues to be refined in that context (Anderson, Hogarty, & Reiss, 1980; Anderson & Reiss, 1982; Gallagher & Nazarian, 1995; Goldstein, 1991; Munich, 1996). Didactic material emphasizes the biological etiology of schizophrenia, reassuring family members that they are not the *cause* of the illness, while helping them understand how patterns of interaction in the family may influence the *course* of the illness. Although the family receives the education, the patient's functioning is the primary target, the goal being to minimize the likelihood of relapse. Outcome studies consistently support the effectiveness of this intervention (Simon, 1997).

Having demonstrated success in the treatment of schizophrenia, clinicians have extended the psychoeducational approach to the treatment of a wide range of other disorders, including depression, bipolar disorder, obsessive-compulsive disorder, chemical dependency, eating disorders, BPD, and medical illness (Anderson, 1995; Garner, 1997; Gunderson, Berkowitz, & Ruiz-Sancho, 1997; Holder & Anderson, 1990). In an important development, psychoeducation has gone beyond educating the family to educating the patient, even in the context of schizophrenia (Gallagher & Nazarian, 1995). Advocating this patient-centered focus, Siegmann and Long (1995) recently delineated a model of psychoeducational group therapy for individuals with a wide range of problems and disorders.

The extension of psychoeducational approaches to the treatment of trauma-related psychopathology is a natural evolution, and it is especially fitting because of the bewildering and controversial nature of many trauma-related symptoms. Linehan's dialectical behavior therapy for BPD provides a precedent for trauma education insofar as trauma and BPD overlap, affect regulation and self-injurious behavior are a primary focus, and the therapy includes a strong educational component (Linehan, 1993a, 1993b; Linehan et al., 1991). Whereas Linehan's interventions focus on the individual client, Gunderson and colleagues (Gunderson et al., 1997) have extended the psychoeducational approach to family members of clients with BPD.

Educational interventions also have been prominent in Critical Incident Stress Debriefing, a group intervention intended to ameliorate stress in the immediate aftermath of traumatic events so as to decrease risk of developing PTSD and other trauma-related problems. Mitchell and Everly (1995) stated that 'no other CISM [Critical Incident Stress Management] component can match education for its importance' (p. 58). Although debriefings are widely used and positively valued by participants such as emergency service personnel (Robinson & Mitchell, 1993), reviewers of this literature have consistently pointed to the absence of controlled research supporting the preventive value of the intervention (Bisson & Deahl, 1994; Gore-Felton, Gill, Koopman, & Spiegel, 1999; Rose & Bisson, 1998; Wilson, Raphael, Meldrum, Bedosky, & Sigman, 2000). Furthermore, indications of potential negative effects of debriefings have prompted concern and caution about the routine use of this intervention (Raphael, Wilson, Meldrum, & McFarlane, 1996).

This chapter reviews the literature on educational approaches to traumatized adults, then describes the range of programs my colleagues and I have developed as well as the process of conducting educational groups. After I review our programs for traumatized adult patients, AnnMarie Glodich describes our extension of the educational approach to adolescents, and Kay Kelly discusses its applications to partners and family members.

CLIENT EDUCATION IN TRAUMA TREATMENT

Patient education is now firmly rooted in the field of trauma treatment. Therapists of diverse theoretical orientations have advocated education as beneficial in the treatment of a wide range of traumas, and a number of authors have developed systematic educational interventions.

Incorporating education into standard treatments

Educating clients helps build a therapeutic alliance in cognitive-behavioral approaches to treating trauma (Meichenbaum, 1994; Resick & Schnicke, 1993). In their protocol for rape-related trauma, for example, Foa and Rothbaum (1998) provide extensive information about trauma-related symptoms and also educate clients in a step-by-step fashion about each facet of treatment. They hand out written materials and discuss them with clients. They review the core symptoms of PTSD (reexperiencing, hyperarousal, avoidance, numbing), associated emotions (anger, guilt, shame, depression), and the impact of trauma on cognitions, self-esteem, and relationships. Their compelling rationale for exposure therapy is essential, because exposure is a highly aversive procedure that can lead to significant resistance (e.g., avoiding sessions or dropping out prematurely), which reinforces the avoidance symptoms of PTSD. The authors introduce in vivo and imaginal exposure by educating clients about the costs of avoidance and the need for exposure and habituation. They assure clients, ' you will find out that even if you are very anxious in certain situations, exposing yourself repeatedly to these situations and staying in them long enough will result in a gradual decrease in your anxiety and distress' (p. 145). Therapists who encourage clients to talk about traumatic experiences might consider giving a similar rationale.

Dynamically oriented therapists also incorporate education into treatment. Van der Kolk and colleagues (van der Kolk, McFarlane et al., 1996), for example, discuss the importance of providing clients with a cognitive framework that helps them to feel less crazy and provides some emotional distance from the traumatic experience. Regardless of the therapist's theoretical orientation, several trauma-related problems routinely call for education. For example, therapists must help clients understand the basis of bewildering dissociative symptoms (van der Hart et al., 1998). Clients grappling with confusion about the historical accuracy of memories can be educated about the limitations of memory (Allen, 1995a, 1995b). Educational interventions also may help disabuse clients of the wish for healing by catharsis (Chu, 1992). And persons in the midst of domestic violence require information about means of maintaining safety (Enns et al., 1997).

Psychoeducational interventions

Although education is part of routine practice, some therapists have developed systematic educational interventions. Benham (1995) described a psychoeducational intervention conducted by members of the nursing staff in an inpatient program for women with a history of childhood abuse. The program fosters containment by helping patients cope with flashbacks, dissociative states, and self-injurious impulses. In inpatient settings, nurses are in the best position to help patients monitor their emotional states and implement constructive coping strategies such as grounding, relapse plans, and forming a support network.

Similarly, Talbot and colleagues (Talbot et al., 1998) implemented a psychoeducational group in a short-term inpatient and partial hospital setting that treats women with a history of childhood sexual abuse. The group emphasizes safety and control, strategies for self-care, and here-and-now problems in the women's lives. Patients are discouraged from disclosing details of their trauma history in the group. The group meets three times weekly for one hour, and members are typically in the group for three weeks, with the focal topic varying from week to week (i.e., body image and physical health, safety and control of the environment, emotional regulation).

Empirical studies support the effectiveness of psychoeducational interventions for trauma. Resnick and colleagues (Resnick, Acierno, Holmes, Kilpatrick, & Jager, 1999) developed a focal intervention to alleviate women's anxiety in the context of forensic rape examinations. These authors produced a 17-minute videotape that provided information about the examination procedures, showed a woman undergoing the procedures calmly and successfully, and presented strategies for coping with post-traumatic symptoms. Compared to a control group of women who received the standard briefing, the women who watched the video presentation reported less stress after the exam. The authors are conducting a follow-up study to determine if the intervention reduces the risk for post-traumatic symptoms. In light of the potential hazards of routine management of rape trauma (Campbell et al., 1999), Resnick's approach bears emulating.

Zlotnick and colleagues (Zlotnick, Shea, Rosen et al., 1997) developed a 15-week affect management group for women with a history of childhood sexual abuse, and the group had a substantial educational focus. Compared to those in a wait-list control group, women who received the intervention had a lower level of post-traumatic symptoms at the end of treatment. Stalker and Fry (1999) compared individual and group formats for a psychoeducational approach focusing on childhood sexual abuse and its sequelae. The women discussed their trauma and were given information about PTSD and dissociation. They were encouraged to reframe their symptoms as efforts to adapt to overwhelming events. Clients in both individual and group treatment reported fewer symptoms and improved functioning at follow-up, and the two formats were equally effective.

Lubin and colleagues (Lubin & Johnson, 1997; Lubin, Loris, Burt, & Johnson, 1998) developed a 16-week psychoeducational group in which multiply traumatized women meet once a week for 90 minutes. The program is divided into three four-week modules, the first focusing on the impact of trauma on the self, the next focusing on interpersonal relationships, and the last focusing on finding meaning in life despite the trauma. Participants are encouraged to disclose the trauma at a level of detail comfortable for them and, at the end of the group, they invite members of their social network (including family members) to participate in sharing of a creative project that captures their experience in the group. Participants also place writings and artwork in a Breaking the Silence book. Each session includes brief educational presentations at the beginning and end that focus the discussion. The therapists provide written material summarizing the educational lectures and highlight key points on a blackboard.

Lubin and colleagues (Lubin et al., 1998) investigated the effectiveness of their psychoeducational intervention for a group of participants with a history of multiple traumas in childhood as well as adulthood. Many clients had been in extensive treatment, and half had been hospitalized, attempted suicide, or both. Most clients were prescribed medication. The psychoeducational group was added to their ongoing standard treatment. The researchers excluded clients in acute crises and those with substance abuse problems, psychotic symptoms, or current suicidality. Although the study did not include a control group, the investigators tracked clients' symptoms over one-month intervals during the course of the treatment, and they included a six-month follow-up assessment. Pre-treatment and post-treatment comparisons revealed decreases in PTSD symptoms, depression, dissociation, and overall distress, although follow-up assessments showed some return toward baseline in depression and overall distress. Half the group showed clinically meaningful reductions in PTSD symptoms. Considering the severity of the trauma and extensiveness of prior treatment, these results are encouraging.

A CLINIC-WIDE PSYCHOEDUCATIONAL PROGRAM FOR ADULTS

I began developing an educational program for patients in the early 1990s, when a long-term general psychiatry unit at the Menninger Clinic began to specialize in the treatment of trauma and dissociative disorders. Treating a subgroup of patients with DID in the midst of patients with other psychiatric disorders proved challenging in the inpatient milieu. The patients with DID were bewildered, as were others interacting with them. Thus I instituted a group to explain the nature and origins of dissociative symptoms to all interested patients. When we subsequently formalized a specialty program for the treatment of trauma-related disorders, I developed a comprehensive educational intervention. Ultimately, my colleagues and I extended trauma education into the entire range of clinical services.

Specialized inpatient treatment

The trauma education group in the specialized trauma treatment program met twice weekly for one hour. Developing this intervention in a teaching hospital had the advantage that psychiatric residents, fellows in psychology and social work, and student nurses could also participate. Interested staff members from other clinical services also attended. At its inception, this was a relatively novel endeavor that fostered a spirit of learning for all involved—patients, trainees, other staff members, and myself. My background in teaching undergraduate abnormal psychology led me to develop a college-like curriculum. Yet this was not a lecture course but rather an amalgam of an educational seminar and group psychotherapy. I briefly introduced various topics, then invited patients to discuss their personal experience. I provided the conceptual framework, and patients presented the clinical detail. Throughout each group, we alternated between didactic material and group discussion. I kept track of the discussion by writing the central points and conclusions on the blackboard, making ample use of impromptu diagrams. Many patients who felt alienated stated that it was eye opening—and disconcerting—to 'see' themselves so starkly on the board.

As would befit a college course, I presented extensive material on trauma and its treatment. Often, owing to the extensiveness of group discussion, we took many months to cover the curriculum. The group was open ended, and many patients hospitalized for shorter durations attended only a portion of the course. I compensated for this limited exposure in various ways. I invited patients to bring up whatever concern was on their mind at any time, regardless of its ostensible fit with the current topic. Given the dense interrelationships between various aspects of the course content, patients' immediate concerns rarely derailed the focus. I also provided patients with a manuscript that covered the essential points in considerable detail. After the limitations of the manuscript material became apparent, I wrote a textbook for the course (Allen, 1995a). Later I made videotapes that provide an overview of the course content (Allen, 1999, 2000). Many patients who have difficulty with attention and concentration find the videotapes easier to assimilate than the written material. My colleagues also use the videotapes for patient education in a wide range of clinical services, and patients' family members also find them helpful.

The emotional climate of the specialized inpatient group was highly variable. Teaching traumatized patients about their disturbance is a far cry from lecturing college students. After passing through an initial anxiety-provoking period of flying by the seat of the pants, the group settled into a familiar routine and evolved a generally pleasant climate. We covered painful material, and there were many occasions when members became tearful or frightened—or struggled with dissociative states. For some, the eruption of intrusive symptoms required that they leave the group and seek support from members of the nursing staff. Yet these were the exceptions rather than the rule. Lighthearted interchanges and humor offset the emotional distress. Quite regularly, a spirit of inquisitiveness prevailed in which the patients and I actively formulated understanding together. At its best, the group became a think tank to which the patients and I each contributed a different kind of expertise. Most patients consistently valued the group and looked forward to it.

General principles

Over the years, I have developed a set of general principles to guide this educational work.

First, I organize the educational content into a relatively *simple, coherent conceptual framework*. Such a framework enables patients to organize their traumatic experience and to feel less crazy.

Second, to the extent that they are willing and able, *I involve patients as active participants* in the educational process. I encourage patients to apply the concepts to their own experience. These concrete applications make the educational material meaningful. By their participation, patients actively engage in the process of self-understanding, which fosters their capacity for reflection.

Third, by providing a conceptual framework and encouraging active participation, I help patients *learn to communicate* their difficulties to others. Then they can rely more on words than actions, and they are in a better position to explain their problems and treatment needs to others.

Fourth, I endeavor to *foster a group climate conducive to self-disclosure, exploration, and learning*—a secure base that fosters reflection. I approach group members with an attitude of acceptance, curiosity, and inquisitiveness. I convey respect for their knowledge and continually encourage them to teach each other—and me. We all pool our expertise. I use praise liberally. I remark, 'That's a crucial point,' 'That's a great insight!' 'That's a good topic for this group.' 'I can't think of how you could have handled it any better.' 'That's what I'd call a heroic effort to cope.' I also continually refer back to points that patients have made. For example, 'As Beth said, sometimes the best you can do is get out of the situation,' 'That reminds me of Sam's point that being put down constantly can be worse than being hit.'

Fifth, *I address resistance before encouraging change*. When I make it clear to patients that I understand the problems they face when following our therapeutic suggestions, as well as their fear of change, they realize we are on the same wavelength, and they are more open to exploring new ways of coping.

Sixth, while giving problems and challenges their due, I make an effort to *keep treatment and constructive coping in view*. Focusing on problems without solutions can be demoralizing. Despite my best efforts, some groups sink into a depressive morass—an experience I assiduously try to avoid. Thus, alongside destructive means of regulation emotion, I always put constructive alternatives on the board, at least in the general form of social support and self-regulation.

Seventh, I convey a sober appreciation for the severity of the problems and difficulty overcoming them while also *fostering hope*. You may have noticed that I often refer to states of mind—for example, unbearable emotional states, which are the fulcrum for educating patients about coping. Hope is implicit in my emphasis on states: *states change*. Too, my unshakable conviction that we can make sense of the problems conveys some hope. But perhaps most important, I have the benefit of a long-term perspective on treatment that informs my conviction that severely traumatized patients can benefit substantially from sustained treatment. Sometimes I mention, for example, that I have worked with patients who were determined to die for a long period, then were glad to be alive years later. I always acknowledge, however, that treatment is likely to be slow, difficult, and characterized by many ups and downs—as well as serious relapses. I regularly reiterate my belief that the most demoralizing experience that patients face is suffering relapses despite their best efforts in treatment. Recognizing their hopelessness in this context mitigates it. Acknowledging this reality helps patients feel hopeful, because it matches their experience.

Extensions to other clinical services

Having attended the specialized inpatient group, my colleague Kay Kelly initiated its implementation in the partial hospital service for patients with a wide range of psychiatric disorders. She and I conducted once-weekly sessions that covered the same broad range of content as the inpatient group. Because these patients were living in the community (some in halfway houses), the group emphasized coping with trauma-related problems in daily living. In addition, given that we conducted the group in an open setting rather than an inpatient unit, we highlighted the capacity for self-containment in selecting patients for the group. Despite careful screening, some members occasionally became highly distressed. Thus we found it helpful to work as co-therapists, such that one of us could attend to a distressed member who needed to leave the group. We also find co-therapy to be useful in that one of us can attend to the group process while the other is concentrating on educational content. Often one or more members may begin showing signs of distress in response to a particular topic, and the distress must be addressed therapeutically to provide support and containment so as to avoid its escalation throughout the group. Just remarking, 'Tom, it looks like this discussion is upsetting to you . . .' can launch a group process that provides containment.

In a similar extension, my colleague Janis Huntoon and I developed a group for day hospital patients who had been discharged from the specialized inpatient trauma program. Most of these patients had been exposed to the inpatient trauma education, and this became an advanced group. We shifted from focusing on acute symptoms to considering personality disturbance, that is, the impact of trauma on the self and relationships. In addition, as patients struggled with the prospect of returning home, we devoted considerable attention to resistance to change and the temptation to cling to familiar ways of thinking, feeling, and behaving. For example, the group developed the metaphor of a wall, with problematic but comfortably familiar ways of functioning on one side, and healthy but anxiety-provoking ways of functioning on the other side. As discussion evolved, the group began to construe resistance as a permeable membrane rather than a brick wall, allowing for back and forth movement and a less anxiety-provoking process of gradual change.

My colleagues Kay Kelly and Lisa Lewis also developed a protocol for educating patients with trauma-related problems in a residential program for professionals in crisis. Patients in this program have a history of highly successful functioning despite a significant trauma history, and many present with acute and severe psychiatric disorders to which the trauma has made a significant contribution. The program for professionals is a relatively structured eight-session intervention that provides a broad overview of trauma, reviewing stress management exercises, the psychology and biology of PTSD, the impact of trauma on self and relationships, and treatment approaches. The intervention begins with individual goal setting, and patients are given homework assignments pertinent to the topic. Each session begins with an opening meditation, for example, employing a passage from a poem or book.

Consistent with the increasing recognition of the role of trauma in psychotic disorders, my colleague Ella Squyres invited me to collaborate in developing a trauma education group on an inpatient and residential service for persons with chronic psychotic disorders (acutely psychotic patients do not attend). The group meets twice weekly for one hour, and the content of the education is broadly similar to the other groups we have conducted. Yet problems with impulse control loom large in this patient population, and we often have occasion to highlight the need for self-restraint. We focus on the desired psychological space between the affectively charged impulse and the ensuing destructive action. My colleague Maria Holden, a postdoctoral fellow who assists us in leading the group, usefully presented the analogy of pressing the pause button in this context. The pause button concretizes the need to interpose reflection between emotion (e.g., anger) and action (e.g., self-harm). In using this analogy, we draw patients' attention to the need to tolerate emotional distress while opening up the psychological space required to engage in constructive coping.

Kay Kelly and I also developed a once-weekly outpatient group that clients attend on an open-ended basis. The group is an adjunct to individual psychotherapy, and most clients who enter the group have had some prior trauma education. Like those in day hospital and partial hospital groups, clients in this group are primarily interested in applying the educational material to problems in daily functioning and coping. Perhaps most important, this group offers mutual support by providing a setting in which members can feel less isolated as well as being able to learn daily coping skills from each other. Yet the additional support of the individual psychotherapy is also crucial in the outpatient setting. Individual therapy provides containment for emotions evoked by the group, and it is a setting in which the details of individuals' trauma can be discussed. We find that group tolerance for discussion of individuals' traumatic experiences varies widely, depending on group composition and the group climate at a given point.

Explicit discussion of trauma is not needed to evoke traumatic memories. Although all these psychoeducational groups are highly structured and supportive, many participants are thinking about their individual traumatic experiences during these groups—whether or not they are talking about them. Thus they benefit from whatever containment the group and individual therapy can provide. Furthermore, despite our emphasis on support and containment, some participants find that the group evokes more distress than they can tolerate, and we discourage them from attending while this is the case.

Single-session educational groups

Adapting the trauma education intervention to an acute general psychiatry inpatient unit has been my greatest challenge. Owing to the extremely short lengths of hospital stay, I conduct the group four times a week. The group is open-ended, with a high level of patient turnover. Nearly every session includes a mixture of patients who have been in the group one or more times and a patient new to the group. Some patients attend one or a few times, whereas others are in the group for several sessions. I do not systematically move through predetermined educational content but rather focus on the most pressing issues raised by group members on a session-by-session basis. Often a particular theme of interest will provide a focus for several sessions running, with some continuity in group membership. Such themes include depression, dissociation, self-destructive behavior and suicide, problems with social support, trauma treatment, and the like. Yet this is almost always a single-session intervention insofar as the group membership changes on a daily basis. By necessity, process becomes more prominent than content. I encourage patients to take an active role in learning about their illness and make available the resources for them to do so.

To orient new group members, I make them aware of our written and videotaped educational material, encourage them to raise questions, and give a brief overview of relevant topics. In outline, the main domains consist of traumatic stress, painful emotional states, destructive coping, and constructive coping. Using the stress pile-up model (see Figure 1.1), I begin by noting that the accumulation of past trauma and recent stressors may lead to unbearably painful emotional states. I distinguish two paths that patients may take from these painful states. Coping that backfires entails retreat (isolation, depression, dissociation), self-destructive behavior (substance abuse, self-harm, suicidal behavior), and outwardly destructive behavior (aggression, violence, rages). Effective coping entails making use of supportive relationships and self-regulation. With this outline as a prompt, patients may take the discussion in any direction, and any of the material in this book is fair game. The following paragraphs give examples of the gist of educational content that might be covered in any given session.

In response to questions about trauma, I distinguish between interpersonal and impersonal trauma. I emphasize the core of trauma as feeling afraid and alone, and patients may then comment on feelings of being neglected and their inability to talk about the trauma in childhood and adulthood. Sometimes a group will expand on various features of trauma that we summarize on the board, such as feeling overpowered, trapped, out of control, and paralyzed. We do not generally discuss details of any individual's trauma, although sometimes this is possible and productive. Some patients will merely mention that they were 'sexually abused' or 'physically abused.' Others will describe a series of traumatic losses. A number mention recent stressors.

Given an opening to do so, I draw attention to various aspects of unbearably painful emotional states. Often a group will delineate a wide range of emotions that can be listed under this heading, such as anxiety, fear, panic, pain, shame, guilt, fight-or-flight, sadness, depression, rejection, despair, emptiness, confusion, disorientation, and the like. One patient summarized a long list of painful emotions as 'Hell,' which served as useful shorthand for the range of dysphoria associated with trauma. *Stimulus overload* is a useful concept, as many patients are extremely distressed by crowds or other stimulating environments such as shopping malls and grocery stores. Given a list of painful states, I emphasize that the initial step in regulating emotion is to label your feelings, such as we have just done. Then we discuss the importance of accepting your feelings, with the caveat that *all feelings are valid*. We discuss the importance of being able to sit with feelings, pressing the 'pause button' rather than plunging into counterproductive actions.

I differentiate among different categories of destructive coping or encourage patients to generate a discursive list. Such lists include suicide attempts, alcohol and drug abuse, overeating, excessive spending, gambling, promiscuous sexual behavior, self-cutting, rages, and so forth. I then elaborate the theme that such behaviors are intended to interrupt unbearably painful emotional states but draw attention to their stressful consequences, which brings us to an explicit consideration of vicious circles. Many patients usefully describe how their destructive behavior damages their self-esteem and undermines their functioning. I generally emphasize how destructive coping exacerbates stress in close relationships, leading to rejection and feelings of abandonment.

Whatever the topic, I attempt to keep constructive coping in the foreground, emphasizing a balance between social support and self-regulation. Patients in educational groups can readily generate a relatively long list of potentially helpful self-regulating activities. I write these long lists down on the blackboard. Such lists may include deep breathing, journaling, painting, walking, crafts, listening to music, watching a movie, gardening, taking a warm bath, and sleeping. I often add the possible benefit of the simplest way to change your state of mind, *getting up and moving to a different place*. This elementary behavior has the advantage of requiring no thought or concentration as well as affording a sense of freedom of movement that counters the feeling of being trapped and helpless. Delineating such self-regulating activities enables patients to learn from each other and also highlights individual differences—what helps one patient may backfire for another. I encourage each patient in the group to develop an individualized list, in the group or afterward.

Whenever the topic of social support comes up, I attempt to give equal weight to hazards and benefits, and I always start with the former to head off the inevitable—and well-founded—'Yes, but . . .' resistance. When we broach the topic of social support, patients often complain about others admonishing them to 'Just put the past behind you,' 'Get over it,' 'Focus on the future,' 'Stop feeling sorry for yourself,' and 'Move on.' I list these statements on the board, encouraging members to examine their feasibility and to consider what might prompt other persons to admonish them in this way. And I point out that many of these admonishments are also self-criticisms: 'I should be over this by now!' I contend that any admonishment beginning with 'Just . . .' is likely to be inflammatory. 'Just put it out of your mind!' The person in the throes of PTSD cannot simply do this. Nor is putting it out of mind desirable insofar as treatment entails being able to remember without reliving or avoiding. Of course patients often wish to do as others admonish, but they do not know *how* to do so. 'Just move on!' Yes, but *how*? The answer may be the whole of treatment, in all its complexity. I encourage patients not to internalize others' unrealistic expectations and point out that sometimes the best they can do is to become 'wiser than others' about the challenges in coping with trauma. These educational groups are intended to provide them with some of the needed wisdom.

Beyond adult educational groups

Although psychoeducational interventions for trauma are proliferating, most trauma education takes place in the context of therapies that are not primarily educational. Having adopted a penchant for education, I bring the sort of material just discussed into any suitable clinical context, be it psychological assessment, diagnostic consultation, or psychotherapy. I use a pad of paper while I am meeting with an individual client, just as I use a blackboard in working with a group. I may just summarize key points or, in a more didactic fashion, draw illustrative diagrams. I find that shifting gears between support, exploration, and education can be as smooth in individual work as it is in groups. Many traumatized clients have difficulty taking in information and remembering it, such that written notes from individual sessions can be a useful record for them.

In any therapeutic context, making use of the client's expertise and endeavoring to enhance it facilitates a treatment alliance. Many of our clients know far more than we do about trauma. The best we can do is learn from them, encourage them to learn from each other, and spread the knowledge we acquire. Having learned from our adult clients, we recognized the potential value of educating adolescents as well as family members.

EDUCATING ADOLESCENTS
AnnMarie Glodich

The full range of post-traumatic symptoms and syndromes evident in adulthood also have been identified in childhood and adolescence (Pynoos et al., 1996; Pynoos, Steinberg et al., 1995). Our clinical work in inpatient and residential treatment programs for adolescents provided ample evidence for the pervasiveness of trauma as a contributing factor to severe psychopathology in that age group. Adolescent patients being treated for mood disorders, conduct problems, substance abuse, psychotic symptoms, and self-injurious behavior gave histories of abuse and neglect as well as striking exposure to violence in their homes and communities. Many clients had witnessed or been directly involved in shootings and stabbings, as victims or perpetrators, in gangs and in families.

As awareness of the extent of exposure to trauma and its relation to symptoms in the adolescent client population grew, the clinical staff appreciated the need for an intervention focusing on trauma. In collaboration with Jon

Allen, I extended the educational approach into the adolescent services. In the course of that clinical work, I gradually became aware of the paramount significance of reenactment and reexposure to trauma in the adolescent clients, as well as the potentially traumatic impact of many adolescents' continual exposure to violence in the community. Accordingly, I further extended what began as a clinical service into the community in the form of a school-based trauma education program focused on prevention of further trauma and exposure to violence in particular.

Inpatient and residential group

I began with the assumption that a group treatment approach would be best, given the paramount role of peer relationships in adolescent development (Kymissis, 1993). As it does with adults, the group provides adolescents with the opportunity to normalize their experience and to gain insight into their symptoms. Furthermore, the educational focus was an ideal way to introduce trauma-focused interventions into the adolescent services, because it emphasizes structure, support, and containment. In addition, the educational approach is relatively non-threatening insofar as individuals are not expected to discuss their trauma history in any detail.

As is true in the treatment of adults, many therapists include an educational component in their treatment of traumatized adolescents (Blechman, Dumas, & Prinz, 1994; Lindon & Nourse, 1992; Steinberg & Sunkenberg, 1994; Trolley, 1995). Schamess (1993), for example, described trauma-focused activity–discussion groups that are psychoeducational in nature, with the therapist assuming multiple roles of 'activities director, educator about adaptive functioning in the aftermath of trauma, and protective symbolic parent' (p. 569). Other authors have developed effective psychoeducational groups for adolescent sex offenders (Hains, Herrman, Baker, & Graber, 1986) and children exposed to community violence (Jones & Selder, 1996).

Our adolescent group includes members with a wide range of traumas. The group meets twice weekly for one-hour sessions. Our colleague, Cindy Arnold, is a member of the inpatient unit nursing staff who assists in running the group and also fosters integration of the group with the inpatient milieu by informing other staff members about events in the group and following up with members who are distressed. We planned the curriculum around core concepts, including the symptoms of PTSD, dissociation, and depression; the importance of attachment and the impact of trauma on the self and peer relationships; and ways of coping constructively with painful emotions evoked by stress and reminders of trauma. Following the model of the adult groups, we began with the intention of introducing a topic for discussion, then inviting participants to raise questions and share experiences with one another. On occasion, this strategy was effective. More often, however, the group members spontaneously began talking amongst themselves, often on matters of immediate concern, such as events of the day and relationship problems. Often their conversations did not relate directly to our agenda of teaching them about trauma. Sometimes we were able to steer the discussion in the direction of a trauma-related topic. At other times, their immediate concerns prevailed.

Rather than being able to structure the process consistently around our educational agenda, we discovered the concept of the *teachable moment*—one that is all too familiar to public school teachers. That is, at opportune junctures, we endeavored to hold participants' attention for a few minutes to present a trauma-related concept in conjunction with their current concerns. We might focus for a short time, for example, on dissociative detachment, nightmares, panicky feelings, depression, self-harm, or coping with intense aggressive impulses. The process became more important than the content. We attempted to establish a respectful climate in which the adolescents could listen to each other's emotional experience and empathize with it. We endeavored to help them become more aware of trauma-related states of mind, in themselves and in their peers, and we attempted to marshal sufficient containment in the group so that they could develop greater tolerance for trauma-related thoughts, images, and emotions.

We incorporate activities into the group to provide structure and foster containment so as to modulate the level of tension. Each client has a folder with pencils and paper to write notes, draw, or doodle. We summarize points on the blackboard and invite participants to use it as well, for example, drawing a picture of a mood state. Borrowing from James (1989) we write various emotions associated with violence and abuse on slips of paper and place the slips in a paper bag. Then we circulate the bag among the members of the group, asking each one to draw out a slip of paper and to discuss their experience with the particular emotion. Among the most powerful activities is role playing. Using the traumatic reenactment diagram (see Figure 3.2), we invite members of the group to role-play scenarios involving a perpetrator, victim, rescuer, and witnessing bystander. Participants as well as observers find these role-plays to be emotionally evocative, and making links between the role playing and their daily interactions enables them to begin thinking about their behavior in relation to traumatic reenactments.

In developing an educational agenda and structuring group activities, we had intended to help the adolescents appreciate the impact of trauma on their experience and behavior, to foster more adaptive coping skills, and to nurture a supportive group climate that would counter their sense of alienation. We sought to help them with *post*-traumatic symptoms. Yet we were increasingly impressed by the paramount role of ongoing exposure to trauma in their daily life. We felt we were swimming against the tide in emphasizing post-traumatic symptoms in the face of their continual re-exposure to trauma by virtue of their poor impulse control and risk-taking behavior. The adolescents were continually placing themselves in danger, whether by getting into fights, using weapons, or driving drunk. Substance abuse looms especially large in revictimization in this adolescent population, as intoxication compromises cognitive functioning and judgment, thereby increasing vulnerability to rape, other forms of assault, and accidents.

Focus on reenactment: trauma begets trauma

Our appreciation of ongoing trauma exposure led us to place major emphasis on risk-taking behavior from the perspective of reenactment of traumatic relationship patterns. We came to recognize the value of the trauma perspective not only for helping the adolescents find meaning in their current symptoms but also for underscoring the psychological cost of their trauma reenactments and the associated cumulative trauma exposure. Although therapists have given a great deal of consideration in recent years to a host of post-traumatic symptoms in childhood and adolescence, they have given insufficient attention to reenactment and risk taking. Notable exceptions, however, are adolescent groups that include education about the dynamics of abuse and revictimization (Hazzard, 1993; Pescosolido, 1993; Rice-Smith, 1993; Steinberg & Sunkenberg, 1994).

As described in the context of attachment (Chapter 3), in the earliest years of life trauma is associated with extremely unbalanced relationships as evident in a hostile–helpless pattern (Lyons-Ruth et al., 1999). These polarizations can evolve into stable traits, with some children becoming more aggressive and others more passive (Perry et al., 1995; Pfefferbaum & Allen, 1998; Terr, 1991). Both extreme aggression and passivity can be construed as reenactments that increase the risk of further trauma exposure. Aggression begets aggression and the likelihood of being traumatized by violence (Lynch & Cicchetti, 1998; Pfefferbaum & Allen, 1998). Passivity also may expose the adolescent to further victimization. For example, one group member who witnessed her mother being battered by a series of violent men, although abhorring her mother's behavior, sought out relationships with abusive boyfriends and girlfriends. Another adolescent consistently had dated kind and considerate boys until she was raped. Thereafter she began dating abusive boys, remaining completely unaware of the connection between the rape and the altered quality of her subsequent relationships. Passive reenactment is also evident in the failure of self-protection. For example, adolescents in our groups report remaining at parties where they know others are carrying weapons, or they ride in cars with drivers who are intoxicated. As trauma exposure accumulates, they feel increasingly inadequate, helpless, and desperate. At worst, sensitization contributes to escalating post-traumatic symptoms, destructive efforts to defuse tension, and additional trauma exposure.

Containment entails a balance of social support and self-regulation, and we attempt to foster these capacities in the group process. By providing a climate of understanding and acceptance, the group is a model of social support. Members not only have an opportunity to be supported but also learn to be supportive. We not only discuss self-regulation but also endeavor to foster it within the group setting. Oftentimes members have difficulty containing the anxiety aroused by topics we or their peers introduce. The process of providing social support—listening attentively, endeavoring to understand, and responding empathically—fosters their capacity for containment.

The goal of helping traumatized adolescents to move from the realm of action to mentalization and reflection is ambitious and challenging. In our view, the primary value of the group intervention is in providing the adolescents with an opportunity to reflect upon their own and others' mental states as they relate to trauma. Providing them with knowledge about trauma is helpful in itself to the degree that it counters feelings of alienation and of being crazy. The unspeakable gets a name. Yet information alone carries little weight. Introducing concepts is valuable only insofar as the concepts foster reflection about matters of personal significance. Many adolescents have not had an opportunity to discuss emotionally charged problems with adults in a calm climate. Yet, in these groups, adults are explaining in a matter-of-fact way what the adolescents might be experiencing. Some become curious about—and even fascinated by—the wide-ranging effects of trauma on their behavior. They see themselves in the trauma reenactment roles. They begin to feel understood. Most of the adolescents do not think about their experience in the group as fostering a capacity to be reflective, even though this might be happening. They describe the group as a place where others can 'hang with' them, explain some experiences, explore meanings, and not force an agenda on them. One adolescent gave a metaphor for her accumulating knowledge: 'It's like someone gives me a quarter each time I come to the group. You know, you save your quarters for a new outfit. I feel like I get a quarter every time I come and this will help me to have a new outfit, to think differently.'

I also have found it helpful to foster reflection by encouraging the adolescents to anticipate the impact of trauma on their future. I bring an intergenerational perspective into the educational process by using a *future family diagram*, modeled after the family genogram pioneered by Bowen (1978, 1980). Rather than focusing on the past, however, I ask the adolescents to construct a family tree for the future and to draw it on the blackboard. I guide the construction of the diagram by several questions pertinent to reenactment in relationships. Do you want to have a committed relationship? If so, at what age? What type of committed relationship do you want to have? Do you want to have children? Do love and abuse go together? Do you want your partner to hit you or your children? If not, what steps can you take to avoid this? I have been impressed repeatedly by the extent to which these imagined future families include dysfunction and trauma—substance abuse, violence, divorce, and death. Lively discussions ensue as these future scenarios are linked to the past and the group members begin to think about the possibility of developing relationships in the future that differ from those in the past.

I ask other questions pertinent to self-development and goal setting. If you could have any job you wanted, what would that job be? Do you need to finish high school? Do you plan to attend college? If so, how can you go about doing this? Where can you go to receive help? Do you have funding sources available to you? How can you find out about this? A concrete diagram fosters reflection that counters the sense of a foreshortened future so characteristic of PTSD—and likely to be a concrete consequence of dangerous reenactments.

The violence epidemic

An epidemic of trauma and violence among young people is sweeping across the United States, creating a public health crisis of unprecedented proportions (Garbarino, 1995; Osofsky, 1997a). Many children and adolescents are living in potentially traumatizing situations—in their homes as well as on the streets and even in their schools. Some experience pervasive and chronic threats to their safety, whereas others encounter only a single incident. Yet even single incidents of violence can be traumatic, leaving behind a trail of insecurity, helplessness, and hopelessness. Moreover, witnessing violence can be just as traumatizing as being physically injured (Eth & Pynoos, 1994).

Empirical research and clinical reports document the potentially profound impact of exposure to violence. Over time, such exposure can lead to a wide range of adverse consequences, including depression, anxiety, detachment, dissociation, reexperiencing, hyperarousal, hypervigilance, post-traumatic stress disorder, risk-taking behavior, substance abuse, sexual acting out, pregnancy, delinquency, violence, school failure, self-injurious behavior, and even suicide (Amayala-Jackson & March, 1993; Arroyo & Eth, 1996; Eth & Pynoos, 1985; Garbarino, 1995; Garbarino & Kostelny, 1997; Jenkins & Bell, 1997; Marans & Adelman, 1997; Nader & Pynoos, 1993; Perry, 1997; Prothrow-Stith, 1991; Pynoos, 1990; Pynoos, Steinberg et al., 1995; Terr, 1991; Yule & Williams, 1990).

Although our appreciation of the relationship between trauma and the violence epidemic grew in the context of a clinical intervention for adolescents in inpatient and residential treatment, we began to recognize the potential value of bringing the trauma perspective to bear on violence prevention efforts in the schools. If we could contribute to forestalling reenactment and trauma exposure, we might aid in preventing adolescents from developing psychopathology that would require clinical intervention. Moreover, we might reach adolescents who needed mental health services but did not have access to them or might feel stigmatized by seeking them.

School-based trauma education

Schools are increasingly recognized as the optimal setting in which to provide interventions for adolescents exposed to violence and abuse (Allen-Meares, Washington, & Welsch, 1990; Murphy, Pynoos, & James, 1997; Osofsky, 1997b; Pynoos, Goenjian, & Steinberg, 1995). School-based interventions do not carry the stigmatizing potential associated with mental health facilities (Scannapieco, 1994). Psychoeducational approaches, in particular, are tailor made for the schools, which naturally place children and adolescents in an environment where they expect to attend classes and learn (Herz, Goldberg, & Reis, 1984). Pynoos and Nader (1988) pioneered a school-based debriefing model for single-event trauma. They provide a cognitive framework for the exploration of feelings and increase individuals' sense of mastery over trauma-related distress. Yet Wallen (1993) pointed out that debriefing models do not adequately address the impact of chronic exposure to family and community violence. She contended that the long-term effects of ongoing violence exposure require interventions that promote the development of self-protective strategies and focus on increasing competence and self-esteem.

As part of a broader community-wide violence prevention effort, we developed a protocol for time-limited, trauma-focused psychoeducational groups in the high school setting. School social workers and counselors serve as referral sources and also as group co-leaders. To be referred to the group, the adolescent must have experienced or witnessed violent events that were stressful or traumatizing. Such events include witnessing or participating in an attempted or actual shooting or stabbing; rape; traumatic accidents; and traumatic loss. Also referred are adolescents who are exposed to family violence or abuse as well as those distressed by living in a high crime area where community violence is a daily occurrence.

The group is designed to foster awareness of the traumatic impact of exposure to violence and its relation to reenactment and risk-taking behaviors. The eight-session protocol entails a specific topic for each session along with a concrete activity or task that promotes coping. Session topics include prevalence of violence and trauma; post-traumatic stress symptoms and defenses; reenactment and further trauma exposure; combating helplessness; self-protective strategies to decrease victimization, including ways of avoiding and defusing violence; and the role of the family in coping with trauma.

A controlled study of the effectiveness of the psychoeducational intervention showed promising results (Glodich, 1999). Forty-seven adolescents from a local high school were randomly assigned to an intervention group or a wait-list control group. Both groups were assessed immediately before and after the eight-week protocol, and wait-list participants were offered the intervention subsequently. All participants completed a tailor-made trauma-knowledge test assessing their understanding of trauma concepts, role reenactment, and the relation between trauma and self-endangering behavior. Participants also completed a measure of attitudes toward risk-taking behavior (Busen, 1991). As intended, the intervention had a significant effect on knowledge about trauma. Although the intervention group showed a slight increase in healthy attitudes toward risk taking compared to a decrease in the wait-list control group, the contrast was not statistically significant. Yet, at post-test, there was a significant correlation for all subjects between level of trauma knowledge and healthy attitudes toward risk taking.

Since the initial study was completed, we have extended the intervention into three schools; increased the number of sessions from eight to twelve; refined the assessment to include newly developed measures of trauma exposure and post-traumatic symptoms; and included an instrument to measure self-reported change in risk-taking *behavior*. In addition we have increased the proportion of structured activities in relation to didactic education. For example, we are including sessions with police officers who not only share their experience with violence and trauma but also role-play potentially dangerous interactions with the adolescents. These role-plays are intended to help the participants avoid traumatic confrontations in the context of law enforcement. In this respect we are building on the work of others who have involved police officers in violence prevention efforts with children and adolescents (Marans & Adelman, 1997; Murphy et al., 1997; Osofsky, 1997b).

Thus we are in the process of enhancing the intervention, expanding the target population, and refining the methodology for assessing its effectiveness. The collaboration we have forged between clinical services and the law enforcement system, school district administration, and school personnel has been challenging and gratifying. In the process we have fostered greater community awareness of the impact of trauma and its role in violence prevention.

EDUCATING PARTNERS AND FAMILY MEMBERS
Kay A. Kelly

The need for systematic family education in the field of trauma became apparent to us when a member of our psychoeducational group in the partial hospital services spontaneously exclaimed, 'I wish my husband could hear this!' Other members agreed and implored us to include family members in the group. To preserve group cohesiveness and maintain confidentiality, we declined to make this change. Instead we developed a family-focused intervention. This section reviews literature on family education and working with couples, then describes the format of our *Partners in Trauma* workshop.

Family education

Traditional psychoeducational approaches endeavor to help family members understand the patient's illness and to interact with the patient in such a way as to minimize the likelihood of relapse. Tarrier and colleagues have shown that this approach is as applicable to trauma as it is to schizophrenia, insofar as high expressed emotion (e.g., hostility and criticism) characterizes the interactions of a substantial proportion of family members of persons with PTSD (Tarrier, 1996), and such interactions have a demonstrably adverse impact on treatment outcome (Tarrier, Sommerfield et al., 1999).

Yet a number of authors have argued cogently that the mental health profession must go beyond psychoeducational approaches aimed at minimizing patients' relapses. The substantial emotional and practical burden that family members experience in caring for individuals with serious mental disorders is well documented (Fadden, 1998; Marsh & Johnson, 1997; Solomon & Draine, 1995). To reduce this burden, *family education* targets family members themselves as the primary beneficiaries of intervention, aiming to provide education and support that will increase the family members' well-being and quality of life (Hatfield, 1994; Simon, 1997; Solomon, 1996).

Yet the term, burden, fails to capture the extent of potential stress associated with severe mental disorder in a family member. Marsh and Johnson (1997) characterized the eruption of serious mental disorder as a *catastrophic* event to families. Such illness not only entails a host of responsibilities and burdens associated with caregiving but also severe emotional strain associated with loss, grief, chronic sorrow, and living on an emotional roller coaster. In light of the extreme stress associated with severe mental illness, Burland (1998) advocated a *trauma-and-recovery model* of family education.

No doubt, trauma-related disorders can be just as traumatizing to family members as primary psychotic disorders (Figley, 1989). Trauma-related disorders carry all the potential strains of other serious mental disorders, and they also entail exposure to emotional contagion and involvement in traumatic reenactment (Chapter 3). In the context of trauma-related disorders or other severe mental disorders, self-harm and suicidal behavior are potentially traumatic events that meet criterion A for PTSD, which includes being confronted with events that involve a threat to the physical integrity of others (APA, 1994). Family members may also develop PTSD and other trauma-related disorders (Brende & Goldsmith, 1991). For example, spouses sensitized by repeated suicide attempts may become hypervigilant and extremely reactive to reminders of suicide attempts or to cues that foreshadow additional attempts. Moreover, spouses of combat veterans with PTSD not only may be dealing with a host of illness-related stressors but also the traumatized veteran's threatening and violent behavior (Matsakis, 1996; Nelson & Wright, 1996; Rabin, 1995). Thus family education employing a trauma perspective is especially pertinent to trauma-related disorders.

Working with couples

The burdens of mental illness are somewhat different for partners and spouses than for parents and other members of the patient's family of origin (Goldstein & Miklowitz, 1994). Mannion and colleagues (Mannion, Mueser, & Solomon, 1994), for example, demonstrated the effectiveness of a spouse coping skills workshop that addressed multiple difficulties, including 'maintaining a sense of partnership, raising children, running a household, managing finances and maintaining a social life with a mate whose illness often involves chronic or episodic psychosis, impulsivity, unreliability, self-absorption, lethargy and social withdrawal' (p. 180). Such problems pertain to trauma-related disorders as well as to other psychiatric disorders. Nelsen (1994) noted that incest-related trauma calls for couples treatment that addresses many problem areas. These include overcoming denial and acknowledging the client's illness and need for treatment; establishing open communication and dealing with a range of feelings, including anxiety, anger, sadness, and guilt; negotiating responsibilities in relation to the client's limitations; and forgoing one's own needs, sometimes including sexual satisfaction and control over the sexual relationship.

Compton and Follette (1998) delineated a substantial list of challenges that face couples exposed to trauma. These include problems with emotional expressiveness and intimacy; conflict and emotional turbulence; physical violence and revictimization; dissatisfaction with the relationship; and high rates of separation and divorce. Often the couple is isolated from other persons. Conflicts over closeness in the relationship are common, and this is particularly true in the case of sexual trauma, which may be associated with decreased sexual desire and satisfaction, difficulty communicating about sexual matters, and sexual promiscuity. These authors note that relationship problems can be particularly intense in dual trauma couples, where both members have a trauma history. They advocate a behavioral approach to couples treatment that includes trauma education and focuses on specific interactional problems.

All persons in close relationships with traumatized clients will experience some degree of emotional contagion and reenactment. Yet these problems are most salient in primary attachment relationships, which are likely to involve couples. Maltas (Maltas & Shay, 1995; Maltas, 1996) discussed contagion and reenactment in couples in which one member has a history of childhood sexual abuse. Partners of sexually abused women may themselves be traumatized. For example, they may struggle with shattered assumptions; become distrusting, numb, and detached; and engage in self-destructive coping (e.g., substance abuse) to quell their distress. Maltas (1996) likened contagion to a viral infection and described the transition to reenactment as 'a malevolent transformation from savior to someone who is seductive, neglectful, and/or abusive, a transformation that can destroy the relationship and its opportunity for healing' (p. 352). At a minimum, partners in such relationships need education, and self-help books are available (Cameron, 1994; Davis, 1991; Engle, 1991). As Maltas (1996) recommended, however, adequate treatment often will require individual, group, and couples therapy—the latter being especially critical to provide a balanced perspective of each individual's contribution to role reenactments.

As previous authors have proposed, I find it helpful to approach couples from the perspective that both members are sensitized to trauma. To concretize the concept of sensitization in work with trauma survivors and their partners, I use the concept of a *90/10 reaction*, in which an intense emotional reaction stems 90% from the past and 10% from the present (see Figure 13.1). The partner, with an eye on only the present 10%, cannot understand the basis of the survivor's response, which is embedded largely in the accumulation of stress and trauma from the past. Hence the partner's irritation and criticism may be seen as abusive, or the partner's desire for sexual intimacy may be experienced as exploitative or coercive. The 90/10 figures are arbitrary but set the stage for considering first that there is inevitably some realistic basis for the reaction in the present (e.g., the 10%). The proportions of

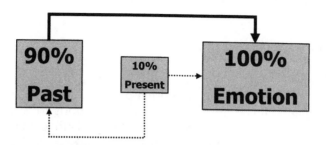

Figure 13.1 Sensitization as a '90/10 response'

present and past provocation can vary (e.g., an intense reaction to current violence may be better characterized as a 10/90 reaction). Moreover, to the extent that both members of the couple are struggling with past trauma, both may be showing a 90/10 response in a process of mutual escalation of emotion. Caught in the throes of reactions that fit poorly with the present and are not understandable in light of the past, both members feel helpless and out of control and, ultimately, cut off from one another.

The 90/10 reaction dovetails with the diagram we developed to help individual clients understand the phenomenon of reenactment (see Figure 3.2), and this reenactment diagram is especially useful in working with couples. The diagram reflects the process of sensitization in reenactment. That is, ordinary interactions characterized by helping, hurting, and distancing can escalate into rescuing, abusing, and neglecting. Each member of the couple—or both members—may, in effect, spin out from ordinary conflict to a traumatic reenactment. As it is in individual work, the role of neglect bears emphasis in couples therapy. Just as trauma survivors respond intensely to feelings of neglect, so do their partners. The following is a common pattern: the partner is highly committed to the relationship and desires to provide help and support. When the survivor's disturbance intensifies, the partner is drawn into escalating efforts to provide rescue. The partner eventually becomes frustrated, fatigued, and depressed, and then withdraws (e.g., into detachment, work, or substance abuse). Then the survivor feels neglected—as does the partner, who has lost the intimacy and gratification that the relationship previously provided.

I find that educating couples about these patterns—the 90/10 reaction and its relation to role reenactments—helps normalize their emotional reactions and relationship conflicts, thereby diminishing blame and guilt feelings. Normalizing their experience sets the stage for helping them to reconnect in their relationship, to identify their contributions to the conflicts and disentangle them from their past, and to marshal their resources so as to increase the level of mutual support in the relationship. Without reconnection, both partners are left feeling abandoned and neglected. Ultimately, both members must be helped to care for themselves and for each other, through psychoeducational and other therapeutic modalities.

Partners in trauma workshop

We have been fortunate to work in a clinical setting that places a premium on family intervention and has supported psychoeducational interventions on chronic mental illness for decades. Thus our efforts to educate family members about trauma were a natural evolution. Throughout the clinical services, social workers and other therapists make available to family members the written material and bibliographies we have developed, as well as the related videotapes (Allen, 1999, 2000). Yet clients, family members, and colleagues consistently expressed a wish for an educational intervention for family members, which prompted us to offer periodic *Partners in Trauma* workshops.

Staff members and therapists who are working with traumatized clients refer workshop participants. Most participants are spouses, although close friends and parents occasionally attend. Prospective participants are screened by contact with the referring therapist as well as by telephone contact. Appropriate participants complete a brief questionnaire that includes questions about what they want to learn. Prospective participants raise a wide range of concerns, including questions about PTSD and other psychiatric disorders; medication management; dealing with flashbacks; coping with anger toward abusers; as well as dealing with relationship problems such as intimacy, sexuality, and parenting. They also wonder how to manage their own needs while not neglecting their partner, how to strengthen the relationship, and how to move forward. One prospective participant merely wrote, 'Tell me everything!' 'Is there hope?' is a critical question that is also raised continually by clients.

The three-hour workshop, with membership typically ranging from five to ten participants, is divided into two parts. The first part is relatively didactic, including information on the characteristics of trauma and the process of sensitization; symptoms of PTSD, dissociation, and self-harm; the impact of trauma on the self and relationships, the latter emphasizing reenactment; and various aspects of treatment. As is true of our client education groups, the presentation is relatively informal, and we encourage questions on any and all topics. As we do with traumatized clients, we provide handouts with brief articles and diagrams we have developed as well as bibliographies on trauma.

The second half of the workshop engages participants in discussing with each other the problems they face as well as their coping strategies. This section of the workshop is highly supportive in fostering a sense of universality, that is, a feeling of commonality. We are eager to have participants learn from each other, as they exchange coping strategies that have been helpful and effective. An important theme that has emerged in these discussions is the need to move beyond having your life revolve around trauma. Nelsen (1994) pointed out that

> An especially difficult long-term issue is that the unimpaired partner cannot be expected to continue indefinitely giving his or her needs a lower priority than those of the mate. Asking the impaired partner who is still suffering from a serious illness or condition to meet more of these needs can produce guilt in the one who is unimpaired, yet not asking and not having major needs met leads to anger and despair. . . . Workers can help by acknowledging that the unimpaired partner's needs are legitimate, whether or not the mate can fully meet them. (p. 195)

Consistent with Nelsen's view, members of these groups encourage each other not to isolate themselves but rather to seek a broader social support network, to take time for themselves, and to enjoy individual pursuits. We also encourage partners to be mindful of post-traumatic symptoms in themselves and other family members and to seek individual treatment as needed.

Evaluation forms that participants complete after the Partners in Trauma workshops have indicated consistently positive responses to the material presented as well as appreciation for the opportunity to share experience with persons in similar situations. Yet their responses also make plain that we have merely scratched the surface in interventions for family members. In a relatively brief, one-session intervention, we only cover a limited range of content, emphasizing symptoms, disorders, and treatment.

More intensive focus on relationship challenges, for example, including problems with intimacy and sexuality as well as parenting, would be valuable, as would help in managing crises. Many participants express a need for an ongoing support group. We have focused primarily on partners and spouses, and there is a need for comparable interventions for parents and members of the family of origin. In addition, groups in which clients participate along with their family members might also be beneficial. As Figley's (1989) work exemplifies, there is a great need for trauma-related interventions at the family-system level, and this is wide-open territory for creative interventions.

REFLECTION

A colleague once asked me, 'Don't you get bored, running these same groups, day after day?' If I were just lecturing, I would have quit years ago. But I am always challenged, always learning, and always trying to figure out better ways of explaining things. When I am trying to understand a particular trauma-related problem better, I seize the opportunity to explore it with patients in a group. And trying to keep abreast of the burgeoning literature so as to provide patients with current knowledge is a sure antidote to boredom. This work is painful, anxiety provoking, and discouraging. But it is always *interesting*—never boring. And it can be enjoyable and gratifying.

Chapter 14

THERAPISTS AT RISK

We are the tools of our trade. (Pearlman & Saakvitne, 1995a, p. 185)

Becoming a therapist confers no immunity from psychiatric disorder. As Menninger (1963) stated decades ago,

> Gone forever is the notion that the mentally ill person is an exception. It is now accepted that most people have some degree of mental illness at some time, and many of them have a degree of mental illness most of the time. This really should not surprise anyone, for do not most of us have some physical illness some of the time, and some of us much of the time? (p. 33)

We therapists are not exempted.

Working intensively with severely traumatized clients is a highly stressful occupation, and it can be detrimental to our mental and physical health. Throughout this book, I have examined the consequences of severe and prolonged stress from the client's point of view. In closing, I use this developmental framework as a mirror, applying it to us therapists. This chapter considers a few key questions. How common is a history of childhood trauma among us? What is the impact of a trauma history on our functioning and practices? What can we do to protect ourselves? Thanks to colleagues who have researched these questions on our behalf, we are in a position to be well informed about our own risk and protective factors.

CHILDHOOD ADVERSITY

We therapists are subject to all the risk factors that pertain to our clients, including genetic vulnerabilities (e.g., to anxiety, depression, alcohol abuse), family history of psychiatric disorder, and our own individual history of behavioral, emotional, and physical disorders. Fortunately, just as we are not excluded from risk factors, we are not excluded from protective factors, among the most important of which is a history of supportive relationships and secure attachments.

Like everyone else, we who grew up to become therapists were at significant risk for childhood trauma. A substantial number of surveys document the prevalence of a trauma history among therapists. Pearlman and MacIan (1995) asked a multidisciplinary group of self-identified trauma therapists, 'Do you have a trauma history?' Sixty percent answered yes. Two surveys revealed that a substantial proportion of psychologists report a history of childhood trauma. Polusny and Follette (1996) found that 32% of their respondents (42% of women and 23% of men) reported a history of childhood sexual abuse. Feldman-Summers and Pope (1994) found that 29% of women and 18% of men reported a history of childhood sexual abuse, physical abuse, or both, and that 40% of these psychologists with an abuse history reported a period of forgetting their abuse. Conducting psychotherapy for trauma survivors is one context that prompts remembering abuse (Pearlman & Saakvitne, 1995a).

Little and Hamby (1996) studied a multidisciplinary group of therapists and found that 33% of women and 20% of men reported a history of childhood sexual abuse. Among therapists working with sex offenders, Hilton and colleagues (Hilton, Jennings, Drugge, & Stephens, 1995) found that 37% of women and 27% of men reported a history of childhood sexual abuse. Nuttall and Jackson (1994) surveyed a multidisciplinary group of professionals responsible for evaluating childhood sexual abuse allegations and found that 20% of women and 13% of men reported a history of childhood sexual abuse. In addition, 7% of women and 7% of men reported a history of childhood physical abuse.

Without comparison groups it is difficult to know if childhood trauma is more or less common among therapists than the general population. Two studies have begun to address this question. Follette and colleagues (Follette, Polusny, & Milbeck, 1994) contrasted mental health professionals (psychologists and marriage and family therapists) with law enforcement professionals, finding a history of childhood abuse to be reported by 36% of women and 23% of men among the mental health professionals and 40% of women and 17% of men among the law enforcement professionals. The authors did not report whether the differences between professional groups were statistically significant. They not only studied sexual and physical abuse but also emotional abuse. Among the mental health professionals, 19% of women and 11% of men reported sexual abuse; 24% of women and 18% of men reported physical abuse; and 51% of women and 39% of men reported emotional abuse.

Elliott and Guy (1993) contrasted a multidisciplinary sample of women mental health professionals from various disciplines (a majority being licensed clinical social workers) with women in a wide range of other professions. They found significantly higher levels of childhood adversity among the mental health professionals, including physical abuse, sexual molestation, parental alcoholism, hospitalization of a parent for mental illness, and death of a parent or sibling. They also found the family environment reported by mental health professionals to be more dysfunctional, with significant differences on scales measuring conflict, cohesion, independence, achievement orientation, and moral–religious emphasis. Of course one cannot know if the mental health professionals were more likely to experience adversity or more open to remembering and reporting it.

CURRENT STRESS

Just as therapists are not protected from childhood adversity, they are not immune to the full array of adulthood stressors and traumas. Follette and colleagues (Follette et al., 1994) documented a wide range of adulthood trauma exposure among therapists, including the finding that 16% of women and 5% of men reported abuse in relationships with partners or spouses. Therapists also face the occupational hazard of assaults by clients, which plainly qualify as potentially traumatic events (Caldwell, 1992; Miller, 1998). As Pearlman and Saakvitne (1995a) noted, it is extremely stressful—and potentially traumatic—to work closely with clients who are chronically suicidal and who engage in deliberate self-harm. Moreover the current litigious climate regarding false memories (D. Brown et al., 1998; Scheflin, 2000) presents stresses unique to the trauma field. Putting it simply, 'It is dismaying to enter a field in order to help people and then be accused of harming them' (Pearlman & Saakvitne, 1995a, p. 343). As trauma therapists, we are in a highly stressful niche of a highly stressful profession.

A key component of the stress pile-up that therapists face is indirect exposure from listening to clients' traumatic experiences. The definition of traumatic events in DSM-IV (APA, 1994) includes not only direct exposure and witnessing trauma but also *learning about* traumatic events to which others were exposed: 'Events experienced by others that are learned about include, but are not limited to, violent personal assault, serious accident, or serious injury experienced by a family member or a close friend' (p. 424). It is a small extrapolation to consider clients with whom one has worked closely to be akin to 'a close friend.' The more intensive the therapy, and the stronger the attachment, the greater the stressful impact of hearing about a client's trauma. Yet interviewing research subjects also can carry significant risk of vicarious traumatization (Urquiza, Wyatt, & Goodlin-Jones, 1997).

Consider what goes on in your mind when you bear witness as your client talks about traumatic experience. Owing to your brain's gift for vivid visual imagery (Kosslyn, 1994), you are likely to picture what your client went through. Like your client, you may later be haunted by these images, during the daytime or during your sleep (Pearlman & Saakvitne, 1995a). Owing to your empathy and penchant for emotional contagion (Hatfield et al., 1994), you will experience some degree of distress, potentially sharing in the full range of emotions—fear, anger, despair, and the rest. Like your client, you may feel guilty about your emotional and physiological responses (e.g., feeling guilty for your vengeful fantasies or sexual arousal). Like your client, your cognitive assumptions may be shattered (Janoff-Bulman, 1992). Like your client, you may become sensitized, more reactive rather than less reactive to subsequent stressors. Just as it is for your client, the therapeutic work you are doing may constitute a reminder of your past trauma.

IMPACT OF SECONDARY TRAUMATIC STRESS

The stress of clinical work—sometimes compounded by a personal history of childhood trauma—can exact a personal toll, and it can affect your clinical practice.

Impact on the therapist

Figley (1995a, 1995b) usefully distinguished between secondary traumatic *stress* and secondary traumatic stress *disorder*. Emphasizing the cost of caring, he also referred to these two phenomena as *compassion stress* and *compassion fatigue* (Figley, 1995a). Figley (1995a) defined secondary traumatic stress as 'the natural consequent behaviors and emotions resulting from knowing about a traumatizing event experienced by a significant other—the stress resulting from helping or wanting to help a traumatized or suffering person' (p. 7). The concept of compassion stress implies that empathy, albeit our most valuable resource for helping, also puts us at risk.

Compassion stress is an inevitable concomitant of the cost of caring, but it may evolve into compassion fatigue (secondary traumatic stress disorder). Compassion fatigue is the therapist's symptomatic counterpart to the client's PTSD, resulting from prolonged exposure and manifested in exhaustion and dysfunction (Figley, 1995b). Figley (1995a) distinguished compassion stress from *burnout*, the latter referring to a more gradual process of exhaustion associated with chronic emotional strain. Pearlman and Saakvitne (1995a) noted that burnout may be the therapist's counterpart to clients' numbing and avoidance. Consistent with Figley's thinking, most studies demonstrate a dose–response relationship. More extensive trauma work is associated with more therapist distress (Pearlman & MacIan, 1995), although not all findings are consistent on this point (Follette et al., 1994).

Pearlman and colleagues (McCann & Pearlman, 1990; Pearlman & MacIan, 1995; Pearlman & Saakvitne, 1995a) went beyond the symptomatic perspective to examine the *existential impact* of working with traumatized persons. They defined vicarious traumatization as 'the transformation in the inner experience of the therapist that comes about as a result of empathic engagement with clients' trauma material' (Pearlman & Saakvitne, 1995a, p. 31). Vicarious traumatization is an adverse transformation in the sense that it disrupts the therapist's cognitive schemas relating to safety, trust, self-esteem, intimacy, and sense of control. The concept of transformation is crucial here. Vicarious traumatization is not a matter of becoming acutely symptomatic; rather the therapist's worldview is fundamentally altered. Hence vicarious trauma reflects a process of gradual adaptation to cumulative clinical experience with a range of trauma survivors.

To what extent is the impact of trauma work mediated by the therapist's personal trauma history? Research findings are highly variable. Therapists working with sex offenders reported minimal adverse effects of a trauma history (Hilton et al., 1995). Follette and colleagues (Follette et al., 1994) found that law enforcement professionals reported more post-traumatic symptoms and general distress than mental health professionals, perhaps because the latter were more likely to avail themselves of personal therapy. Moreover, among mental health professionals, personal trauma history was *not* associated with extent of trauma symptoms or with negative responses to clinical work (e.g., dissociating during therapy). Trauma history aside, however, negative coping inside and outside of therapy as well as general level of personal stress were positively associated with post-traumatic symptoms. As described earlier, Elliott and Guy (1993) found a higher prevalence of childhood trauma among women mental health professionals than they did among women from other professions. Yet these authors found a *lower* level of symptoms (anxiety, depression, dissociation, sleep disturbance), as well as *less impaired* interpersonal functioning (interpersonal discomfort, interpersonal hypersensitivity, and maladaptive interpersonal patterns) among mental health professionals.

On the other hand, in their study of trauma therapists of various professional disciplines, Pearlman and MacIan (1995) found that those who reported a history of any trauma showed *higher* levels of vicarious traumatization, as well as post-traumatic symptoms and general symptomatology. Furthermore, in their study of a multidisciplinary group of therapists, all of whom reported a history of childhood sexual abuse, Little and Hamby (1999) found that women reported greater adverse impact of the childhood trauma than men (i.e., on body image, eating habits, self-esteem, trust, relationships, work, and coping with stress).

Pearlman and MacIan (1995) found that, among therapists with a trauma history, those new to trauma work showed the highest level of vicarious traumatization. At greatest risk were therapists with little experience and no supervision who worked in hospital settings (i.e., with the most acutely distressed survivors). On the other hand, for those therapists without a trauma history, doing trauma work for a longer period of time was associated with somewhat more symptoms of vicarious traumatization, perhaps reflecting an insidious process of disillusionment.

Impact on practice

A history of childhood trauma might have positive and negative effects on clinical practice. Hilton and colleagues (Hilton et al., 1995) reported that the majority of clinicians felt that their abuse history had a positive influence on their ability and motivation to work with sex offenders. Conversely, these professionals believed that their work had a positive impact on how they felt about their history. Pearlman and Saakvitne (1995a) observed that 'Incest survivors can be outstanding therapists for incest survivor clients. Their own experiences and personal healing can make them deeply empathic and strong advocates for their clients' (p. 188). Yet they introduced an important caveat:

> empathy without technique and good intentions without training are especially dangerous to clients with seriously disturbed family histories. There are many survivors of child sexual abuse across the many disciplines of psychotherapists and mental health workers. These therapists need treatment, training, and supervision in order to be sensitive and responsive to the complicated issues of technique and countertransference in their clinical work. (pp. 188–189)

Does the therapist's abuse history have a demonstrable impact on practice? Follette and colleagues (Follette et al., 1994) did not find that a history of abuse was associated with either the pattern of clinical activity (e.g., specializing in abuse) or negative responses to survivors of sexual abuse. Similarly, Little and Hamby (1999) did not find a history of sexual abuse to be associated with screening practices, diagnostic formulations, or estimations of extent of harm stemming from sexual abuse. Polusny and Follette (1996) did not find therapists' abuse history to be associated with reported use of memory retrieval techniques. Yet therapists with an abuse history more strongly believed in the importance of remembering trauma for decreasing clients' distress, and they were more likely to suggest that survivors read books about sexual abuse. Researchers also found that persons who investigate childhood abuse allegations and who have a history of childhood sexual abuse are more likely to believe the allegations (Nuttall & Jackson, 1994).

Pearlman and MacIan (1995) found evidence for greater vicarious traumatization in clinicians with a history of sexual abuse, and Pearlman and Saakvitne (1995a) described how vicarious traumatization and countertransference may exacerbate each other. Little and Hamby (1996) specifically examined the impact of a history of sexual abuse on countertransference responses to survivors of sexual abuse. Therapist survivors differed from those without a trauma history only on three of seventeen items (crying with clients, sharing their own experience of sexual abuse, and boundary mistakes). Gender differences were more striking than trauma history in influencing practice. For example, women reported screening more frequently for sexual abuse as well as viewing sexual abuse as having more long-term harmful effects. Women also reported more intense feelings (protectiveness, tearfulness, anger, hopelessness, and disgust) as well as making more boundary mistakes. Men were more likely to report sexual arousal and blaming of clients. These findings are merely one facet of the profound role that gender may play in the treatment of sexual abuse (Pearlman & Saakvitne, 1995a).

PREVENTION AND INTERVENTION

With increasing recognition of potential adverse effects of trauma work comes a substantial literature on coping and preventive strategies for therapists (Cerney, 1995; Munroe et al., 1995; Pearlman & Saakvitne, 1995a; Saakvitne et al., 2000; Saakvitne & Pearlman, 1996; Yassen, 1995). Therapists with a history of abuse employ a range of coping strategies. For example, Follette and colleagues (Follette et al., 1994) found that therapists with a trauma history reported significantly more positive coping to deal with sexual abuse cases than did their non-abused counterparts. Little and Hamby (1996) found that therapist survivors of sexual abuse were more likely than those without a sexual abuse history to be involved in community prevention, to pursue more education and supervision, to discuss cases with colleagues, and to engage in personal therapy. Little and Hamby (1999) found that, although therapists with a history of childhood sexual abuse reported a wide array of coping and healing strategies to be beneficial, *the single most helpful recovery experience was personal therapy.*

The framework presented in the last three chapters applies to therapists as well as it does to clients. Just as our clients do, we need containment in the form of a treatment frame, social support, and self-regulation strategies. Just as we need to educate our clients, we need to educate ourselves. Just as our clients do, we need to come to terms with our experience by talking about it. We must follow all our own prescriptions.

Treatment frame

Maintaining a treatment frame protects the therapist as well as the client. Boundary violations, for example, are not only damaging to clients but also to therapists. Gross boundary violations such sexual relationships spell disaster for both therapist and client. But therapists also must be aware of the potential cost of less glaring failures to maintain boundaries and set appropriate limits (Pearlman & Saakvitne, 1995a).

Intensive and prolonged contact with traumatized clients poses greatest risk of secondary traumatic stress and burnout. The treatment frame, which provides a consistent structure for therapeutic contact, regulates the degree of work stress. Well-meaning therapists may exceed these limits in an effort to be helpful. Paradoxically, as we become more distressed, we become less available and less helpful. The treatment frame preserves our consistency and reliability for our clients, the most important thing we have to offer them. At worst, our failure to maintain the treatment structure can lead to a level of overload—intertwined with our clients' escalating regression—that can eventuate in our being unable to continue the treatment. In our heroic efforts to help our clients, we are liable to abandon them.

Social support

In many respects, co-workers can provide the most effective social support for job-related stress (Argyle, 1992). Thus trauma therapists can benefit from being part of a treatment team (Munroe et al., 1995) and joining support or supervision groups composed of therapists engaged in similar work (Pearlman & Saakvitne, 1995a). Trauma therapists may have difficulty finding social support outside of work relationships. Not only do we face limits associated with confidentiality but also the horrific nature of the clinical material precludes our discussing it in other relationships. Just like our clients, we may burden and alienate prospective sources of social support. Yet, relying on colleagues for social support is a double-edged sword. Exclusive reliance on colleagues can lead to an imbalance, short-changing non-work-related relationships (Pearlman & Saakvitne, 1995b). Just as our clients need a broad network of supportive relationships to maintain their physical and mental health, so do we.

Self-regulation

To care for our clients (or anyone else), we must care for ourselves. In the domain of work, we must balance trauma-related practice with other professional activities so as to regulate the extent of vicarious trauma exposure. Moreover, work must be balanced with rest and play. As Pearlman and Saakvitne (1995a) aver, 'Probably the most important recommendation we make to our colleagues about their personal lives is to have one' (p. 393). Saakvitne and colleagues (Saakvitne et al., 2000; Saakvitne & Pearlman, 1996) have provided extensive guidance for therapists in the realm of self-care. They constructed instruments that therapists can use to assess their level of vicarious traumatization and to evaluate their range of self-care activities. They also devised a set of exercises to promote self-awareness and self-care as it relates to working with traumatized clients. Self-regulation is an ancient art, and the stresses of our contemporary work require that we practice it.

Education

Like social support and self-care, knowledge and understanding serve a containing function. Intellectual understanding can promote optimal detachment, which is one crucial element in mitigating compassion stress and fatigue (Figley, 1995b). In this vein, Miller (1998) noted that 'Theoretical understanding through continued training or scholarly review of the relevant professional literature may be valuable to trauma therapists by providing healthy emotional insulation through intellectual structure and distance' (p. 139). For example, my colleagues and I find it easier to absorb clients' accounts of trauma having the conceptual framework outlined in Chapter 2 to bring coherence to this experience. A number of studies have pointed to the value of education as a valuable coping strategy for trauma therapists (Follette et al., 1994; Little & Hamby, 1999; Little & Hamby, 1996). Pearlman and Saakvitne (1995a) commented how education and supervision is especially important for those therapists who are new to the work; yet lack of adequate supervision is unfortunately common.

Education not only provides some measure of intellectual detachment but also contributes to therapeutic effectiveness. Figley (1995b) pointed out that, along with optimal detachment, a sense of efficacy in relieving suffering is a crucial antidote to compassion fatigue. But education goes beyond knowledge of therapeutic processes. A thorough understanding of the developmental impact of trauma also plays a central role in formulating realistic therapeutic expectations and goals. The countertransference literature offers help to therapists working with clients who are difficult to *treat*. But I think our clinical literature gives insufficient attention to the stress we encounter in working with clients who are difficult to *help*. Slow progress toward goals can be depressing (Carver & Scheier, 1998). Much of this book has documented the difficulty inherent in working on trauma-related problems. Like our clients, we must accommodate ourselves to modest goals and slow progress. We also must remain mindful of clients' vulnerability to relapse, despite our best efforts. Our sense of efficacy—and hope—depends on informed expectations and realistic goals, as well as a capacity to tolerate failure. In the latter regard, trauma therapists may fall back on the wise counsel of the Dalai Lama:

> If you are motivated by a wish to help on the basis of kindness, compassion, and respect, then you can carry on any kind of work, in any field, and function more effectively with less fear or worry, not being afraid of what others think or whether you ultimately will be successful in reaching your goal. Even if you fail to achieve your goal, you can feel good about having made the effort. (Dalai Lama & Cutler, 1998, p. 272)

Trauma narratives

Like our clients, we should follow the ancient prescription: talk about it. We too must create ever-changing trauma narratives in relation to our work. Research findings suggest that, like others, therapists who have a history of childhood trauma use and benefit from psychotherapy (Cerney, 1995; Little & Hamby, 1999; Pearlman & Saakvitne, 1995a). Yet it is not just our past history that bears processing but also our ongoing vicarious exposure to trauma. The simple prescription, 'Talk about it,' applies to coping with vicarious trauma exposure as well as direct trauma exposure. Constraints of confidentiality limit the extent to which we therapists are able to 'talk about it.' Psychotherapy is one context in which we can talk about the impact of the work as well as our own history. Supervision and consultation also afford an opportunity to process the impact of the work (Pearlman & Saakvitne, 1995a).

Like our clients, we need more than desensitization. We must transform the experience of hearing about trauma so as to find meaning in it. Herman (1992b) pointed to the value of a survivor mission for traumatized clients, and many trauma therapists find purpose in social activism (Miller, 1998). As Pearlman and Saakvitne (1995a) put it, 'The work of the trauma therapist is the work of a revolutionary' (p. 405). While giving full attention to the psychological and physiological havoc wreaked by trauma, we must remain mindful of its potentially positive effects (Tedeschi, 1999). As Pearlman and Saakvitne (1995a) documented, treating traumatized persons not only leads to vicarious trauma but also may have a positive impact on the therapist:

> One significant reward of doing trauma therapy has been our increased sense of connection with people who suffer everywhere, across time and across cultures. People who are able to complete graduate training and become therapists in this country are relatively privileged. We give back something meaningful from this place of privilege when we choose to enter the world of pain and to acknowledge our deep human connection with those who suffer. While it is a dark path, it is a spiritual journey, into the darkest recesses of people's private experience, and one which deepens our humanity in increasing our awareness of all aspects of life. In this way, it is indeed a gift, a reward of doing this work. (pp. 405–406)

To maintain the hope we need to sustain ourselves and our clients, we must cultivate such positive effects. While facing the tragedy of trauma, we can learn from it. And we can pass on what we have learned to our clients, to each other, and to those in the public sector who are in a position to help prevent and ameliorate trauma.

REFERENCES

Abbott, J., Johnson, R., Koziol-McLain, J., & Lowenstein, S. R. (1995). Domestic violence against women: Incidence and prevalence in an emergency department population. *Journal of the American Medical Association, 273,* 1763–1767.

Acierno, R., Resnick, H., Kilpatrick, D. G., Saunders, B., & Best, C. L. (1999). Risk factors for rape, physical assault, and posttraumatic stress disorder in women: Examination of differential multivariate relationships. *Journal of Anxiety Disorders, 13,* 541–563.

Adam, K. S., Sheldon Keller, A. E., & West, M. (1995). Attachment organization and vulnerability to loss, separation, and abuse in disturbed adolescents. In S. Goldberg, R. Muir, & J. Kerr (Eds.), *Attachment theory: Social, developmental, and clinical perspectives* (pp. 309–341). Hillsdale, NJ: Analytic Press.

Ainsworth, M. D. S. (1989). Attachments beyond infancy. *American Psychologist, 44,* 709–716.

Ainsworth, M. D. S., Blehar, M. C., Waters, E., & Wall, S. (1978). *Patterns of attachment: A psychological study of the strange situation.* Hillsdale, NJ: Erlbaum.

Akiskal, H. S. (1997). Overview of chronic depressions and their clinical management. In H. S. Akiskal & G. B. Cassano (Eds.), *Dysthymia and the spectrum of chronic depressions* (pp. 1–34). New York: Guilford.

Akiskal, H. S., & Cassano, G. B. (Eds.). (1997). *Dysthymia and the spectrum of chronic depressions.* New York: Guilford.

Alarcon, R. D., Glover, S. G., & Deering, C. G. (1999). The cascade model: An alternative to comorbidity in the pathogenesis of posttraumatic stress disorder. *Psychiatry, 62,* 114–124.

Albarracin, D., Repetto, M. J., & Albarracin, M. (1997). Social support in child abuse and neglect: Support functions, sources, and contexts. *Child Abuse and Neglect, 21,* 607–615.

Alexander, P. C. (1993). The differential effects of abuse characteristics and attachment in the prediction of long-term sexual abuse. *Journal of Interpersonal Violence, 8,* 346–362.

Alexander, P. C., Anderson, C. L., Brand, B., Schaffer, C. M., Grelling, B. Z., & Kretz, L. (1998). Adult attachment and longterm effects in survivors of incest. *Child Abuse and Neglect, 22,* 45–61.

Alexander, P. C., Neimeyer, R. A., Follette, V. M., Moore, M. K., & Harter, S. (1989). A comparison of group treatments of women sexually abused as children. *Journal of Consulting and Clinical Psychology, 57*, 479–483.

Allen, J. G. (1977). Ego states and object relations. *Bulletin of the Menninger Clinic, 41*, 522–538.

Allen, J. G. (1980). Adaptive functions of affect and their implications for therapy. *Psychoanalytic Review, 67*, 217–230.

Allen, J. G. (1995a). *Coping with trauma: A guide to self-understanding.* Washington, DC: American Psychiatric Press, Inc.

Allen, J. G. (1995b). The spectrum of accuracy in memories of childhood trauma. *Harvard Review of Psychiatry, 3*, 84–95.

Allen, J. G. (1996). Loosening traumatic bonds. *Renfrew Perspective, 2*(2), 7–8, 13.

Allen, J. G. (1997). *Sexual harassment from the trauma perspective.* Topeka, KS: Menninger Clinic/Office of Army Chief of Chaplains.

Allen, J. G. (1998). The return of the dissociated. *Contemporary Psychology, 43*, 74–75.

Allen, J. G. (1999). *The Catch 22s of depression.* Topeka, KS: Menninger Video Productions.

Allen, J. G. (2000). *Understanding trauma and its treatment.* Topeka, KS: Menninger Video Productions.

Allen, J. G., Console, D. A., Brethour, J. R., Jr., Huntoon, J., Fultz, J., & Stein, A. B. (2001). Screening for trauma-related sleep disturbance in women admitted for specialized inpatient treatment. *Journal of Trauma and Dissociation, 1*, 59–86.

Allen, J. G., Console, D. A., & Lewis, L. (1999). Dissociative detachment and memory impairment: Reversible amnesia or encoding failure? *Comprehensive Psychiatry, 40*, 160–171.

Allen, J. G., & Coyne, L. (1995). Dissociation and vulnerability to psychotic experience: The Dissociative Experiences Scale and the MMPI-2. *Journal of Nervous and Mental Disease, 183*, 615–622.

Allen, J. G., Coyne, L., & Console, D. A. (1996). Dissociation contributes to anxiety and psychoticism on the Brief Symptom Inventory. *Journal of Nervous and Mental Disease, 184*, 639–641.

Allen, J. G., Coyne, L., & Console, D. A. (1997). Dissociative detachment relates to psychotic symptoms and personality decompensation. *Comprehensive Psychiatry, 38*, 327–334.

Allen, J. G., Coyne, L., & Console, D. A. (2000). Course of illness following specialized inpatient treatment for women with trauma-related psychopathology. *Bulletin of the Menninger Clinic, 64*, 235–256.

Allen, J. G., Coyne, L., & Huntoon, J. (1998a). Complex posttraumatic stress disorder in women from a psychometric perspective. *Journal of Personality Assessment, 70*, 277–298.

Allen, J. G., Coyne, L., & Huntoon, J. (1998b). Trauma pervasively elevates Brief Symptom Inventory profiles in inpatient women. *Psychological Reports, 83*, 499–513.

Allen, J. G., Gabbard, G. O., Newsom, G. E., & Coyne, L. (1990). Detecting patterns of change in patients' collaboration within individual psychotherapy sessions. *Psychotherapy, 27*, 522–530.

Allen, J. G., Huntoon, J., & Evans, R. B. (1999a). Complexities in complex posttraumatic stress disorder in inpatient women: Evidence from cluster analysis of MCMI-III personality disorder scales. *Journal of Personality Assessment, 73*, 449–471.

Allen, J. G., Huntoon, J., & Evans, R. B. (1999b). A self-report measure to screen for trauma history and its application to women in inpatient treatment for trauma-related disorders. *Bulletin of the Menninger Clinic, 63*, 429–442.

Allen, J. G., Huntoon, J., Fultz, J., Stein, H., Fonagy, P., & Evans, R. B. (in press). A model for brief assessment of attachment and its application to women in inpatient treatment for trauma-related psychiatric disorders. *Journal of Personality Assessment.*

Allen, J. G., Keller, M. W., & Console, D. A. (1999). *EMDR: A closer look (videotape program manual).* New York: Guilford.

Allen, J. G., Kelly, K. A., & Glodich, A. (1997). A psychoeducational program for patients with trauma-related disorders. *Bulletin of the Menninger Clinic, 61,* 222–239.

Allen, J. G., & Lewis, L. (1996). A conceptual framework for treating traumatic memories and its application to EMDR. *Bulletin of the Menninger Clinic, 60,* 238–263.

Allen, J. G., Newsom, G. E., Gabbard, G. O., & Coyne, L. (1984). Scales to assess the therapeutic alliance from a psychoanalytic perspective. *Bulletin of the Menninger Clinic, 48,* 383–400.

Allen, J. G., & Smith, W. H. (1993). Diagnosing dissociative disorders. *Bulletin of the Menninger Clinic, 57,* 328–343.

Allen, J. P., & Land, D. (1999). Attachment in adolescence. In J. Cassidy & P. R. Shaver (Eds.), *Handbook of attachment: Theory, research, and clinical applications* (pp. 319–335). New York: Guilford.

Allen-Meares, P., Washington, R., & Welsch, B. (1990). *Social work services in schools.* Boston: Allyn & Bacon.

Alpert, J. L., Brown, L. S., Ceci, S. J., Courtois, C. A., Loftus, E. F., & Ornstein, P. A. (1996). *Working group on investigation of memories of childhood abuse: Final report.* Washington, DC: American Psychological Association.

Amayala-Jackson, L., & March, J. S. (1993). Post-traumatic stress disorder in children and adolescents. *Child and Adolescent Psychiatric Clinics of North America, 2,* 639–654.

Amick-McMullan, A., Kilpatrick, D. G., & Resnick, H. S. (1991). Homicide as a risk factor for PTSD among surviving family members. *Behavior Modification, 15,* 545–559.

Anderson, C. L., & Alexander, P. C. (1996). The relationship between attachment and dissociation in adult survivors of incest. *Psychiatry, 59,* 240–254.

Anderson, C. M. (1995). Psychoeducation. In M. H. Sacks, W. H. Sledge, & C. Warren (Eds.), *Core readings in psychiatry: An annotated guide to the literature* (pp. 503–511). Washington, DC: American Psychiatric Press.

Anderson, C. M., Hogarty, G. E., & Reiss, D. J. (1980). Family treatment of adult schizophrenic patients: A psycho-educational approach. *Schizophrenia Bulletin, 6,* 490–505.

Anderson, C. M., & Reiss, D. J. (1982). Approaches to psychoeducational family therapy. *International Journal of Family Psychiatry, 3,* 501–517.

Andrade, J., Kavanagh, D., & Baddeley, A. (1997). Eye movements and visual imagery: A working memory approach to the treatment of post-traumatic stress disorder. *British Journal of Clinical Psychology, 36,* 209–223.

Andreski, P., Chilcoat, H., & Breslau, N. (1998). Post-traumatic stress disorder and somatization symptoms: A prospective study. *Psychiatry Research, 79,* 131–138.

Andrews, B., Brewin, C. R., Rose, S., & Kirk, M. (2000). Predicting PTSD symptoms in victims of violent crime: The role of shame, anger, and childhood abuse. *Journal of Abnormal Psychology, 109,* 69–73.

Angst, J. (1997). Minor and recurrent brief depression. In H. S. Akiskal & G. B. Cassano (Eds.), *Dysthymia and the spectrum of chronic depressions* (pp. 183–190). New York: Guilford.

Ansfield, M. E., & Wegner, D. M. (1996). The feeling of doing. In P. M. Gollwitzer & J. A. Bargh (Eds.), *The psychology of action: Linking cognition and motivation to behavior* (pp. 482–506). New York: Guilford.

Antleman, S. M., & Yehuda, R. (1994). Time-dependent change following acute stress: Relevance to the chronic and delayed aspects of PTSD. In M. M. Murburg (Ed.), *Catecholamine function in posttraumatic stress disorder* (pp. 87–98). Washington, DC: American Psychiatric Press.

Antoni, M. H., Millon, C. M., & Millon, T. (1997). The role of psychological assessment in health care: The MBHI, MBMC, and beyond. In T. Millon (Ed.), *The Millon inventories: Clinical and personality assessment* (pp. 409–448). New York: Guilford.

APA (1980). *Diagnostic and statistical manual of mental disorders, 3rd edition.* Washington, DC: American Psychiatric Press.

APA (1994). *Diagnostic and statistical manual of mental disorders, 4th edition.* Washington, DC: American Psychiatric Press.

Ards, S., & Harrell, A. (1993). Reporting of child maltreatment: A secondary analysis of the national incidence surveys. *Child Abuse and Neglect, 17,* 337–344.

Argyle, M. (1992). Benefits produced by supportive relationships. In H. O. F. Veiel & U. Baumann (Eds.), *The meaning and measurement of social support* (pp. 13–32). New York: Hemisphere.

Armony, J. L., & LeDoux, J. E. (1997). How the brain processes emotional information. In R. Yehuda & A. C. MacFarlane (Eds.), *Psychobiology of posttraumatic stress disorder* (Vol. 821, pp. 259–270). New York: New York Academy of Sciences.

Armstrong, D. (1997). What is consciousness? In N. Block, O. Flanagan, & G. Guzeldere (Eds.), *The nature of consciousness: Philosophical debates* (pp. 721–728). Cambridge, MA: MIT Press.

Arroyo, W., & Eth, S. (1996). Post-traumatic stress disorder and other stress reactions. In R. Apfel & B. Simon (Eds.), *Minefields in their hearts* (pp. 52–74). New Haven: Yale University Press.

Asch, S. S. (1988). The analytic concepts of masochism: A reevaluation. In R. A. Glick & D. I. Meyers (Eds.), *Masochism: Current psychoanalytic perspectives* (pp. 93–115). Hillsdale, NJ: Analytic Press.

Astin, J. A. (1997). Stress reduction through mindfulness meditation: Effects on psychological symptomatology, sense of control, and spiritual experiences. *Psychotherapy and Psychosomatics, 66,* 97–106.

Aston-Jones, G., Valentino, R. J., Van Bockstaele, E. J., & Meyerson, A. T. (1994). Locus coeruleus, stress, and PTSD: Neurobiological and clinical parallels. In M. M. Murburg (Ed.), *Catecholamine function in posttraumatic stress disorder: Emerging concepts* (pp. 17–62). Washington, DC: American Psychiatric Press.

Austin, J. H. (1998). *Zen and the brain.* Cambridge, MA: MIT Press.

Baars, B. J. (1988). *A cognitive theory of consciousness.* New York: Cambridge University Press.

Bachman, R., & Pillemer, K. A. (1992). Epidemiology and family violence involving adults. In R. T. Ammerman & M. Hersen (Eds.), *Assessment of Family Violence: A clinical and legal sourcebook* (pp. 108–120). New York: Wiley.

Bahrick, L. E., & Watson, J. S. (1985). Detection of intermodal proprioceptive–visual contingency as a potential basis of self-perception in infancy. *Developmental Psychology, 21,* 963–973.

Barach, P. M. (1993). Draft of 'recommendations for treating dissociative identity disorder'. *International Society for the Study of Multiple Personality and Dissociation, 11*(5), 14–19.

Barach, P. M. M. (1991). Multiple personality disorder as an attachment disorder. *Dissociation, 6,* 117–123.

Barclay, C. R. (1986). Schematization of autobiographical memory. In D. C. Rubin (Ed.), *Autobiographical memory* (pp. 82–99). New York: Cambridge University Press.

Barclay, C. R., & Wellman, H. M. (1986). Accuracies and inaccuracies in auto-biographical memories. *Journal of Memory and Language, 25*, 93–103.

Bargh, J. A., & Chartrand, T. L. (1999). The unbearable automaticity of being. *American Psychologist, 54*, 462–479.

Bargh, J. A., Raymond, P., Pryor, J. B., & Strack, F. (1995). Attractiveness of the underling: An automatic power–sex association and its consequences for sexual harassment and aggression. *Journal of Personality and Social Psychology, 68*, 768–781.

Barnett, D., Manly, J. T., & Cicchetti, D. (1991). Continuing toward an operational definition of psychological maltreatment. *Development and Psychopathology, 3*, 19–29.

Barnett, D., Manly, J. T., & Cicchetti, D. (1993). Defining child maltreatment: The interface between policy and research. In D. Cicchetti & S. L. Toth (Eds.), *Child abuse, child development, and social policy: Advances in applied developmental psychology* (Vol. 8, pp. 7–73). Norwood, NJ: Ablex Publishing Corporation.

Bartholomew, K., & Horowitz, L. M. (1991). Attachment styles among young adults: A test of a four-category model. *Journal of Personality and Social Psychology, 61*, 226–244.

Bartlett, F. C. (1932). *Remembering: A study in experimental and social psychology.* New York: Cambridge University Press.

Bateman, A., & Fonagy, P. (1999). Effectiveness of partial hospitalization in the treatment of borderline personality disorder: A randomized controlled trial. *American Journal of Psychiatry, 156*, 1563–1569.

Bateman, A., & Fonagy, P. (in press). Follow-up of psychoanalytically oriented partial hospitalization treatment of borderline personality disorder. *American Journal of Psychiatry.*

Baumeister, R. F. (1990). Suicide as escape from self. *Psychological Review, 97*, 90–113.

Baumeister, R. F., Bratslavsky, E., Muraven, M., & Tice, D. M. (1998). Ego depletion: Is the active self a limited resource? *Journal of Personality and Social Psychology, 74*, 1252–1265.

Bears, J. O. (1994). Why dissociative disordered patients are fundamentally responsible: A master class commentary. *International Journal of Clinical and Experimental Hypnosis, 42*, 93–96.

Beck, A. T. (1991). Cognitive therapy: A 30-year retrospective. *American Psychologist, 46*, 368–375.

Beckham, J. C., Moore, S. D., Feldman, M. E., Hertzberg, M. A., Kirby, A. C., & Fairbank, J. A. (1998). Health status, somatization, and severity of posttraumatic stress disorder in Vietnam combat veterans with posttraumatic stress disorder. *American Journal of Psychiatry, 155*, 1565–1569.

Bedi, R. P. (1999). Depression: An inability to adapt to one's perceived life distress? *Journal of Affective Disorders, 54*, 225–234.

Beer, M. D. (1996). Psychosis: A history of the concept. *Comprehensive Psychiatry, 37*, 273–291.

Belsky, J. (1999a). Interactional and contextual determinants of attachment security. In J. Cassidy & P. R. Shaver (Eds.), *Handbook of attachment: Theory, research, and clinical applications* (pp. 249–264). New York: Guilford.

Belsky, J. (1999b). Modern evolutionary theory and patterns of attachment. In J. Cassidy & P. R. Shaver (Eds.), *Handbook of attachment: Theory, research, and clinical applications* (pp. 141–161). New York: Guilford.

Belsky, J., Rosenberger, K., & Crnic, K. (1995). The origins of attachment security: 'Classical' and contextual determinants. In S. Goldberg, R. Muir, & J. Kerr (Eds.), *Attachment theory: Social, developmental, and clinical perspectives* (pp. 153–183). Hillsdale, NJ: Analytic Press.

Benham, E. (1995). Coping strategies: A psychoeducational approach to posttraumatic symptomatology. *Journal of Psychosocial Nursing, 33,* 30–35.

Benoit, D., & Parker, K. C. H. (1994). Stability and transmission of attachment across generations. *Child Development, 65,* 1444–1456.

Benson, H. (1975). *The relaxation response.* New York: William Morrow.

Bercez, J. M. (1992). *Understanding Tourette syndrome, obsessive-compulsive disorder, and related problems: A development and catastrophe theory perspective.* New York: Springer.

Berman, S. M., & Noble, E. P. (1997). The D2 dopamine receptor (DRD2) gene and family stress: Interactive effects on cognitive functions in children. *Behavior Genetics, 27,* 33–43.

Berne, E. (1961). *Transactional analysis in psychotherapy.* New York: Grove Press.

Bernstein, E. M., & Putnam, F. W. (1986). Development, reliability, and validity of a dissociation scale. *Journal of Nervous and Mental Disease, 174,* 727–735.

Bifulco, A., Brown, G. W., & Adler, Z. (1991). Early sexual abuse and clinical depression in adult life. *British Journal of Psychiatry, 159,* 115–122.

Bifulco, A., Brown, G. W., & Harris, T. O. (1994). Childhood Experience of Care and Abuse (CECA): A retrospective interview measure. *Journal of Child Psychology and Psychiatry, 35,* 1419–1435.

Bifulco, A., Brown, G. W., Lillie, A., & Jarvis, J. (1997). Memories of childhood neglect and abuse: Corroboration in a series of sisters. *Journal of Child Psychology and Psychiatry, 38,* 365–374.

Bifulco, A., Brown, G. W., Moran, P., Ball, C., & Campbell, C. (1998). Predicting depression in women: The role of past and present vulnerability. *Psychological Medicine, 28,* 39–50.

Bifulco, A., Brown, G. W., Neubauer, A., Moran, P. M., & Harris, T. O. (1994). *Childhood Experience of Care and Abuse (CECA) training manual.* London: Royal Holloway, University of London.

Bifulco, A., Harris, T., & Brown, G. W. (1992). Mourning or early inadequate care? Reexamining the relationship of maternal loss in childhood with adult depression and anxiety. *Development and Psychopathology, 4,* 433–439.

Bifulco, A., & Moran, P. (1998). *Wednesday's Child: Research into women's experience of neglect and abuse in childhood, and adult depression.* London: Routledge.

Bifulco, A., Moran, P. M., Stanford, K., Baines, R., & Bunn, A. (2000). Psychological abuse in childhood II: Association with adult major depression. *Submitted for publication.*

Billard, M., Partinen, M., Roth, T., & Shapiro, C. (1994). Sleep and psychiatric disorders. *Journal of Psychosomatic Research, 38,* 1–2.

Binder, R. L., McNiel, D. E., & Goldstone, R. L. (1994). Patterns of recall of childhood sexual abuse as described by adult survivors. *Bulletin of the American Academy of Psychiatry and the Law, 22,* 357–366.

Bisson, J. I., & Deahl, M. P. (1994). Psychological debriefing and prevention of posttraumatic stress. *British Journal of Psychiatry, 165,* 717–720.

Blake, D. D., & Sonnenberg, R. T. (1998). Outcome research on behavioral and cognitive-behavioral treatments for trauma survivors. In V. M. Follette, J. I. Ruzek, & F. R. Abueg (Eds.), *Cognitive-behavioral therapies for trauma* (pp. 15–47). New York: Guilford.

Blanchard, E. B., Buckley, T. C., Hickling, E. J., & Taylor, A. E. (1998). Posttraumatic stress disorder and comorbid major depression: Is the correlation an illusion? *Journal of Anxiety Disorders, 12,* 21–37.

Blanchard, E. B., Hickling, E. J., Mitnick, N., Taylor, A. E., Loos, W. R., & Buckley, T. C. (1995). The impact of severity of physical injury and perception of life threat in the development of post-traumatic stress disorder in motor vehicle accident victims. *Behavior Research and Therapy, 33*, 529–534.

Blanchard, E. B., Hickling, E. J., Vollmer, A. J., Loos, W. R., Buckley, T. C., & Jaccard, J. (1995). Short-term follow-up of post-traumatic stress symptoms in motor vehicle accident victims. *Behavior Research and Therapy, 33*, 369–377.

Blank, A. S., Jr. (1993). The longitudinal course of posttraumatic stress disorder. In J. R. T. Davidson & E. B. Foa (Eds.), *Posttraumatic stress disorder: DSM-IV and beyond* (pp. 3–22). Washington, DC: American Psychiatric Press.

Blatt, S. J., Auerbach, J. S., & Levy, K. N. (1997). Mental representations in personality development, psychopathology, and the therapeutic process. *Review of General Psychology, 1*, 351–374.

Blatt, S. J., & Blass, R. B. (1990). Attachment and separateness: A dialectic model of the products and processes of development throughout the life cycle. *Psychoanalytic Study of the Child, 45*, 107–127.

Blatt, S. J., & Blass, R. B. (1992). Relatedness and self-definition: Two primary dimensions in personality development, psychopathology, and psychotherapy. In J. W. Barron, M. N. Eagle, & D. L. Wolitzky (Eds.), *Interface of psychoanalysis and psychology* (pp. 399–428). Washington, DC: American Psychological Association.

Blatt, S. J., & Homann, E. (1992). Parent-child interaction in the etiology of dependent and self-critical depression. *Clinical Psychology Review, 12*, 47–91.

Blechman, E., Dumas, J., & Prinz, R. (1994). Prosocial coping by youth exposed to violence. *Journal of Child and Adolescent Group Therapy, 4*, 208–227.

Bliss, E. L. (1986). *Multiple personality, allied disorders, and hypnosis.* New York: Oxford University Press.

Blum, K., Cull, J. G., Braverman, E. R., & Comings, D. E. (1996). Reward deficiency syndrome. *American Scientist, 84*, 132–145.

Bogdan, R. J. (1997). *Interpreting minds.* Cambridge, MA: MIT Press.

Bolin, R. (1993). Natural and technological disasters: Evidence of psychopathology. In A. L. A. Ghadirian & H. E. Lehmann (Eds.), *Environment and psychopathology* (pp. 121–140). New York: Springer.

Bonanno, G. A., & Keuler, D. J. (1998). Psychotherapy without repressed memory: A parsimonious alternative based on contemporary memory research. In S. J. Lynn & K. M. McConkey (Eds.), *Truth in memory* (pp. 437–463). New York: Guilford.

Boon, S., & Draijer, N. (1993). The differentiation of patients with MPD or DDNOS from patients with a cluster B personality disorder. *Dissociation, 6*, 126–135.

Boudewyn, A. C., & Liem, J. H. (1995). Childhood sexual abuse as a precursor to depression and self-destructive behavior in adulthood. *Journal of Traumatic Stress, 8*, 445–459.

Boudewyns, P. A., & Hyer, L. A. (1996). Eye Movement Desensitization and Reprocessing (EMDR) as treatment for post-traumatic stress disorder (PTSD). *Clinical Psychology and Psychotherapy, 3*, 185–195.

Boudewyns, P. A., Hyer, L., Peralme, L., Touze, J., & Kiel, A. (1995). *Eye Movement Desensitization and Reprocessing (EMDR) and exposure therapy in the treatment of combat-related PTSD: An early look.* Paper presented at the American Psychological Association Convention, New York.

Boudreaux, E., Kilpatrick, D. G., Resnick, H. S., Best, C. L., & Saunders, B. E. (1998). Criminal victimization, posttraumatic stress disorder, and comorbid psychopathology among a community sample of women. *Journal of Traumatic Stress, 11*, 665–678.

Bowen, M. (1978). *Family therapy in clinical practice.* New York: Aronson.

Bowen, M. (1980). Key to the use of the genogram (family diagram). In E. A. Carter

& M. McGoldrick (Eds.), *The family life cycle: A framework for family therapy* (p. xxiii). New York: Gardner Press.

Bower, B. (1995). Promise and dissent: New research enters debate over a highly touted trauma therapy. *Science News, 148,* 270–271.

Bower, G. H. (1981). Mood and memory. *American Psychologist, 36,* 129–148.

Bower, G. H., & Sivers, H. (1998). Cognitive impact of traumatic events. *Development and Psychopathology, 10,* 625–653.

Bower, M. E., & Knutson, J. F. (1996). Attitudes toward physical discipline as a function of disciplinary history and self-labeling as physically abused. *Child Abuse and Neglect, 20,* 689–699.

Bowers, K. S. (1990). Unconscious influences and hypnosis. In J. L. Singer (Ed.), *Repression and dissociation: Implications for personality theory, psychopathology, and health* (pp. 143–179). Chicago: Chicago University Press.

Bowlby, J. (1973). *Attachment and loss, Volume 2: Separation.* New York: Basic Books.

Bowlby, J. (1982). *Attachment and loss, 2nd Edition, Vol 1: Attachment* (2nd edn.). New York: Basic Books.

Bowlby, J. (1988). *A secure base: Parent–child attachment and healthy human development.* New York: Basic Books.

Bowman, E. S. (1993). Etiology and clinical course of pseudoseizures: Relationship to trauma, depression, and dissociation. *Psychosomatics, 34,* 333–341.

Bowman, E. S., & Coons, P. M. (2000). The differential diagnosis of epilepsy, pseudoseizures, dissociative identity disorder, and dissociative disorder not otherwise specified. *Bulletin of the Menninger Clinic, 64,* 164–180.

Bowman, E. S., & Markland, O. N. (1999). The contribution of life events to pseudoseizure occurrence in adults. *Bulletin of the Menninger Clinic, 63,* 70–88.

Bradley, J. J. (1998). Medical negligence and post traumatic stress disorder. *Medicine and the Law, 17,* 225–228.

Brady, K., Pearlstein, T., Asnis, G. M., Baker, D., Rothbaum, B., Sikes, C. R., & Farfel, G. M. (2000). Efficacy and safety of sertraline treatment of posttraumatic stress disorder. *Journal of the American Medical Association, 283,* 1837–1844.

Brady, K. T., Dansky, B. S., Sonne, S. C., & Saladin, M. E. (1998). Posttraumatic stress disorder and cocaine dependence: Order of onset. *American Journal on Addictions, 7,* 128–135.

Braun, B. G. (1988). The BASK model of dissociation. *Dissociation, 1,* 4–23.

Braun, B. G., & Sachs, R. G. (1985). The development of multiple personality disorder: Predisposing, precipitating and perpetuating factors. In R. P. Kluft (Ed.), *Childhood antecedents of multiple personality disorder* (pp. 37–64). Washington, DC: American Psychiatric Press.

Bremner, J. D. (1999). Does stress damage the brain? *Biological Psychiatry, 45,* 797–805.

Bremner, J. D., & Brett, E. (1997). Trauma-related dissociative states and long-term psychopathology in posttraumatic stress disorder. *Journal of Traumatic Stress, 10,* 37–49.

Bremner, J. D., Narayan, M., Staib, L. H., Southwick, S. M., McGlashan, T., & Charney, D. S. (1999). Neural correlates of memories of childhood sexual abuse in women with and without posttraumatic stress disorder. *American Journal of Psychiatry, 156,* 1787–1795.

Bremner, J. D., Randall, P., Scott, T. M., Bronen, R. A., Seibyl, J. P., Southwick, S. M., Delaney, R. D., McCarthy, G., Chaney, D. S., & Innis, R. B. (1995). MRI-based measurement of hippocampal volume in patients with combat-related posttraumatic stress disorder. *American Journal of Psychiatry, 152,* 973–981.

Bremner, J. D., Randall, P., Vermetten, E., Staib, L., Bronen, R. A., Mazure, C., Capelli, S., McCarthy, G., Innis, R. B., & Charney, D. S. (1997). Magnetic resonance imaging-based measurement of hippocampal volume in posttraumatic stress disorder related to childhood physical and sexual abuse: A preliminary report. *Biological Psychiatry, 41,* 23–32.

Bremner, J. D., Scott, T. M., Delaney, R. C., Southwick, S. M., Mason, J. W., Johnson, D. R., Innis, R. B., McCarthy, G., & Charney, D. S.(1993). Deficits in short-term memory in posttraumatic stress disorder. *American Journal of Psychiatry, 150,* 1015–1019.

Bremner, J. D., Southwick, S. M., & Charney, D. S. (1995). Etiological factors in the development of posttraumatic stress disorder. In C. M. Mazure (Ed.), *Does stress cause psychiatric illness* (pp. 149–185). Washington, DC: American Psychiatric Press.

Bremner, J. D., Southwick, S. M., Darnell, A., & Charney, D. S. (1996). Chronic PTSD in Vietnam combat veterans: Course of illness and substance abuse. *American Journal of Psychiatry, 153,* 369–375.

Bremner, J. D., Staib, L. H., Kaloupek, D., Southwick, S. M., Soufer, R., & Charney, D. S. (1999). Neural correlates of exposure to traumatic pictures and sound in Vietnam combat veterans with and without posttraumatic stress disorder: A positron emission tomography study. *Biological Psychiatry, 45,* 806–811.

Bremner, J. D., Steinberg, M., Southwick, S. M., Johnson, D. R., & Charney, D. S. (1993). Use of the Structured Clinical Interview for DSM-IV Dissociative Disorders for systematic assessment of dissociative symptoms in posttraumatic stress disorder. *American Journal of Psychiatry, 150,* 1011–1014.

Brende, J. (1983). A psychodynamic view of character pathology in Vietnam combat veterans. *Bulletin of the Menninger Clinic, 47,* 193–216.

Brende, J. O., & Goldsmith, R. (1991). Post-traumatic stress disorder in families. *Journal of Contemporary Psychotherapy, 21,* 115–124.

Brennan, K. A., Clark, C. L., & Shaver, P. R. (1998). Self-report measurement of adult attachment: An integrative overview. In J. A. Simpson & W. S. Rholes (Eds.), *Attachment theory and close relationships* (pp. 46–75). New York: Guilford.

Brenner, I. (1996). The characterological basis of multiple personality. *American Journal of Psychotherapy, 50,* 154–166.

Breslau, N. (1998). Epidemiology of trauma and posttraumatic stress disorder. In R. Yehuda (Ed.), *Psychological trauma* (pp. 1–29). Washington, DC: American Psychiatric Press.

Breslau, N., Chilcoat, H. D., Kessler, R. C., & Davis, G. C. (1999). Previous exposure to trauma and PTSD effects of subsequent trauma: Results from the Detroit area survey of trauma. *American Journal of Psychiatry, 156,* 902–907.

Breslau, N., Davis, G., Andreski, P., Fe'derman, B., & Anthony, J. C. (1998). Epidemiological findings on posttraumatic stress disorder and co-morbid disorders in the general population. In B. P. Dohrenwend (Ed.), *Adversity, stress, and psychopathology* (pp. 319–330). New York: Oxford University Press.

Breslau, N., Davis, G. C., Andreski, P., & Peterson, E. (1991). Traumatic events and posttraumatic stress disorder in an urban population of young adults. *Archives of General Psychiatry, 48,* 216–222.

Bretherton, I., & Munholland, K. A. (1999). Internal working models in attachment relationships. In J. Cassidy & P. R. Shaver (Eds.), *Handbook of attachment: Theory, research, and clinical applications* (pp. 89–111). New York: Guilford.

Brett, E. A. (1993). Classifications of posttraumatic stress disorder in DSM-IV: Anxiety disorder, dissociative disorder, or stress disorder? In J. R. T. Davidson & E. B. Foa (Eds.), *Posttraumatic stress disorder: DSM-IV and beyond* (pp. 191–204). Washington, DC: American Psychiatric Press.

Breuer, J., & Freud, S. (1895/1957). *Studies on hysteria.* New York: Basic Books.

Brewer, W. F. (1986). What is autobiographical memory? In D. C. Rubin (Ed.), *Auto-biographical memory* (pp. 25–49). New York: Cambridge University Press.

Brewin, C. R., & Andrews, B. (1998). Recovered memories of trauma: Phenomenology and cognitive mechanisms. *Clinical Psychology Review, 18*, 949–970.

Brewin, C. R., Andrews, B., & Gotlib, I. H. (1993). Psychopathology and early experience: A reappraisal of retrospective reports. *Psychological Bulletin, 113*, 82–98.

Brewin, C. R., Andrews, B., Rose, S., & Kirk, M. (1999). Acute stress disorder and posttraumatic stress disorder in victims of violent crime. *American Journal of Psychiatry, 156*, 360–366.

Brewin, C. R., Dalgleish, T., & Joseph, S. (1996). A dual representation theory of posttraumatic stress disorder. *Psychological Review, 103*, 670–686.

Briere, J., & Conte, J. (1993). Self-reported amnesia for abuse in adults molested as children. *Journal of Traumatic Stress, 6*, 21–31.

Briere, J., & Elliott, D. M. (1993). Sexual abuse, family environment, and psychological symptoms: On the validity of statistical control. *Journal of Consulting and Clinical Psychology, 61*, 284–288.

Briere, J., & Runtz, M. (1990). Differential adult symptomatology associated with three types of child abuse histories. *Child Abuse and Neglect, 14*, 357–364.

Brodsky, B. S., Dulit, R., & Cloitre, M. (1995). Relationship of dissociation to self-mutilation and childhood abuse in borderline personality disorder. *American Journal of Psychiatry, 152*, 1788–1792.

Brom, D., Kleber, R. J., & Defares, P. B. (1989). Brief psychotherapy for posttraumatic stress disorders. *Journal of Consulting and Clinical Psychology, 57*, 607–612.

Bronisch, T., & Mombour, W. (1998). The modern assessment of personality disorders. Part 2: Reliability and validity of personality disorders. *Psychopathology, 31*, 293–301.

Brown, D., Scheflin, A. W., & Hammond, D. C. (1998). *Memory, trauma treatment, and the law*. New York: W. W. Norton & Co.

Brown, D. P., & Fromm, E. (1986). *Hypnotherapy and hypnoanalysis*. Hillsdale, NJ: Erlbaum.

Brown, G. R., & Anderson, B. (1991). Psychiatric morbidity in adult inpatients with childhood histories of sexual and physical abuse. *American Journal of Psychiatry, 148*, 55–61.

Brown, G. W. (1992). Social support: An investigator-based approach. In H. O. F. Veiel & U. Baumann (Eds.), *The meaning and measurement of social support* (pp. 235–258). New York: Hemisphere.

Brown, G. W. (1998). Loss and depressive disorders. In B. P. Dohrenwend (Ed.), *Adversity, stress, and psychopathology* (pp. 358–370). New York: Oxford University Press.

Brown, L. (1993). *The new shorter Oxford English dictionary*. Oxford: Clarendon Press.

Brown, L. S. (1996). On the construction of truth and falsity: Whose memory, whose history. In K. Pezdek & W. P. Banks (Eds.), *The recovered memory/false memory debate* (pp. 341–352). New York: Academic Press.

Brown, P. J., Stout, R. L., & Gannon-Rowley, J. (1998). Substance use disorder-PTSD comorbidity: Patients' perceptions of symptom interplay and treatment issues. *Journal of Substance Abuse Treatment, 15*, 445–448.

Brown, R., & Kulick, J. (1977). Flashbulb memories. *Cognition, 5*, 73–99.

Brown, S.-E., & Katcher, A. H. (1997). The contribution of attachment to pets and attachment to nature to dissociation and absorption. *Dissociation, 10*, 125–129.

Browne, A. (1993). Violence against women by male partners: Prevalence, outcomes, and policy implications. *American Psychologist, 48*, 1077–1087.

Browne, A., & Finkelhor, D. (1986). Impact of child sexual abuse: A review of the research. *Psychological Bulletin, 99*, 66–77.

Bryant, R. A., & Harvey, A. G. (1996). Visual imagery in posttraumatic stress disorder. *Journal of Traumatic Stress, 9*, 613–619.

Bryer, J. B., Nelson, B. A., Miller, J. B., & Krol, P. A. (1987). Childhood sexual and physical abuse as factors in adult psychiatric illness. *American Journal of Psychiatry, 144*, 1426–1430.

Buchanan, A. (1998). Intergenerational child maltreatment. In Y. Danieli (Ed.), *International handbook of multigenerational legacies of trauma* (pp. 535–552). New York: Plenum.

Buchele, B. J. (1993). Group psychotherapy for persons with multiple personality and dissociative disorders. *Bulletin of the Menninger Clinic, 57*, 362–370.

Buchholz, E. S., & Helbraun, E. (1999). A psychobiological developmental model for an 'alonetime' need in infancy. *Bulletin of the Menninger Clinic, 63*, 143–158.

Burgess, A. W., & Holmstrom, L. L. (1974). Rape trauma syndrome. *American Journal of Psychiatry, 131*, 981–986.

Burgess, A. W., & Roberts, A. R. (1996). Family violence against women and children: Prevalence of assaults and fatalities, family dynamics, and intervention. *Crises Intervention, 3*, 65–80.

Burland, J. (1998). Family-to-Family: A trauma-and-recovery model of family education. In H. P. Lefley (Ed.), *Families coping with mental illness: The cultural context: New directions for mental health services, No. 77* (pp. 33–41). San Francisco: Jossey-Bass.

Burnstein, A. (1985). Posttraumatic flashbacks, dream disturbances, and mental imagery. *Journal of Clinical Psychiatry, 46*, 374–378.

Busen, N. (1991). Development of an adolescent risk-taking instrument. *Journal of Child and Adolescent Psychiatric and Mental Health Nursing, 4*, 143–149.

Butler, R. W., Mueser, K. T., Sprock, J., & Braff, D. L. (1996). Positive symptoms of psychosis in posttraumatic stress disorder. *Biological Psychiatry, 39*, 839–844.

Byrne, R. W., & Whiten, A. (Eds.). (1988). *Machiavellian intelligence: Social expertise and the evolution of intellect in monkeys, apes, and humans.* New York: Oxford University Press.

Cabib, S., & Puglisi-Allegra, S. (1996). Stress, depression and the mesolimbic dopamine system. *Psychopharmacology, 128*, 331–342.

Cadoret, R. J., Yates, W. R., Troughton, E., Woodworth, G., & Stewart, M. A. (1995). Genetic–environmental interaction in the genesis of aggressivity and conduct disorders. *Archives of General Psychiatry, 52*, 916–924.

Cahill, S. P., Carrigan, M. H., & Frueh, B. C. (1999). Does EMDR work? And if so, Why? A critical review of controlled outcome and dismantling research. *Journal of Anxiety Disorders, 13*, 5–33.

Caldwell, M. F. (1992). Incidence of PTSD among staff victims of patient violence. *Hospital and Community Psychiatry, 43*, 838–839.

Calhoun, K. S., & Resick, P. A. (1993). Post-traumatic stress disorder. In D. H. Barlow (Ed.), *Clinical handbook of psychological disorders: A step-by-step treatment manual* (pp. 48–98). New York: Guilford.

Cameron, C. (1996). Comparing amnesic and nonamnesic survivors of childhood sexual abuse: A longitudinal study. In K. Pezdek & W. P. Banks (Eds.), *The recovered memory/false memory debate* (pp. 41–68). New York: Academic Press.

Cameron, G. (1994). *What about me? A guide for men helping female partners deal with child sexual abuse.* Carp, Ontario: Creative Bound.

Campbell, R., Sefl, T., Barnes, H. E., Ahrens, C. E., Wasco, S. M., & Zaragoza-Diesfeld, Y. (1999). Community services for rape survivors: Enhancing psychological well-being or increasing trauma? *Journal of Consulting and Clinical Psychology,* 67, 847–858.

Cannon, W. B. (1953). *Bodily changes in pain, hunger, fear and rage: An account of recent researches into the function of emotional excitement.* Boston: Charles T. Branford.

Cardeña, E. (2000). Hypnosis in the treatment of trauma: A promising, but not fully supported, efficacious intervention. *International Journal of Clinical and Experimental Hypnosis, 48,* 225–237.

Cardeña, E., & Spiegel, D. (1993). Dissociative reactions to the San Francisco bay area earthquake of 1989. *American Journal of Psychiatry, 150,* 474–478.

Cardeña, E., & Spiegel, D. (1996). Diagnostic issues, criteria, and comorbidity of dissociative disorders. In L. K. Michelson & W. J. Ray (Eds.), *Handbook of dissociation: Theoretical, empirical, and clinical perspectives* (pp. 227–250). New York: Plenum.

Carlier, I. V. E., Lamberts, R. D., Fouwels, A. J., & Gersons, B. P. R. (1996). PTSD in relation to dissociation in traumatized police officers. *American Journal of Psychiatry, 153,* 1325–1328.

Carlson, E. A. (1998). A prospective longitudinal study of attachment disorganization/disorientation. *Child Development, 69,* 1107–1128.

Carlson, E. B. (1994). Studying the interaction between physical and psychological states with the Dissociative Experiences Scale. In D. Spiegel (Ed.), *Dissociation: Culture, mind, and body* (pp. 41–58). Washington, DC: American Psychiatric Press.

Carlson, E. B., & Armstrong, J. (1994). The diagnosis and assessment of dissociative disorders. In S. J. Lynn & J. W. Rhue (Eds.), *Dissociation* (pp. 159–174). New York: Guilford.

Carlson, E. B., Armstrong, J., Loewenstein, R., & Roth, D. (1998). Relationships between traumatic experiences and symptoms of posttraumatic stress, dissociation, and amnesia. In J. D. Bremner & C. R. Marmar (Eds.), *Trauma, memory, and dissociation* (pp. 205–227). Washington, DC: American Psychiatric Press.

Carlson, E. B., & Putnam, F. W. (1993). An update on the Dissociative Experiences Scale. *Dissociation, 6,* 16–27.

Carlson, V., Cicchetti, D., Barnett, D., & Braunwald, K. G. (1989). Finding order in disorganization: Lessons from research on maltreated infants' attachments to their caregivers. In D. Cicchetti & G. V. Carlson (Eds.), *Child maltreatment: Theory and research on the causes and consequences of child abuse and neglect* (pp. 494–528). New York: Cambridge University Press.

Cartwright, R. D. (1981). The contribution of research on memory and dreaming to a 24-hour model of cognitive behavior. In W. Fishbein (Ed.), *Sleep, dreams, and memory* (pp. 239–247). New York: Spectrum Publications.

Carver, C. S., & Scheier, M. F. (1998). *On the self-regulation of behavior.* Cambridge, UK: Cambridge University Press.

Casada, J. H., Amdur, R., Larsen, R., & Liberzon, I. (1998). Psychophysiologic responsivity in posttraumatic stress disorder: Generalized hyperresponsiveness versus trauma specificity. *Biological Psychiatry, 44,* 1037–1044.

Cassidy, J. (1999). The nature of the child's ties. In J. Cassidy & P. R. Shaver (Eds.), *Handbook of attachment: Theory, research, and clinical applications* (pp. 3–20). New York: Guilford.

Caul, D., Sachs, R. G., & Braun, B. G. (1986). Group therapy in the treatment of multiple personality disorder. In B. G. Braun (Ed.), *Treatment of multiple personality disorder* (pp. 143–156). Washington, DC: American Psychiatric Press.

Cerney, M. S. (1995). Treating the 'heroic treaters'. In C. R. Figley (Ed.), *Compassion fatigue: Coping with secondary traumatic stress disorder in those who treat the traumatized* (pp. 131–149). New York: Brunner/Mazel.

Charney, D., & Russell, R. (1994). An overview of sexual harassment. *American Journal of Psychiatry, 151,* 10–17.

Charney, D. S., Deutch, A. Y., Krystal, J. H., Southwick, S. M., & Davis, M. (1993). Psychobiologic mechanisms of posttraumatic stress disorder. *Archives of General Psychiatry, 50,* 294–305.

Charney, D. S., Deutch, A. Y., Southwick, S. M., & Krystal, J. H. (1995). Neural circuits and mechanisms of post-traumatic stress disorder. In M. J. Friedman, D. S. Charney, & A. Y. Deutch (Eds.), *Neurobiological and clinical consequences of stress: From normal adaptation to post-traumatic stress disorder* (pp. 271–287). Philadelphia: Lippincott-Raven.

Cheit, R. E. (1998). Consider this, skeptics of recovered memory. *Ethics and Behavior, 8,* 141–160.

Chekhov, A. (1998). *The cherry orchard* (S. Mulrine, Trans.). London: Nick Hern.

Chilcoat, H. D., & Breslau, N. (1998). Posttraumatic stress disorder and drug disorders: Testing causal pathways. *Archives of General Psychiatry, 55,* 913–917.

Christian, C. W., Scribano, P., Seidl, T., & Pinto-Martin, J. A. (1997). Pediatric injury resulting from family violence. *Pediatrics, 99,* 1–4.

Chrousos, G. P., & Gold, P. W. (1992). The concepts of stress and stress system disorders. *Journal of the American Medical Association, 267,* 1244–1252.

Chu, J. (1991). The repetition compulsion revisited: Reliving dissociated trauma. *Psychotherapy, 28,* 327–332.

Chu, J. A. (1992). The therapeutic roller coaster: Dilemmas in the treatment of childhood abuse survivors. *Journal of Psychotherapy: Practice and Research, 1,* 351–370.

Chu, J. A. (1998). Dissociative symptomatology in adult patients with histories of childhood physical and sexual abuse. In J. D. Bremner & C. R. Marmar (Eds.), *Trauma, memory, and dissociation* (pp. 179–203). Washington, DC: American Psychiatric Press.

Chu, J. A., Frey, L. M., Ganzel, B. L., & Mathhews, J. A. (1999). Memories of childhood abuse: Dissociation, amnesia, and corroboration. *American Journal of Psychiatry, 156,* 749–755.

Cicchetti, D., & Cohen, D. J. (1995). Perspectives on developmental psychopathology. In D. Cicchetti & D. J. Cohen (Eds.), *Developmental psychopathology. Volume 1: Theory and methods* (pp. 3–20). New York: Wiley.

Cicchetti, D., & Toth, S. L. (1995). A developmental psychopathology perspective on child abuse and neglect. *Journal of the American Academy of Child and Adolescent Psychiatry, 34,* 541–565.

Clark, L. A., Watson, D., & Mineka, S. (1994). Temperament, personality, and the mood and anxiety disorders. *Journal of Abnormal Psychology, 103,* 103–116.

Cloitre, M. (1998). Sexual revictimization: Risk factors and prevention. In V. M. Follette, J. I. Ruzek, & F. R. Abueg (Eds.), *Cognitive-behavioral therapies for trauma* (pp. 278–304). New York: Guilford.

Cloitre, M., Scarvalone, P., & Difede, J. (1997). Posttraumatic stress disorder, self- and interpersonal dysfunction among sexually retraumatized women. *Journal of Traumatic Stress, 10,* 437–452.

Cloitre, M., Tardiff, K., Marzuk, P. M., Leon, A. C., & Portera, L. (1996). Childhood abuse and subsequent sexual assault among female inpatients. *Journal of Traumatic Stress, 9,* 473–482.

Coccaro, E. F., & Kavoussi, R. J. (1997). Fluoxetine and impulsive aggressive behavior in personality-disordered subjects. *Archives of General Psychiatry, 54,* 1081–1088.

Cohen, N. J. (1996). Functional retrograde amnesia as a model of amnesia for childhood sexual abuse. In K. Pezdek & W. Banks (Eds.), *The recovered memory/false memory debate* (pp. 81–95). New York: Academic Press.

Collins, N. L. (1996). Working models of attachment: Implications for explanation, emotion, and behavior. *Journal of Personality and Social Psychology, 71,* 810–832.

Collins, N. L., & Read, S. J. (1990). Adult attachment, working models, and relationship quality in dating couples. *Journal of Personality and Social Psychology, 58,* 644–663.

Collins, N. L., & Read, S. J. (1994). Cognitive representations of attachment: The structure and function of working models. In K. Bartholomew & D. Perlman (Eds.), *Attachment processes in adulthood* (pp. 53–90). London: Jessica Kingsley.

Comijs, H. C., Pot, A. M., Smit, J. H., Bouter, L. M., & Jonker, C. (1998). Elder abuse in the community: Prevalence and consequences. *Journal of the American Geriatric Society, 46,* 885–888.

Comings, D. E. (1998). Why different rules are required for polygenic inheritance: Lessons from studies of the DRD2 gene. *Alcoholism, 16,* 61–70.

Comings, D. E., Muhleman, D., & Gysin, R. (1996). Dopamine D2 receptor (DRD2) gene and susceptibility to posttraumatic stress disorder: A study and replication. *Biological Psychiatry, 40,* 368–372.

Compton, A., & Goldberg, D. A. (1985). A reexamination of the concept 'object' in psychoanalysis. *Journal of the American Psychoanalytic Association, 33,* 167–185.

Compton, J. S., & Follette, V. M. (1998). Couples surviving trauma: Issues and interventions. In V. M. Follette, J. I. Ruzek, & F. R. Abueg (Eds.), *Cognitive-behavioral therapies for trauma* (pp. 321–352). New York: Guilford.

Connor, K. M., & Davidson, J. R. T. (1997). Familial risk factors in posttraumatic stress disorder. In R. Yehuda & A. C. McFarlane (Eds.), *Psychobiology of posttraumatic stress disorder* (Vol. 821, pp. 35–51). New York: New York Academy of Sciences.

Connors, R. (1996). Self-injury in trauma survivors: 1. Functions and meanings. *American Journal of Orthopsychiatry, 66,* 197–206.

Constans, J. I., Lenhoff, K., & McCarthy, M. (1997). Depression subtyping in PTSD patients. *Annals of Clinical Psychiatry, 9,* 235–240.

Coons, P. M. (1996). Depersonalization and derealization. In L. K. Michelson & W. J. Ray (Eds.), *Handbook of dissociation: Theoretical, empirical, and clinical perspectives* (pp. 291–305). New York: Plenum.

Coons, P. M., & Bradley, K. (1985). Group psychotherapy with multiple personality patients. *Journal of Nervous and Mental Disease, 173,* 515–521.

Cooper, A. M. (1988). The narcissistic–masochistic character. In R. A. Glick & D. I. Meyers (Eds.), *Masochism: Current psychoanalytic perspectives* (pp. 117–138). Hillsdale, NJ: Analytic Press.

Cormier, J. F., & Thelen, M. H. (1998). Professional skepticism of multiple personality disorder. *Professional Psychology: Research and Practice, 29,* 163–167.

Cottler, L. B., Compton, W. M. I., Mager, D., Spitznagel, E. L., & Janca, A. (1992). Posttraumatic stress disorders among substance users from the general population. *American Journal of Psychiatry, 149,* 664–670.

Cowan, N. (1988). Evolving conceptions of memory storage, selective attention, and their mutual constraints within the human information-processing system. *Psychological Bulletin, 104,* 163–191.

Coyne, J. C. (1990). Interpersonal processes in depression. In G. I. Keitner (Ed.), *Depression and families: Impact and treatment* (pp. 31–53). Washington, DC: American Psychiatric Press.

Coyne, J. C., Ellard, J. H., & Smith, D. A. F. (1990). Social support, interdependence, and the dilemmas of helping. In B. A. Sarason, I. G. Sarason, & G. R. Pierce (Eds.), *Social support: An interactional view* (pp. 129–149). New York: Wiley.

Craighead, W. E., Craighead, L. W., & Ilardi, S. S. (1998). Psychosocial treatments for major depressive disorder. In P. E. Nathan & J. M. Gorman (Eds.), *A guide to treatments that work* (pp. 226–239). New York: Oxford University Press.

Craske, M. G., & Rowe, M. K. (1997). Nocturnal panic. *Clinical Psychology: Science and Practice, 4*, 153–174.

Crime Victims Research and Treatment Center (1992). *Rape in America: A report to the nation*. Charleston, SC: Department of Psychiatry and Behavioral Sciences, Medical University of South Carolina.

Crittenden, P. M. (1995). Attachment and psychopathology. In S. Goldberg, R. Muir, & J. Kerr (Eds.), *Attachment theory: Social, developmental, and clinical perspectives* (pp. 367–406). Hillsdale, NJ: Analytic Press.

Crittenden, P. M., & Ainsworth, M. D. S. (1989). Child maltreatment and attachment theory. In D. Cicchetti & V. Carlson (Eds.), *Child maltreatment: Theory and research on the causes and consequences of child abuse and neglect* (pp. 432–463). Cambridge, UK: Cambridge University Press.

Crowell, J. A., Fraley, R. C., & Shaver, P. R. (1999). Measurement of individual differences in adolescent and adult attachment. In J. Cassidy & P. R. Shaver (Eds.), *Handbook of attachment: Theory, research, and clinical applications* (pp. 434–465). New York: Guilford.

Crowell, J. A., & Treboux, D. (1995). A review of adult attachment measures: Implications for theory and research. *Social Development, 4*, 294–327.

Csibra, G., & Gergely, G. (1998). The teleological origins of mentalistic action explanations: A developmental hypothesis. *Developmental Science, 1*, 255–259.

Csibra, G., Gergely, G., Biro, S., Koos, O., & Brockbank, M. (1999). Goal attribution without agency cues: The perception of 'pure reason' in infancy. *Cognition, 72*, 237–267.

Cummings, E. M., Hennessy, K. D., Rabideau, G. J., & Cicchetti, D. (1994). Response of physically abused boys to interadult anger involving their mothers. *Development and Psychopathology, 6*, 31–41.

Cusack, K., & Spates, C. R. (1999). The cognitive dismantling of Eye Movement Desensitization and Reprocessing (EMDR) treatment of posttraumatic stress disorder (PTSD). *Journal of Anxiety Disorders, 13*, 87–99.

Cutrona, C. E., & Russell, D. W. (1990). Type of social support and specific stress: Toward a theory of optimal matching. In B. R. Sarason, I. G. Sarason, & G. R. Pierce (Eds.), *Social support: An interactional view* (pp. 319–366). New York: Wiley.

Dalai Lama, & Cutler, H. C. (1998). *The art of happiness*. New York: Penguin Putnam.

Damasio, A. (1999). *The feeling of what happens: Body and emotion in the making of consciousness*. New York: Harcourt Brace.

Damasio, A. R. (1994). *Descartes' error: Emotion, reason, and the human brain*. New York: Avon.

Dancu, C. V., Riggs, D. S., Hearst-Ikeda, D., Shoyer, B. G., & Foa, E. B. (1996). Dissociative experiences and posttraumatic stress disorder among female victims of criminal assault and rape. *Journal of Traumatic Stress, 9*, 253–267.

Dansky, B. S., Brady, K. T., & Saladin, M. E. (1998). Untreated symptoms of PTSD among cocaine-dependent individuals: Changes over time. *Journal of Substance Abuse Treatment, 15*, 499–504.

Dansky, B. S., Brewerton, T. D., Kilpatrick, D. G., & O'Neil, P. M. (1997). The National Women's Study: Relationship of victimization and posttraumatic stress disorder to bulimia nervosa. *International Journal of Eating Disorders, 21*, 231–228.

Darwin, C. (1872/1965). *The expression of emotion in man and animals*. Chicago: University of Chicago Press.

Davidson, J., Allen, J. G., & Smith, W. H. (1987). Complexities in the hospital treatment of a patient with multiple personality disorder. *Bulletin of the Menninger Clinic, 51,* 561–568.

Davidson, J. R. T., & Fairbank, J. A. (1993). The epidemiology of posttraumatic stress disorder. In J. R. T. Davidson & E. B. Foa (Eds.), *Posttraumatic stress disorder: DSM-IV and beyond* (pp. 147–169). Washington, DC: American Psychiatric Press.

Davidson, J. R. T., & Foa, E. B. (1993). Epilogue. In J. R. T. Davidson & E. B. Foa (Eds.), *Posttraumatic stress disorder: DSM-IV and beyond* (pp. 229–235). Washington, DC: American Psychiatric Press.

Davidson, J. R. T., Tupler, L. A., Wilson, W. H., & Connor, K. M. (1998). A family study of chronic post-traumatic stress disorder following rape trauma. *Journal of Psychiatric Research, 32,* 301–309.

Davies, J. M., & Frawley, M. G. (1994). *Treating the adult survivor of childhood sexual abuse.* New York: Basic Books.

Davis, L. (1991). *Allies in healing: When the person you love was sexually abused as a child.* New York: HarperCollins.

Davis, M. (1992). The role of the amygdala in fear and anxiety. *Annual Review of Neuroscience, 15,* 353–375.

de Waal, F. (1989). *Peacemaking among primates.* Cambridge, MA: Harvard University Press.

de Waal, F. B. M., & Aureli, F. (1999). Conflict resolution and distress alleviation in monkeys and apes. In C. S. Carter, I. I. Lederhendler, & B. Kirkpatrick (Eds.), *The integrative neurobiology of affiliation* (pp. 119–130). Cambridge, MA: MIT Press.

DeBell, C., & Jones, R. D. (1997). As good as it seems? A review of EMDR experimental research. *Professional Psychology: Research and Practice, 28,* 153–163.

Deffenbacher, J. L. (1999). Cognitive-behavioral conceptualization and treatment of anger. *Journal of Clinical Psychology, 55,* 295–300.

Dell, P. F. (1998). Axis II pathology in outpatients with dissociative identity disorder. *Journal of Nervous and Mental Disease, 186,* 352–356.

Dement, W. C. (1999). *The promise of sleep.* New York: Random House.

Dennett, D. C. (1987). *The intentional stance.* Cambridge, MA: MIT Press.

Dennett, D. C. (1991). *Consciousness explained.* Boston: Little, Brown.

Depue, R. A., Luciana, M., Arbisi, P., Collins, P., & Leon, A. (1994). Dopamine and the structure of personality: Relation of agonist-induced dopamine activity to positive emotionality. *Journal of Personality and Social Psychology, 67,* 485–498.

Deutch, A. Y., & Young, C. D. (1995). A model of the stress-induced activation of prefrontal cortical dopamine systems: Coping and the development of post-traumatic stress disorder. In M. J. Friedman, D. S. Charney, & A. Y. Deutch (Eds.), *Neurobiological and clinical consequences of stress: From normal adaptation to post-traumatic stress disorder* (pp. 163–175). Philadelphia: Lippincott-Raven.

deVegvar, M.-L., Siever, L. J., & Trestmen, R. L. (1994). Impulsivity and serotonin in borderline personality disorder. In K. R. Silk (Ed.), *Biological and neurobehavioral studies of borderline personality disorder* (pp. 23–40). Washington, DC: American Psychiatric Press.

Devilly, G. J., & Spence, S. H. (1999). The relative efficacy and treatment distress of EMDR and a cognitive-behavior trauma treatment protocol in the amelioration of posttraumatic stress disorder. *Journal of Anxiety Disorders, 13,* 131–157.

Devilly, G. J., Spence, S. H., & Rapee, R. M. (1998). Statistical and reliable change with Eye Movement Desensitization and Reprocessing: Treating trauma within a veteran population. *Behavior Therapy, 29,* 435–455.

Dinwiddie, S., Heath, A. C., Dunne, M. P., Bucholz, K. K., Madden, P. A. F., Slutske, W. S., Bierut, L. J., Statham, D. B., & Martin, N. G. (2000). Early sexual abuse and lifetime psychopathology: A co-twin control study. *Psychological Medicine, 30,* 41–52.

Dohrenwend, B. P., Shrout, P. E., Link, B. G., Skodol, A. E., & Stueve, A. (1995). Life events and other possible psychosocial risk factors for episodes of schizophrenia and major depression: A case–control study. In C. M. Mazure (Ed.), *Does stress cause psychiatric illness?* (pp. 43–65). Washington, DC: American Psychiatric Press.

Dozier, M. (1990). Attachment organization and treatment use for adults with serious psychopathological disorders. *Development and Psychopathology, 2*, 47–60.

Dozier, M., Cue, K. L., & Barnett, L. (1994). Clinicians as caregivers: Role of attachment organization in treatment. *Journal of Consulting and Clinical Psychology, 62*, 793–800.

Dozier, M., Stovall, K. C., & Albus, K. E. (1999). Attachment and psychopathology in adulthood. In J. Cassidy & P. R. Shaver (Eds.), *Handbook of attachment: Theory, research, and clinical applications* (pp. 497–519). New York: Guilford.

Draijer, N., & Langeland, W. (1999). Childhood trauma and perceived parental dysfunction in the etiology of dissociative symptoms in psychiatric inpatients. *American Journal of Psychiatry, 156*, 379–385.

Dubo, E. D., Zanarini, M. C., Lewis, R. E., & Williams, A. A. (1997). Childhood antecedents of self-destructiveness in borderline personality disorder. *Canadian Journal of Psychiatry, 42*, 63–69.

Dubovsky, S. L. (1997). *Mind–body deceptions: The psychosomatics of everyday life.* New York: W. W. Norton.

DuBreuil, S. C., Garry, M., & Loftus, E. F. (1998). Tales from the crib: Age regression and the creation of unlikely memories. In S. J. Lynn & K. M. McConkey (Eds.), *Truth in memory* (pp. 137–160). New York: Guilford.

Duman, R. S., Heninger, G. R., & Nestler, E. J. (1997). A molecular and cellular theory of depression. *Archives of General Psychiatry, 54*, 597–606.

Duman, R. S., & Nestler, E. J. (2000). Role of gene expression in stress and drug-induced neural plasticity. *The Economics of Neurobiology, 2*, 53–70.

Duncan, R. D., Saunders, B. E., Kilpatrick, D. G., Hanson, R. F., & Resnick, H. S. (1996). Childhood physical assault as a risk factor for PTDS, depression, and substance abuse: Findings from a national survey. *American Journal of Orthopsychiatry, 66*, 437–448.

Dunmore, E., Clark, D. M., & Ehlers, A. (1999). Cognitive factors involved in the onset and maintenance of posttraumatic stress disorder (PTSD) after physical or sexual assault. *Behaviour Research and Therapy, 37*, 809–829.

Dunn, A. L., & Dishman, R. K. (1991). Exercise and the neurobiology of depression. In J. O. Holloszy (Ed.), *Exercise and sport sciences reviews* (pp. 41–98). Baltimore: Williams & Wilkins.

Dunn, J. (1996). The Emanuel Miller Memorial Lecture 1995: Children's relationships: Bridging the divide between cognitive and social development. *Journal of Child Psychology and Psychiatry, 37*, 507–518.

Dutton, D., & Painter, S. L. (1981). Traumatic bonding: The development of emotional attachments in battered women and other relationships of intermittent abuse. *Victimology, 6*, 139–155.

Echeburua, E., Corral, P. D., Zubizarreta, I., & Sarasua, B. (1997). Psychological treatment of chronic posttraumatic stress disorder in victims of sexual aggression. *Behavior Modification, 21*, 433–456.

Edelman, G. M. (1989). *The remembered past: A biological theory of consciousness.* New York: Basic Books.

Edelman, G. M. (1992). *Bright air, brilliant fire: On the matter of the mind.* New York: Basic Books.

Edelman, G. M., & Tononi, G. (2000). *A universe of consciousness: How matter becomes imagination.* New York: Basic Books.

Egeland, B. (1997). Mediators of the effects of child maltreatment on developmental adaptation in adolescence. In D. Cicchetti & S. L. Toth (Eds.), *Developmental perspectives on trauma: Theory, research, and intervention* (Vol. 8, pp. 403–434). Rochester, NY: University of Rochester Press.

Ehlers, A., Maercker, A., & Boos, A. (2000). Posttraumatic stress disorder following political imprisonment: The role of mental defeat, alienation, and perceived permanent change. *Journal of Abnormal Psychology, 109*, 45–55.

Ehrenberg, D. B. (1992). *The intimate edge: Extending the reach of psychoanalytic interaction*. New York: Norton.

Eisen, S. A., Neuman, R., Goldberg, J., True, W. R., Rice, J., Scherrer, J. F., & Lyons, M. J. (1998). Contribution of emotionally traumatic events and inheritance to the report of current physical health problems in 4042 Vietnam era veteran twin pairs. *Psychosomatic Medicine, 60*, 533–539.

Ellason, J. W., Ross, C. A., & Fuchs, D. L. (1996). Lifetime axis I and II comorbidity and childhood trauma history in dissociative identity disorder. *Psychiatry, 59*, 255–266.

Ellenberger, H. F. (1970). *The discovery of the unconscious: The history and evolution of dynamic psychiatry*. New York: Basic Books.

Elliott, D. M. (1997). Traumatic events: Prevalence and delayed recall in the general population. *Journal of Clinical and Consulting Psychology, 65*, 811–820.

Elliott, D. M., & Guy, J. D. (1993). Mental health professionals versus non-mental-health professionals: Childhood trauma and adult functioning. *Professional Psychology: Research and Practice, 24*, 83–90.

Ellsberg, M. (1999). Domestic violence and emotional distress among Nicaraguan women. *American Psychologist, 54*, 30–36.

Elster, J. (1999). *Strong feelings: Emotion, addiction, and human behavior*. Cambridge, MA: MIT Press.

Engle, B. (1991). *Partners in recovery: How mates, lovers and other prosurvivors can learn to support and cope with adult survivors of childhood sexual abuse*. New York: Fawcett Columbine.

Enns, C. Z., Campbell, J., & Courtois, C. A. (1997). Recommendations for working with domestic violence survivors, with special attention to memory issues and posttraumatic processes. *Psychotherapy, 34*, 459–477.

Epstein, J. N., Saunders, B. E., Kilpatrick, D. G., & Resnick, H. S. (1998). PTSD as a mediator between childhood rape and alcohol use in adult women. *Child Abuse and Neglect, 22*, 223–234.

Erdelyi, M. H. (1996). *The recovery of unconscious memories*. Chicago: University of Chicago Press.

Erickson, M. F., & Egeland, B. (1996). Child neglect. In J. Briere, L. Berliner, J. A. Bulkley, C. Jenny, & T. Reid (Eds.), *The APSAC handbook on child maltreatment* (pp. 4–20). Thousand Oaks, CA: Sage.

Erickson, M. T. (1993). Rethinking Oedipus: An evolutionary perspective of incest avoidance. *American Journal of Psychiatry, 150*, 411–416.

Erickson, M. T. (1999). Incest avoidance: Clinical implications of the evolutionary perspective. In J. J. McKenna, W. Trevathan, & E. O. Smith (Eds.), *Evolutionary medicine* (pp. 165–181). New York: Oxford University Press.

Erikson, K. T. (1976). Loss of communality at Buffalo Creek. *American Journal of Psychiatry, 133*, 302–305.

Esman, A. H. (1991). Child abuse and multiple personality disorder [Letter]. *American Journal of Psychiatry, 151*, 948.

Eth, S., & Pynoos, R. S. (1985). *Post-traumatic stress disorder in children*. Washington, DC: American Psychiatric Press.

Eth, S., & Pynoos, R. S. (1994). Children who witness the homicide of a parent. *Psychiatry, 57,* 287–306.

Fadden, G. (1998). Family intervention in psychosis. *Journal of Mental Health, 7,* 115–122.

Fahrion, S. L., & Norris, P. A. (1990). Self-regulation of anxiety. *Bulletin of the Menninger Clinic, 54,* 217–231.

Fahy, T. A. (1988). The diagnosis of multiple personality disorder: A critical review. *British Journal of Psychiatry, 153,* 597–606.

Fallon, P., & Wonderlich, S. A. (1997). Sexual abuse and other forms of trauma. In D. M. Garner & P. E. Garfinkel (Eds.), *Handbook of treatment for eating disorders* (2nd edn.,) (pp. 394–414). New York: Guilford.

Falsetti, S. A., Resnick, H. S., Dansky, B. S., Lydiard, R. B., & Kilpatrick, D. G. (1995). The relationship of stress to panic disorder: Cause or effect? In C. M. Mazure (Ed.), *Does stress cause psychiatric illness?* (pp. 111–147). Washington, DC: American Psychiatric Press.

Fanselow, M. S., & Lester, L. S. (1988). A functional behavioristic approach to aversively motivated behavior: Predatory imminence as a determinant of the topography of defensive behavior. In R. C. Bolles & M. D. Beecher (Eds.), *Evolution and learning* (pp. 185–212). Hillsdale, NJ: Erlbaum.

Fantuzzo, J., Boruch, R., Beriama, A., Atkins, M., & Marcus, S. (1997). Domestic violence and children: Prevalence and risk in five major US cities. *Journal of the American Academy for Child and Adolescent Psychiatry, 36,* 116–122.

Favazza, A. R. (1987). *Bodies under siege: Self-mutilation in culture and psychiatry.* Baltimore, MD: Johns Hopkins University Press.

Favazza, A. R., & Conterio, K. (1989). Female habitual self-mutilators. *Acta Psychiatrica Scandanavica, 79,* 283–289.

Favazza, A. R., & Rosenthal, R. J. (1993). Diagnostic issues in self-mutilation. *Hospital and Community Psychiatry, 44,* 134–140.

Fawcett, G. M., Heise, L. L., Isita-Espejel, L., & Pick, S. (1999). Changing community responses to wife abuse: A research and demonstration in Iztacalco, Mexico. *American Psychologist, 54,* 41–49.

Feeny, N. C., Zoellner, L. A., & Foa, E. B. (2000). Anger, dissociation, and posttraumatic stress disorder among female assault victims. *Journal of Traumatic Stress, 13,* 89–100.

Feindel, W. (1961). Response patterns elicited from the amygdala and deep temporoinsular cortex. In D. E. Sheer (Ed.), *Electrical stimulation of the brain: An interdisciplinary survey of neurobehavioral integrative systems* (pp. 519–532). Austin, TX: University of Texas Press.

Feldman, M. D. (1988). The challenge of self-mutilation: A review. *Comprehensive Psychiatry, 29,* 252–269.

Feldman, W., Feldman, E., Goodman, J. T., McGrath, P. J., Pless, R. P., Corsini, L., & Bennett, S. (1991). Is childhood sexual abuse really increasing in prevalence? An analysis of the evidence. *Pediatrics, 88,* 29–33.

Feldman-Summers, S., & Pope, K. S. (1994). The experience of 'forgetting' childhood abuse: A national survey of psychologists. *Journal of Consulting and Clinical Psychology, 62,* 636–639.

Fenichel, O. (1945). *The psychoanalytic theory of neurosis.* New York: Norton.

Ferenczi, S. (1949). Confusion of tongues between the adult and the child. *International Journal of Psycho-Analysis, 30,* 225–230.

Ferguson, K. S., & Dacey, C. M. (1997). Anxiety, depression, and dissociation in women health care providers reporting a history of childhood psychological abuse. *Child Abuse and Neglect, 21,* 941–952.

Field, T. (1985). Attachment as psychobiological attunement: Being on the same wavelength. In M. Reite & T. Field (Eds.), *The psychobiology of attachment and separation* (pp. 415–454). New York: Academic Press.

Field, T., & Reite, M. (1985). The psychobiology of attachment and separation: A summary. In M. Reite & T. Field (Eds.), *The psychobiology of attachment and separation* (pp. 455–479). New York: Academic Press.

Figley, C. R. (1989). *Helping traumatized families*. San Francisco: Jossey-Bass.

Figley, C. R. (1995a). Compassion fatigue as secondary traumatic stress disorder: An overview. In C. R. Figley (Ed.), *Compassion fatigue: Coping with secondary traumatic stress disorder in those who treat the traumatized* (pp. 1–20). New York: Brunner/Mazel.

Figley, C. R. (1995b). Epilogue: The transmission of trauma. In C. R. Figley (Ed.), *Compassion fatigue: Coping with secondary traumatic stress disorder in those who treat the traumatized* (pp. 248–254). New York: Brunner/Mazel.

Figueroa, E., & Silk, K. R. (1997). Biological implications of childhood sexual abuse in borderline personality disorder. *Journal of Personality Disorders, 11*, 71–92.

Finkelhor, D. (1984). *Child sexual abuse: New theory and research*. New York: Free Press.

Finkelhor, D., Hotaling, G., Lewis, I. A., & Smith, C. (1990). Sexual abuse in a national survey of adult men and women: Prevalence, characteristics, and risk factors. *Child Abuse & Neglect, 14*, 19–28.

Fitzgerald, L. (1993). Sexual harassment: Violence against women in the workplace. *American Psychologist, 48*, 1070–1076.

Fitzgerald, S. G., & Gonzalez, E. (1994). Dissociative states induced by relaxation training in a PTSD combat veteran: Failure to identify trigger mechanisms. *Journal of Traumatic Stress, 7*, 111–115.

Foa, E. B. (1997). Psychological processes related to recovery from a trauma and effective treatment for PTSD. In R. Yehuda & A. C. McFarlane (Eds.), *Psychobiology of posttraumatic stress disorder* (Vol. 823, pp. 410–424). New York: New York Academy of Sciences.

Foa, E. B. (1998). *Obsessive-compulsive disorder and post-traumatic stress disorder*. Kansas City, MO: Institute for Behavioral Healthcare.

Foa, E. B., Dancu, C. V., Hembree, E. A., Jaycox, L. H., Meadows, E. A., & Street, G. P. (1999). A comparison of exposure therapy, stress inoculation training, and their combination for reducing posttraumatic stress disorder in female assault victims. *Journal of Consulting and Clinical Psychology, 67*, 194–200.

Foa, E. B., Ehlers, A., Clark, D. M., Tolin, D. F., & Orsillo, S. M. (1999). The posttraumatic cognitions inventory (PTCI): Development and validation. *Psychological Assessment, 11*, 303–314.

Foa, E. B., & Hearst-Ikeda, D. (1996). Emotional dissociation in response to trauma: An information-processing approach. In L. K. Michelson & W. J. Ray (Eds.), *Handbook of dissociation: Theoretical, empirical, and clinical perspectives* (pp. 207–224). New York: Plenum.

Foa, E. B., & Kozak, M. J. (1986). Emotional processing of fear: Exposure to corrective information. *Psychological Bulletin, 99*, 20–35.

Foa, E. B., & Kozak, M. J. (1991). Emotional processing: Theory, research, and clinical implications for anxiety disorders. In J. D. Safran & L. S. Greenberg (Eds.), *Emotion, psychotherapy, and change* (pp. 21–49). New York: Guilford.

Foa, E. B., & McNally, R. J. (1996). Mechanisms of change in exposure therapy. In R. M. Rapee (Ed.), *Current controversies in the anxiety disorders* (pp. 329–343). New York: Guilford.

Foa, E. B., & Meadows, E. A. (1997). Psychosocial treatments for posttraumatic stress disorder: A critical review. *Annual Review of Psychology, 48*, 449–480.

Foa, E. B., & Riggs, D. S. (1993). Posttraumatic stress disorder and rape. In J. M. Oldham, M. B. Riba, & A. Tasman (Eds.), *American Psychiatric Press Review of Psychiatry* (Vol. 12, pp. 273–303). Washington, DC: American Psychiatric Press.

Foa, E. B., Riggs, D. S., & Gershuny, B. S. (1995). Arousal, numbing, and intrusion: Symptom structure of PTSD following assault. *American Journal of Psychiatry, 152,* 116–120.

Foa, E. B., Riggs, D. S., Massie, E. D., & Yarczower, M. (1995). The impact of fear activation and anger on the efficacy of exposure treatment for posttraumatic stress disorder. *Behavior Therapy, 26,* 487–499.

Foa, E. B., & Rothbaum, B. O. (1998). *Treating the trauma of rape: Cognitive-behavioral therapy for PTSD.* New York: Guilford.

Foa, E. B., Rothbaum, B. O., & Molnar, C. (1995). Cognitive-behavioral therapy for post-traumatic stress disorder. In M. J. Friedman, D. S. Charney, & A. Y. Deutch (Eds.), *Neurobiological and clinical consequences of stress: From normal adaptation to PTSD* (pp. 483–494). Philadelphia: Lippincott-Raven.

Foa, E. B., Rothbaum, B. O., Riggs, D. S., & Murdock, T. B. (1991). Treatment of post-traumatic stress disorder in rape victims: A comparison between cognitive-behavioral procedures and counseling. *Journal of Consulting and Clinical Psychology, 59,* 715–723.

Foa, E. B., Zinbarg, R., & Rothbaum, B. O. (1992). Uncontrollability and unpredictability in post-traumatic stress disorder: An animal model. *Psychological Bulletin, 112,* 218–238.

Follette, V. M., Polusny, M. M., & Milbeck, K. (1994). Mental health and law enforcement professionals: Trauma history, psychological symptoms, and impact of providing services to child sexual abuse survivors. *Professional Psychology: Research and Practice, 25,* 275–282.

Fonagy, P. (1995). Playing with reality: The development of psychic reality and its malfunction in borderline personalities. *International Journal of Psycho-Analysis, 76,* 39–44.

Fonagy, P. (1998). An attachment theory approach to treatment of the difficult patient. *Bulletin of the Menninger Clinic, 62,* 147–169.

Fonagy, P. (1999a). Memory and therapeutic action. *International Journal of Psycho-Analysis, 80,* 215–223.

Fonagy, P. (1999b). *Pathological attachments and therapeutic action.* Paper presented at the Annual Meeting of the California Branch of the American Academy of Child and Adolescent Psychiatry, Yosemite Valley, CA.

Fonagy, P. (1999c). Process and outcome in mental health care delivery: A model approach to treatment evaluation. *Bulletin of the Menninger Clinic, 63,* 288–304.

Fonagy, P. (1999d). *Transgenerational consistencies of attachment: A new theory.* Paper presented at the Annual Meeting of the California Branch of the American Academy of Child and Adolescent Psychiatry, Yosemite Valley, CA.

Fonagy, P., Leigh, T., Steele, M., Steele, H., Kennedy, R., Mattoon, G., Target, M., & Gerber, A. (1996). The relation of attachment status, psychiatric classification, and response to psychotherapy. *Journal of Consulting and Clinical Psychology, 64,* 22–31.

Fonagy, P., Moran, G. S., Edgcumbe, R., Kennedy, H., & Target, M. (1993). The roles of mental representations and mental processes in therapeutic action. In A. J. Solnit, P. B. Neubauer, S. Abrams, & A. S. Dowling (Eds.), *The psychoanalytic study of the child* (Vol. 48, pp. 9–48). New Haven: Yale University Press.

Fonagy, P., Steele, H., & Steele, M. (1991). Maternal representations of attachment during pregnancy predict the organization of infant–mother attachment at one year of age. *Child Development, 62,* 891–905.

Fonagy, P., Steele, M., Steele, H., Leigh, T., Kennedy, R., Mattoon, G., & Target, M.

(1995). Attachment, the reflective self, and borderline states: The predictive specificity of the Adult Attachment Interview and pathological emotional development. In S. Goldberg, R. Muir, & J. Kerr (Eds.), *Attachment theory: Social, developmental, and clinical perspectives* (pp. 233–278). New York: Analytic Press.

Fonagy, P., & Stein, H. B. (1999). *The long-term effects of the quality of parenting on adolescent and adult functioning: A research proposal* (Technical Report No. 99-0006). Topeka, KS: Menninger Clinic, Research Department.

Fonagy, P., & Target, M. (1997a). Attachment and reflective function: Their role in self-organization. *Development and Psychopathology, 9,* 679–700.

Fonagy, P., & Target, M. (1997b). Perspectives on the recovered memories debate. In J. Sandler & P. Fonagy (Eds.), *Recovered memories of abuse: True or false?* (pp. 183–237). Madison, CT: International Universities Press.

Fonagy, P., Target, M., & Gergely, G. (2000). Attachment and borderline personality disorder: A theory and some evidence. *Psychiatric Clinics of North America, 23,* 103–122.

Fossati, A., Madeddu, F., & Maffei, C. (1999). Borderline personality disorder and childhood sexual abuse: A meta-analytic study. *Journal of Personality Disorders, 13,* 268–280.

Fox, N. A., & Card, J. A. (1999). Psychophysiological measures in the study of attachment. In J. Cassidy & P. R. Shaver (Eds.), *Handbook of attachment: Theory, research, and clinical applications* (pp. 226–245). New York: Guilford.

Foy, D. W., Resnick, H. S., Sipprelle, R. C., & Carooll, E. M. (1989). Premilitary, military, and postmilitary factors in the development of combat-related posttraumatic stress disorder. *Behavior Therapist, 10,* 3–9.

Fraley, R. C., & Waller, N. G. (1998). Adult attachment patterns: A test of the typological model. In J. A. Simpson & W. S. Rholes (Eds.), *Attachment theory and close relationships* (pp. 77–114). New York: Guilford.

Frankel, F. H. (1990). Hypnotizability and dissociation. *American Journal of Psychiatry, 147,* 823–829.

Frankel, F. H. (1993). Adult reconstruction of childhood events in the multiple personality literature. *American Journal of Psychiatry, 150,* 954–958.

Frankel, F. H. (1994a). The concept of flashbacks in historical perspective. *International Journal of Clinical and Experimental Hypnosis, 42,* 321–336.

Frankel, F. H. (1994b). Dissociation in hysteria and hypnosis: A concept aggrandized. In S. J. Lynn & J. W. Rhue (Eds.), *Dissociation: Clinical and theoretical perspectives* (pp. 80–93). New York: Guilford.

Frazier, P., & Cohen, B. (1992). Research on the sexual victimization of women: Implications for counselor training. *The Counseling Psychologist, 20,* 141–158.

Freed, S., Craske, M. G., & Greher, M. R. (1999). Nocturnal panic and trauma. *Depression and Anxiety, 9,* 141–145.

Freedman, S. A., Brandes, D., Peri, T., & Shalev, A. (1999). Predictors of chronic posttraumatic stress disorder. *British Journal of Psychiatry, 174,* 353–359.

Freud, S. (1914/1958). Remembering, repeating, and working-through. In J. Strachey (Ed.), *The standard edition of the complete psychological works of Sigmund Freud* (Vol. 12, pp. 147–156). London: Hogarth Press.

Freud, S. (1920/1955). Beyond the pleasure principle. In J. Strachey (Ed.), *The standard edition of the complete psychological works of Sigmund Freud* (Vol. 18, pp. 7–64). London: Hogarth Press.

Freyd, J. J. (1996). *Betrayal trauma: The logic of forgetting childhood abuse.* Cambridge, MA: Harvard University Press.

Freyd, J. J. (1998). Science in the memory debate. *Ethics and Behavior, 8,* 101–113.

Friedman, M. (1997). Drug treatment for PTSD: Answers and questions. In R. Yehuda & A. C. McFarlane (Eds.), *Psychobiology of posttraumatic stress disorder* (Vol. 821, pp. 359–371). New York: New York Academy of Sciences.

Friedman, M. J. (1990). Interrelationships between biological mechanisms and pharmacotherapy of posttraumatic stress disorder. In M. E. Wolf & A. D. Mosnaim (Eds.), *Posttraumatic stress disorder: Etiology, phenomenology, and treatment* (pp. 204–225). Washington, DC: American Psychiatric Press.

Friedman, M. J., & Schnurr, P. P. (1995). The relationship between trauma, post-traumatic stress disorder, and physical health. In M. J. Friedman, D. S. Charney, & A. Y. Deutch (Eds.), *Neurobiological and clinical consequences of stress: From normal adaptation to post-traumatic stress disorder* (pp. 507–524). Philadelphia: Lippincott-Raven.

Friedman, M. J., & Southwick, S. M. (1995). Towards pharmacotherapy for post-traumatic stress disorder. In M. J. Friedman, D. S. Charney, & A. Y. Deutch (Eds.), *Neurobiological and clinical consequences of stress: From normal adaptation to post-traumatic stress disorder* (pp. 465–481). Philadelphia: Lippincott-Raven.

Friedman, M. J., & Yehuda, R. (1995). Post-traumatic stress disorder and comorbidity: Psychobiological approaches to differential diagnosis. In M. J. Friedman, D. S. Charney, & A. Y. Deutch (Eds.), *Neurobiological and clinical consequences of stress: From normal adaptation to post-traumatic stress disorder* (pp. 429–445). New York: Lippincott-Raven.

Frieswyk, S. H., Colson, D. B., & Allen, J. G. (1984). Conceptualizing the therapeutic alliance from a psychoanalytic perspective. *Psychotherapy, 21*, 460–464.

Fromm, E. (1973). *The anatomy of human destructiveness* (Fawcett Paperbacks edn.). New York: Holt, Rinehart, & Winston.

Frueh, B. C., De Arellano, M. A., & Turner, S. M. (1997). Systematic desensitization as an alternative exposure strategy for PTSD [Letter]. *American Journal of Psychiatry, 154*, 287–288.

Gabbard, G. O. (1997). Challenges in the analysis of adult patients with histories of childhood sexual abuse. *Canadian Journal of Psychoanalysis, 5*, 1–25.

Gabbard, G. O. (2000). *Psychodynamic psychiatry in clinical practice* (3rd edn.). Washington, DC: American Psychiatric Press.

Gabbard, G. O., Coyne, L., Allen, J. G., Spohn, H., Colson, D. B., & Vary, M. (2000). Evaluation of intensive inpatient treatment of patients with severe personality disorders. *Psychiatric Services, 51*, 893–898.

Gabbard, G. O., & Twemlow, S. W. (1984). *With the eyes of the mind: An empirical analysis of out-of-body states.* New York: Praeger.

Gabbard, G. O., & Wilkinson, S. M. (1994). *Management of countertransference with borderline patients.* Washington, DC: American Psychiatric Press.

Gallagher, R. E., & Nazarian, J. (1995). A comprehensive cognitive-behavioral/educational program for schizophrenic patients. *Bulletin of the Menninger Clinic, 59*, 357–371.

Gallup, G. G. J. (1974). Animal hypnosis: Factual status of a fictional concept. *Psychological Bulletin, 81*, 836–853.

Ganaway, G. K. (1989). Historical versus narrative truth: Clarifying the role of exogenous trauma in the etiology of MPD and its variants. *Dissociation, 2*, 205–220.

Garbarino, J. (1995). *Raising children in a socially toxic environment.* San Francisco: Jossey-Bass.

Garbarino, J., & Kostelny, K. (1997). What children can tell us about living in a war zone. In J. Osofsky (Ed.), *Children in a violent society* (pp. 32–41). New York: Guilford.

Garland, A. F., Landsverk, J. L., Hough, R. L., & Ellis-MacLeod, E. (1996). Type of maltreatment as a predictor of mental health service use for children in foster care. *Child Abuse & Neglect, 20*, 675–688.

Garner, D. M. (1997). Psychoeducational principles in treatment. In D. M. Garner & P. E. Garfinkel (Eds.), *Handbook of treatment for eating disorders* (2nd edn., pp. 145–177). New York: Guilford.

Gazzaniga, M. S. (1992). *Nature's mind: The biological roots of thinking, emotions, sexuality, language, and intelligence.* New York: Basic Books.

Gelernter, J., Southwick, S., Goodson, S., Morgan, A., Nagy, L., & Charney, D. S. (1999). No association between D2 dopamine receptor (DRD2) 'A' system alleles, or DRD2 haplotypes, and posttraumatic stress disorder. *Biological Psychiatry, 45,* 620–625.

Gelinas, D. J. (1993). Relational patterns in incestuous families, malevolent variations, and specific interventions with the adult survivor. In P. L. Paddison (Ed.), *Treatment of adult survivors of incest* (pp. 1–34). Washington, DC: American Psychiatric Press.

George, C., & Solomon, J. (1999). Attachment and caregiving: The caregiving behavioral system. In J. Cassidy & P. R. Shaver (Eds.), *Handbook of attachment: Theory, research, and clinical applications* (pp. 649–670). New York: Guilford.

Gergely, G. (1999, March 19–20). *The development of the representation of self and others.* Paper presented at the Institute for Psychoanalytic Training and Research Conference on the Evolution and Dissolution of the Self, New York.

Gergely, G. (in press). Reapproaching Mahler: New perspectives on normal autism, symbiosis, splitting and libidinal object constancy from cognitive developmental theory. *Journal of the American Psychoanalytic Association.*

Gergely, G., Nadasdy, Z., Csibra, G., & Biro, S. (1995). Taking the intentional stance at 12 months of age. *Cognition, 56,* 165–193.

Gergely, G., & Watson, J. S. (1996). The social biofeedback theory of parental affect-mirroring: The development of emotional self-awareness and self-control in infancy. *International Journal of Psycho-Analysis, 77,* 1181–1212.

Gergely, G., & Watson, J. S. (1999). Early social–emotional development: Contingency perception and the social biofeedback model. In P. Rochat (Ed.), *Early social cognition: Understanding others in the first months of life* (pp. 101–137). Hillsdale, NJ: Erlbaum.

Gershon, M. D. (1998). *The second brain.* New York: HarperCollins.

Gershuny, B. S., & Thayer, J. F. (1999). Relations among psychological trauma, dissociative phenomena, and trauma-related distress: A review and integration. *Clinical Psychology Review, 19,* 631–657.

Gilbert, P. (1992). *Depression: The evolution of powerlessness.* New York: Guilford.

Gleaves, D. H., & Eberenz, K. P. (1994). Sexual abuse histories among treatment-resistant bulimia nervosa patients. *International Journal of Eating Disorders, 15,* 227–231.

Gleaves, D. H., Eberenz, K. P., & May, M. C. (1998). Scope and significance of posttraumatic symptomatology among women hospitalized for an eating disorder. *International Journal of Eating Disorders, 24,* 147–156.

Glodich, A. (1999). *Psychoeducational groups for adolescents exposed to violence and abuse: Assessing the effectiveness of increasing knowledge of trauma to avert reenactment and risk-taking behaviors.* Unpublished Ph.D., thesis, Smith College, Northampton, MA.

Glover, H. (1992). Emotional numbing: A possible endorphin-mediated phenomenon associated with post-traumatic stress disorders and other allied psychopathologic states. *Journal of Traumatic Stress, 5,* 643–675.

Glover, H., Lader, W., Walker-O'Keefe, J., & Goodnick, P. (1997). Numbing scale scores in female psychiatric inpatients diagnosed with self-injurious behavior, dissociative identity disorder, and major depression. *Psychiatry Research, 70,* 115–123.

Goldberg, J., True, W. R., Eisen, S. A., & Henderson, W. G. (1990). A twin study of the effects of the Vietnam War on posttraumatic stress disorder. *Journal of the American Medical Association, 263,* 1227–1232.

Goldberg, S. (1991). Recent developments in attachment theory and research. *Canadian Journal of Psychiatry, 36,* 393–400.

Golding, J. M. (1994). Sexual assault history and physical health in randomly selected Los Angeles women. *Health Psychology, 13*, 130–138.

Goldman, J. D. G., & Padayachi, U. K. (1997). The prevalence and nature of child sexual abuse in Queensland, Australia. *Child Abuse & Neglect, 21*, 489–498.

Goldstein, M. J. (1991). Psychosocial (nonpharmacologic) treatments for schizophrenia. In A. Tasman & S. M. Goldfinger (Eds.), *American Psychiatric Press annual review of psychiatry* (Vol. 10, pp. 116–135). Washington, DC: American Psychiatric Press.

Goldstein, M. J., & Miklowitz, D. J. (1994). Family intervention for persons with bipolar disorder. In A. B. Hatfield (Ed.), *Family interventions in mental illness: New directions for mental health services, No. 62* (pp. 23–35). San Francisco: Jossey-Bass.

Goldstein, M. Z. (1996). Elder maltreatment and posttraumatic stress disorder. In P. E. Ruskin & J. A. Talbott (Eds.), *Aging and posttraumatic stress disorder* (pp. 127–135). Washington, DC: American Psychiatric Press.

Gollwitzer, P. M. (1999). Implementation intentions: Strong effects of simple plans. *American Psychologist, 54*, 493–503.

Good, M. I. (1993). The concept of an organic dissociative syndrome: What is the evidence? *Harvard Review of Psychiatry, 1*, 145–157.

Goodman, G. S., Quas, J. A., Batterman-Faunce, J. M., Riddlesberger, M. M., & Kuhn, J. (1996). Predictors of accurate and inaccurate memories of traumatic events experienced in childhood. In K. Pezdek & W. P. Banks (Eds.), *The recovered memory/false memory debate* (pp. 3–28). New York: Academic Press.

Goodwin, J. M. (1993a). Human vectors of trauma: Illustrations from the Marquis de Sade. In J. M. Goodwin (Ed.), *Rediscovering childhood trauma: Historical casebook and clinical applications* (pp. 95–111). Washington, DC: American Psychiatric Press.

Goodwin, J. M. (1993b). Sadistic abuse: Definition, recognition, and treatment. *Dissociation, 6*, 181–187.

Gore-Felton, C., Gill, M., Koopman, C., & Spiegel, D. (1999). A review of acute stress reactions among victims of violence: Implications for early intervention. *Aggression and Violent Behavior, 4*, 293–306.

Gorey, K. M., & Leslie, D. R. (1997). The prevalence of child sexual abuse: Integrative review adjustment for potential response and measurement biases. *Child Abuse and Neglect, 21*, 391–398.

Graham, D. L. R., Rawlings, E., & Rimini, N. (1988). Survivors of terror: Battered women, hostages, and the Stockholm Syndrome. In K. Yllo & M. Bograd (Eds.), *Feminist perspectives on wife abuse* (pp. 217–233). London: Sage.

Greaves, G. B. (1993). A history of multiple personality disorder. In R. P. Kluft & C. G. Fine (Eds.), *Clinical perspectives on multiple personality disorder* (pp. 355–380). Washington, DC: American Psychiatric Press.

Green, B. L. (1993). Disasters and posttraumatic stress disorder. In J. R. T. Davidson & E. B. Foa (Eds.), *Posttraumatic stress disorder: DSM-IV and beyond* (pp. 75–97). Washington, DC: American Psychiatric Press.

Green, B. L., Lindy, J. D., Grace, M. C., Gleser, G. C., Leonard, A. C., Korol, M., & Winget, C. (1990). Buffalo Creek survivors in the second decade: Stability of stress symptoms. *American Journal of Orthopsychiatry, 60*, 43–54.

Greenberg, L. S., & Safran, J. D. (1989). Emotion in psychotherapy. *American Psychologist, 44*, 19–29.

Greenberg, M. A., Wortman, C. B., & Stone, A. A. (1996). Emotional expression and physical health: Revising traumatic memories of fostering self-regulation? *Journal of Personality and Social Psychology, 71*, 588–602.

Greenberg, M. T. (1999). Attachment and psychopathology in childhood. In J. Cassidy

& P. R. Shaver (Eds.), *Handbook of attachment: Theory, research, and clinical applications* (pp. 469–496). New York: Guilford.

Greenspan, G. S., & Samuel, S. E. (1989). Self-cutting after rape. *American Journal of Psychiatry, 146,* 789–790.

Greenwald, R. (1999). The power of suggestion: Comment on EMDR and Mesmerism: A comparative historical analysis. *Journal of Anxiety Disorders, 13,* 611–615.

Griffin, D., & Bartholomew, K. (1994). Models of the self and other: Fundamental dimensions underlying measures of adult attachment. *Journal of Personality and Social Psychology, 67,* 430–445.

Griffin, D. W., & Bartholomew, K. (1994). The metaphysics of measurement: The case of adult attachment. In K. Bartholomew & D. Perlman (Eds.), *Attachment processes in adulthood* (Vol. 5, pp. 17–52). London: Jessica Kingsley.

Griffin, M. G., Resick, P. A., & Mechanic, M. B. (1997). Objective assessment of peritraumatic dissociation: Psychophysiological indicators. *American Journal of Psychiatry, 154,* 1081–1088.

Grillon, C., & Morgan, C. A. I. (1999). Fear-potentiated startle conditioning to explicit and contextual cues in Gulf War veterans with posttraumatic stress disorder. *Journal of Abnormal Psychology, 108,* 134–142.

Grinker, R. R., & Spiegel, J. P. (1945). *Men under stress.* Philadelphia: Blakiston.

Grinker, R. R., Werble, B., & Drye, R. C. (1968). *The borderline syndrome: A behavioral study of ego-functions.* New York: Basic Books.

Grossmann, K. E., Grossmann, K., & Zimmermann, P. (1999). A wider view of attachment and exploration: Stability and change during the years of immaturity. In J. Cassidy & P. R. Shaver (Eds.), *Handbook of attachment: Theory, research, and clinical applications* (pp. 760–786). New York: Guilford.

Gunderson, J. G. (1996). The borderline patient's intolerance of aloneness: Insecure attachments and therapist availability. *American Journal of Psychiatry, 153,* 752–758.

Gunderson, J. G., Berkowitz, C., & Ruiz-Sancho, A. (1997). Families of borderline patients: A psychoeducational approach. *Bulletin of the Menninger Clinic, 61,* 446–457.

Gurvits, T. V., Shenton, M. E., Hokama, H., Ohta, H., Lasko, N. B., Gilbertson, M. W., Orr, S. P., Kikinis, R., Jolesz, F. A., McCarley, R. W., & Pitman, R. K. (1996). Magnetic resonance imaging study of hippocampal volume in chronic, combat-related posttraumatic stress disorder. *Biological Psychiatry, 40,* 1091–1099.

Gutek, B. (1993). Responses to sexual harassment. In S. Oskamp & M. Costanzo (Eds.), *Gender issues in contemporary society: Claremont symposium on applied social psychology* (Vol. 6, pp. 197–216). Newbury Park, CA: Sage.

Gutheil, T. G. (1993). True or false memories of sexual abuse? A forensic psychiatric view. *Psychiatric Annals, 23,* 527–531.

Gutheil, T. G., & Gabbard, G. O. (1993). The concept of boundaries in clinical practice: Theoretical and risk-management dimensions. *American Journal of Psychiatry, 150,* 188–196.

Guzeldere, G. (1997). The many faces of consciousness: A field guide. In N. Block, O. Flanagan, & G. Guzeldere (Eds.), *The nature of consciousness: Philosophical debates* (pp. 1–67). Cambridge, MA: MIT Press.

Haines, J., Williams, C. L., Brain, K. L., & Wilson, G. V. (1995). The psychophysiology of self-mutilation. *Journal of Abnormal Psychology, 104,* 471–489.

Hains, A., Herrman, L., Baker, K., & Graber, S. (1986). The development of a psychoeducational group program for adolescent sex offenders. *Journal of Offender Counseling, 11,* 63–76.

Halgren, E. (1992). Emotional neurophysiology of the amygdala within the context of human cognition. In J. P. Aggleton (Ed.), *The amygdala: Neurobiological aspects of emotion, memory, and mental dysfunction* (pp. 191–228). New York: Wiley.

Halleck, S. L. (1990). Dissociative phenomena and the question of responsibility. *International Journal of Clinical and Experimental Hypnosis, 38,* 298–314.

Hammen, C., & Gitlin, M. (1997). Stress reactivity in bipolar patients and its relation to prior history of disorder. *American Journal of Psychiatry, 154,* 856–857.

Hammen, C. L. (1995). Stress and the course of unipolar and bipolar disorders. In C. M. Mazure (Ed.), *Does stress cause psychiatric illness?* (pp. 87–110). Washington, DC: American Psychiatric Press.

Hamner, M. B. (1997). Psychotic features and combat-associated PTSD. *Depression and Anxiety, 5,* 34–38.

Hamner, M. B., Frueh, C., Ulmer, H. G., & Arana, G. W. (1999). Psychotic features and illness severity in combat veterans with chronic posttraumatic stress disorder. *Biological Psychiatry, 45,* 846–852.

Harber, K. D., & Pennebaker, J. W. (1992). Overcoming traumatic memories. In S. Christianson (Ed.), *The handbook of emotion and memory: Research and theory* (pp. 359–387). Hillsdale, NJ: Erlbaum.

Harris, T. O. (1992). Some reflections on the process of social support and the nature of unsupportive behaviors. In H. O. F. Veiel & U. Baumann (Eds.), *The meaning and measurement of social support* (pp. 171–190). New York: Hemisphere.

Hart, S. N., Binggeli, N. J., & Brassard, M. R. (1998). Evidence for the effects of psychological maltreatment. *Journal of Emotional Abuse, 1,* 27–58.

Hart, S. N., & Brassard, M. R. (1987). A major threat to children's mental health: Psychological maltreatment. *American Psychologist, 42,* 160–165.

Hart, S. N., & Brassard, M. R. (1991). Psychological maltreatment: Progress achieved. *Development and Psychopathology, 3,* 61–70.

Harter, S. (1999). *The construction of the self: A developmental perspective.* New York: Guilford.

Hartmann, E. (1998). Nightmare after trauma as a paradigm for all dreams: A new approach to the nature and functions of dreaming. *Psychiatry, 61,* 223–238.

Hartsough, D. M., & Savitsky, J. C. (1984). Three Mile Island: Psychology and environmental policy at a crossroads. *American Psychologist, 39,* 1113–1122.

Harvey, A. G., & Bryant, R. A. (1998a). The effect of attempted thought suppression in acute stress disorder. *Behaviour Research and Therapy, 36,* 583–590.

Harvey, A. G., & Bryant, R. A. (1998b). The relationship between acute stress disorder and posttraumatic stress disorder: A prospective evaluation of motor vehicle accident survivors. *Journal of Consulting and Clinical Psychology, 66,* 507–512.

Harvey, A. G., & Bryant, R. A. (1999). The relationship between acute stress disorder and posttraumatic stress disorder: A 2-year prospective evaluation. *Journal of Consulting and Clinical Psychology, 67,* 985–988.

Harvey, A. G., Bryant, R. A., & Dang, S. T. (1998). Autobiographical memory in acute stress disorder. *Journal of Consulting and Clinical Psychology, 66,* 500–506.

Hatfield, A. B. (1994). Family education: Theory and practice. In A. B. Hatfield (Ed.), *Family interventions in mental illness: New directions for mental health services, No. 62* (pp. 3–11). San Francisco: Jossey-Bass.

Hatfield, E., Cacioppo, J. T., & Rapson, R. (1993). Emotional contagion. *Current Directions in Psychological Science, 2,* 96–99.

Hatfield, E., Cacioppo, J. T., & Rapson, R. L. (1994). *Emotional contagion.* Paris: Cambridge University Press.

Hazan, C., & Shaver, P. (1987). Romantic love conceptualized as an attachment process. *Journal of Personality and Social Psychology, 52,* 511–524.

Hazan, C., & Shaver, P. R. (1994). Attachment as an organizational framework for research on close relationships. *Psychological Inquiry, 5,* 1–22.

Hazan, C., & Zeifman, D. (1999). Pair bonds as attachments: Evaluating the evidence. In J. Cassidy & P. R. Shaver (Eds.), *Handbook of attachment: Theory, research, and clinical applications* (pp. 336–354). New York: Guilford.

Hazzard, A. (1993). Psychoeducational groups to teach children about sexual abuse prevention skills. *Journal of Child and Adolescent Group Therapy, 3,* 13–23.

Hazzard, A., Rogers, J. H., & Angert, L. (1993). Factors affecting group therapy outcome for adult sexual abuse survivors. *International Journal of Group Psychotherapy, 43,* 453–468.

Heatherton, T. F., & Baumeister, R. F. (1991). Binge eating as escape from self-awareness. *Psychological Bulletin, 110,* 86–108.

Heim, C., Ehlert, U., Hanker, J. P., & Hellhammer, D. H. (1998). Abuse-related post-traumatic stress disorder and alterations of the hypothalamic–pituitary–adrenal axis in women with chronic pelvic pain. *Psychosomatic Medicine, 60,* 309–318.

Heim, C., Owens, M. J., Plotsky, P. M., & Nemeroff, C. B. (1997). Endocrine factors in the pathophysiology of mental disorders. *Psychopharmacology Bulletin, 33,* 185–192.

Henderson, A. J. Z., Bartholomew, K., & Dutton, D. G. (1997). He loves me; he loves me not: Attachment and separation resolution of abused women. *Journal of Family Violence, 12,* 169–191.

Herbert, J. D., & Mueser, K. T. (1995). What is EMDR? *Harvard Mental Health Letter,* August, 8.

Herman, J., & Schatzow, E. (1984). Time-limited group therapy for women with a history of incest. *International Journal of Group Psychotherapy, 34,* 605–616.

Herman, J. L. (1981). *Father–daughter incest.* Cambridge, MA: Harvard University Press.

Herman, J. L. (1992a). Complex PTSD: A syndrome in survivors of prolonged and repeated trauma. *Journal of Traumatic Stress, 5,* 377–391.

Herman, J. L. (1992b). *Trauma and recovery.* New York: Basic Books.

Herman, J. L. (1993). Sequelae of prolonged and repeated trauma: Evidence for a complex posttraumatic syndrome (DESNOS). In J. R. T. Davidson & E. B. Foa (Eds.), *Posttraumatic stress disorder: DSM-IV and beyond* (pp. 213–228). Washington, DC: American Psychiatric Press.

Herman, J. L., & Schatzow, E. (1987). Recovery and verification of memories of childhood sexual trauma. *Psychoanalytic Psychology, 4,* 1–14.

Herz, E., Goldberg, W., & Reis, J. (1984). Family life education for young adolescents: A quasi-experiment. *Journal of Youth and Adolescence, 16,* 309–327.

Hesse, E. (1999). The Adult Attachment Interview: Historical and current perspectives. In J. Cassidy & P. R. Shaver (Eds.), *Handbook of attachment: Theory, research, and clinical applications* (pp. 395–433). New York: Guilford.

Hesse, E., & Van IJzendoorn, M. H. (1998). Parental loss of close family members and propensities towards absorption in offspring. *Developmental Science, 1,* 299–305.

Hilgard, J. R. (1970). *Personality and hypnosis: A study of imaginative involvement.* Chicago: University of Chicago Press.

Hill, J., Davis, R., Byatt, M., Burnside, E., Rollinson, L., & Fear, S. (in press). Childhood sexual abuse and affective symptoms in women: A general population study. *Psychological Medicine.*

Hill, J., Fudge, H., Harrington, R., Pickles, A., & Rutter, M. (1995). The Adult Personality Functioning Assessment (APFA): Factors influencing agreement between subject and informant. *Psychological Medicine, 25,* 263–275.

Hill, J., Harrington, R., Fudge, H., Rutter, M., & Pickles, A. (1989). Adult Personality

Functioning Assessment (APFA): An investigator-based standardised interview. *British Journal of Psychiatry, 155*, 24–35.

Hill, J., Pickles, A., Burnside, E., Byatt, M., Rollinson, L., Davis, R., & Harvey, K. (in press). Child sexual abuse, poor parental care and adult depression: Evidence for different mechanisms. *British Journal of Psychiatry.*

Hilton, N. Z., Jennings, K. T., Drugge, J., & Stephens, J. (1995). Childhood sexual abuse among clinicians working with sex offenders. *Journal of Interpersonal Violence, 10*, 525–532.

Hobson, J. A. (1994). *The chemistry of conscious states: How the brain changes its mind.* Boston: Little, Brown.

Hofer, M. A. (1970). Cardiac and respiratory function during sudden prolonged immobility in wild rodents. *Psychosomatic Medicine, 32*, 633–647.

Hofer, M. A. (1984). Relationships as regulators: A psychobiologic perspective on bereavement. *Psychosomatic Medicine, 46*, 183–197.

Hofer, M. A. (1995). Hidden regulators: Implications for a new understanding of attachment, separation, and loss. In S. Goldberg, R. Muir, & J. Kerr (Eds.), *Attachment theory: Social, developmental, and clinical perspectives* (pp. 203–230). New York: Academic Press.

Hoffman, K. J., & Sasaki, J. E. (1997). Comorbidity of substance abuse and PTSD. In C. S. Fullerton & R. J. Ursano (Eds.), *Posttraumatic stress disorder: Acute and long-term responses to trauma* (pp. 159–174). Washington, DC: American Psychiatric Press.

Holder, D., & Anderson, C. (1990). Psychoeducational family intervention for depressed patients and their families. In G. I. Keitner (Ed.), *Depression and families: Impact and treatment* (pp. 159–184). Washington, DC: American Psychiatric Press.

Holmes, D. S. (1990). The evidence for repression: An examination of sixty years of research. In J. L. Singer (Ed.), *Repression and dissociation: Implications for personality theory, psychopathology, and health* (pp. 85–102). Chicago: University of Chicago Press.

Holmes, J. (1999). Defensive and creative uses of narrative in psychotherapy: An attachment perspective. In G. Roberts & J. Holmes (Eds.), *Healing stories: Narrative in psychiatry and psychotherapy* (pp. 49–66). London: Oxford University Press.

Holtzworth-Munroe, A., Smutzler, N., Bates, L., & Sandin, E. (1997). Husband violence: Basic facts and clinical implications. In W. K. Halford & H. J. Markman (Eds.), *Clinical handbook of marriage and couple interventions* (pp. 129–156). Chichester: Wiley.

Horne, S. (1999). Domestic violence in Russia. *American Psychologist, 54*, 55–61.

Horowitz, L. M., Rosenberg, S. E., Baer, B. A., Ureno, G., & Villasenor, V. S. (1988). Inventory of Interpersonal Problems: Psychometric properties and clinical applications. *Journal of Consulting and Clinical Psychology, 56*, 885–892.

Horowitz, M. J. (1986). Stress–response syndromes: A review of posttraumatic and adjustment disorders. *Hospital and Community Psychiatry, 37*, 241–249.

Horowitz, M. J. (1988). Psychodynamic phenomena and their explanation. In M. J. Horowitz (Ed.), *Psychodynamics and cognition* (pp. 3–20). Chicago: University of Chicago Press.

Horowitz, M. J. (1991a). Person schemas. In M. J. Horowitz (Ed.), *Person schemas and maladaptive interpersonal patterns* (pp. 13–31). Chicago: University of Chicago Press.

Horowitz, M. J. (Ed.). (1991b). *Person schemas and maladaptive interpersonal patterns.* Chicago: University of Chicago Press.

Horowitz, M. J. (1997). *Stress response syndromes: PTSD, grief, and adjustment disorders* (3rd edn.). Northvale, NJ: Aronson.

Horowitz, M. J., Siegel, B., Holen, A., Bonanno, G. A., Milbrath, C., & Stinson, C. H.

(1997). Diagnostic criteria for complicated grief disorder. *American Journal of Psychiatry, 154,* 904–910.

Horwitz, L. (1974). *Clinical prediction in psychotherapy.* New York: Aronson.

Horwitz, L. (1983). Projective identification in dyads and groups. *International Journal of Group Psychotherapy, 33,* 259–279.

Horwitz, L., Gabbard, G. O., Allen, J. G., Frieswyk, S. H., Colson, D. B., Newsom, G. E., & Coyne, L. (1996). *Borderline personality disorder: Tailoring the therapy to the patient.* Washington, DC: American Psychiatric Press.

Howe, M. L., & Courage, M. L. (1993). On resolving the enigma of infantile amnesia. *Psychological Bulletin, 113,* 305–326.

Howell, E. F. (1997). Masochism: A bridge to the other side of abuse. *Dissociation, 10,* 240–245.

Howes, C. (1999). Attachment relationships in the context of multiple caregivers. In J. Cassidy & P. R. Shaver (Eds.), *Handbook of attachment: Theory, research, and clinical applications* (pp. 671–687). New York: Guilford.

Hoyer, A. (1994). Sexual harassment: Four women describe their experiences—background and implications for the clinical nurse specialist. *Archives of Psychiatric Nursing, 8,* 177–183.

Hudson, J., & Nelson, K. (1986). Repeated encounters of a similar kind: Effects of familiarity on children's autobiographic memory. *Cognitive Development, 1,* 253–271.

Hudson, J. E., Manoach, D. S., Sabo, A. N., & Sternbach, S. E. (1991). Recurrent nightmares in post-traumatic stress disorder: Association with sleep paralysis, hypnopompic hallucinations, and REM sleep. *Journal of Nervous and Mental Disease, 179,* 572–573.

Humphrey, N. K. (1988). The social function of intellect. In R. W. Byrne & A. Whiten (Eds.), *Machiavellian intelligence: Social expertise and the evolution of intellect in monkeys, apes, and humans* (pp. 13–26). New York: Oxford University Press.

Hyer, L., Brandsma, J., & Boyd, S. (1997). The MCMIs and posttraumatic stress disorder. In T. Millon (Ed.), *The Millon inventories: Clinical and personality assessment* (pp. 191–216). New York: Guilford.

Hyman, I. E., & Billings, F. J. (1998). Individual differences and the creation of false memories. *Memory, 6,* 1–20.

Hyman, S. E., & Nestler, E. J. (1993). *The molecular foundations of psychiatry.* Washington, DC: American Psychiatric Press.

Ilardi, S. S., Craighead, W. E., & Evans, D. D. (1997). Modeling relapse in unipolar depression: The effects of dysfunctional cognitions and personality disorders. *Journal of Consulting and Clinical Psychology, 65,* 381–391.

Inman, D. J., Silver, S. M., & Doghramji, K. (1990). Sleep disturbance in posttraumatic stress disorder: A comparison with non-PTSD insomnia. *Journal of Traumatic Stress, 3,* 429–437.

Irwin, H. J. (1994). Proneness to dissociation and traumatic childhood events. *Journal of Nervous and Mental Disease, 182,* 456–460.

Irwin, H. J. (1996). Traumatic childhood events, perceived availability of emotional support, and the development of dissociative tendencies. *Child Abuse and Neglect, 20,* 701–707.

Izard, C. E. (1977). *Human emotions.* New York: Plenum.

Jacobs, S. (1993). *Pathologic grief: Maladaptation to loss.* Washington, DC: American Psychiatric Press.

Jaffe, P. G., Sudermann, M., & Reitzel, D. (1992). Child witnesses of marital violence. In R. T. Ammerman & M. Hersen (Eds.), *Assessment of family violence: A clinical and legal sourcebook* (pp. 313–331). New York: Wiley.

James, B. (1989). *Treating traumatized children.* New York: Lexington Books.

James, W. (1890/1950). *The principles of psychology* (Vol. 1). New York: Dover.

Jang, K. L., Paris, J., Zweig-Frank, H., & Livesley, W. J. (1998). Twin study of dissociative experience. *Journal of Nervous and Mental Disease, 186,* 345–351.

Janoff-Bulman, R. (1992). *Shattered assumptions: Towards a new psychology of trauma.* New York: Free Press.

Janov, A. (1970). *The primal scream.* New York: Dell.

Jaycox, L. H., Foa, E. B., & Morral, A. R. (1998). Influence of emotional engagement and habituation on exposure therapy for PTSD. *Journal of Consulting and Clinical Psychology, 66,* 185–192.

Jenkins, E., & Bell, C. (1997). Exposure and response to community violence among children and adolescents. In J. Osofsky (Ed.), *Children in a violent society* (pp. 9–31). New York: Guilford.

Johnson, J. G., Cohen, P., Brown, J., Smailes, E. M., & Bernstein, D. P. (1999). Childhood maltreatment increases risk for personality disorders during early adulthood. *Archives of General Psychiatry, 56,* 600–606.

Johnson, S. L., & Roberts, J. E. (1995). Life events and bipolar disorder: Implications from biological theories. *Psychological Bulletin, 117,* 434–449.

Jones, F., & Selder, F. (1996). Psychoeducational groups to promote effective coping in school age children living in violent communities. *Issues in Mental Health Nursing, 17,* 559–571.

Jones, I., & Daniels, B. A. (1996). An ethological approach to self-injury. *British Journal of Psychiatry, 169,* 263–267.

Josephs, L. (1992). *Character structure and the organization of the self.* New York: Columbia University Press.

Kabat-Zinn, J. (1990). *Full catastrophe living.* New York: Delta.

Kabat-Zinn, J. (1994). *Wherever you go, there you are: Mindfulness meditation in everyday life.* New York: Hyperion.

Kabat-Zinn, J., Massion, A. O., Kristeller, J., Peterson, L. G., Fletcher, K. E., Pbert, L., Lenderking, W. R., & Santorelli, S. F. (1992). Effectiveness of a meditation-based stress reduction program in the treatment of anxiety disorders. *American Journal of Psychiatry, 149,* 936–943.

Kagan, J. (1989). *Unstable ideas: Temperament, cognition, and self.* Cambridge, MA: Harvard University Press.

Kalin, N. H., Shelton, S. E., & Takahashi, L. K. (1991). Defensive behaviors in infant rhesus monkeys: Ontogeny and context-dependent selective expression. *Child Development, 62,* 1175–1183.

Kaplan, L. J. (1991). *Female perversions: The temptations of Emma Bovary.* New York: Doubleday.

Kaplan, S. J. (1996). Physical abuse of children and adolescents. In S. J. Kaplan (Ed.), *Family violence: A clinical and legal guide* (pp. 1–35). Washington, DC: American Psychiatric Press.

Kaplan, S. J., Pelcovitz, D., Salzinger, S., Weiner, M., Mandel, F. S., Lesser, M. L., & Labruna, V. E. (1998). Adolescent physical abuse: Risk for adolescent psychiatric disorders. *American Journal of Psychiatry, 155,* 954–959.

Kardiner, A. (1941). *The traumatic neuroses of war.* Washington, DC: National Research Council.

Kasim, M. S., Cheah, I., & Shafie, H. M. (1995). Childhood deaths from physical abuse. *Child Abuse and Neglect, 19,* 847–854.

Kaufman, J., & Zigler, E. (1987). Do abused children become abusive parents? *American Journal of Orthopsychiatry, 57,* 186–192.

Keane, T. M. (1998). Psychological and behavioral treatments of post-traumatic stress disorder. In P. E. Nathan & J. M. Gorman (Eds.), *A guide to treatments that work* (pp. 398–407). New York: Oxford University Press.

Keane, T. M., Fairbank, J. A., Caddell, J. M., & Zimering, R. T. (1989). Implosive (flooding) therapy reduces symptoms of PTSD in Vietnam combat veterans. *Behavior Therapy, 20,* 245–260.

Kemp, A., Rawlings, E. I., & Green, B. L. (1991). Post-traumatic stress disorder (PTSD) in battered women: A shelter sample. *Journal of Traumatic Stress, 4,* 137–148.

Kempe, C. H., Silverman, F. N., Steele, B. F., Droegemueller, W., & Silver, H. K. (1962). The battered-child syndrome. *Journal of the American Medical Association, 181,* 105–112.

Kemperman, I., Russ, M. J., Clark, W. C., Kakuma, T., Zanine, E., & Harrison, K. (1997). Pain assessment in self-injurious patients with borderline personality disorder using signal detection theory. *Psychiatry Research, 70,* 175–183.

Kemperman, I., Russ, M. J., & Shearin, E. (1997). Self-injurious behavior and mood regulation in borderline patients. *Journal of Personality Disorders, 11,* 146–157.

Kendall-Tackett, K. A., Williams, L. M., & Finkelhor, D. (1993). Impact of sexual abuse on children: A review and synthesis of recent empirical studies. *Psychological Bulletin, 113,* 164–180.

Kendler, K. S. (1997). Social support: A genetic–epidemiological analysis. *American Journal of Psychiatry, 154,* 1398–1404.

Kendler, K. S., Karkowski, L. M., & Prescott, C. A. (1999). Causal relationships between stressful life events and the onset of major depression. *American Journal of Psychiatry, 156,* 837–841.

Kendler, K. S., Neale, M., Kessler, R., Heath, A., & Eaves, L. (1993). A twin study of recent life events and difficulties. *Archives of General Psychiatry, 50,* 789–796.

Kent, A., Waller, G., & Dagnan, D. (1999). A greater role for emotional than physical or sexual abuse in predicting disordered eating attitudes: The role of mediating variables. *International Journal of Eating Disorders, 25,* 159–167.

Kernberg, O. F. (1976). *Object relations theory and clinical psychoanalysis.* New York: Aronson.

Kernberg, O. F. (1988). Clinical dimensions of masochism. *Journal of the American Psychoanalytic Association, 36,* 1005–1029.

Kessler, R. C., Kendler, K. S., Heath, A., Neale, M. C., & Eaves, L. J. (1992). Social support, depressed mood, and adjustment to stress: A genetic epidemiologic investigation. *Journal of Personality and Social Psychology, 62,* 257–272.

Kessler, R. C., Sonnega, A., Bromet, E., Hughes, M., & Nelson, C. B. (1995). Posttraumatic stress disorder in the National Comorbidity Survey. *Archives of General Psychiatry, 52,* 1048–1060.

Kessler, R. C., & Zhao, S. (1999). The prevalence of mental illness. In A. V. Horwitz & T. L. Scheid (Eds.), *A handbook for the study of mental health: Social contexts, theories, and systems* (pp. 58–78). Cambridge: Cambridge University Press.

Kihlstrom, J. F. (1984). Conscious, subconscious, unconscious: A cognitive perspective. In K. S. Bowers & D. Meichenbaum (Eds.), *The unconscious reconsidered* (pp. 149–211). New York: Wiley.

Kihlstrom, J. F. (1994). One hundred years of hysteria. In S. J. Lynn & J. W. Rhue (Eds.), *Dissociation: Clinical and theoretical perspectives* (pp. 365–394). New York: Guilford.

Kihlstrom, J. F. (1998). Exhumed memory. In S. J. Lynn & K. M. McConkey (Eds.), *Truth in memory* (pp. 3–31). New York: Guilford.

Kihlstrom, J. F., & Barnhardt, T. M. (1993). The self-regulation of memory: For better or for worse, with and without hypnosis. In D. M. Wegner & J. W. Pennebaker (Eds.), *Handbook of mental control* (pp. 88–125). Englewood Cliffs, NJ: Prentice Hall.

Kihlstrom, J. F., & Hoyt, I. P. (1990). Repression, dissociation, and hypnosis. In J. L. Singer (Ed.), *Repression and dissociation: Implications for personality theory, psychopathology, and health* (pp. 181–208). Chicago: Chicago University Press.

Kihlstrom, J. F., & Schacter, D. L. (1995). Functional disorders of autobiographical memory. In A. D. Baddeley, B. A. Wilson, & F. N. Watts (Eds.), *Handbook of memory disorders* (pp. 337–364). New York: Wiley.

Kilpatrick, D. G., & Resnick, H. S. (1993). Posttraumatic stress disorder associated with exposure to criminal victimization in clinical and community populations. In J. R. T. Davidson & E. B. Foa (Eds.), *Posttraumatic stress disorder: DSM-IV and beyond* (pp. 113–143). Washington, DC: American Psychiatric Press.

Kim, Y., Pilkonis, P. A., & Barkham, M. (1997). Confirmatory factor analysis of the personality disorder subscales from the Inventory of Interpersonal Problems. *Journal of Personality Assessment, 69,* 284–296.

Kinzie, J. D., Denney, D., Rile, C., Boehnlein, J., McFarland, B., & Leung, P. (1998). A cross-cultural study of reactivation of posttraumatic stress disorder symptoms: American and Cambodian psychophysiologial response to viewing traumatic video scenes. *Journal of Nervous and Mental Disease, 186,* 670–676.

Kirby, J. S., Chu, J. A., & Dill, D. L. (1993). Correlates of dissociative symptomatology in patients with physical and sexual abuse histories. *Comprehensive Psychiatry, 34,* 258–263.

Kirsch, I., & Lynn, S. J. (1999). Automaticity in clinical psychology. *American Psychologist, 54,* 504–515.

Klein, D. N., & Miller, G. A. (1997). Depressive personality: Relationship to dysthymia and major depression. In H. S. Akiskal & G. B. Cassano (Eds.), *Dysthymia and the spectrum of chronic depressions* (pp. 87–95). New York: Guilford.

Kline, N. A., & Rausch, J. L. (1985). Olfactory precipitants of flashbacks in posttraumatic stress disorder: Case reports. *Journal of Clinical Psychiatry, 46,* 383–384.

Klohnen, E. C., & John, O. P. (1998). Working models of attachment: A theory-based prototype approach. In J. A. Simpson & W. S. Rholes (Eds.), *Attachment theory and close relationships* (pp. 115–140). New York: Guilford.

Kluft, R. P. (1987). First-rank symptoms as a diagnostic clue to multiple personality disorder. *American Journal of Psychiatry, 144,* 293–298.

Kluft, R. P. (1990a). Incest and subsequent revictimization: The case of therapist–patient sexual exploitation, with a description of the sitting duck syndrome. In R. P. Kluft (Ed.), *Incest-related syndromes of adult psychopathology* (pp. 263–287). Washington, DC: American Psychiatric Press.

Kluft, R. P. (Ed.). (1990b). *Incest-related syndromes of adult psychopathology.* Washington, DC: American Psychiatric Press.

Kluft, R. P. (1991). Multiple personality disorder. In A. Tasman & S. M. Goldfinger (Eds.), *American Psychiatric Press review of psychiatry* (Vol. 10, pp. 161–188). Washington, DC: American Psychiatric Press.

Kluft, R. P. (1992). Discussion: A specialist's perspective on multiple personality disorder. *Psychoanalytic Inquiry, 12,* 139–171.

Kluft, R. P. (1993). Basic principles in conducting the psychotherapy of multiple personality disorder. In R. P. Kluft & C. G. Fine (Eds.), *Current perspectives on multiple personality disorder* (pp. 19–50). Washington, DC: American Psychiatric Press.

Kluft, R. P. (1995). The confirmation and disconfirmation of memories of abuse in DID patients: A naturalistic clinical study. *Dissociation, 8,* 253–258.

Kluft, R. P. (1996). Dissociative identity disorder. In L. K. Michelson & W. J. Ray (Eds.), *Handbook of dissociation: Theoretical, empirical, and clinical perspectives* (pp. 337–366). New York: Plenum.

Kobak, R. R., Cole, H. E., Ferenz-Gilles, R., Fleming, W. S., & Gamble, W. (1993). Attachment and emotion regulation during mother–teen problem solving: A control theory analysis. *Child Development, 61*, 231–245.

Koch-Hattem, A., Hattem, D. M., & Plummer, L. P. (1987). The role of mental-health resources in explaining family adaptation to stress: A preliminary analysis. *Family Systems Medicine, 5*, 206–219.

Koob, G. F., & Nestler, E. J. (1997). The neurobiology of drug addiction. In S. Salloway, P. Malloy, & J. L. Cummings (Eds.), *The neuropsychiatry of limbic and subcortical structures* (pp. 179–194). Washington, DC: American Psychiatric Press.

Koopman, C., Classen, C., & Spiegel, D. (1994). Predictors of posttraumatic stress symptoms among survivors of the Oakland/Berkeley, Calif., Firestorm. *American Journal of Psychiatry, 151*, 888–894.

Koopman, C., Classen, C., & Spiegel, D. (1997). Multiple stressors following a disaster and dissociative symptoms. In C. S. Fullerton & R. J. Ursano (Eds.), *Posttraumatic Stress Disorder: Acute and long-term responses to trauma and disaster* (pp. 21–35). Washington, DC: American Psychiatric Press.

Koss, M. P. (1993). Rape: Scope, impact, interventions, and public policy responses. *American Psychologist, 48*, 1062–1069.

Koss, M. P., Figueredo, A. J., Bell, I., Tharan, M., & Tromp, S. (1996). Traumatic memory characteristics: A cross-validated mediational model of response to rape among employed women. *Journal of Abnormal Psychology, 105*, 421–432.

Kosslyn, S. M. (1994). *Image and brain: The resolution of the imagery debate.* Cambridge, MA: MIT Press.

Koutstaal, W., & Schacter, D. L. (1997). Intentional forgetting and voluntary thought suppression: Two potential methods for coping with childhood trauma. In L. J. Dickstein, M. B. Riba, & J. M. Oldham (Eds.), *Review of Psychiatry* (Vol. 16, pp. 79–121). Washington, DC: American Psychiatric Press.

Kozu, J. (1999). Domestic violence in Japan. *American Psychologist, 54*, 50–54.

Kraemer, G. W. (1999). Psychobiology of early social attachment in Rhesus monkeys: Clinical applications. In C. S. Carter, I. I. Lederhendler, & B. Kirkpatrick (Eds.), *The integrative neurobiology of affiliation* (pp. 373–390). Cambridge, MA: MIT Press.

Krakow, B., Germain, A., Tandberg, D., Koss, M., Schrader, R., Hollifield, M., Cheng, D., & Edmond, T. (2000). Sleep breathing and sleep movement disorders masquerading as insomnia in sexual-assault survivors. *Comprehensive Psychiatry, 41*, 49–56.

Krystal, H. (1988). *Integration and self-healing: Affect, trauma, alexithymia.* Hillsdale, NJ: Analytic Press.

Krystal, J. H., Bennett, A., Bremner, J. D., Southwick, S. M., & Charney, D. S. (1995). Toward a cognitive neuroscience of dissociation and altered memory functions in post–traumatic stress disorder. In M. J. Friedman, D. S. Charney, A. Y. Deutch (Eds.), *Neurobiological and clinical consequences of stress: From normal adaptation to posttraumatic stress disorder* (pp. 239–269). New York: Lippincott-Raven.

Krystal, J. H., Bremner, J. D., Southwick, S. M., & Charney, D. S. (1998). The emerging neurobiology of dissociation: Implications for treatment of posttraumatic stress disorder. In J. D. Bremner & C. R. Marmar (Eds.), *Trauma, memory, and dissociation* (pp. 321–363). Washington, DC: American Psychiatric Press.

Krystal, J. H., Kosten, R. R., Southwick, S., Mason, J. W., Perry, B. D., & Geller, E. L. (1989). Neurobiological aspects of PTSD: Review of clinical and preclinical studies. *Behavior Therapy, 20*, 177–198.

Krystal, J. H., Southwick, S. M., & Charney, D. S. (1995). Posttraumatic stress disorder: Psychobiological mechanisms of traumatic remembrance. In D. L. Schacter (Ed.), *Memory distortion: How minds, brains, and societies reconstruct the past* (pp. 150–172). Cambridge, MA: Harvard University Press.

Kubany, E. (1998). Cognitive therapy for trauma-related guilt. In V. M. Follette, J. I. Ruzek, F. R. Abueg (Eds.), *Cognitive-behavioral therapies for trauma* (pp. 124–161). New York: Guilford.

Kudryavtseva, N. N., & Avgustinovich, D. F. (1998). Behavioral and physiological markers of experimental depression induced by social conflicts (DISC). *Aggressive Behavior, 24*, 271–286.

Kulka, R. A., Schlenger, W. E., Fairbank, J. A., Hough, R. L., Jordan, B. K., Marmar, C. R., & Weiss, D. S. (1990). *Trauma and the Vietnam war generation: Report of findings from the National Vietnam Veterans Readjustment Study.* New York: Brunner/Mazel.

Kunzendorf, R. G., Hulihan, D. M., Simpson, W., Pritykina, N., & Williams, K. (1998). Is absorption a diathesis for dissociation in sexually and physically abused patients? *Imagination, Cognition, and Personality, 17*, 277–282.

Kymissis, P. (1993). Group psychotherapy with adolescents. In H. Kaplan & B. Sadock (Eds.), *Comprehensive group psychotherapy* (3rd edn., pp. 577–584). Baltimore: Williams & Wilkins.

Lacey, J. H. (1993). Self-damaging and addictive behaviour in bulimia nervosa: A catchment area study. *British Journal of Psychiatry, 163*, 190–194.

Lachs, M. S., Williams, C. S., O'Brien, S., Pillemer, K. A., & Charlson, M. E. (1998). The mortality of elder mistreatment. *JAMA, 280*, 428–342.

LaMothe, R. (1999). The absence of cure: The core of malignant trauma and symbolization. *Journal of Interpersonal Violence, 14*, 1193–1210.

Lang, P. J. (1977). Imagery in therapy: An information processing analysis of fear. *Behavior Therapy, 8*, 862–886.

Lang, P. J. (1985). The cognitive psychophysiology of emotion: Fear and anxiety. In A. H. Tuma & J. Maser (Eds.), *Anxiety and the anxiety disorders* (pp. 131–170). Hillsdale, NJ: Erlbaum.

Laporte, L., & Guttman, H. (1996). Traumatic childhood experiences as risk factors for borderline and other personality disorders. *Journal of Personality Disorders, 10*, 247–259.

LeDoux, J. (1996). *The emotional brain.* New York: Simon & Schuster.

LeDoux, J. E. (1992). Emotion and the amygdala. In J. P. Aggleton (Ed.), *The amygdala: Neurobiological aspects of emotion, memory, and mental dysfunction* (pp. 339–351). New York: Wiley.

LeDoux, J. E. (1995). Setting 'stress' into motion: Brain mechanisms of stimulus evaluation. In M. J. Friedman, D. S. Charney, & A. Y. Deutch (Eds.), *Neurobiological and clinical consequences of stress: From normal adaptation to post-traumatic stress disorder* (pp. 125–134). Philadelphia: Lippincott-Raven.

LeDoux, J. E., Romanski, L., & Xagoraris, A. (1989). Indelibility of subcortical emotional memories. *Journal of Cognitive Neuroscience, 1*, 238–243.

Leibenluft, E., Gardner, D. L., & Cowdry, R. W. (1987). The inner experience of the borderline self-mutilator. *Journal of Personality Disorders, 1*, 317–324.

Leitenberg, H., Greenwald, E., & Cado, S. (1992). A retrospective study of long-term methods of coping with having been sexually abused during childhood. *Child Abuse and Neglect, 16*, 399–407.

Lenhart, S. (1996). Physical and mental health aspects of sexual harassment. In D. Schrier (Ed.), *Sexual harassment in the workplace and academia: Psychiatric issues* (pp. 21–38). Washington, DC: American Psychiatric Press.

Leslie, A. M. (1987). Pretense and representation: The origins of 'theory of mind'. *Psychological Review, 94*, 412–426.

Leslie, A. M. (1994). ToMM, ToBy, and agency: Core architecture and domain specificity. In L. A. Hirschfeld & S. A. Gelman (Eds.), *Mapping the mind: Domain specificity in cognition and culture* (pp. 119–148). Cambridge, UK: Cambridge University Press.

Levy, K. N., Blatt, S. J., & Shaver, P. R. (1998). Attachment styles and parental representations. *Journal of Personality and Social Psychology, 74,* 407–419.

Lewinsohn, P. M. (1974). A behavioral approach to depression. In R. J. Friedman & M. M. Katz (Eds.), *The psychology of depression: Contemporary research and theory* (pp. 157–178). New York: Wiley.

Lewis, D. O. (1992). From abuse to violence: Psychophysiological consequences of maltreatment. *Journal of the American Academy of Child and Adolescent Psychiatry, 31,* 383–391.

Lewis, J. L. (1996). Two paradigmatic approaches to borderline patients with a history of trauma. *Journal of Psychotherapy Practice and Research, 5,* 1–19.

Liberzon, I., Taylor, S. F., Amdur, R., Jung, T. D., Chamberlain, K. R., Minoshima, S., Koeppe, R. A., & Fig, L. M. (1999). Brain activation in PTSD in response to trauma-related stimuli. *Biological Psychiatry, 45,* 817–826.

Lichtenberg, J. D. (1989). *Psychoanalysis and motivation.* Hillsdale, NJ: Analytic Press.

Lieberman, A. F., & Zeanah, C. H. (1999). Contributions of attachment theory to infant–parent psychotherapy and other interventions with infants and young children. In J. Cassidy & P. R. Shaver (Eds.), *Handbook of attachment: Theory, research, and clinical applications* (pp. 555–574). New York: Guilford.

Lindon, J., & Nourse, C. (1992). A multi-dimensional model of group work for adolescent girls who have been sexually abused. *Child Abuse and Neglect, 18,* 341–348.

Linehan, M. M. (1993a). *Cognitive-behavioral treatment of borderline personality disorder.* New York: Guilford.

Linehan, M. M. (1993b). *Skills training manual for treating borderline personality disorder.* New York: Guilford.

Linehan, M. M., Armstrong, H. E., Suarez, A., Allmon, D., & Heard, H. L. (1991). Cognitive-behavioral treatment of chronically parasuicidal borderline patients. *Archives of General Psychiatry, 48,* 1060–1064.

Liotti, G. (1995). Disorganized/disoriented attachment in the psychotherapy of dissociative disorders. In S. Goldberg, R. Muir, & J. Kerr (Eds.), *Attachment theory: Social, developmental, and clinical perspectives* (pp. 343–363). Hillsdale, NJ: Analytic Press.

Liotti, G. (1999). Disorganization of attachment as a model for understanding dissociative psychopathology. In J. Solomon & C. George (Eds.), *Attachment disorganization* (pp. 291–317). New York: Guilford.

Lipschitz, D. S., Kaplan, M. L., Sorkenn, J., Chorney, P., & Asnis, G. M. (1996). Childhood abuse, adult assault, and dissociation. *Comprehensive Psychiatry, 37,* 261–266.

Little, L., & Hamby, S. (1999). Gender differences in sexual abuse outcomes and recovery experiences: A survey of therapist–survivors. *Professional Psychology: Research and Practice, 30,* 378–385.

Little, L., & Hamby, S. L. (1996). Impact of a clinician's sexual abuse history, gender, and theoretical orientation on treatment issues related to childhood sexual abuse. *Professional Psychology: Research and Practice, 27,* 617–625.

Littrell, J. (1998). Is the reexperience of painful emotion therapeutic? *Clinical Psychology Review, 18,* 71–102.

Litz, B. T., Schlenger, W. E., Weathers, F. W., Caddell, J. M., Fairbank, J. A., & LaVange, L. M. (1997). Predictors of emotional numbing in posttraumatic stress disorder. *Journal of Traumatic Stress, 10,* 607–618.

Livesley, W. J., Jackson, D. N., & Schroeder, M. L. (1992). Factorial structure of traits delineating personality disorders in clinical and general population samples. *Journal of Abnormal Psychology, 101,* 432–440.

Loewenstein, R. J. (1991). Psychogenic amnesia and psychogenic fugue: Comprehensive review. In A. Tasman & S. M. Goldfinger (Eds.), *American Psychiatric Press review of psychiatry* (Vol. 10, pp. 189–221). Washington, DC: American Psychiatric Press.

Loewenstein, R. J. (1996). Dissociative amnesia and dissociative fugue. In L. K. Michelson & W. J. Ray (Eds.), *Handbook of dissociation: Theoretical, empirical, and clinical perspectives* (pp. 307–336). New York: Plenum.

Loftus, E. F. (1993). The reality of repressed memories. *American Psychologist, 48,* 518–537.

Loftus, E. F., & Loftus, G. R. (1980). On the permanence of stored information in the human brain. *American Psychologist, 35,* 409–420.

Loftus, E. F., Polansky, S., & Fullilove, M. T. (1994). Memories of childhood sexual abuse: Remembering and repressing. *Psychology of Women Quarterly, 18,* 67–84.

Loftus, E. F., & Rosenwald, L. A. (1993). Buried memories, shattered lives. *American Bar Association Journal, 79,* 70–73.

Lohr, J. M., Tolin, D. F., & Lilienfeld, S. O. (1998). Efficacy of Eye Movement Desensitization and Reprocessing: Implications for behavior therapy. *Behavior Therapy, 29,* 123–156.

Lubin, H., & Johnson, D. R. (1997). Interactive psychoeducational group therapy for traumatized women. *International Journal of Group Psychotherapy, 47,* 271–290.

Lubin, H., Loris, M., Burt, J., & Johnson, D. R. (1998). Efficacy of psychoeducational group therapy in reducing symptoms of posttraumatic stress disorder among multiply traumatized women. *American Journal of Psychiatry, 155,* 1172–1177.

Luborsky, L. (1976). Helping alliances in psychotherapy. In J. L. Claghorn (Ed.), *Successful psychotherapy* (pp. 92–116). New York: Brunner/Mazel.

Luborsky, L., Crits-Christoph, P., Alexander, L., Margolis, M., & Cohen, M. (1983). Two helping alliance methods for predicting outcomes of psychotherapy: A counting signs vs. a global rating method. *Journal of Nervous and Mental Disease, 171,* 480–491.

Ludwig, A. M. (1983). The psychobiological functions of dissociation. *American Journal of Clinical Hypnosis, 26,* 93–99.

Lumley, M. A., Stettner, L., & Wehmer, F. (1996). How are alexithymia and physical illness linked? A review and critique of pathways. *Journal of Psychosomatic Research, 41,* 505–518.

Luntz, B. K., & Widom, C. S. (1994). Antisocial personality disorder in abused and neglected children grown up. *American Journal of Psychiatry, 151,* 670–674.

Lynch, M., & Cicchetti, D. (1998). An ecological–transactional analysis of children and contexts: The longitudinal interplay among child maltreatment, community violence and children's symptomatology. *Development and psychopathology, 10,* 235–257.

Lynn, S. J., & Rhue, J. W. (1988). Fantasy proneness: Hypnosis, developmental antecedents, and psychopathology. *American Psychologist, 43,* 35–44.

Lyons, J. A., & Keane, T. M. (1989). Implosive therapy for the treatment of combat-related PTSD. *Journal of Traumatic Stress, 2,* 137–152.

Lyons, M. J., Goldberg, J., Eisen, S. A., True, W., Tsuang, M. T., Meyer, J. M., & Henderson, W. G. (1993). Do genes influence exposure to trauma? A twin study of combat. *American Journal of Medical Genetics (Neuropsychiatric Genetics), 48,* 22–27.

Lyons-Ruth, K., & Block, D. (1996). The disturbed caregiving system: Relations among childhood trauma, maternal caregiving, and infant affect and attachment. *Infant Mental Health Journal, 17,* 257–275.

Lyons-Ruth, K., Bronfman, E., & Atwood, G. (1999). A relational diathesis model of hostile–helpless states of mind: Expressions in mother–infant interaction. In

J. Solomon & C. George (Eds.), *Attachment disorganization* (pp. 33–70). New York: Guilford.

Lyons-Ruth, K., & Jacobvitz, D. (1999). Attachment disorganization: Unresolved loss, relational violence, and lapses in behavioral and attentional strategies. In J. Cassidy & P. R. Shaver (Eds.), *Handbook of attachment: Theory, research, and clinical applications* (pp. 520–554). New York: Guilford.

Lystad, M., Rice, M., & Kaplan, S. J. (1996). Domestic violence. In S. J. Kaplan & H. A. Davidson (Eds.), *Family violence: A clinical and legal guide* (pp. 139–180). Washington, DC: American Psychiatric Press.

MacCarthy, D. (1979). Recognition of signs of emotional deprivation: A form of child abuse. *Child Abuse and Neglect, 3,* 423–428.

Macklin, M. L., Metzger, L. J., Lasko, N. B., Berry, N. J., Orr, S. P., & Pitman, R. K. (2000). Five-year follow-up study of Eye Movement Desensitization and Reprocessing therapy for combat-related posttraumatic stress disorder. *Comprehensive Psychiatry, 41,* 24–27.

Mackner, L. M., Starr, R. H., & Black, M. M. (1997). The cumulative effect of neglect and failure to thrive on cognitive functioning. *Child Abuse and Neglect, 21,* 691–700.

MacLean, P. D. (1985). Brain evolution relating to family, play, and the separation call. *Archives of General Psychiatry, 42,* 405–417.

MacLean, P. D. (1990). *The triune brain in evolution: Role in paleocerebral functions.* New York: Plenum.

MacMillan, H. L., Fleming, J. E., Trocme, N., Boyle, M. H., Wong, M., Racine, Y. A., Beardslee, W., & Offord, D. R. (1997). Prevalence of child physical and sexual abuse in the community. *Journal of the American Medical Association, 278,* 131–135.

Maes, M., Lin, A., Verkerk, R., Delmeire, L., Gastel, A. V., Van der Planken, M., & Scharpe, S. (1999). Serotonergic and noradrenergic markers of post-traumatic stress disorder with and without major depression. *Neuropsychopharmacology, 20,* 188–197.

Maestripieri, D., Schino, G., Aureli, F., & Troisi, A. (1992). A modest proposal: Displacement activities as an indicator of emotions in primates. *Animal Behaviour, 44,* 967–979.

Magarions, A. M., McEwen, B. S., Flugge, G., & Fuchs, E. (1996). Chronic psychosocial stress causes apical dendritic atrophy of hippocampal CA3 pyramidal neurons in subordinate tree shrews. *Journal of Neuroscience, 16,* 3534–3540.

Mahoney, P., & Williams, L. M. (1998). Sexual assault in marriage: Prevalence, consequences, and treatment of wife rape. In J. L. Jasinski & L. M. Williams (Eds.), *Partner violence: A comprehensive review of 20 years of research* (pp. 113–161). Thousand Oaks, CA: Sage.

Main, M. (1995a). Discourse, prediction, and recent studies in attachment: Implications for psychoanalysis. In T. Shapiro & R. N. Emde (Eds.), *Research in psychoanalysis: Process, development, outcome* (pp. 209–244). Madison, CT: International Universities Press.

Main, M. (1995b). Recent studies in attachment: Overview, with selected implications for clinical work. In S. Goldberg, R. Muir, & J. Kerr (Eds.), *Attachment theory: Social, developmental, and clinical perspectives* (pp. 407–474). Hillsdale, NJ: Analytic Press.

Main, M. (1999). Attachment theory: Eighteen points with suggestions for future studies. In J. Cassidy & P. R. Shaver (Eds.), *Handbook of attachment: Theory, research, and clinical applications* (pp. 845–887). New York: Guilford.

Main, M., & Goldwyn, R. (1994). *Adult attachment scoring and classification systems (unpublished scoring manual).* Berkeley, CA: Department of Psychology, University of California, Berkeley.

Main, M., & Hesse, E. (1990). Parents' unresolved traumatic experiences are related to infant disorganized attachment status: Is frightened and/or frightening parental behavior the linking mechanism? In M. T. Greenberg, D. Cicchetti, & E. M. Cummings (Eds.), *Attachment in the preschool years: Theory, research, and intervention* (pp. 161–182). Chicago: University of Chicago Press.

Main, M., Kaplan, N., & Cassidy, J. (1985). Security in infancy, childhood, and adulthood: A move to the level of representation. In I. Bretherton & E. Waters (Eds.), *Growing points of attachment theory and research (Monographs of the Society for Research in Child Development)* (Vol. 50, 1–2, Serial No. 209, pp. 66–104). Chicago: University of Chicago Press.

Main, M., & Morgan, H. (1996). Disorganization and disorientation in infant Strange Situation behavior: Phenotypic resemblance to dissociative states. In L. K. Michelson & W. J. Ray (Eds.), *Handbook of dissociation: Theoretical, empirical, and clinical perspectives* (pp. 107–138). New York: Plenum.

Main, M., & Solomon, J. (1990). Procedures for identifying infants as disorganized/disoriented during the Ainsworth Strange Situation. In M. T. Greenberg, D. Cicchetti, & E. M. Cummings (Eds.), *Attachment in the preschool years: Theory, research, and intervention* (pp. 121–160). Chicago: University of Chicago Press.

Maker, A. H., Kemmelmeier, M., & Peterson, C. (1998). Long-term psychological consequences in women of witnessing parental physical conflict and experiencing abuse in childhood. *Journal of Interpersonal Violence, 13,* 574–589.

Maldonado, J. R., & Spiegel, D. (1998). Trauma, dissociation, and hypnotizability. In J. D. Bremner & C. R. Marmar (Eds.), *Trauma, memory, and dissociation* (pp. 57–106). Washington, DC: American Psychiatric Press.

Malinosky-Rummell, R., & Hansen, D. J. (1993). Long-term consequences of childhood physical abuse. *Psychological Bulletin, 114,* 68–79.

Mallinckrodt, B., McCreary, B. A., & Robertson, A. K. (1995). Co-occurrence of eating disorders and incest: The role of attachment, family environment, and social competencies. *Journal of Counseling Psychology, 42,* 178–186.

Maltas, C., & Shay, J. (1995). Trauma contagion in partners of survivors of childhood sexual abuse. *American Journal of Orthopsychiatry, 65,* 529–539.

Maltas, C. P. (1996). Reenactment and repair: Couples therapy with survivors of childhood sexual abuse. *Harvard Review of Psychiatry, 3,* 351–355.

Mannion, E., Mueser, K., & Solomon, P. (1994). Designing psychoeducational services for spouses of persons with serious mental illness. *Community Mental Health Journal, 30,* 177–190.

Marans, S., & Adelman, A. (1997). Experiencing violence in a developmental context. In J. Osofsky (Ed.), *Children in a violent society* (pp. 202–222). New York: Guilford.

March, J. S. (1993). What constitutes a stressor? The 'Criterion A' issue. In J. R. T. Davidson & E. B. Foa (Eds.), *Posttraumatic stress disorder: DSM-IV and beyond* (pp. 37–54). Washington, DC: American Psychiatric Press.

Marcus, S. V., Marquis, P., & Sakai, C. (1997). Controlled study of treatment of PTSD using EMDR in an HMO setting. *Psychotherapy, 34,* 307–315.

Markovitz, P. (1995). Pharmacotherapy of impulsivity, aggression, and related disorders. In E. Hollander & D. J. Stein (Eds.), *Impulsivity and aggression* (pp. 263–287). Chichester: Wiley.

Marks, I., Lovell, K., Noshirvani, H., Livanou, M., & Thrasher, S. (1998). Treatment of posttraumatic stress disorder by exposure and/or cognitive restructuring. *Archives of General Psychiatry, 55,* 317–325.

Marmar, C. R., Weiss, D. S., & Metzler, T. J. (1997). The peritraumatic dissociative experiences questionnaire. In J. P. Wilson & T. M. Keane (Eds.), *Assessing psychological trauma and PTSD* (pp. 412–428). New York: Guilford.

Marmar, C. R., Weiss, D. S., Metzler, T. J., & Delucchi, K. (1996). Characteristics of emergency services personnel related to peritraumatic dissociation during critical incident exposure. *American Journal of Psychiatry, 153,* 94–102.

Marmar, C. R., Weiss, D. S., Metzler, T. J., Delucchi, K. L., Best, S. R., & Wentworth, K. A. (1999). Longitudinal course and predictors of continuing distress following critical incident exposure in emergency services personnel. *Journal of Nervous and Mental Disease, 187,* 15–22.

Marmar, C. R., Weiss, D. S., Metzler, T. J., Ronfeldt, H. M., & Foreman, C. (1996). Stress responses of emergency services personnel to the Loma Prieta earthquake inter-state 880 freeway collapse and control traumatic incidents. *Journal of Traumatic Stress, 9,* 63–85.

Marmar, C. R., Weiss, D. S., Schlenger, W. E., Fairbank, J. A., Jordan, B. K., Kulka, R. A., & Hough, R. L. (1994). Peritraumatic dissociation and posttraumatic stress in male Vietnam theater veterans. *American Journal of Psychiatry, 151,* 902–907.

Marmar, S. S., & Fink, D. (1994). Rethinking the comparison of borderline personal-ity disorder and multiple personality disorder. *Psychiatric Clinics of North America, 17,* 743–771.

Marsh, D. T., & Johnson, D. L. (1997). The family experience of mental illness: Implications for intervention. *Professional Psychology: Research and Practice, 28,* 229–237.

Marshall, R. D., Davidson, J. R. T., & Yehuda, R. (1998). Pharmacotherapy in the treat-ment of posttraumatic stress disorder and other trauma-related syndromes. In R. Yehuda (Ed.), *Psychological trauma* (pp. 133–177). Washington, DC: American Psychiatric Press.

Marshall, R. D., Spitzer, R., & Liebowitz, M. R. (1999). Review and critique of the new DSM-IV diagnosis of acute stress disorder. *American Journal of Psychiatry, 156,* 1677–1685.

Mason, J. W., Wang, S., Yehuda, R., Bremner, J. D., Riney, S. J., Lubin, H., Johnson, D. R., Southwick, S. M., & Charney, D. S. (1995). Some approaches to the study of the clinical implications of thyroid alterations in post-traumatic stress disorder. In M. J. Friedman, D. S. Charney, & A. Y. Deutch (Eds.), *Neurobiological and clinical consequences of stress: From normal adaptation to post-traumatic stress disorder* (pp. 367–379). Philadelphia: Lippincott-Raven.

Masserman, J. H. (1943). *Behavior and neurosis: An experimental psychoanalytic approach to psychobiologic principles.* Chicago: University of Chicago Press.

Matsakis, A. (1996). *Vietnam wives: Facing the challenges of life with veterans suffering post-traumatic stress.* Lutherville, MD: Sidran.

Mayne, T. J., & Ambrose, T. K. (1999). Research review on anger in psychotherapy. *Journal of Clinical Psychology, 55,* 353–363.

McCabe, P. M., & Schneiderman, N. (1985). Physiological reactions to stress. In N. Schneiderman & J. T. Tapp (Eds.), *Behavioral medicine: The biopsychosocial approach* (pp. 99–131). Hillsdale, NJ: Erlbaum.

McCann, L., & Pearlman, L. A. (1990). Vicarious traumatization: A framework for understanding the psychological effects of working with victims. *Journal of Traumatic Stress, 3,* 131–149.

McCarthy, G., & Taylor, A. (1999). Avoidant/ambivalent attachment style as a mediator between abusive childhood experiences and adult relationship difficulties. *Journal of Child Psychology and Psychiatry, 40,* 465–477.

McCauley, J., Kern, D. E., Kolodner, K., Dill, L., Schroeder, A. F., DeChant, H. K., Ryden, J., Derogatis, L. R., & Bass, E. B. (1997). Clinical characteristics of women with a history of childhood abuse. *Journal of American Medical Association, 277,* 1362–1368.

McEwen, B. S. (1995). Adrenal steroid actions on brain: Dissecting the fine line between protection and damage. In M. J. Friedman, D. S. Charney, & A. Y. Deutch (Eds.), *Neurobiological and clinical consequences of stress: From normal adaptation to posttraumatic stress disorder* (pp. 135–147). New York: Lippincott-Raven.

McEwen, B. S., & Magarinos, A. M. (1997). Stress effects on morphology and function of the hippocampus. In R. Yehuda & A. C. MacFarlane (Eds.), *Psychobiology of posttraumatic stress disorder* (Vol. 821, pp. 271–284). New York: New York Academy of Sciences.

McFarlane, A. C. (1994). Individual psychotherapy for post-traumatic stress disorder. *Psychiatric Clinics of North America, 17,* 393–408.

McFarlane, A. C. (1997). The prevalence and longitudinal course of PTSD: Implications for neurophysiological models of PTSD. In R. Yehuda & A. C. McFarlane (Eds.), *Psychobiology of posttraumatic stress disorder* (Vol. 821, pp. 10–23). New York: New York Academy of Sciences.

McFarlane, A. C. (1998). Epidemiological evidence about the relationship between PTSD and alcohol abuse: The nature of the association. *Addictive Behaviors, 23,* 813–825.

McFarlane, A. C., & De Girolamo, G. (1996). The nature of traumatic stressors and the epidemiology of posttraumatic reactions. In B. A. van der Kolk, A. C. McFarlane, & L. Weisaeth (Eds.), *Traumatic stress: The effects of overwhelming experience on mind, body, and society* (pp. 129–154). New York: Guilford.

McFarlane, A. C., & van der Kolk, B. A. (1996). Conclusions and further directions. In B. A. van der Kolk, A. C. McFarlane, & L. Weisaeth (Eds.), *Traumatic stress: The effects of overwhelming experience on mind, body, and society* (pp. 559–575). New York: Guilford.

McGaugh, J. L. (1995). Emotional activation, neuromodulatory systems, and memory. In D. L. Schacter (Ed.), *Memory distortion: How minds, brains, and societies reconstruct the past* (pp. 255–273). Cambridge, MA: Harvard University Press.

McGaugh, J. L., Introini-Collison, I. B., Cahill, L., Kim, M., & Liang, K. C. (1992). Involvement of the amygdala in neuromodulatory influences on memory storage. In J. P. Aggleton (Ed.), *The amygdala: Neurobiological aspects of emotion, memory, and mental dysfunction* (pp. 431–451). New York: Wiley.

McGee, R. A., & Wolfe, D. A. (1991). Psychological maltreatment: Toward an operational definition. *Development and Psychopathology, 3,* 3–18.

McHugh, P. R. (1995a). Affirmative rebuttal. *Journal of the American Academy of Child and Adolescent Psychiatry, 34,* 962–963.

McHugh, P. R. (1995b). Resolved: Multiple personality disorder is an individually and socially created artifact: Affirmative. *Journal of the Academy of Child and Adolescent Psychiatry, 34,* 957–959.

McNally, R. J. (1999a). EMDR and Mesmerism: A comparative historical analysis. *Journal of Anxiety Disorders, 13,* 225–236.

McNally, R. J. (1999b). On eye movements and animal magnetism: A reply to Greenwald's defense of EMDR. *Journal of Anxiety Disorders, 13,* 617–620.

McNally, R. J., & Ricciardi, J. N. (1996). Suppression of negative and neutral thoughts. *Behavioural and Cognitive Psychotherapy, 24,* 17–25.

McWhirter, P. T. (1999). Domestic violence in Chile—La violencia privada. *American Psychologist, 54,* 37–40.

Mead, G. H. (1934). *Mind, self, and society.* Chicago: University of Chicago Press.

Meadows, E. A., & Foa, E. B. (1998). Intrusion, arousal, and avoidance: Sexual trauma survivors. In V. M. Follette, J. I. Ruzek, & F. R. Abueg (Eds.), *Cognitive-behavioral therapies for trauma* (pp. 100–123). New York: Guilford.

Meichenbaum, D. (1994). *A clinical handbook/practical therapist manual for assessing and treating adults with posttraumatic stress disorder (PTSD)*. Waterloo, Ontario: Institute Press.

Meissner, W. W. (1978). *The paranoid process*. New York: Aronson.

Mellman, T. A., & Davis, G., C. (1985). Combat-related flashbacks in posttraumatic stress disorder: Phenomenology and similarity to panic attacks. *Journal of Clinical Psychiatry, 46*, 379–382.

Mellman, T. A., Kulick-Bell, R., Ashlock, L. E., & Nolan, B. (1995). Sleep events among veterans with combat-related posttraumatic stress disorder. *American Journal of Psychiatry, 152*, 110–115.

Melson, G. F. (1988). Studying children's attachment to their pets: A conceptual and methodological review. *Anthrozoos, 4*, 91–99.

Menninger, K. (1963). *The vital balance*. New York: Viking Press.

Menninger, K. A. (1938). *Man against himself*. New York: Harcourt, Brace.

Merskey, H. (1992). The manufacture of personalities: The production of multiple personality disorder. *British Journal of Psychiatry, 160*, 327–340.

Michelson, D., Licinio, J., & Gold, P. W. (1995). Mediation of the stress response by the hypothalamic–pituitary–adrenal axis. In M. J. Friedman, D. S. Charney, & A. Y. Deutch (Eds.), *Neurobiological and clinical consequences of stress: From normal adaptation to post-traumatic stress disorder* (pp. 225–238). Philadelphia: Lippincott-Raven.

Michelson, L., June, K., Vives, A., Testa, S., & Marchione, N. (1998). The role of trauma and dissociation in cognitive-behavioral psychotherapy outcome and maintenance for panic disorder with agoraphobia. *Behaviour Research and Therapy, 36*, 1011–1050.

Miller, L. (1998). Our own medicine: Traumatized psychotherapists and the stresses of doing therapy. *Psychotherapy, 35*, 137–146.

Miller, S. D., & Triggiano, P. J. (1992). The psychophysiological investigation of multiple personality disorder: Review and update. *American Journal of Clinical Hypnosis, 35*, 47–61.

Millon, T. (1996). *Disorders of personality: DSM-IV and beyond*. New York: Wiley.

Mischel, W. (1996). From good intentions to willpower. In P. M. Gollwitzer & J. A. Bargh (Eds.), *The psychology of action: Linking cognition and motivation to behavior* (pp. 197–218). New York: Guilford.

Mitchell, J. T., & Everly, G. S. (1995). *Critical incident stress debriefing: An operations manual for the prevention of traumatic stress among emergency services and disaster workers* (2nd edn.). Ellicott City, MD: Chevron.

Modell, A. H. (1991). A confusion of tongues or whose reality is it? *Psychoanalytic Quarterly, 60*, 227–244.

Modestin, J., Ebner, G., Junghan, M., & Erni, T. (1996). Dissociative experience and dissociative disorders in acute psychiatric inpatients. *Comprehensive Psychiatry, 37*, 355–361.

Modestin, J., Oberson, B., & Erni, T. (1998). Possible antecedents of DSM-III-R personality disorders. *Acta Psychiatrica Scandinavica, 97*, 260–266.

Mollon, P. (1998). *Remembering trauma: A psychotherapist's guide to memory and illusion*. Chichester: Wiley.

Monroe, S. M., & Steiner, S. (1986). Social support and psychopathology: Interrelations with preexisting disorder, stress, and personality. *Journal of Abnormal Psychology, 95*, 29–39.

Montgomery, R. W., & Ayllon, T. (1994). Eye movement desensitization across subjects: Subjective and physiological measures of treatment efficacy. *Journal of Behavior Therapy and Experimental Psychiatry, 25*, 217–230.

Montgomery, S. A. (1997). Suicide in chronic and recurrent depressions. In H. S. Akiskal & G. B. Cassano (Eds.), *Dysthymia and the spectrum of chronic depressions* (pp. 191–197). New York: Guilford.

Moran, P. M., Bifulco, A., Ball, C., & Jacobs, C. (2000). Psychological abuse in childhood I: Definition and measurement. *Submitted for publication.*

Morgan, H. G., Burns-Cox, C. J., Pocock, H., & Pottle, S. (1975). Deliberate self-harm: Clinical and socio-economic characteristics of 368 patients. *British Journal of Psychiatry, 127,* 564–574.

Morton, J. (1991). Cognitive pathologies of memory: A headed records analysis. In W. Kessen, A. Ortony, & F. Craik (Eds.), *Memories, thoughts, and emotions: Essays in honor of George Mandler* (pp. 199–210). Hillsdale, NJ: Erlbaum.

Morton, J. (1994). Cognitive perspectives on memory recovery. *Applied Cognitive Psychology, 8,* 389–398.

Morton, J., Andrews, B., Bekerian, D., Brewin, C., & Mollon, P. (1996). Recovered memories: The report of the working party of the British Psychological Society. In K. Pezdek & W. P. Banks (Eds.), *The recovered memory/false memory debate* (pp. 373–392). New York: Academic Press.

Moscovitch, M. (1994). Memory and working with memory: Evaluation of a component process model and comparisons with other models. In D. L. Schacter & E. Tulving (Eds.), *Memory systems 1994* (pp. 269–310). Cambridge, MA: MIT Press.

Moscovitch, M. (1995). Confabulation. In D. L. Schacter (Ed.), *Memory distortion: How minds, brains, and societies reconstruct the past* (pp. 226–251). Cambridge, MA: Harvard University Press.

Mueser, K. T., Goodman, L. B., Trumbetta, S. L., Rosenberg, S. D., Osher, F. C., Vidaver, R., Auciello, P., & Foy, D. W. (1998). Trauma and posttraumatic stress disorder in severe mental illness. *Journal of Consulting and Clinical Psychology, 66,* 493–499.

Mulder, R. T., Beautrais, A. L., Joyce, P. R., & Fergusson, D. M. (1998). Relationship between dissociation, childhood sexual abuse, childhood physical abuse, and mental illness in a general population sample. *American Journal of Psychiatry, 155,* 806–811.

Muller, R. T. (2000). Relationship between attachment style and posttraumatic stress symptomatology among adults who report the experience of childhood abuse. *Journal of Traumatic Stress, 13,* 321–332.

Munich, R. L. (1996). Contemporary treatment of schizophrenia. *Bulletin of the Menninger Clinic, 61,* 189–221.

Munroe, J. F., Shay, J., Fisher, L., Makary, C., Rapperport, K., & Zimering, R. (1995). Preventing compassion fatigue: A team treatment model. In C. R. Figley (Ed.), *Compassion fatigue: Coping with secondary traumatic stress disorder in those who treat the traumatized* (pp. 209–231). New York: Brunner/Mazel.

Murburg, M. M. (Ed.). (1994). *Catecholamine function in posttraumatic stress disorder: Emerging concepts.* Washington, DC: American Psychiatric Press.

Murburg, M. M., Ashleigh, E. A., Hommer, D. W., & Veith, R. C. (1994). Biology of catecholaminergic systems and their relevance to PTSD. In M. M. Murburg (Ed.), *Catecholamine function in posttraumatic stress disorder: Emerging concepts* (pp. 3–15). Washington, DC: American Psychiatric Press.

Murdoch, M., & Nichols, K. (1995). Women veterans' experiences with domestic violence and sexual harassment while in the military. *Archives of Family Medicine, 4,* 411–418.

Murphy, L., Pynoos, R. S., & James, C. B. (1997). The trauma/grief focused group psychotherapy module of an elementary school-based violence prevention/intervention program. In J. Osofsky (Ed.), *Children in a violent society* (pp. 223–255). New York: Guilford.

Muscat, R., Papp, M., & Willner, P. (1992). Antidepressant-like effects of dopamine agonists in an animal model of depression. *Biological Psychiatry, 31,* 937–946.

Nader, K., & Pynoos, R. S. (1993). School disaster: Planning and initial interventions. *Journal of Social Behavior and Personality, 8,* 299–320.

Nader, K. O. (1998). Violence: Effects of parent's previous trauma on currently trau-matized children. In Y. Danieli (Ed.), *International handbook of multigenerational legacies of trauma* (pp. 571–583). New York: Plenum.

Najavits, L. M., Gastfriend, D. R., Barber, J. P., Reif, S., Muenz, L. R., Blaine, J., Frank, A., Crits-Christoph, P., Thase, M., & Weiss, R. D. (1998). Cocaine dependence with and without PTSD among subjects in the National Institute on Drug Abuse Collaborative Cocaine Treatment Study. *American Journal of Psychiatry, 155,* 214–219.

Najavits, L. M., Weiss, R. D., Shaw, S. R., & Muenz, L. R. (1998). 'Seeking safety': Outcome of a new cognitive-behavioral psychotherapy for women with posttrau-matic stress disorder and substance dependence. *Journal of Traumatic Stress, 11,* 437–456.

Nash, M. R., Hulsey, T. L., Sexton, M. C., Harralson, T. L., & Lambert, W. (1993a). Long-term sequelae of childhood sexual abuse: Perceived family environment, psychopathology, and dissociation. *Journal of Consulting and Clinical Psychology, 61,* 276–283.

Nash, M. R., Hulsey, T. L., Sexton, M. C., Harralson, T. L., & Lambert, W. (1993b). Reply to comment by Briere and Elliott. *Journal of Consulting and Clinical Psychol-ogy, 61,* 289–290.

Nathan, D. M. (1997). *Diabetes.* New York: Random House.

Nathanson, D. L. (1992). *Shame and pride: Affect, sex, and the birth of the self.* New York: W. W. Norton.

Nayak, M. B., Resnick, H. S., & Holmes, M. M. (1999). Treating health concerns within the context of childhood sexual assault: A case study. *Journal of Traumatic Stress, 12,* 101–109.

Neese, R. M. (2000). Is depression an adaptation? *Archives of General Psychiatry, 57,* 14–20.

Neisser, U. (1986). Nested structure in autobiographical memory. In D. C. Rubin (Ed.), *Autobiographical memory* (pp. 71–81). New York: Cambridge University Press.

Neisser, U. (1988a). Five kinds of self-knowledge. *Philosophical Psychology, 1,* 35–59.

Neisser, U. (1988b). Time present and time past. In M. M. Gruneberg, P. E. Morris, & R. N. Sykes (Eds.), *Practical aspects of memory: Current research and issues* (pp. 545–560). New York: Wiley.

Nelsen, J. C. (1994). One partner impaired: Implications for couple treatment. *Family Therapy, 21,* 185–196.

Nelson, B. S., & Wright, D. W. (1996). Understanding and treating post-traumatic stress disorder symptoms in female partners of veterans with PTSD. *Journal of Marital and Family Therapy, 22,* 455–467.

Nelson, C. A., & Carver, L. J. (1998). The effects of stress and trauma on brain and memory: A view from developmental cognitive neuroscience. *Development and Psychopathology, 10,* 793–809.

Nelson, D. E., Higginson, G. K., & Grant-Worley, J. A. (1995). Physical abuse among high school students: Prevalence and correlation with other health behaviors. *Archives of Pediatric and Adolescent Medicine, 149,* 1254–1258.

Nelson, K. (1993). The psychological and social origins of autobiographical memory. *Psychological Science, 4,* 7–14.

Newman, L. S., & Baumeister, R. F. (1998). Abducted by aliens: Spurious memories of interplanetary masochism. In S. J. Lynn & K. M. McConkey (Eds.), *Truth in memory* (pp. 284–303). New York: Guilford.

Nijenhuis, E. R. S., Spinhoven, P., van Dyck, R., van der Hart, O., & Vanderlinden, J. (1999). Degree of somatoform and psychological dissociation in dissociative dis-order is correlated with reported trauma. *Journal of Traumatic Stress, 11,* 711–730.

Nijenhuis, E. R. S., Spinhoven, P., Vanderlinden, J., van Dyck, R., & van der Hart, O. (1998). Somatoform dissociative symptoms as related to animal defensive reactions to predatory imminence and injury. *Journal of Abnormal Psychology, 107*, 63–73.

Nijenhuis, E. R. S., Vanderlinden, J., & Spinhoven, P. (1998). Animal defensive reactions as a model for trauma-induced dissociative reactions. *Journal of Traumatic Stress, 11*, 243–260.

Ninan, P. T., Insel, T. M., Cohen, R. M., Cook, J. M., Skolnick, P., & Paul, S. M. (1982). Benzodiazepine receptor-mediated experimental 'anxiety' in primates. *Science, 218*, 1332–1334.

Nishith, P., Mechanic, M. B., & Resick, P. A. (2000). Prior interpersonal trauma: The contribution to current PTSD symptoms in female rape victims. *Journal of Abnormal Psychology, 109*, 20–25.

Norman, D. A., & Shallice, T. (1986). Attention to action: Willed and automatic control of behavior. In R. J. Davidson, G. E. Schwartz, & D. Shapiro (Eds.), *Consciousness and self-regulation: Advances in research and theory* (Vol. 4, pp. 1–18). New York: Plenum.

Norris, F. (1992). Epidemiology of trauma: Frequency and impact of different potentially traumatic events on different demographic groups. *Journal of Clinical and Consulting Psychology, 60*, 409–418.

North, C. S., Smith, E. M., & Spitznagel, E. L. (1997). One-year follow-up of survivors of a mass shooting. *American Journal of Psychiatry, 154*, 1696–1702.

Novaco, R. W., & Chemtob, C. M. (1998). Anger and trauma: Conceptualization, assessment, and treatment. In V. M. Follette, J. I. Ruzek, & F. R. Abueg (Eds.), *Cognitive-behavioral therapies for trauma* (pp. 162–190). New York: Guilford.

Novotny, P. (1972). Self-cutting. *Bulletin of the Menninger Clinic, 36*, 505–514.

Nuttall, R., & Jackson, H. (1994). Personal history of childhood abuse among clinicians. *Child Abuse and Neglect, 18*, 455–472.

Ogden, T. H. (1985). On potential space. *International Journal of Psycho-Analysis, 66*, 129–141.

O'Hagan, K. P. (1995). Emotional and psychological abuse: Problems of definition. *Child Abuse and Neglect, 19*, 449–461.

Oldham, J. M., Skodol, A. E., Kellman, H. D., Hyler, S. E., Rosnick, L., & Davies, M. (1992). Diagnosis of DSM-III-R personality disorders by two structured interviews: Patterns of comorbidity. *American Journal of Psychiatry, 149*, 213–220.

O'Leary, K. M., & Cowdry, R. W. (1994). Neuropsychological testing results in borderline personality disorder. In K. R. Silk (Ed.), *Biological and neurobehavioral studies of borderline personality disorder* (pp. 127–157). Washington, DC: American Psychiatric Press.

Olio, K. A. (1996). Are 25% of clinicians using potentially risky therapeutic practices? A review of the logic and methodology of the Poole, Lindsay et al. study. *Journal of Psychiatry and Law, 24*, 277–298.

Oliver, J. E. (1993). Intergenerational transmission of child abuse: Rates, research, and clinical implications. *American Journal of Psychiatry, 150*, 1315–1324.

Olson, D. H., Lavee, Y., & McCubbin, H. I. (1988). Types of families and family response to stress across the family life cycle. In D. M. Klein & J. Aldous (Eds.), *Social stress and family development* (pp. 16–43). New York: Guilford.

Osofsky, J. (1997a). Children and youth violence: An overview of the issues. In J. Osofsky (Ed.), *Children in a violent society* (pp. 3–8). New York: Guilford.

Osofsky, J. (1997b). The violence intervention project for children and families. In J. Osofsky (Ed.), *Children in a violent society* (pp. 256–260). New York: Guilford.

Osofsky, J. D. (1995). Children who witness domestic violence: The invisible victims. *Social Policy Report of the Society for Research in Child Development, 9*(3), 1–16.

Osuch, E. A., Noll, J. G., & Putnam, F. W. (1999). The motivations for self-injury in psychiatric inpatients. *Psychiatry, 62,* 334–346.

Panksepp, J., Nelson, E., & Bekkedal, M. (1999). Brain systems for the mediation of social separation-distress and social-reward: Evolutionary antecedents and neuropeptide intermediaries. In C. S. Carter, I. I. Lederhendler, & B. Kirkpatrick (Eds.), *The integrative neurobiology of affiliation* (pp. 221–243). Cambridge, MA: MIT Press.

Pao, P.-N. (1969). The syndrome of delicate self-cutting. *British Journal of Medical Psychiatry, 42,* 195–206.

Parens, H. (1992). A view of the development of hostility in early life. In T. Shapiro & R. N. Emde (Eds.), *Affect: Psychoanalytic perspectives* (pp. 75–108). Madison, CT: International Universities Press.

Parens, H. (1993). Rage toward self and others in early childhood. In R. A. Glick & S. P. Roose (Eds.), *Rage, power, and aggression* (pp. 123–147). New Haven, CT: Yale University Press.

Paris, J. (1994). *Borderline personality disorder: A multidimensional approach.* Washington, DC: American Psychiatric Press.

Paris, J. (1997). Childhood trauma as an etiological factor in the personality disorders. *Journal of Personality Disorders, 11,* 34–49.

Paris, J. (1998a). Does childhood trauma cause personality disorder in adults? *Canadian Journal of Psychiatry, 43,* 148–153.

Paris, J. (1998b). Psychotherapy for the personality disorders: Working with traits. *Bulletin of the Menninger Clinic, 62,* 287–297.

Park, L. C., Imboden, J. B., Park, T. J., Hulse, S. H., & Unger, H. T. (1992). Giftedness and psychological abuse in borderline personality disorder: Their relevance to genesis and treatment. *Journal of Personality Disorders, 6,* 226–240.

Parker, G., & Barrett, E. (2000). Personality and personality disorder: Current issues and directions. *Psychological Medicine, 30,* 1–9.

Patrick, M., Hobson, R. P., Castle, D., Howard, R., & Maughan, B. (1994). Personality disorder and the mental representation of early experience. *Development and Psychopathology, 6,* 375–388.

Pattison, E. M., & Kahan, J. (1983). The deliberate self-harm syndrome. *American Journal of Psychiatry, 140,* 867–872.

Paulsen, S. (1995). Eye Movement Desensitization and Reprocessing: Its cautious use in the dissociative disorders. *Dissociation, 8,* 32–44.

Payne, D. G., & Blackwell, J. M. (1998). Truth in memory: Caveat emptor. In S. J. Lynn & K. M. McConkey (Eds.), *Truth in memory* (pp. 32–61). New York: Guilford.

Pearlman, L. A., & MacIan, P. S. (1995). Vicarious traumatization: An empirical study of the effects of trauma work on trauma therapists. *Professional Psychology: Research and Practice, 26,* 558–565.

Pearlman, L. A., & Saakvitne, K. W. (1995a). *Trauma and the therapist: Countertransference and vicarious traumatization in psychotherapy with incest survivors.* New York: W. W. Norton.

Pearlman, L. A., & Saakvitne, K. W. (1995b). Treating therapists with vicarious traumatization and secondary traumatic stress disorders. In C. R. Figley (Ed.), *Compassion fatigue: Coping with secondary traumatic stress disorder in those who treat the traumatized* (pp. 150–177). New York: Brunner/Mazel.

Peebles, M. J. (1989). Through a glass darkly: The psychoanalytic use of hypnosis with post-traumatic stress disorder. *International Journal of Clinical and Experimental Hypnosis, 37,* 192–206.

Peniston, E. G., & Kulkosky, P. J. (1991). Alpha–theta brainwave neuro-feedback for Vietnam veterans with combat-related post-traumatic stress disorder. *Medical Psychotherapy, 4,* 1–14.

Peniston, E. G., Marrinan, D. A., Deming, W. A., & Kulkosky, P. J. (1993). EEG alpha–theta brainwave synchronization in Vietnam theater veterans with post-traumatic stress disorder and alcohol abuse. *Advances in Medical Psychotherapy, 6,* 37–50.

Pennebaker, J. W. (1997). Writing about emotional experiences as a therapeutic process. *Psychological Science, 8,* 162–166.

Perry, B. (1997). Incubated in terror: Neurodevelopmental factors in the 'cycle of violence'. In J. Osofsky (Ed.), *Children in a violent society* (pp. 124–149). New York: Guilford.

Perry, B. D. (1994). Neurobiological sequelae of childhood trauma: PTSD in children. In M. M. Murburg (Ed.), *Catecholamine function in posttraumatic stress disorder* (pp. 233–255). Washington, DC: American Psychiatric Press.

Perry, B. D., Pollard, R. A., Blakley, T. L., Baker, W. L., & Vigilante, D. (1995). Child-hood trauma, the neurobiology of adaptation, and 'use-dependent' development of the brain: How 'states' become 'traits'. *Infant Mental Health Journal, 16,* 271–289.

Perry, J. C., Banon, E., & Ianni, F. (1999). Effectiveness of psychotherapy for person-ality disorders. *American Journal of Psychiatry, 156,* 1312–1321.

Pescosolido, F. J. (1993). Clinical considerations related to victimization dynamics and post-traumatic stress in the group treatment of sexually abused boys. *Journal of Child and Adolescent Group Therapy, 3,* 49–73.

Peterson, J. A. (1996). Hypnotherapeutic techniques to facilitate psychotherapy with PTSD and dissociative clients. In L. K. Michelson & W. J. Ray (Eds.), *Handbook of dissociation: Theoretical, empirical, and clinical perspectives* (pp. 449–474). New York: Plenum.

Pezdek, K., Finger, K., & Hodge, D. (1997). Planting false childhood memories: The role of event plausibility. *Psychological Science, 8,* 437–441.

Pfefferbaum, B., & Allen, J. (1998). Stress in children exposed to violence: Reenact-ment and rage. *Child and Adolescent Clinics of North America, 7,* 121–136.

Phillips, K. A., Gunderson, J. G., Triebwasser, J., Kimble, C. R., Faedda, G., Lyoo, I. K., & Renn, J. (1998). Reliability and validity of depressive personality disorder. *American Journal of Psychiatry, 155,* 1044–1048.

Piaget, J. (1962). *Play, dreams and imitation in childhood* (C. Gattegno & F. M. Hodgson, Trans.). New York: Norton.

Pilkonis, P. A., Kim, Y., Proietti, J. M., & Barkham, M. (1996). Scales for personality disorders developed from the Inventory of Interpersonal Problems. *Journal of Personality Disorders, 10,* 355–369.

Pillemer, D. B. (1998). *Momentous events, vivid memories.* Cambridge, MA: Harvard University Press.

Pillemer, D. B., & White, S. H. (1989). Childhood events recalled by children and adults. In H. W. Reese (Ed.), *Advances in child development and behavior* (Vol. 21, pp. 297–340). New York: Academic Press.

Piper, A. J. (1994). Multiple personality disorder. *British Journal of Psychiatry, 164,* 600–612.

Pitman, R. (1990). Self-mutilation in combat-related PTSD [letter]. *American Journal of Psychiatry, 147,* 123–124.

Pitman, R. K., Altman, B., Greenwald, E., Longpre, R. E., Macklin, M. L., Poire, R. E., & Steketee, G. S. (1991). Psychiatric complications during flooding therapy for post-traumatic stress disorder. *Journal of Clinical Psychiatry, 52,* 17–20.

Pitman, R. K., Orr, S. P., Altman, B., Longpre, R. E., Poire, R. E., & Macklin, M. L. (1996). Emotional processing during Eye-Movement Desensitization and Repro-cessing therapy of Vietnam veterans with chronic posttraumatic stress disorder. *Comprehensive Psychiatry, 37,* 419–429.

Pitman, R. K., Orr, S. P., Altman, B., Longpre, R. E., Poire, R. E., Macklin, M. L., Michaels, M. J., & Steketee, G. S. (1996). Emotional processing and outcome of imaginal flooding therapy in Vietnam veterans with chronic posttraumatic stress disorder. *Comprehensive Psychiatry, 37*, 409–418.

Pitman, R. K., Orr, S. P., van der Kolk, B. A., Greenberg, M. S., Meyerhoff, J. L., & Mougey, E. H. (1990). Analgesia: A new dependent variable for the biological study of posttraumatic stress disorder. In M. E. Wolf & A. D. Mosnaim (Eds.), *Posttraumatic stress disorder: Etiology, phenomenology, and treatment* (pp. 140–147). Washington, DC: American Psychiatric Press.

Plakun, E. M. (1998). Enactment and the treatment of abuse survivors. *Harvard Review of Psychiatry, 5*, 318–325.

Plutchik, R. (1962). *The emotions: Facts, theories and a new model.* New York: Random House.

Polan, H. J., & Hofer, M. A. (1999). Psychobiological origins of infant attachment and separation responses. In J. Cassidy & P. R. Shaver (Eds.), *Handbook of attachment: Theory, research, and clinical applications* (pp. 162–180). New York: Guilford.

Polusny, M. A., & Follette, V. M. (1995). Long-term correlates of child sexual abuse: Theory and review of the empirical literature. *Applied and Preventive Psychology, 4*, 143–166.

Polusny, M. A., & Follette, V. M. (1996). Remembering childhood sexual abuse: A national survey of psychologists' clinical practices, beliefs, and personal experiences. *Professional Psychology: Research and Practice, 27*, 41–52.

Poole, D. A., Lindsay, D. S., Memon, A., & Bull, R. (1995). Psychotherapy and the recovery of memories of childhood sexual abuse: U.S. and British practitioners' opinions, practices, and experiences. *Journal of Consulting and Clinical Psychology, 63*, 426–437.

Pope, H. G., & Hudson, J. I. (1992). Is childhood sexual abuse a risk factor for bulimia nervosa? *American Journal of Psychiatry, 149*, 455–463.

Pope, H. G., & Hudson, J. I. (1995). Can memories of childhood sexual abuse be repressed? *Psychological Medicine, 25*, 121–126.

Pope, H. G., Oliva, P. S., Hudson, J. I., Bodkin, J. A., & Gruber, A. J. (1999). Attitudes toward DSM-IV dissociative disorder diagnoses among board-certified American psychiatrists. *American Journal of Psychiatry, 156*, 321–323.

Post, R. M. (1992). Transduction of psychosocial stress into the neurobiology of recurrent affective disorder. *American Journal of Psychiatry, 149*, 999–1010.

Post, R. M., Weiss, S. R. B., Li, H., Smith, M. A., Zang, L. X., Xing, G., Osuch, E. A., & McCann, U. D. (1998). Neural plasticity and emotional memory. *Development and Psychopathology, 10*, 829–855.

Post, R. M., Weiss, S. R. B., Smith, M., Li, H., & McCann, U. (1997). Kindling versus quenching: Implications for the evolution and treatment of posttraumatic stress disorder. In R. Yehuda & A. C. McFarlane (Eds.), *Psychobiology of posttraumatic stress disorder* (Vol. 823, pp. 285–295). New York: New York Academy of Sciences.

Post, R. M., Weiss, S. R. B., & Smith, M. A. (1995). Sensitization and kindling: Implications for the evolving neural substrates of post-traumatic stress disorder. In M. J. Friedman, D. S. Charney, & A. Y. Deutch (Eds.), *Neurobiological and clinical consequences of stress: From normal adaptation to post-traumatic stress disorder* (pp. 203–224). Philadelphia: Lippincott-Raven.

Post, R. M., Weiss, S. R. B., Smith, M. A., & Leverich, G. S. (1996). Impact of psychosocial stress on gene expression: Implications for PTSD and recurrent affective disorder. In T. W. Miller (Ed.), *Theory and assessment of stressful life events* (pp. 37–91). Madison, CT: International Universities Press.

Price, J., Sloman, L., Gardner, R., Gilbert, P., & Rhode, P. (1994). The social competition hypothesis of depression. *British Journal of Psychiatry, 164,* 309–315.

Prince-Embury, S., & Rooney, J. F. (1995). Psychological adaptation among residents following restart of Three Mile Island. *Journal of Traumatic Stress, 8,* 47–59.

Prins, A., Kaloupek, D. G., & Keane, T. M. (1995). Psychophysiological evidence for autonomic arousal and startle in traumatized adult populations. In M. J. Friedman, D. S. Charney, & A. Y. Deutch (Eds.), *Neurobiological and clinical consequences of stress: From normal adaptation to post-traumatic stress disorder* (pp. 291–314). Philadelphia: Lippincott-Raven.

Prothrow-Stith, D. (1991). *Deadly consequences.* New York: HarperCollins.

Pruyser, P. W. (1987). Maintaining hope in adversity. *Bulletin of the Menninger Clinic, 51,* 463–474.

Putnam, F. W. (1988). The switch process in multiple personality disorder and other state-change disorders. *Dissociation, 1,* 24–32.

Putnam, F. W. (1991). Recent research on multiple personality disorder. *Psychiatric Clinics of North America, 14,* 489–502.

Putnam, F. W. (1992). Discussion: Are alter personalities fragments or figments? *Psychoanalytic Inquiry, 12,* 95–111.

Putnam, F. W. (1995a). Negative rebuttal. *Journal of the American Academy of Child and Adolescent Psychiatry, 34,* 963.

Putnam, F. W. (1995b). Resolved: Multiple personality disorder is an individually and socially created artifact: Negative. *Journal of the American Academy of Child and Adolescent Psychiatry, 34,* 960–962.

Putnam, F. W., & Carlson, E. B. (1998). Hypnosis, dissociation, and trauma: Myths, metaphors, and mechanisms. In J. D. Bremner & C. R. Marmar (Eds.), *Trauma, memory, and dissociation* (pp. 27–55). Washington, DC: American Psychiatric Press.

Putnam, F. W., Helmers, K., Horowitz, L. A., & Trickett, P. K. (1995). Hypnotizability and dissociativity in sexually abused girls. *Child Abuse and Neglect, 19,* 645–655.

Putnam, F. W., & Trickett, P. K. (1997). Psychobiological effects of sexual abuse: A longitudinal study. In R. Yehuda & A. C. MacFarlane (Eds.), *Psychobiology of post-traumatic stress disorder* (Vol. 821, pp. 150–159). New York: New York Academy of Sciences.

Pynoos, R. S. (1990). Post-traumatic stress disorder in children and adolescents. In B. Garfinkel, G. Carlson, & E. Weller (Eds.), *Psychiatric disorders in children and adolescents* (pp. 48–63). Philadelphia: Saunders.

Pynoos, R. S., Goenjian, A., & Steinberg, A. M. (1995). Strategies of disaster intervention for children and adolescents. In S. E. Hobfoll & M. deFries (Eds.), *Extreme stress and communities: Impact and interventions* (pp. 445–471). Dordrecht, The Netherlands: Kluwer.

Pynoos, R. S., & Nader, K. (1988). Psychological first aid and treatment approach to children exposed to community violence: Research implications. *Journal of Traumatic Stress, 1,* 445–473.

Pynoos, R. S., & Nader, K. (1989). Case study: Children's memory and proximity to violence. *Journal of the American Academy Child and Adolescent Psychiatry, 28,* 236–241.

Pynoos, R. S., Steinberg, A. M., & Goenjian, A. (1996). Traumatic stress in childhood and adolescence: Recent developments and current controversies. In B. A. van der Kolk, A. C. McFarlane, & L. Weisaeth (Eds.), *Traumatic stress: The effects of overwhelming experience on mind, body, and society* (pp. 331–358). New York: Guilford.

Pynoos, R. S., Steinberg, A. M., Ornitz, E. M., & Goenjian, A. K. (1997). Issues in the developmental neurobiology of traumatic stress. In R. Yehuda & A. C. MacFarlane

(Eds.), *Psychobiology of posttraumatic stress disorder* (Vol. 821, pp. 176–193). New York: New York Academy of Sciences.

Pynoos, R. S., Steinberg, A. M., & Wraith, R. (1995). A developmental model of childhood traumatic stress. In D. Cicchetti & D. Cohen (Eds.), *Developmental psychopathology. Volume 2: Risk, disorder, and adaptation* (pp. 72–95). New York: Wiley.

Qin, J., Goodman, G. S., Bottoms, B. L., & Shaver, P. R. (1998). Repressed memories of ritualistic and religion-related child abuse. In S. J. Lynn & K. M. McConkey (Eds.), *Truth in memory* (pp. 260–283). New York: Guilford.

Rabin, C. (1995). The use of psychoeducational groups to improve marital functioning in high risk Israeli couples: A stage model. *Contemporary Family Therapy, 17,* 503–515.

Rachman, S. (1980). Emotional processing. *Behaviour Research and Therapy, 18,* 51–60.

Rapaport, D. (1953). On the psychoanalytic theory of affects. *International Journal of Psycho-Analysis, 34,* 177–198.

Raphael, B., Wilson, J., Meldrum, L., & McFarlane, A. C. (1996). Acute preventive interventions. In B. A. van der Kolk, A. C. McFarlane, & L. Weisaeth (Eds.), *Traumatic stress: The effects of overwhelming experience on mind, body, and society* (pp. 463–479). New York: Guilford.

Rauch, J. L., Geyer, M. A., Jenkins, M. A., Breslin, C., & Braff, D. L. (1994). Neurobiology of startle response abnormalities in PTSD. In M. M. Murburg (Ed.), *Catecholamine function in posttraumatic stress disorder* (pp. 279–292). Washington, DC: American Psychiatric Press.

Rauch, S. L., van der Kolk, B. A., Fisler, R. E., Alpert, N. M., Orr, S. P., Savage, C. R., Fischman, A. J., Jenicke, M. A., & Pitman, R. K. (1996). A symptom provocation study of posttraumatic stress disorder using positron emission tomography and script-driven imagery. *Archives of General Psychiatry, 53,* 380–387.

Read, J. D., & Lindsay, D. S. (2000). 'Amnesia' for summer camps and high school graduation: Memory work increases reports of prior periods of remembering less. *Journal of Traumatic Stress, 13,* 129–147.

Reader, F. (1998). Medico-legal implications of sexual and relationship sequelae following trauma, surgery or childbirth. *Sexual and Marital Therapy, 13,* 159–167.

Regehr, C., & Marziali, E. (1999). Response to sexual assault: A relational perspective. *Journal of Nervous and Mental Disease, 187,* 618–623.

Reiker, P. P., & Carmen, E. (1986). The victim-to-patient process: The disconfirmation and transformation of abuse. *American Journal of Orthopsychiatry, 56,* 360–370.

Reiss, D., Hetherington, E. M., Plomin, R., Howe, G. W., Simmens, S. J., Henderson, S. H., O'Connor, T. J., Bussell, D. A., Anderson, E. R., & Saw, T. (1995). Genetic questions for environmental studies: Differential parenting and psychopathology in adolescence. *Archives of General Psychiatry, 52,* 925–936.

Renfrey, G., & Spates, C. R. (1994). Eye Movement Desensitization and Reprocessing: A dismantling study. *Journal of Behavior Therapy and Experimental Psychiatry, 25,* 231–239.

Resick, P. A., Jordan, C. G., Girelli, S. A., Hutter, C. K., & Marhoefer-Dvorak, S. (1988). A comparative outcome study of behavioral group therapy for sexual assault victims. *Behavior Therapy, 19,* 385–401.

Resick, P. A., & Schnicke, M. K. (1992). Cognitive processing therapy for sexual assault victims. *Journal of Consulting and Clinical Psychology, 60,* 748–756.

Resick, P. A., & Schnicke, M. K. (1993). *Cognitive processing therapy for rape victims: A treatment manual.* London: Sage.

Resnick, H., Acierno, R., Holmes, M., Kilpatrick, D. G., & Jager, N. (1999). Prevention of post-rape psychopathology: Preliminary findings of a controlled acute rape treatment study. *Journal of Anxiety Disorders, 13,* 359–370.

Resnick, H. S., Kilpatrick, D. G., Dansky, B. S., Saunders, B. E., & Best, C. L. (1993). Prevalence of civilian trauma and posttraumatic stress disorder in a representative national sample of women. *Journal of Consulting and Clinical Psychology*, *61*, 984–991.

Resnick, H. S., Yehuda, R., & Acierno, R. (1997). Acute post-rape plasma cortisol, alcohol use, and PTSD symptom profile among recent rape victims. In R. Yehuda & A. C. McFarlane (Eds.), *Psychobiology of posttraumatic stress disorder* (Vol. 821, pp. 433–436). New York: New York Academy of Sciences.

Revelle, W., & Loftus, D. A. (1992). The implications of arousal effects for the study of affect and memory. In S. Christianson (Ed.), *The handbook of emotion and memory: Research and theory* (pp. 113–149). Hillsdale, NJ: Erlbaum.

Rhodes, R. (1995). *How to write*. New York: William Morrow.

Rhue, J. W., & Lynn, S. J. (1987). Fantasy proneness and psychopathology. *Journal of Personality and Social Psychology*, *53*, 327–336.

Riccio, D. C., Rabinowitz, V. C., & Axelrod, S. (1994). Memory: When less is more. *American Psychologist*, *49*, 917–926.

Rice-Smith, E. (1993). Group psychotherapy with sexually abused children. In H. Kaplan & B. Sadock (Eds.), *Comprehensive group psychotherapy* (3rd edn., pp. 531–550). Baltimore: Williams & Wilkins.

Richards, J. M., Beal, W. E., Seagal, J. D., & Pennebaker, J. W. (2000). Effects of disclosure of traumatic events on illness behavior among psychiatric prison inmates. *Journal of Abnormal Psychology*, *109*, 156–160.

Rifkin, A., Ghisalbert, D., Dimatou, S., Jin, C., & Sethi, M. (1998). Dissociative identity disorder in psychiatric inpatients. *American Journal of Psychiatry*, *155*, 844–855.

Rind, B., Tromovitch, P., & Bauserman, R. (1998). A meta-analytic examination of assumed properties of childhood sexual abuse using college samples. *Psychological Bulletin*, *124*, 22–53.

Roberts, G. (1999). Introduction: A story of stories. In G. Roberts & J. Holmes (Eds.), *Healing stories: Narrative in psychiatry and psychotherapy* (pp. 3–26). London: Oxford University Press.

Robins, S., & Novaco, R. W. (1999). Systems conceptualization and treatment of anger. *Journal of Clinical Psychology*, *55*, 325–337.

Robinson, R. C., & Mitchell, J. T. (1993). Evaluation of psychological debriefings. *Journal of Traumatic Stress*, *6*, 367–382.

Roche, D. N., Runtz, M. G., & Hunter, M. (1999). Adult attachment: A mediator between child sexual abuse and later psychological adjustment. *Journal of Interpersonal Violence*, *14*, 184–207.

Roche, S. M., & McConkey, K. M. (1990). Absorption: Nature, assessment, and correlates. *Journal of Personality and Social Psychology*, *59*, 91–101.

Rockland, L. H. (1989). *Supportive therapy: A psychodynamic approach*. New York: Basic Books.

Roemer, L., Orsillo, S. M., Borkovec, T. D., & Litz, B. T. (1998). Emotional response at the time of a potentially traumatizing event and PTSD symptomatology: A preliminary retrospective analysis of the DSM-IV criterion A-2. *Journal of Behavior Therapy and Experimental Psychiatry*, *29*, 123–130.

Romans, S. E., Martin, J. L., Anderson, J. C., Herbison, G. P., & Mullen, P. E. (1995). Sexual abuse in childhood and deliberate self-harm. *American Journal of Psychiatry*, *152*, 1336–1342.

Rook, K. (1992). Detrimental aspects of social relationships: Taking stock of an emerging literature. In H. O. F. Veiel & U. Baumann (Eds.), *The meaning and measurement of social support* (pp. 157–169). New York: Hemisphere.

Rorty, M., & Yager, J. (1996). Histories of childhood trauma and complex-posttraumatic sequelae in women with eating disorders. *Psychiatric Clinics of North America, 19,* 773–791.

Rose, D. S. (1993). Sexual assault, domestic violence, and incest. In D. E. Stewart & N. L. Stotland (Eds.), *Psychological aspects of women's health care* (pp. 447–483). Washington, DC: American Psychiatric Press.

Rose, S., & Bisson, J. (1998). Brief early psychological interventions following trauma: A systematic review of the literature. *Journal of Traumatic Stress, 11,* 697–710.

Rosenblum, L. A., Coplan, J. D., Friedman, S., Bassoff, T., Gorman, J. M., & Andrews, M. W. (1994). Adverse early experiences affect noradrenergic and serotonergic functioning in adult primates. *Biological Psychiatry, 35,* 221–227.

Rosenheck, R., & Fontana, A. (1998). Transgenerational effects of abusive violence on the children of Vietnam combat veterans. *Journal of Traumatic Stress, 11,* 731–742.

Ross, C. A., Anderson, G., Fleisher, W. P., & Norton, G. R. (1991). The frequency of multiple personality disorder among psychiatric inpatients. *American Journal of Psychiatry, 148,* 1717–1720.

Ross, C. A., & Joshi, S. (1992). Schneiderian symptoms and childhood trauma in the general population. *Comprehensive Psychiatry, 33,* 269–273.

Ross, C. A., Miller, S. D., Reagor, P., Bjornson, L., Fraser, G. A., & Anderson, G. (1990). Schneiderian symptoms in multiple personality disorder and schizophrenia. *Comprehensive Psychiatry, 31,* 111–118.

Ross, R. J., Ball, W. A., Dinges, D. F., Kribbs, N. B., Morrison, A. R., Silver, S. M., & Mulvaney, F. D. (1994). Motor dysfunction during sleep in posttraumatic stress disorder. *Sleep, 17,* 723–732.

Ross, R. J., Ball, W. A., Sullivan, K. A., & Caroff, S. N. (1989). Sleep disturbance as the hallmark of posttraumatic stress disorder. *American Journal of Psychiatry, 146,* 697–707.

Ross, S. M. (1996). Risk of physical abuse to children of spouse abusing parents. *Child Abuse and Neglect, 20,* 589–598.

Roth, A., & Fonagy, P. (1996). *What works for whom? A critical review of psychotherapy research.* New York: Guilford.

Roth, M., & Mountjoy, C. Q. (1997). The need for the concept of neurotic depression. In H. S. Akiskal & G. B. Cassano (Eds.), *Dysthymia and the spectrum of chronic depressions* (pp. 96–129). New York: Guilford.

Rothbaum, B. O. (1997). A controlled study of Eye Movement Desensitization and Reprocessing in the treatment of posttraumatic stress disorder. *Bulletin of the Menninger Clinic, 61,* 317–334.

Rothbaum, B. O., & Foa, E. B. (1993). Subtypes of posttraumatic stress disorder and duration of symptoms. In J. R. T. Davidson & E. B. Foa (Eds.), *Posttraumatic stress disorder: DSM-IV and beyond* (pp. 23–35). Washington, DC: American Psychiatric Press.

Rubin, D. C. (1982). On the retention function for autobiographical memory. *Journal of Verbal Learning and Verbal Behavior, 21,* 21–28.

Rubonis, A. V., & Bickman, L. (1991). Psychological impairment in the wake of disaster: The disaster–psychopathology relationship. *Psychological Bulletin, 109,* 384–399.

Russ, M. J., Clark, W. C., Cross, L. W., Kemperman, I., Kakuma, T., & Harrison, K. (1996). Pain and self-injury in borderline patients: Sensory decision theory, coping strategies, and locus of control. *Psychiatry Research, 63,* 57–65.

Russ, M. J., Shearin, E. N., Clarkin, J. F., Harrison, K., & Hull, J. W. (1993). Subtypes of self-injurious patients with borderline personality disorder. *American Journal of Psychiatry, 150,* 1869–1871.

Rutter, M. (1987). Temperament, personality, and personality disorder. *British Journal of Psychiatry, 150,* 443–458.

Rutter, M. (1989). Pathways from childhood to adult life. *Journal of Child Psychology and Psychiatry, 30,* 23–51.

Rutter, M. (1995). Clinical implications of attachment concepts: Retrospect and prospect. *Journal of Child Psychology and Psychiatry, 36,* 549–571.

Rutter, M. (1999). Resilience concepts and findings: Implications for family therapy. *Journal of Family Therapy, 21,* 119–144.

Rutter, M., & Maughan, B. (1997). Psychosocial adversities in childhood and adult psychopathology. *Journal of Personality Disorders, 11,* 4–18.

Rutter, M., & O'Connor, T. G. (1999). Implications of attachment theory for child care policies. In J. Cassidy & P. R. Shaver (Eds.), *Handbook of attachment: Theory, research, and clinical applications* (pp. 823–844). New York: Guilford.

Rutter, M., & Rutter, M. (1993). *Developing minds: Challenge and continuity across the lifespan.* London: Penguin.

Ruzek, J. I., Polusny, M. A., & Abueg, F. R. (1998). Assessment and treatment of concurrent posttraumatic stress disorder and substance abuse. In V. M. Follette, J. I. Ruzek, & F. R. Abueg (Eds.), *Cognitive-behavioral therapies for trauma* (pp. 226–255). New York: Guilford.

Saakvitne, K. W., Gamble, S., Pearlman, L. A., & Lev, B. T. (2000). *Risking connection: A training curriculum for working with survivors of childhood abuse.* Lutherville, MD: Sidran.

Saakvitne, K. W., & Pearlman, L. A. (1996). *Transforming the pain: A workbook on vicarious traumatization.* New York: Norton.

Sabo, A. N., Gunderson, J. G., Najavits, L. M., Chauncey, D., & Kisiel, C. (1995). Changes in self-destructiveness of borderline patients in psychotherapy: A prospective follow-up. *Journal of Nervous and Mental Disease, 183,* 370–376.

Safran, J. D., Muran, J. C., & Samstag, L. W. (1994). Resolving therapeutic alliance ruptures: A task analytic investigation. In A. O. Horvath & L. S. Greenberg (Eds.), *The working alliance: Theory, research, and practice* (pp. 225–255). New York: Wiley.

Sagi, A., & Hoffman, M. L. (1976). Empathic distress in the newborn. *Developmental Psychology, 12,* 175–176.

Saigh, P. A. (1998). Effects of flooding on memories of patients with posttraumatic stress disorder. In J. D. Bremner & C. R. Marmar (Eds.), *Trauma, memory, and dissociation* (pp. 285–320). Washington, DC: American Psychiatric Press.

Salzman, C., Wolfson, A. N., Schatzberg, A., Looper, J., Henke, R., Albanese, M., Schwartz, J., & Miyawaki, E. (1995). Effect of fluoxetine on anger in symptomatic volunteers with borderline personality disorder. *Journal of Clinical Psychopharmacology, 15,* 23–29.

Sanitioso, R., Kunda, Z., & Fong, G. T. (1990). Motivated recruitment of autobiographical memories. *Journal of Personality and Social Psychology, 59,* 229–241.

Sapolsky, R. M. (1997). Stress, glucocorticoids, and damage to the nervous system. In R. Yehuda & A. C. McFarlane (Eds.), *Psychobiology of posttraumatic stress disorder* (Vol. 821, pp. 1–19). New York: New York Academy of Sciences.

Sarason, B. A., Sarason, I. G., & Pierce, G. R. (Eds.). (1990). *Social support: An interactional view.* New York: Wiley.

Sarason, B. R., Pierce, G. R., & Sarason, I. G. (1990). Social support: The sense of acceptance and the role of relationships. In B. R. Sarason, I. G. Sarason, & G. R. Pierce (Eds.), *Social support: An interactional view* (pp. 97–128). New York: Wiley.

Sarason, I. G., Levine, H. M., Basham, R. B., & Sarason, B. R. (1983). Assessing social support: The social support questionnaire. *Journal of Personality and Social Psychology, 44,* 127–139.

Sartre, J.-P. (1957). *The transcendence of the ego: An existentialist theory of consciousness* (F. Williams & R. Kirkpatrick, Trans.). New York: Farrar, Straus, & Giroux.

Saunders, E. A., & Arnold, F. (1993). A critique of conceptual and treatment approaches to borderline psychopathology in light of findings about childhood abuse. *Psychiatry, 56*, 188–203.

Saxe, G. N., van der Kolk, B. A., Berkowitz, R., Chinman, G., Hall, K., Lieberg, G., & Schwartz, J. (1993). Dissociative disorders in psychiatric inpatients. *American Journal of Psychiatry, 150*, 1037–1042.

Scannapieco, M. (1994). School-linked programs for adolescents from high-risk, urban environments: A review of research and practice. *School Social Work Journal, 18*, 16–27.

Schacter, D. L. (1989). Memory. In M. I. Posner (Ed.), *Foundations of cognitive science* (pp. 683–725). Cambridge, MA: MIT Press.

Schacter, D. L. (1994). Priming and multiple memory systems: Perceptual mechanisms of implicit memory. In D. L. Schacter & E. Tulving (Eds.), *Memory systems 1994* (pp. 233–268). Cambridge, MA: MIT Press.

Schacter, D. L. (1995). Memory distortion: History and current status. In D. L. Schacter (Ed.), *Memory distortion: How minds, brains, and societies reconstruct the past* (pp. 1–43). Cambridge, MA: Harvard University Press.

Schacter, D. L. (1996). *Searching for memory: The brain, the mind, and the past.* New York: Basic Books.

Schacter, D. L. (1999). The seven sins of memory: Insights from psychology and cognitive neuroscience. *American Psychologist, 54*, 182–203.

Schacter, D. L., & Kihlstrom, J. F. (1989). Functional amnesia. In F. Goller & J. Grafman (Eds.), *Handbook of neuropsychology* (Vol. 3, pp. 209–231). New York: Elsevier.

Schacter, D. L., & Tulving, E. (1994). *Memory systems 1994.* Cambridge, MA: MIT Press.

Schafer, J., Caetano, R., & Clark, C. L. (1998). Rates of intimate partner violence in the United States. *American Journal of Public Health, 88*, 1702–1704.

Schamess, G. (1993). Group psychotherapy with children. In H. Kaplan & B. Sadock (Eds.), *Comprehensive group psychotherapy* (3rd edn., pp. 560–577). Baltimore: Williams & Wilkins.

Scharfe, E., & Bartholomew, K. (1994). Reliability and stability of adult attachment patterns. *Personal Relationships, 1*, 23–43.

Scheck, M. M., Schaeffer, J. A., & Gillette, C. (1998). Brief psychological intervention with traumatized young women: The efficacy of Eye Movement Desensitization and Reprocessing. *Journal of Traumatic Stress, 11*, 25–44.

Scheflin, A. W. (2000). The evolving standard of care in the practice of trauma and dissociative disorder therapy. *Bulletin of the Menninger Clinic, 64*, 197–234.

Schmale, A. H. (1972). Depression as affect, character style, and symptom formation. In R. R. Holt & E. Peterfeund (Eds.), *Psychoanalysis and contemporary science: An annual of integrative interdisciplinary studies. Volume 1, 1972* (pp. 327–351). New York: Macmillan.

Schoenberger, N. E. (1999). Expectancy and fear. In I. Kirsch (Ed.), *How expectancies shape experience* (pp. 125–144). Washington, DC: American Psychological Association.

Schouten, R. (1994). Allegations of sexual abuse: A new area of liability risk. *Harvard Review of Psychiatry, 1*, 350–352.

Schuengel, C., Bakermans-Kranenburg, M. J., & van IJzendoorn, M. H. (1999). Frightening maternal behavior linking unresolved loss and disorganized infant attachment. *Journal of Consulting and Clinical Psychology, 67*, 54–63.

Schwartz, H. L. (1994). From dissociation to negotiation: A relational psychoanalytic perspective on multiple personality disorder. *Psychoanalytic Psychology, 11*, 189–231.

Scott, J. P. (1987). The emotional basis of attachment and separation. In J. L. Sacksteder, D. P. Schwartz, & Y. Akabane (Eds.), *Attachment and the therapeutic processes: Essays in honor of Otto Allen Will, Jr., M.D.* (pp. 43–62). Madison, CT: International Universities Press.

Segal, Z. V., Williams, J. M., Teasdale, J. D., & Gemar, M. (1996). A cognitive science perspective on kindling and episode sensitization in recurrent affective disorder. *Psychological Medicine, 26,* 371–380.

Segrin, C., & Abramson, L. Y. (1994). Negative reactions to depressive behaviors: A communication theories analysis. *Journal of Abnormal Psychology, 103,* 655–668.

Seligman, M. E. P. (1975). *Helplessness: On depression, development and death.* San Francisco: W. H. Freeman.

Seligman, S. (1999). Integrating Kleinian theory and intersubjective infant research observing projective identification. *Psychoanalytic Dialogues, 9,* 129–159.

Shalev, A. Y. (1996). Stress versus traumatic stress: From acute homeostatic reactions to chronic psychopathology. In B. A. van der Kolk, A. C. McFarlane, & L. Weisaeth (Eds.), *Traumatic stress: The effects of overwhelming experience on mind, body, and society* (pp. 77–101). New York: Guilford.

Shalev, A. Y. (1997a). Acute to chronic: Etiology and pathophysiology of PTSD—A biopsychosocial approach. In C. S. Fullerton & R. J. Ursano (Eds.), *Posttraumatic stress disorder: Acute and long-term responses to trauma and disaster* (pp. 209–240). Washington, DC: American Psychiatric Press.

Shalev, A. Y. (1997b). Discussion: Treatment of prolonged posttraumatic stress disorder—Learning from experience. *Journal of Traumatic Stress, 10,* 415–423.

Shalev, A. Y. (1997c). Treatment failure in acute PTSD: Lessons learned about the complexity of the disorder. In R. Yehuda & A. C. McFarlane (Eds.), *Psychobiology of posttraumatic stress disorder* (Vol. 821, pp. 372–387). New York: New York Academy of Sciences.

Shalev, A. Y., Freedman, S., Tuvia, P., Brandes, D., Sahar, T., Orr, S. P., & Pitman, R. K. (1998). Prospective study of posttraumatic stress disorder and depression following trauma. *American Journal of Psychiatry, 155,* 630–637.

Shalev, A. Y., Peri, T., Brandes, D., Freedman, S., Orr, S. P., & Pitman, R. K. (2000). Auditory startle response in trauma survivors with posttraumatic stress disorder: A prospective study. *American Journal of Psychiatry, 157,* 255–261.

Shalev, A. Y., Peri, T., Canetti, L., & Schreiber, S. (1996). Predictors of PTSD in injured trauma survivors: A prospective study. *American Journal of Psychiatry, 153,* 219–225.

Shalev, A. Y., Peri, T., Gelpin, E., Orr, S. P., & Pitman, R. K. (1997). Psychophysiologic assessment of mental imagery of stressful events in Israeli civilian posttraumatic stress disorder patients. *Comprehensive Psychiatry, 38,* 269–273.

Shapiro, B. L., & Schwarz, J. C. (1997). Date rape: Its relationship to trauma symptoms and sexual self-esteem. *Journal of Interpersonal Violence, 12,* 407–419.

Shapiro, D. H. (1982). Overview: Clinical and physiological comparison of meditation with other self-control strategies. *American Journal of Psychiatry, 139,* 267–274.

Shapiro, F. (1989). Efficacy of Eye Movement Desensitization procedure in the treatment of traumatic memories. *Journal of Traumatic Stress, 2,* 199–223.

Shapiro, F. (1995a). *EMDR: Level I training manual.* Pacific Grove, CA: EMDR Institute.

Shapiro, F. (1995b). *Eye Movement Desensitization and Reprocessing: Basic principles, protocols, and procedures.* New York: Guilford.

Shapiro, F. (1996). Eye Movement Desensitization and Reprocessing (EMDR): Evaluation of controlled PTSD research. *Journal of Behavior Therapy and Experimental Psychiatry, 27,* 209–218.

Shaver, P. R., & Hazan, C. (1993). Adult romantic attachment: Theory and evidence. In D. Perlman & W. Jones (Eds.), *Advances in personal relationships* (pp. 29–70). Greenwich, CT: JAI.

Shaw, K., McFarlane, A., & Bookless, C. (1997). The phenomenology of traumatic reactions to psychotic illness. *Journal of Nervous and Mental Disease, 185,* 434–441.

Shea, M. T., Zlotnick, C., & Weisberg, R. B. (1999). Commonality and specificity of personality disorder profiles in subjects with trauma histories. *Journal of Personality Disorders, 13,* 199–210.

Shearer, S. L. (1994). Dissociative phenomena in women with borderline personality disorder. *American Journal of Psychiatry, 151,* 1324–1328.

Sherman, J. J. (1998). Effects of psychotherapeutic treatments for PTSD: A meta-analysis of controlled clinical trials. *Journal of Traumatic Stress, 11,* 413–435.

Shin, L. M., Kosslyn, S. M., McNally, R. J., Alpert, N. M., Thompson, W. L., Rauch, S. L., Macklin, M. L., & Pitman, R. K. (1997). Visual imagery and perception in posttraumatic stress disorder: A positron emission tomographic investigation. *Archives of General Psychiatry, 54,* 233–241.

Shoham, V., & Rohrbaugh, M. (1997). Interrupting ironic processes. *Psychological Science, 8,* 151–153.

Shore, J. H., Tatum, E. L., & Vollmer, W. M. (1986). Psychiatric reactions to disaster: The Mount St. Helens experience. *American Journal of Psychiatry, 143,* 590–595.

Siegmann, R. M., & Long, G. M. (1995). Psychoeducational group therapy changes the face of managed care. *Journal of Practical Psychiatry and Behavioral Health, 1,* 29–36.

Silver, R. C., Wortman, C. B., & Crofton, C. (1990). The role of coping in support provision: The self-presentational dilemma of victims of life crises. In B. R. Sarason, I. G. Sarason, & G. R. Pierce (Eds.), *Social support: An interactional view* (pp. 397–426). New York: Wiley.

Silverman, R. C., & Lieberman, A. F. (1999). Negative maternal attributions, projective identification, and the intergenerational transmission of violent relational patterns. *Psychoanalytic Dialogues, 9,* 161–186.

Sime, W. E. (1984). Psychological benefits of exercise training in the healthy individual. In J. D. Matarazzo, S. M. Weiss, J. A. Herd, N. E. Miller, & S. M. Weiss (Eds.), *Behavioral health: A handbook of health enhancement and disease prevention* (pp. 488–508). New York: Wiley.

Simeon, D., Gross, S., Guralnik, O., Stein, D. J., Schmeidler, J., & Hollander, E. (1997). Feeling unreal: 30 cases of DSM-III-R depersonalization disorder. *American Journal of Psychiatry, 154,* 1107–1113.

Simeon, D., Stanley, B., Frances, A., Jann, J. J., Winchel, R., & Stanley, M. (1992). Self-mutilation in personality disorders: Psychological and biological correlates. *American Journal of Psychiatry, 149,* 221–226.

Simner, M. L. (1971). Newborn's response to the cry of another infant. *Developmental Psychology, 5,* 136–150.

Simon, C. (1997). Psychoeducation: A contemporary approach. In T. R. Watkins & J. W. Callicutt (Eds.), *Mental health policy and practice today* (pp. 129–145). London: Sage.

Simon, R. I. (1999). Chronic posttraumatic stress disorder: A review and checklist of factors influencing prognosis. *Harvard Review of Psychiatry, 6,* 304–312.

Simons, R. L., & Johnson, C. (1998). An examination of competing explanations for the intergenerational transmission of domestic violence. In Y. Danieli (Ed.), *International handbook of multigenerational legacies of trauma* (pp. 553–570). New York: Plenum.

Simpson, J. A. (1999). Attachment theory in modern evolutionary perspective. In

J. Cassidy & P. R. Shaver (Eds.), *Handbook of attachment: Theory, research, and clinical applications* (pp. 115–140). New York: Guilford.

Simson, P. E., & Weiss, J. M. (1994). Altered electrophysiology of the locus coeruleus following uncontrollable stress: Relationship to anxiety and anxiolytic action. In M. M. Murburg (Ed.), *Catacholamine function in posttraumatic stress disorder: Emerging concepts* (pp. 63–86). Washington, DC: American Psychiatric Press.

Singer, J. L., & Salovey, P. (1991). Organized knowledge structures and personality: Person schemas, self-schemas, prototypes, and scripts. In M. J. Horowitz (Ed.), *Person schemas and maladaptive interpersonal patterns* (pp. 33–79). Chicago: University of Chicago Press.

Slade, A. (1999). Attachment theory and research: Implications for the theory and practice of individual psychotherapy with adults. In J. Cassidy & P. R. Shaver (Eds.), *Handbook of attachment: Theory, research, and clinical applications* (pp. 575–594). New York: Guilford.

Slade, A., & Aber, J. L. (1992). Attachments, drives, and development: Conflicts and convergences in theory. In J. W. Barron, M. N. Eagle, & D. L. Wolitzkly (Eds.), *Interface of psychoanalysis and psychology* (pp. 154–185). Washington, DC: American Psychological Association.

Sloman, L., Price, J., Gilbert , P., & Gardner, R. (1994). Adaptive function of depression: Psychotherapeutic implications. *American Journal of Psychotherapy, 48,* 401–416.

Sluzki, C. E. (1993). Toward a model of family and political victimization: Implications for treatment and recovery. *Psychiatry, 56,* 178–187.

Smith, W. H. (1993a). Hypnotherapy with rape victims. In J. W. Rhue, S. H. Lynn, & I. Kirsch (Eds.), *Handbook of clinical hypnosis* (pp. 479–491). Washington, DC: American Psychological Association.

Smith, W. H. (1993b). Incorporating hypnosis into the psychotherapy of patients with multiple personality disorder. *Bulletin of the Menninger Clinic, 57,* 344–354.

Solomon, J., & George, C. (1999). The measurement of attachment security in infancy and childhood. In J. Cassidy & P. R. Shaver (Eds.), *Handbook of attachment: Theory, research, and clinical applications* (pp. 287–316). New York: Guilford.

Solomon, P. (1996). Moving from psychoeducation to family education for families of adults with serious mental illness. *Psychiatric Services, 47,* 1364–1370.

Solomon, P., & Draine, J. (1995). Subjective burden among family members of mentally ill adults: Relation to stress, coping, and adaptation. *American Journal of Orthopsychiatry, 65,* 419–427.

Solomon, R. L. (1980). The opponent-process theory of motivation: The costs of pleasure and the benefits of pain. *American Psychologist, 35,* 691–712.

Solomon, Z., Laror, N., & McFarlane, A. C. (1996). Acute posttraumatic reactions in soldiers and civilians. In B. A. van der Kolk, A. C. McFarlane, & L. Weisaeth (Eds.), *Traumatic stress: The effects of overwhelming experience on mind, body, and society* (pp. 102–114). New York: Guilford.

Sorg, B. A., & Kalivas, P. W. (1995). Stress and neuronal sensitization. In M. J. Friedman, D. S. Charney, & A. Y. Deutch (Eds.), *Neurobiological and clinical consequences of stress: From normal adaptation to post-traumatic stress disorder* (pp. 83–102). Philadelphia: Lippincott-Raven.

Southwick, S. M., Morgan, C. A., III, Bremner, A. D., Grillon, C. G., Krystal, J. H., Nagy, L. M., & Charney, D. S. (1997). Noradrenergic alterations in posttraumatic stress disorder. In R. Yehuda & A. C. McFarlane (Eds.), *Psychobiology of posttraumatic stress disorder* (Vol. 821, pp. 125–141). New York: New York Academy of Sciences.

Southwick, S. M., Yehuda, R., & Giller, E. L. (1993). Personality disorders in treatment-seeking combat veterans with posttraumatic stress disorder. *American Journal of Psychiatry, 150,* 1020–1023.

Southwick, S. M., Yehuda, R., & Morgan, C. A. I. (1995). Clinical studies of neurotransmitter alterations in post-traumatic stress disorder. In M. J. Friedman, D. S. Charney, & A. Y. Deutch (Eds.), *Neurobiological and clinical consequences of stress: From normal adaptation to post-traumatic stress disorder* (pp. 335–349). Philadelphia: Lippincott-Raven.

Spangler, G., & Grossman, K. (1999). Individual and physiological correlates of attachment disorganization in infancy. In J. Solomon & C. George (Eds.), *Attachment disorganization* (pp. 95–124). New York: Guilford.

Spanos, N. P. (1996). *Multiple identities and false memories: A sociocognitive perspective.* Washington, DC: American Psychological Association.

Spence, D. L. (1994). Narrative truth and putative child abuse. *International Journal of Clinical and Experimental Hypnosis, 42,* 289–303.

Spence, D. P. (1982). *Narrative truth and historical truth: Meaning and interpretation in psychoanalysis.* New York: Norton.

Sperling, M. B., Foelsch, P., & Grace, C. (1996). Measuring adult attachment: Are self-report instruments congruent? *Journal of Personality Assessment, 76,* 37–51.

Spiegel, D. (1988). Dissociation and hypnosis in post-traumatic stress disorders. *Journal of Traumatic Stress, 1,* 17–33.

Spiegel, D. (1990a). Hypnosis, dissociation, and trauma: Hidden and overt observers. In J. L. Singer (Ed.), *Repression and dissociation: Implications for personality theory, psychopathology, and health* (pp. 121–142). Chicago: Chicago University Press.

Spiegel, D. (1990b). Trauma, dissociation, and hypnosis. In R. P. Kluft (Ed.), *Incest-related syndromes of adult psychopathology* (pp. 247–261). Washington, DC: American Psychiatric Press.

Spiegel, D. (1995). Hypnosis and suggestion. In D. L. Schacter (Ed.), *Memory distortion: How minds, brains, and societies reconstruct the past* (pp. 129–149). Cambridge, MA: Harvard University Press.

Spiegel, D. (1997). Trauma, dissociation, and memory. In R. Yehuda & A. C. McFarlane (Eds.), *Psychobiology of posttraumatic stress disorder* (Vol. 821, pp. 225–237). New York: New York Academy of Sciences.

Spiegel, D., & Cardeña, E. (1991). Disintegrated experience: The dissociative disorders revisited. *Journal of Abnormal Psychology, 100,* 366–378.

Spiegel, D., Frischholz, E. J., & Spira, J. (1993). Functional disorders of memory. In J. M. Oldham, M. B. Biba, & A. Tasman (Eds.), *The American Psychiatric Press review of psychiatry* (Vol. 12, pp. 747–782). Washington, DC: American Psychiatric Press.

Spiegel, D., & Scheflin, A. W. (1994). Dissociated or fabricated? Psychiatric aspects of repressed memory in criminal and civil cases. *International Journal of Clinical and Experimental Hypnosis, 42,* 411–432.

Spivak, B., Vered, Y., Graff, E., Blum, I., Mester, R., & Weizman, A. (1999). Low platelet–poor plasma concentrations of serotonin in patients with combat-related posttraumatic stress disorder. *Biological Psychiatry, 45,* 840–845.

Sprang, S., & McNeil, J. (1998). Post-homicide reactions: Grief, mourning and posttraumatic stress disorder following a drunk driving fatality. *Omega, 37,* 41–58.

Squire, L. R. (1987). *Memory and brain.* New York: Oxford University Press.

Squire, L. R. (1995). Biological foundations of accuracy and inaccuracy in memory. In D. L. Schacter (Ed.), *Memory distortion: How minds, brains, and societies reconstruct the past* (pp. 197–225). Cambridge, MA: Harvard University Press.

Squire, L. R., & Zola-Morgan, S. (1991). The medial temporal lobe memory system. *Science, 253,* 1380–1386.

Sroufe, L. A. (1997). Psychopathology as an outcome of development. *Development and Psychopathology, 9*, 251–268.

Stalker, C. A., & Davies, F. (1995). Attachment organization and adaptation in sexually-abused women. *Canadian Journal of Psychiatry, 40*, 234–240.

Stalker, C. A., & Fry, R. (1999). A comparison of short-term group and individual therapy for sexually abused women. *Journal of Canadian Psychiatry, 44*, 168–174.

Stallones, L., Marx, M. B., Garrity, T. F., & Johnson, T. P. (1988). Pet ownership and attachment in relation to the health of U.S. adults, 21 to 64 years of age. *Anthrozoos, 4*, 100–112.

Steele, H., Steele, M., & Fonagy, P. (1996). Associations among attachment classifications of mothers, fathers, and their infants. *Child Development, 67*, 541–555.

Stein, H., Jacobs, N. J., Ferguson, K. S., Allen, J. G., & Fonagy, P. (1998). What do adult attachment scales measure? *Bulletin of the Menninger Clinic, 62*, 33–82.

Stein, H. B., Allen, D., Allen, J. G., Koontz, A. D., & Wisman, M. (2000). *Supplementary manual for scoring Bifulco's Childhood Experience of Care and Abuse Interview (M-CECA): Version 2.0* (Technical Report No. 00-0024). Topeka, KS: Menninger Clinic, Research Department.

Stein, H. B., Allen, J. G., Brand Bartlett, A., & Gabbard, G. O. (1999). *Childhood risk and adulthood functioning: A research proposal* (Technical Report No. 00-0022). Topeka, KS: Menninger Clinic, Research Department.

Stein, H. B., Fonagy, P., Ferguson, K. S., & Wisman, M. (2000). Lives through time: An ideographic approach to the study of resilience. *Bulletin of the Menninger Clinic, 64*, 281–305.

Stein, H. B., Koontz, A. D., Allen, J. G., Fultz, J., Brethour, J. R., Jr., Allen, D., Evans, R. B., & Fonagy, P. (2000). *Adult attachment questionnaires: Disagreement rates and construct and criterion validity* (Technical Report No. 00-0022). Topeka, KS: Menninger Clinic, Research Department.

Stein, M. B., Koverola, C., Hanna, C., Torchia, J. G., & McClarty, B. (1997). Hippocampal volume in women victimized by child abuse. *Psychological Medicine, 27*, 951–959.

Stein, M. B., Walker, J. R., Anderson, G., Hazen, A. L., Ross, C. A., Eldridge, G., & Forde, D. R. (1996). Childhood physical and sexual abuse in patients with anxiety disorders and in a community sample. *American Journal of Psychiatry, 153*, 275–277.

Stein, M. B., Walker, J. R., Hazen, A. L., & Forde, D. R. (1997). Full and partial posttraumatic stress disorder: Findings from a community survey. *American Journal of Psychiatry, 154*, 1114–1119.

Steinberg, B. J., Trestman, R. L., & Siever, L. J. (1994). The cholinergic and noradrenergic neurotransmitter systems and affective instability in borderline personality disorder. In K. R. Silk (Ed.), *Biological and neurobehavioral studies of borderline personality disorder* (pp. 41–62). Washington, DC: American Psychiatric Press.

Steinberg, M. (1993). *Interviewer's guide to the Structured Clinical Interview for DSM-IV Dissociative Disorders (SCID-D)*. Washington, DC: American Psychiatric Press.

Steinberg, M. (1995). *Handbook for the assessment of dissociation: A clinical guide*. Washington, DC: American Psychiatric Press.

Steinberg, M. (2000). Advances in the clinical assessment of dissociation: The SCID-D-R. *Bulletin of the Menninger Clinic, 64*, 146–163.

Steinberg, M., Rounsaville, B., & Cicchetti, D. (1991). Detection of dissociative disorders in psychiatric patients by a screening instrument and a structured diagnostic interview. *American Journal of Psychiatry, 148*, 1050–1054.

Steinberg, M., Rounsaville, B., & Cicchetti, D. V. (1990). The Structured Clinical Interview for DSM-III-R Dissociative Disorders: Preliminary report on a new diagnostic instrument. *American Journal of Psychiatry, 147*, 76–82.

Steinberg, R., & Sunkenberg, M. (1994). A group intervention model for sexual abuse: Treatment and education in an inpatient child psychiatric setting. *Journal of Child and Adolescent Group Therapy, 4*, 61–73.

Stern, D. N. (1985). *The interpersonal world of the infant: A view from psychoanalysis and developmental psychology.* New York: Basic Books.

Stern, D. N. (1989). The representation of relational patterns: Developmental considerations. In A. J. Sameroff & R. N. Emde (Eds.), *Relationship disturbances in early childhood* (pp. 52–69). New York: Basic Books.

Stern, D. N., Sander, L. W., Nahum, J. P., Harrison, A. M., Lyons-Ruth, K., Morgan, A. C., Bruschweiler-Stern, N., & Tronick, E. Z. (1998). Non-interpretive mechanisms in psychoanalytic therapy: The 'something more' than interpretation. *International Journal of Psycho-Analysis, 79*, 903–921.

Stevens-Simon, C., & Reichert, S. (1994). Sexual abuse, adolescent pregnancy, and child abuse. *Archives of Pediatric Adolescent Medicine, 148*, 23–27.

Stewart, S. H., Pihl, R. O., Conrod, P. J., & Dongier, M. (1998). Functional associations among trauma, PTSD, and substance-related disorders. *Addictive Behaviors, 23*, 797–812.

Stine, S. M., & Kosten, T. R. (1995). Complications of chemical abuse and dependency. In M. J. Friedman, D. S. Charney & A. Y. Deutch (Eds.), *Neurobiological and clinical consequences of stress: From normal adaptation to post-traumatic stress disorder* (pp. 447–464). Philadelphia: Lippincott-Raven.

Stout, S. C., Kilts, C. D., & Nemeroff, C. B. (1995). Neuropeptides and stress: Preclinical findings and implications for pathophysiology. In M. J. Friedman, D. S. Charney, & A. Y. Deutch (Eds.), *Neurobiological and clinical consequences of stress: From normal adaptation to post-traumatic stress disorder* (pp. 103–123). Philadelphia: Lippincott-Raven.

Strentz, T. (1982). The Stockholm Syndrome: Law enforcement policy and hostage behavior. In F. M. Ochberg & D. A. Soskis (Eds.), *Victims of terrorism* (pp. 149–163). Boulder, CO: Westview Press.

Suomi, S. J. (1999). Attachment in Rhesus monkeys. In J. Cassidy & P. R. Shaver (Eds.), *Handbook of attachment: Theory, research, and clinical applications* (pp. 181–197). New York: Guilford.

Swann, W. B., Jr. (1997). The trouble with change: Self-verification and allegiance to the self. *Psychological Science, 8*, 177–180.

Swirsky, D., & Mitchell, V. (1996). The binge–purge cycle as a means of dissociation: Somatic trauma and somatic defense in sexual abuse and bulimia. *Dissociation, 9*, 18–27.

Symonds, M. (1982). Victim responses to terror: Understanding and treatment. In F. M. Ochberg & D. A. Soskis (Eds.), *Victims of terrorism* (p. 95). Boulder, CO: Westview Press.

Talbot, N. L., Houghtalen, R. P., Cyrulik, S., Betz, A., Barkun, M., Duberstein, P. R., & Wynne, L. (1998). Women's safety in recovery: Group therapy for patients with a history of childhood sexual abuse. *Psychiatric Services, 49*, 213–217.

Tang, C. S.-K. (1998). The rate of physical child abuse in Chinese families: A community survey in Hong Kong. *Child Abuse & Neglect, 22*, 381–391.

Target, M. (1998). Outcome research on the psychosocial treatment of personality disorders. *Bulletin of the Menninger Clinic, 62*, 215–230.

Target, M., & Fonagy, P. (1996). Playing with reality: II. The development of psychic reality from a theoretical perspective. *International Journal of Psycho-Analysis, 77*, 459–479.

Tarrier, N. (1996). An application of expressed emotion to the study of PTSD: Preliminary findings. *Clinical Psychology and Psychotherapy, 3*, 220–229.

Tarrier, N., Pilgrim, H., Sommerfield, C., Faragher, B., Reynolds, M., Graham, E., & Barrowclough, C. (1999). A randomized trial of cognitive therapy and imaginal exposure in treatment of chronic posttraumatic stress disorder. *Journal of Consulting and Clinical Psychology, 67*, 13–18.

Tarrier, N., Sommerfield, C., & Pilgrim, H. (1999). Relatives' expressed emotion (EE) and PTSD treatment outcome. *Psychological Medicine, 29*, 801–811.

Taylor, G. J. (1992). Psychosomatics and self-regulation. In J. W. Barron, M. N. Eagle, & D. L. Wolitsky (Eds.), *Interface of psychoanalysis and psychology* (pp. 464–488). Washington, DC: American Psychological Association.

Taylor, S., Koch, W. J., & McNally, R. J. (1992). How does anxiety sensitivity vary across the anxiety disorders? *Journal of Anxiety Disorders, 6*, 249–259.

Taylor, S., Kuch, K., Koch, W. J., Crockett, D. J., & Passey, G. (1998). The structure of posttraumatic symptoms. *Journal of Abnormal Psychology, 197*, 154–160.

Tedeschi, R. G. (1999). Violence transformed: Posttraumatic growth in survivors and their societies. *Aggression and Violent Behavior, 4*, 319–341.

Teicher, M. H., Ito, Y., Glod, C. A., Andersen, S. L., Dumont, N., & Ackerman, E. (1997). Preliminary evidence for abnormal cortical development in physically and sexually abused children using EEG coherence and MRI. In R. Yehuda & A. C. MacFarlane (Eds.), *Psychobiology of posttraumatic stress disorder* (Vol. 821, pp. 160–175). New York: New York Academy of Sciences.

Teicher, M. H., Ito, Y., Gold, C. A., Schiffer, F., & Gelbard, H. A. (1994). Early abuse, limbic system dysfunction, and borderline personality disorder. In K. R. Silk (Ed.), *Biological and neurobehavioral studies of borderline personality disorder* (pp. 177–207). Washington, DC: American Psychiatric Press.

Tellegen, A., & Atkinson, G. (1974). Openness to absorbing and self-altering experiences ('absorption'), a trait related to hypnotic susceptibility. *Journal of Abnormal Psychology, 83*, 268–277.

Tellegen, A., Lykken, D. T., Bouchard, T. J., Wilcox, K. J., Segal, N. L., & Rich, S. (1988). Personality similarity in twins reared apart and together. *Journal of Personality and Social Psychology, 54*, 1031–1039.

Terr, L. (1988). What happens to early memories of trauma? A study of twenty children under age five at the time of documented traumatic events. *Journal of the Academy of Child and Adolescent Psychiatry, 27*, 96–104.

Terr, L. (1994). *Unchained memories: True stories of traumatic memories, lost and found.* New York: Basic Books.

Terr, L. C. (1991). Childhood traumas: An outline and overview. *American Journal of Psychiatry, 148*, 10–20.

Thakkar, R. R., & McCanne, T. R. (2000). The effects of daily stressors on physical health in women with and without a history of childhood sexual abuse. *Child Abuse and Neglect, 24*, 209–221.

Thompson, A. E., & Kaplan, C. A. (1996). Childhood emotional abuse. *British Journal of Psychiatry, 168*, 143–148.

Thompson, R. A. (1999). Early attachment and later development. In J. Cassidy & P. R. Shaver (Eds.), *Handbook of attachment: Theory, research, and clinical applications* (pp. 265–286). New York: Guilford.

Thompson, R. F. (1993). *The brain: A neuroscience primer* (2nd edn.). New York: Freeman.

Tichenor, V., Marmar, C. R., Weiss, D. S., Metzler, T. J., & Ronfeldt, H. M. (1996). The relationship of peritraumatic dissociation and posttraumatic stress: Findings in female Vietnam theater veterans. *Journal of Consulting and Clinical Psychology, 64*, 1054–1059.

Tobias, B. A., Kihlstrom, J. F., & Schacter, D. L. (1992). Emotion and implicit memory.

In S. Christianson (Ed.), *The handbook of emotion and memory: Research and theory* (pp. 67–92). Hillsdale, NJ: Erlbaum.

Torem, M. S. (1989). Recognition and management of dissociative regressions. *Hypnos, 16,* 197–213.

Trickett, P. K., Reiffman, A., Horowitz, L. A., & Putnam, F. W. (1997). Characteristics of sexual abuse trauma and the prediction of developmental outcomes. In D. Cicchetti & S. L. Toth (Eds.), *Developmental perspectives on trauma: Theory, research, and intervention* (Vol. 8, pp. 289–311). Rochester, NY: University of Rochester Press.

Trolley, B. (1995). Group issues and activities for female teen survivors of sexual abuse. *Child and Adolescent Social Work Journal, 12,* 101–118.

Tromp, S., Koss, M. P., Figueredo, A. J., & Tharan, M. (1995). Are rape memories different? A comparison of rape, other unpleasant, and pleasant memories among employed women. *Journal of Traumatic Stress, 8,* 607–627.

True, W. R., Rice, J., Eisen, S. A., Heath, A. C., Goldberg, J., Lyons, M. J., & Nowak, J. (1991). A twin study of genetic and environmental contributions to liability for posttraumatic stress symptoms. *Archives of General Psychiatry, 50,* 257–264.

Tryon, W. W. (1999). A bidirectional associative memory explanation of posttraumatic stress disorder. *Clinical Psychology Review, 19,* 789–818.

Tulving, E. (1972). Episodic and semantic memory. In E. Tulving & W. Donaldson (Eds.), *Organization of memory* (pp. 381–403). New York: Academic Press.

Turell, S. C., & Armsworth, M. W. (2000). Differentiating incest survivors who self-mutilate. *Child Abuse and Neglect, 24,* 237–249.

Twemlow, S. W., Sacco, F. C., & Williams, P. (1996). A clinical and interactionist perspective on the bully–victim–bystander relationship. *Bulletin of the Menninger Clinic, 60,* 296–313.

Tyrrell, C. L., Dozier, M., Teague, G. B., & Fallot, R. D. (1999). Effective treatment relationships for persons with serious psychiatric disorders: The importance of attachment states of mind. *Journal of Consulting and Clinical Psychology, 67,* 725–733.

Uhl, G. R., Persico, A. M., & Smith, S. S. (1992). Current excitement with D2 dopamine receptor gene alleles in substance abuse. *Archives of General Psychiatry, 49,* 157–160.

Urquiza, A. J., Wyatt, G. E., & Goodlin-Jones, B. L. (1997). Clinical interviewing with trauma victims. *Journal of Interpersonal Violence, 12,* 759–772.

Ursano, R. J., Fullerton, C. S., Epstein, R. S., Crowley, B., Kao, T.-C., Vance, K., Craig, K., Dougall, A., & Baum, A. (1999). Acute and chronic posttraumatic stress disorder in motor vehicle accident victims. *American Journal of Psychiatry, 156,* 589–595.

Ursano, R. J., Fullerton, C. S., Epstein, R. S., Crowley, B., Vance, K., Kao, T.-C., & Baum, A. (1999). Peritraumatic dissociation and posttraumatic stress disorder following motor accidents. *American Journal of Psychiatry, 156,* 1808–1810.

Usher, J. A., & Neisser, U. (1993). Childhood amnesia and the beginnings of memory for four early life events. *Journal of Experimental Psychology General, 122,* 155–165.

van der Hart, O., & Brown, P. (1992). Abreaction re-evaluated. *Dissociation, 5,* 127–140.

van der Hart, O., & Friedman, B. (1989). A reader's guide to Pierre Janet on dissociation: A neglected intellectual heritage. *Dissociation, 2,* 3–16.

van der Hart, O., van der Kolk, B. A., & Boon, S. (1998). Treatment of dissociative disorders. In J. D. Bremner & C. R. Marmar (Eds.), *Trauma, memory, and dissociation* (pp. 253–283). Washington, DC: American Psychiatric Press.

van der Kolk, B. A. (1987). The role of the group in the origin and resolution of the trauma response. In B. A. van der Kolk (Ed.), *Psychological trauma* (pp. 153–171). Washington, DC: American Psychiatric Press.

van der Kolk, B. A. (1989). The compulsion to repeat the trauma: Reenactment, revictimization, and masochism. *Psychiatric Clinics of North America, 12,* 389–411.

van der Kolk, B. A. (1994). The body keeps the score: Memory and the evolving psychobiology of posttraumatic stress. *Harvard Review of Psychiatry, 1,* 253–265.

van der Kolk, B. A. (1996). Trauma and memory. In B. A. van der Kolk, A. C. McFarlane, & L. Weisaeth (Eds.), *Traumatic stress: The effects of overwhelming experience on mind, body, and society* (pp. 279–302). New York: Guilford.

van der Kolk, B. A., Burbridge, J. A., & Suzuki, J. (1997). The psychobiology of traumatic memory: Clinical implications of neuroimaging studies. In R. Yehuda & A. C. McFarlane (Eds.), *Psychobiology of posttraumatic stress disorder* (Vol. 821, pp. 99–113). New York: New York Academy of Sciences.

van der Kolk, B. A., Dreyfuss, D., Michaels, M., Shera, D., Berkowitz, R., Fisler, R., & Saxe, G. (1994). Fluoxetine in posttraumatic stress disorder. *Journal of Clinical Psychiatry, 55,* 517–522.

van der Kolk, B. A., & Fisler, R. E. (1994). Child abuse and neglect and loss of self-regulation. *Bulletin of the Menninger Clinic, 58,* 145–168.

van der Kolk, B. A., Greenberg, M. S., Orr, S. P., & Pitman, R. K. (1989). Endogenous opioids, stress induced analgesia, and posttraumatic stress disorder. *Psychopharmacology Bulletin, 25,* 417–420.

van der Kolk, B. A., & McFarlane, A. C. (1996). The black hole of trauma. In B. A. van der Kolk, A. C. McFarlane, & L. Weisaeth (Eds.), *Traumatic stress: The effects of overwhelming experience on mind, body, and society* (pp. 3–23). New York: Guilford.

van der Kolk, B. A., McFarlane, A. C., & van der Hart, O. (1996). A general approach to treatment of posttraumatic stress disorder. In B. A. van der Kolk, A. C. McFarlane, & L. Weisaeth (Eds.), *Traumatic stress: The effects of overwhelming experience on mind, body, and society* (pp. 417–440). New York: Guilford.

van der Kolk, B. A., Pelcovitz, D., Roth, S., Mandel, F. S., McFarlane, A., & Herman, J. L. (1996). Dissociation, somatization, and affect dysregulation: The complexity of adaptation to trauma. *American Journal of Psychiatry, 153,* 83–93.

van der Kolk, B. A., Perry, J. C., & Herman, J. L. (1991). Childhood origins of self-destructive behavior. *American Journal of Psychiatry, 148,* 1666–1671.

Van Etten, M. L., & Taylor, S. (1998). Comparative efficacy of treatments for posttraumatic stress disorder: A meta-analysis. *Clinical Psychology and Psychotherapy, 5,* 126–144.

van IJzendoorn, M. H. (1995). Adult attachment representations, parental responsiveness, and infant attachment: A meta-analysis on the predictive validity of the Adult Attachment Interview. *Psychological Bulletin, 117,* 387–403.

van IJzendoorn, M. H., & Bakermans-Kranenburg, M. J. (1996). Attachment representations in mothers, fathers, adolescents, and clinical groups: A meta-analytic search for normative data. *Journal of Consulting and Clinical Psychology, 64,* 8–21.

van IJzendoorn, M. H., & Schuengel, C. (1996). The measurement of dissociation in normal and clinical populations: Meta-analytic validation of the Dissociative Experiences Scale (DES). *Clinical Psychology Review, 16,* 365–382.

van IJzendoorn, M. H., Schuengel, C., & Bakermans-Kranenburg, M. J. (1999). Disorganized attachment in early childhood: Meta-analysis of precursors, concomitants, and sequelae. *Development and Psychopathology, 11,* 225–249.

van Reekum, R., Links, P. S., & Federov, C. (1994). Impulsivity in borderline personality disorder. In K. R. Silk (Ed.), *Biological and neurobehavioral studies of borderline personality disorder* (pp. 1–22). Washington, DC: American Psychiatric Press.

Vaughan, S. C. (1997). *The talking cure: The science behind psychotherapy.* New York: Putnam.

Vaughn, B. E., & Bost, K. K. (1999). Attachment and temperament: Redundant, independent, or interacting influences on interpersonal adaptation and personality development? In J. Cassidy & P. R. Shaver (Eds.), *Handbook of attachment: Theory, research, and clinical applications* (pp. 198–225). New York: Guilford.

Vermetten, E., Bremner, J. D., & Spiegel, D. (1998). Dissociation and hypnotizability: A conceptual and methodological perspective on two distinct concepts. In J. D. Bremner & C. R. Marmar (Eds.), *Trauma, memory, and dissociation* (pp. 107–159). Washington, DC: American Psychiatric Press.

Vinogradov, S., King, R. J., & Huberman, B. A. (1992). An associationist model of the paranoid process: Application of phase transitions in spreading activation networks. *Psychiatry, 55,* 79–94.

Viviano, T. F., & Schill, T. (1996). Relation of reports of sexual abuse to scores on the self-defeating personality scale. *Psychological Reports, 79,* 615–617.

Wagner, A. W., & Linehan, M. M. (1997). Biosocial perspective on the relationship of childhood sexual abuse, suicidal behavior, and borderline personality disorder. In M. C. Zanarini (Ed.), *Role of sexual abuse in the etiology of borderline personality disorder* (pp. 203–223). Washington, DC: American Psychiatric Press.

Wagner, A. W., & Linehan, M. M. (1998). Dissociative behavior. In V. M. Follette, J. I. Ruzek, & F. R. Abueg (Eds.), *Cognitive-behavioral therapies for trauma* (pp. 191–225). New York: Guilford.

Wakefield, H., & Underwager, R. (1992). Recovered memories of alleged sexual abuse: Lawsuits against parents. *Behavioral Science and the Law, 10,* 483–507.

Waldinger, R. J. (1994). Boundary crossings and boundary violations: Thoughts on navigating a slippery slope. *Harvard Review of Psychiatry, 2,* 225–227.

Waldinger, R. J., Swett, C., Frank, A., & Miller, K. (1994). Levels of dissociation and histories of reported abuse among women outpatients. *Journal of Nervous and Mental Disease, 182,* 625–630.

Walker, L. E. (1979). *The battered woman.* New York: Harper & Row.

Walker, L. E. (1999). Psychology and domestic violence around the world. *American Psychologist, 54,* 21–29.

Wallen, J. (1993). Protecting the mental health of children in dangerous neighborhoods. *Children Today, 22*(3), 24–28.

Waller, G. (1991). Sexual abuse as a factor in eating disorders. *British Journal of Psychiatry, 159,* 664–671.

Waller, N. G., Putnam, F. W., & Carlson, E. B. (1996). Types of dissociation and dissociative types: A taxometric analysis of dissociative experiences. *Psychological Methods, 1,* 300–321.

Waller, N. G., & Ross, C. A. (1997). The prevalence and biometric structure of pathological dissociation in the general population: Taxometric and behavior genetic findings. *Journal of Abnormal Psychology, 106,* 499–510.

Walsh, B. W., & Rosen, P. M. (1988). *Self-mutilation: Theory, research, and treatment.* New York: Guilford.

Ward, M. J., & Carlson, E. A. (1995). Associations among adult attachment representations, maternal sensitivity, and infant–mother attachment in a sample of adolescent mothers. *Child Development, 66,* 69–79.

Watson, C. G., Barnett, M., Nikunen, L., Schultz, C., Randolph-Elgin, T., & Mendez, C. M. (1997). Lifetime prevalences of nine common psychiatric/personality disorders in female domestic abuse survivors. *Journal of Nervous and Mental Disease, 185,* 645–647.

Watson, C. G., Tuorila, J. R., Vickers, K. S., Gearhart, L. P., & Mendez, C. M. (1997). The efficacies of three relaxation regimens in the treatment of PTSD in Vietnam war veterans. *Journal of Clinical Psychology, 53,* 917–923.

Watson, D. (2000). *Mood and temperament*. New York: Guilford.

Watson, D., & Clark, L. A. (1997). Extraversion and its positive emotional core. In R. Hogan, J. A. Johnson, & S. Briggs (Eds.), *Handbook of personality psychology* (pp. 767–793). San Diego, CA: Academic Press.

Watson, J. S. (1994). Detection of self: The perfect algorithm. In S. T. Parker, R. W. Mitchell, & M. L. Boccia (Eds.), *Self-awareness in animals and humans* (pp. 131–148). Cambridge, UK: Cambridge University Press.

Watts, A. (1957). *The way of Zen*. New York: Random House.

Weary, G., & Gannon, K. (1996). Depression, control motivation, and person perception. In P. M. Gollwitzer & J. A. Bargh (Eds.), *The psychology of action: Linking cognition and motivation to behavior* (pp. 146–167). New York: Guilford.

Weaver, T. L., & Clum, G. A. (1993). Early family environments and traumatic experiences associated with borderline personality disorder. *Journal of Consulting and Clinical Psychology, 61*, 1068–1075.

Webster (1979). *Webster's new twentieth century dictionary of the English language, unabridged* (2nd edn.). New York: Simon & Schuster.

Wechselblatt, T., Gurnick, G., & Simon, R. (2000). Autonomy and relatedness in the development of anorexia nervosa: A clinical case series using grounded theory. *Bulletin of the Menninger Clinic, 64*, 91–123.

Wegner, D. M. (1994). Ironic processes of mental control. *Psychological Review, 101*, 34–52.

Wegner, D. M. (1997). When the antidote is the poison: Ironic mental control processes. *Psychological Science, 8*, 148–150.

Wegner, D. M., & Erber, R. (1992). The hyperaccessibility of suppressed thoughts. *Journal of Personality and Social Psychology, 63*, 903–912.

Weiner, H. (1992). *Perturbing the organism: The biology of stressful experience*. Chicago: University of Chicago Press.

Weiner, H. (1998). Notes on an evolutionary medicine. *Psychosomatic Medicine, 60*, 510–520.

Weinfield, N. S., Sroufe, L. A., Egeland, B., & Carlson, E. A. (1999). The nature of individual differences in infant–caregiver attachment. In J. Cassidy & P. R. Shaver (Eds.), *Handbook of attachment: Theory, research, and clinical application* (pp. 68–88). New York: Guilford.

Weiss, D., & Marmar, C. R. (1997). The Impact of Event Scale–Revised. In J. P. Wilson & T. M. Keane (Eds.), *Assessing psychological trauma and PTSD* (pp. 399–411). New York: Guilford.

Weiss, E. L., Longhurst, J. G., & Mazure, C. M. (1999). Childhood sexual abuse as a risk factor for depression in women: Psychosocial and neurobiological correlates. *American Journal of Psychiatry, 156*, 816–828.

Welch, S. L., & Fairburn, C. G. (1994). Sexual abuse and bulimia nervosa: Three integrated case control comparisons. *American Journal of Psychiatry, 151*, 402–407.

Welch, S. L., & Fairburn, C. G. (1996). Impulsivity or comorbidity in bulimia nervosa: A controlled study of deliberate self-harm and alcohol and drug misuse in a community sample. *British Journal of Psychiatry, 169*, 451–458.

Westerlund, E. (1992). *Women's sexuality after childhood incest*. New York: W. W. Norton.

Wexler, B. E., Lyons, L., Lyons, H., & Mazure, C. M. (1997). Physical and sexual abuse during childhood and development of psychiatric illness during adulthood. *Journal of Nervous and Mental Disease, 185*, 522–524.

Whalen, J. E., & Nash, M. R. (1996). Hypnosis and dissociation: Theoretical, empirical, and clinical perspectives. In L. K. Michelson & W. J. Ray (Eds.), *Handbook of dis-*

sociation: Theoretical, empirical, and clinical perspectives (pp. 191–206). New York: Plenum.

Whiffen, V. E., Judd, M. E., & Aube, J. A. (1999). Intimate relationships moderate the association between childhood sexual abuse and depression. *Journal of Interpersonal Violence, 14*, 940–954.

Whipple, E. E., & Richey, C. A. (1997). Crossing the line from physical discipline to child abuse: How much is too much? *Child Abuse and Neglect, 21*, 431–444.

Whiten, A., & Byrne, R. W. (1988). The Machiavellian intelligence hypothesis: Editorial. In R. W. Byrne & A. Whiten (Eds.), *Machiavellian intelligence: Social expertise and the evolution of intellect in monkeys, apes, and humans* (pp. 1–9). New York: Oxford University Press.

Widom, C. S. (1989). The cycle of violence. *Science, 244*, 160–166.

Widom, C. S. (1999a). Childhood victimization and the development of personality disorders: Unanswered questions remain. *Archives of General Psychiatry, 56*, 607–608.

Widom, C. S. (1999b). Posttraumatic stress disorder in abused and neglected children grown up. *American Journal of Psychiatry, 156*, 1223–1229.

Widom, C. S., Ireland, T., & Glynn, P. J. (1995). Alcohol abuse in abused and neglected children: Are they at increased risk? *Journal of Studies on Alcohol, 56*, 207–217.

Widom, C. S., & Kuhns, J. B. (1996). Childhood victimization and subsequent risk for promiscuity, prostitution, and teenage pregnancy: A prospective study. *American Journal of Public Health, 86*, 1607–1612.

Widom, C. S., & Morris, S. (1997). Accuracy of adult recollections of childhood victimization: Part 2. Childhood sexual abuse. *Psychological Assessment, 9*, 34–46.

Widom, C. S., & Shepard, R. L. (1996). Accuracy of adult recollections of childhood victimization: Part 1. Childhood physical abuse. *Psychological Assessment, 8*, 412–421.

Widom, C. S., Weiler, B. L., & Cottler, L. B. (1999). Childhood victimization and drug abuse: A comparison of prospective and retrospective findings. *Journal of Consulting and Clinical Psychology, 67*, 867–880.

Williams, L. M. (1994). Recall of childhood trauma: A prospective study. *Journal of Consulting and Clinical Psychology, 62*, 1167–1176.

Williams, L. M. (1995). Recovered memories of abuse in women with documented child sexual victimization. *Journal of Traumatic Stress, 8*, 649–673.

Williams, L. M., & Banyard, V. L. (1997). Perspectives on adult memories of childhood sexual abuse: A research review. In L. J. Dickstein, M. B. Riba, & J. M. Oldham (Eds.), *American Psychiatric Press review of psychiatry* (Vol. 16, pp. 123–151). Washington, DC: American Psychiatric Press.

Wilson, A., Calhoun, K. S., & Bernat, J. (1999). Risk recognition and trauma-related symptoms among sexually revictimized women. *Journal of Consulting and Clinical Psychology, 67*, 705–710.

Wilson, J. P., Raphael, B., Meldrum, L., Bedosky, C., & Sigman, M. (2000). Preventing PTSD in trauma survivors. *Bulletin of the Menninger Clinic, 64*, 181–196.

Wilson, S. A., Becker, L. A., & Tinker, R. H. (1995). Eye Movement Desensitization and Reprocessing (EMDR) treatment for psychologically traumatized individuals. *Journal of Consulting and Clinical Psychology, 63*, 928–937.

Wilson, S. A., Becker, L. A., & Tinker, R. H. (1997). Fifteen-month follow-up of Eye Movement Desensitization and Reprocessing (EMDR) treatment for posttraumatic stress disorder and psychological trauma. *Journal of Consulting and Clinical Psychology, 65*, 1047–1056.

Wilson, S. C., & Barber, T. X. (1983). The fantasy-prone personality: Implications for understanding imagery, hypnosis, and parapsychological phenomena. In A. A.

Sheikh (Ed.), *Imagery: Current theory, research, and application* (pp. 340–387). New York: Wiley.

Winnicott, D. W. (1953). Transitional objects and transitional phenomena: A study of the first not-me possession. *International Journal of Psycho-Analysis, 34*, 89–97.

Winnicott, D. W. (1971). *Playing with reality*. London: Routledge.

Winokur, G. (1990). The concept of secondary depression and its relationship to comorbidity. *Psychiatric Clinics of North America, 13*, 567–583.

Witvliet, C. V. (1997). Traumatic intrusive imagery as an emotional memory phenomenon: A review of research and explanatory information processing theories. *Clinical Psychology Review, 17*, 509–536.

Wolfe, J., & Schlesinger, L. K. (1997). Performance of PTSD patients on standard tests of memory: Implications for trauma. In R. Yehuda & A. C. McFarlane (Eds.), *Psychobiology of posttraumatic stress disorder* (Vol. 821, pp. 208–218). New York: New York Academy of Sciences.

Wolff, P. H. (1987). *The development of behavioral states and the expression of emotions in early infancy: New proposals for investigation*. Chicago: Chicago University Press.

Wolfner, G. D., & Gelles, R. J. (1993). A profile of violence toward children: A national study. *Child Abuse and Neglect, 17*, 197–212.

Wolock, I., & Horowitz, B. (1984). Child maltreatment as a social problem: The neglect of neglect. *American Journal of Orthopsychiatry, 54*, 530–542.

Wonderlich, S. A., Brewerton, T. D., Jocic, J., Dansky, B. S., & Abbott, D. W. (1997). Relationship of childhood sexual abuse and eating disorders. *Journal of the American Academy of Child and Adolescent Psychiatry, 36*, 1107–1115.

Woodward, S. H. (1995). Neurobiological perspectives on sleep in post-traumatic stress disorder. In M. J. Friedman, D. S. Charney, & A. Y. Deutch (Eds.), *Neurobiological and clinical consequences of stress: From normal adaptation to PTSD* (pp. 315–333). Philadelphia: Lippincott-Raven.

Worden, J. W. (1991). *Grief counseling and grief therapy: A handbook for the mental health practitioner* (2nd edn.). New York: Springer.

Wright, K., Ursano, R. J., Ingraham, L., & Bartone, P. (1990). Individual and community responses to an aircraft disaster. In M. E. Wolf & A. D. Mosnaim (Eds.), *Posttraumatic stress disorder: Etiology, phenomenology, and treatment* (pp. 126–138). Washington, DC: American Psychiatric Press.

Wyatt, G., & Riederle, M. (1994). Sexual harassment and prior sexual trauma among African-American and white American women. *Violence and Victims, 9*, 233–247.

Wylie, M. S. (1993). The shadow of a doubt. *Family Therapy Networker, 17*, 18–29, 70, 73.

Yalom, I. D. (1970). *The theory and practice of group psychotherapy*. New York: Basic Books.

Yassen, J. (1995). Preventing secondary traumatic stress disorder. In C. R. Figley (Ed.), *Compassion fatigue: Coping with secondary traumatic stress disorder in those who treat the traumatized* (pp. 178–208). New York: Brunner/Mazel.

Yehuda, R. (1997). Sensitization of the hypothalamic–pituitary–adrenal axis in posttraumatic stress disorder. In R. Yehuda & A. C. McFarlane (Eds.), *Psychobiology of posttraumatic stress disorder* (Vol. 821, pp. 57–75). New York: New York Academy of Sciences.

Yehuda, R. (1998). Neuroendocrinology of trauma and posttraumatic stress disorder. In R. Yehuda (Ed.), *Psychological trauma* (pp. 97–131). Washington, DC: American Psychiatric Press.

Yehuda, R., Giller, E. L., Jr., Levengood, R. A., Southwick, S. M., & Siever, L. J. (1995). Hypothalamic–pituitary–adrenal functioning in post-traumatic stress disorder: Expanding the concept of the stress response spectrum. In M. J. Friedman, D. S.

Charney, & A. Y. Deutch (Eds.), *Neurobiological and clinical consequences of stress: From normal adaptation to post-traumatic stress disorder* (pp. 351–365). Philadelphia: Lippincott-Raven.

Yehuda, R., Marshall, R., & Giller, E. L. (1998). Psychopharmacological treatment of post-traumatic stress disorder. In P. E. Nathan & J. M. Gorman (Eds.), *A guide to treatments that work* (pp. 377–397). New York: Oxford University Press.

Yehuda, R., & McFarlane, A. C. (1995). Conflict between current knowledge about posttraumatic stress disorder and its original conceptual basis. *American Journal of Psychiatry, 152,* 1705–1713.

Yehuda, R., & McFarlane, A. C. (1997). Introduction. In R. Yehuda & A. C. McFarlane (Eds.), *Psychobiology of posttraumatic stress disorder* (Vol. 821, pp. xi–xv). New York: New York Academy of Sciences.

Yehuda, R., McFarlane, A. C., & Shalev, A. Y. (1998). Predicting the development of posttraumatic stress disorder from the acute response to a traumatic stressor. *Biological Psychiatry, 44,* 1305–1313.

Young, W. C., & Young, L. J. (1996). Inpatient treatment of dissociative disorders. In L. K. Michelson & W. J. Ray (Eds.), *Handbook of dissociation: Theoretical, empirical, and clinical perspectives* (pp. 499–524). New York: Plenum.

Yuille, J. C., & Tollestrup, P. A. (1992). A model of the diverse effects of emotion on eyewitness testimony. In S.-A. Christianson (Ed.), *The handbook of emotion and memory: Research and theory* (pp. 201–215). Hillsdale, NJ: Erlbaum.

Yule, W., & Williams, R. M. (1990). Post-traumatic stress reactions in children. *Journal of Traumatic Stress, 3,* 279–295.

Zacharko, R. M. (1994). Stressors, the mesocorticolimbic system, and anhedonia: Implications for PTSD. In M. M. Murburg (Ed.), *Catacholamine function in posttraumatic stress disorder* (pp. 99–130). Washington, DC: American Psychiatric Press.

Zanarini, M. C. (1993). Borderline personality disorder as an impulse spectrum disorder. In J. Paris (Ed.), *Borderline personality disorder: Etiology and treatment* (pp. 67–85). Washington, DC: American Psychiatric Press.

Zanarini, M. C. (Ed.). (1997). *Role of sexual abuse in the etiology of borderline personality disorder.* Washington, DC: American Psychiatric Press.

Zanarini, M. C., & Frankenburg, F. R. (1997). Pathways to the development of borderline personality disorder. *Journal of Personality Disorders, 11,* 93–104.

Zanarini, M. C., Frankenburg, F. R., DeLuca, C. J., Hennen, J., Khera, G. S., & Gunderson, J. G. (1998). The pain of being borderline: Dysphoric states specific to borderline personality disorder. *Harvard Review of Psychiatry, 6,* 201–207.

Zanarini, M. C., Frankenburg, F. R., Dubo, E. D., Sickel, A. E., Trikha, A., Levin, A., & Reynolds, V. (1998). Axis I comorbidity of borderline personality disorder. *American Journal of Psychiatry, 155,* 1733–1739.

Zanarini, M. C., Kimble, C. R., & Williams, A. A. (1994). Neurological dysfunction in borderline patients and Axis II control subjects. In K. R. Silk (Ed.), *Biological and neurobehavioral studies of borderline personality disorder* (pp. 159–175). Washington, DC: American Psychiatric Press.

Zanarini, M. C., & Weinberg, E. (1996). Borderline personality disorder: Impulsive and compulsive features. In J. M. Oldham, E. Hollander, & A. E. Skodol (Eds.), *Impulsivity and compulsivity* (pp. 37–58). Washington, DC: American Psychiatric Press.

Zanarini, M. C., Williams, A. A., Lewis, R. E., Reich, R. B., Soledad, C. V., Marino, M. F., Levin, A., Yong, L., & Frankenburg, F. R. (1997). Reported pathological childhood experiences associated with the development of borderline personality disorder. *American Journal of Psychiatry, 154,* 1101–1106.

Zatzick, D. F., Marmar, C. R., Weiss, D. S., & Metzler, T. (1994). Does trauma-linked dissociation vary across ethnic groups? *Journal of Nervous and Mental Disease, 182,* 576–582.

Zeanah, C. H., & Zeanah, P. D. (1989). Intergenerational transmission of maltreatment: Insights from attachment theory and research. *Psychiatry, 52,* 177–196.

Zerbe, K. J. (1993a). *The body betrayed: Women, eating disorders, and treatment.* Washington, DC: American Psychiatric Press.

Zerbe, K. J. (1993b). Selves that starve and suffocate: The continuum of eating disorders and dissociative phenomena. *Bulletin of the Menninger Clinic, 57,* 319–327.

Zerbe, K. J. (1993c). Whose body is it anyway? Understanding and treating psychosomatic aspects of eating disorders. *Bulletin of the Menninger Clinic, 57,* 161–177.

Zerbe, K. J. (1995). The emerging sexual self of the patient with an eating disorder: Implications for treatment. *Eating Disorders, 3,* 197–215.

Zerbe, K. J. (1999). *Women's mental health in primary care.* Philadelphia: Saunders.

Zetzel, E. R. (1965). Depression and the incapacity to bear it. In M. Schur (Ed.), *Drives, affects, behavior* (Vol. 2, pp. 243–274). New York: International Universities Press.

Zigmond, M. J., Finlay, J. M., & Sved, A. F. (1995). Neurochemical studies of central noradrenergic responses to acute and chronic stress: Implications for normal and abnormal behavior. In M. J. Friedman, D. S. Charney, & A. Y. Deutch (Eds.), *Neurobiological and clinical consequences of stress: From normal adaptation to post-traumatic stress disorder* (pp. 45–60). Philadelphia: Lippincott-Raven.

Zimmerman, M., & Mattia, J. I. (1999). Psychotic subtyping of major depressive disorder and posttraumatic stress disorder. *Journal of Clinical Psychiatry, 60,* 311–314.

Zlotnick, C. (1999). Antisocial personality disorder, affect dysregulation and childhood abuse among incarcerated women. *Journal of Personality Disorders, 13,* 90–95.

Zlotnick, C., Begin, A., Shea, M. T., Pearlstein, T., Simpson, E., & Costello, E. (1994). The relationship between characteristics of sexual abuse and dissociative experiences. *Comprehensive Psychiatry, 35,* 465–470.

Zlotnick, C., Mattia, J. I., & Zimmerman, M. (1999). Clinical correlates of self-mutilation in a sample of general psychiatric patients. *Journal of Nervous and Mental Disease, 187,* 296–301.

Zlotnick, C., & Pearlstein, T. (1997). Validation of the structured interview for disorders of extreme stress. *Comprehensive Psychiatry, 38,* 243–247.

Zlotnick, C., Shea, M. T., Pearlstein, T., Begin, A., Simpson, E., & Costello, E. (1996). Differences in dissociative experiences between survivors of childhood incest and survivors of assault in adulthood. *Journal of Nervous and Mental Disease, 184,* 52–54.

Zlotnick, C., Shea, M. T., Pearlstein, T., Simpson, E., Costello, E., & Begin, A. (1996). The relationship between dissociative symptoms, alexithymia, impulsivity, sexual abuse, and self-mutilation. *Comprehensive Psychiatry, 37,* 12–16.

Zlotnick, C., Shea, M. T., Recupero, P., Bidadi, K., Pearlstein, T., & Brown, P. (1997). Trauma, dissociation, impulsivity, and self-mutilation among substance abuse patients. *American Journal of Orthopsychiatry, 67,* 650–654.

Zlotnick, C., Shea, M. T., Zakriski, A., Costello, E., Begin, A., Pearlstein, T., & Simpson, E. (1995). Stressors and close relationships during childhood and dissociative experiences in survivors of sexual abuse among inpatient psychiatric women. *Comprehensive Psychiatry, 36,* 207–212.

Zlotnick, C., Shea, T. M., Rosen, K., Simpson, E., Mulrenin, K., Begin, A., & Pearlstein, T. (1997). An affect-management group for women with posttraumatic stress disorder and histories of childhood sexual abuse. *Journal of Traumatic Stress, 10,* 425–436.

Zlotnick, C., Warshaw, M., Shea, M. T., Allsworth, J., Pearlstein, T., & Keller, M. B. (1999). Chronicity in posttraumatic stress disorder (PTSD) and predictors of course of comorbid PTSD in patients with anxiety disorders. *Journal of Traumatic Stress, 12,* 89–99.

Zweig-Frank, H., Paris, J., & Guzder, J. (1994a). Dissociation in female patients with borderline and non-borderline personality disorder. *Journal of Personality Disorders, 8,* 203–209.

Zweig-Frank, H., Paris, J., & Guzder, J. (1994b). Dissociation in male patients with borderline and non-borderline personality disorders. *Journal of Personality Disorders, 8,* 210–218.

INDEX